ECONOMIC DEVELOPMENT AND SOCIAL CHANGE

THE MODERNIZATION OF VILLAGE COMMUNITIES

EDITED BY GEORGE DALTON

AMERICAN MUSEUM SOURCEBOOKS IN ANTHROPOLOGY

PUBLISHED FOR

THE AMERICAN MUSEUM OF NATURAL HISTORY

THE NATURAL HISTORY PRESS

1971 GARDEN CITY, NEW YORK

EDITOR'S NOTE

Twenty-two of the readings in this volume are reprinted at the full length of their original publication. Those by Wolf, Geertz, and Smith are each lengthy excerpts drawn from several chapters of a book. Those by Sahlins, Wharton, and Lewis are excerpts from a single chapter, report, or journal article. In all but one reading the original footnotes and bibliographical references are retained in their entirety. (In the excerpts from Smith's book, references to works in Japanese have been omitted.) The date and place of original publication are cited on the first page of each essay.

I am grateful to John Adams, Irma Adelman, David Brokensha, Percy Cohen, Raymond Mack, Peter McLoughlin, and Walter Neale for giving me suggestions on readings to include in this volume.

The illustrations for this book
were prepared by the Graphic Arts Division
of The American Museum of Natural History.

CONTENTS

Dualism and Foreign Investment

GEORGE DALTON holds a joint appointment as a Professor in the Departments of Economics and Anthropology at Northwestern University and is a staff member of its Program of African Studies. In 1961–62 he spent fifteen months in West Africa, and is co-author of *Growth Without Development: An Economic Survey of Liberia* (Clower, Dalton, Harwitz, and Walters 1966). With Paul Bohannan, he edited *Markets in Africa* (1962; abridged edition, 1965). He has edited a book of readings in economic anthropology, *Tribal and Peasant Economies* (1967), and a collection of the essays of Karl Polanyi, *Primitive, Archaic, and Modern Economies* (1968). A volume of his own essays will appear in 1971, entitled *Economic Anthropology and Development.*

AMERICAN MUSEUM SOURCEBOOKS
IN ANTHROPOLOGY

LAW AND WARFARE:
Studies in the Anthropology of Conflict
PAUL BOHANNAN

TRIBAL AND PEASANT ECONOMIES:
Readings in Economic Anthropology
GEORGE DALTON

PERSONALITIES AND CULTURES:
Readings in Psychological Anthropology
ROBERT HUNT

COMPARATIVE POLITICAL SYSTEMS:
Studies in the Politics of Preindustrial Societies
RONALD COHEN and JOHN MIDDLETON

MYTH AND COSMOS:
Readings in Mythology and Symbolism
JOHN MIDDLETON

GODS AND RITUALS:
Readings in Religious Beliefs and Practices
JOHN MIDDLETON

MAGIC, WITCHCRAFT, AND CURING:
JOHN MIDDLETON

BEYOND THE FRONTIER:
Social Process and Cultural Change
PAUL BOHANNAN and FRED PLOG

MARRIAGE, FAMILY, AND RESIDENCE:
PAUL BOHANNAN and JOHN MIDDLETON

KINSHIP AND SOCIAL ORGANIZATION
PAUL BOHANNAN and JOHN MIDDLETON

ENVIRONMENT AND CULTURAL BEHAVIOR:
Ecological Studies in Cultural Anthropology
ANDREW P. VAYDA

FROM CHILD TO ADULT:
Studies in the Anthropology of Education
JOHN MIDDLETON

ANTHROPOLOGY AND ART:
Readings in Cross-Cultural Aesthetics
CHARLOTTE M. OTTEN

ECONOMIC DEVELOPMENT AND SOCIAL CHANGE

We must beware . . . of regarding our own system as the only good one. . . . Societies which are at present engaged in the processes of economic development and industrialization may with the help of their own specific cultural wealth build up their own systems of motivations and incentives; and before these are criticized by reference to criteria peculiar to the industrial societies of the West, they must be subjected to minute examination. They also offer us a rewarding field of study.

Claude Lévi-Strauss

Little else is requisite to carry a state to the highest degree of opulence from the lowest barbarism, but peace, easy taxes, and a tolerable administration of justice.

Adam Smith

It is only our Western societies that quite recently turned man into an economic animal.

Marcel Mauss

God loves the truth,
The African grain
And the White Man money   *Wolof saying*

INTRODUCTION[1]

George Dalton

THIS BOOK contains several kinds of literature on transforming village communities. The first section consists of theoretical and empirical essays on tribal and peasant economies. One must know their salient characteristics in order to understand how and why they changed in the colonial period and after. It also introduces the student to some of the older themes in economic anthropology and to conceptual issues relating to economy and society that have engaged anthropologists and others in recent years.

The second group of readings contains descriptions and analayses of the initial impacts and long-run consequences of colonialism. Colonial situations of varying sorts and durations were almost ubiquitous in Third World countries. Even the few areas that were never European or American colonies were influenced nevertheless by European commerce, investment, or religion.

The third and longest section is concerned with present-day modernization. Like the previous sections, it too consists of writings on different parts of the world, by economists, sociologists, and historians, as well as anthropologists. One of the themes of this book is that modernization is a field of social science; that the questions of interest to anthropologists are answered in part by economists and sociologists, and vice versa. Another is that it must be studied in historical depth. A third is that macro- and micro-development are complementary: to understand how and why villages are changing, one must know their formative experiences over the past, but also the develop-

[1] This Introduction is a revised and expanded version of a paper given at Syracuse University in April, 1969. I am grateful to David Brokensha, Walter Neale, Frederick Pryor, and Manfred Stanley for their critical comments on an earlier draft. Irma Adelman and I completed a research project on micro-development, under NSF grant GS1235, just before I began the compilation of this anthology. The project allowed me to do a good deal of reading which is reflected in this Introduction and in the choice of readings included in this book.

ment programs of the nation-states of which they are now a part. Finally, as in other branches of anthropology (and social science), one must study theoretical work and empirical cases.

THE SCOPE OF ECONOMIC ANTHROPOLOGY

Economic anthropology has only recently become a field of special interest within social and cultural anthropology. Its subject is thousands of small-scale communities in Africa, Asia, Latin America, Oceania, and the Middle East.[2] Its principal method of research is personal observation during fieldwork. The anthropologist usually works alone, lives in the small community he studies for a year or two, and supplements the data he himself collects by reading whatever literature exists on the social group and the cultural area he is studying. Anthropologists are professionally sensitive to the mutual interaction of cultural, social, and economic forces. Indeed, anthropology differs from the other social sciences in its overwhelming reliance on the fieldwork technique of face-to-face immersion in the community life of the people studied, its focus on village-level communities in the non-Western world, and its wide interests in all the principal activities, institutions, and relationships in the small communities studied. It is rare for an anthropologist to concentrate exclusively on economic matters because the *Gemeinschaft* structure of the small societies anthropologists study require them to analyze kinship, religion, technology, ecology, and polity, in order to say interesting things about economy.

The economic anthropologist is also interested in two different dimensions of economy, organization and performance, and in economies under three sets of conditions: their aboriginal condition before European contact and colonization, their changed condition during the colonial period of European presence and control, and their presently changing condition in the post-colonial period, which, for Africa and much of Asia, is barely one generation old.[3] Anthropology is a complicated subject not be-

---

[2] A relatively small number of anthropologists study communities in Japan and Europe, principally the less developed rural parts (e.g., Yugoslavia, Spain), or special sorts of communities such as Kibbutzim in Israel.

[3] For the study of communities in Europe, e.g., Pitt-Rivers (1954) and Arensberg (1937), an appropriate distinction is before and since the beginnings of industrialization and the modern nation-state.

cause it has developed a body of abstract theory—as with physics and economics—but because its subject matter is so varied. If the topics of interest to economic anthropologists were translated into the counterpart interests of economists (as fields in economics are demarcated in the study of industrial capitalism), the list would be formidable: economic history, comparative economic systems, industrial organization, agricultural economics, national income accounting, industrial sociology, and economic development.

Anthropologists, moreover, use two approaches, two professional emphases in portraying real-world societies. One is an artistic approach which shares much with psychological and sociological fiction (e.g., Alan Sillitoe's *The Loneliness of the Long Distance Runner;* Eugene O'Neill's *Long Day's Journey into Night*). The aim here is to convey the inward meaning of events, actions, and relationships within the small tribal or village community—folkviews, attitudes, values, and individual behavior. Like the playwright and novelist, the anthropologist becomes a sensitive translator of personality, world-views, and social events (compare Colin Turnbull, *The Forest People* and his *The Lonely African,* with Laura Bohannan, *Return to Laughter,* and Isak Dinesen, *Out of Africa*). There is much to be learned from such portrayals of personal views and community life in other cultures. All the great ethnographers convey such artistic essence in some of their writings.

The social science approach, however, now dominates. Here, the emphasis is on concepts, analytical conclusions, generalizations, and comparisons: to show how a given economic system works, how it compares with other economic systems, and how it relates to culture and society. But until recently, little was done to create an analytical framework for economic anthropology. Malinowski's pioneer work—and, indeed, brilliant work—remained the dominating format: rich ethnographic description of activities and organization; sensitive portrayals of the perceptions of the people and the inward meaning they attributed to land, work, and treasure items. The themes stressed were the interpenetration of economic and social organization and the special regard people had for the prestige sectors of economy (kula, pig tusks, potlatch, bridewealth). Works such as these continue to supply us with factual raw materials necessary for analysis, but not with analysis itself. Rather little was done from the more technical social science viewpoint: to contrive conceptual categories, to draw analytical conclusions, to make systematic comparisons, to quantify, and to derive policy prescriptions.

In the last ten years the social science emphasis in economic anthropology has been influenced from three directions. A group of economists and anthropologists, associated with the economic historian Karl Polanyi, have argued the need for a special analytical framework and conceptual vocabulary to study the socio-economic organization of pre-industrial systems, and have begun to construct such theory.[4] Another group of economists and anthropologists have argued the need to incorporate the conceptual vocabulary, leading ideas, and methodology of conventional economic analysis, and to measure the economic performance of primitive and peasant economies.[5]

The third happening which has affected the scope and theory of economic anthropology consists of two events. One is the Colonial Revolution, begun with India's achievement of political independence in 1947, and followed by nation-statehood for some fifty or more countries, principally in Africa and Asia, accompanied by policies to initiate national economic development and modernization. The related event is the rapid establishment of sub-fields in all the social sciences concerned with the new nations. For the first time ever, I believe, large groups of professionals from all the social sciences came to have a common focus of interest in the same set of processes and problems—structural transformation in the developing world.

ECONOMICS AND DEVELOPMENT

Of all the social sciences concerned with development and modernization, economics has achieved the most in generating theory and policy prescriptions. The reasons are worth examining. We

---

[4] Polanyi (1944: ch. 4, 5, 6); Polanyi, Arensberg and Pearson (1957); Polanyi (1966). P. Bohannan (1959); P. and L. Bohannan (1968); P. Bohannan and G. Dalton (1962). Sahlins (1965; 1968). Dalton (1961; 1962; 1965a; 1967; 1968a; 1969c). The most extensive evaluation of Polanyi's work yet to appear is Humphreys (1969).

[5] Firth (1966b; 1967; 1964a); LeClair (1962); Burling (1962); Salisbury (1962); Hill (1963; 1965); Epstein (1962); Deane (1953). On the very important topic of physical environment (ecology) as it relates to traditional and changing primitive and peasant communities, see Vayda (1969).

may be able to see why other social sciences (including cultural
and economic anthropology) have a more difficult task than
economics when they consider modernization. It is the nature of
that segment of social reality that economists deal with and the
greater power of their methods and theories that accounts for their
performance.

The glaring fact of the underdeveloped world is its material
poverty. The fact is glaring to the leaders and an increasing
number of ordinary people in Africa, Asia, and Latin America;
to the governments and people of the developed countries; to the
international civil service of the UN; to the social scientists in
the universities on all the continents; and to the great private
philanthropies of the United States. Poverty means not only
insufficient food, but also disease, early death, and a life sentence
of ignorance, immobility, and meanness for hundreds of millions
of people. The overriding priority, therefore, is to increase incomes of persons, village communities, and nations. So it is
economic analysis, economic planning, economic policy, and economic aid that appear paramount.

It is not only the pressing need for material improvement
that accounts for the prominence of economists in the subject of
modernization. There are reinforcing reasons attributable to the
kinds of theory and measurement used in economics, and ultimately to the quantifiable nature of that special sphere of
social reality economists deal with. It is probably so that the
extent of success each social science has in analyzing development
and modernization reflects its ability to employ its conventional
methods and theories—the theoretical and policy achievements of
the subject *before* development came to be a focus of interest.
Economists who turn to development studies are able to employ
a good deal of their ordinary analyses and measurements. Herein
lies one of its strengths.

Economists bring to their work on development a strong conviction that they must create theory in order to derive policy
prescriptions. The tradition is deeply imbedded in economics.
Adam Smith, David Ricardo, Karl Marx, and Maynard Keynes
were theoreticians and policymakers. Good theory makes clear
the strategic relationships determining real-world processes of importance, and suggests policy levers to direct the processes toward
desired goals. Good theory is an essential tool to transform what
is into what ought to be. One reason then for the effectiveness

of economics in development studies is the ability of economists to create persuasive theory as a rationale for policy guidelines. Another is their ability to quantify. Economic theory and policy are most powerful when economists can establish the numerical dimensions of economic structure, performance, processes, and transactions, from hard data series.

Other social sciences consider spheres of human activity and social organization which are not as amenable to statistical specification. Anthropology and political science have very little quantified information equivalent to national income accounts, input-output tables, and balance of payments components. I need hardly add that it is not the superior genes of economists which make them effective analyzers of development. It is the quantifiable nature of the portion of social reality they deal with and their ability to build theoretical models depicting strategic functional relationships. The economist is more fortunate than the anthropologist for the same reason that the surgeon is more fortunate than the psychiatrist: the symptoms of illness can be more exactly ascertained; the essential causes can be more assuredly established; and therefore the alleviation of pain can be more confidently prescribed and implemented.[6]

Economists spoke development from 1776 to 1870—from Adam Smith to Karl Marx—forgot it for the next seventy years, but resumed speaking a mandarin dialect called growth theory just before the Colonial Revolution made economists remember their childhood tongue. In the late 1930s, Keynes answered the questions, what makes the size of the aggregate national income for a developed capitalist country what it is for any one year, and what accounts for its short-run fluctuations? In the late 1940s, Harrod and Domar asked what determines the long-run growth of aggregate national income for such countries? And Schumpeter stressed the strategic roles in the process played by entrepreneurs and innovations. The econometricians measured national eco-

---

[6] I do not mean to overstate the case. For many problems and processes of national development, conventional economic analysis is necessary but certainly not sufficient. There is a growing literature of contention on the relevance and adequacy of conventional economics to studies of modernization and development. See Myrdal (1957); Seers (1963); Martin and Knapp (1967); Adelman and Morris (1967); and Dalton (1968b). On the need for development economists to engage in wider social analyses, see the essays by Myrdal and Sawyer in this volume, also, Dalton (1965c).

nomic structure and performance. They filled in the theoretical skeleton with the flesh of numbers and transactional facts. Macroeconomic theory, inter-industry analysis, and the use of national income statistics to measure performance, were established before economists turned to the development of Africa and Asia.

Economists were equipped in other ways as well to undertake development studies. The economic historians and specialists in Soviet economy quickly discovered they too had been speaking development all their lives. Rostow and Gerschenkron, among others, pointed out that we could learn things of interest about the current transformation of India and Nigeria by re-examining the historical transformation of England and Germany, and the deliberate development efforts of Soviet Russia and Japan.[7]

We have always had with us, moreover, our Veblens and Galbraiths—semi-pariahs within the profession, heroes to the rest of the world—lecturing us on the social implications of economic organization and performance, and the need to study institutions and the cultural framework within which the economy functions. The lesson was remembered by a few economists who set out to investigate the interpenetration of socio-political institutions, or personality and culture, with economic activity in the process of development.[8] It seems easier for economists to cross over into politics, sociology, and anthropology than for the other social scientists to incorporate economics in their formal analyses. Almost certainly it is because economics is less easily self-taught than the other social sciences. In part, perhaps, it is also due to an older tradition in economics of pragmatic engagement. Some economists have always chosen real problems to investigate, and used whatever methods produce interesting results, even, as with Everett Hagen, if it required them to put down their surgeon's tools and take up the psychiatrist's.

Finally, real world events in Europe and America prepared the economists to undertake modern development analysis and plan-

---

[7] Japan should be of special interest to all the social sciences because it is the most successful non-European country in its economic and technological development. The extent to which Japan retained its traditional culture while undergoing its Industrial Revolution should make it of very special interest to anthropology (see Smith 1959).

[8] Lewis (1954; 1955); Myrdal (1957); Hagen (1962); Adelman-Morris (1967); Seers (1963); Singer (1950); Clower, Dalton, Harwitz, Walters (1966).

ning. The Great Depression of the 1930s killed laissez-faire in practice and in ideology, and Keynesian economics killed its theoretical rationale. Central government was to "intervene" in the private market economy to assure something close to full employment. Government was to be not only the sporadic compensator in emergency, but the institutionalized governor and regulator. Central planning in capitalist countries during World War II proved that Keynes was right, and also that governmental policies could increase the national growth rate. (We also came to understand what the Russians had been up to since 1928. During the war, Britain and the United States also displaced market autonomy with central planning in order to produce quickly a narrow range of high priority goods.) We emerged from the war with knowledge and experience in economic planning, and perhaps, as well, a fresh appreciation of the developmental power of technological innovation. Radar was converted to television, jet propulsion to commercial aviation, and military rocketry to space research. The Marshall Plan to help European reconstruction was the last of these preparations for development planning and analysis.[9]

ANTHROPOLOGY AND MODERNIZATION

Anthropology has catalogued and described many strange societies always with scrupulous care not to disturb them, with its focus of interest on culture rather than on social change, its powerful instrument the notion of the validity of all cultures. More than any other social science it has seen institutions in context; it has striven always to penetrate the mode of thought of the group under study.

Economics on the other hand has sought out the mechanism of change. It has been very close to business and government; economic thinking everywhere influences major decisions (Keyfitz 1959:46).

_____

[9] The quick and dramatic success of the Marshall Plan probably had the unfortunate consequence of creating over-optimism about the potential effectiveness of economic aid for developing nations. Europe and Japan needed only short-run aid, principally food and capital equipment to repair the devastation of war and the overworking of physical plant during the war. They were already industrialized and developed. Africa and Asia require much more than food and capital transfers. The problems of structural transformation they now confront had no real counterpart in the countries receiving Marshall aid.

Just as the economist's approach to development was in large measure shaped by the working methods of economics and the problems and processes it addressed before the Colonial Revolution, so too with anthropology and modernization. But the circumstances here were entirely different. Anthropologists were not well prepared to undertake post-colonial studies of micro-development.

Anthropology has many fewer practicing professionals than does economics and was established as a university subject much later. As an international subject it is much less uniform than economics. Swedish, Italian, and American economists have in common not only a large base of economic theory and techniques of statistical measurement, but also a common focus of empirical interest: the structure and performance of the industrial capitalism of their own national economies. National traditions in anthropology, however, were shaped principally by colonial experience. In those European nations which were not important colonial powers, archeology and physical anthropology rather than social anthropology were likely to be stressed. In England, which had primitive societies intact and functioning in its colonies in Africa, Oceania, and Asia, social anthropology studied them as living social systems. In the United States, where American Indian tribes were already radically changed from their aboriginal condition by 1875, cultural anthropology became established with different emphases.

Until quite recently, moreover, social and cultural anthropologists concentrated their studies in tribal rather than the Latin American and Asian peasant societies which comprise the bulk of today's underdeveloped world (Geertz 1962a). Classic ethnographies, such as Boas on Eskimos and northwest coast Indians, Malinowski on the Trobriands, and Evans-Pritchard on the Nuer, were on small, stateless, relatively isolated groups, whose language and religion were not widely shared. The village communities of India and Latin America received much less attention.

When anthropologists studied socio-economic change, they frequently studied situations which were different from those typifying today's modernization. Aside from grand theories of evolution concerned with unobserved early change in archaic and ancient societies, anthropologists studied acculturation of American Indians, or the early generations of culture contact under colonial conditions (Broom et al. 1954). Many of those engaged in applied anthropology tried to introduce innovations piecemeal in village communities before national development programs came to be established with political independence (Spicer 1952).

APPLIED ANTHROPOLOGY AND AGRICULTURAL ECONOMICS

If the economist's model of behavior tends to be the prizefight, the sociologist's model tends to be the quilting bee (Moore 1955: 158).

Economists and anthropologists also have somewhat different conceptions of development. When economists turn to the problem of inducing rural peoples to undertake new economic activities (e.g., planting new cash crops), and using new technology (e.g., chemical fertilizers), they think in terms of providing sufficient material incentives (profitable prices for cash crops), needed skills, resources, and equipment to undertake the activities (agricultural extension services, farm to market roads and transport, and credit). The economist, moreover, views development as a long-run continuing process of new, improved, and diversified activities and technology, so that community income rises continually with the village's ever-deepening and widening interaction with its national economy and society.

The conception of micro-development contained in many studies of applied anthropology is both different and a special case. Many of the studies consider problems of introducing one or two specific innovations—improved seed, mosquito control—into a village community.[10] Overwhelmingly, the case studies of applied anthropology entail the special situation of the visiting expert ("change agent") in temporary residence, as the initiator of the one or few innovations to be introduced. The literature describes cases of success and failure in introducing innovations piecemeal and draws analytical and policy conclusions from them (Spicer 1952; Erasmus 1961). It stresses the need for the visiting expert to know the history and the present organization of the community. Above all, it stresses the *cultural* complexity of innovations—the many resistances to innovation stemming from the

---

[10] The case of Vicos, described by Holmberg and Vázquez in this volume, is an unusual example of applied anthropology for several reasons, including the comprehensiveness of the changes and innovations introduced in a short period of time.

peoples' values, attitudes, social relationships, and past experiences; and the *social* consequences of innovations: that the adoption of a steel axe can induce a train of unforeseen changes in social relationships, and even new conflict situations (Sharp 1952).

The literature of applied anthropology is useful to agricultural extension agents, public health fieldworkers, Peace Corps volunteers, and other visiting experts charged with introducing specific innovations in their short-run visits. But its relevance to the study of modernization is limited. For theoretical and policy reasons it should be supplemented in several ways. In studying present-day development we must include the new socio-economic conditions and policies created by the ending of colonialism and the new knowledge brought forth by the several subjects now analyzing development processes.

One supplementary field of analysis is agricultural economics (see the articles by Allan, Fogg, and Wharton in this volume). These agronomists and economists show the *ecological, economic,* and *technological* complexity of agricultural innovation: the monetary costs, new skills, soil and water conditions, and enlarged labor requirements entailed in successful innovation. It is almost certainly so nowadays that developmental projects fail more frequently because of faulty ecological, economic, and technical analysis than because of cultural resistances: that the soil or rainfall conditions are unsuitable to the innovation; that the profitable use of chemical fertilizer requires more labor than is physically available in the community; that irrigation equipment requires a package of complementary innovations simultaneously introduced as a condition for its successful employment.

> Difficulties were encountered in harvesting groundnuts because the soil becomes incredibly hard when it dries. Sugar cane suffered from lack of irrigation facilities . . . the herbicides presently in use are ineffective in controlling the local weeds; techniques for irrigating wheat are scarcely understood; insecticides are misused . . . In 1909 cultivators reportedly gave three reasons for not transplanting their paddy [rice]: insufficient irrigation, poor soils, and scattered holdings. Farmers contacted during the 1963–64 farm survey claimed they did not transplant because their draft animals were too weak for puddling, labor was insufficient, and grazing was not controlled (Weaver 1968:194, 199).

It should also be understood that most socio-economic change currently goes on without the entrepreneurial presence of visiting experts transmitting innovative skills (see, for example, the two articles by Epstein in this volume). Nowdays, new opportunities for income growth, new modes of production, and new cultural achievement are frequently provided by *impersonal* agencies and facilities which link the village to the region and nation by creating whole new sets of economic and cultural transactions: all-weather roads and regular bus service, electricity, radios and newspapers, postal savings facilities. The applied anthropologists who were in the field before 1950 studied village economies at a time when the regions and nations of which they were a part were relatively static, economically. They are no longer so. With an end to semi-isolation comes mobility, new alternatives, and new activities—development from above. It is this movement of people, goods, and ideas within the post-colonial framework of new regional and national institutions, policies, and capital facilities which is central to modernization.

DIFFICULTIES IN STUDYING MICRO-DEVELOPMENT

The empirical data and analyses of micro-development are spread over several branches of social science. Anyone who attempts to create a theoretical framework has to read deeply in several subjects other than his own. Consider the relevant sources one would turn to in constructing models of socio-economic change, development, and modernization of village communities.

The anthropological literature is very large indeed, and appears under the headings of evolution, adaptation to physical environment, culture contact, acculturation, applied anthropology, culture change, and, recently, the anthropology of modernization. The common focus of interest is change at the village community level, but the underlying conditions, the historical periods, and the kinds of change studied vary enormously (see the survey articles by Spindler 1959; Rubin 1962; Voget 1963).

Several fields within economics contribute to the study of micro-development. The agricultural economists have long been interested in measuring and analyzing rural development (Jones 1961; Miracle 1962; Allan 1965; Mellor et al. 1968). Several national income statisticians have measured the performance of village economies in the hinterland of developing nations (Deane 1953; Samuels 1963). The literature of the economic and social history of already developed nations in Europe and Asia contains much that is relevant to current experiences, particularly, as with Japan and eastern Europe, where pre-modernization economy and society—peasantries, pronounced social stratification—bore striking similarities to structures of the nations developing today (Smith 1959; Polanyi 1944; Coulborn 1956; Duby 1968). The industrial sociologists also have made some notable contributions in their studies of social change accompanying European industrialization (Bendix 1956; Smelser 1958).

Finally, there is the institutional literature of economic development concerned with the interaction of economic, social, and political forces in the processes of modernization. I shall have more to say later in this Introduction about the insights into micro-development to be got from the works of Myrdal, Hagen, Smelser, and Adelman and Morris.

Anthropologists and others who work on the theoretical and policy aspects of micro-development are handicapped by the absence of hard data series relating to village economies (Hill 1966). There are very few village or tribal economies for which comparable data series exist of the sort economists find essential to analyze national economic development: the composition and totals of community income and output; balance of payments figures; the data to construct input-output matrices; productivity measurements for various lines of production; price series, figures on investment, etc.[11] (Fogg 1965; Lewis 1953; Stolper 1966).

There is insufficient theory of socio-economic change and development at the village level. There are some leading ideas, insights, and the beginnings of a conceptual vacabulary, but little in the way of verbal or mathematical models depicting strategic relationships. We are only beginning to discern the important regularities that underlie the transformation sequence for village communities, and to understand what are the prime inducers of modernization. And we now look for the general lessons to be learned from the empirical studies of unusual success or unusual failure, and to expect that it is *both* cultural heredity and economic and physical environment which induce success or failure.

---

[11] There seems to be no equivalent in the conventional subjects of anthropological inquiry, such as kinship, religion, and polity, to what is here meant by the quantifiable performance of an economy. The closest one comes is simple enumeration: for example, the frequency of murder, theft, or divorce.

NEW METHODS OF INVESTIGATION

The circumstances under which economic development and cultural modernization of village communities now proceeds require new techniques of investigation in addition to the traditional field excursion of one man studying one village for one year. The socio-economic changes we call modernization occur as sequential processes which take place over generations—they are not once-and-for-all changes. Enlarged commercialization, the use of new technology, the growth of literacy and its consequences, the transactional and institutional links created between hinterland communities and the new central governments and cities since the former colonies became independent nation-states, are very long-run changes.

These complicated changes never occur evenly. Some are always lagged and occur piecemeal over many generations, for at least three disparate reasons. One is personality formation, which conditions the ability of different age groups during any one time period to absorb new skills and values and undertake new activities (Hagen 1962). Another is capital formation, that lengthy and expensive process of building private and public investment goods (Singer 1952). To equip a nation with machine-using factories, roads, power facilities, and schools, requires the work and savings of generations. A third is the inevitable lags in reforming political and social institutions to enable them to undertake the tasks of development and the provision of social services (Myrdal 1960). We in industrialized, modernized, developed America should learn from our national strife over Vietnam and the restructuring of Negro life in our society, that the reform of political and social institutions is neither simple nor painless. The tenacity, the inertia, the resistance to deep reform seems shakable —lamentably—only when shocked by undeniable signs of malaise, expressed forcibly. We in America who are seeing years of strife in Berkeley, Watts, and Chicago in pursuit of social and political reform, should not be surprised at African and Latin American coups. Nor should the Russians after Prague. One of the least understood aspects of modernization is what determines time rates of change, especially change in political and social institutions.

The new technology, and the new economic and cultural activities that comprise modernization, mutually interact and displace the old, thereby affecting individuals and networks of social groupings. Not only are traditional economies changing, but also cultures and social relationships; not only are social and economic organization changing, but also economic and cultural performance. Individual persons are changing, their relationships in and to social groupings are changing, and the local community's transactions—economic, cultural, political—with the region, the nation, and the rest of the world, are changing. To measure and analyze these changes requires more than one man working one year in one community. The processes at work are altogether more complicated than a single innovation working itself out within a traditional culture otherwise intact. Modernization is not the same as the introduction of the horse among the Plains Indians, or the steel axe among aboriginal Australians.[12]

Modernization at the village level now takes place within the larger settings of regional and national development. Frequently we are dealing with local communities being vitally affected by new taxes, new goods, new experts, new roads, new political parties, all originating outside the local community. If anthropologists are to understand the causes and consequences of change in the rural community they must enlarge their studies these days to include the region and the nation whose policies, activities, and personnel now impinge on the local community in unprecedented ways and with unprecedented frequency.

In recent years anthropologists have developed new methods to study change in reaction to the more complicated circumstances and longer time horizon which characterize economic development and cultural modernization. A few older anthropologists have restudied communities they first visited twenty or thirty years earlier in order to record and analyze the intervening change. Raymond Firth's excellent restudies of Tikopia and Malay fishermen are works of this sort (Firth 1959; 1966b).

---

[12] One of several ways in which agricultural economics supplements applied anthropology is in showing how more complicated modern innovations in agricultural technology are compared to the famous case of the steel axe displacing the stone axe. Note that the steel axe is a simple innovation because it requires no complementary resources in order to be used effectively. Chemical fertilizer is a complicated innovation because its effective usage requires several associated resources and labor redeployment: more water, more labor in weeding, and sometimes different methods in preparing the soil. See Mellor et al. (1968).

T. Scarlett Epstein's work (1962) deserves wide reading both for its substance and its methods. She used the traditional fieldwork approach but chose a strategic field situation: two agricultural village communities in India within six miles of one another, only one of which got irrigation facilities (some twenty-five years earlier). She analyzed the socio-economic changes occurring in both villages. Enough time had elapsed so that important changes were discernible. Her training in economics allowed her to measure productivity, income, and expenditure, so as to buttress her qualitative analysis of socio-economic organization with statistical data on comparative economic performance. Her work should be recognized as a model of how the traditional fieldwork approach of anthropologists can be adapted to study the social and cultural consequences of technological and economic change.[13]

Clifford Geertz's work in Indonesia on entrepreneurs (1962b; 1963a), and on agricultural change (1963b), is noteworthy for the fruitful combination of historical, ecological, and anthropological analysis and for his study of the economic growth of towns. (His more recent field work in Morocco is designed to study change in depth by frequent residence over a ten-year period.)

Collaborative fieldwork is another method of coping with the complicated processes of social and economic change. Several kinds of teams of researchers have done useful work in the field. A group of anthropologists from Cornell (Holmberg et al. 1965), in residence over several years, studied minutely the socio-economic transformation of Vicos, a peasant hacienda community in Peru. Their work is unusual because of the quick success the group had in initiating technological, economic, and socio-cultural innovations. The theoretical sophistication brought to bear, moreover, together with the depth and breadth of description and analysis, allow the reader to learn some important lessons from Vicos.

A different kind of collaborative effort is a recent piece of work sponsored by the World Bank (de Wilde et al. 1967). A group of economists and anthropologists studied problems of transforming agriculture in tropical Africa. They did brief field

---

[13] See her two essays (including the statistical appendix to the second one) reprinted in this book.

investigations in thirteen areas of varying ecological, cultural, economic, and technological conditions.

MICRO-DEVELOPMENT AND HISTORICAL SEQUENCE

Any planned growth is embedded in a set of institutions and attitudes which come from the past (Keyfitz 1959:34).

The study of modernization at the local community level should begin with two leading ideas: that the communities we observe undergoing social and economic change today were importantly shaped by their social and economic organization, physical environment, and contact experiences in the pre-colonial and colonial periods. Anthropological analysis therefore should be done within a conscious framework of historical time periods. Secondly, that the characteristic forces of change were different in the pre-colonial, colonial, and post-colonial periods. The essays in this volume by Wolf, Geertz, and Smith, are particularly noteworthy because they show so clearly how the past shaped the present.

Pre-colonial Africa, Asia, and Latin America (like pre-industrial Europe) were not static, but the characteristic changes which moved people and restructured social, political, and economic life were principally ravages of nature and ravages of man: famine, pestilence, war, and conquest. These brought change, but not the sorts of change induced by industrialization and mass literacy. The changes were like those caused by the external shocks of the bubonic plague in fourteenth-century Europe, the Viking raids on Britain and France in the tenth century, and the Norman Conquest of England in the eleventh. Frequently, the culture and polity of the conquerors were not of a different order of complexity or economic achievement from those of the conquered (Roman civilization confronting barbarians was a rare thing). As with Christianity in Europe, the spread of new religions, such as Islam in Africa, also brought important change. Occasionally, foreign trade—and most dramatically, the slave trade—brought important change. But here too, frequently, the cultural contacts it entailed were confined to trade goods, the goods few and the trade sporadic, and the trading parties represented socio-economic systems at roughly the same level of technology and economic performance (Hogbin 1958; Polanyi et al. 1957).

With European colonization from the sixteenth through the nineteenth centuries (when the European powers themselves began and then intensified their industrialization and economic growth), came new kinds of change with irreversible consequences for what we now call the developing areas. It is, perhaps, a commonplace among historians of colonialism that one must know what was happening in the European home country to understand its policies and actions in its colonies (Simpson 1950). Europeans who established overseas colonies before industrialization was importantly begun in their home countries (e.g., the Spanish), viewed the potential economic benefits to themselves differently from those who colonized after industrialization had burgeoned at home. Geertz (1963b:105) contrasts the economic policies of the Dutch in the Outer Islands of Indonesia, after 1863, with their earlier policies in Java:

> . . . rather than being focused on condiments [e.g., pepper], confections [e.g., sugar], and stimulants [coffee and tobacco], the development centered on the production of industrial raw materials —a reflex, as Wertheim [1956:67, 97] has pointed out, of the alteration in world market conditions attendant upon the spectacular growth of large-scale manufacturing in the West after the middle of the nineteenth century. In 1900, rubber, tin, and petroleum—almost entirely Outer Island products—accounted for about 17 percent of Indonesia's export value . . . in 1930 about 37 percent; in 1940, after the collapse of sugar in the depression, about 66 percent [see Furnivall 1944:36–37].

The colonial powers moved and resettled peoples. Slaves were taken out of Africa and resettled in utterly different circumstances in the Caribbean, and North and South America. Indians in Latin America were moved to haciendas and settled as serfs under Spanish overlords (see the articles by Wolf and Holmberg in this volume). Some American Indians and Africans were moved to reservations. Chinese and Asian Indian laborers formed overseas enclaves in societies as radically different from their own as Hawaii, the Fiji Islands, East Africa, and British Guiana. White Europeans settled everywhere, either as colonial administrators or missionaries doing tours of duty, or, as with merchants and farmers, as permanent settlers with families.

Colonial policies and decrees forbade specific activities and practices thereby disrupting indigenous culture and social organization. Public health measures and the curtailment of tribal warfare set in motion long-run changes such as population growth and land shortages. Colonial administration and European commerce and industry brought new political institutions and the beginnings of new economic activities. Colonialism created dual economies by establishing European commercial enclaves of mining and agricultural production for export alongside of traditional societies producing subsistence goods with homemade technology (see the essays by Geertz, Singer, and Jaspan in this volume). What Geertz (1963b:120) says about the social and psychological changes which accompanied the rapid commercialization of agricultural production in the Outer Islands of Indonesia around 1910, holds widely:

> This [economic, or market-capitalist] mentality has had its customary sociocultural accompaniments: increasing flexibility of land tenure; growth of individualism and slackening of extended family ties; greater class differentiation and conflict, intensified opposition between young and old, modern and conservative; weakening of traditional authority and wavering of traditional social standards; and even the growth of "Protestant ethic" religious ideologies (see Schrieke 1955:107 ff.). What changed here (as in Java though in a different way) was not just a pattern of land use or a set of productive techniques but a system of functionally interrelated adaptively relevant institutions, practices and ideas—a "cultural core."

The post-colonial period (except in Latin America) is a scant generation old, but it is already clear that the changes begun with political independence are in part qualitatively and in part quantitatively different from the changes experienced in the pre-colonial and colonial periods. What is new is not the general fact of "change," but the initiation of particular, structural changes: the beginnings of national political integration, national market integration, industrialization and the application of science to agricultural production, and the beginnings of mass literacy and education. The governments of India and the Ivory Coast are now able to mobilize their nation's resources through national plans and budgets, and to participate as sovereign nations in international economic institutions. The small communities in which anthropologists have traditionally focused their interest cannot be studied in isolation from the developing national institutions and activities in which they now participate.

THEORETICAL GUIDELINES

Which are the promising ideas or lines of analysis in the study of socio-economic change, development, and modernization at the village level? Which concepts and generalizations contribute to the formulation of theory? Which published works on micro-development should be read for the theoretical guidelines they provide? What are the interesting questions to be answered about processes and problems of socio-economic change?

In a subject as vast and complex as the causes and consequences of social and economic change in village communities in Africa, Asia, Latin America, Oceania, and the Middle East, in the pre-colonial, colonial, and post-colonial periods, it is well to specify which of a large set of questions are most worth answering. Indeed, it is essential to do so. What we call theory in the social sciences—leading ideas, concepts, specification of functional relationships, and analytical conclusions and generalizations— can always be regarded as addressed to specific questions. If we want to invent good theory in order to understand and direct processes of modernization, it is sensible to specify the questions such theory should be able to answer.

1. Are there typical sequences of socio-economic change at the village level? Are there underlying regularities in the transformation sequence?

2. Which features of traditional economy, society, and culture make for receptivity or resistance to innovations of a modernizing sort? How are receptivity and resistance to modernizing innovations related to earlier experiences of intrusion (e.g., by missionaries, colonial government, the slave trade)?

3. Once modernizing activities have begun, such as producing export crops, using improved technology, establishing modern schools, how and why do traditional social organization and culture change? What do such changes tell us about traditional society?

4. What comprises "successful" village development? Can we define it? Can we construct models of successful village development from case studies of real-world experience? What analytical lessons are to be learned from case studies of unusual success and definite failure in development? Does success or failure de-

pend on the sequence in which economic as compared to non-economic innovations are introduced? What analytical time dimension is most useful in studying socio-economic change?

5. To what extent are processes of social and economic change at the village level the small-scale counterparts of economic development and cultural modernization at the national level? What theoretical benefits would accrue to anthropological analysis by considering the work of economists, political scientists, and sociologists, on national modernization?

I turn now to a few of the theoretical guidelines, concepts, analytical insights, and lines of research that I think most fruitful.

THE MUTUAL INTERACTION OF ECONOMIC AND CULTURAL FORCES

Modernization is a sequential process of cumulative change over time, generated by the interaction of economic and cultural innovations impinging on traditional economy, polity, and society, with feedback effects on the innovating activities. To put it this way is to point up the problem of inventing analytical categories which reveal the strategic workings of such a complicated process in the real world of developing areas. The conceptual categories must include both economic and non-economic attributes; they must show how the attributes mutually affect one another in changing traditional society; and in what sequence, over what period of time, and with what consequences.

Gunnar Myrdal's *Rich Lands and Poor* (especially chapters 1–3)[14] speaks to all the social sciences in his insistence on the need to include all relevant variables regardless of which social science jurisdiction they traditionally have been under. His points are additionally persuasive because they illuminate development processes and problems of several sorts characterized by the mutual interaction of diverse forces. We learn from Myrdal, moreover, some useful language with which to talk about modernization—cumulative causation, spread effects, backwash effects—and why piecemeal change (the attempt to introduce a single innovation into traditional societies) frequently fails to generate more comprehensive structural change.

---

[14] Chapters 2 and 3 are reprinted in this volume.

. . . the principle of interlocking circular interdependence within a process of cumulative causation has validity over the entire field of social relations. It should be the main hypothesis when studying economic underdevelopment and development (1957:23).

Myrdal argues that complicated social situations, such as the position of Negroes in America, and underdevelopment, share crucial characteristics of a sort which require a special kind of analysis. The social reality underlying these situations consists of interlocking, mutually dependent and mutually reinforcing economic, social, political, historical, and cultural forces. There is no single cause of underdevelopment, there are many, and they are not independent of each other; they are integral, not additive. The essential idea is of a vicious circle of numerous and different causes mutually reinforcing each other, working in the same direction to produce the same result.

Several analytical and policy conclusions follow from Myrdal's work: (1) Underdevelopment does not mean simply a shortage of capital, or an absence of entrepreneurial initiative. Whole sets of disparate forces are determining the outcome we perceive as underdevelopment. (2) No single social science provides all the data or conceptual apparatus necessary to analyze underdevelopment. Rather than identify "economic" or "cultural" forces, the analyst must identify all relevant forces at work, regardless of which sector of social reality they come from. (3) Development is a dynamic and complicated process which takes place over time. If sufficient improvement in the several spheres of activity that comprise development can be successfully initiated, they too will be mutually reinforcing. Development is a cumulative process upward: improvements in income make improvements in health, education, and technology easier, and vice versa.

Myrdal recognizes that there is a great deal we do not know about these processes. From the large set of potential development improvements—income, health, education, new lines of production—can we identify a smaller set of strategic factors and specific policies, which, if successful, produce large multiplier effects; or policies which work more quickly than others?[15] What are the most powerful levers of change that are available to policy makers; how, why, and how long do they take to work, and with what induced effects?

---

[15] See Adelman and Morris (1968a; 1968b).

The writings of Boeke (1942), Furnivall (1948), Lewis (1954), and Singer (1950) on dual economies analyzes the mutual inter- action of economic and non-economic forces under the special conditions of colonialism: the transactional flows between the European, commercial-industrial sector and the traditional primi- tive or peasant hinterland. Much of this sort of analysis remains relevant for the post-colonial period in those least developed nations where there remains a sharp dichotomy between the urban-commercial-export sector and traditional village subsistence economies.[16]

In extremely clear terms, Smelser (1963), describes the typical kinds of social change that accompany economic and tech- nological development: from subsistence farming to production of agricultural commodities for markets; from the use of simple tools and traditional techniques to the application of scientific knowledge and advanced technology; from the use of human and animal power to the kinds of inanimate power and mechanized techniques entailed in industrialization; from farm and village life toward increased urbanization; from apprentice training within the family and farm to formal schooling.[17]

---

[16] See Dalton (1965c). There is a rich anthropological literature of ethnographic description and analysis which properly belongs under the heading of dualism, particularly empirical works such as Watson (1958) and Gulliver (1965), on the response of tribal groups to the penetration of European commercial economy.

[17] Smelser (1963) is reprinted in this volume. A succinct summary of the secular changes entailed in the national transformation towards greater development, from the viewpoint of an economist, is the following: "Coun- tries which have attained high levels of per capita income have experi- enced rather drastic changes in the relative importance of different indus- trial sectors—a sharp decline in agriculture, a growth in the manufacturing sector, and a later, more pronounced expansion of transportation, com- munication, and the service sectors generally (retailing, finance, govern- ment, and so on). Associated with this have been declines in numbers of unskilled workers, proprietors, and managers (largely in the farm sector) and increases in numbers of clerical, professional, and technical workers. These [labor] input changes in large part reflect the differential impact of technical change and the changing composition of output associated with rising incomes, such as the rising proportion of government ex- penditures in total output and the major compositional changes in con- sumer expenditures—growth in the relative importance of durable goods and in the provision of services, such as education, medical care, and recreation. Superimposed on these changes are the decline of the household as a nucleus of productive activity and the increasing importance of the

His point is that all these modernizing activities induce similar changes away from the base of traditional society. Smelser addresses himself particularly to two questions: How exactly do development activities and values change traditional society and economy? What are the new forms of social organization created in the course of economic, technological, and cultural modernization?

The process of change in traditional economy and society induced by modern activities is what Smelser (following Parsons) calls "structural differentiation."

> The concept of structural differentiation can be employed to analyze what is frequently termed the "marked break in established patterns of social and economic life" in periods of development . . . "differentiation" is the evolution from a multi-functional role structure to several more specialized structures (Smelser 1963: 35).

Agricultural production for sale, the use of modern technology, factory work, urbanism, modern education, all involve activities carried on with persons outside the family household or local village, and create what might be called new dependency relationships, external to the family and village. A more familiar way to put these points is to say that impersonal market forces and contractual relationships displace local dependence on kin and status. And, indeed, people come to move physically and occupationally in new orbits of economic and cultural activity. Production and education are no longer carried on exclusively within the family; new specialized agencies carry on activities in the modern sector:

> During a society's transition from domestic to factory industry the division of labor increases and the economic activities previously lodged in the family move to the firm. As a formal educational system emerges, the functions previously performed by the family and church are established in a more specialized unit, the school. The modern political party has a more complex structure than do tribal factions, and the former is less likely to be fettered with kinship loyalties, competition for religious leadership, etc. . . . structural differentiation is a process whereby one social role or

market nexus, an increase in leisure time, and a massive shift of the population from a primarily rural to a primarily urban environment" (Rosenberg 1964:660).

organization . . . differentiates into *two or more* roles or organizations which function more effectively in the new historical circumstances. The new social units are structurally distinct from each other, but taken together are functionally equivalent to the original unit (Smelser 1963:35).

Differentiation characterizes the changes in traditional economy and society induced by modernizing activities. Following Durkheim (*Division of Labor in Society*, ch. 3–8), Smelser calls "integration" the institutions and mechanisms ". . . for coordinating and solidifying the interaction among individuals whose interests are becoming progressively more diversified" (Smelser 1963:41). Durkheim emphasizes the role of the legal system as an integrative or coordinating device. Smelser points to many such devices and institutions that accompany development and modernization, e.g., ". . . trade unions, associations, political parties, and a mushrooming state apparatus" (p. 41).

The work of Irma Adelman and Cynthia Taft Morris (1965; 1967; 1968a; 1968b) is pathbreaking in its use of statistical techniques to investigate how social and political organization interact with economic and technological performance in the transformation sequences of development. They draw their data from seventy-four developing nations.[18] The work is noteworthy for its methodology, its analytical conclusions, and for the policy guidelines its conclusions suggest. It draws widely on comparable data, so that its conclusions are of general significance. Its statistical techniques cluster inter-correlated variables and show the importance of different clusters as the process of development advances.

Aside from their statistical methods, which are most certainly applicable to micro-analysis of village development (see the essay by Adelman and Dalton in this volume), the Adelman-Morris work shows that cultural, political, and economic components of development vary sharply in their importance depending on the level of modernization achieved: the lower the level of

---

[18] Adelman and Morris are presently engaged in a complementary study of historical development using the same kinds of statistical techniques. They attempt to answer the following questions: considering the structure of society, polity, and economy of some twenty-five nations in 1870 (most of which have since become highly developed) could one—on the bases of these structures and performances in 1870—have predicted their development paths and rates?

achieved development the more powerfully do non-economic characteristics of traditional society, polity, and culture act as obstacles to economic development; but it is nevertheless economic and technological innovations, such as the enlargement of production for sale, the use of improved technology, and the establishment of modern financial institutions, that are the most powerful levers that change traditional society. For its methods and its substance, the work is important to all social scientists interested in national and village development and modernization.

DIFFERENTIATION AND INTEGRATION:

CHANGING THE TRADITIONAL VILLAGE COMMUNITY AND

LINKING IT WITH THE NEW NATIONAL ECONOMY AND SOCIETY

The transformation sequence we call modernization is an interaction process in two senses. Not only do economic and sociocultural activities and relationships interact, but also *old* economic activities, social relationships and cultural practices change in reaction to *new* ones becoming instituted. We described how Smelser characterized the process of changing the old as "differentiation," and instituting the new as "integration." These are central ideas, and I should like to show their power in an anthropological context.

Empirical studies of modernization teach us a good deal about traditional societies that was not obvious before they began to modernize.[19] For example, a rather common characteristic of primitive and peasant agricultural economies was their material insecurity, the sporadic experience of famine or months of hunger due to the failure of the principal food staple relied upon (see the essays in this volume by Sahlins, Allan, Wharton, and Epstein). The simple technology employed had two principal consequences. One was low average productivity; the other was

---

[19] There are many examples from our own social and economic history of how a changed situation brings to light features of the earlier condition which were insufficiently appreciated. The structure of nineteenth-century capitalism appeared different to us when it changed in the 1930s and 1940s with increasing government participation in response to depression, Keynesian analysis, and economic planning during World War II. The traditional position of Negroes in U.S. life has been made very clear to us in the fifteen years since the Supreme Court decision on school integration and the momentous episodes of civil strife, agitation for reform, and growing integration of Negroes into all areas of national life.

its inability to compensate for or control plant disease, insects, soil deficiencies, or adverse weather. Too little rain, too many insects, a blighting plant disease or a decimating animal disease, meant hunger.[20] The village or tribal segment was relatively isolated economically, that is, frequently it had no access to markets. In pre-colonial times, frequently there was physical isolation as well due to tribal enmities and the consequent risks of travel (see the essay by Douglas). It is important to note that the condition of material insecurity—the threat of sporadic famine—was the combined result of different forces working in the same direction: poor technology, physical isolation, absence of market organization, and the absence of real alternatives to secure material livelihood aside from the few agricultural production lines or hunting and gathering activities in the home community.

So too with the traditional practices employed to mitigate the ever-present threat of starvation; they too are several and of different sorts. One is the people's minute knowledge of its natural environment (which plants are edible, the habits of game animals, etc.). Another is the practice of planting too much of the preferred staple crop in the hope that if bad weather or insects decimate the crop a sufficient amount will be harvestable to stave off hunger. Another is to plant a less preferred crop which is eaten only if the preferred crop fails. But social and cultural contrivance are also used to cope with material uncertainty: the use of magic and ritual to induce agricultural success (Malinowski 1935); and, of course, several sharing devices based upon reciprocal social relationships. If a single household suffers disaster while the local community is not similarly afflicted, it receives gifts from kin, friends, neighbors, lineage heads, chiefs. If the local community is similarly afflicted, it calls upon distant kin, allies, and gift-friends for emergency support; and if these fail or are unavailable, it resorts to money-lenders and debt-bondage, or infanticide, abortion, or migration.

To say that traditional primitive and peasant economies were economically self-sufficient is to say they were not integrated into any larger economy outside the local community; there were

---

[20] We see immediately that aside from yielding greater productivity, modern technology and applied science also confer much greater material *security and certainty* in their ability to counteract fluctuations in weather and the depredation of insects and plant disease.

external trade transactions, but, with rare exceptions, they were sporadic and not relied upon for basic livelihood. Subsistence producers depend for livelihood on *local* ecology, *local* technology, and *local* social organization.

Economic development and cultural modernization comprise activities and institutions which radically change local dependence and local self-sufficiency. The interlocking characteristics of traditional economies produce local social security systems, turned inward, so to speak. Commercialization and cash earning, literacy and education, and new technology turn them outward. Material income and security come to depend on transactions and institutions outside the village. Above all, modern activities create new income alternatives, and modern technology allows control over the physical environment. Irrigation equipment creates its own rainy season.

> At primitive levels, man has to struggle for subsistence. With great drudgery he succeeds in wresting from the soil barely enough to keep himself alive. Every year he passes through a starvation period for several months, because the year's crop barely lasts out until the next harvest. Regularly he is visited by famine, plague or pestilence. Half his children die before reaching the age of ten, and at forty his wife is wrinkled and old. Economic growth enables him to escape from this servitude. Improved techniques yield more abundant and more varied food for less labor. Famine is banished, the infant mortality rate falls . . . the death rate [falls] . . . Cholera, smallpox, malaria, hookworm, yellow fever, plague, leprosy, and tuberculosis disappear altogether. Thus life itself is freed from some of nature's menaces (Lewis 1955:420, 421).

Modernization consists of displacing local dependence with external dependence on markets, and by so doing integrating the village community into the region, the nation, and through foreign trade transactions, the rest of the world. Almost all the principal innovations that comprise modernization reduce household dependence on the local village community, its physical environment and network of social relationships, and increase household dependence on local, national, and international market organization. From the viewpoint of individual persons, real alternatives and mobility, as well as real income, are increased with the new and diversified transactions.

What distinguishes post-colonial modernization from the changes which occurred in the pre-colonial and colonial periods is the establishment of the sovereign nation-state and its initiation of nation-wide development activities and institutions: principally widespread commercialization of production processes, the beginning of industrialization and the use of improved technology, and the inculcation of mass education and training. These are watershed changes for Africa and Asia, as indeed they were in the eighteenth and nineteenth centuries for Europe and Japan (see the essays by Sawyer and Smith). They are also mutually reinforcing changes that work in the same direction to change more or less self-sufficient village economies and societies into interacting sectors of national economy, culture, and polity. Integration means two-way transactional flows which create mutual dependence between villages and national markets and national government.[21] The structure of traditional village society becomes undermined because its traditional functions become displaced once superior economic and technological alternatives become available. Persons no longer have to rely on social relationships for daily livelihood or emergency support.

SUMMARY AND CONCLUSION

The systematic study of national economic development came into being only since the former colonies in Asia and Africa achieved their political independence, beginning with India in 1947.[22] The geographical scope of the subject is extraordinarily wide. It includes some eighty countries containing most of the

---

[21] "Integration" means several things all of which occur in the course of successful development. Its *economic* meaning is best stated in terms of the growth and diversification of purchase, sale, financial and capital transactions between village-based households and firms, and those based outside the village, in cities, the region, and the nation. Social overhead capital, such as roads, power facilities, and regional irrigation works, play an important implemental role in increasing and diversifying such transactions. So too do new institutional facilities, such as banks and agricultural experiment stations. "Integration" also has socio-political expressions, which consist of new political transactions, such as village participation in national elections, and growth in common cultural identity, as when regional and ethnic differences diminish with the national use of a common language, and national access to the same school system, newspapers, and radio programs.

[22] For theories of growth and development in the literature of classical and neo-classical economics, see Adelman (1961) and Robbins (1968).

world's population. The range of processes and problems entailed
in the structural transformation of these countries is also very
great. To say that all the social sciences have an interest in the
subject is an understatement. Economics, for example, contains
a dozen or more sub-fields many of which now have counterpart interests in the study of developing countries: economic
history (Rostow 1960; Gerschenkron 1962), international trade
(Chenery 1965; Levin 1960), national income accounting,
statistics, and econometrics (Deane 1953; Samuels 1963; Adelman and Morris 1967), agricultural economics (De Wilde et al.
1968; Mellor et al. 1968), are some examples. Others could be
added in economics and within other social sciences. The common focus of interest in Africa or Asia has also generated interdisciplinary research and programs of area studies.

The profound impact of development studies is felt beyond
the social science subjects in the universities on all the continents. An international civil service of development research,
planning, and project implementation is now also in being. The
Ford and Rockefeller Foundations, governments of the industrialized developed nations, agencies of the United Nations and the
World Bank, are very much engaged. The wide and deep concern with development comes from the pragmatic urgency for
income growth, which, in turn, requires the theoretical understanding of the transformation processes and sequences that comprise modernization. The developing countries need good policies
and planning. To formulate them they need good theory and
measurement.

Most social scientists, and economists in particular, are concerned with development from above—national, macro-develop-
ment—or with impersonal problems and sectors, such as capital
formation and foreign trade. These are necessary and important
concerns. Many fewer social scientists study development from
below—village community, or micro-development; traditionally,
only anthropologists, agricultural economists, and rural sociologists. Yet, some of the most intractable problems of development exist at the rural community level: how to increase agricultural productivity, village literacy, and vocational skills.

We know from European and Japanese history that pre-industrial economic structure and the early decades of modernization bear importantly on current structure and performance of
developed national economies (Rostow 1960; Smith 1959). So

too for developing village economies. Hacienda communities in Peru still reflect the Spanish Conquest four hundred years ago (see the articles by Wolf and Holmberg), and African communities, the coming of the Dutch and English three hundred years ago (see the article by Jaspan; also Schapera 1928; Hunter 1961).

Modernization is an historical subject because of the way in which sequential events in pre-colonial and colonial times shaped the present; and it is a subject for all the social sciences—and some of the physical sciences, (see Vayda 1969)—because of the way in which economic, political, and social forces interact in development and modernization (Adelman and Morris 1967; Dalton 1965c). What used to be almost the exclusive preserve of anthropologists a generation ago is now a field of wide professional interest to economists, sociologists, psychologists, and others, all over the world, in universities, governments, and research institutes. Recent anthropological studies of community change and development reflect the changes brought by the Colonial Revolution in their use of new fieldwork methods and new techniques of analysis. Anthropology will continue to figure prominently in micro-development studies, but theories of village development as well as policy formulation must now draw on all the social sciences.

A number of economists have written works bearing directly on socio-economic development at the local community level (and on the cultural and social aspects of national economic development). The work of Myrdal (1957:ch. 1–3), Hagen (1962), and Adelman and Morris (1967) in particular, is of wide application because it is concerned with the mutual interaction of economic and non-economic forces over long periods of time—the essence of development. In what must be the most imaginative departure from conventional economics ever attempted by an economist, Hagen employs psychoanalytical theory to trace out the inter-generational changes in personality formation necessary to produce persons of entrepreneurial initiative. With an utterly different approach, Adelman and Morris use the statistical technique of factor analysis to show the varying influence of social, cultural, and economic forces at different levels of national development.

Several economists have written on the problems of transforming subsistence agriculture and increasing agricultural productivity in underdeveloped areas (Yudelman 1964a; 1964b; Schultz 1964; Jones 1961; Fogg 1965; Hill 1963). Others consider the important question of how to widen the scope of conventional economics so as to bring formal analysis to bear on the special problems and processes of development (Seers 1963; Myint 1965; Hill 1966; Martin and Knapp 1967). Boeke (1953), of course, in his analysis of "dualism" was one of the first to point out how traditional primitive and peasant societies existed side by side with colonially implanted commercial production for export. Lewis (1954), in a classic article, showed how development proceeded in dualistic economies.

As with the anthropologists and economists, the sociologists, psychologists, and political scientists perceive the processes of transformation from their special viewpoints: Smelser (1958) has written on the social changes that accompanied the British Industrial Revolution, and the similar changes in the present-day transformations of underdeveloped areas (Smelser 1963, reprinted in this volume). The rural sociologists have extended their interests from Europe and America to the underdeveloped world (Rogers 1960; see especially his bibliography). The psychologist McClelland (1961) has started a special line of investigation with his work on achievement motivation. Apter (1960), a very perceptive political scientist, has written on the connections between traditional and modern political leadership in the new context of politically independent African states.

Economic anthropology considers the structure and performance of tribal and peasant village economies under pre-colonial, colonial, and post-colonial conditions. It differs from counterpart subjects in other social sciences, such as comparative economic systems, economic development, and industrial sociology, in several ways. Its principal focus of interest is the small economy of village or tribal segment; its predominant concern is with such communities outside of Western Europe and the United States, today's developing areas. The bulk of its literature consists of field-work studies of traditional systems, or their changing condition under European colonialism. Economic anthropologists have analyzed socio-economic organization more extensively than quantifiable economic performance, and they emphasize the systematic relationships between economy, ecology, culture, and society. Applied anthropology—action programs to initiate and implement community development projects—is a rapidly growing interest among anthropologists.

All these segments of economic anthropology—structure, performance, primitive, peasant, traditional, modernizing, theory, policy—have received relatively little systematic formulation. But the prospects for more intensive and extensive theoretical treatment are good because of the rapidly burgeoning interest in the subject, due primarily to the social science concern with development and modernization. The two branches of the subject, traditional and modernizing economies, are complementary: the more we learn about either, the more we can learn about the other.

Anthropologists in training who intend to specialize in economic anthropology should do a great deal of library research, particularly to read deeply in European and Asian economic history (e.g., Smith 1959), economic development (e.g., Adelman and Morris 1967), and comparative economic systems (e.g., Carr 1951; Myrdal 1960; Nove 1962). If economic anthropologists are to pursue comparative analysis, then studying historical and contemporary economies becomes important. The utility of doing so is obvious when one considers topics such as slavery, feudalism, or peasantry (see the essays by Finley, Goody, and Polanyi). So too with money, markets, external trade, land tenure, and, indeed, many others within both branches of economic anthropology.

India alone has half a million village communities, and Africa probably another several hundred thousand. They vary enormously with regard to size of population, physical resource endowment, quality of technology, extent of commercialization, access to transport and to urban areas, access to education and health facilities, in basic social organization and culture, and in historical experiences shaping their present structures. There are people in New Guinea who had their first contact with Europeans only thirty years ago (Salisbury 1962), while others in India felt the impact of European commerce, culture, and administration three hundred years ago. A good deal of useful work is yet to be done in formulating analytical classifications and historical demarcations to cope with such diversity.

The more anthropologists are concerned with economic development, the more important measurement of economic performance becomes. Indeed, as commercial production, cash income, and modern technology displace subsistence production and traditional techniques, the more scope there is for using ordinary economic terms, concepts of measurement, and conventional economic analysis. One branch of economic anthropology will move toward the economist's fields of economic development and agricultural economics (Joy 1967a; 1967b). Such analysis would be facilitated if anthropologists in the field collected hard data series—statistical information on village structure and performance (see the statistical appendix to Epstein's second essay).

Tribal and village communities have special and tenacious problems of development which stem from their traditional condition of material insecurity: the sporadic threat of hunger due to reliance on one or two staple foodstuffs produced with technology of low quality under circumstances of relative economic isolation and uncontrolled physical environment. Much of traditional social organization may be regarded as a social security system to assure access to labor, land, and emergency support.

What an older generation of anthropologists called the tenacity of custom was in part due to the cultural and physical isolation of the communities studied; many had no firsthand knowledge of alternative ways of producing, especially when the larger regions of which they were a part were economically stagnant (see Foster 1965). But it was also due to the high risk of adopting innovations which might fail and cause hunger. To innovate, moreover, might require new activities, new skills, new outlays of time and effort, movement outside the community, which made it impossible to fulfill obligations to kin, neighbors, community, or chief, those upon whom one traditionally relied for material security.

Modernization and development inevitably restructure the economy and society of village communities because the principal innovations that comprise modernization are new economic, cultural, and political transactions, activities, and institutions which connect the village to the outside world, thereby undoing local socio-economic dependence, autonomy, and isolation. What anthropologists sometimes call the increase in scale that accompanies modernization means new mobility and alternatives; new activities and occupations; new transactional flows. These integrate local communities with the nation, economically, and create a new common cultural identity—shared values and attitudes— as well as new equipment and diversified lines of production.

Village development involves complex processes of world-wide scope taking place over long periods of time. The need for anthropologists and other social scientists to confront these special difficulties has brought forth new approaches, interdisciplinary sophistication, and some fruitful results. It is to be hoped that an increasing number of the young social scientists emerging from university training with a specialist's interest in the subject will be New Men, combining the several talents necessary. They should be fieldworkers and historians, anthropological economists and economic anthropologists, theoreticians and practitioners. The readings contained in this volume were chosen with this hope in mind.

Part I | PRIMITIVE AND PEASANT ECONOMIES:
BEFORE MODERNIZATION

[In the Solomon Islands] there are three main interests in life, women, pigs, and money, but money comes last, not first.

A. H. Quiggin

1 PREFACE, TO THE PRIMITIVE ECONOMICS OF THE NEW ZEALAND MAORI [1929]

R. H. Tawney

THE FOLLOWING PAGES contain an account by a young New Zealand scholar of the social and economic organisation of the Maori people, before that organisation was transformed by contact with Western civilisation—of its class structure, its land system, its industry, its methods of co-operative labour, exchange, and distribution, and of the psychological foundations upon which the fabric of its social arrangements rested. In spite of the work of pioneers like Professor Hobhouse, Dr Rivers, and Professor Malinowski, English books on the economic institutions of primitive communities are few, and books written with the imaginative insight shown by Dr Raymond Firth are fewer still. A society, like an individual, reveals the secrets of its inner life only to those who bring to its study not merely scientific curiosity and a mastery of technique, but respect and affection. Of Dr Firth's technical qualifications it would be presumptuous for a layman to speak. But he was evidently found in the life of the race whom he has studied a quality which not only interested him as a sociologist, but moved, and even charmed him, as a man. So his book is charming and illuminating even to one who is unversed in the controversies discussed in its opening chapter. It is a picture of a society which, within the boundaries drawn by natural resources and its own inherent limitations, had achieved a kind of simple equilibrium—a culture primitive, indeed, but yet not wholly immature, not wholly incompatible with a widespread sense of personal dignity and of collective satisfaction. What are called primitive peoples are not necessarily, it appears, uncivilised. Some of them, of whom the

SOURCE: R. H. Tawney, "Preface," pages xiii–xvii, in Raymond Firth, *Primitive Economics of the New Zealand Maori*, Routledge, 1929. Reprinted by permission of the publisher.

Maori were one, are merely peoples with a different kind of civilisation.

If the only result of economic anthropology were to establish that fact, its practical importance would, nevertheless, be considerable. Though the injury caused by the application to non-European societies of the legal and economic conceptions of Western civilisation is now a commonplace, there are parts of the world in which it continues almost unabated, with results which, in the long run, are likely to be as disastrous to those who inflict it as to those on whom it is inflicted. It is the disposition of mankind, especially when it is driven by the compulsion of strong economic interests, to condemn what it does not understand, and the natural result of a failure to grasp the economic psychology of races which have not been through the peculiar discipline of modern industrial societies is to cause those who have to bring against them charges of precisely the same kind as were brought against the working classes in Europe itself in the age when that discipline was not yet firmly established—to lead them to denounce "the natives" as idle, thriftless, self-indulgent, and capable of being rendered serviceable only by judicious turns of the economic screw. Such charges are, doubtless, often justified. But communities survive because of their virtues, not because of their failings, and the removal of the failings depends upon an appreciation of the virtues which is possible only to those who have penetrated the complex of beliefs, traditions, and habits which finds expression in both. The layman cannot penetrate it unaided, for he does not command the resources of comparative investigation which are necessary if the riddle is to be read. If he is wise, therefore, if he desires to understand, and not merely to dominate and use, he will consult an anthropologist who has studied the economic institutions of primitive peoples. And the anthropologist, as Dr Firth's book shows, can supply him with material and methods of interpretation, in the light of which those institutions, instead of appearing an impenetrable jungle of follies and vices, are seen to possess a significance from which he must start in his effort to improve them, if he feels called upon to attempt their improvement.

It is not only, however, its practical utility to those in contact with the economic life of primitive peoples which gives its value to a study such as that of Dr Firth. There is also the contribution which anthropology brings to economic science, and the influence which, as a consequence, it may exercise upon thought concerning the social problems and economic issues of regions less remote from Europe than Polynesia. Inference may be as exact and dispassionate as logic can make it, but it is a wise philosopher who knows the source of his own premises. Like other sciences, economic science tends normally to take for granted the assumptions from which it starts, for, unless it did so, it would find it difficult to start at all. These assumptions, however, have not always been submitted to a very rigorous criticism. They are apt to reflect the views as to the manner in which man may be expected to behave that happen to be accepted, or rather—for they are often somewhat belated—to have been accepted, by a particular society at a particular moment; and, while the economist is aware that they are provisional and abstract, the publicist who popularises him not seldom treats them as established truths, which it is irrational, or even immoral, to question. Thus there develops a kind of economic fundamentalism, which, like religious fundamentalism, preserves itself from mental disturbance by wearing blinkers, and is sometimes indignant at the discoveries reported and scepticisms hinted by those who allow their eyes to rove over a wider field. It regards the institutions and habits of thought of its own age and civilisation as in some peculiar sense natural to man, dignifies with the majestic name of economic laws the generalisations which describe the conduct of those who conform to its prejudices, and dismiss as contrary to human nature the suggestion that such conduct might be other than it is.

Economic fundamentalism of this kind is less tyrannous than it was, but, outside the ranks of economists themselves, it is still a power. The assumption that effort is always a "cost", and that the "motive" which causes the cost to be incurred is the desire of the individual to "satisfy his wants"; the crude antithesis between "self-interest", which is supposed to be all-powerful, and "altruism", which is supposed to be weak; the common assertion that no one will work except under the spur of immediate economic necessity, and the whole elaborate mythology of rewards and penalties which Dr Burns, in his interesting book on *Industry and Civilisation,* describes as derived from an obsolete psychology—"the psychology of the individual seeker after pleasure, whose first mental activities are regarded as the reception of certain stimuli"—how familiar it all is in current discussions of industrial policy! And how fantastic and remote from human realities! Dr Firth is justified in suggesting that the wealth of new evidence offered by anthropology as to the organisation and psychology of races on a different plane of economic civilisation contains suggestions which even the student interested primarily in the issues presented by more advanced societies cannot afford to regard with indifference.

To understand our own problems, it is sometimes expedient to stand outside them, in a world with different standards and presuppositions. Civilised peoples are disposed, perhaps, both to underestimate the part played by economic rationalism in primitive society, and to exaggerate that which it plays in their own. Studies such as that contained in the following pages, by correcting the first error, help indirectly to remove the second. Not that Dr Firth restores to Polynesia the economic man who has been expelled from the textbooks of Europe. On the contrary, the whole tendency of his book is to emphasise—it is not only in dealing with the Maori that the emphasis is appropriate—how immensely more complex than is often supposed are the forces that produce the activities commonly described as economic. The life of the Maori, he insists, cannot be explained on the assumption that economic interests and needs have created their social structure. Though modified by them, that structure had biological and social foundations of its own, which fixed the channels along which economic effort should flow and determined the form which it should assume. The economic activities of the Maori were developed, in short, within a framework set by the family, the tribe, the class system, the institution of property, the powers and duties of chiefs. To isolate it from these social institutions is to give a quite abstract and misleading picture even of the economic aspects of Maori society.

It was a society, as Dr Firth points out, which was very far from being the victim of the economic helplessness and squalor that are sometimes supposed to be the lot of all primitive communities. Nor, again, was it relieved by the wealth of its natural endowments from the necessity of strenuous labour. It was compelled by its environment to work, and it worked, on the whole, with success. Not only did it attain a high excellence in the individual craftsmanship of the weaver and the carver, but it carried out considerable undertakings, for example in building, which demanded leadership and organisation. What were the forces which made possible the comparatively high standard of life which it attained? They were partly economic, in the narrowest and most limited sense of the term: food must be secured, and birds must be snared and fish caught in order to provide it. But the economic motive was intertwined with motives which were social and religious, and if the Maori, like Europeans, worked in order to satisfy hunger, the manner in which he worked and the co-operation with his fellows on which the result of his work depended, were determined less by his own expectation of the gain to be secured than by the pressure of the community to which he belonged. "Social motives", writes Dr Firth, "formed the great spur to individual action." By "social motives" he means, as he explains, the influence of tradition, of religious sanctions, of emulation and the desire for prestige, of pride in achievement and pleasure in work, of the public condemnation of idleness and public recognition of useful achievement. Thus effort directed to economic ends derived its vigour and achieved its success partly, he seems to suggest, from the fact that, at the moment when it was being undertaken, the considerations impressed on the minds of participants were not purely, or even primarily, economic. It was at once intensified and lightened by the social ritual surrounding it, and by the emotions which that ritual evoked.

It was the fashion among some writers in the eighteenth century to use pictures of the imaginary felicity of primitive races as a vehicle for criticisms upon contemporary European civilisation. It was the fashion among some writers in the nineteenth to describe such races as separated from civilised man by an impassable gulf. Dr Firth, as becomes a scientist, is as free from the one illusion as from the other. The people whom he describes with so much sympathy, yet with so much realism, appear, after all, to have been neither noble savages nor inhuman brutes, but men; and, if their differences from man as he is known to the Western world of to-day are significant and instructive, it is partly, at least, because in so much they are seen to have resembled him. Of those who reveal new affinities between different branches of the human family we are all the debtors. One who has been charmed and enlightened by Dr Firth's book may be allowed to confess that the sentiment uppermost in his mind, as he lays it down, is the desire that an equally gifted Maori anthropologist should write an equally faithful account of the people of Great Britain.

2 TRIBAL ECONOMICS

Marshall Sahlins

ALTHOUGH CONCERNED with "economics," the present chapter discusses families as much as production; where it speaks of exchange it is preoccupied with kinship, and when it deals with consumption it is all about chiefs. Something more is involved than the simple point that economics is functionally related to the social and political arrangements of tribal societies. Economics is not distinguishable from these arrangements. The economy is organized by just such generalized institutions as families and lineages—"embedded" in them, as the economic historian says (Polanyi 1957a; 1957b).

An exchange of goods appears as a momentary episode in a continuous social relation. The terms of the exchange are governed by the relation of the parties to it. Different relationships, different terms. What are in the conventional wisdom of economic science "exogenous" or "noneconomic" factors, such as kinship and politics, are in the tribal reality the very organization of the economic process. Anthropological economics cannot conceive them as external, impinging upon "the economy" from somewhere outside it. They *are* the economy, essential elements of the economic calculus and of any proper analysis of it. The matter is generally as Evans-Pritchard said of the Nuer: "One cannot treat Nuer economic relations by themselves, for they always form part of direct social relations of a general kind" (Evans-Pritchard 1940:90).

THE FAMILIAL MODE OF PRODUCTION

Thus in tribal societies the "mode of production"—taking the phrase to include relations of production as well as material

---

SOURCE: Marshall D. Sahlins, "Tribal Economics," chapter 5 in *Tribesmen*, copyright 1968. Reprinted by permission of the author and the publisher, Prentice-Hall, Inc., Englewood Cliffs, New Jersey. The excerpts reprinted here comprise two-thirds of the original chapter.

means—should be styled "domestic" or "familial," in light of
the strategic position assumed by individual households. The
family is to the tribal economy as the manor to the medieval
European economy, or the industrial corporation to modern capitalism: each of these is the central production-institution of its
time. Each, moreover, is a special way of producing, involving
a characteristic division of labor and type of technology, certain
property relations, definite objectives of production, and customary social and material relations with similar groups.

The domestic groups of tribal societies have not yet suffered
demotion to a mere consumption status. Nor is human labor
power detached from the family and, employed in an external
realm, made subject to an alien organization and purpose. Production is a domestic function. The family is *as such* directly
engaged in the economic process, and largely in control of it.
Its own inner relations, as between husband and wife, parent
and child, are relations of production. What goods the people
produce, as well as how their labor is allocated, are for the
most part domestic stipulations. The decisions are taken with a
view to domestic needs: production is geared to familial requirements.

I hasten to add that domestic groups are not self-sufficient,
although they often do produce most of what they consume.
Household production is not precisely described as "production for
use"; i.e., for direct consumption. Families may also produce
for exchange, thus indirectly getting what they need. Still, it is
"what they need" that governs output, not how much profit
they can make. The interest in exchange remains a consumer
interest, not a capitalist one. Perhaps the best phrase is "production for provisioning."

It would be wrong, too, to suppose that the family is necessarily a self-contained work group. Its members frequently co-
operate with individuals of other households, and some tasks may
be undertaken collectively at higher levels, as by lineage or
village groups. "Familial mode of production" is not synonymous
with "familial production." It is the regulation of production
which is at issue, and its orientation or purpose. Production
is principally organized by and for families, if it is not always
carried on as a domestic activity.

The sovereignty of domestic groups in the domain of production rests on this: that they are constituted, equipped, entitled,

and empowered to determine and fashion the societal output. Families are *constituted* for production primarily by the sexual division of labor, the sole full-time specialization in the run of primitive societies. Complementary and nearly exhaustive of society's tasks, a man's work together with a woman's can provide most of the customary Good Things. Families are *equipped* to govern production by possession of the necessary tools and skills; they generally hold the everyday technical means. This control is consistent with a certain simplicity of the means, one might say a certain democracy of technology: implements that are easily made and widely available; technical skills that are common, public knowledge; uncomplicated tools that can be wielded by individuals or small groups; and productive processes that are often unitary, such that the same interested party can carry through the whole job from extraction of the natural resource to completion of the consumable product. Finally, the family is *entitled* and *empowered* to act autonomously by its access to resources of production. Not that it is the exclusive private owner of farmlands, pastures, and other natural resources. More commonly these are held by larger corporate groups, such as lineages or villages, and the family's rights are contingent on its membership in the proprietary group. The family has *usufructuary privilege*—including control of the manner of use of its share, and of disposition of the product. Rather than an impediment to family enjoyment, the investment of ownership in a larger group gives member families something of an inalienable guarantee of livelihood. No household is in the normal course excluded from direct access to the means of its own survival, any more than it is excluded from participation in the greater social structure. No expropriated class of landless paupers is characteristic of tribal societies. If expropriation occurs, it is by way of accident—as a cruel fortune of war, for instance—and not as a constituted condition of the economy. . . .

Organizing a vast division of labor, the competitive market economy [in contrast] embodies at least continuous action and reaction, systematic adjustments in production set off by variations in price. Nor is "glut" occasioned by a headlong rush of independent entrepreneurs toward profitable lines the recurrent weakness of primitive anarchy. If anything, the tribal crisis is underproduction—not enough goods forthcoming from the several domestic establishments, not enough for their own good, or for the good of society. . . . The small domestic labor force—in the first place, perhaps unfavorably constituted, with too many unproductive dependents relative to productive workers—is often sorely beset. Its working adults are vulnerable to incapacitating injury, disease, and an early death, and the women to an occasional pregnancy. These handicaps, or even slight disadvantages in luck or skill, translate themselves into serious food shortages. If left to "go it alone," the household economy proves inadequate: some families at any given time, and any given family at some times, can probably look forward to the prospect of an empty granary.

Contributing to this dismal outlook is another factor, the importance of which cannot be exaggerated: the economy is not organized for sustained production even in normal times. A domestic mode of production is a mode of *domestic* production. Directed toward supplying the family with its customary stock of consumables, it has built-in limits on output, and no inherent propensity to evoke continuous work or surpassing wealth. In more familiar terms, incentive to produce a surplus is lacking. On the contrary, the domestic mode of production would inhibit surplus production. When no household need is in sight, or none that could not be met by some future effort, the normal tendency is to leave off working. Production ceases when the domestic quota is filled for the time being. The economic organization implies this definite ceiling on output—beyond that it is "a fetter on the means of production."

Here the classic distinction between "production for use" (i.e., provisioning) and "production for exchange" (i.e., profit) becomes meaningful. The competitive market is an eternal dynamo, perhaps not always in working order, but at least designed to generate intensive currents of output. On the producer's side, the incentive to profitable enlargement is continuous, as a matter of jungle survival. But perhaps most of us are more familiar with the push (and pull) on the consumer. The market makes available a dazzling array of products, good things in unlimited quantity and variety, each with its clarion price-tag call: "this is all it takes to have me." A man's reach is then inevitably beyond his grasp, for one never has enough to buy everything. Before the judgment of the market, the consumer stands condemned to *scarcity,* and so to a life sentence at hard labor. Nor is there any reprieve in acquiring things. To participate in a market economy is an inevitable tragedy: what began in inadequacy will end in

deprivation. For every acquisition is simultaneously a deprivation
—of something else that could have been had instead. To buy
one thing is to deny yourself another. . . .

The competitive market combines scarcity, demand, work, and
supply in a riotous turmoil of creation. Now let thoughts rest on
this serene contrast, derived from observation of the Indonesian
village economy, a peasant system to be sure but in the particulars
at issue not different from a tribal economy.

> Another respect in which an Eastern differs from a Western society
> is the fact that *needs are very limited*. This is connected with the
> limited development of exchange, with the fact that most people
> have to provide for themselves, that families have to be content
> with what they are able to produce themselves, so that needs
> necessarily have to remain modest in quantity and quality. Another
> consequence of this is that the economic motive does not work
> continuously. Therefore . . . economic activity is also intermittent.
> Western economy tends in a diametrically opposite direction, its
> starting point being the idea of limitless needs in comparison
> with which means are always limited, so that the economic subject
> must always, when, satisfying his wants, make a choice and impose
> limits on himself (Boeke 1953:39).

The constraints of the household economy are, however, overcome in tribal societies—or else the society is overcome. It is,
after all, a matter of survival. Families that do not support themselves are either supplied by others or go under. The need for
a public economy may be just as serious; that is, some means of
subsidizing and organizing such collective enterprises as irrigation
construction and such activities as religious ceremony and warfare. A society can expire for lack of these too, and the domestic
stranglehold on production bids fair to arrange just such an end—
were it not for counteracting institutions such as kinship, or
chieftainship.

The kinship nexus relegates economic anarchy to a contradiction
lurking in the background. Caught up with others in a community
of kinship, a family is hard-pressed to maintain the luxury of
domestic self-interest, especially when relatives next door haven't
enough to eat. If the familial mode of production generates
centripetal economic forces, kinship sets off centrifugal ones, pro-
pelling goods out of the household for remedial distribution to the
destitute. Urgent goods flow along kinship lines from the haves
to the have-nots. Nor does the "feedback" necessarily come in

the form of grateful reciprocation, but perhaps in additional
production by the donor, now saddled with the upkeep of others
as well as his own house. In other words, kinship responsibilities
may force effective producers to extend their output above and
beyond the call of domestic duty. More than an incentive to
charity, kinship gives the spur to productivity.

The organization of authority likewise stands against the organization of production. Power invades the humble home, sub-
verting familial economic autonomy and contending successfully
against domestic underproduction. The public economic role of
tribal authorities demands that they thus impose upon the underlying population. Big-men and chiefs are compelled to relieve
shortages among the people—just like ordinary kinsmen but even
more so, for the tribal leader is a paragon among kinsmen and
his concern for community welfare is a kind of centralization of
kinship morality. Besides bread, there are certain circuses. Here
local authorities play the impresario, putting on main community
events: the spectacular rituals, public works, ceremonious exchanges with other groups. "I think that throughout the world,"
Malinowski wrote, "we would find that the relations between
economics and politics are of the same type. The chief, everywhere, acts as a tribal banker, collecting food, storing it, and
protecting it, and then using it for the benefit of the whole
community" (Malinowski 1937:232).

To function in this capacity, a chief must apply pressure on the
household economies within his sphere, forcing them to raise their
production sights or summoning labor from them "for the benefit
of the whole community." Leadership is one of the great productive
forces. It acts to intensify familial production, to congeal by
political pressure a material surplus, and, in disposing of this
fund, to float the community as a going concern. Different systems of tribal authority, as we shall see, develop varying impacts
on the domestic economy, thus different coefficients of production
and surplus accumulation. Quite apart from technological improvements, political transformation can play the decisive role in
economic development. . . .

Regular, repetitive work, the "daily grind," is the American
plan. Here again tribal peoples differ from us notably. Their
labor is more episodic and diversified. It is in total less than ours.
It is also not so inhuman. In a household economy, as Boeke
says, the economic motive does not work continuously; therefore,

neither do people. There are after all two roads to satisfaction, to reducing the gap between means and ends: producing much or desiring little. Oriented toward providing a modest supply of consumables, the household economy takes the latter, Zen course. Their needs, we say, are limited. Economic activity therefore does not break into a galloping compulsion, goaded by an interminable sense of inadequacy (i.e., a "scarcity of means"). Work is instead intermittent, sporadic, discontinuous, ceasing for the moment when not required for the moment. To this ordinary irregularity a neolithic economy adds long periods of "seasonal unemployment" following the harvest, or at least a depressed level of activity implying a "concealed unemployment." . . .

Nor is tribal labor alienated labor. We have seen it is not alienated from the means of production or from the product. Indeed, the tribesman's relation to productive means and finished products often exceeds ownership as we understand it, moving beyond mundane possession to a mystic attachment. The land is a spiritual value, a beneficent Source—the home of the ancestors, "the plain of one's bones," Hawaiians say. And the things a man makes and habitually uses are expressions of himself, perhaps so imbued with his genius that their ultimate disposition can be only his own grave.

These mystical associations reflect another aspect of labor: that it is not alienated from man himself, detachable from his social being and transactable as so many units of depersonalized labor-power. A man works, produces, in his capacity as a social person, as a husband and father, brother and lineage mate, member of a clan, a village. Labor is not implemented apart from these existences, as if it were a different existence. "Worker" is not a status in itself, nor "labor" a true category of tribal economics. Said differently, work is organized by relations "noneconomic" in the conventional sense, belonging rather to the general organization of society. Work is an expression of pre-existing kin and community relations, the exercise of these relations. This remains true of arrangements that seem otherwise like hire, where a man engages to work for another. "The situation is phrased [by the Abelam of New Guinea] in terms of kinship obligation, 'she is my sister, therefore I prepare the sago with her,' and *not* in some such phrase as 'she will give me sago, therefore I help her'" (Kaberry 1940–41:351).

But then, a man is what he does, and what he does is what he is. Incapable of selling himself as independent of himself, a man is not by work detached from his existence as a dutiful kinsman, citizen of the community, and an intelligent being capable of art and joy. Work is not divorced from life. There is no "job," no time and place where one spends most of one's time not being oneself. Nor are work and life related as means to end (as they often are for us): the former a necessary evil tolerated for the sake of the latter, "living," which is something to do after business hours, on your *own* time, if you have the energy. The Industrial Revolution split work from life. The reintegration has not yet been achieved. In the interim, the loss of primitive human integration is a justifiable lament of romantic criticism, and the alienation of labor a penetrating cry of revolutionary pain:

> What, then, constitutes the alienation of labour? First, the fact that labour is *external* to the worker, i.e., it does not belong to his essential being; that in his work, therefore, he does not affirm himself but denies himself, does not feel content but unhappy, does not develop freely his physical and mental energy but fortifies his body and ruins his mind. The worker therefore only feels himself outside his work, and in his work he feels outside himself. He is at home when he is not working, and when he is working he is not at home. His labour is therefore not voluntary, but coerced; it is *forced labour*. It is therefore not the satisfaction of a need; it is merely a *means* to satisfy needs external to it. Its alien character emerges clearly in the fact that as soon as no physical or other compulsion exists, labour is shunned like the plague. . . . Lastly, the external character of labour for the worker appears in the fact that it is not his own, but someone else's, that it does not belong to him, that in it he belongs . . . to another. Just as in religion the spontaneous activity of the human imagination, of the human brain and the human heart, operates independently of the individual—that is, operates on him as an alien, divine or diabolical activity—in the same way the worker's activity is not his spontaneous activity. It belongs to another; it is the loss of his self (Marx 1961:72–73). . . .

EXCHANGE AND KINSHIP

Exchange in tribal societies is, like work, governed by "direct social relations of a general kind." It is instigated often as an expression of such relations, and constrained always by the kinship and community standing of the parties concerned. The greater part of tribal exchange, therefore, is like the lesser part of our own—in a class with the gift-giving and hospitality we practice with social intimates. Contaminated as they are by social considerations, these reciprocal gestures are conceived by us as "noneconomic," qualitatively different from the main run of proper exchange and confined to a sphere where whoever saw fit to do business on the principle of devil-take-the-hindmost would be cordially directed to go to the devil himself. But in the tribes, just as "labor" does not exist as a differentiated activity independent of the worker's other social capacities, so exchange does not exist apart from "noneconomic" relations. Better said, there is an economic aspect to every social relationship. Father-son, maternal uncle-nephew, chief-follower: each implies a mode of exchange of one kind or another, consistent in its material terms with its social terms. Thus, from a relative "you can get it wholesale," and, from a close relative, perhaps for free.

On a more abstract level: the tribal exchange scheme is constructed from the scheme of social segmentation. Each group in the segmentary hierarchy is in the perspective of its participants a sector of social relationships, more or less solidary and sociable —more in the inner spheres of home and community, progressively less as one proceeds toward the intertribal outer darkness. As I suggested in an earlier passage, each sector implies appropriate norms of reciprocity. Differences thus appear in the way people deal with each other, according to the way they are socially divided from each other. The tribal scheme of segmentation sets up a sectoral scheme of reciprocities.

But is this not poorly stated? Normally the term "reciprocity" does not admit of degrees. Yet ethnography will support us here. Reciprocity is not always a one-for-one exchange. There is, in fact, a complex continuum of variations in the directness and equivalence of exchange. The subtleties of reciprocal exchange appear especially when one concentrates singularly on the material transaction, leaving aside "reciprocity" in the sense of a broad social principle or moral norm of give-and-take. Observable at one end of the spectrum is assistance freely given, the small currency of everyday kinship, friendship, and neighborly relations, the "pure gift" Malinowski called it, regarding which an explicit demand for reciprocation would be as unthinkable as it is unsociable—although it would be equally bad form not to bestow similar casual favors in return, if and when it is possible.

Toward the middle of the continuum stand balanced exchanges, in which a fair and immediate trade is right behavior, as for example when kinsmen come from a distance seeking food and bearing gifts. And at the far end of the spectrum: self-interested seizure, appropriation by chicane or force requited only by an equal and opposite reaction on the principle of *lex talionis*— "negative reciprocity," Alvin Gouldner calls it (Gouldner 1960). Consider that the extremes are notably positive and negative in a moral sense, and the intervals between them not only so many gradations of material balance but of sociability. The distance between the poles of reciprocity is social distance. "Unto a stranger," says the Old Testament, "thou mayest lend upon usury; but unto thy brother thou shalt not lend upon usury." The same applies in the wilds of New Guinea: "A trader always cheats people. For this reason intra-regional trade is rather frowned upon while intertribal trade gives to the [Kapauku] businessman prestige as well as profit" (Pospisil 1958:127). Thorstein Veblen framed the common underlying principle. "Gain at the cost of other communities," he wrote, "particularly communities at a distance, and more especially such as are felt to be aliens, is not obnoxious to the standards of homebred use and wont."

In his book *The Hunters*, Professor Service defined the end points on the continuum of reciprocity—"generalized" and "negative" reciprocity—and also the mid-point—"balanced" reciprocity (Service 1966). In the interest of describing the sectoral economy of tribal societies, we briefly recapitulate this typology:

1. *Generalized reciprocity*. These transactions are at least putatively altruistic, on the lines of assistance given and, if possible and necessary, assistance returned. Aside from the "pure gifts" mentioned before, other concrete forms of generalized reciprocity appear in ethnographic accounts as "sharing," "hospitality," "token gifts," "mutual aid," and "generosity." Obligatory gifts to kinsmen and chiefs ("kinship dues" and "chiefly dues") as well as *noblesse oblige* are less sociable but, without stretching the point too much, in the same class.

At the extreme, say voluntary food-sharing among very close relatives—or for its logical value one might think of a mother suckling her child—the expectation of a direct material return is unseemly, at the most implicit. The social side of the relation overwhelms the material and in a way conceals it, as if it were of no account. Reckoning is simply not proper. Not that there is no obligation to reciprocate, but the expectation of reciprocity is left indefinite, unspecified as to time, quantity, and quality. As it works in practice, the time of reciprocation and the value of return gifts are not only conditional on what the donor gave, but also on what he needs and when, and likewise what the recipient can afford to give him and when. The obligation to reciprocate is diffuse: when necessary to the donor and/or possible for the recipient. The requital thus may be very soon, or then again, never. There are people—the widowed, the old, the impaired—who in the fullness of time remain incapable of helping themselves or others. Yet the obligations to them of close kin may not falter. A sustained one-way flow is a good pragmatic sign of generalized reciprocity. Failure to reciprocate, or to give just as much as was received, does not cause the original giver of things to stop: the goods move one way, in favor of the have-not, for a long time.

2. *Balanced reciprocity.* Direct exchange: the return is made straight off and is equivalent in value to the goods received. The perfect type of balanced reciprocity, a simultaneous exchange of identical things, is not only conceivable but ethnographically documented in certain marital transactions between bride's and groom's kinsmen, blood-brotherhood pacts, and peace agreements. More loosely, "balanced reciprocity" may be applied where goods of commensurate worth or utility should be given in return within a customary finite period or short run. Many of the "gift-exchanges" of which ethnographers write, as well as much of the "trade," "barter," and "buying" with "primitive money" belong in this class of reciprocity.

Balanced reciprocity is less "personal" than generalized reciprocity, so from our distorted vantage, "more economic." The people deal as parties of separate economic and social interests. The material aspect of the bargain is as important as the social, and there has to be some reckoning, more or less precise, because accounts have to be balanced. So the pragmatic test here is an inability to tolerate one-way flows: the relations between people are disrupted when one reneges, fails to make a *quid pro quo* within a limited time period—like the feeling a hostess gets when a fairly distant acquaintance she has invited once or twice to dinner doesn't "in all this time" invite her. Among close friends there would not be the same calculation.

3. *Negative reciprocity.* This is the attempt to get something for nothing: transactions opened and conducted toward net utilitarian advantage. In other words, what we might consider sound business principles. It appears on the ethnographic record occasionally as

"bargaining" or "haggling," or even in more unsociable forms as "gambling," "chicanery," "theft," and other varieties of seizure. The participants in all instances confront each other not merely as distinct but opposed interests, each looking to maximize his position at the other's expense. Bargaining with an eye to the main chance is one of the more sociable forms. From this, negative reciprocity ranges through various degrees of cunning, guile, stealth, and violence to the finesse of a well-conducted horse raid. Like generalized reciprocity, the "reciprocation" is conditional again, but in an opposite way: contingent on mustering enough countervailing pressure or guile to serve or, better, enhance one's own interests.

It is a long way from a suckling child to a Plains Indian horse-raid. But the exchanges of even a single tribal society can grade into each other along the whole span. Not, however, in a random way. After all, one suckles one's own child and steals horses from some other outfit. The disposition to practice one or another mode of reciprocity is sectorally organized. It is close kin who are inclined to share, to enter into generalized reciprocity, and distant and non-kin who trade and horse-trade. The need to strike a balance becomes compulsory in proportion to kinship distance, lest relations break off altogether, for with distance and separation of interests there can be little tolerance for gain and loss, even as there is little inclination to extend oneself on another's behalf. As far as non-kinsmen are concerned—those "other people" who are perhaps not even "people"—no quarter need be given and none is asked; but let the buyer beware.

The play of sectoral distinctions on reciprocity is complicated by the influence of spatial distance on measures of "kinship distance." Close kinsmen usually live nearby and distant kinsmen far away, because kinsmen who live nearby are reckoned close in a sociological sense whereas those who live at a distance are distant kinsmen. The rule is subject to several exceptions; *e.g.,* fellow-clansmen or genealogically close relatives who happen to reside in other places. These may be treated economically as if in a nearer social sphere. Otherwise, reciprocity marches in character with segmentary distance.

Probably all this has been easy to understand—because in fact it is perfectly applicable to our own society. It is only more significant in tribal society. Partly because kinship is more significant there. Even the category "non-kinsman" is defined by kinship, that is, as the logical boundary of the class. Among ourselves, non-kinsman is usually also a positive status relation of some kind: doctor-patient, policeman-citizen, classmates, professional colleagues, etc. But for them non-kinsman is ordinarily the negation of community or tribalism—thus often synonymous with "stranger" and "enemy." The economic relation is accordingly a simple negation of kinship reciprocities; other institutional norms need not be invoked.

For a general appreciation, then, of the play of reciprocity among tribesmen, we superimpose the society's sectoral plan on the reciprocity continuum (Fig. 1). The relations of each social sphere are more solidary than relations of the next, more peripheral sector. Reciprocity thus tends toward balance and chicane in proportion to sectoral distance. In each sector, certain modes of exchange are dominant or characteristic. Generalized reciprocity prevails in the narrower spheres and plays out in the wider; balanced reciprocity is characteristic of intermediate segmentary relations; negative reciprocity is the mode of peripheral, especially inter-tribal, exchange.

This profile of exchange is purely hypothetical. Incorporated within the particular segmentary structures of particular societies, the spectrum of reciprocities is variously modified. To adjust our standardized conception to the variations posed by real societies, it will be necessary to move the balanced reciprocity "mid-point" inward in some cases, outward in others, reflecting narrower or wider fields of generalized exchange. Indeed, just such pulsations of generosity may materialize within the same tribe over a period of time and changing circumstance. Beset by declining food supplies, it is common for tribesmen (and not only tribesmen) to meet the threat by a double-barreled intensification of community solidarity and economic cooperation. People help each other out as they can and, during the shortage, generalized reciprocity is stretched beyond its normal social sphere. Yet, if the shortage proves prolonged and severe, the structure of solidarities may prove unable to bear the strain: in the final crisis households reassert their self-interest, and people who had shared food through the first stages of disaster display now indifference to each others' plight, if they do not hasten a mutual downfall by guile, haggle, and theft.

Even as a normal rule, different societies draw the line on helpful sharing at different points. Some peoples, we are tempted to say, are selfish, willing perhaps to render assistance to a few

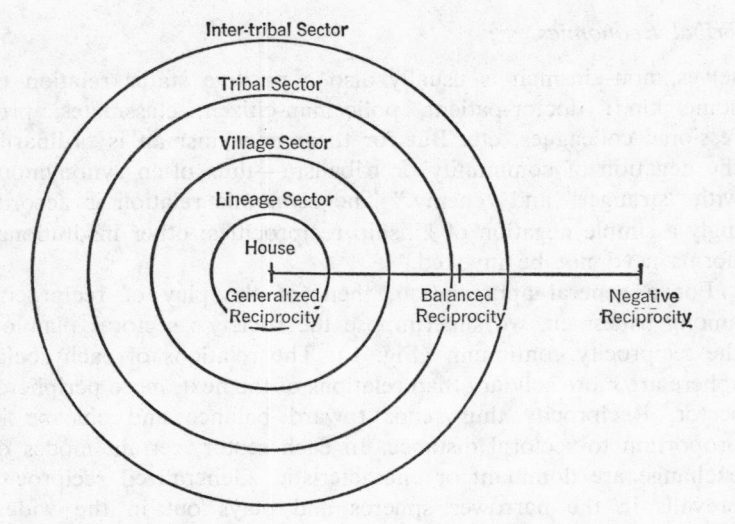

Figure 1   Reciprocity and kinship-residential sectors.

intimates while reluctant to make even a *quid pro quo* with anyone else, including kinsmen of nearby places. Said in sociology,
the segmentary system develops marked cleavages at lower levels,
such that small local groups of kinsmen, highly solidary within,
maintain a posture of sustained hostility toward all others. The
people's selfishness, which is to say, the limited compass of
generalized reciprocity, reflects then their splintered social condition. On the other hand, inter-tribal symbiosis involving regular
exchange of important specialized products may inhibit the propensity to "gain at the cost of communities at a distance—especially such as are felt to be aliens," and instead extend fair
dealing (balanced reciprocity) into peripheral zones. . . .

POLITICAL ECONOMY

Differences of rank, as much as distances of kinship, suppose
an economic relation and an appropriate mode of exchange. Not
the least among nobility's privileges is the economic one, the
lord's due; nor is *noblesse oblige* the least of obligations. Thus
the dues and duties fall on both sides of a relation of rank: both
high and low have their claims on each other. . . .

The tribal leader's claims on his followers and theirs on him are inter-dependent. A chief's demand for goods and services in turn obligates him, opens him to requests from those who answer his. Conversely, the chief's assistance to his people is his lien on them. In a word, the economic relation between mighty and lowly is reciprocal. And it is in the genre of generalized reciprocity, phrased as assistance with the return left indefinite, but tempered often by power, for goods are in truth *yielded* to people in authority and their favors may have to be humbly *solicited*. It seems good sociology if bad punning to say the mode of exchange is "akin" to generalized reciprocity, with the chief acting in a capacity of superior kinsman—the "father of his people." On the other hand, a moderate exposure to Westerners may put the people in mind of another institution, the self-same as occurred to Malinowski when he described the chief as "a tribal banker": thus, the Solomon islander explained to the missionary that the chief's store of wealth is "the 'panga,' the 'bank' of the village because it is drawn on for communal purposes such as feasts or the payments of blood money" (Ivers 1927:32).

The "economic basis" of tribal politics is chiefly generosity, at one stroke an act of positive morality and a laying of indebtedness upon the underlying population. Or, to take a more complete view, the political order is underwritten by a centralized circulation of goods, flowing toward the top of the social pyramid and down again, with each presentation not only implying a relation of rank but, as a generalized gift not directly requited, compelling a loyalty. . . .

Getting a faction together is the key. Any ambitious man who can gather a following can inaugurate a societal career. The up-and-coming Melanesian big-man depends initially on a small core of followers, mainly his own household and nearest relatives. Upon these people he can prevail economically: he capitalizes in the beginning on kinship dues and by finessing the relations of generalized reciprocity appropriate among close kinsmen. At an early phase, a big-man will seek to enlarge his own household, especially by getting more wives. The more wives he has, the more pigs. (The connection between wives and pigs is functional, not identical: with more women gardening there will be more pig-feed and more swine-herds.) Each new marriage also creates another set of affinal relatives from whom he can exact support.

But a leader's career goes into "take-off" when he is able to bring other men and their households into his faction, harnessing their production to his ambition. Usually this is done by helping them in some big way, as to put them forever in his debt. Paying bridewealth on behalf of a young man is a common technique.

Malinowski had a felicitous phrase for what the big-man is doing: amassing a "fund of power." A big-man is one who uses and creates social relations that give him leverage on others' production and the ability to siphon off an excess product. He transcends the fragmented household economy and, impelled by his own ambition, promotes society's interests. For in the public distribution of his funds of power, the big-man initiates a combination of groups and an organization of functions quite beyond ordinary ken. The context of the giveaway may be a religious ceremony, the construction of a local clubhouse, a ritual exchange between groups or a dance. These testaments to a big-man's status happen to bring together people from all around: the big-man fashions supralocal organization. In tribes normally segmented into small independent groups, he at last temporarily widens the sphere of economics, politics, and ceremony. Yet always this greater societal organization depends on the lesser factional organization, and especially it depends on the ceilings on economic mobilization set by relations between big-men and their subordinates. . . .

The accumulation of funds of power and their redistribution was the underpinning of Polynesian politics. I use Polynesian examples here because the descriptions are good and I am familiar with them, but in respect of their redistributive activities Polynesian chiefs are at most exemplary and not at all unique. With a few minor modifications, the following eighteenth-century account of the Creek Indians (Southeast United States) could be interpolated in a book on the Maori of New Zealand:

> [When] all the grain is ripe, the whole town again assemble, and every man carries off the fruits of his labour, from the part [of the town field] first allotted to him, which he deposits in his own granary. . . . But previous to their carrying off their crops from the field, there is a large crib or granary, erected in the plantation, which is called the king's crib; and to this each family carries and deposits a certain quantity, according to his [*sic*] ability or inclination, or none at all if he so chooses, this in appearance seems

a tribute or revenue to the mico [chief], but in fact is designed for another purpose, i.e. that of a public treasury [v. Malinowski], supplied by a few and voluntary contributions, and to which every citizen has the right of free and equal access, when his own private stores are consumed, to serve as a surplus to fly to for succour, to assist neighboring towns whose crops have failed, accommodate strangers, or travellers, afford provisions or supplies, when they go forth on hostile expeditions, and for all other exigencies of the state; and this treasure is at the disposal of the king or mico; which is surely a royal attribute to have an exclusive right and ability in a community to distribute comfort and blessings to the necessitous (Bartram 1958:326).

In Polynesia, uses of the chiefly fund were quite similar. Chiefs provided lavish entertainments for visiting dignitaries and succored the local people in times of need. Chiefs subsidized craft production, initiated major technical works, such as irrigation projects, built temples, sponsored ceremonies, and organized support for military campaigns. . . .

Like Melanesian big-man systems, the development of Polynesian chiefdoms was eventually short-circuited by an overload on the relation of chiefs to people. Still the Polynesian cut-off point was higher. Different structures have different coefficients of economic productivity and political power, as well as different limits. The comparative success of chieftainship comes of its greater impact on the household economy, its more effective mobilization of domestic production. And the limits of chieftainship are the limits of primitive society itself. Where kinship is king, the king is in the last analysis only kinsman, and something less than royal. The same bonds that link a chief to the underlying population and give him his authority, in the end tie his hands.

This parochial comparison of Pacific Island societies can be put to the service of another general point: chiefdom formation alters the social profile of exchange, the incidence of different modes of reciprocity, just as segmentary tribes introduce changes in this respect by comparison with hunting bands.

In the isolated camps of marginal food collectors, the uncertainties of the chase are mitigated by a collective emphasis on share and share alike. "Their culture insists that they share with each other, and it has never happened that a Bushman failed to share objects, food or water with other members of his band, for without very rigid co-operation Bushmen could not

survive the famines and droughts the Kalahari offers them"
(Thomas 1959:22; see also, Service 1966). This demand of co-
operation, combined with but few opportunities of direct trade
with outsiders, puts generalized reciprocity in the position of
the dominant mode of exchange.

By contrast, the social horizons of tribesmen are usually broader,
the range of their transactions wider, and the balanced reciprocity enjoined in the world beyond competes now with homebred
generosity for importance in the tribal scheme of things. To the
local organization of band society the segmentary tribe adds new
dimensions of peripheral structure, and to local exchange new
economic relations in the intercommunity and inter-tribal sectors.
Development takes place precisely in the areas where balanced
exchange is appropriate, whether in pursuit of goods from a
distance or of peace and alliance with other communities. By
comparison with bands, segmentary tribes show an increase,
greater or less in different circumstances, in the proportion of
balanced to generalized exchange. In the line of this development, perhaps the most complete expression of it, is the appearance of "primitive money" in some tribal regions; e.g., the
shell currencies of Melanesia and aboriginal California. Functioning as customary standards of equivalence and media of
exchange, these monies both reflect and facilitate a heavy balanced traffic.[1] Not all segmentary tribes have money, but tribes
that have money are typically segmentary tribes. Primitive money
is rare or nonexistent in the less developed band economies.
And also in the more developed chiefdoms—however much
that goes against our own views of economic progress.

But in the chiefdom the internal economy regains predominance over the external, partly a process of sheer displacement.
The progression from segmentary tribe to chiefdom is in one
sense a transformation of external into internal relations, as adjacent local groups are integrated under the aegis of powerful
chiefs and (often) extensive descent groups. Balanced reciprocity

---

[1] They are especially useful where seasonal differences in production
render difficult the direct exchange of local commodities. But it should be
cautioned I use "primitive money" in a restricted sense: goods primarily of
exchange-value rather than inherent use-value and employed (in peripheral
sectors) as means of exchange against a variety of other goods—whatever
else their purpose. For a broader conception of "money" and its distribution, see Dalton (1965a).

falls off in consequence. Its incidence is restricted, first, by the "internalization" of exchange relationships; the drawing-together of people in major political and descent associations tend to generalize reciprocity between them. Second, it is restricted by the prevalence of rank. Rank becomes a factor in the calculus of almost every transaction, imposing elements of imbalance out of considerations of status. Third and most significant is the centralization of exchange in a public economy. Reciprocities focus on the ruling chiefs, to whom all must give their due and from whom flow "comforts and blessings to the necessitous." Thus integrated politically, reciprocity changes in quality. It re-appears in a higher form, the collective pooling and reallocation of goods by powers-that-be, a process deserving its own name— *redistribution.*

Malinowski saw in the chief's accumulation and disbursement of goods, ". . . the prototype of the public finance system and the organization of State treasuries of to-day." The prototype, however, has its own prototypes, not only in the chiefdom itself but at all stages of primitive society. Redistribution—in this form it is also known as "pooling" and "householding"—is what families do everywhere, their individual members contributing to the common hearth and receiving therefrom a due share. It is ordinary practice as well in connection with cooperative food production, such as impounding buffalo in the northern Plains or net fishing in a Polynesian lagoon, where the catch is collected and then divided among all participants. Chiefly redistribution must derive some of its political efficacy by analogy with these more humble forms, but even more from the fact that this integration of reciprocities changes the whole sociology of exchange. In its simpler form, reciprocity is a *between* relation, the action and response of two parties. Although the exchange may establish harmony between them, the differentiation of parties, the distinction of interests, is here inescapable. But where reciprocity separates, redistribution combines. Redistribution is a *within* relation, the collective action of a group, and of a group, moreover, with a social center where goods are concentrated and thence flow outward. Redistribution is chieftainship said in economics.

3 LELE ECONOMY COMPARED WITH THE BUSHONG

A STUDY OF ECONOMIC BACKWARDNESS

Mary Douglas

THE LELE[1] and the Bushong[2] are separated only by the Kasai River. The two tribes recognize a common origin, their houses, clothes and crafts are similar in style, their languages are closely related.[3] Yet the Lele are poor, while the Bushong are rich. The Lele produce only for subsistence, sharing their goods, or distributing them among themselves as gifts and fees. The Bushong have long been used to producing for exchange, and their native economy was noted for its use of money and its specialists and markets. Everything that the Lele have or can do, the Bushong have more and can do better. They produce more, live better, and populate their region more densely.

SOURCE: Mary Douglas, "Lele Economy Compared with the Bushong—A Study of Economic Backwardness," in *Markets in Africa*, Paul Bohannan and George Dalton, editors, Northwestern University Press, 1962. Reprinted by permission of the author and publisher.

[1] The Lele are a tribe, inhabiting the west border of the Bakuba Empire. They are divided into three chiefdoms, of which only the most westerly has been studied. The Chief of the eastern Lele, at Perominenge, apes Kuba fashions in his little capital; the men wear basketry hats held on with metal pins, the chief has some of the dress and paraphernalia of the Nyimi. How much deeper this resemblance goes, it is impossible to say, since conditions at the time of field work were not favorable for study of this chiefdom. Everything that is said here concerning the Lele refers to the western Lele, whose chief, when visits were made in 1949–50 and 1953, was Norbert Pero Mihondo. The field work was carried out under the generous auspices of the International African Institute, and of the *Institut de Recherche Scientifique en Afrique Centrale.*

[2] The Bushong are the ruling tribe of the Kuba Kingdom. They were studied in 1953–56 by Dr. Vansina, to whom I am deeply indebted for his collaboration and for supplying unpublished information for this paper.

[3] According to the Lexico-statistical survey conducted by Dr. Vansina, there is an 80 per cent similarity between the two languages.

The first question is whether there are significant differences in the physical environment of the two peoples. Both live in the lat. 5 Degrees, in the area of forest park merging into savannah, which borders the south of the Congo rain forest. They both have a heavy annual rainfall of 1400 to 1600 mm. (40 to 60 inches) per annum. The mean annual temperature is about 78° F. (25° C.). As we should expect from their proximity, the climatic conditions are much the same for both tribes.

Nonetheless, a curious discrepancy appears in their respective assessments of their climate. The Bushong, like the local Europeans, welcome the dry season of mid-May to mid-August as a cold season, whereas the Lele regard it as dangerously hot. The Bushong in the north tend to have a dry season ten days shorter (Bultot 1954) than most of the Lele (see Figure 2), and the Lele soils retain less moisture, and the vegetation is thinner, so that the impression of drought is more severe, but otherwise there seems no objectively measurable difference in the climate to account for their attitudes.

There are certainly important differences in the soil, drainage and vegetation. The Lele are distinctly less fortunate. Their soils

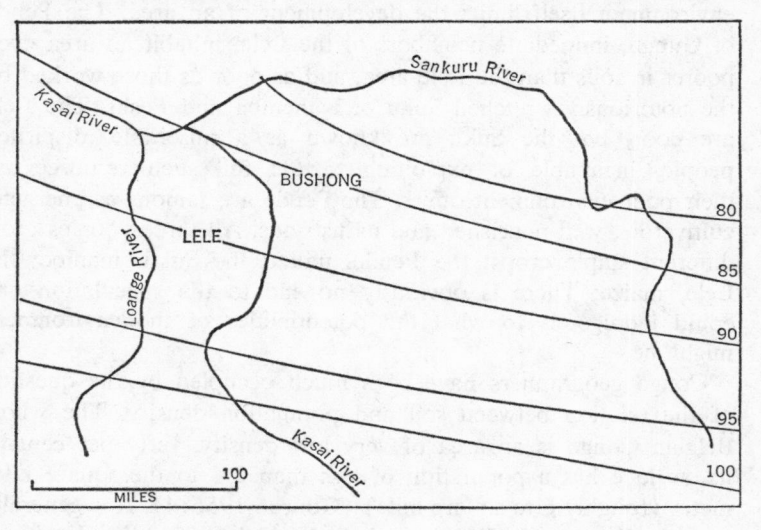

Figure 2 Average length of dry season expressed in days (From: F. Buitot — "Saisons et Périodes Sèches et Pluvieuses au Congo Belge" Bruxelles, 1954).

belong to the most easterly extension of the Kwango plateau system, and to some extent share in the sterility characteristic of that region. On that plateau, the soils are too poor to support anything but a steppe-like vegetation in spite of the ample rainfall. The soils consist of sands, poor in assimilable minerals of any kind, lacking altogether in ferro-magnates or heavy minerals, and so permeable that they are incapable of benefiting from the heavy rainfall[4] (see Figure 3). On the Bushong side of the Kasai River the soil is altogether richer, and mineral deposits, particularly of iron ore, occur. Whereas Lele country is characterized by rolling grasslands with forest galleries along the river banks, Bushong country is relatively well-forested, although the sketch map tends to exaggerate the forested area on their side of the Kasai.

With such important differences in their basic natural resources, we are not surprised that Lele country is poorer and more sparsely populated. But how much poverty and how low a density can be attributed to the environmental factor? Can we leave the matter here?

There is no certain method of estimating the extent to which environment itself limits the development of an area. The Pende of Gungu, immediate neighbors of the Lele, inhabit an area even poorer in soils than the Lele area, and as poor as those worked by the notoriously wretched Suku of Kahemba and Feshi. The Lele are poor, but the Suku are known as a miserable, dispirited people, incapable of exploiting to the full such resources as their poor environment offers. The Pende are famous as energetic cultivators, well-nourished and industrious. All three peoples grow different staple crops; the Pende, millet; the Suku, manioc; the Lele, maize. There is obviously no end to the speculation one could indulge as to what the potentialities of the environment might be.

Congo geographers have been much occupied by the question of the relation between soil and population density. The whole Belgian Congo is an area of very low density. Fifty per cent of its surface has a population of less than 2.4 to the square kilometer (roughly 6 to square mile) (Gourou 1955:4). It is generally agreed (Gourou 1955 cities Cohen; Nicolai 1952:247) that there is a rough correlation of poor sandy soils with low densities, inso-

---
[4] We are very grateful to M. L. Cahen, Director of the *Musée du Congo Belge,* Tervuren, for guidance on the physical environment of the two tribes.

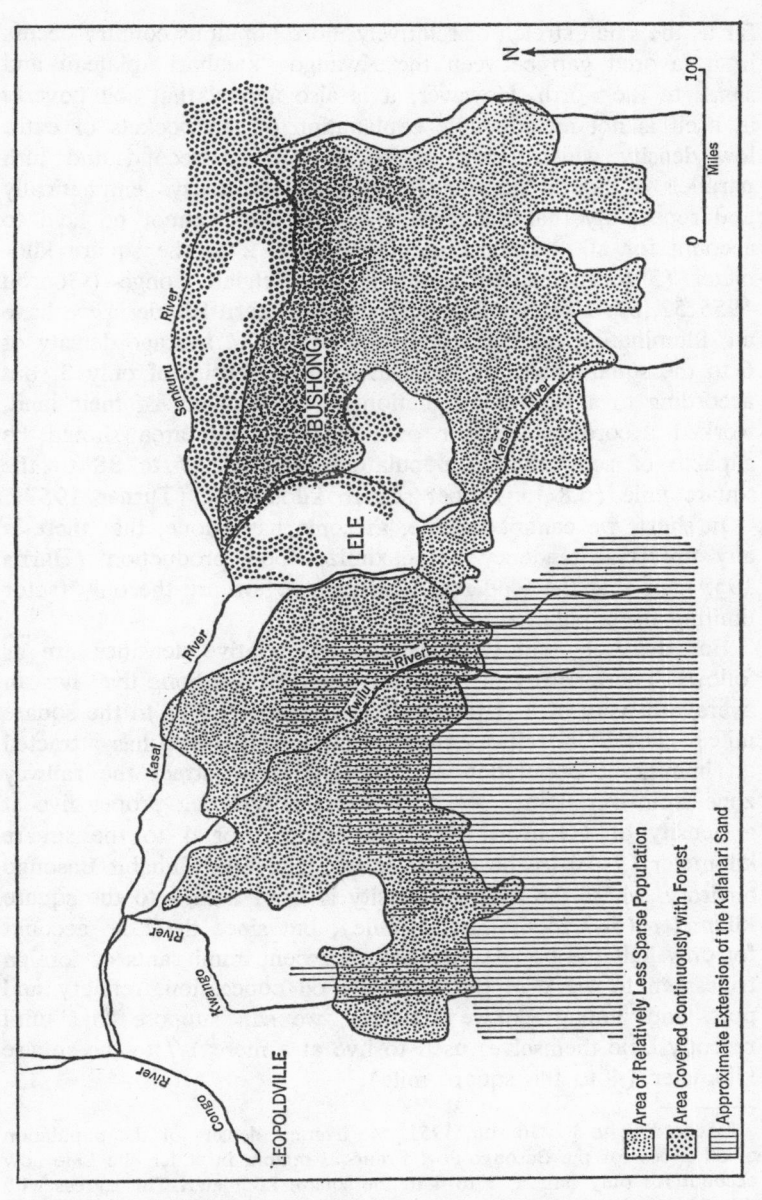

Figure 3 Population density and forest cover (Lele and Bushong).
(From: H. Nicolai & J. Jacques—"La transformation du paysage
Congolais par Chemin de Fer" 1954 p. 112.)

far as the small stretch of relatively more populous country occurs in a favored gap between the Kwango "kalahari" plateau and sands to the north. However, it is also agreed that soil poverty in itself is not an adequate explanation of the pockets of extra low density which occur, especially on the second and fifth parallels of South latitude. Professor Gourou says emphatically and repeatedly that the sterility of the soils cannot be held to account for all the densities of less than 2 to the square kilometer (5 to the square mile) in the Belgian Congo (Gourou 1955:52, 57, 109; Nicolai 1952). In Northern Rhodesia we have an illuminating case. The Ndembu live at an average density of 6 to the square mile, in many areas at a density of only 3, but according to a careful calculation of the capacity of their land, worked according to their own methods, the area should be capable of supporting a population of from 17 to 38 to the square mile (6.8 to 15 per square kilometer) (Turner 1957).

In short, we cannot assume, as some have done, that there is any universal tendency to maximize food production (Harris 1959), or that the food resources of a region are the only factor limiting its population.

For the Lele and the Bushong the relative densities are as follows. The territory of Mweka, where the Bushong live, has an average density of 4–5 to the square kilometer (11 to the square mile). The BCK railway running through the area has attracted an immigrant population of Luba. If we abstract the railway zone from our figures, we find that the Bushong proper live at a density of (Gourou 1955:109) only 3 or 4 to the square kilometer (7–10 to the square mile). The Lele[5] inhabit Basongo territory, where the average density is from 2 to 4 to the square kilometer (5–7 to the square mile), but since the Lele account for only half the population (among recent immigrants of foreign tribesmen to work in the Brabanta oil concession, refinery and port, and among Cokwe hunters), we can suppose that until recently Lele themselves used to live at a mere 1.7 to the square kilometer (4 to the square mile).

---

[5] According to P. Gourou, 1951, the average density of the population of all tribes for the Basongo-Port Francqui region, in which the Lele now account for only half, is 3 to 4 to the square kilometer. This agrees with calculations based on the total number of Lele in that area, about 26,000, and the extent of their territory, about 63 by 110 miles, which give a Lele density of roughly 4 to the square mile, or 1.7 to the sq. km.

When the geographers agree that poverty of soil is not a sufficient explanation for the degree of poverty prevailing in similar areas, we are justified in looking for a sociological explanation to supplement the effect of environmental factors. For one thing, it is obvious that the demographic factor works two ways. Low density is partly the result of inferior technology, applied to inferior resources, but it may also inhibit development by hampering enterprises which need large-scale collaboration.

If we now consider technology, we find many suggestive differences. In certain processes marked superiority would be likely to increase output. Others are proof of a higher standard of living. Surveying these, we find that in hunting, fishing and housebuilding, the Bushong worker uses more specialized materials and equipment than the Lele, and in cultivation he spends more energy and time.

Take hunting first, since the Lele are passionately interested in it and pride themselves on their skill (Douglas 1954). In the eyes of their neighbors, it seems that they are notorious as inefficient hunters, particularly because they do not use nets, and only rarely make pit traps.

Hunting is the only occupation in which large numbers of Lele men regularly combine. They reckon that fifteen to twenty men and ten dogs are necessary for a good hunt. Using nets, the Bushong need a team of only ten men, and can hope to do well with five. In short, the Bushong hunter uses better capital equipment, and his hours of hunting are more productive.

Why should the Lele not have nets? The materials are present in the forest on both sides of the river, and the Lele know what nets are. Making a net is presumably a long task. In view of the local deforestation and the resulting paucity of game, it may be a case in which costly capital equipment is simply not worthwhile. Bushong nets are made by their women. Perhaps the rest of the answer lies in the different division of labor between men and women in each tribe, and the larger proportion of the total agricultural work which Lele leave to their women. Whatever the reason, we note that the absence of nets is consistent with a general Lele tendency not to invest time and labor in long-term equipment.

The same applies to pit-traps. Lele know how to make these, and frequently talk about them. The task requires a stay in the forest of several days and nights, or regular early dawn journeys and late returns. The traps are hard work to dig with only a blunt matchet for spade, and once set, they need to be watched. In practice few men ever trouble to make them. I suspect that the reason in this case is again that the amount of game caught by pit-traps tends to be disappointing in relation to the effort of making them, and that the Lele have felt discouraged when using a technique which is more productive in the thicker forests on the other side of the river.

Lest it be thought that the Lele neglect capital-intensive aids because hunting is a sport, a pleasure, and a religious activity, let me deny any parallel with English fox-hunting. The Lele would have applauded the French Brigadier of fiction who used his sabre to slay the fox. Their eager purchase of firearms whenever they can get the money and the license shows that their culture does not restrict them to inferior techniques when these do not require long-term collaboration and effort.

In fishing the Lele are also inferior. Their country is well watered by streams and rivers, and bounded on two sides by the great Kasai, and on the west by the swift-flowing Loange. Along the banks of the Kasai are fishing villages, whose men dot the river with elaborate traps and fishing platforms. These fishermen are mostly Dinga, or Bushong, and not often Lele. In one northern village, near the Kasai, Lele women used to go every two days to the nearest Dinga village where, lacking claims of kinship, they obtained fish by bartering manioc. Compared with the Bushong the Lele as a whole are not good at fishing, nor at canoe making. There is no need to describe in detail the diversity and elaborate character of Bushong fishing equipment, but it is worth noting that in some types of fishing, using several canoes trailing nets, the team may consist of twenty men or more. These skills may be a legacy from their distant past, since the Bushong claim to have entered their territory in canoes along the Kasai river, while the Lele claim to have travelled overland (Vansina 1956) and to have found the river banks already occupied by Dinga fishing villages.

If the Lele were originally landsmen, and the Bushong originally fishermen, this might account for more than the latter's present technical superiority in fishing. For primitive fishermen are necessarily more heavily equipped than are primitive hunters and cultivators. The need for fishing tackle, nets, lines, hooks, traps, curing platforms, and for watercraft as well as for weirs and dams makes quite a different balance in the allocation of time between consumers' and producers' goods. If they started in this area with the typical balance of a fishing economy, this may have meant an initial advantage for the Bushong in the form of a habit of working for postponed consumption.

Be that as it may, Lele mostly leave fishing to their women. Their simple method is to block a slow-moving stream, so as to turn the nearest valley into a marsh. In this they make mud banks and ponds, where they set traps for fish scarcely bigger than minnows. A morning's work draining out such a pond and catching the fish floundering in the mud yields a bare pint or so of fish. In the dry season they make a two-day expedition to the Lumbundji, where they spread a saponaceous vegetable poison over the low waters, and pull out the suffocated fish by hand, or in baskets.

As to housing, Lele and Bushong huts look much alike. They are low rectangular huts, roofed with palm thatch. The walls are covered with rows of split bamboos or palm ribs, lashed onto layers of palm leaf, on a frame of strong saplings. Deceptive in appearance, Lele huts when new look much sturdier than those of the Bushong, but in practice they last less well: the Lele hut is more roughly and quickly made. A well-built one will last about six years without repair, and, as they are capable of being renewed piecemeal, by the substitution of new walls or roof thatch, they are not replaced until the whole village is moved to a new site, and the owner decides that he has neglected his hut so long that it will not stand removal. A hut in good condition is transported to a new site, with from six to eight men carrying the roof, and four at a time carrying the walls.

Bushong huts are also transportable. They are made with slightly different materials. For the roof thatch, they use the leaves of the raffia palm, as do the Lele. For the walls, they use the reputedly more waterproof leaves of a dwarf palm growing in the marshes. Over this, instead of palm ribs split in half, they sew narrow strips of bamboo, where available. Lele consider bamboo to be a tougher wood than palm, but it is rare in their region. The narrow strips are held in place by stitching in pleasing geometric patterns (Nicolai & Jacques 1954:272 ff). A rich Bushong man, who can command labor, can build a hut that will last much longer than the ordinary man's hut, up to fifteen years without major repairs. The palace of the Nyimi at Mushenge, which was still in good condition in 1956, had been originally built in 1920.

The Bushong use an ingenious technique of ventilation, a movable flap between the roof and the walls, which lets out smoke. It is impossible to say whether they do this because their building is too solid to let the smoke filter through the walls, or whether they are more fastidious and painstaking about their comfort than the Lele, whose huts do certainly retain some of the smoke of their fires.

Within the hut, the furnishings illustrate the difference in material wealth, for the Bushong have a much greater refinement of domestic goods. They sit on stools, lay their heads on carved neck rests (often necessary to accommodate an elaborate hair style). They eat from basketry plates, with iron or wooden spoons. They have a bigger range of specialized basketry or wooden containers for food, clothing, cosmetics. A man who has more than one hat needs a hat box and a place for his metal hat pins. Lele do not make fibre hats, and only a few men in a village may possess a skin hat. The beautiful Bushong caskets for cosmetics are prized objects in many European museums. When a Lele woman has prepared some cosmetic from camwood, she uses it at once, and there is rarely enough left over for it to be worth storing in a special container. Only a young mother who, being cared for by her own mother after her delivery, has nothing else to do but grind camwood for herself and the baby, stores the prepared ointment in a little hanging basket hooked into the wall, enough for a few days.

Dr. Vansina was impressed with the high protein content of the Bushong diet, with the large quantities of fish and meat they ate, and the variety in their food. The Lele give an impression of always being hungry, always dreaming of meat, often going to bed fasting because their stomach revolts at the idea of a vegetable supper. They talk a lot about hunger, and *ihiobe,* an untranslatable word for meatlessness and fishlessness. The Bushong cultivate a wider range of crops and also grow citrus fruits, pineapples, pawpaws, mangoes, sugar cane and bananas, which are either rare or completely absent in the Lele economy.

In short, the Bushong seem to be better sheltered, better fed, better supplied with goods, and with containers for storing what they do not immediately need. This is what we mean by saying that the Bushong are richer than the Lele. As to village-crafts, such as carving and smithing, the best of the Lele products can compete in quality with Bushong manufacture, but they are much scarcer. The Lele are more used to eating and drinking out of folded green leaves than from the basket plates and carved beakers common among the Bushong. Their medical instruments, too, are simpler. If, instead of cutting down a gourd top, they carve a wooden enema funnel for a baby, they make it as fine and thin as they can, but do not adorn it with the elaborate pattern found on some Bushong examples.

Before considering agriculture, we should mention the method of storing grain, for this is a rough index of output. Both Lele and Bushong houses are built with an internal grain store, suspended from the roof or supported on posts over the hearth. Here grain and even fish and meat can be preserved from the ravages of damp and of insects by the smoke of the fire. Most Lele women have no other grain store. Bushong women find this too small and use external granaries, built like little huts, raised a few feet above ground. These granaries, of which there may be one or two in a Lele village, are particularly characteristic of the southern Bushong villages, while in the north the huts which are built in the fields for a man to sleep in during the period of heaviest agricultural work are used as temporary granaries. The Lele are not in the habit of sleeping in their fields, except to shoot wild pig while the grain is ripening. This may be another indication that they do less agricultural work than the Bushong.

When we examine the techniques of cultivation, we find many contrasts. The Bushong plant five crops in succession in a system of rotation that covers two years. They grow yams, sweet potatoes, manioc, beans, and gather two and sometimes three maize harvests a year. The Lele practice no rotation and reap only one annual maize harvest. If we examine the two agricultural cycles, we see that the Bushong work continuously all the year, and that the Lele have one burst of activity, lasting about six weeks, in the height of the dry season.

Here is the probable explanation of their dread of the dry season. There is, in fact, surprisingly little range in the average monthly temperatures through the year. For the coldest month, July, it is only 2° C. less than the hottest month, January (Vandenplas 1947:33–38). Nonetheless, the Europeans and the Bushong welcome the period from mid-May to mid-August as the "cold season", probably because they enjoy the cooler nights and the freedom from humidity. But the Lele, enduring the sun beating on them from a cloudless sky while they are trying to do enough agricultural work for the whole year, suffer more from the dust and impurities in the atmosphere and from the greatly increased insolation. The relatively cooler nights may make them feel the day's heat even more intensely.

Apart from the differences in crops cultivated, we may note some differences in emphasis. Lele give hunting and weaving a high priority throughout the year, while the Bushong think of them as primarily dry-season activities. Traditionally, the Lele used to burn the grassland for big hunts (in which five or six villages combined for the day) at the end of the dry season, when the bulk of their agricultural work was done. If the first rains had already broken, so much the better for the prospects of the hunt, they said, as the animals would leave their forest watering places to eat the new shoots. As the end of the dry season is the time in which the firing could do the maximum damage to the vegetation, it has been forbidden by the administration, and if permission is given at all, the firing must be over by the beginning of July. The Bushong used to burn the grassland in mid-May or early June, at the beginning of the dry season, when the sap had not altogether died down in the grass.

The cycle of work described for the Lele is largely what the old men describe as their traditional practice. It was modified by the agricultural officers of the Belgian Congo. Lele are encouraged to sow maize twice, for harvesting in November, and in April. Manioc is now mainly grown in the grassland, instead of in the forest clearings. There are some changes in the plants cultivated. Voandzeia has been replaced by groundnuts, some hill rice is sown, and beans in some parts. These are largely treated as cash crops by the Lele, who sell them to the Europeans to earn money for tax. The other occupation which competes for their time is cutting oil-palm fruits to sell to the *Huileries du Congo Belge,* whose lorries collect weekly from the villages. Lele complain that they are now made to work harder than before, to clear more land, keep it hoed, grow more crops. They never complain that cutting oil-palm fruits interferes with their agricultural program, only that the total of extra work interferes with their hunting.

This is not the place for a detailed study of Bushong agriculture. It is enough to have shown that it is more energetically pursued and is more productive. One or two details of women's work are useful indications of a different attitude to time, work and food. Lele like to eat twice a day: in the morning at about 11 o'clock or midday, and in the evening. They complain that their wives are lazy, and only too often the morning meal consists of cold scraps from the previous night; they compare themselves unfavorably with Cokwe, who are reputed to have more industrious wives. In practice the Lele women seem to be very hard-working, but it is possible that the absence of labor-saving devices may make their timetable more arduous.

ANNUAL CYCLE OF WORK

	Bushong			Lele
Dry Season				
Mid-May	Harvest beans, maize II, yams. Clear forest	Hunt, weave draw wine		Clear forest for maize
	Burn grassland for hunt			
June	Hunt, fish, weave, repair huts	"	"	
Mid-July to Aug. 15th	Burn forest clearings, gather bananas and pineapple. Plant hemp	"	"	Women fish in low waters
	Hunt, fish, plant sugar cane and bananas			Burn forest clearings Sow maize
	Send tribute to capital period of plenty			
Wet Season				
Mid-August	Lift ground nuts	"	"	Fire grassland for hunting
Sept.	Sow ground nut. Sow Maize I Collect termites	"	"	Sow voandzeia, plant manioc, bananas,
Oct.		"	"	peppers; sugar cane, pineapples
Nov.		"	"	(occasional) and raffia palms in
Mid-Dec.		"	"	forest clearings, with maize
Little Dry Season				
Mid-Dec.	Sow maize II; sow voandzeia	"	"	Green maize can be plucked
Jan.	Sow tobacco, sow maize II	"	"	Maize harvest
Wet Season				
Feb.	Lift ground nuts, sow beans, collect termites and grubs	"	"	Lift voandzeia
	Reap maize I (Main crop)			
March	Reap maize I. Sow tobacco, beans, yams, manioc	"	"	
April to Mid-May	Gather beans, sow voandzeia and tobacco	"	"	

For example, one of their daily chores is to fetch water from the stream. At the same time, they carry down a heavy pile of manioc roots to soak for a few days before carrying them back to the village. Bushong women, on the other hand, are equipped with wooden troughs, filled with rain water from the roofs, so that they can soak their manioc in the village, without the labor of transporting it back and forth. Bushong women also cultivate mushrooms indoors for occasional relish, while Lele women rely on chance gathering.

Bushong women find time to do the famous raffia embroidery, perhaps because their menfolk help them more in the fields. Lele men admiring the Bushong *Velours,* were amazed to learn that women could ever be clever enough to use needle and thread, still less make this elaborate stitching. The Bushong culinary tradition is more varied than that of the Lele. This rough comparison suggests that Lele women are less skilled and industrious than Bushong women, but it is probable that a time-and-motion study of women's and men's work in the two economies would show that Lele men leave a relatively heavier burden of agricultural work to their women, for reasons which we shall show later.

Another difference between Bushong and Lele techniques is in the exploitation of palms for wine. Lele use only the raffia palm for wine. Their method of drawing it kills the tree; in the process of tapping, they cut out the whole of the crown of the palm just at the time of its first flowering. During the few years before the palm has matured to this point, they take the young yellow fronds for weaving, and after drawing the sap for wine, the stump is stripped and left to rot down. Lele have no use for a tree which has once been allowed to flower, except for fuel and building purposes. The life of a palm, used in this way, is rarely more than five years, although there seems to be some range in the different times at which individual palms mature.

The Bushong also use this method on raffia palms, but they have learnt to tap oil palms by making an incision at the base of the large inflorescene, a technique which does not kill the tree. Presumably this technique could be adapted to raffia palms, since the Yakö of Cross River, Nigeria use it (Forde 1937). But neither Lele nor Bushong attempt to preserve the raffia palm in this way, and Lele do not draw any wine from oil palms, although these grow plentifully in the north of their territory.

According to Lele traditions oil palms were very scarce in their country until relatively recently, and this may account for their not exploiting it for wine. But here again, consistently with other tendencies in their economy, their techniques are directed to short-term results, and do not fully use their resources.

To balance this picture of Lele inefficiency, we should mention the weaving of raffia, for here, at least, they are recognized as the better craftsmen. Their raffia cloth is of closer texture than Bushong cloth, because they use finer strands of raffia, produced by combing in three stages, whereas the Bushong only comb once. Incidentally, the fine Lele cloth is not suitable for velours embroidery.

Lele take pride in producing cloth of a regular and fine weave, and they refuse inferior cloth if it is proffered for payment. A length of woven raffia is their normal standard of value for counting debts and dues of all kinds. How little it has even now become a medium of exchange has been described elsewhere (Douglas 1958). Raffia cloth is not the medium of exchange for the Bushong, who freely used cowries, copper units, and beads before they adopted Congolese francs as an additional currency. Raffia cloth is the principal export for the Lele, whereby they obtain knives, arrowheads and camwood. This may explain why unadorned raffia cloth holds a more important place in the admittedly simpler economy of the Lele than its equivalent in the diversified economy of the Bushong.

If we ask now why one tribe is rich and the other poor, the review of technology would seem to suggest that the Lele are poorer not only because their soil is less fertile, but because they work less at the production of goods. They do not build up producer's capital, such as nets, canoes, traps and granaries. Nor do they work so long at cultivation, and their houses wear out quicker. Their reduced effort is itself partly a consequence of their poorer environment. It is probable that their soil could not be worked by the intensive methods of Bushong agriculture without starting a degenerative cycle. Hunting nets and pit-traps are less worthwhile in an area poor in forest and game. But certain other features of their economy cannot be fully explained as adaptations to the environment.

When Lele timetables of work are compared with those of the Bushong, we see no heavy schedules which suggest that there would be any shortage of labor. Yet, their economy is characterized paradoxically by an apparent shortage of hands, which confronts anyone who seeks collaborators. When a sick man wants to send a message, or needs help to clear his fields, or to repair his hut, or to draw palm wine for him, he will often be hard put to find anyone whose services he can command. *"Kwa itangu bo—No time,"* is a common reply to requests for help. His fields may lie uncleared, or his palm trees run to seed for lack of hands. This reflects the weakness of the authority structure in Lele society, and does not imply that every able-bodied man is fully employed from dawn to dusk.

Some anthropologists write as if the poorer the environment and the less efficient the techniques for exploiting it, the more the population is forced to work hard to maintain itself in existence; more productive techniques produce a surplus which enables a part of the population to be supported as a "leisure class."[6] It is not necessary to expose the fallacies of this approach, but it is worth pointing out that, poor as they are, the Lele are less fully employed than the Bushong. They do less work.

"Work," of course, is here used in a narrow sense, relevant to a comparison of material wealth. Warfare, raiding, ambushing, all planning of offensive and defensive actions, as also abductions, seductions, and reclaiming of women, making and rebutting of sorcery charges, negotiations for fines and compensations and for credit—all these absorbingly interesting and doubtless satisfying activities of Lele social life must, for this purpose of measuring comparative prosperity, be counted as alternatives to productive work. Whether we call them forms of preferred idleness, or leisure activities, or "non-productive work," no hidden judgment of value is implied. The distinction between productive work and other activities is merely used here as rough index of material output.

If we wish to understand why the Lele work less, we need to consider whether any social factors inhibit them from exploiting their resources to the utmost. We should be prepared to find in a backward economy (no less than in our own economy) instances of decisions influenced by short-term desires which, once taken, may block the realization of long-term interests.

First, we must assess in a very general way, the attitudes

---

[6] For the most widely read statement of this view, see Herskovits 1952a (Part V, The Economic Surplus) and for a list of reputed subscribers to this view, see Harris 1959.

shown by the Lele towards the inconveniences and rewards of work.

For the Bushong, work is the means to wealth, and wealth the means to status. They strongly emphasize the value of individual effort and achievement, and they are also prepared to collaborate in numbers over a sustained period when this is necessary to raise output. Nothing in Lele culture corresponds to the Bushong striving for riches. The Bushong talk constantly and dream about wealth, while proverbs about it being the steppingstone to high status are often on their lips. Riches, prestige, and influence at court are explicitly associated together (Vansina 1954).

On the other hand, Lele behave as if they expect the most satisfying roles of middle and old age to fall into the individual's lap in the ripeness of time, only provided that he is a real man—that is, normally virile. He will eventually marry several wives, beget children, and so enter the Begetter's cult. His infant daughters will be asked in marriage by suitors bearing gifts and ready to work for him. Later, when his cult membership is bringing in a revenue of raffia cloth from fees of new initiates, his newborn daughter's daughters can be promised in marriage to junior clansmen, who will strengthen his following in the village. His wives will look after him in his declining years. He will have stores of raffia to lend or give, but he will possess this wealth because, in the natural course of events, he reached the proper status for his age. He would not be able to achieve this status through wealth.

The emphasis on seniority means that, among the Lele, work and competitiveness are not geared to their longings for prestige. Among the Bushong, largely through the mechanism of markets, through money, and through elective political office, the reverse is true. It also means that Lele society holds out its best rewards in middle life and after. Those who have reached this period of privilege have an interest in maintaining the *status quo*.

All over the world it is common for the privileged sections of a community to adopt protective policies, even against their own more long-term interests. We find traces of this attitude among old Lele men. They tend to speak and behave as if they held, collectively, a position to be defended against the encroachments of the young men. Examples of this attitude have been published elsewhere (Douglas 1959). Briefly, secrets of ritual and healing are jealously guarded, and even knowledge of the debts and

marriage negotiations of their own clans are deliberately withheld
from the young men, as a technique for retarding their adulthood.
The old are realistic enough to know that they are dependent
ultimately on the brawn and muscle of the young men, and this
thought is regularly brought up in disputes, when they are pressing
defense of their privileges too far: "What would happen to us,
if we chased away the young men? Who would hunt with us,
and carry home the game? Who would carry the European's
luggage?" The young men play on this, and threaten to leave
the village until eventually the dispute is settled. Although it
does not directly affect the levels of production that we have
been discussing, this atmosphere of jealousy between men's age-
groups certainly inhibits collaboration and should probably not
be underestimated in its long-term effects.

Lele also believe in restricting competition. At the beginning of
the century, the Lele chief NgomaNvula tried to protect the
native textile industry by threatening death for anyone who wore
European cloth (Simpson 1911:310). If a Lele man is asked
why women do not weave or sew, he instantly replies: "If a
woman could sew her own clothes, she might refuse to cook for
the men. What could we give them instead of clothes to keep
them happy?" This gives a false picture of the male contribution
to the domestic economy, but it is reminiscent of some modern
arguments against "equal pay" for both sexes.

Within the local section of a clan, restrictions on entry into the
skilled professions are deliberately enforced. A young boy is not
allowed to take up a craft practiced by a senior clansman, unless
the latter agrees to retire. In the same clan, in the same village,
two men rarely specialize in the same skill. If a man is a good
drummer, or carver, or smith, and he sees an aptitude for the
same craft in his son or nephew, he may teach the boy all he
knows and work with him until he thinks the apprenticeship
complete. Then, ceremonially, he hands over his own position,
with his tools, and retires in favour of the younger man. This
ideal is frequently practiced. The accompanying convention, that
a boy must not compete with his elder kinsman, is also strong
enough to stop many a would-be specialist from developing his
skill. Lele openly prefer reduced output. Their specialist craftsmen
are few and far between because they are expected to make
matters unpleasant for rivals competing for their business. Con-

sequently the Lele as a whole are poorer in metal or wooden objects for their own use, or for export.

Lastly, it seems that Lele old men have never been able to rely on their junior clansmen for regular assistance in the fields. As a junior work-mate, a son-in-law is more reliable than a fellow-clansman. This is so for reasons connected with the pattern of residence and the weak definition of authority within the clan (Douglas 1957). An unmarried youth has no granary of his own to fill. Work which he does to help his maternal uncles, father, or father's brothers, is counted in his favor, but he can easily use the claims of one to refuse those of another, and escape with a minimum of toil. Boys would be boys, until their middle thirties. They led the good life, of weaving, drinking, and following the manly sports of hunting and warfare, without continuous agricultural responsibilities.

The key institution in which the old men see their interests as divorced from those of the young men is polygyny. Under the old system, since the young girls were pre-empted by the older men, the age of marriage was early for girls (eleven or twelve), and late for men (in their thirties). It would be superficial to suppose that these arrangements were solely for the sexual gratification of the old men. One should see them as part of the whole economic system, and particularly as one of the parts which provide social security for the old.

The division of labor between the sexes leaves the very old men with little they can do. An old woman, by contrast, can earn her keep with many useful services. But old men use their rights over women to secure necessary services, both from women and from men. Through polygyny, the principles of male dominance and of seniority are maintained to the end. To borrow an analogy from another sphere, we could almost say that the Lele have opted for an ambitious old-age pensions scheme at the price of their general standards of living. We shall see that the whole community pays for the security in old age which polygyny represents.

In the kingdom of ends peculiar to the Lele, various institutions seem to receive their justification because they are consistent with polygyny of the old men and delayed marriage of the young. The latter were reconciled to their bachelorhood, partly by the life of sport and ease, and partly by the institution of wife-sharing by age-sets. They were encouraged to turn their attention away from the young wives in their own villages by the related custom of abducting girls from rival villages (Douglas 1951). Intervillage feuding therefore appears to be an essential part of the total scheme, which furthermore commits the Lele to small-scale political life. The diversion of young men's energies to raiding and abducting from rival villages was a major cause of the low levels of production, for its effects were cumulative. The raiding gave rise to such insecurity that at some times half the able-bodied males were engaged in giving armed escort to the others. Men said that in the old days a man did not go to the forest to draw palm wine alone, but his age-mate escorted him and stood with his back to the tree, bowstring taut, watching for ambush.

Coming from Bushong country in 1907, Torday was amazed at the fortified condition of Lele villages:

> Here, too, we found enclosures, but instead of the leaf walls which are considered sufficient among the Bushongo, the separations were palisades formed by solid stakes driven into the ground. Such a wall surrounded the whole village, and the single entrance was so arranged that no more than one person was able to enter at one time (Torday 1925:231).

Simpson also remarked that Lele men, asked to carry his baggage from their own village to the next, armed as if going into strange country. Such insecurity is obviously inimical to trade.

We have started with polygyny as the primary value to which other habits have been adjusted, because the Lele themselves talk as if all relations between men are defined by rights to women.

The point is the more effective since the Bushong are monogamous. We know well that polygyny elsewhere does not give rise to this particular accumulation of effects. Are there any features peculiar to Lele polygyny? One is the proportion of polygynous old men, indicated by the high rate of bachelorhood. Another is in the solutions they have adopted for the problems of late marriage. In some societies with extensive polygyny, the institutions which exist for the sexual satisfaction of the young men[7] are either wholly peaceful, or directed to warfare with other tribes and not to hostilities between villages. Thirdly, where

---

[7] For example, Tiv "sister-marriage" or the "manyatta" of the Masai.

the chain of command is more sharply defined (as in patrilineal systems, or in matrilineal societies in which offices are elective or carry recognizable political responsibilities, as among the Bushong), then polygyny of older men is less likely to be accompanied by attitudes of suspicion and hostility between men's age-groups.

Having started our analysis with polygyny and the high rate of bachelorhood, tracing the various interactions, we find the Lele economy constantly pegged down to the same level of production. Something like a negative feedback appears in the relations of old to young men: the more the old men reserve the girls for themselves, the more the young men are resentful and evasive; the more the young men are refractory, the more the old men insist on their prerogatives. They pick on the most unsatisfactory of the young men, refuse to allot him a wife, refuse him cult membership; the other note his punishment, and either come to heel or move off to another village. There cannot be an indefinite worsening in their relations because, inevitably, the old men die. Then the young men inherit their widows, and, now not so young, see themselves in sight of polygynous status, to be defended by solidarity of the old.

So we find the Lele, as a result of innumerable personal choices about matters of immediate concern, committed to all the insecurity of feuding villages, and to the frustrations of small-scale political life and ineffective economy.

If we prefer to start our analysis at the other end, not with polygyny but with scale of political organization, we come to the same results. For whatever reason, the Bushong developed a well organized political system (Vansina 1957), embracing 70,000 people. Authority is decentralized from the Nyimi, or paramount chief, to minor chiefs, and from these to canton heads, and from these to village heads. Judicial, legislative, and administrative powers are delegated down these channels, with decisions concerning war and peace held at the center by the Nyimi. Political office is elective or by appointment. Appropriate policing powers are attached to leaders at each point in the hierarchy. Leaders are checked by variously constituted councils, whom they must consult. The Nyimi maintains his own army to quell rebellions. Tribute of grain, salt, dried foods, and money is brought into the capitals, and redistributed to loyal subjects and officials. The chiefly courts provide well-rewarded markets for craftsmen's wares so that regional specialities are salable far from their sources. Even before the advent of Europeans there was a food-market at Musenge, the Nyimi's capital. No doubt the Kasai River, protecting them from the long arm of the Bushong Empire, is partly responsible for the Lele's never having been drawn, willy-nilly, into its orbit, and accepting its values.

The Lele village, which is their largest autonomous unit, is not so big as the smallest political unit in the Bushong system. (The Lele villages average a population of 190, and the Bushong villages 210.) True, there are Lele chiefs, who claim relationship with Bushong chiefs. Each village is, indeed, found within a chiefdom —that is, an area over which a member of the chiefly clan claims suzerainty. But in practice his rights are found to be ritual and social. Each village is completely independent. The chief has no judicial or military authority. He claims tribute, but here we have no busy palace scene in which tribute payers flock in and are lavishly fed by the special catering system which chiefly polygyny so often represents.

When a chief visited a village, he was given raffia cloths, as many as could be spared. Then the villagers asked what woman he would give them in return. He named one of his daughters, and they settled a day to fetch her. The girl became the communal wife of one of the age-sets, the whole village regarding itself as her legal husband and as son-in-law to the chief. Son-in-lawship expressed their relation to him until the day that he claimed the girl's first daughter in marriage. Then the relation became reversed, the chief being son-in-law to the village. The raffia gifts and women which went back and forth between the chief and village were not essentially different from those which linked independent villages to one another in peaceful exchange. None of this interfered with the autonomy of the village.

The simple factor of scale alone has various repercussions. There is no ladder of status up which a man may honorably climb to satisfy his competitive ambitions. There is no series of offices for which age and experience qualify a man, so that in his physical decline he can enjoy respect and influence and material rewards. The Bushong lay great emphasis on individual effort and achievement, but the Lele try to damp it down. They avoid overt roles of leadership and fear the jealousy which individual success arouses. Their truncated status system turns the Lele village in on itself, to brood on quarrels and sorcery accusations, or turns it, in hostility, against other villages, so promoting the general feeling of insecurity. The latter makes markets impossible, and renders pointless ambition to produce above home needs. The old, in such an economy, unable to save, or to acquire dignity in their declining years by occupying high political office, bolster their position by claiming the marriageable women, and building up a system of rewards reserved for those who begat in wedlock. And so we are back again to polygyny and prolonged bachelorhood.

This picture has been partly based on deductions about what Lele society must have been like twenty years before fieldwork was begun. Before 1930 they could still resort to ordeals, enslave, raid and counterraid, abduct women, and pursue blood-vengeance with barbed arrows. They still needed to fortify their villages against attacks. By 1949 the scene had changed. The young men had broken out of their restraining social environment—by becoming Christians. They enjoyed protection, from mission and government, from reprisals by pagans. They could marry young Christian girls who, similarly, were able to escape their expected lot as junior wives of elderly polygynists. Raiding was ended, age-sets were nearly finished. Old men had less authority even than before. The young Christians tended to seek employment with Europeans to escape the reproaches and suspicions which their abstention from pagan rituals engendered.[8]

It would be interesting to compare their performance as workers in the new and freer context. One might expect that, away from the influence of their old culture, Lele performance might equal or surpass that of Bushong. Unfortunately the framework for such a comparison is lacking. Neither tribe has a high reputation for industry with its respective employers, compared with immigrant Cokwe, Luba and Pende workers. This may simply be because the best reputations are earned by tribes which have longest been accustomed to wage-labor.

One is tempted to predict that, in so far as it is due to social factors, Lele are likely to change their name for idleness and lack of stamina before long. In 1949–50 they were not forthcoming in numbers for plantation labor or for cutting oil-palm nuts. By 1954, when a scattering of small shops through the territory had put trade goods within their reach, they had become eager to

---

[8] This process has been described in Douglas (1959b).

earn money. The restrictive influence of the old social system was already weaker.

We may now look again at the demographic factor, and distinguish some effects on it of the economy and the political system. It is obvious that in different types of economy, the active male contribution may have different time spans according to the nature of the work. If there were a modern community whose bread-winners were international skating champions, footballers, or miners at the coal-face, their period of active work would be briefer than in economies based on less physically exacting tasks. A primitive economy is, by definition, one based on a rudimentary technology, and the more rudimentary, the more the work consists of purely individual physical effort. Moreover, the simpler the economy, the smaller the scope for managerial roles and ancillary sedentary work. The result, then, is that the period of full, active contribution to the economy is shorter.[9]

If we compare Lele and Bushong economies on these lines, we see that the "age of retirement" is likely to be earlier for the Lele.

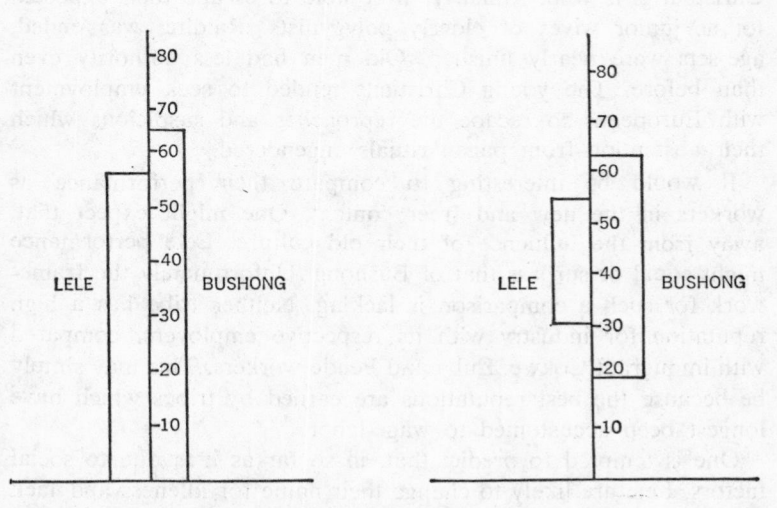

Figure 4 *Age of retirement from work.*

Figure 5 *Period of full work, showing age of entry into full agricultural responsibility.*

[9] This approach was suggested by Linton (1940).

The typical Bushong man is able, long after he has passed his physical prime, to make a useful contribution to production, either by using his experience to direct the collaboration of others or in various administrative roles which are important in maintaining the security and order necessary for prosperity. The Lele economy, on the other hand, with its emphasis on individual work, gives less weight to experience and finds less productive work for the older man to do. We can only guess at the differences, but it is worth presenting the idea visually, as in Figures 4 and 5.

Furthermore, at the other end of the life span, the same trend is increased because of the late entry into agricultural work of Lele men. The young Lele is not fully employed in agriculture until he is at least thirty and married, the Bushong man when he is twenty.

Figure 5 illustrates the idea that the active labor force in the Lele economy, as a proportion of the total population, is on both scores smaller than it is with the Bushong. The total output of the economy has to be shared among a larger population of dependents.

The comparison of the two economies has shown up something like the effects of "backwash" described by Professor Myrdal (1957). First we see that in the environment there are initial disadvantages which limit development. Secondly, we find that in the social organization itself there are further inhibiting effects which are cumulative, and which work one on another and back again on the economy, technology and population, to intensify the initial disadvantages. We have tried to present the interaction of these tendencies in a simplified form in Figure 6.

"Nothing succeeds like success." Somehow, sometime, the Bushong took decisions which produced a favorable turn in their fortunes and set off interactions which resulted in their political hegemony and their wealth. The Lele missed the benefits of this civilization because of their location on the other side of the Kasai River, their poorer soils, their history. The decisions they took amounted to an accommodation of their life to a lower political and economic level. Their technology was inferior, so their efforts were backed with less efficient equipment, and their economy was less productive. Their old social system barred many of the chances which might have favored economic growth.

Anthropologists sometimes tend to discuss the adoption or rejection of new techniques in terms of a cultural mystique, as if dealing with irreducible principles, of which no analysis is feasi-

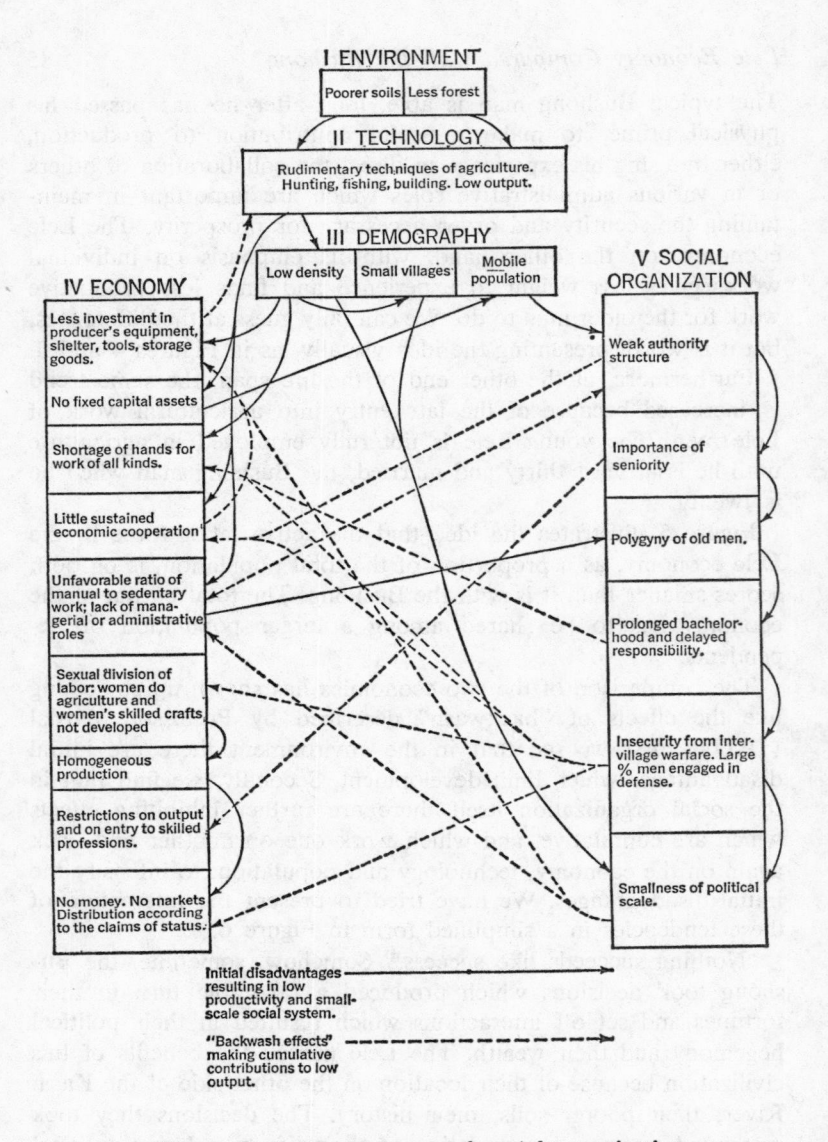

I ENVIRONMENT

Poorer soils | Less forest

II TECHNOLOGY

Rudimentary techniques of agriculture.
Hunting, fishing, building. Low output.

III DEMOGRAPHY

Low density | Small villages | Mobile population

IV ECONOMY

Less investment in producer's equipment, shelter, tools, storage goods.

No fixed capital assets

Shortage of hands for work of all kinds.

Little sustained economic cooperation

Unfavorable ratio of manual to sedentary work; lack of managerial or administrative roles

Sexual division of labor: women do agriculture and women's skilled crafts not developed

Homogeneous production

Restrictions on output and on entry to skilled professions.

No money. No markets Distribution according to the claims of status.

V SOCIAL ORGANIZATION

Weak authority structure

Importance of seniority

Polygyny of old men.

Prolonged bachelorhood and delayed responsibility.

Insecurity from Inter-village warfare. Large % men engaged in defense.

Smallness of political scale.

Initial disadvantages resulting in low productivity and small-scale social system.

"Backwash effects" making cumulative contributions to low output.

Figure 6 Lele economy and social organization.

ble.[10] The Lele may be taken as a case in point. Their preference for their own inferior techniques, in spite of awareness of better methods used across the river, depend on certain institutions, and these again on their history and environment. Through economic analysis we can break down the effect of choices, each made reasonably enough in its own restricted context. By following up the interactions of these choices, one upon another, we can see how the highly idiosyncratic mold of Lele culture is related to a certain low level of production.

---

[10] See Benedict (1956:187): "Among primitive peoples, this lack of interest in 'progress' has been proverbial . . . Every primitive tribe has its own cultural arrangements which ensure its survival . . . They may be culturally uninterested in labor-saving devices. Often the value they put on time is extremely low, and 'wisdom' is far more valued than efficiency. Our cultural system and theirs are oriented around different ideals."

4 THE NORMAL SURPLUS
OF SUBSISTENCE AGRICULTURE

W. Allan

I T WOULD appear to be a reasonable—if not axiomatic—proposition that subsistence cultivators, dependent entirely or almost entirely on the produce of their gardens, tend to cultivate an area large enough to ensure the food supply in a season of poor yields. Otherwise the community would be exposed to frequent privation and grave risk of extermination or dispersal by famine, more especially in regions of uncertain and fluctuating rainfall.[1] One would, therefore, expect the production of a "normal surplus" of food in the average year.

SALES OF AFRICAN-PRODUCED MAIZE IN NORTHERN RHODESIA

This simple and obvious idea first occurred to me as the result of a study of a practical problem in Northern Rhodesia. The story goes back to the 1930s when world prices for maize fell far below the level remunerative for the European producer. Maize production was then in excess of local demand, which came mainly from the copper mines, and the stability—indeed, the existence—of the European farming industry of Northern Rhodesia was seriously threatened. To meet this situation marketing legislation was introduced. The grain price on the internal market was fixed and a Maize Control Board was set up to purchase and market all maize offered for sale, the final price paid to the producer being

SOURCE: W. Allan, "The Normal Surplus of Subsistence Agriculture," chapter 4 of *The African Husbandman*, Oliver and Boyd, 1965. Reprinted by permission of the publisher.

[1] Records for Cyprus, extending over 80 years, show that the wheatgrowers of the Mesaoria, which is such a region, may expect three good seasons, four average seasons, two poor seasons, and one crop failure in each decade.

determined by the relationship between the quantity sold at the controlled local price and exported at the low world price. Some African cultivators in Reserves near the railway line, mainly the Tonga, were already selling considerable quantities of maize to traders and the remunerative local market was divided between European and African producers on what was thought to be an equitable proportion based on sales over the three previous years. The share of the African producers was estimated, on this basis, to be 58,000 bags (one bag=200 lb of grain) and there was therefore considerable surprise and consternation when, in 1936, the first year of maize control, no less then 234,000 bags of maize were delivered by Africans.

The equity of the market division was, of course, called in question, but it appeared probable that a discrepancy even of this order could be explained on the assumption that the African producers, or the great majority of them, were in fact selling the normal surplus of subsistence cultivation. Data from sampling surveys indicated that the average "producing unit" might be regarded as a family group cultivating approximately six acres of maize and requiring about thirteen bags of grain to meet domestic requirements.[2] By assessing the total number of "producing units"—about 17,000 as nearly as could be estimated—from population figures for the areas from which maize was then sold, and using the simple formula $P(6Y-13)$ to estimate the expectation of total sales, where P is the number of Producing Units and Y the mean Yield for the season in bags per acre, the following conjectures were formulated:

(a) For each increase of one bag per acre in excess of 2.17 bags per acre, the minimum domestic requirement, approximately 100,000 bags of maize would be sold by African producers.

(b) Annual deliveries would fluctuate within very wide limits, probably from a minimum of 20,000 bags to a maximum of about 340,000 bags, assuming a static producing population.

(c) Average deliveries over a long series of years might be expected to approximate to 85,000 bags, again assuming a static producing population.

---

[2] See *The Annual Report of the Dept. of Agriculture,* Northern Rhodesia, Lusaka, 1938.

These very tentative conclusions involved assumptions, based on very slight yield data, that the mean maize yield of any season would be unlikely to fall much below 2.5 bags per acre or to exceed 5.5 bags, and that the mean yield of the "average" season might approximate to 3 bags per acre. It was intended that they should be checked against the results of more adequate sampling and reliable field estimates of yields, but this could not be done on account of other preoccupations and the changes that came with the outbreak of war. It was not until 1943 that an estimate of yield was made from reasonably adequate field sampling, and then only in part of the Tonga country and for a different purpose. The purpose of this survey was to assess the maize yields obtained by paid demonstrators cultivating their own holdings on an improved system devised by the Agricultural Department, and to compare them with the general yield. Maize grown in the Demonstrators' gardens gave an average yield of 5.25 bags per acre, compared with an estimated general average of 2.75 bags per acre for that season. At this general yield level, on the basis of the original conjectures, expected deliveries would be 59,000 bags: actual deliveries in 1943 amounted to 60,000 bags.

The possibility that the original hypothesis and the conjectures deriving from it were not very far from reality, in spite of the inadequacy of the data, is supported by the fact that for fourteen years, from 1936 to 1949, and until there was a radical alteration of the whole picture, deliveries of African-produced maize fell within the predicted limits (Figure 7). Johnson (1956) has described the period 1938–44 as one of declining production "following the low prices of the middle and late thirities." This must mean either that the Tonga maize-growers sold less of their surplus or that the number of farmers—in the sense of families cultivating significantly more than a subsistence acreage—declined. There is, however, no very convincing reason to suppose that the Tonga, accustomed to selling their surplus at "low" prices and with no criterion of price other than that paid to the European producer, to which the African price was related, suddenly reduced their sales; and the data collected by the 1945 survey (Allan and Gluckman 1948) indicate an increase rather than a decline in the number of "farmers." In 1945 the great majority of the maize sellers were still subsistence cultivators deriving most of their cash income not from maize sales but from sales of livestock, poultry, and eggs, and from the wages of labour, to whom the selling of the maize surplus, when they happened to have one, was a convenient method of storage and any profit from it, a gift of the season. It may, I think, be more accurate to regard 1936–49 as a relatively static period. Until the latter part of this period new ploughs, carts, and spare parts were in short supply and the marketing area remained much the same. The main factor determining the pattern of maize sales over the period was the effect of weather on the amount of surplus produced by a more-or-less static number

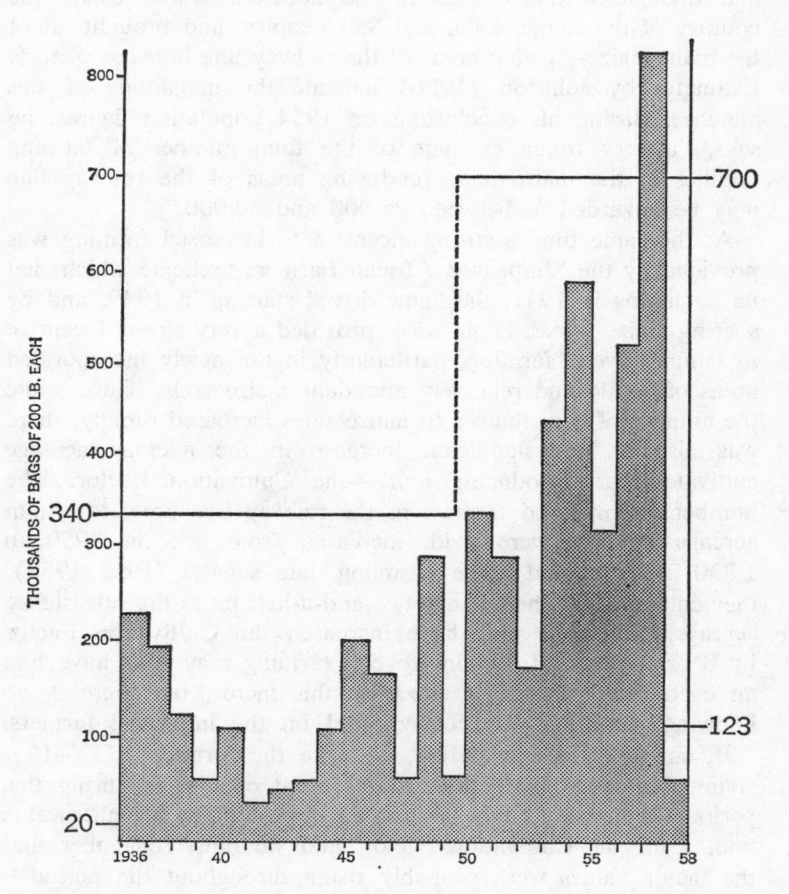

Figure 7   Sales of African produced maize: Northern Rhodesia Railway lines areas only.

of subsistence and semi-subsistence cultivators, and it happened
that there was no very good season in the period 1938–44. One
does not expect a six to turn up in every seven throws of a die.

The new pattern of the 1950s is to be accounted for by a
number of factors, of which a great increase in the number of
"producing units" was probably the most important. The marketing area was greatly extended, by the setting up of buying points
and provision of transport. This not only expanded the original
area but tapped the "normal surplus" of a large belt of fertile
and undepleted maize soils in the northern Kafue basin, the
country of the Lenje, Sala, and Soli peoples, and brought all of
the main maize-growing areas of the railway line into the picture.
Estimates by Johnson (1956) indicate the magnitude of this
increase. Basing his conclusions on 1954 population figures, he
says, "a very rough estimate of the total number of farming
families in the main maize-producing areas of the railway line
may be hazarded at between 25,000 and 30,000."

At the same time a strong incentive to increased farming was
provided by the "Improved African Farmers" scheme which had
its beginning in 1947, the "new drive" starting in 1949, and by
soaring maize prices. High prices provided a very strong incentive
to "unimproved" farming, particularly in the newly incorporated
areas of fertile and relatively abundant maize soils. Thus, while
the number of contributors to maize sales increased rapidly, there
was also a very significant increase in the average acreage
cultivated per "producing unit"—the Cultivation Factor. The
number of improved farmers in the railway line area, to whom
acreage bonuses were paid, increased from 455 in 1950 to
1,830 in 1958, and if, as sampling data suggest (Rees 1958),
they cultivated on the average two-and-a-half times the subsistence
acreage, this alone may have increased the Cultivation Factor
by 8 or 9 per cent. "Unimproved" farming may well have had
an even more significant effect on this factor, but there is no
knowing; attention was concentrated on the improved farmers.

If, simply as a speculation, we take the formula $P(7Y-13)$,
giving P a value of 27,500, to represent conditions during this
period—though we might be justified in postulating a higher value
than 7 for the Cultivation Factor, and we must remember that
the factor values were probably rising throughout the period—
the expectation of maize deliveries then falls within the limits
123,000 and 700,000 bags. Seven of the nine events conform to

this expectation and two do not, the deliveries of the remarkable and contrasting years 1957 and 1958 when purchases amounted to 832,000 and 55,000 bags respectively (see Figure 7). The exceptions, however, serve to emphasise the point.

The forecasts or expectations of maize deliveries were based on certain hypothetical yield levels which might generally be expected, but exceptionally good and bad seasons are certain to occur in the long run. It happened that two such seasons followed each other. The first, 1956–7, was the near-perfect year, almost certainly the best for thirty years or more; while in 1957–8, according to report, "the season was the worst on record."[3] To explain the seemingly remarkable deliveries of 1957 it is only necessary to postulate the quite unremarkable maize yield, for such a season, of about 6 bags an acre—or less if one assumes a higher value for the Cultivation Factor at that time; while in 1958, one may reasonably assume, the mean yield approximated to subsistence level and the great majority of cultivators had little or no surplus. It was a very bad year but not a famine year; and, quite possibly, it was not the worst on record. On my own recollection, the 1932–3 season, when vast swarms of the red locust, then at the peak of the last great swarm cycle, destroyed almost entirely what drought had left of the crop, was probably a great deal worse. Curiously enough, this appalling season had also been preceded by an exceptionally good one, the surplus from which—it had not then been drawn into the money economy to any great extent—served to tide over the year of disaster.

The contrast between European and African deliveries of maize in the two recent years of climatic extremes is interesting and instructive:

	DELIVERIES (*bags of 200 lb*)	
	1957	1958
European	1,176,000	543,000
African (railway line)	832,000	55,000

If the 1957 deliveries are taken as 100 in each case, European and African deliveries in 1958 were 46.2 and 6.6 respectively.

[3] *Annual Report of the Dept. of Agriculture,* Northern Rhodesia, Lusaka, 1958.

African yields must, of course, have fallen to a greater extent (for the area of European production consists almost entirely, and the African area only partly, of good maize soils; while the technical skill, equipment, and "farming awareness" of the European are unquestionably superior): but the difference is mainly that to be expected between the saleable product of commercial farming, which is simply and directly related to the seasonal yield, and the surpluses of subsistence of semi-subsistence cultivation, in which the bulk of the crop in a normal year is used to meet domestic requirements. European and African yields probably fell to, roughly, 46 per cent and 36 per cent of those of the previous year.

THE ROLE OF THE BEER PARTY IN TRADITIONAL AGRICULTURE

Further evidence of the general existence of a grain surplus is to be found in the practice, almost universal throughout Africa, of the working "beer party." Beer-making played an essential part in the economies of most of the traditional systems of food-production, and the changes of recent years have not greatly diminished its importance. The more laborious operations, such as tree-felling, bush-clearing, opening new land, heavy hoeing, and harvesting, are still commonly carried out by collective work parties of kinsfolk and neighbours, to whom beer—or, sometimes, game meat in hunting regions—is offered as incentive and reward. In effect, since agricultural production is individualistic, the majority of men in a group work collectively for each other in turns, the output of work varying with the quantity of beer provided. If much beer is offered much work will be done: but if the quantity is parsimonious or the quality poor the work output will be reduced in proportion. Women too initiate beer-parties, taking part when the work is hoeing, and this practice may be on the increase in regions of migrant labour. Such an increase, attributed to the absence of men, has been recorded among the Nsenga of Petauke.

De Schlippe (1956) has described the role of the working beer party among the Zande of the southern Sudan[4] and pointed out that the practice tends to maintain some degree of social inequality. Households who act as generous hosts, because they

---

[4] Turner (1957) has described its operation in Ndembu society.

happen to have a considerable surplus of cereals, will acquire the most extensive cultivations and are therefore most likely to produce a surplus again in subsequent years. He adds that "the incentive to thrift and foresight which is provided by prestige as well as by profit from work paid for in beer is very important."

OTHER USES OF THE NORMAL SURPLUS

There were other uses for the food surplus. It was used in the fulfilment of social obligations, to acquire prestige by the display of hospitality and generosity, and to honour important people, while in some societies it entered into barter trade and played a part in religious ritual. Lynn (1937), writing in the 1930s of the Mamprusi in what is now Northern Ghana, says that their surplus of grain in a good year was "used lavishly in religious ceremonies"; so lavishly, it seems, that some enthusiasts found themselves short of seed by the start of the next season.

The obligation to offer customary gifts to political superiors, in acknowledgment of the right to hold or allocate land, sometimes amounted to a form of taxation which diverted part of the normal surplus to the maintenance of elaborate social and political hierarchies. This appears to have been true of the Chagga, who live on the moist southern slopes of Kilimanjaro [in Kenya] in a region of highly fertile volcanic soils and reliable climate. Their chiefs once maintained elaborate courts, supported by customary gifts, where the heads of powerful clans—"nobles," as my Chagga informants called them—lived throughout the year, and to which any subject of the Chief might go in expectation of hospitality. This organisation was possible because soil and climate permitted a high population density, and ensured a surplus that did not vary greatly from year to year and could be collected within a relatively small area. In contrast with the Chagga, the Tonga— with their highly variable surplus, liable to vanish altogether— had no such organisation and, indeed, no political chiefs.

HUNGER MONTHS AND FAMINE YEARS

The conclusion that fully agricultural peoples normally produced a surplus of food is not necessarily contradicted by the fairly frequent occurrence of "hunger months" in some African societies. No doubt, individual lack of foresight and too lavish use of

the surplus were common enough: but where general and regular
food shortages occur they are, I suggest, commonly associated with
systems in which hunting and food gathering, pastoralism or
tribute formerly made an important contribution to the food supply, or with fully agricultural systems in process of degeneration.
The Bemba of Northern Rhodesia [see Richards 1948], who
certainly have "hunger months," are a case in point. They preserve
a strong hunting cult—as do the Ndembu, the Zande, and many
others—which may well indicate the former economic importance
of game meat. Bemba men will still point north to the country
of the Mambwe [see Watson 1958] on whom they levied
tribute, and say, "Our gardens were there"; and they have long
been involved in the migrant labour nexus with its effects on
man-power and production. The fact that, with the diminution
of game, a hunting cult may no longer derive its importance
from contribution to the food supply, but from the identification
of hunting with masculinity and social status, explains its survival
but does not disprove an economic origin.

People who are primarily pastoralists frequently cultivate too
small an acreage to yield a normal surplus, and when the numbers
of their livestock in relation to population fall below a certain
level, recurrent food shortages are inevitable unless there is an
adequate increase of acreage. This appears to be the situation of
the Gogo of Dodoma in Tanganyika, a semi-arid region better
suited to livestock than crop production. They are still described
as "essentially pastoral," but the average household owns only
about 8.25 livestock units, which is clearly well below the requirements of a pastoral economy, and they also cultivate. Rounce
(1946) has attributed the "prevalence of famine" in Dodoma
partly to the small acreage cultivated "per adult": he says that
four adults cultivate on the average only 4.5 acres, and one may
hazard a guess, based on his figures, that this represents 0.7 of an
acre or less per head of population, an area which may be too
small to yield a normal surplus in this environment, particularly
on depleted soils. Degeneration may also be regarded as a contributing factor, since there is serious over-stocking and over-
cultivation and the fallow period has fallen below the level
required for the maintenance of fertility. General population
density is probably well above the critical point, in relation to
the natural poverty of the environment and the weakness of the
system—though there have been compensating innovations, such

as conservation of crop residues for dry season feed (a Dodoma Native Authority rule specifies 100 bundles per household) and the use of manure: but the quality of manure is poor and, since it has usually to be transported in headloads, the quantity applied to the land is small.

People who relied partly on tribute or pillage are also very liable to find themselves short of food when these sources are no longer open to them. Such were the Ngoni, whose history Barnes has described as "essentially that of an armed nation on the march." Their settlements were on a military pattern, closely grouped, and this, together with their attitude to cultivation as an occupation fit only for women and slaves, necessarily implied a weak and inadequate agriculture. Priestley and Greening (1956) estimate that as early as 1898 Ngoni lands in Fort Jameson were carrying a population three or four times greater than they could sustain in perpetuity under traditional methods of cultivation, and it is hardly surprising that food shortages appeared when tribute and raiding ended. The reverse of this situation is to be seen among the Matengo in the north of the Livingstone Mountains, between Songea and Lake Nyasa, who still cultivate about twice as much as they require for their own needs, a survival of the time when they had to provide not only for themselves but also for their Ngoni overlords.

For the people who lived wholly by their agriculture there were strong incentives and compulsions to cultivate more than the bare subsistence minimum, and among these the incentive of security was compelling. The food surplus was an essential safeguard and an important element in the economic and social structure of tribal societies. But this safeguard was never complete. In most years there was food to spare and in poor years a sufficiency that ensured survival, but, unless it had been preceded by an exceptionally good season, a year of catastrophe—by drought, flood, locusts, or other pests—meant famine, and, if not the destruction of the community, at least temporary dispersal and a reduction of its numbers. Twice in the last half of the nineteenth century the Lamba of Northern Rhodesia came near to extinction. In 1891, the year after Joseph Thomson's visit to Mushiri's country, the crops failed and there was famine, while the crops of the following year were destroyed by great swarms of the red locust. The plight of the Lamba was desperate, but in this crisis many were able to save themselves by fleeing to the Lenje country where the crops had escaped destruction. Of those who remained behind, in the hope of subsisting on wild fruits and famine foods, only a few survived. This was their second major catastrophe within fifty years. There had been an earlier locust famine in the decade 1850–60 so severe that the Lamba were almost wiped out (Dore 1931). Many tribes must have suffered a similar fate and some may have perished. Even with the safeguard of the normal surplus, existence was precarious enough for the subsistence cultivator; without it, Africa would have been an even more sparsely populated continent when the Europeans first came there.

The existence of a surplus of the main food crop—cereals, cassava, yams, or whatever it might be—or an abundance in the good seasons, does not, of course, imply that the diet was adequate or balanced throughout the year. The well-known diet deficiencies of Africa are common to the cultivating peoples. Except in the years of disaster, food was generally adequate in terms of calories, but there were, and are, in almost every agricultural society periods of "hidden hunger" due to vitamin and mineral deficiencies and a diet with too low a protein/carbohydrate ratio.

One of the earlier effects of European administration and settlement in Africa was to make the food surplus less essential as a safeguard and to attract it within the orbit of the money economy. Suzerain governments could generally be relied upon to provide famine relief in times of catastrophe and they did their best to control locust outbreaks—with final success, it appears, in the case of the red locust—and to mitigate their effects. The first markets for the surplus were administrative centres and mission stations whose small needs were easily supplied: but, as increasing demand came from industry, mining, and other enterprises employing African labour on a large scale, the very unreliable nature of the surplus—or, as it was usually expressed, the inadequacy of "native farming"—became apparent in the regions of unreliable climate. We must, however, leave this aspect of the matter aside for the present, since our main concern is with the factors influencing the area cultivated by subsistence producers following their traditional methods of land-use. The incentive to produce a surplus must be counted as one such factor, and it will be evident that climate, operating directly on crop yields and indirectly through its effects on staple crops and agricultural practices, may well exert a decisive influence.

5 CUSTOMARY SYSTEMS OF REWARDS IN RURAL SOUTH INDIA

Scarlett Epstein

INTRODUCTION

ECONOMICS is concerned with the phenomena of production and distribution. Market and non-market economies alike have to meet the same problems: goods have to be produced and distributed among the population. It is on the former that economists have concentrated their attention. At the same time they have tended to neglect the interactions and conflicts between the market and other social institutions. However, in the study of societies which are changing over from non-market to market economies such factors cannot be so easily ignored. Since the majority of the world's population lives in societies where this transition is now occurring, the development of underdeveloped areas has become a central problem in world affairs, and a central concern of economists and others. Ways and means have to be devised to increase output so as to allow for surplus to be sold, by which the economy is incorporated in the market system. Economic development involves here not only the use of new and more productive methods, it also depends on the presence of appropriate incentives which will induce the population to adopt the new techniques. In these circumstances, therefore, the recognition of the interplay of all social institutions becomes particularly important. This probably explains why economists have developed so few models to show the working of traditional non-market economies. They have concentrated their attention rather on the emerging and growing capitalist sector (Lewis, 1954:139–

SOURCE: Scarlett Epstein, "Productive Efficiency and Customary Systems of Rewards in Rural South India," in *Themes in Economic Anthropology,* Raymond Firth, editor, Tavistock Publications Limited, 1967. Reprinted by permission of the author and publisher.

191, and 1958:1–32). Yet in order to establish the conditions for
the emergence and growth of a capitalist sector in underdeveloped
countries an understanding of the principles underlying the customary non-market economies is essential. Apart from its purely
theoretical interest, this is necessary to explain why some development schemes are successful and others fail; why the indigenous
population of underdeveloped areas is prepared to react positively
to some new economic opportunities and not to others.

Here I seek to explore some of these issues by focusing on
hereditary labour relationships as they operate in India. My
analysis is concerned to examine the implications of this system
for productive efficiency, for the principles that underlie it and the
way in which these differ from forms of capitalist economic organization. I shall show the importance of average productivity in
underdeveloped Indian villages as opposed to the emphasis placed
on marginal productivity in industrial economies.

THE JAJMANI SYSTEM

Economists sometimes assume that all farming economies are
composed of self-sufficient owner-occupier households (e.g.
Lewis 1954:148). However, there are many rural societies in
which members perform specialized functions: Indian farming
communities with their complex division of labour provide a
good example. The character of economic relationships in Indian villages is largely determined by the high degree of specialization that exists and by the particular sets of beliefs and ob-
servances that underlie and perpetuate this division of labour. It
is in fact the caste system that throws into relief the complex
division of labour in Indian society. A major feature of the caste
system is that labour relationships between the landowning castes
and their dependent servicing castes are usually hereditary and
rewards are paid annually in the form of fixed quantities of farming produce.

In the past, villages were largely self-sufficient; goods and
services were mutually exchanged by the different specialist castes
within small rural communities. Services and duties which the
various castes performed for one another and the rewards associated with these were regulated by a socio-economic system
known as the *jajmani* system. According to Sanscritic Indian
usage, *'jajmani'* refers to a client who receives religious services

and gives gifts in return for them. But, following Wiser, the term *jajmani* has come to be accepted for the system as a whole. He defined *jajmani* as follows: 'These service relationships reveal that the priest, bard, accountant, goldsmith, florist, vegetable grower, etc. etc. are served by all the other castes. They are the *jajmans* of these other castes. In turn each of these castes has a form of service to perform for the others. Each in turn is master. Each in turn is servant. Each has his own clientele comprising members of different castes which is his *"jajmani"* or *"birt"*. This system of interrelatedness in service within the Hindu community is called the Hindu *"jajmani* system"' (Wiser 1958:xxi). Beidelman has criticized Wiser for describing a Hindu caste village as a system of idyllic mutuality, whereas in reality castes are linked in unequal relationships based upon power (1959:6). This asymmetrical dimension of the *jajmani* system had its roots in land tenure, numerical predominance, political influence, and ritual differentiation in the caste hierarchy. From this point of view, Gould has described *jajmani* as 'a matter of landowning, wealth and power controlling castes providing a structurally fixed share of their agricultural produce along with numerous "considerations", in exchange for craft and menial services rendered by the mainly landless impoverished, politically weak lower castes' (1958:431). Similarly, Beidelman speaks of *jajmani* as 'a feudalistic system of prescribed hereditary obligations of payment and of occupational and ceremonial duties between two or more specific families of different castes in the same locality' (1959:6). In short, where Wiser talks of mutual rights and obligations, Beidelman and Gould emphasize the high degree of economic and political differentiation characteristic of India's customary system of labour relations. On the face of it, these views of the *jajmani* system are plainly inconsistent. I shall try to show later, however, that both are in a sense correct; the inconsistency arises from the fact that each stresses only one aspect of the total system.

All writers on the *jajmani* system stress the point that rewards and duties were strictly defined. The interdependence between the different caste occupations was based on hereditary ties. Rewards were in terms of agricultural produce, and quantities were fixed. As a result, methods of work were handed down from generation to generation and a certain rhythm of productive activities became a fixed aspect of the Indian villager's life.

TYPES OF TRADITIONAL LABOUR RELATIONS

In order to understand the traditional economic relationships
which have been described as falling within the *jajmani* system,
their component parts and variations in different places and under different conditions must be made clear. The extreme form
of *jajmani,* that is the prescribed hereditary relationship involving
all castes in any one rural settlement, appears to have been
largely limited to certain areas in North India. Yet the division
of labour supported by the caste system, and expressed in the
hereditary ties between different caste households, occurred to
some extent in most Indian villages. Thus in Mysore in South
India I found two types of hereditary link in the villages: one
between Peasant[1] masters and their Untouchable labourers, the
other between Peasants and certain functionary castes, such as
Washerman, Barber, and Blacksmith, whose services were continually required. Village craftsmen, such as the Goldsmith and
Potter, whose services were not in regular demand, had no
hereditary relationship with Peasant caste households; they were
not rewarded annually, but rather on the occasions when their
services were required. In these Mysore villages landholding was
vested in Peasants, who possessed what Srinivas has called 'decisive dominance' (1959:1–16), that is they dominated numerically, economically, politically, and also largely ritually. (There
were no Brahmins in this village.) Though most of the servicing
caste households had some land of their own, their holdings were
too small to suffice for their subsistence. Therefore the castes with
little land contributed their labour and/or skills to the life of the
community and in return received a fixed share of the total
agricultural output produced. These economic relations were,
however, only one aspect of the multiple relations which linked
the different caste households in the Indian village. For instance,
the hereditary relationship between a Peasant master and his
Untouchable labourer operated not only in the economic but also
in the political and ritual spheres. If an Untouchable was involved in a dispute with another, whether Untouchable or not,
his Peasant master had to come to his support. Similarly, the

---

[1] Caste names are written with capital initials: thus a Peasant is a
member of the Peasant caste, whereas a peasant is a farmer.

Untouchable allied himself with his Peasant master in disputes. He was expected to be prepared to fight for the latter, even against Untouchables aligned with other Peasants in conflict with his own master. Perhaps even more important, the Untouchable had to perform a number of ritual services for his Peasant master, such as carrying a torch ahead of a funeral procession from his master's household. These different types of relations—political, economic, and ritual—reinforced each other and in turn helped to ensure the stability of Indian peasant economies. Furthermore, the Hindu concepts of Karma (destiny) and Dharma (innate endowment), as well as beliefs in ritual pollution, stressed the maintenance of the *status quo*. Caste indeed pervaded the total complex of Indian society. There are, therefore, many aspects to caste relations. For the purpose of the present argument, however, we need concern ourselves only with the way in which the different aspects of the hereditary ties affected the purely economic part of the relationship. The more general social and political advantages, which, as we have seen, are part of the system of customary labour relationships, acted as additional incentive to landowners to meet their economic liabilities in good and bad harvest years alike. The non-economic aspects of labour relations are probably even more important from the workers' point of view. Not only are Untouchable labourers assured of a minimum subsistence level in bad harvests, but the hereditary relationship provides them with a benevolent master who is expected to look after them as a father provides for his children. In fact, the customary relationship between Peasant masters and Untouchable labourers is couched in kinship terms; a Peasant calls his Untouchable labourer his 'Old Son' (*Hale maga*). Moreover, by leading the good life of an Untouchable, a labourer can hope to be reborn into a higher caste in his next existence.

The caste system incorporated two types of economic relationship. There were strictly hereditary ties between landowners and their servicing castes; these were highly prescribed. There were also the less prescribed but more personally contractual relationships between landowners and certain artisan castes, such as Basketmaker and Potter, whose services were not in regular demand. The establishment of links with outside markets brought new economic opportunities to Indian villages. The possibility of selling crops and labour offered incentives to enterprising men to improve their productive efficiency. We can investigate, therefore, whether these different types of socio-economic relationship produced different reactions to the new opportunities. I shall illustrate my discussion mainly with material from two villages: Wangala, with its strictly prescribed hereditary system of rewards; and Dalena, where the diversification of economic activities had already largely undermined the traditional relationships (Epstein 1962).

CUSTOMARY SYSTEMS OF REWARDS
AND IMPROVED PRODUCTION TECHNIQUES

Following irrigation, Wangala lands required more and deeper ploughing. Farmers, therefore, had to replace their customary wooden ploughs with iron ones. Not only did these need more maintenance than wooden ploughs, but repairs also demanded greater skill. Wangala's Blacksmith, who had hereditary relations with Peasant farmers in the village, found that he had to learn how to repair the new iron ploughs. He also found that he was kept busier by his Peasant clients than he had been prior to irrigation. Yet his annual reward in kind remained the same. When he approached Peasant elders about an increase in the customary reward, they flatly refused it. They argued that it had been fixed by elders in the distant past and they saw no reason to increase the quantity of agricultural produce given annually to the Blacksmith, since it was still adequate to feed him.

The Blacksmith then carefully considered his position and came to the conclusion that it would be in his best interest to discontinue his hereditary relations with Peasant households altogether and work instead for cash. However, when he proposed this to Wangala's Peasant elders, who composed the village *panchayat,* they opposed his suggestion most strongly. They pointed out to him that relations which had lasted through generations could not be broken off at one stroke. It was, of course, in their own interest that the traditional arrangement should be maintained. They threatened that if the Blacksmith refused to perform his customary duties they would make his life in the village pretty much impossible. Since he had a small landholding in Wangala he was reluctant to move to another village. Nevertheless, being a very enterprising man, he was determined to be rid of his customary obligations, which he regarded as obstacles in his way to success. He wanted to be able to branch out into other activities, not directly connected with his craft, such as making doors and window-frames. He continued to argue with the Peasant elders until they finally offered a compromise. They suggested that if he could find some other Blacksmith prepared to carry on the traditional relations on customary terms, he himself would then be free to work as he liked. Wangala's Blacksmith managed to find a classificatory brother from another village who, as the youngest of a large family, was pleased to be able to take over the position which Wangala's Blacksmith had come to find so burdensome. Thereafter the new Blacksmith repaired wooden ploughs and other traditional tools belonging to the Peasants for which he received his annual reward of a fixed quantity of agricultural produce; the indigenous Blacksmith repaired their more recently acquired iron ploughs, for which he was paid in cash. Whereas Peasant farmers had at first not been prepared to grant even a small increase in the quantity of annual reward in kind the blacksmith received, they were now quite ready to pay extra cash for the services, which they had previously expected from him as part of their customary arrangements. Though this behaviour may appear strange, I shall show that the rationale and the principles on which it was based are quite clear.

Admittedly irrigation had increased the productivity of land. However, Peasants tended to regard the greater yield as part of the normal windfall profits which had been associated with the system of prescribed hereditary rewards. They rationalized their argument in terms of subsistence requirements and told the Blacksmith that the customary reward was still sufficient to feed him and his family. But the expansion of a cash sector induced the Blacksmith to hold out for higher rewards; this meant that he was no longer prepared to work for a minimum of subsistence. After the Blacksmith had managed to disentangle himself from his customary obligations and had provided a substitute for himself, Peasants were quite prepared to pay different amounts of cash for the various jobs he performed for them and which his substitute was not able to do. As soon as the hereditary ties between Wangala's indigenous Blacksmith and his Peasant clients had been broken as a result of the contact with the wider cash economy, Wangala Peasants acted as typical entrepreneurs in advanced economies. They were prepared to pay extra for the blacksmith's work because it could be associated with a considerable increase in total output.

In the case of Wangala's Blacksmith we are dealing with an extremely enterprising man: he designed a new and improved iron plough and started making it himself; he branched out into house-building and other activities for which the growing prosperity in the area produced a demand. However, before he could take advantage of the new economic opportunities he had to disentangle himself from his hereditary relationship with his Peasant clients. Peasant elders, village *panchayat* members, had used their political influence and power to force the indigenous Blacksmith to provide a substitute for himself to carry out his traditional duties. Thus the customary system of rights and duties continued to exist and exert pressures to ensure conformity. Customary ties are obligatory not only for workers but also and equally, for employers. 'Workers were entitled to their rights from every villager, according to the rules of the village communities; and if the villagers declined to employ their services to which they were entitled, they must still pay the *bullcottee hucks* (reward in kind)' (Wiser, 1958:xxvi). What is also worth noting, incidentally, is how this system of relationships is modified to operate in India's large and rapidly growing cities. I became aware of this when I stayed with one of my English friends in Bombay. It appears that individual Washermen managed to establish a system of 'customary' relationships with tenants in particular blocks of flats. The Washerman washes all the clothes for the resident families and in turn receives a fixed monthly reward from each of them. When my hosts' Washerman decided to return to his natal village for a few months a year, he arranged for one of his kin to carry on his duties during his absence. Though my hosts were satisfied with their 'own' Washerman, they found the services of his substitute highly unsatisfactory; they therefore wanted to find a different Washerman. However, none of the many underemployed Washermen in Bombay was prepared to take on the job. They all regarded it as the prerogative of the 'customary' Washerman, who in turn had the right and duty to provide a substitute in his stead, if he went absent. In fact my hosts were boycotted by Bombay's Washermen, because they had attempted to change their 'customary' Washerman. The system of customary relationships in this way gives labour relations great stability and tends to eliminate competition, even in a highly competitive urban environment.

Similarly, Wangala's new Blacksmith continued to work according to long-established rules and was completely unaffected by the new economic opportunities in his environment. The existence of hereditary labour relations and fixed annual rewards, therefore, acted as a force to maintain the *status quo* and accordingly as an obstacle to economic growth and expansion. Wiser reports that 'there is very little stimulus for better work. The Washerman has no desire to buy a flat iron to iron his *jajmani's* clothes. If he were to get one, he would simply increase his own labour and get very little, if any more, pay for it' (1958:142).

Craftsmen who have no such prescribed and highly formalized relations with their clients can much more easily branch out into new activities than those who, like Wangala's Blacksmith, are subject to traditional labour relations. For example, in Dalena there were a number of immigrant craftsmen caste households, such as the Basketmaker, whose enterprise was not in any way hampered by traditional agreements. When the growing urban demand for more colourful and nicely shaped mats and baskets became effective, Dalena's Basketmaker changed his products and methods of production. (There was no Basketmaker in Wangala with which to compare him but a comparable craftsman there, a Jeweller, preferred to cultivate his own small plot of land instead of seeking the advantage of the new urban market.) Moreover, the Basketmaker's close links with the nearby urban centre made him realize there was a big demand for pork—which may be eaten by lower-caste Hindus. Accordingly, he started rearing pigs in Dalena itself and sold them with considerable profit at the nearest urban market. His enterprise proved so successful that he even sent word to his brother to join him. The latter came and they continued to expand their business. A comparison of the case of Wangala's indigenous Blacksmith with that of Dalena's Basketmaker clearly indicates the drawback of a prescribed system of rewards and obligations when it comes to economic expansion. This point can be further illustrated by the reaction of Wangala Peasants to the introduction of improved production techniques.

Wangala had had some tank-irrigated lands even before canal irrigation reached the village. Thus some of Wangala's peasants were already accustomed to growing paddy (rice) long before canal irrigation made the growing of wet crops a practical proposition. Traditionally, a *gumpu* group of ten or twelve women was employed as a team to transplant the paddy seedlings from the nursery to the paddy fields. Each *gumpu* had a leader, whose responsibility it was to see that her co-workers turned up on the day arranged between her and the Peasant: the leader also received a certain fixed amount of crops per acre of paddy her group transplanted. She gave equal shares of this agricultural produce to each member of her *gumpu* while she kept a slightly larger proportion for herself. Each Peasant always employed the *gumpu* of the wife of the Untouchable with whom he had hereditary relations. Accordingly, there was a traditional relationship between a Peasant farmer and his *gumpu,* involving fixed customary rewards. About 20 years after canal irrigation reached Wangala, the Agricultural Department tried to introduce the Japanese method of paddy cultivation to Wangala farmers. The officials stressed the considerable increase in yield which would result from the new method. Though farmers were quite prepared to believe this, only a few were ready to experiment with the new method, which involved a more laborious way of spacing plants properly. First of all, farmers were not prepared to pay the *gumpu* more for transplanting the new way, because there was pressure from the more conservative farmers against raising the fixed reward for the services of a group of women. Secondly, the few more enterprising men who were prepared to offer a higher reward to their *gumpu* found that the women had developed a certain rhythm of work and were reluctant to change it; besides no one was prepared to pay them for re-training. Similarly, when officials from the Agricultural Department tried to introduce a cheap and most efficient weeding hook, the use of which would have considerably reduced the cultivation labour required, Wangala farmers were not prepared to employ the new tool. At first sight their reaction appears difficult to understand, but it becomes more readily explicable when viewed in the context of hereditary relationships. These make them responsible for providing a minimum of subsistence for their Untouchable labourers. If they substituted tools for labour and therefore saved some agricultural produce in terms of rewards, they might then have to give in charity what they had initially saved. They would therefore have no net gain. Besides, they would be criticized for being mean and selfish.

In these instances we see the Peasants of Wangala rejecting new techniques which would have increased output. But their response cannot be attributed simply to conservatism—which in any case often indicates a recognition of diffuse benefits not seen on the surface. For in other spheres, which were not covered by the hereditary system of rewards, Wangala Peasant farmers displayed a considerable degree of enterprise. They were, for example, extremely progressive in their attitude towards sugarcane cultivation, an entirely new venture to them. Since sugarcane had not been one of the traditionally cultivated crops, there were no customary production techniques or traditional rewards associated with it. Thus farmers felt free to experiment with the new techniques and methods and adopted those that proved most productive and efficient. They paid their labourers in cash on a daily basis. The number of labourers any one farmer employed was largely determined by the interaction between the wage-rate and marginal productivity, as is the case in any capitalist system. Since the problem of the subsistence for the village population was taken care of by the system of hereditary labour relations, a Wangala farmer could operate in spheres outside the customary system like any 'rational' employer in an industrial society: he attempted to maximize his returns by equating marginal returns with marginal costs. A Peasant's hereditary obligation to provide a minimum of subsistence for his dependent households provides an obstacle to improving productive efficiency and maximizing returns. Wherever this obligation is not in existence or has been abandoned, we can expect a more positive reaction to new economic opportunities. This becomes clear when we examine Dalena's economic activities.

Dalena lands had remained dry even after irrigation had reached the area. Dalena farmers therefore sought to participate in the growing prosperity of the region by diversifying their economic activities and by purchasing wet lands in neighbouring villages. This resulted in the breakdown of hereditary ties between Peasant farmers and their Untouchable labourers. In turn, this meant that farmers were left free to employ labourers with whom they had no customary arrangements. Nor were they bound by customary rewards in the form of a fixed quantity of agricultural produce. Unlike his Wangala counterpart, a Dalena Peasant farmer was thus able to select his labourers, who worked for him according to his instructions and under his supervision. His re-

lationship with his labourers was mainly contractual; he paid
them in cash on a daily basis. The better worker received a
higher daily wage. Moreover, since his hereditary obligation to
provide a minimum of subsistence for his dependent Untouchable
households had already disappeared, he was keen to employ the
new weeding hook, which Wangala farmers were reluctant to
accept. This resulted in a considerable saving of labour and
therefore in a sizeable gain. Paddy was a new crop to Dalena
farmers. But, unlike Wangala landowners, Dalena Peasants were
not tied to any customary techniques and arrangements for
paddy cultivation, and they showed themselves eager to experiment with the Japanese method of paddy cultivation, which
promised them greater returns. In fact, the adoption of the new
method of paddy cultivation enabled Dalena farmers to get a
considerably higher output per acre of paddy than Wangala
farmers with their customary method. According to a stratified
random sample, which I compiled in the same way in both villages in 1955 and 1956, the average output per acre of paddy
cultivation by Dalena farmers was as much as Rs. 362 (1962:
218), while it amounted to only Rs. 281 in Wangala (1962:47).
Thus the average yield per acre of paddy was about 30 per cent
higher for Dalena than for Wangala farmers. As a matter of fact,
Dalena's village headman won the prize in 1953 for the best
yield per acre of paddy in the whole district. Although Dalena
farmers have less wet land and have to walk longer distances to
their fields than Wangala Peasant farmers, yet the disappearance
of the prescribed hereditary system of labour relations enabled
them to adopt more efficient and productive methods of paddy
cultivation and therefore ensured them a considerably higher
yield.

AVERAGE PRODUCT AND CUSTOMARY REWARDS

Having discussed the operation of customary systems of reward
and shown that they provide serious obstacles to increasing productivity and economic growth in general I want now to attempt
an analysis of the principles underlying these labour relations in
stagnant village economies. Here I seek to suggest answers to
such questions as: What determined the number of masters any
one craftsman or agricultural labourer sought? What determined
the number of customary labour relationships any one farmer was

prepared to continue? And, again, what determined the amount of the fixed annual reward?

Since hereditary labour relationships still operate in Wangala, I shall utilize the numerical data I collected there as the basis for this discussion. Prior to irrigation, *ragi* (*Eleusine corocana,* a millet) used to be the major crop in Wangala; it also provided the staple diet for the villagers. The population was composed of 128 Peasant, 28 Untouchable, 2 Washerman, and 1 Blacksmith households. The total area of dry land cultivated by Wangala villagers was about 540 acres. Output of *ragi* varied from year to year according to climatic conditions. Bad years were those when rainfall was insufficient or fell at the wrong time; famine years were those when most crops failed and a considerable proportion of the population had to go hungry and many even died. Informants told me that bad years used to occur with a frequency of about one in every five or six years; this is borne out by Mysore rainfall statistics. Accordingly, we find that the output per acre of *ragi* varied from a minimum of just over two *pallas* (one *palla* of *ragi* equals 208 lb) in bad seasons to a maximum of about eight or nine *pallas* in good ones. The average daily subsistence requirement of *ragi* per household is just under two *seers* (one *seer* is one-hundredth of one *palla,* or 2 lb); this makes the annual *ragi* requirements for each household about seven *pallas* and for the whole village composed of 159 households 1,113 *pallas.* In bad years Wangala's total *ragi* output of approximately 1,300 pallas was thus slightly more than sufficient to keep all the households fed, provided it was distributed equally among all of them. The average output per household in bad seasons was, therefore, an important factor in determining the size of any one settlement. I shall subsequently return to the importance of the average in stagnant economies. At this stage in the argument it is sufficient to note that in bad years the total product of the village had to be distributed equally among all households in order to keep the population alive. Yet the discrepancy in the landholding by Peasants and their dependent Untouchable labouring households was, and still is, considerable. The average landholding per Untouchable household was about 1½ acres, while that of Peasants was about 4 acres. This meant that in bad years Wangala Untouchable households managed to produce only approximately 3½ *pallas of ragi,* while each needed at least 7 *pallas* to survive. By contrast, the average Peasant household produced

over 9 *pallas* of *ragi*. Average labour requirements per acre of
ragi amount to about 35 labour days in bad years. The average
Peasant household thus needed a minimum of about 120 labour
days to cultivate its *ragi* fields. As cultivation of *ragi* is concentrated into a short period in the year—*ragi* is a two to four
months crop—each Peasant farmer needed at least one or two
helpers. It is extremely difficult for the Indian farmer to know
the marginal product of his labour, i.e. the addition to total output
produced by the last unit of labour employed: sometimes two men
produce as much as three do, at other times there are differences in
return. For the Peasant farmer it is much easier and more reliable
to calculate the average product per labourer: this can readily be
done by sharing the output equally among all cultivators. In bad
years Wangala villagers, Peasants and their dependent households
alike, all received an equal share of the total quantity of *ragi* produced. This meant that each Peasant had to give 50 *seers* of *ragi*
to each of his two dependent Untouchable households. Fifty
seers of *ragi* is in fact the quantity of fixed annual reward given
by Wangala Peasant masters to their Untouchable servants. Each
Untouchable household had to have hereditary relationships with
about eight or nine Peasant masters in order to make up the
deficiency in bad years between his family's food requirements
and his own output of *ragi*.

Clearly, in bad years Peasants had no more *ragi* supplies than
their dependent Untouchables. However, masters were prepared
to accept this egalitarian distribution always in the hope of better
seasons. In years of bumper crops the average Peasant farmer
could produce a surplus of about 25 *pallas* of *ragi* over and
above his subsistence needs including the fixed rewards to his
Untouchable labourers. This surplus enabled him to throw large
feasts, arrange for elaborate weddings, invest in better bullocks or
houses, etc. (cash saving was very rare). Good harvests, therefore,
provided Peasants with the means with which to conduct their
struggle for prestige. Economic differentiation was clearly taking
place in good years, whereas in bad seasons the emphasis was on
egalitarianism. In order to maximize his total product the Peasant
farmer needed helpers; he needed them even more in good years
than in bad. To make certain that his helpers were on the spot
when required, he in turn was prepared to maintain hereditary
relationships with them and give them fixed annual rewards. Other
considerations besides the purely economic, such as ritual and

political, reinforced the Peasant's preparedness to maintain his customary relationships.

Good years meant better yields also for Untouchables. However, since their landholdings were so much smaller than those of Peasants and their masters had prior claim on their work performance, their own output never reached the village maximum. Labour requirements per acre of *ragi* were higher in good than in bad years: bumper crops needed more weeding and more harvesting. Therefore, in good years Untouchables had even less time for their own fields than in bad seasons. The major part of their food requirements was always provided by their Peasant masters in the form of fixed quantities of annual rewards. Untouchables were prepared to accept the system of fixed rewards because it provided them with security even in bad years. Though no dependent Untouchable ever managed to have a surplus even approaching that of Peasant households in good seasons, the servicing castes did also benefit indirectly from good harvests: they watched the Peasants' lavish weddings and collected food at feasts. They could also get loans from their masters to help purchase cattle. Moreover, the hereditary relationships offered to the dependent Untouchables a number of advantages of more diverse economic and social nature: each Untouchable could count on his Peasant masters to help him in arranging and conducting weddings and in settling disputes and to give him some degree of social security in general.

In our Wangala example we have seen how the small landholdings of the Untouchables buttressed the system of fixed customary rewards. On the basis of this, we may postulate that the quantity of fixed annual rewards will vary according to the total village produce in bad years, the size of the labourers' landholdings, and the number of labour relations any one of them can maintain. This statement may be verified in different ways: first, by examining the fixed annual rewards of landless dependent households; second, by finding out whether there is any correlation between the quantity of fixed rewards and the size of the dependent household's acreage; and, third, by establishing whether or not there are differences in the quantity of fixed rewards in different villages in the same area.

We can satisfy the first point by examining the hereditary relationships in which Wangala's two Washerman households were involved. Prior to irrigation they were completely landless. Each had hereditary relationships with 64 Peasant masters. In turn each Peasant gave his Washerman 15 *seers* of *ragi* per year. This meant that the Washerman households' annual income in terms of *ragi* amounted to 9½ *pallas,* which in bad years was probably more than the *ragi* intake in Peasant households. However, since these Washerman households were completely dependent for their own requirements on their annual rewards, which did not vary at all according to bad or good seasons, Peasants as a group were prepared to let them have slightly more than the average *ragi* output of a bad year. By contrast, the Blacksmith, who owned one acre of dry land and had hereditary relationships with all 128 Peasant households, received only 5 *seers* of *ragi* annually from each of them. Since one Blacksmith could quite easily meet the work requirements of 128 Peasant households and since he owned some land himself, his annual reward from each of his masters was only one-third of that of the Washerman. This clearly indicates that annual rewards were fixed regardless of the service involved.

Furthermore, neighbouring villages in the Wangala area, where the landholding pattern as well as the caste composition of the population is different, also had different quantities of *ragi* making up the annual rewards given by Peasant masters to their dependent households.

The importance of the average product in underdeveloped economies has already been emphasized by Lewis, when he referred to it as setting an objective standard for wages in the capitalist sector; 'men will not leave the family farm to seek employment if the wage is worth less than they would be able to consume if they remained at home' (1954:148–149). However, this is not entirely true, because other incentives besides wages may attract men to cities and often they do not understand how much subsistence costs in money terms. In any case, since Lewis's main concern at the time was to show how a newly emerging capitalist sector operates, rather than to analyse the subsistence sector, he did not pursue the point further.

In order to throw into relief the importance of the average product in Indian village economies I shall now describe the operation of a customary system of rewards by a composite picture of a traditional large settlement made up of one Peasant farmer, controlling 50 acres of dry land, and 14 dependent Untouchable households. The output of approximately 120 *pallas* of *ragi* in bad seasons was slightly more than sufficient to keep the small community alive—7 *pallas* of *ragi* being the annual subsistence minimum per household. The Peasant master, who always hoped for better harvests, wanted to retain his labour force and, therefore, in bad years distributed his total product equally: his own as well as each of his 14 dependent households received 8 *pallas* each.

If, owing to the improvement in climatic conditions, a number of good harvests were experienced in succession, more labour was required to cope with cultivation and, in particular, with harvesting so as to maximize the total product. Thus one or more servicing households may have been attracted to join the 14 Untouchables' households. However, it probably took quite some time before the news of the more favourable harvests spread to less fortunate areas. Furthermore, time had to elapse before putative kinship ties—since hereditary labour relations are couched in kinship terms—could be manipulated so as to arrange for a grafting on to the system of hereditary labour relationships, as in the case of the Blacksmith cited earlier. Conversely, if after an increase in the number of dependent households once more some bad harvests occurred which reduced the output again to 120 *pallas* per year, pressures will have begun to operate on the last accepted member of the group to migrate and lighten the burden of the Peasant's obligation to provide subsistence for his labourers. The time-lag between the variations in harvests and the appropriate adjustment in the size of the labour force helps to explain cases of zero or even negative marginal productivity, as well as incidents of strains and stress in the political and social system of Indian villages.

The share of the Peasant landholder, who himself participated in cultivating, was in bad sessions no larger than the annual reward he had to give to each of his dependent Untouchable households. By contrast, good harvests gave him a surplus of as much as 300 *pallas* of *ragi* over and above the rewards he had to pay to his labourers. He could utilize this surplus to throw large feasts and establish status and prestige for himself. Labourers, on the other hand, were prepared to accept the system of fixed annual rewards, because it assured them of their subsistence requirements, even in bad seasons. Thus, it was the expectation of good harvests which induced the Peasant master to accept in bad years a share equal to the annual rewards his labourers

received, whereas the continued threat of bad harvests induced
Untouchable labourers to accept a reward which did not vary
according to labour performed or according to harvest. The system was, therefore, maintained by the chance occurrences of good
and bad harvests. Its essence was chance of profit for the Peasant and assurance of security for the Untouchable. It broke
down only in extremely bad harvests, when the total product was
not sufficiently large to provide a minimum of subsistence for all
the members of the society. Such years were famine periods,
during which the customary system of rewards had to be completely suspended. But in normal times, when bad and good
harvests occurred fairly regularly, the fixed rewards for customary services were based on the average product produced in
bad seasons.

Indian villagers, rich and poor alike, used to be largely at the
mercy of climatic conditions. In bad seasons 'share and share
alike' was their motto, whereas good harvests facilitated large
feasting and economic differentiation with its concomitant struggle
for prestige. This may help to explain the contradictory views
of the *jajmani* system expressed by Wiser, on the one hand, and
by Gould and Beidelman, on the other. Wiser may have examined the *jajmani* system as it operated in bad seasons with its
emphasis on equal distribution of output, while Gould and Beidelman may have concentrated their attention on good harvests
when extreme economic differentiation occurred and when masters appeared to exploit their dependent helpers as capitalists
are supposed to exploit their workers. But the difference may also
be due to different philosophical approaches. However, while the
success of a capitalist enterprise is largely due to the foresight
and organizing ability of its managers, traditional Indian landowners and landless alike relied completely on favourable climatic
conditions to provide them with good harvests. No one, of Wiser,
Gould, or Beidelman, seems to appreciate that Indian villagers,
rich and poor alike, were all subject to the hazards of their
environment, over which they had very little control. Mere survival was therefore of the utmost importance to the population
of these underdeveloped economies. Indian villagers did not have
the technological know-how nor did they have any incentives to
initiate growth in these economies, which were geared to stability.

In traditional Indian village economies with hereditary systems
of reward, landowners were chiefly concerned with the quantity of

the average product in bad years—or to put it in time-perspective: they were interested in the long-term average product, rather than in the marginal addition to total output which any one worker might contribute. This emphasis on the average is noticeable not only in economic relations; it pervades many other aspects of the culture. Beliefs in sorcery and witchcraft sanction 'average' behaviour. For instance, when a Wangala Peasant builds a new house with the surplus he produced in good years, he always hangs a broken pot on to the outside. This is done to protect the new house from evil and jealous spirits. The broken mudpot is supposed to give the impression that the house is not new but really old like all the other houses in the vicinity.

As soon as external forces break down the isolation of Indian villages and new economic opportunities are introduced, innovations and changes at the margin tend to become important. This is precisely what happened in Wangala after irrigation had facilitated cash cropping. As we have seen, Wangala Peasant farmers were not prepared to grant the Blacksmith even a small increase in his customary fixed reward of five *seers* per household. This had been based on the average product in bad years and was regarded as more than sufficient for subsistence. However, as soon as the Blacksmith managed to disentangle himself from his hereditary obligations, Peasants started to think of his work in terms of the contribution it made to the cultivation of their lands. The Blacksmith was obviously an innovator: he designed an improved plough and became a housing contractor. Peasants then began to appreciate their Blacksmith and his contribution to their output, i.e. wet crops, the cultivation of which necessitated iron ploughs in place of the customary wooden ones. Thus the transition from a non-market to a market economy involves a change from emphasis on average productivity to one on marginal productivity. However, before such change in emphasis can take place customary labour relations must be eliminated. Planners would be well advised to bear in mind that it may be easier to improve productivity efficiency by introducing entirely new crops or products, rather than by attempting to change the traditional methods and techniques of production. For example, in Saurashtra 'attempts were made to introduce improved methods of cultivation like the Russian method of *bajri* cultivation and the Japanese method of paddy cultivation. Only 34 acres were brought under the Russian method of *bajri* cultivation against the overall target of about 2,600 acres and for the Japanese method, the respective figures were 52 acres and 865 acres' (Government of India 1954:247). If the agricultural officials responsible for this programme had appreciated the principles underlying the traditional organization of labour, they would never have attempted to introduce improved methods for cultivating customary crops, but would have tried to introduce entirely new crops, which could then have been cultivated outside the system of traditional labour relations.

This change-over from emphasis on the average product to stress on the marginal product is not only a symbol of important changes in the economic organization of previously isolated economies, but is also marked by radical changes in the social and political systems. In non-market economies nonconformity is usually penalized. By contrast, economic growth necessitates innovation and needs men who are prepared to take risks. These new entrepreneurs who try to take advantage of the new economic opportunities then want to translate their wealth into social status. They want to replace the system of ascribed social status with one in which status can be achieved. This has been happening in Dalena (Epstein 1962:276–293) and is evidenced in a great number of societies which are in the process of being integrated into the wider economy and polity. The strains and stresses associated with these changes provide a fascinating field for study and analysis.

CONCLUSION

A prescribed hereditary system of rights and duties of the kind I have been describing is a mark of a stagnant rather than a developing economy. India's customary systems of rewards and obligations placed great emphasis on stability. In a country such as India, with low soil fertility and little and/or irregular rainfall, there are usually great fluctuations in harvests occurring side by side with small margins of agricultural profits. Accordingly, the security value offered by the stable system of prescribed rights and duties was of great importance. Landowners knew in advance the exact quantity of agricultural produce they had to give as reward for services rendered them throughout the year. A good harvest brought them windfall profits. However, making allowances for differences of individual skill—and some were very adept in getting the best yield out of a poor soil—the greater yield was due primarily not to any positive efforts of their own, but to more favourable climatic conditions. On the other hand, a good harvest also meant more work for labourers, as well as for certain functionaries, for which they received no extra rewards, though they did get greater fringe benefits. Yet a poor harvest still provided the dependent castes with a minimum of subsistence. Since Indian villagers, landowners and landless alike, were all subject to the hazards of their climate and environment, they were all prepared to participate in a system which offered all of them at least the minimum necessities of life, except in times of extreme crop failure and general famine. There were, therefore, no incentives to initiate growth in these stagnant economies. The relative isolation of traditional Indian villages and the absence of outside markets helped to perpetuate the system of hereditary relationships, which defined most obligations and rewards.

The equal distribution of the total output in bad seasons may help to explain migration whenever population increased to such an extent that the average product in bad years became insufficient to provide a minimum standard of subsistence for villagers. There may be also some correlation with infanticide and the frequency of abortion though this is much more difficult to measure. Moreover, the appreciation of fixed annual rewards, i.e. fixed labour costs, associated with variations in output may clarify the fact of economic differentiation in traditional non-market peasant economies as well as the forms such differentiation has taken.

If my analysis of traditional Indian peasant economies is valid —and I hope I have shown that it is—it may also be relevant to other pre-industrial societies. For instance, we may find that many societies with a low level of technological knowledge and consequent inability to control their environment tend to distribute produce in a standard pattern equally in bad as in good seasons. What good seasons do is to facilitate economic differentiation. This tentative suggestion gains support from a study of African farming practices. Allan, an agriculturalist, reckons that before the introduction of cash crops to Africa, men cultivated enough land to bring them in a small surplus in normal years—he calls this a normal surplus. However, in good seasons, when there were favourable climatic conditions, they had bumper harvests

with a large surplus; in bad years they went on short commons.
Allan worked this out in trying to explain the considerable annual
variations in the crops that African tribes now sell on the open
market. Before the creation of this external European market,
the bumper seasons presumably produced large-scale feasting,
while bad harvests involved mutual assistance in terms of the
same relations (Allan 1965:38–49). Though African landholding patterns and labour relations differ from those in India, there
seems to be a general similarity. The emphasis on average productivity in bad seasons may also help to throw light on witchcraft beliefs and sorcery in many primitive societies. These are
but a few of the many interesting problems raised by the preceding analysis of Indian village economies.

I

I HAVE TAKEN my title from the *Onomastikon* or *Word-Book* of an Alexandrian Greek of the second century of our era named Julius Pollux. At the end of a longish section (3.73–83) listing, and sometimes exemplifying, the Greek words which meant "slave" or "enslave", in certain contexts at least, Pollux noted that there were also men like the helots in Sparta or the *penestae* in Thessaly who stood "between the free men and the slaves". It is no use pretending that this work is very penetrating or systematic, at least in the abridged form in which it has come down to us, but the foundation was laid in a much earlier work by a very learned scholar, Aristophanes of Byzantium, who flourished in the first half of the third century B.C. The interest in the brief passage I have cited is that it suggests in so pointed a way that social status could be viewed as a continuum or spectrum; that there were statuses which could only be defined, even if very crudely, as "between slavery and freedom". Customarily Greek and Roman writers were not concerned with such nuances. To be sure, the Romans had a special word for a freedman,

SOURCE: M. I. Finley, "Between Slavery and Freedom," *Comparative Studies in Society and History*, Vol. 6, 1965, pages 233–49. Reprinted by permission of the author and the Cambridge University Press.

[1] This is the text, slightly modified, of a lecture I gave to the Royal Anthropological Institute in London on May 30, 1963. I have kept annotation to a bare minimum. For Graeco-Roman slavery, see the bibliographical essay in the volume of articles I edited, *Slavery in Classical Antiquity* (Cambridge, Eng., 1960). My colleague, Mr. E. R. Leach of King's College, kindly read and criticized the manuscript. I have also benefited from the opportunity to discuss the *servi Caesaris* with Mr. P. R. C. Weaver of the University of Western Australia, and problems of American slavery with Professor A. A. Sio of Colgate University.

libertus, as distinguished from *liber,* a free man. When it came
to political status, furthermore, distinctions of all kinds were
made, necessarily so. But for social status (which I trust I may
be permitted, at this stage, to distinguish from political status),
and often for purposes of private law, they were satisfied with
the simple antinomy, slave or free, even though they could hardly
have been unaware of certain gradations.

There is a Greek myth which neatly exemplifies the lexical
point, a myth certainly much older than its first surviving literary
reference in the *Agamemnon* of Aeschylus produced at Athens
in 458 B.C. Hercules was afflicted with a disease which persisted
until he went to Delphi to consult Apollo about it. There the
oracle informed him that his ailment was a punishment for his
having killed Iphitus by treachery, and that he could be cured
only by having himself sold into slavery for a limited number of
years and handing over the purchase price to his victim's kinsmen. Accordingly he was sold to Omphale, queen of the Lydians
(but originally a purely Greek figure), and he worked off his
guilt in her service. The texts—which are fairly numerous and
scattered over a period of many centuries—disagree on several
points: for example, whether Hercules was sold to Omphale by
the god Hermes or by friends who accompanied him to Asia for
the purpose; whether his term of servitude was one year or
three, and so on.[2]

One has no right to expect neatness in a myth, of course, nor
for that matter, in the legal institutions of the archaic society
in which this particular myth arose. The ancient texts all speak
of Hercules being "sold", and to describe his status while in
Omphale's service they employ either *doulos,* the most common
Greek word for "chattel slave", or *latris,* a curious word that
meant "hired man" and "servant" as well as "slave". The word
latris upsets modern lexicographers and legal historians, but the
historical situation behind the lexical "confusion" is surely that
in earlier Greece, as in other societies, "service" and "servitude"
did in fact merge into each other. The Biblical code was explicit
(*Deuteronomy* 15.12–17): "If thy brother . . . be sold unto
thee and serve thee six years; then in the seventh year thou
shalt let him go free from thee . . . And it shall be, if he say

---

[2] The most important sources are Sophocles, *Trach.* 68–72, 248–54,
274–76 (with scholia); Apollodorus, *Bibl.* 2.6.2–3; Diodorus 4.31.5–8.

unto thee, I will not go out from thee; because he loveth thee and thy house, because he is well with thee; then thou shalt take an awl, and thrust it into his ear unto the door, and he shall be thy servant for ever."

Cynical remarks are tempting. Quite apart from the very real possibility that the six-year limitation was, as one distinguished authority has phrased it, "a social programme rather than actually functioning law",[3] there is an odd ring about "if he say unto thee, I will not go out from thee; because he loveth thee and thy house". One suspects that the transition from a more limited bondage to outright slavery was neither so gentle nor so voluntary; that, unlike Hercules, the victims in real life, once caught up in bondage, had little hope of release; that, as in peonage, their masters could find devices enough by which to hold them in perpetuity. The sixth-century Athenian statesman Solon, referring to debt-bondsmen, used these words: "I set free those here [in Athens] who were in unworthy enslavement, trembling at the whim of their masters."[4] And the Greek words he employed were precisely those which became the classical terminology of chattel slavery: *douleia*—slavery; *despotes*—master; *eleutheros* —a free man. Modern scholars, too, regularly speak of enslavement for debt. Why not? Why play with words? Why draw elaborate, abstract distinctions?

The men Solon liberated belonged to a restricted though numerous class: they were Athenians who had fallen into bondage to other Athenians in Athens. His programme did not extend to non-Athenians, outsiders, who were slaves in Athens, just as the Biblical six-year limitation was restricted to "thy brother", a fellow-Hebrew, and did not extend to the Gentile. Nor was this merely a sentimental distinction, empty rhetoric holding up vain hopes to the in-group, pretending that they were different from the outsiders when in fact they shared the latter's fate. The whole story of Solon (like the closely analogous struggles in early Roman history) proves that the distinction was meaningful, though it may have been in abeyance in any individual case or in any given span of time. For Solon was able to abolish debt-bondage

---

[3] D. Daube, *Studies in Biblical Law* (Cambridge, Eng., 1947), p. 45; cf. the important recent article of E. E. Urbach, "The Laws regarding Slavery . . . of the Period of the Second Temple, the Mishnah and Talmud", *Annual of Jewish Studies*, 1 (London, 1963), pp. 1–54.

[4] Quoted in Aristotle, *Const. of Athens* 12.4.

—indeed, he had been brought to power for that express purpose—following a political struggle that bordered on civil war.
Athenian bondsmen had remained Athenians; now they re-
asserted their rights as Athenians, and they forced an end to
the institution—servitude for debt—which had deprived them
de facto of all or most of those rights. They were not opposed
to slavery as such, only to the subjection of Athenians by other
Athenians. Hence, whatever the superficial similarity, this was
not a slave revolt; nor did ancient commentators ever make such
a connection, despite their resort to slave terminology.

I am not now concerned with the history of debt-bondage and
its abolition or of clientage in Athens or Rome, nor for the
moment with giving precise content to the notion of "rights".
I am merely trying, as a preliminary, to establish the need to
distinguish among kinds of servitude, even though contemporaries
were themselves not concerned to do so, at least not in their
vocabulary. The matter of revolts is worth pursuing a little further
in this connection. The debt-revolt syndrome was one of the most
significant factors in the early history of both Greece and Rome,
and it even survived into classical history. Helot revolts were
equally important and very persistent in the history of Sparta.
Chattel slaves, on the other hand, showed no such tendency at
any time in Greek history and only for a brief period, between
about 135 and 70 B.C., were there massive slave revolts in
Roman history.[5] Towards the end of antiquity, finally, there
was more or less continual revolt in Gaul and Spain by depressed
and semi-servile peasants and slaves acting in concert (Thompson
1952).

To explain the differences in the revolt pattern, and particularly
in the propensity to revolt, by the differences in treatment, by
the relative harshness or mildness of the masters, will not do.
The one distinction which stands out most clearly is this, that the
chattels, who were both the most rightless of all the servile types
and the most complete outsiders in every sense, were precisely
those who showed the weakest tendency to cohesive action, the

---

[5] The basic, though brief, study is now Joseph Vogt, *Struktur der
antiken Sklavenkriege* (Akad. d. Wiss. u. d. Lit., Mainz, *Abhandlungen*,
1957, no. 1). See also Peter Green, "The First Sicilian Slave War", *Past &
Present*, 20 (1961), pp. 10–29, with discussion in no. 22 (1962), pp. 87–92;
Claude Mossé, "Le rôle des esclaves dans les troubles politiques du monde
grec . . .", *Cahiers d'histoire*, 6 (Lyon, 1961), pp. 353–60.

weakest drive to secure freedom. Under certain conditions individual slaves were permitted considerable latitude and eventual emancipation was often held out as an incentive to them. That is another matter, however. Slaves as slaves showed no interest in slavery as an institution. Even when they did revolt, their objective was either to return to their native lands or to reverse the situation where they were, to become masters themselves and to reduce to slavery their previous masters or anyone else who came to hand. Insofar as they thought about freedom, in other words, they accepted the prevailing notion completely: freedom for them, as individuals, included the right to possess other individuals as slaves. Debt-bondsmen and helots, in contrast, fought —when they fought—not only to transfer themselves, as individuals, from one status to the other, but to abolish that particular type of servitude altogether (though not, significantly, to abolish all forms, and particularly not chattel slavery).

II

To a Greek in the age of Pericles or a Roman in Cicero's day, "freedom" had become a definable concept, and the antinomy, slave-free, a sharp, meaningful distinction. We are their heirs, and also their victims. Sometimes the results are amusing, as in the first efforts in the Far East in the nineteenth century to cope with the word "freedom" for which they had no synonym and which till then was "scarcely possible" in, say, Chinese (Pulleyblank 1958:204–5). And sometimes the results are very unfunny, as when western colonial administrators and well-meaning international organizations decree the immediate abolition of such practices as the payment of bride-wealth or the "adoption" of debtors on the ground that they are devices for enslavement (Stevenson 1943:175–80). My subject, however, is not current social or political policy but history; the simple slave-free antinomy, I propose to argue, has been equally harmful as a tool of analysis when applied to some of the most interesting and seminal periods of our history. "Freedom" is no less complex a concept than "servitude" or "bondage"; it is a concept which had no meaning and no existence for most of human history; it had to be invented finally, and that invention was possible only under very special conditions. Even after it had been invented, furthermore, there remained large numbers of men who could not

be socially located as either slave or free, who were "between
slavery and freedom", in the loose language of Aristophanes of
Byzantium and Julius Pollux.

Let us look at one particular case which came before the
royal court of Babylonia in the middle of the sixth century
B.C., in the so-called neo-Babylonian or Chaldaean period.[6] A
man borrowed a sum of money from a woman who was head
of a religious order, and gave her his son as a debt-bondsman.
After four years the woman died and both the debt and the
debt-bondsman were tranferred to her successor. The debtor also
died and his son, now his heir, found himself in the position of
being simultaneously the debtor and the debt-bondsman (an
oddity in the ancient Near East, I may add parenthetically,
where the transfer of wives and children for debt was common,
but the transfer of the debtor himself was rare, unlike the Graeco-
Roman practice). After ten years the bondsman paid over a
quantity of barley from his own resources and went to court.
The judges made a calculation, according to the conventional
ratios, translating each day's service into barley and then translating the barley (both the real barley and the fictitious barley)
into money; this arithmetic produced a sum which was equal to
the original loan plus 20% interest per annum for ten years;
the court ruled, accordingly, that the debt was now paid up and
the bondsman was liberated.

During his ten years of service was the bondsman who was
working off his father's debt (which became his debt) a free
man or a slave? Were the Israelites in Egypt slaves because
they were called upon, as were most native Egyptians, to perform
compulsory labor for the Pharaoh? The answer seems clearly
to be "Neither"; or better still, "Yes and no". In analogous
situations the Greeks and Romans defined such service obligations
as "slave-like", and that catches the correct nuance. There were
in Babylonia and Egypt chattel slaves in the strict property sense,
whose services were not calculated at so much barley or so
much anything per day, who could not inherit, own property
or take a matter to court. But there was no word in the languages
of these regions to encompass all the others, those who were

---

[6] V. Scheil, "La libération juridique d'un fils donné en gage . . . en
558 av. J.-C.", *Rev. d'Assyriologie*, 12 (1915), pp. 1–13; cf. H. Petschow,
Neubabylonisches Pfandrecht (*Abh.* Akad. Leipzig, Phil.-hist. K1., 48,
no. 1, 1956), pp. 63–65.

not chattel slaves. To call them all "free" makes no sense because it wipes out the significant variations in status, including the presence of elements of unfreedom, among the bulk of the population.

If one examines the various law codes of the ancient Near East, stretching back into the third millennium B.C., whether Babylonian or Assyrian or Hittite, the central fact is the existence of a hierarchy of statuses from the king at the top to the chattel slaves at the bottom, with rules—in the penal law, for example —differentiated among them. Translators often enough employ the term "a free man", but I believe this to be invariably a mistranslation in the strict sense, the imposition of an anachronistic concept on texts in which that concept is not present. It is enough to read the commentaries appended to the translations to appreciate the error: each such rendition requires the most complex contortions in the commentary if the various clauses of the codes are not to founder in crass inner contradictions once "free man" has been inserted. What the codes actually employ are technical status-terms, which we are unable to render precisely because in our tradition the hierarchy and differentiation of statuses had been different. Hence, for example, careful Hittitologists resort to such conventional renditions as "man of the tool", which may not be very lucid but has the great advantage of not being downright misleading. The English word "slave" is a reasonable translation of one such status-term, but it is then necessary to emphasize the fact that slaves were never very significant and never indispensable in the ancient Near East, unlike Greece or Rome.

The neo-Babylonian case I have discussed took place 60 or 70 years before the Persian Wars, by which time the Greek city-state had achieved its classical form, in Asia Minor and the Aegean islands as well as on the mainland of Greece, in southern Italy and Sicily. Proper analysis of classical Greece would require far more space than I have at my disposal, for the society was not nearly so homogeneous throughout the many scattered and independent Greek communities as we often pretend.[7] I shall confine myself to two cities, Athens and Sparta, in the fifth and

---

[7] On this point see Finley, "The Servile Statuses of Ancient Greece", *Rev. int. des droits de l'antiq.*, 3rd ser., 7 (1960), pp. 165–89; D. Lotze, *Metaxy eleutheron kai doulon. Studien zur Rechtsstellung unfreier Landbevölkerungen in Griechenland . . .* (Berlin, 1959).

fourth centuries B.C., the two cities which the Greeks themselves considered the best exemplars of two sharply contrasting social systems and ideologies.

Athens is, of course, the Greek city that comes first to mind in association with the word "freedom". And Athens was the Greek city which possessed the largest number of chattel slaves. The actual number is a matter of dispute—as are nearly all ancient statistics or, better, statistical guesses—but much of the debate is largely irrelevant since no one can seriously deny that they constituted a critical sector of the labour force (in a way which slaves never did in the ancient Near East). My own guess is of the order of 60–80,000, which would give a ratio to the free population about the same as in the southern states of the United States in the first half of the nineteenth century, but with a different distribution pattern. Proportionally more Athenians than Southerners owned slaves, but there were few if any great concentrations in single hands because there were no plantations, no Roman *latifundia*.

For our present concern there are a number of points to be made about slavery in Athens, which I shall run through briefly.

1. There were no activities in which slaves were not engaged other than political and military, and even those two categories must be understood very narrowly, for slaves predominated in the police and in what we should call the lower civil service. Contrariwise, there were no activities in which free men were not engaged, which slaves monopolized: they came nearest to achieving that in mining and domestic service. In other words, it was not the nature of the work which distinguished the slave from the free man but the status of the man performing the work.

2. Slaves were outsiders in a double sense. After Solon's abolition of debt bondage, no Athenian could be a slave in Athens. Hence all slaves to be found there had either been imported from outside the state or had been born within to a slave mother. "Outside the state" could mean a neighboring Greek state as well as Syria or southern Russia—the law never forbade Greeks to enslave other Greeks, as distinct from Athenians and Athenians —but the evidence seems to show that the great majority were in fact non-Greeks, "barbarians" as they called them, and that is why I say "outsiders in a double sense".

3. Slaveowners had the right, essentially without restriction, to free their slaves, a right which seems to have been exercised

with some frequency, especially among domestic servants and skilled craftsmen, though, as usual, we are unable to express the pattern numerically.

4. The contemporary attitude was summed up by Aristotle when he wrote (*Rhetoric* 1367a32): "The condition of the free man is that he does not live under the restraint of another." In that sense, manumitted slaves were free men, if we ignore, as we legitimately may in this outline analysis, conditional manumissions and minor obligations towards the ex-master. But in another sense "free man" is an excessively loose category. The distinction between citizens and free non-citizens was not merely political—the right to vote or hold office—but went much deeper: a non-citizen could not own real property, for example, except by special grant of that privilege by the popular assembly, a grant which was rarely made. Nor, for much of the period under consideration, could a non-citizen marry a citizen; their children were by definition bastards, subject to various legal disabilities and excluded from the citizen-body. Manumitted slaves were not citizens, though free in the loose sense, and hence they suffered all the limitations on freedom I have just mentioned. In addition, it should be noted that insofar as slaves were often freed relatively late in life, and insofar as any children born to them were not freed along with them—practices which existed though we do not know in what proportion of the cases—to that extent freed women were effectively denied the right to procreate free children.

Now let us look at Sparta in the same period, the fifth and fourth centuries B.C., and in the same schematic way.

1. The Spartiates proper were a relatively small group, perhaps never more than 10,000 adult males and declining from that figure more or less steadily during our period.

2. Such chattel slaves as existed were wholly insignificant. In their place there existed a relatively numerous servile population known as helots (a word with a disputed etymology) who were scattered over extensive territories in the southern and western Peloponnese, in the districts of Laconia and Messenia. Again we lack figures, but it is certain that the helots outnumbered the Spartiates, perhaps several times over (in contrast to Athens where the proportion of slaves to free was probably of the order of 1:4, of slaves to citizens less than 1:1).

3. Who the helots were in origin is disputed. They may even

have been Greeks to begin with, but whether so or not, they were the people of Laconia and Messenia, respectively, whom the Spartans subjugated and then kept in subjection in their own home territories. That immediately distinguished them—and distinguished them sharply—from the chattel slave "outsiders", not only genetically but also in later history, for they were bound together by something far more than just the weak negative factor of sharing a common fate, by ties of kinship, nationhood (if I may use the term) and tradition, all perpetually reinforced through their survival on their native soil.

4. Insofar as it makes any sense to use the terminology of property, the helots belonged to the state and not to the individual Spartiates to whom they were assigned. (Parenthetically I should say that the word "belonged", which explains the willingness of the Greeks to call the helots "slaves", is justified by the existence of a further Peloponnesian population who were politically subject to Sparta but were at the same time free and citizens of their own communities, the *perioeci,* whom I am ignoring in this discussion.)

5. It follows from the previous point that only the state could manumit helots. They did so only in one type of situation: when military service by helots was unavoidable, those selected were freed, either beforehand or as a subsequent reward. Once freed they did not become Spartiates but acquired a curious and distinct status, as did Spartiates who lost their standing for one reason or another, so that, as in Athens, the category of "free men" was a conglomeration, not a homogeneous single group.

These points do not exhaust the picture, nor do they by any means exhaust the range of differences between Athens and Sparta, but I trust I have said enough to make it clear not only that the differences were very sharp but also that the number of status possibilities was very considerable. It remains to add that whereas for our subject Athens was typical of the more highly urbanized Greek communities on the mainland of Greece and in the Aegean islands, Sparta was, taken whole, unique. However, if we narrow our focus solely to the helots, then parallels were far from uncommon, less so in Greece proper than in the areas of Greek dispersion east and west, such as Sicily or the regions bordering on the Black Sea, where native populations were reduced to a status sufficiently like that of the helots to warrant their being bracketed with them, as Pollux did, under the rubric "between the free men and the slaves".[8]

Now, merely to illustrate the variety which actually existed, I want to look briefly at the institution we know from the so-called law code of Gortyn in Crete.[9] The text we have was inscribed on stone in the fifth century B.C. but the provisions may be much older. The code is far from complete, and there are some devilishly difficult problems in interpretation. It is clear, however, that there was a servile population which in some sense "belonged" to individual Gortynians who could buy and sell them (apparently with restrictions hinted at, but not clarified, in the code), unlike the situation in Sparta with which too easy comparisons are often made. Yet this same servile population had rights which slaves in Athens lacked. For example, the rules regarding adultery and divorce and the provisions regulating relations between bondsmen and free women leave no doubt that it is proper to speak of marriage, of a relationship which was more than the Roman *contubernium* between slaves, because it created enforceable rights, but which was at the same time far less than a marriage between free persons. For one thing, an unfree husband was not his wife's tutor; that role was fulfilled by her master. For another, such a marriage did not lead to the creation of a kinship group, although it created the elementary family for certain purposes. Hence a composition payment for adultery could be arranged with the kinsmen of a free woman, but only with the master of a servile woman. (Parenthetically, I should also note that debt-bondsmen are clearly differentiated in the code from the bondsmen I have been discussing.)

After the conquests of Alexander the Great, finally, when Greeks and Macedonians became the ruling class in Egypt, Syria and other lands of the ancient Near East, they found no difficulty in adapting themselves to the social structure which had been in existence there for millennia, modifying the top of the pyramid more than the bottom. A city in the Greek style like Alexandria had its chattel slaves just as in Athens; in the

---

[8] In addition to Lotze, *op cit.*, see D. M. Pippidi, "Die Agrarverhältnisse in den griechischen Städten der Dobrudscha in vorrömischer Zeit", in *Griechische Städte und einheimische Völker des Schwarzmeergebietes* (Berlin, 1961), pp. 89–105.

[9] See the works cited in n. 6 and D. Lotze, "Zu den *woikees* von Gortyn", *Klio*, 40 (1962), pp. 32–43.

Egyptian countryside, however, the peasantry remained in its traditional status, neither free nor unfree. Royal grants of land to favorite ministers included whole villages along with their inhabitants. Compulsory labor services of various kinds were imposed on them, precisely as on the Israelites a thousand years earlier. Our greatest historian of this era, Rostovtzeff, (1953, I:320) has written of this peasantry that "they possessed a good deal of social and economic freedom in general and of freedom of movement in particular, . . . And yet they were not entirely free. They were bound to the government and could not escape from this bondage, because on it depended their means of subsistence. This bondage was real, not nominal." Which both makes my point and illustrates, in the vagueness and inadequacy of its formulations, how far we still are from a proper analysis of the social pattern.

The Romans, who eventually replaced the Greeks as rulers of this whole area, had a history of servitude more like that of Athens than of Sparta or the Near East, but with features of their own worth our notice. They, too, had an internal crisis in the archaic period brought about by massive debt-bondage. They, too, then turned to chattel slaves on a large scale, the form of dependent labor which was characteristic of Rome in what I shall arbitrarily define as its classic period, roughly speaking, the three centuries between 150 B.C. and 150 A.D. "Rome" is here ambiguous: we normally use it to refer both to the city on the Tiber and to the whole of the Roman Empire, which by the end of the classical age extended from the Euphrates to the Atlantic. I want to focus on neither, however, but on Italy, the Latin heartland of the Empire, which had become sufficiently uniform socially and culturally to warrant our treating it as a unit. And I want to single out a few characteristics of slavery in Italy which contribute new dimensions to the picture I have drawn so far.

1. The great landed estates of Italy, the *latifundia,* which specialized in ranching, olive- and wine-production, remained, at least until the American South replaced them, the western model of slave agriculture *par excellence.* Slave numbers there, and in the rich urban households, reached proportions far exceeding anything in Greece. In the final struggle between Pompey and Caesar, for example, Pompey's son enlisted 800 slaves from his shepherds and personal attendants to add to his father's army (Caesar, *Bell. civ.* 3.4.4.). In a law of 2 B.C., Augustus

restricted to 100 the number of slaves a man could manumit in his will, and only an owner of 500 or more was permitted to free that many (Gaius, *Inst.* 1.43). A certain Pedanius Secundus, who was prefect of the city in A.D. 61, maintained 400 slaves (Tacitus, *Ann.* 14.43.4). These are examples at the upper end of the scale, to be sure, but they help fix the whole level.

2. Upon manumission a freedman acquired the status of his ex-master, so that the freed slave of a Roman citizen became a citizen himself, distinguished by certain minor disabilities (chiefly with respect to his former master) but none the less a citizen with the right to vote and to marry in the citizen class. This last had interesting and amusing implications. Within the Roman imperial territory there was a complicated variety of free statuses in the sense that there were numerous non-Romans, free and citizens of their communities, who lacked both the political rights of Roman citizenship and the *ius conubii,* the right to contract a marriage with a Roman citizen. But an ex-slave, by the mere private act of manumission, which required no approval from the government, automatically jumped the queue, in law at any rate, provided his master was a Roman citizen.

3. A significant proportion of the industrial and business activity in Rome and other cities was carried on by slaves acting independently, controlling and managing property known as a *peculium.* This was a legal device invented in the first instance to permit adults to function independently while still technically in *patria potestas,* the tenacity of which in Rome is one of the most remarkable features of the social history of that civilization. The extension of *peculium* to slaves created legal problems of great complexity—in the event of a lawsuit, to give the most obvious example—but they do not concern me now, apart from one notable anomaly. It was possible, and by no means rare, that a *peculium* included one or more slaves, leaving the slave in charge of the *peculium* in the position of owning other slaves *de facto,* though not *de jure.* The reason I have singled out *peculium* can perhaps best be clarified by some rhetorical questions. In what sense were a slave loaded with chains in one of the notorious agricultural *ergastula* and a slave managing a sizeable tannery which was his *peculium* both members of the same class we (and the Romans) call "slaves"? Who was more free, or more unfree, a slave with a *peculium* or a "free" debt-bondsman?

Can the concept of freedom be usefully employed at all in such comparisons?

4. In order to insure their administrative control, the early emperors, beginning with Augustus and reaching a crescendo under Claudius and Nero, made extensive use of their own *familiae* in running the Empire. The *servi* and *liberti Caesaris,* the emperor's own slaves and freedmen, took charge of the bureaus and even headed them for a time. Careful investigation has shown that even among these imperial slaves their children were not as a rule freed along with them if they were also slaves—there are complications here, arising from the status of the mothers, which I need not go into—but stayed on as *servi Caesaris,* advancing in the service if they were capable and earning their own freedom in time. Hence the interesting situation was created in which important civil servants not only came out of the slave class but left their children behind in that class. And more interesting still, the generalization may be made that in Rome of the first century of our era, much the greatest opportunity for social mobility lay among the imperial slaves. No one among the free poor could have risen to a status like that of head of the bureau of accounts, or, for that matter, to anything like the many lower posts in the administration. I doubt if I need make further comment.

III

All the societies I have been discussing, from those of the Near East in the third millennium B.C. to the end of the Roman Empire, shared without exception, and throughout their history, a need for dependent, involuntary labor. Structurally and ideologically, dependent labor was integral, indispensable. In the first book of the Pseudo-Aristotelian *Oeconomica* we read: "Of property, the first and most necessary kind, the best and most manageable, is man. Therefore the first step is to procure good slaves. Of slaves there are two kinds, the overseer and the worker." Just like that, without justification or embellishment. There is no need to pile on the quotations; it is simpler to note that not even the ancient believers in the brotherhood of man were opponents of slavery: the best that Seneca the Stoic and St Paul the Christian could offer was some variation on the theme, "status doesn't matter". Diogenes the Cynic, it is said, was once seized by pirates and taken to Corinth to be sold. Standing on the auction block he pointed to a certain Corinthian among the buyers and said: "Sell me to him; he needs a master." (Diogenes Laertius 6.74).

Most revealing of all is the firm implication in many ancient texts, and often the explicit statement, that one element of freedom was the freedom to enslave others. Aristotle wrote the following in the *Politics* (1333b38ff., translated by Barker): "Training for war should not be pursued with a view to enslaving men who do not deserve such a fate. Its objects should be these—first, to prevent men from ever becoming enslaved themselves; secondly, to put men in a position to exercise leadership . . . ; and thirdly, to enable men to make themselves masters of those who naturally deserve to be slaves." It may be objected that I am unfair to select a text from Aristotle, the most forthright exponent of the doctrine of natural slavery, a doctrine which was combatted in his own day and generally rejected by philosophers in later generations. Let us then try another text. About the year 400 B.C. an Athenian cripple who had been taken off the dole on the ground that the amount of property he owned made him ineligible, appealed formally to the Council for reconsideration of his case. One of his arguments was that he could not yet afford to buy a slave who would support him though he hoped eventually to do so (Lysias 24.6). Here was no theorist but a humble Athenian addressing a body of his fellow-citizens in the hope of gaining a pittance from them. The implications—and the whole psychology —could scarcely be brought out more sharply.

I do not propose to revive the old question of the origin of the inequality of classes, to ask why dependent labor was indispensable. My starting-point is the fact that everywhere in the civilizations under consideration, as far back as our documentation goes (including the new documentation provided by the Linear B tablets), there was well established reliance on dependent labor. All these societies, as far back as we can trace them, were already complex, articulated, hierarchical, with considerable differentiation of functions and division of labor, with extensive foreign trade and with well-defined political and religious institutions.

It is rather what happened thereafter which interests me now: the essentially different development as between the Near East and the Graeco-Roman world, and, in the latter, the sharp

differences in different periods as well as the unevenness of
development in different sectors. I have already indicated the
most fundamental difference, namely, the shift among Greeks
and Romans from reliance on the half-free within to reliance
on chattel slaves from outside, and as a corollary, the emergence
of the idea of freedom. A wholly new social situation emerged,
in which not only some of the components were different from
anything known before but also the relationships and spread
among them, and the thinking. We may not be able to trace
the process but we can mark its first literary statement beyond
any doubt, in the long poem, the *Works and Days,* in which
Hesiod, an independent Boeotian landowner of the seventh century B.C., presumed freely to criticize his betters, the "bribe-
devouring princes" with their "crooked judgments".

In another poem, the *Theogony,* also attributed to Hesiod—
and it does not matter whether the attribution is right or not,
for the *Theogony* and the *Works and Days* were approximately
contemporary, which is enough for this discussion—the same
new social situation found expression in another area of human
behavior, in man's relations with his gods. As Frankfort phrased
it, the author of the *Theogony* "is without oriental precedent in
one respect: the gods and the universe were described by him
as a matter of private interest. Such freedom was unheard of in
the Near East . . ." (Frankfort 1949:250) It was a firm doctrine
in the ancient Near East that man was created for the sole
and specific purpose of serving the gods: that was the obvious
extension by one further step of the hierarchical structure of
society. Neither Greek nor Roman religion shared that idea. Man
was created by the gods, of course, and he was expected to
serve them in a number of ways, as well as to fear them, but his
purpose, his function, was not that, and surely not that alone.
Institutionally the distinction may be expressed this way: whereas
in the Near East government and politics were a function of the
religious organization, Greek and Roman religion was a function of the political organization.

Hesiod is often called a peasant-poet, which is inexact, for
Hesiod was not only himself an owner of slaves but he assumes
slavery as an essential condition of life for his class. From the
first, therefore, the slave-outsider was as necessary a condition
of freedom as the emancipation of clients and debt-bondsmen

within. The methods by which outsiders were introduced into the society need not concern us. But it is worth a moment to consider one aspect of the outsider situation, the "racial" one, which is being much discussed today, both by historians and sociologists, chiefly with reference to the American South. It is important to fix in mind that "outsiders" were often neighbors of similar stock and culture; that though the Greeks tried to denigrate the majority of their slaves with the "barbarian" label and though Roman writers (and their modern followers) are full of contemptuous references to "Orientals" among their slaves and freedmen, the weaknesses of this simple classification and its implications were apparent enough even to them. The decisive fact is that widespread manumission and the absence of strict endogamy together destroy all grounds for useful comparison with the American South on this score. I need not go into the variations in antiquity with respect to rights of marriage—I have already indicated the significance of the Roman practice which granted freedmen full rights of *conubium,* for example, and that should be enough to show that the "racial" element in the concept of the outsider, though not zero, was essentially irrelevant, both in fact and in the ideology. When the Roman lawyers agreed on the formulation, "Slavery is an institution of the *ius gentium* whereby someone is subject to the *dominium* of another, contrary to nature," (*Digest* 1.5.4.1) they were saying in effect that slavery was indispensable, that it was defensible only on that ground, and that one was liable to be enslaved just because one was an outsider. An outsider, in short, was an outsider. That tautological definition is the best we can offer. Hence the expansion of the Roman Empire, for example, automatically converted blocks of outsiders to free insiders.

Why, we must then ask, was the historical trend in some Greek communities, such as Athens, and in Rome towards the polarity of the free insider and the slave outsider, while elsewhere no comparable development occurred (or where incipient signs appeared, they soon proved abortive)? Max Weber suggested that the answer lay in the loosening of the royal grip on trade and the consequent emergence of a free trading class who acted as social catalysts (Weber 1924:99–107). I have no great confidence in this hypothesis, which can neither be verified nor falsified from Greek or Roman evidence. The decisive changes occurred precisely in the centuries for which we lack documentation, and for which there is no realistic prospect of new documentation being discovered. I must confess immediately that I have no alternative explanation to offer. Reexamination of the body of Greek and Roman myth may help, but the hope lies, in my opinion, in the very extensive documentation of the ancient Near East.

I say "hope", and no more, because it is no use pretending that study of Near Eastern servitude has taken us very far. One reason is the primitive classification into slave and free which has been my theme, and I now want to return to this and suggest an approach. Merely to say, as I have thus far, that there were statuses between slavery and freedom is obviously not enough. How does one proceed to formulate the differences between a Biblical bondsman who hoped for release and the man who chose to remain a slave in perpetuity and had his ear bored to mark his new status? Or between a helot in Sparta and a chattel in Athens?

The Sicilian Greek historian Diodorus, writing as a contemporary of Julius Caesar, gives us the following variation on the Hercules-Omphale myth. Hercules, he says, produced two children during the period of his stay with the Lydian queen, the first by a slave-woman while he was in servitude, the second by Omphale herself after he had been restored to freedom. Unwittingly Diodorus has pointed the way. All men, unless they are Robinson Crusoes, are bundles of claims, privileges, immunities, liabilities and obligations with respect to others. A man's status is defined by the total of these elements which he possesses or which he has (or has not) the potential of acquiring. Actual and potential must both be considered: the potential of the *servi Caesaris,* for example, was always a factor in the psychology of status in the early Roman Empire, and sometimes it became an actuality, when one of them climbed high enough on the civil service ladder and was freed. Obviously none of this can be expressed in numerical, quantitative terms: it is not a matter of one man having one more privilege or one more liability than another. Rather it is a matter of location on a spectrum or continuum of status; the *servi Caesaris* as a class, in this language, stood nearer the freedom end than did the *servi* of any private owner in Rome.

It is possible, furthermore, to work out a typology of rights and duties. By way of illustration, I suggest the following rough scheme.[10]

1. Claims to property, or power over things—a category which is itself complex and requires further analysis: for example, the difference between the power of a slave over his *peculium* and the power of an owner in the strict sense; or differences according to the different categories of things, land, cattle, money, personal possessions, and so forth.

2. Power over human labor and movements, whether one's own or another's—including, of course, the privilege of enslaving others.

3. Power to punish, and, conversely, immunity from punishment.

4. Privileges and liabilities in judicial process, such as immunity from arbitrary seizure or the capacity to sue and be sued.

5. Privileges in the area of the family: marriage, succession and so on—involving not only property rights and rights of *conubium,* but, at one step removed, the possibility of protection or redemption in case of debt, ransom or blood-feud.

6. Privileges of social mobility, such as manumission or enfranchisement, and their converse: immunity from, or liability to, bondage, penal servitude and the like.

7. Privileges and duties in the sacral, political and military spheres.

I have said enough, I trust, to forestall any suggestion that I am proposing a mechanical procedure. In Athens chattel slaves and wealthy free non-citizens (Aristotle, for example) were equally barred from marriage with a citizen; in terms of my typology, they both lacked the privilege of *conubium*. It would be absurd, however, to equate them in a serious sense just on that score. Or to take a more meaningful instance of quite another kind: Athenian slaves and Spartan helots both belonged to someone, but the fact that the someone was a private individual in the one case, the Spartan state in another, introduced a very important distinction. These various combinations must be weighed and judged in terms of the whole structure of the individual society under examination.

If I am then asked, What has become of the traditional

---

[10] This is substantially the scheme I first formulated in the article cited in n. 6.

property definition of a slave? Where on your continuum do you draw the line between free and slave, free and unfree?—my answer has to be rather complicated. To begin with, the idea of a continuum or spectrum is metaphorical: it is too smooth. Nevertheless, it is not a bad metaphor when applied to the ancient Near East or to the earliest periods of Greek and Roman history. There one status did shade into another. There, although some men were the property of others and though the gap between the slave and the king was as great as social distance can be, neither the property-definition nor any other single test is really meaningful. There, in short, freedom is not a useful category and therefore it is pointless to ask where one draws the line between the free and the unfree.

In classical Athens and Rome, on the other hand, the traditional dividing line, the traditional distinction according to whether a man is or is not the property of another, remains a convenient rule of thumb for most purposes. For them the metaphor of a continuum breaks down. But the problem has not been to understand those two, relatively atypical societies, but the others, societies which we have not understood very well just because, in my view, we have not emancipated ourselves from the slave-free antinomy. And if my approach proves useful, I suggest it will lead to a better understanding of Athens and Rome, too, where the category of "free man" needs precise subdivision.

I might close with a highly schematic model of the history of ancient society. It moved from a society in which status ran along a continuum towards one in which statuses were bunched at the two ends, the slave and the free—a movement which was most nearly completed in the societies which most attract our attention for obvious reasons. And then, under the Roman Empire, the movement was reversed; ancient society gradually returned to a continuum of statuses and was transformed into what we call the medieval world.

7 PRIMITIVE FEUDALISM AND
THE FEUDALISM OF DECAY
[1950]

Karl Polanyi

WHILE FEUDALISM in the classical sense, or feudalism proper, is a phenomenon, the interest of which lies for us mainly in its role in the history of our own civilization, feudalism in the broad sense is more or less universal, not restricted to one type of society, nor even to civilized society withal.

In this latter sense of a universal institution, we will distinguish two forms of feudalism: the one, a progressive, healthy development in early society, connected with its territorial expansions; the other associated with the dissolution of empires. The first we call primitive feudalism; the second, feudalism of decay. Classical [European] feudalism, then, was a compound of the two. Such a fully fledged form of feudalism is exceptional. It amounts to much more than an institutional system; it is a type of society, including a military, political and economic system of a particular kind. The existence of such a social system was one of the great features of Western European history; although very exceptional, it was not unique. One of our tasks is to explain this rare event. The answer lies, as indicated, in the meeting of primitive feudalism and feudalism of decay. In effect, in other instances of such a conjuncture, we are met with a civilization similar to that of Western feudalism.

PRIMITIVE FEUDALISM

Primitive feudalism is found the world over as a definite phase

---

SOURCE: This short essay, "Primitive Feudalism and the Feudalism of Decay," is one of a number of unpublished manuscripts and sets of lecture notes by Karl Polanyi given to Columbia University by Mrs. Polanyi. It is published here by permission of Ilona Polanyi.

in the development of an expanding tribal society. It is closely connected with the requirements of government ruling a larger territorial entity under conditions of an economy 'in kind.' The expansion may have occurred through the intervention of foreigners, as is the case in Polynesia and Micronesia, where a larger island inhabited by various tribes is united under one rule; or through the original tribe extending its dominance into neighboring territories, as in Africa. This, again, may take place through shepherds and herdsmen settling peacefully in the interstices of cultivators' and hunters' communities, or through outright conquest and subjugation (which, on the whole, appears to be rarer). But, whatever the stimulus to the uniting of agglomerations of settlements, and whatever form of the extension of political government, it mostly is accompanied by (1) the emergence of leadership and some degree of central control, and (2) the cattle or land (whichever is scarcer) remains the exclusive property of the new rulers. Indeed, ownership of cattle may be the source of their superiority as well as its symbol. The only way of making use of the cattle or land may lie in organizing political rule along economic lines, as in the case of the fief by which the vassal becomes possessor of cattle or land in exchange for the pledge of loyalty (mainly of a military nature).

According to the manner in which the larger territory came under a single rule, the vassals may be recruited in different ways. If the foreign aristocracy was established peacefully, or the expansion into foreign territory was peaceful, the vassals may well belong to the kin of the ruling clan or tribe (as in Samoa; or with the Banyankole and their cattle fiefs), or made into kin (Trobrianders). But if the exploit was definitely warlike the war leader's band may be recruited irrespective of kinship or clan, and a different type of vassal is met with: the "follower" of the war leader who is recompensed by allotment of land (an estate or land-holding) in the conquered territory.

Yet the elements are always fairly similar. The political organization is based on economic organization both being embedded in a new type of social relationship. Even if the vassal is of the kin of the ruling race (e.g. with the Banyankole) the tie is not that of blood, but of personal fealty or office. In principle, heredity of the fief is incompatible with the feudal tie; even where the son inherits the fief, he is usually reappointed to office.

Traces of such a development can be found in its first stage with the Trobrianders, where the Kiriwina chiefs enjoy superior prestige, and the other villagers make voluntary deliveries of yams to him. His privilege of polygamy bridges the gap between the egalitarian tribal tradition and the aristocratic superiority enjoyed by him.

With the Samoan, the feudal duty is fairly developed, but with many remnants of prior forms. The subsistence of the chief is provided by his dependent vassals, while tribute gifts are still reciprocated by counter-gifts (as with the Trobrianders). If the chief receives more than he can use up, he is bound to give a feast. If this overtaxes the chief's capacity, his family or village will help him out (as with the Manus). Thus the element of feudal lordship is qualified by traditions of reciprocity.

Goldenweiser, in his *Anthropology* (1922), describes the Baganda as being in the process of "disintegration of clan and transformation into something akin to feudalism." He says: "What we find now is a gentile system in the process of transmutation from its more primitive and regular pattern to one more nearly compatible with a vastly greater population and the requirements of a centralized political system."

This primitive feudalism is a progressive development; it makes for larger economic integration, greater military power, and the establishment of government (which contains the germs of law and justice).

FEUDALISM OF DECAY

An entirely different meaning of feudalism describes a condition of dissolution of a unitary state or empire. The term came into use in 18th-century France, and especially because of the French Revolution. The legion d'honneur was established in 1802, and its statutes committed every wearer of the pink rosette to fight all attempts to return to the feudal system. What was meant was the supposed fragmentation of the country into territories, patrimonial powers, regional customs, decentralization of government, and the appropriation of public powers by private individuals—in short, the alleged breakup of an organized empire into semi-independent sovereignties. Actually, they meant something like the political condition of Germany before the Napoleonic reforms, a country consisting of several hundred sovereign or semi-sovereign entities. This feudal condition of political Europe gave rise to the term feudalism whenever in history the decomposition of central government showed similar symptoms of decay. The criteria are these: the prerogatives of sovereignty are appropriated by private individuals. Justice, taxation, tolls and customs, coinage, and offices, are appropriated by the former servants of the central government. Public law is dissolved into private law. This is the inevitable concomitant of the breakdown of an empire. For government must be carried on, police, military safety, law and order, economic life must be maintained, and once the central government is unable to do so, by devolution, the rights fall to the local potentate, whoever he may be. This happened in the so-called feudal period of ancient Egypt, and there is hardly an ancient Oriental Empire which has not passed through such a 'feudal' period. Feudalism in this sense, is synonymous with decay of central government.

PRIMITIVE FEUDALISM AND FEUDALISM OF DECAY: A CONTRAST

Let us now enlarge somewhat on the meaning of the terms "primitive feudalism" and "feudalism of decay."

Feudalism, in the classical sense in which we know it in Western Europe, was the result of the interaction of two components: The primitive feudalism of the expansionist Germanic tribes, and the feudalism of decay resulting from the dissolution of the Roman Empire.

Let us briefly compare and contrast the two:

A. Primitive feudalism of the Germanic tribes which intersettled with the Roman population of the provinces.

1. The nuclear institution may have been most often the war-gang, the band of followers of the war leader. The organization of the gang involved

   (a) either keeping the gang at headquarters, feeding them, clothing them, investing them with arms and a horse, and giving them a good time. This is the *provende,* the Latin *prebenda* i.e. emoluments in kind given at headquarters;

   (b) or they were settled away from headquarters, provided with land and maybe some people on it, to support themselves and their horse. By this time this was mainly agricultural population used to tilling the land, or at least to supervise the work of agricultural labourers.

2. The role of land is important for their's was an economy of kind lacking trade, markets, and money. Land alone can support a person. At the same time it means the disappearance of the communal ownership of land by the clan, where it still existed. Private property in land is thus extended, and the basis of 'householding' broadened.

3. A new sort of social relationship makes its appearance. Military service is linked with the war leader's person, and land tenure is derived not from status in the clan but from the personal relation to a chief or leader.

In this manner the tribal organization is adapted to cope with problems arising out of extension of the political entity and the need to govern the new territory. However, only 'up to a point':

—a territory much too extensive for the forces at its disposal. (Bloch 1931)

What we find now is a clan system, [among the Baganda] in the process of transmutation from its more primitive and regular pattern to one more nearly compatible with a vastly greater population and the requirements of a centralized political system. (Goldenweiser 1922)

The barbarian kingdoms could *not* handle the mechanisms of administration that they had inherited. . . . the institutions were ill suited to huge kingdoms whose needs and whose size were *utterly* different from those of the little tribes and tribal leagues of yesterday. (Bloch 1941)

what we call feudal *particularism* is simply *"incomplete integration"* of the diverse parts of the country into one state. (Hintze n.d.)

The barbarian kingdom did not represent full-scale independent government but a halfway house between an awkward guestship and an equally dubious conquest. These settlers were sometimes pushing, sometimes apologetic. They did not know whether their contempt or their secret admiration for the natives was greater. For the environment into which they moved was, in most cases, civilized. They usually settled in the mild forms of military billeting in peace time, but sometimes with a radical expropriation of the Roman landowners, and amidst awful carnage. In this environment they found still existing:

    (a) the Roman householding system practiced on a large
        scale
    (b) in what remained of the cities, markets and trade and
        the use of money
    (c) a surviving municipal administration and the incipient
        functioning of the Church, while the center of the
        empire had ceased to function.

B. With feudalism of decay, the other component factor in the
development of Western European feudalism, this civilized environment showed signs of all-round decomposition.

    (a) politically, territorial disintegration—breakup of gov-
        ernment into provincial units.
    (b) economically, a return to economy of kind with the
        gradual disappearance of trade, markets, and money.
    (c) the reappearance of a social tie, reminiscent of the primi-
        tive tribal society of early Rome, which had been later
        discarded, namely the relations of patron and client
        as it existed in Republican times. Essentially it was an
        exchange of protection against fealty (*fides*). (You will
        see presently whence this great need for protection
        arose).

We can now attempt to compare and contrast the two:
Clearly, there was a resemblance between the situation arising
out of the positive achievements of a progressive [expansionist]
primitive feudalism and the negative results of a regressive
[decentralizing] development accompanying the disintegration of
a civilization of enormous extent, such as the Roman Empire was.
The similarity consists in the role played by (a) a multiplicity
of local units (particularism), (b) an economy of kind, and
(c) the emergence of a personal tie of protection and loyalty.

The contrast between primitive feudalism and feudalism of
decay centers on this:

    1. Tribal society in its growth is faced only with problems
       which are, so as to speak, of its own making. As Marx
       once wrote, human societies as a rule set themselves only
       such problems as they are capable of solving. Normally
       this is true. Tribal society has normally to cope with the
       problem of territory only to the extent to which territory
       has been settled, conquered or in some other way, already
       brought under control.
    2. As a rule, it is moving into territory of a *lower material*

culture, which is, on that account, unable to resist the incursion, or even welcomes it. This is the case with the numerous instances of herdsmen or shepherds moving into the interstices of cultivator or hunter groups, so frequent in Africa, or superior navigating races reaching islands populated by natives with less skill and organizing experience, as was so often the case in Polynesia and Micronesia. It follows that the problem facing tribal organization is how to govern a large expanse of territory. This compels them to create new means of administrative and economic integration mainly based on the localizing of both. Usually the enfeoffment of cattle or later, land, offers the solution.

In the circumstances of feudalism of decay, the *opposite* conditions obtain:

1. The tribal organization has to cope with a *sudden* vast expansion of governmental functions which it must perform or perish. The boundaries are not set by the impetus which carried the tribe into new territory, but by pre-existing boundaries of those territories.
2. A *higher* not a lower material and intellectual culture is found in being.
3. The *unequal rate of disintegration* creates an acute problem of insecurity. For the permanent means of communication and the indestructible roads, survive and outlive by centuries, the decay of government and economy. Distance, which is the great obstacle to law and order on a primitive level, offers no obstacle to the raider, the marauder, the pirate, the bullying neighbor. Within weeks invading armed parties cover hundred of miles; and inside of days forays, robberies, violent incursions of neighbors can occur. *Acute insecurity of life is the result of the combination of decay of law and order in a large territory while the means of communication [facilitate] the forces of lawlessness and disorder.* (On a small scale something akin was experienced in this country [U.S.] in the 1920's when, for a short time, gangs and rackets used modern means for criminal purposes; and on a world scale today, the means of communication having been developed on a planet from which law and government is receding).

The classical feudalism of the Middle Ages was the result of such a [dual] development.

8 FEUDALISM IN AFRICA?[1]

Jack Goody

Was feudalism a purely Western phenomenon? Is it a universal stage in man's history, emphasizing replacement of kinship by ties of personal dependence which further social development required? If it is neither a universal prerequisite nor yet exclusively Western, what are the conditions under which it is found? A host of such questions are raised by the consistent use both by historians and sociologists of the term 'feudal' as a description of the societies they are studying. Here I want to inquire into the implications and value of the concept as applied to African societies.

First used, apparently, in the seventeenth century,[2] the word

source: Jack Goody, "Feudalism in Africa?" *Journal of African History* Vol. IV, No. 1, 1963. Reprinted by permission of the author and Cambridge University Press.

[1] An earlier version of this paper was read to the African History Seminar of the University of London in May 1962, and I am grateful not only for the comments of those who attended, but also to the other contributors, whose papers were later circulated to me. Some of these, like Dr Mair and Mrs Chilver, were certainly better qualified to discuss the African studies, and I had already made use of their work. Others like Professor Helen Cam, who wrote on English feudalism, dealt much more adequately with the non-African material. My thanks are particularly due to Dr John Fage, who raised with me a problem I touch upon in the course of this essay, namely, what contribution a medieval historian could make to the study of African society were he to immerse himself in that material. For an illuminating treatment of some of the general problems that lie behind this discussion, the reader should turn to E. E. Evans-Pritchard, *Anthropology and History* (Manchester, 1961).

[2] In the sense of 'pertaining to the feudal system'. Of related words, some like feudary were used much earlier while others like feudalism were neologisms of the nineteenth century. The historian's discovery of the feudal system dates from the time of Cujas and Hotman in the sixteenth century. See J. G. A. Pocock, *The Ancient Constitution and the Feudal Law; a Study of English Historical Thought in the Seventeenth Century* (Cambridge, 1957), 70 ff.

feudal has since served an astounding variety of purposes, in everyday speech as well as in the writings of historians and sociologists. The primary referent is of course to a particular historical period, to Western Europe between the ninth and thirteenth centuries, to the social systems that on the one hand superseded the Roman Empire and the 'tribal' régimes which destroyed it, and that on the other hand preceded first mercantile and then industrial 'capitalism'. But the term has also been used of innumerable societies other than those of the medieval Europe. A recent survey (Coulborn, 1956) includes a comparison of feudalism in Japan, China, Ancient Egypt, India, the Byzantine Empire, and Russia. Nor is this simply an editorial quirk.[3] Many earlier writers on Japan had written of its feudal institutions;[4] Marcel Granet entitled his study *La Féodalité chinoise* (1952); Pirenne and Kees discuss the question in dealing with Egypt; Kovalevski and Baden-Powell do the same with regard to India and Vasiliev for Byzantium.

Historians are not the only persons to use this term in a comparative context. Social anthropologists have employed it in an equally all-embracing way. Roscoe and others have seen the Baganda as 'feudal', Rattray the Ashanti, Nadel the Nupe of northern Nigeria. Indeed it would be difficult to think of any state system, apart from those of Greece and Rome, upon which someone has not at some time pinned the label 'feudal'. And even these archaic societies have not been left entirely alone. Feudal relationships have been found in the Mycenean Greece revealed by the archaeologists and epigraphers, while it is generally agreed that one element in medieval feudalism was the institution of *precarium* of the later Roman Empire.[5]

Unless we assume the term has a purely chronological referent, then, or unless we are to take our smug refuge in the thought that persons, events, and institutions defy comparison be-

---

[3] See also Carl Stephenson, *Mediaeval Feudalism* (1942), 1–2.

[4] See also Marc Bloch, *Feudal Society* (1961), 446–70, and Robert Boutruche, *Seigneurie et féodalité* (1959), 217–97.

[5] The *precarium* was a grant of land to be held by someone during the pleasure of the donor: the land was a boon (*beneficium*) granted as the result of the prayer (*preces*) of the recipient (Stephenson, 1942:7; Pollock and Maitland (2nd ed.), 1898:1, 63 n. 1). This practice has been the subject of an extensive discussion over the relative influence of German and Roman institutions upon feudal Europe.

cause of their uniqueness, the use of any general concept like feudal, more particularly concepts like fief or client, must have comparative implications. Marc Bloch realized this when at the end of his classic study he wrote, 'Yet just as the matrilineal or agnatic clan or even certain types of economic enterprise are found in much the same forms in very different societies, it is by no means impossible that societies different from our own should have passed through a phase closely resembling that which has just been defined. If so, it is legitimate to call them feudal during the phase.' (Bloch, 1961:446.)

There is then a measure of general agreement that 'feudal' should be used in comparative work. Here I want to look briefly at the ways in which it has been employed in the African context. For a large number of political systems of the 'state' type have been called 'feudal', and it seems pertinent to try and find out what the authors are getting at.

There are times when it seems as if people who work in the non-European field use the term 'feudal' in the same spirit that led the composers of the *chansons de geste* to link the histories of their own petty kingdoms on the Atlantic seaboard with the great civilizations of the Mediterranean world; new-comers, up-starts, *nouveaux riches,* thus acquire the aura of respectability that tradition imparts. The danger in this is apparent. If the term has high status in the comparative study of society, there will be a tendency constantly to widen its range of meanings for reasons other than those of analytic utility. Moreover, an attachment to Western European models may turn out to be not the embrace of respectability but the kiss of death, just another version of the old pre-Copernican fallacy of the universe revolving around the earth.

One major difficulty in using the term for comparative purposes is that, even for historians of Europe, it has many meanings. In his introduction to the translation of Bloch, Postan writes of a recent Anglo-Soviet discussion on feudalism in which the two sides 'hardly touched at a single point. The English speaker dwelt learnedly and gracefully on military fiefs, while the Russian speaker discoursed on class domination and exploitation of peasants by landlords' (Bloch, 1961:xiii). These different views represent variants of two rather broader categories of approach which Strayer has summed up in the following words: 'One group of scholars uses the word to describe the technical arrangements by which vassals become dependents of lords, and landed property (with attached economic benefits) become organized as dependent tenures of fiefs. The other group of scholars uses feudalism as a general word which sums up the dominant forms of political and social organization during certain centuries of the Middle Ages' (1956:15).

One can discern two trends in the narrower technological use of the term feudal. The first points to its derivation from 'fee', and hence to dependent land tenure.[6] The second emphasizes the lord-vassal relationship; it was to draw attention to this aspect of 'feudalism' that Pollock and Maitland suggested the term be replaced by 'feudo-vassalism' (1898:1, 67). In general, however, the core institution of feudal society is seen as vassalage associated with the granting of a landed benefit (fief), usually in return for the performance of military duties.[7] In Max Weber's usage, feudalism is 'the situation where an administrative staff exists which is primarily supported by fiefs' (1947:322).

The wider use of the term also has its variants, each with its own body of supporters. Apart from the loose popular turn of phrase that sees all types of hierarchical status (with the possible exception of slavery and bureaucratic office) as 'feudal', there are two main trends, one relating to political structure, the other to economic conditions. Political factors are stressed in the Coulborn symposium, where Strayer summarizes this view in the following words: 'Feudalism is not merely the relationship between lord and man, nor the system of dependent land tenures, for either can exist in a non-feudal society. . . . It is only when rights of government (not mere political influence)

---

[6] e.g. N. D. Fustel de Coulanges, *Les Origines du système féodal: le bénéfice et le patronat pendant l'époque mérovingienne* (*Histoire des institutions politiques de l'ancienne France*), Paris (1890), p. xii.

[7] Although fiefs are usually thought of as based upon the tenure of land, money-fiefs also played an important part in the West; they were of even greater significance in the Crusader Kingdom of Jerusalem (Sir Steven Runciman, *The Families of Outremer* (London, 1960), 5). Kosminsky (and others before him) has pointed out that the bulk of manorial incomes took the form of money-rents rather than 'feudal' services. See E. A. Kosminsky, *Studies in the Agrarian History of England in the Thirteenth Century* (ed. by R. H. Hilton, trans. by Ruth Kisch) (Oxford, 1956) (1st pub. Moscow, 1947) and the review by M. Postan, 'The Manor in the Hundred Rolls', *Economic History Review*, 2nd ser., 3 (1950–1), 119–25.

are attached to lordship and fiefs that we can speak of fully developed feudalism in Western Europe' (1956:16).

The thesis that feudalism is essentially a locally centred form of government is clearly connected with the existence of fiefs. Dependent tenures create (or recognize) a local administration of the fief-holder and those who inhabit his estate; they constitute a devolution of powers and are associated with a weakly centralized government that depends upon vassalage to provide military support.

The other line of thinking stresses the economic aspects and sees these as characteristic of a type of productive system. This was of course Marx's approach. He saw feudalism as one of the stages of pre-capitalistic economies, a 'natural economy' which preceded and led into the commodity market system. Changes in the division of labour were accompanied by different forms of property ('the stage reached in the division of labour . . . determines the relations of individuals to one another with respect to the materials, instruments and product of labour'): the first form is tribal property, the second the communal and State property of antiquity; the third form is feudal or estates property (1845–6:115–19).

Finally, the various political and economic features are clearly linked together in practice (though the analytic nature of the connexion is open to discussion), and there is a comprehensive approach that tries to define feudalism in terms of a number of these associated institutions. Such is the conclusion to Marc Bloch's study of feudal society, where he begins the section entitled 'A cross-section of comparative history' with the words 'A subject peasantry; widespread use of the service tenement (i.e. the fief) instead of a salary, which was out of the question; the supremacy of a class of specialized warriors; ties of obedience and protection which bind man to man and, within the warrior class, assume the distinctive form called vassalage; fragmentation of authority . . . such then seem to be the fundamental features of European feudalism' (1961:446).

Each of these approaches to feudalism has been used by different authors in analysing the pre-colonial régimes of Africa. But the most explicit attempts to compare these political systems with medieval Europe have been in the work on northern Nigeria and the Interlacustrine Bantu, especially in the accounts given by Nadel of Nupe and by Maquet of Ruanda.

A section of Nadel's study, *A Black Byzantium* (1942), is actually entitled 'The Feudal State', and here the author describes the manner in which tribute was collected and how the kingdom was divided into units of different sizes ('counties'), each comprising 'a town with its dependent villages and *tunga* which were administered as fiefs through feudal lords or *egba*' (p. 117). These lords, who were recruited from the royal house, the office nobility, or the Court slaves, were eligible for promotion to more lucrative fiefs, although they continued to reside in the national capital. They constituted a 'feudal nobility' who played an important part in raising military forces for the king, especially through their personal 'clients'.

The institution of clientship (*bara*-ship), which is widespread in the States of northern Nigeria, consists in a voluntary declaration of allegiance for the sake of political protection and often provides the basis for the formation of factions. There are a variety of forms, some of which involve military service, but Nadel sees the institution as essentially comparable to the *patrocinium* of Imperial Rome and medieval Europe (1942:122–3).

In his recent study of one of the Hausa states, M. G. Smith analyses the changes that have occurred over the last hundred and sixty years in a rather similar political system. In the Hausa kingdoms, he writes, government 'is conducted through a system of ranked and titled offices known as *sarautu* . . . each of which can be regarded as an exclusive permanent unit, a corporation sole. These titled offices are characterized by such attributes as fiefs, clients, praise-songs, allocated farmlands, compounds and other possessions . . .' (1960:6).

In Zaria, as in Nupe (but unlike most of the Hausa states), offices were not generally hereditary except for kingship and the major vassal chiefships. The power and ambitions of fief-holders were controlled by the fact that they were clients of the king. Clientage (again there were a number of forms of *bara*-ship) is defined as 'an exclusive relation of mutual benefit which holds between two persons defined as socially and politically unequal and which stresses their solidarity' (1960:8).

There is an interesting difference between the accounts of Nupe and Zaria. Whereas Nadel deliberately speaks of 'a feudal system', as Lombard does for the near-by Bariba of northern Dahomey (1957, 1960), Smith is content to use 'fief' and 'client' as analytic tools without making any overall comparison with medieval Europe.

We find another similar situation in recent accounts of the states of the Interlacustrine Bantu of East Africa. In his study of the Ruanda, *The Premise of Inequality in Ruanda* (1961a),[8] Maquet describes the political system as a feudal structure. He defines a feudality as an organization 'based on an agreement between two individuals who unequally partake in the symbols of wealth and power culturally recognized in their society. The person who, in that respect, is inferior to the other, asks the other for his patronage, and, as a counterpart, offers his services. This is the essence of the feudal régime . . .' (1961a:133). The term 'agreement' here is preferred to contract because the freedom not to enter into clientship was illusory, since no Ruanda could afford to live without a lord. Clients might belong to the ruling estate of cattle-keepers (the *Tutsi*) or to the subordinate group of agriculturalists (the *Hutu*)[9] but in both cases the transaction was established by the loan of cattle to the inferior partner, a transaction which Maquet regards as equivalent to the allocation of a landed fief in feudal Europe (1961a:129, 133).[10] But he claims that the fief itself is only rarely found in Africa, because unlike medieval Europe, the tenure of land is not based upon Roman law (1961b:294). By this I think the author means that a political superior (such as a king) does not 'own' the land in the same way as a feudal lord in Western Europe, i.e. in the same way a *Tutsi* 'owns' cattle, or the Nupe king 'owns' tribute. Hence the characteristic feudal formula of Y holding land of X (*tenere terram de X*) could not be applied. There is a certain truth in this observation, but it should be remembered that in England, at least, the formula of dependence seems to have been applied to a number of very varied conditions. The bundle of rights which we may think of as complete ownership of land

---

[8] See also his general discussion, 'Une hypothèse pour l'étude des féodalités africaines', *Cahiers d'études africaines,* II (1961b), 292–314.

[9] i.e. what Lombard speaks of as the lord-vassal (*liens de vassalité*), as well as the patron-client relationship (*liens de clientèle*) (1960:11). More usually vassalage implies military service; according to Stephenson the term should be restricted to 'an honorable relationship between members of the warrior class' (1954:250, n. 61); see also Boutruche, *Seigneurie et féodalité* (1959), 293 ff.

[10] Mrs Chilver points out that it bears a closer resemblance to the Early Irish form of cattle-clientage, *celsine* (1960:390).

was not always distributed among the actors and groups involved in precisely the same way and the nature of dependence differed in each case. Moreover, such relationships always contained an element of mutuality. From one point of view all higher contracts depended upon the performance of the basic agricultural tasks, and from the evidence concerning the inheritance of land at the village level it would seem that here the idea that conquest put all rights in the hands of the Norman conquerors was something of a fiction. Whatever the legal position on this abstract level, the medieval system in practice appears to display some similarities with African land tenure, especially in states like Nupe.[11]

Clientship in East Africa is also discussed by Lucy Mair in her recent book dealing with the political systems of East Africa (*Primitive Government,* 1962) and in a general paper on 'Clientship in East Africa' (1961).[12] As a minimum definition she suggests: 'a relationship of dependence not based upon kinship, and formally entered into by an act of deliberate choice' (1961:315).[13] She goes on to discuss the institution as it existed both among the cattle-keeping Ruanda and Ankole, and among the predominantly agricultural Ganda and Soga. Ruanda clientship was established by a cattle transaction, initiated by the would-be client with the words 'Give me milk; make me rich; be my father'; but the relationship was entered into because of a universal need for protection rather than for purely economic reasons. Among the Ganda and Soga on the other hand, society was divided into landlords and peasants, the former being subordinate territorial chiefs chosen by the king, who had control of unoccupied land. Mair speaks of the relationship established by the transfer of rights in land from chief to peasant as analogous to that of patron-client (a 'passive clientage', since personal service is absent); but she reserves the use of the term

---

[11] For a discussion of the medieval situation, see Pollock and Maitland (1898:1, 234; II, 4 ff.); for Africa, see Max Gluckman, 'African Land Tenure', *Rhodes-Livingstone Institute Journal,* 5 (1945), 1–12; for the concept of a bundle of rights, see Sir Henry Maine, *Ancient Law* (1861) and *Dissertations on Early Law and Custom* (London, 1883), 344.

[12] For two stimulating studies of particular societies with clientship institutions, see A. W. Southall, *Alur Society,* and L. A. Fallers, *Bantu Bureaucracy* (for the Soga).

[13] Residual categories often give rise to difficulties of analysis and this may prove to be so in the present case, where clientship is defined negatively in respect to kinship.

in the strict sense to the relationships between the king and his territorial rulers ('client-chiefs') and to that between an office-holder and his personal retainers ('private clientship'), from among whom client-chiefs were sometimes recruited (Mair, 1961:322–3; Fallers, n.d.:135).

Dr Mair also observes that clientship is a basis of social differentiation in two ways, firstly because 'it creates formally recognized relationships of superiority and subordination, defined by other criteria than seniority',[14] and secondly because in some societies such as Buganda 'it is the main channel of social mobility' (1961:325).

We earlier saw that historical approaches to the definition of feudalism could be roughly classified into the technical and the general. These two sets of studies of societies in northern Nigeria and in the Interlacustrine region have been concerned with institutions similar or analogous to those which are the subject of the technical analysis of feudalism, namely clientship (or rather vassalage) and fiefs. But whereas Nadel and Maquet feel impelled to describe the societies they have studied as 'feudal', Smith, Fallers, and Mair make at least as adequate an analysis without introducing that concept at all. This second approach seems preferable as a procedure. It is simpler; it minimizes the inevitable Western bias; and it helps to avoid the assumption that because we find vassalage (for example), we necessarily find other institutions associated with it in medieval Europe. It is just these supposed interconnexions which comparative study has to test rather than assume.

I turn now to discussing the way in which the general approach to the study of feudal institutions has been used in work on Africa, beginning with the political. Strayer emphasizes that in medieval Europe many governmental functions were carried out at the local level, and Coulborn goes on to suggest that feudal systems are 'a mode of revival of a society whose polity has gone into extreme disintegration', i.e. after the break-up of a great empire (1956:364; see also Hoyt, 1961). Here is an instance where the Western European starting-point heavily influences the outcome of the analysis. If we are to take as characteristic of feudalism the features that Strayer discusses at the beginning of the volume (i.e. clientship, fiefs, locally

---

[14] See Fallers on the Soga (n.d.:230).

centred government), then it would seem that these institutions are not only to be associated with the revival of government after an earlier collapse. Indeed the African material points clearly to the fact that they may also occur as chiefless communities develop more centralized governments.

Southall touches upon this problem in his study of the Nilotic Alur of East Africa. His general purpose is to examine the 'process of domination' by which Alur dynasties become rulers of neighbouring, chiefless communities. In the course of his book, he discusses 'the embryonic political specialization of the Alur', which he sees as intermediary between chiefless societies on the one hand and state systems on the other (n.d.:234). On the one hand he sees the Alur as introducing 'a new principle in the regulated allegiance of one man to another without any kinship bond existing between them' (p. 234), as in the relation of chiefs with their subjects, of nobles with their domestic serfs, and of chiefs with their various dependents. On the other hand, the Alur have no bureaucracy. 'The embryonic administrative staffs possessed by chiefs in their envoys and courtiers never acquired any formally defined administrative or jural powers, and remained occasional agents, advisers and confidants of their chief' (p.240). Thus this type of political system, he concludes, is intermediary between what Fortes and Evans-Pritchard (1940) spoke of as state systems with an administrative organization (type A) and segmentary lineage systems (type B). Southall calls it the 'segmentary state' (as contrasted with the 'unitary state') and distinguishes as one of its most characteristic features the way in which both local and central authorities exercise very similar powers.[15]

In a section entitled 'The temporal and spatial range of the segmentary state', Southall goes on to consider other societies of this type, among which he includes the Ashanti, the Yoruba, Anglo-Saxon England, and 'feudal France in the eleventh century' (pp. 252–56).[16] While he does not specifically equate feudal

---

[15] Six characteristics are listed by Southall (pp.:248–9), but the distribution of power is basic to them all.

[16] As Stenton notes, the conquest state of Norman England did not display the same local independence in governmental matters that characterized feudal régimes elsewhere in Europe (1961:5, 12–15). Unlike Maitland, Stenton emphasizes the differences in the English social system resulting from the Norman Conquest and asserts that 'only the most

and segmentary state systems, he does include eleventh-century France as an example of the segmentary state and it is his analysis of this kind of system which bears directly upon a central problem of the Coulborn symposium on feudalism; namely, the question of political centralization.[17] And it is clear from the Alur case that we may expect to find such locally centred régimes developing with an increase in administrative centralization as well as after the disintegration of an even more centralized system. This evidence suggests that the latter hypothesis is one of the European derived variety that we have to beware of. True, the sort of breakdown and build-up of central organization that occurred in Western Europe after the withdrawal of Roman rule is likely to give rise to specific institutional forms which warrant comparative treatment (for this situation is not in itself unique). But such comparison needs to include societies like the Alur which are in the initial process of centralization as well as those which are undergoing a secondary process. Only in this way can a satisfactory attempt be made to isolate those institutions that are linked with one process rather than the other, and those that are associated with both.

Clientship (as Southall, Maquet, and Mair see it) can certainly occur in both these situations. Indeed Southall and Mair regard this form of personal dependence as an essential element in the development of centralized institutions (Southall, n.d.:234; Mair, 1962:107 ff.). Mair sees the elements necessary for this process as present even in a chiefless society like the Nuer, an extreme example of polities of type B. The factors crucial to the development of kingship (and so of government which revolves round a single centre-pin) are two: the belief that ritual powers are hereditary and the ability to attract and keep a following. A privileged descent group, privileged perhaps by virtue of first arrival, is able to expand by attracting attached and client groups;

tentative of approaches had been made before the Conquest towards the great feudal principle of dependent tenure in return for definite service' (1961:123). On the other hand, as Barlow remarks, 'most of the features associated with true feudalism can be found in the Old-English Kingdom' (1961:11).

[17] Maquet has a rather different line-up. He sees the coercive sanctions of governments as operating permanently (i.e. in states) or intermittently (i.e. in non-states.) Feudality makes its appearance in both types of systems, but not in states of a despotic kind.

individuals are able to increase the range and extent of their authority by acquiring followers other than their own kin (p. 122). By these and similar processes, diffuse government gives way to minimum government and eventually to yet more centralized forms. Or, as Southall puts it, kin-based, chiefless societies develop into segmentary states and these to unitary states. Certain of the institutions thought of as characteristic of feudal societies, namely, clientship and locally centred government, are characteristic of the second phase of this process.[18]

The discussion which I have outlined in this rather summary way has a direct bearing not only on the question raised in the title to this paper but also to some wider problems that face historians and other students of African societies. But to these points I will return after briefly considering what I have called, for want of a better label, the economic approach to feudalism; that is, the approach which defines feudal institutions primarily with reference to economic features, in particular the mode of land holding.

Any degree of political centralization entails specialized roles and hence some withdrawal of man-power from primary production into administrative activity. To this extent at least all chiefs and lords 'live off the land', and usually have rights in land of a more far-reaching kind. But other more specific features are sometimes regarded as characteristically feudal—certain fiscal arrangements,[19] the seignorial mode of estate management, dependent tenure itself. Here I shall confine my remarks to the approach often adopted by orthodox Marxists, more particularly by I. I. Potekhin in his paper, 'On Feudalism of the Ashanti'.[20]

---

[18] In a similar way L. A. Fallers, using Weber's typology of authority and Parsons's schema of pattern variables, describes the authority structure of the pre-colonial Soga as particularistic in contrast to the universalistic type of social relations that characterize bureaucratic structures; personal clientship is of course a particularistic tie of this kind (Fallers, n.d.:238 ff.).

[19] Mrs Chilver (1960:385) discusses these fiscal arrangements in examining East African states.

[20] Presented at the Twenty-fifth International Congress of Orientalists, Moscow, 1960. See also Basil Davidson, *Black Mother*, 33 ff., where he maintains that writers on African states have often called slavery what was in fact a form of feudal vassalage (p. 38); he speaks of 'African feudalism' (as found, for example, in Ashanti) as 'tribal feudalism' (p. 46). For a contrary view, see Maquet, 1961b:296–8, 307–10.

Potekhin writes that 'Feudal land ownership constitutes the foundation of feudal relations.' Land belongs to a restricted circle of big landowners, while the peasant pays rent or performs services for the right to cultivate his land. In Ashanti, he finds 'the exclusive concentration of land in the hands of the ruling upper strata', together with the conditional land tenure and hierarchies of dependence 'typical of feudal society'. I have earlier commented that the idea of exclusive land tenure is hardly an accurate representation of the medieval evidence; it appears even less satisfactory as an interpretation of the Ashanti situation in the nineteenth century. To deny that 'ownership' of land is exclusively vested in one strata is not of course to assert that Ashanti (or medieval Europe for that matter) was a 'classless' (i.e. unstratified) society. It is simply to state, firstly, that the concept of 'absolute ownership' of land (as distinct from other means of production) is probably applicable only to a society dichotomized into slaves and freemen.[21] Secondly, the splitting of the total quantum of rights in land between two individuals or groups does not necessarily imply a simple relation of dependency; delegation upward or devolution downward would give rise to much the same overall pattern. And lastly, it should be borne in mind that in pre-colonial conditions in Africa land was sometimes of little economic importance; for relatively low population densities (as compared, say, with Europe and Asia) meant that, in many regions, land was not a very scarce resource and hence its tenure could hardly provide the basis of differentiation for the 'class' system.

Before I conclude the discussion of the way in which the broader approaches to feudalism have been applied, let me recapitulate my comments upon the narrower technical approach. I remarked earlier that at this point in our inquiries I could see no great profit (and possibly some loss) in treating the presence of clientship or fiefs as constituting a feudality (e.g. Nadel and Maquet), as against analysing these institutions without inviting any overall identification of these societies with those of medieval Europe (e.g. Smith and Fallers). There seems even less to be gained from the view which sees African societies as feudalities on the basis of wider political or economic criteria. Firstly, there is the

---

[21] On the important analytical difference between land and other property, see Pollock and Maitland, 1898:II, 2, and J. Goody, *Death, Property and the Ancestors* (1962), 292 ff.

ever-present ambiguity of the term itself; and then again the primary referent is to a particular period in European history, and an author employing an analytic tool of this kind tends to focus the whole analysis around the Western situation. The difficulties are nowhere clearer than in the writings of those who see the development of human society in terms of the stages so widely used in the latter half of the nineteenth century. Writers who adhere to the orthodox Marxist doctrine, formulated a hundred years since, are particularly apt to fall back upon the idea of a universal progression from tribalism to slavery, feudalism, capitalism, and finally socialism, each such stage being character-ized by a particular set of social institutions. Most historians assume a rather similar scheme, either explicitly or implicitly, and, like some sociologists, tend to speak of tribal or kinship societies in a way that suggests that they too easily overlook the strength of their own attachments to family and tribe.

Of course, certain general trends of development in political, legal, and economic institutions are rightly accepted by all students of society and the study of these trends has often gained much from the approach associated with the names of Marx and Engels.[22] What blocks advance, here as in other fields of com-parative studies, is a rigid attachment to particular European-based schema, whether this be derived from an explicit ideologi-cal commitment or from an inability to see beyond our own cultural tradition. For an example of the influence exercised by the particular European story, I turn to Davidson's account of the history of slavery in Africa. To support his contention that the servile institutions of indigenous Africa were essentially similar to vassalage in feudal Europe (rather than the slavery of Classical times), he remarks that they coexist with other 'feudal' institutions, namely, 'the titles and rights of great lords, the obligations of the common people, the custom of trade and tribute, the swearing of fealty, the manners of war' (1961:34). Quite apart from the generalized nature of some of these items, a generality which only extensive cross-cultural research could fully reveal, this approach takes the European evidence as its baseline, and as-sumes the very correlations that stand in need of proof.

To suggest that there appears little to be gained by thinking of African societies in terms of the concept of 'feudalism' implies

---

[22] E.g. in the writings of V. Gordon Childe. For a general account of the influence of Marx on the social sciences, see Bottomore and Rubel, 1956.

neither a rejection of comparative work that includes European
society, nor yet of the contribution the European medievalists
can make to the study of African institutions. The last point
first. Although historians of the Middle Ages are dealing with
their own cultural tradition, they are mostly writing about a very
different set of customs from those they have absorbed with
their mother's milk. While their analysis is sometimes inhibited
by the problem of origins, by a preoccupation with medieval
institutions as the germ of contemporary ones, they are, on the
other hand, forced to consider a broader range of human experience than historians who deal with more recent times. In this
task they have been greatly helped by the legal historians who
contributed so much to the study of the medieval period, and
the extent of those whose contribution was due in some measure
to the wide interests of comparative jurisprudence in the latter
half of the nineteenth century. For a direct line runs from Fustel
de Coulanges and Maine to Vinogradoff and Maitland, all men
who had a considerable acquaintance with ethnological studies as
well as with historical material. For Vinogradoff, 'comparative
jurisprudence is one of the aspects of so-called sociology, being
the study of social evolution in the special domain of law';
it draws its material impartially from ancient and modern, civilized
and primitive communities (1911:580). In this way comparative
jurisprudence formed a link between the study of social institutions in primitive, archaic, and medieval societies. And indeed
when Vinogradoff came to list the major figures involved, he
included lawyer-anthropologists like McLennan, Bachofen, and
Morgan, the great Semitic scholar, Robertson Smith, the Romanist
von Ihering, as well as other major figures in the history of
anthropology, such as E. B. Taylor and J. G. Frazer. Frazer's
work has of course influenced many writers on medieval subjects,
particularly in the literary field, and while not all the results
have been entirely happy the author of *The Golden Bough*
can claim some credit for the theme of Marc Bloch's *Les Rois
thaumaturges* (1924). Again the whole body of work on
village communities, in particular the analysis of Early Anglo-
Saxon and Celtic society undertaken by Frederic Seebohm
(1883, 1895, 1902), stemmed from this same tradition.[23]

---

[23] 'Mr Seebohm's *English Village Community* . . . revealed to us, for
the first time, the inner life of mediaeval England.' (W. J. Ashley, 'The
English Manor', introductory chapter to N. D. Fustel de Coulanges, *The*

Thus medieval studies have been influenced in a variety of ways by comparative jurisprudence, which in its turn has had a direct link with social anthropology, or what some of us would prefer to call comparative sociology. The link continues today. Students of anthropology still study Maine, Fustel de Coulanges, and Vinogradoff, as well as the writings of the major figures in sociology. I make this point in order to suggest that the work of some of the outstanding medieval scholars (and of classicists too) has already come into contact with comparative sociology in one form or another, so that one can only expect gains of a limited kind when the insights derived from their work are fed back into studies of African societies.

But, while the reverse is perhaps even more true, Africanists certainly have something to learn from the studies of medieval historians. Firstly, the work of Maitland, for example, is full of acute observations on topics like inheritance, marriage, descent, which provide valuable material for comparative analysis quite apart from the question of whether 'feudal' institutions were present in Africa. Secondly, when dealing with centralized political systems, the anthropologist often acts as a special kind of sociological historian. He records the tables of old men; he may even administer questionnaires, like Maquet did in his Ruanda study. But if it is the indigenous system he is interested in, he cannot do what he does for marriage, household composition, and the like; he cannot go out and observe an independent State in action. It follows that if the anthropologist has to reconstruct the past in this way then he should know something of the procedures of the ordinary graphohistorian.[24] The prospect

---

Origin of Property in Land (1st pub. 1889), trans. by Margaret Ashley, 1891, xii–xiii). There have of course been many criticisms of the 'tribal' school: Fustel de Coulanges's essay on property is one of these. Seebohm's work 'profoundly shocked the learned world of the day' (Stephenson, 1954:241, n. 23) and both Vinogradoff's *Villainage in England* (1892) and Maitland's *Domesday Book and Beyond* (1897) were partly inspired by the desire to refute his thesis that English history 'begins with the serfdom of the masses' (Seebohm, 1883:ix). For a more specific comment on Seebohm's use of sources, see Timothy Lewis, 'Seebohm's Tribal System of Wales', *Economic History Review*, IX (2nd ser., 1956–7), 16–33.

[24] I use this term to make a distinction with the ethnohistorian. Ethnohistory usually refers to a study of the past which involves not only written records but also oral traditions, informant's versions of recent events as well as data of an archaeological and ethnological character. As there is a danger among traditional historians of assuming that a widely based

of this course of indoctrination need not be too overwhelming. As much nonsense is talked about the techniques of the historian as about the methods of the sociologist—and with somewhat less reason.

Today the positive achievements of the writers in the field of historical jurisprudence seems to lie not so much in their grand picture of the development of social organization (although this matter was certainly of considerable importance in their work), but rather in the study of particular customs and concepts in a wide setting and in the attempt to establish interrelationships between the institutions which they isolated in this way. As instances of this work I would cite Maine on the relationship between ancestor-worship and inheritance (1883) and Vinogradoff on the connexions between types of agriculture and family composition (1920:1, 292).

If we are to take up and develop the tradition of comparative work, which has been so neglected in recent years by historians, sociologists and anthropologists alike, then the best strategy at this stage is to avoid the kind of overall comparisons that are invited by words like tribalism, feudalism, capitalism. These abstractions make for too crude a level of analysis. Social anthropologists are sometimes surprised at the sort of statements historians make about the social organization of African societies, just as traditional historians often raise their brows at the kind of remark sociologists make about the Reformation and medieval Europe. We must avoid not only historical particularism, but also ill-considered generalities.

So far progress in the comparative study of centralized insitutions in Africa has not been great;[25] the material is complex

---

study of this kind is in some sense inferior to study resting upon documents alone, it seems desirable (particularly in the context of African studies) to use a word that avoids the opposition 'history-ethnohistory' and at the same time indicates the limitations of a method which ties itself exclusively to writing. Hence 'graphohistory'.

[25] Apart from monographs of theoretical interest and the general works by Fortes and Evans-Pritchard (1940), Schapera (1956), and Mair (1962) some interesting studies have been on a more particular level. There is Beattie's analysis of checks and balances (1959), Colson's discussion of bureaucracy (1958), Gluckman's work on rituals of rebellion (1954) which has led to much discussion and research, Richards's papers on the role of royal relatives (1961) and the social mechanisms for the transfer of political rights (1960).

and compared with the study of lineage systems, for example, it has had little systematic attention. All the more need then for a considered approach.

How should this be tackled? We need first of all to concentrate upon the analysis of particular institutions, so that we can try to select the other factors with which they are associated. This means more than simply offering a definition of, say, 'clientship'. The process of constructing analytic concepts should involve spelling out the range of social behaviour implied and the alternative possibilities for human action.[26] If possible, it should also allow for 'measurement'; that is, for an assessment of gradients of differentiation and thus avoid commitment to a simple typology. And refinements of this kind are necessary, whether we are interested in comparing the differences and similarities of various social systems, or in discerning the sequences and explanation of social change. Until more work of this kind is done, the question 'feudalism in Africa?' has little meaning, except for polemical purposes.

There is, however, a related problem of historical interest where recent sociological studies can help to clear away some of the cobwebs. This is the problem of state formation. African historians, even the 'ethnos', have been more or less exclusively concerned with centralized political systems, and for understandable reasons; in general, societies without rulers are societies without history, and hence without historians. In Fage's *Atlas of African History,* for example, the diagrams are almost entirely of states. Plotted on a map, these units show a clustered but discontinuous distribution which invites questions about their point of origin and manner of diffusion. These are reasonable enough questions. But to answer them we need evidence, and of this there is little. If we have to make do with guesses, then these should be as well informed as possible. Recent studies of African states make it clear that while increased centralization in the political system often results from conquest, it is not only in this way that states arise. The Alur, for example, extend their domination when neighbouring peoples invite their chiefs to come and

---

[26] Boutruche makes a start on this by undertaking the study of 'ties of subordination' in Frankish Europe and outside. He concludes his book with the following remarks upon the general question of feudalism: 'La féodalité est médiévale. Elle ne doit rien à l'Afrique, rien sans doute à l'Asie, le Japon excepté. Elle est fille de l'Occident' (1959:297).

rule over them; we find, in effect, an upward delegation of authority rather than the assumption of power by a military dominant group.

Nor is diffusion, peaceful or violent, the only means. For if we modify the dichotomy between chiefless and state systems by introducing the idea of a gradient of centralization, as has been suggested by M. G. Smith (1956), Easton (1959), Mair (1962), and others, then the nucleus of state systems can be discerned even among the lineages, age-sets, cult-associations, and other basic groupings of acephalous societies.[27] The question of diffusion then assumes less importance in the total picture, for this nucleus needs only the right conditions to develop into a more centralized organization.

A variety of factors suggest themselves here. In West Africa I have been impressed with the apparent ease with which small-scale, temporary systems of a centralized kind arose around (or in opposition to) the raiders for slaves and booty during the period immediately prior to the coming of the Europeans.[28] Then again, while the exchange of goods took place among and across peoples who lacked chiefs, long-distance trade was certainly facilitated by the presence of rulers, and did a good deal to encourage their growth.

These investigations suggest that any idea of the diffusion of kingship or chiefship from a single source, Egypt or elsewhere, should be treated with great reserve. Of course particular state systems have spread and undergone modifications in the process, by conquest and by other means. But before one can seriously entertain a hypothesis of diffusion based simply on the existence

---

[27] I do not mean to suggest, as others have recently done, that the dichotomy between 'acephalous' and 'state' systems is 'almost useless'. Even if one restricts the discussion to the apparatus of authority (in the Weberian sense), there are clearly great differences as one moves between societies at the Tallensi-Nuer end of the continuum, and those at the Ashanti-Nupe end. 'Acephalous' systems are not without holders of authority, but their jurisdiction is limited in terms of the numbers of persons involved and the activities covered; moreover, the methods of social control differ in emphasis from those employed in centralized societies.

[28] The histories of Samori, Babatu, and, on a much smaller scale, Bayuo of Ulu (Dagaba, northern Ghana) provide examples from the Voltic area in the late nineteenth century. Southall describes the case of a man belonging to an acephalous society who entered the slave trade and posed as a chief (n.d.:235–6 n. 1).

of supposed similarities, the criteria of comparison need to be carefully specified. 'Kingship' itself is much too vague. And to add the epithet 'divine' does little to help. We would expect any monarch that arose in Africa to be strongly linked to the religious system, whether it arose in response to local conditions or was created by some process of diffusion.

It is partly this multiplicity of modes of state formation which makes the formulation of the main lines of political development so difficult. That the history of man in the various parts of the world has been marked by a number of broadly similar developments in political institutions is a proposition that few would now wish to deny. In general this progression is seen as one from less to more complex forms of organization; the doctrine that the manners of simple peoples represent decadent remnants cast off by more advanced nations, the customs of those who have fallen from God's grace, no longer occupies the serious attention it did in 1871 when E. B. Tylor published his notable contribution to the study of cultural evolution, *Primitive Culture.*

All would agree now that, despite the hopes of some Utopian writers, there has been a general change from small-scale acephalous polities to large-scale centralized states. Beyond this there is little consensus. The contemporary world situation is in itself a denial of the assumption of many Europeans that there would everywhere be an inevitable progression towards parliamentary democracy.

Then again there is the fact that not all social developments, even in the field of technology, have always been in one direction. For there have been many cases where the useful arts have fallen into decay[29] and where political systems have adopted less centralized forms. In Asia, Leach sees the Kachin of Burma as oscillating in a sort of cyclical fashion between acephaly and monarchy (1954). And in East as in West Africa, slave-raiding gave rise to a number of temporary small-scale, centralized polities which later collapsed. While often, as among the Gonja of northern Ghana, we come across the instance of a conquest state which has become more diffuse and locally centred in its system of government.

But despite these qualifications, and despite the many and

---

[29] See Rivers, 1912. A most striking instance of this process was the apparent disappearance of writing in Greece between 1100 and 800 B.C.

often justified criticisms of the application of evolutionary doctrine to social facts, only a real flat-earther would now regard
the overall history of political systems as static, cyclical, regressive, indeed as anything other than a process of elaboration.

These questions concerning the origin and spread of state institutions and the rise and fall of different types of polity are ones
upon which recent research offers some help. The extent to which
the developments in Africa resembled those that occurred in
Western Europe is certainly worth pursuing and could even shed
some light on the major historical problems that engaged the
attention of Marx and Weber. But in this, as in other comparative
work, we must start with less worn counters, with more operational
concepts. Otherwise the embrace of feudalism, far from leading
to a hypergamous union of the desired respectability, will only
end in an unhappy hypogamy.

9 ARE AFRICAN CULTIVATORS
TO BE CALLED "PEASANTS"?

L. A. Fallers

T HE TERM "peasant" has often been used of African rural
folk, particularly when distinguishing them from political and
religious elites in the larger and more complex societies. The
word for the ordinary peasant cultivator in the kingdom of Buganda—*mukopi*—is commonly translated as "peasant," for example, and the literature of French Africa is full of references
to *"paysans."* But most writers, one suspects, have used the word
rather loosely; if pressed, most of us would be inclined to say:
"Well, perhaps they are not *quite* peasants." Africanists tend to
feel, perhaps, that the common folk of the complex African
polities fall between the categories commonly utilized by those
who have studied "peasant societies" in Latin America, Europe
and Asia, on the one hand, and, on the other, those employed
by students of aboriginal North American "tribes." They strike
us as being not quite peasant, but not quite tribal—something in
between, a *tertium quid*. We may try to understand more clearly
just what this *tertium quid* quality consists in by comparing some
African societies with the notion of the "peasant society" developed during the past twenty years by students of Latin American, Asian and European peoples. The point of this is not, of
course, merely to play with definitions but rather to explore some
of the implications of the fact—of which we are all aware—that
the concept "peasant society" refers to a bundle of features
which do not always go together. In doing this we may hope to
indicate somewhat more precisely how these complex African
societies resemble or differ from the classical peasant societies
—thus satisfying our anthropologist's urge to fit all the peoples

SOURCE: L. A. Fallers, "Are African Cultivators to be called 'Peasants'?"
Current Anthropology, Vol. 2, No. 2, April 1961, pp. 108–10. Reprinted
by permission of the author and publisher.

of the world into a grand classificatory scheme—and to suggest, indirectly, something about the significance of those peasant-like features which Africans do not share.

We may appropriately begin with Kroeber's definition (or description), since it has seemed to Robert Redfield, George Foster, Eric Wolf, and other peasant specialists to best describe their field of interest: "Peasants are definitely rural—yet live in relation to market towns; they form a class segment of a larger population which usually contains urban centers, sometimes metropolitan capitals. They constitute part-societies with part-cultures" (Kroeber 1948:284). This last phrase—"part-societies with part-cultures"—we may take to be the heart of the matter. It can, however, be made somewhat more precise. On the one hand, the phrase *does* quite satisfactorily differentiate peasant societies from the societies we usually describe as "tribal"— societies whose constituent units, or segments, to use Durkheim's phrase, are all much alike and internally more or less homogeneous, in both structure and culture. Peasant societies, as Kroeber's definition suggests, are more differentiated, both socially and culturally. Peasant villages may all be much alike, but they are bound together into a larger whole by structures of a quite different kind, and the persons who man these other structures commonly have a different culture—a "sophisticated" or "urban" or "elite" or "high" culture. On the other hand, Kroeber's definition does not satisfactorily distinguish peasant societies from modern industrial ones, for the constituent units of these latter are also "part-societies with part-cultures"—even more partial than are those of peasant societies, because modern societies are even more differentiated. We may suggest that the single most important difference between peasant and modern industrial societies lies in the nature of their constituent units. Whereas in peasant societies the household and the local community remain the primary units, in modern industrial societies occupational structures dissociated from households and cutting across local community units become important centers of cultural and structural differentiation. It is the vast increase in the differentiation and autonomy of occupational structures which industrialization makes possible above all. Local communities thus lose their semi-self-sufficiency, the semi-detached quality which they still retain in the peasant society and which led Redfield to emphasize— indeed to over-emphasize in his earlier work, as Foster has pointed out—the similarity between the peasant village and the tribal segment (Redfield 1947; Foster 1953). Unlike the latter, the peasant community is not completely isolable, completely capable of self-sufficiency; but neither is it so completely knitted into a larger fabric by criss-crossing occupational structures as is the modern community. The latter cannot possibly be imagined in isolation from the larger society. In contrast, the peasant community is relatively self-sufficient, leading many observers to comment upon its frequent indifference to changes in the political superstructure and hostility to members of the elite. Perhaps we may usefully alter Kroeber's characterization to read as follows: A peasant society is one whose primary constituent units are semi-autonomous local communities with semi-autonomous cultures. In this way we may differentiate the peasant society from both the tribal and the modern industrial varieties. It is perhaps necessary to add that we think of these as ideal, not concrete, types; actual societies will be in varying degrees "tribal," "peasant," and "modern industrial." The types are a means toward greater understanding, not a device for pigeon-holing whole societies.

Now this semi-autonomy of constituent local communities, which we may take to be the differentiating characteristic of the peasant society, may be decomposed into a number of aspects, of which we may here consider three: (1) the economic, (2) the political, and (3) what we may call, perhaps not very satisfactorily, the "cultural." We shall examine each of these briefly, attempting to see how far they find counterparts in the more complex African societies. It should perhaps be repeated that we consider here only trans-Saharan pagan Africa, excluding the Muslim areas and Ethiopia (See Figure 8).

1. In economic terms, a peasant is presumably a man who produces—usually through cultivation—mainly for his own household's consumption, but who also produces something to exchange in a market for other goods and services. This is the economic aspect of the peasant community's semi-autonomy (Firth 1951:87). In this sense, peasants abound in Africa. The vast majority of Africans were cultivators in pre-contact times—in some cases intensive and devoted cultivators. They also traded; the great markets of West Africa are famous, but also in most other parts of the continent there was a good deal of craft specialization and trade aboriginally. Cowrie shells, gold dust, ivory,

iron bars and hoes in different areas provided semi-generalized media of exchange. In the more centralized states there was tribute, and sometimes even regular taxation, to support and augment the authority of the non-agricultural superstructure. In short, in the economic aspect of the matter there appears to be no problem. Economically, most Africans were traditionally peasants and with the opening of the continent to overseas trade they quite easily and naturally took up the cultivation of export crops in exchange for imported goods.

2. Politically, too, the more powerful African states had much in common with the Asian, European and American societies which are commonly classed as "peasant." The political aspect of the peasant society has received relatively little attention from anthropologists, perhaps because so often the societies which the peasant specialists study have long since been "decapitated" politically (to use Kidder's expressive phrase), the indigenous political superstructure being replaced by those of modern colonial or nationalist post-colonial states (Redfield 1956:78). The political aspect is thus the one least accessible to study through the anthropologist's traditional techniques of direct observation. We can learn more about this aspect of the society made up of semi-autonomous peasant local communities from social historians like Marc Bloch, from legal scholars like Maine, Maitland, Seebohm, and Vinogradoff and from comparative sociologists like Max Weber. The legal scholars who unravelled the political structure of medieval Western Europe and its characteristic unit, the manor, divided into two schools, the "Romanists" and the "Germanists," over just this question of the nature of the semi-autonomy of communities which lies at the heart of the peasant type (Vinogradoff 1892:1–39). The Romanists emphasized the vertical relationship of the manor with the political hierarchy, associating it historically with the Roman *latifundiae* established in the area during the time of the Empire. The Germanists, on the other hand, saw in the manor and its surrounding "vill" essentially a development out of the old solidary Germanic village community. If we understand this literature correctly—and it is easy for an anthropologist to go astray in the writings of legal historians—both were right, in the sense that both tendencies were present. They were debating in an historical idiom, the relative importance of the two dimensions which always seem to be present in the peasant society and which constitute the

political aspect of the semi-autonomy of its constituent local communities: On the one hand there is the local community, hostile to the outside, sharing certain common rights in land and governed by local, often informal, mechanisms of social control; and on the other hand there is the hierarchy of patrimonial or feudal relations of personal superiority and responsibility (*noblesse oblige*) and subordinate dependence, which link the local community with the wider polity. Peasant political systems vary with the relative strength of the local community as against that of the vertical structure, as Eric Wolf (1955) has pointed out; and also, as Max Weber (1947:346–58) has shown, with the degree to which the latter is made up of appointed personal retainers as contrasted with hereditary feudal (using the term loosely) vassals.

These political peasant-like features, like the economic ones, are common enough in African states. The village community is a common feature everywhere (though it may be physically dispersed in scattered homesteads) and political hierarchies, where they exist, vary according to the degree to which they consist of appointed officials or hereditary chiefs. Africa is, of course, preeminently the continent of unilineal descent groups and this gives to both village communities and political superstructures a character which is less common in other regions. The village community often contains a core of lineage-mates and its corporate nature may be expressed in the idiom of unilineal descent (Fortes 1953; Smith 1956). There is an interesting range of variation according to whether strangers in such communities are relegated to a kind of second-class citizenship or are fictionally adopted into the core group. These phenomena are not, of course, universal in Africa. In the Interlacustrine area, the lineage is limited to such "domestic" functions as the control of inheritance and exogamy, and the village itself is defined purely territorially (Fallers 1960). In the political superstructure of African states, unilineal descent groups often hold corporate rights to chieftainship; and thus the hierarchy, which in medieval Europe tended to consist of dynasties of individual hereditary lords and vassals, in an African state like Ashanti, or in one of the Southern Bantu states, consists essentially of representatives of corporate descent groups (Busia 1951; Schapera 1955). In some other states, like Dahomey and Buganda, the hierarchy is essentially one of patrimonial retainers, resembling in this respect the states

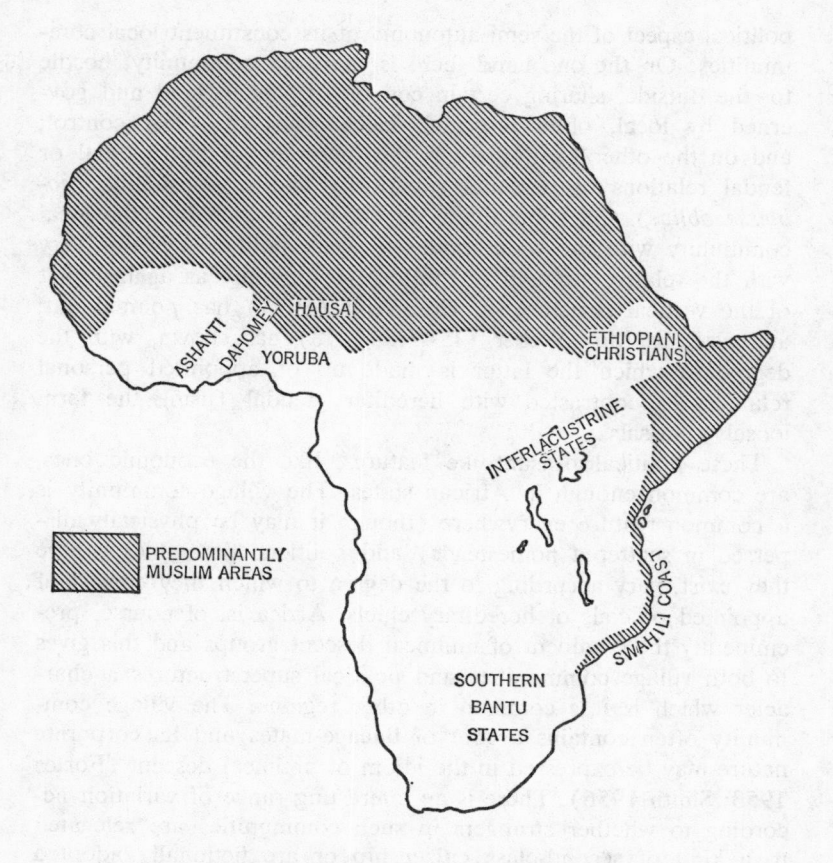

Figure 8 Map showing Islamic areas of Africa and some of the major pagan states.

of the Islamic world and Byzantium more than those of feudal Europe (Herskovits 1938; Fallers 1960). In general, allowing for peculiarities resulting from differences in patterns of descent, the politics of the traditional African states seem to fall well within the peasant range.

3. Thus, there would seem to be no reason why African villagers should not be called "peasants" politically and economically. Doubts arise, however, when we turn to the culture that is characteristic of peasant life—that is, to the tendency, to which Redfield (1956), Foster (1953), and Marriott (1955),

have drawn attention, for the economic and political semi-autonomy of the peasant community to be matched by a cultural semi-autonomy. The culture of the peasant community of the classic conception is a "folk" version of a "high culture"; it is neither the same as the latter nor independent of it, but rather a reinterpretation and reintegration of many elements of the high culture with other elements peculiar to the peasant village. It is this cultural semi-autonomy of the village, it would seem, which above all determines the relations which obtain between social strata in the peasant society. The elite possess, and live by, the high culture to a greater extent than do the peasants. The peasant, accepting the standards of the high culture to some degree, to that degree also accepts its judgment of him as ignorant and uncouth. At the same time, he possesses his own folk culture, containing high culture elements, and this provides him with an independent basis for a sense of self-esteem, together with an ideology within which he may express his partial hostility toward the elite and its version of the common culture. Excellent examples are provided by Homans' account (1940:368–370) of how thirteenth-century English villagers caricatured the behavior of the elite.

Now it would seem to be just the relative absence of this differentiation into high and folk cultures which principally distinguishes the African kingdoms from the societies which have commonly been called "peasant." There is, of course, a substantial degree of cultural differentiation in many African societies. There are craft specialists with highly-developed skills, and there are ritual specialists with great bodies of esoteric knowledge. There are courtly manners and there are recognized degrees of sophistication, ranging from the courtier who is "in the know" politically to the country bumpkin. Nevertheless, there remains an important difference between trans-Saharan pagan Africa in these respects and the differentiation which was possible in medieval Europe, China, India and Islam. The word "peasant" denotes, among other things, a degree of rusticity in comparison with his betters which we do not feel justified in attributing to the African villager.

Lacking the more pronounced degrees of cultural differentiation, the African states characteristically exhibit a somewhat different pattern of stratification. African villagers do not seem to feel the same degree of ambivalence toward the political super-structure that European, Asian and Latin American peasants do because, not standing to the same degree in contrast to the possessors of a differentiated high culture, they do not to the same extent feel judged from above by a set of standards which they cannot attain. Correspondingly, there is less development of a differentiated folk culture as a kind of "counter-culture." Africans very commonly perceive themselves as being differentiated in terms of wealth and power but they do not often, except in the few real composite conquest states, view their societies as consisting of "layers" of persons with differential possession of a high culture. As is well known, they much more characteristically divide in terms of genealogical and territorial segments, even in instances where there are marked "objective class differences" in the Marxian sense. Not even those West African societies in which cities provided a basis for rural-urban cultural differentiation exhibit the degree of folk-high distinction commonly found in what we may now call the real peasant societies. Dahomean and Yoruba villagers were not separated from their urban cousins by a cultural gap of the same magnitude as that which divided medieval European and Asian countrymen from city folk (Herskovits 1938; Bascom 1951; Lloyd 1955).

In large part this difference is due simply to the absence in traditional Africa of the literary religious traditions which formed the bases for the European and Asian high cultures. Written records make possible a vastly greater accumulation and elaboration of high culture. Furthermore, the mere presence of writing places between the literate and the illiterate member of the same society a barrier which cannot easily develop in its absence. The peasant's suspicious hostility toward the member of the urban elite is in large part a product of his realization that the latter, in his ability to read and write, holds a weapon against which the peasant cannot easily defend himself.

Thus the traditional African villager was, we might say, a peasant economically and politically, but was not a peasant culturally. Perhaps it would be better to call him a "proto-peasant" or an "incipient peasant," for wherever literary culture has entered Africa, it has quickly made him more fully a peasant. Thus the Muslim Swahili peoples of the east coast and the Hausa of the Western Sudan were traditionally more peasant-like than their non-literate, pagan neighbors; and the modern Baganda and

Ashanti, with their imported Western Christian high culture, are more fully peasants than were their great-grandfathers. We may suggest that one of the reasons why Christianity, Islam and their accompanying high cultures have been so readily accepted in many parts of Africa is that many African societies were structurally "ready" to receive peasant cultures.

10 THEORETICAL ISSUES
IN ECONOMIC ANTHROPOLOGY[1]

George Dalton

T HE PUBLICATION of *Trade and Market in the Early Empires*
(1957), and other work associated with Karl Polanyi's analytical schema, has intensified theoretical disputes in economic
anthropology having their origins much earlier when the subject
was of interest to many fewer anthropologists (Firth 1939:Chap.
1; Herskovits 1940:Chap. 2; 1941). These disputes are principally over which of several alternative sets of analytical concepts
are best to interpret real world processes and institutions, and
what kinds of analytical questions should be put to primitive
and peasant economies—those asked by economists about our
own economy, or questions having to do with the connections
between economic and social organization.

This paper is addressed to issues raised recently by anthropologists who have criticized the theoretical approach of Polanyi
and myself (LeClair 1962; Burling 1962; Pospisil 1963; Cook
1966). Part I states the positions of Polanyi and his critics
and explains why controversy persists; Part II suggests a theoreti-

SOURCE: George Dalton, "Theoretical Issues in Economic Anthropology,"
Current Anthropology, Vol. 10, No. 1, February 1969, pages 63–80.
Reprinted by permission of the author and the editor of *Current Anthropology*. [The editor of this volume regrets that he cannot reprint here the
twenty double-column pages of *Comment* (written by twenty-four anthropologists and others), and the author's *Reply*, that were originally published together with this article. See *Current Anthropology*, February 1969,
pages 80–99.]

[1] I have been very fortunate in getting critical comments on earlier
drafts of this paper from anthropologists, economists, and others whom
it is a pleasure to thank here: Irma Adelman, Conrad Arensberg, Joseph
Berliner, Paul Bohannan, David Brokensha, Heyward Ehrlich, Everett
Hagen, Thomas Harding, Clifford Geertz, Peter McLoughlin, Sidney
Mintz, Walter Neale, and Ilona Polanyi.

cal framework for economic anthropology which takes account of both sets of ideas. Part III considers the recent extension of economic anthropology to processes of socio-economic change, growth, and development in communities undergoing "modernization".

I. THE CONTROVERSY

Whether one is collecting and analyzing fieldwork information (e.g., Salisbury 1962) or writing a general or comparative work drawing on the extensive ethnographic literature (Herskovits 1952; Belshaw 1965; Nash 1966), one must choose a theoretical approach. Both fieldwork and synthesis in economic anthropology suffer from inadequate theory.

1. Anthropology has devoted less attention to economic organization and performance than to, e.g., kinship or politics. Only two anthropologists, Bronislaw Malinowski and Raymond Firth, have a large corpus of writings in economic anthropology and relatively few—principally Cyril Belshaw, Paul Bohannan, Mary Douglas, Clifford Geertz, Maurice Godelier, Melville Herskovits, Sidney Mintz, Manning Nash, Marshall Sahlins, and Richard Salisbury—have written at length on its theoretical aspects.[2]

2. Anthropologists understand the economic organization and the economic theory of industrial capitalism much less well than they understand European and American politics, kinship, and religion and the theories which explain them. Some anthropologists seem not to understand that conventional economics—the most abstract and mathematical of the social sciences—does not deal with what anthropologists mean by human behavior, and that the concepts of conventional economics relating to economic *organization* are not (with some minor qualifications) fruitfully applicable outside of market systems. What is a serious point of contention among anthropologists (LeClair 1962; Burling 1962; Cook 1966) is dismissed out of hand by a prominent development economist (Lewis 1962:viii):

---

[2] I do not mean to slight the contributions of others, living or dead, (e.g., Mauss 1954) but only to name those who have written at some length on the theoretical aspects of economic anthropology. See Godelier (1965), and Dalton (1967) for further references to theoretical writings.

. . . the economist who studies the non-market economy has to abandon most of what he has learnt, and adopts the techniques of the anthropologist.

3. Economists have not been concerned with primitive and peasant societies and economies. Until recently they had been concerned exclusively with one type of economy, industrial capitalism. The concepts, leading ideas, and causal analyses of price theory, aggregate income theory, and growth theory—as well as fields such as international trade, and money—deal with the structure, performance, and problems of U.S. and West European economies in the 19th and 20th centuries. Economists have had no reason to spell out the content and method of economics in such fashion as to make clear what in conventional economics is and what is not relevant to economic anthropology.

The fact that the attention of economists has been focused so exclusively on just those aspects of our economy least likely to be found among non-literate folk has thus confused anthropologists who turned to economic treatises for clarification of problems and methods in the study of the economic systems of non-literate societies (Herskovits 1952:53).

Very few economists other than myself and those represented in *Trade and Market* (Polanyi, Neale, Pearson, and Fusfeld) have written on these issues. The few economists who have written on the relevance of economics to economic anthropology have done so principally in book reviews (Knight 1941; Rottenberg 1958; Boulding 1957).

The field of comparative economic systems came into being only in the 1930's and '40's (with central planning in the Soviet Union, enlarged governmental spending, borrowing, taxing, and market controls in fascist Germany, the American New Deal, and welfare state reforms in England and Scandinavia). The field remains confined to the study of national industrialized economies. It compares the structure and performance of U.S. and Soviet type economies, and considers the literature of socialism (Gruchy 1966). Comparative economic systems has never included the economies studied by anthropologists nor those described in the literature of pre-industrial economic history of Europe.

The field of economic development, which came into being

after World War II with the achievement of political independence by former colonies in Africa and Asia, brought American and European economists for the first time into those areas of the world in which anthropologists have traditionally centered their interests. Most of the literature of economic development deals, however, with the same impersonal matters of investment and foreign trade relating to the *national* economy (e.g., Nigeria, not the Tiv) that economists are concerned with in analyzing our own national economy. A small part of the development literature written by economists is concerned with social organization and culture (what economists call "institutional matters"), as these relate to national and local community development (Lewis 1955; Myrdal 1957; Hagen 1962; Yudelman 1964*a;* 1964*b;* Adelman and Morris 1965, 1967; Dalton 1965*c*).

With the minor and recent qualifications of comparative economic systems and economic development, conventional economics excludes entirely from its formal analyses matters relating to social organization and culture. Thus the relation of economic to social organization—a problem important in economic anthropology—does not arise in conventional economic theory. It is unfortunate that anthropologists have turned for guidance to post-industrial economic theory rather than to pre-industrial European economic and social history. Pirenne (1936), Bloch (1961; 1966), Bennett (1962), Weber (1950), and Polanyi (who was an economic historian) have more to teach anthropologists about the economies they study than do Marshall (1920), Knight (1941), or Robbins (1935).

4. Almost all the communities anthropologists study in the field are now experiencing some degree of economic, social, cultural, or technological change as parts of newly independent nation-states bent on "modernization" and economic development. The subject of socio-economic change within the context of developing nation-states is extremely complicated and, of course, very recent. We know more about "traditional" systems before Western incursion and about the kinds of change that took place in the 19th century with colonialism. The scope of economic anthropology is now widening considerably. The older focus of interest was the organization and functioning of indigenous economy as it relates to social relationships at one point in time, or under conditions of slow change (Malinowski 1922; 1935). The new focus of interest is modernization. The newly established

political independence of Asian and African nation-states and their governments' explicit intention to create and develop national societies and economies makes the context of present-day community change sufficiently different from that of the early culture contact studies (e.g., on the depopulation of Melanesia or the introduction of the horse among the Plains Indians) to require new theoretical approaches and new policy concerns.

In the absence of adequate theory, controversy persists as to the merits of various alternative frames of reference for the analytical treatment of primitive and peasant societies. The main point of contention has aroused heated controversy: the extent to which anthropologists should adopt conventional economics as the conceptual language with which to analyze primitive and peasant economies (Firth 1958:63). Unlikely Auden's academic warriors who "fight with smiles and Christian names", some of the participants in this dispute display the ferocity of those engaged in theological battle, a battle which has now become a thirty years war (Goodfellow 1939:Chap. 1; Firth 1939:Chap. 1; Herskovits 1940:Chap. 2, 1941, 1952; Knight 1941; Polanyi 1944:Chap. 4; 1947; 1957; Rottenberg 1958; Sahlins 1960; Dalton 1961; 1962; 1965a; LeClair 1962; Burling 1962; Cook 1966; Kaplan 1968; Edel 1969; Humphreys 1969).

The economic anthropologist finds two ready-made bodies of economic theory—concepts, leading ideas, terminology, and generalizations—both created to analyze industrial capitalist economies: conventional economic theory and Marxian theory.[3] The question that confronts him is whether to borrow concepts and leading ideas from these, or to invent a special set of concepts and leading ideas having no counterparts in conventional and Marxian economics—or, indeed, to use some combination of conventional economics, Marxian economics, and a special set of concepts designed for primitive and peasant economies.

The problem seems no longer to arise in other branches of anthropological inquiry. Anthropologists seem to agree that it is inappropriate to borrow concepts and leading ideas from Western religious theory (Christianity and Judaism), and political theory

---

[3] Among those anthropologists who write in English there is only an occasional borrowing of Marxian concepts (such as economic surplus), rather than a systematic attempt to apply Marxian analysis to primitive and peasant economies (Herskovits 1952:Part V; Pearson 1957; Harris 1959; Dalton 1960, 1963).

(democracy and dictatorship) to analyze religious and political organization:

> Nothing is so misleading in ethnographic accounts as the description of facts of native civilizations in terms of our own (Malinowski 1922:176).

> The mistake of judging the men of other periods by the morality of our own day has its parallel in the mistake of supposing that every wheel and bolt in the modern social machine has its counterpart in more rudimentary societies (Maine, quoted in Bohannan 1957:iii).

> . . . most anthropologists have ceased to take their bearings in the study of religion from any religion practiced in their own society (Lienhardt 1956:310).

> One important discovery made in . . . [*African Political Systems*] was that the institutions through which a society organized politically need not necessarily look like the kinds of political institutions with which we have long been familiar in the Western world, and in the great nations of Asia (Gluckman and Cunnison 1962:vi).

In economic anthropology, however, there are those who argue that the leading ideas, concepts, and terminology of conventional economic theory (economizing, maximizing, elasticity, scarcity, supply, demand, capital, etc.) are applicable to primitive as well as peasant economies studied by anthropologists; that the basic similarities between primitive and peasant economies and industrial capitalism are sufficiently close so that some sort of universal economic theory—embracing the very large number of economies studied by anthropologists as well as our own—is achievable; and that anthropologists should learn more conventional economics so as to be able to put the same questions about economic *performance* to their data that economists put to theirs, and (as economists do) to quantify their data when possible (Firth 1957; 1964*a;* 1965; Salisbury 1962:Chaps. 6–9).

With a few exceptions (Bohannan and Dalton 1965; Dalton 1964) Polanyi and the group associated with him have not concerned themselves with *peasant* economies. My own view is that conventional economics is relevant to the commercialized sectors of peasant economic *organization* (i.e., where dependence on purchased land, wage-labor, and the market sale of produce is quantitatively important), and useful in quantifying economic *performance*—the amounts and composition of produce—for any economy, primitive, peasant, industrial capitalist, or industrial communist. But that the differences between primitive economic organization (i.e., where market transactions of resources and produce are absent or present only in petty amounts) and our own are so great that a special set of concepts, leading ideas, and terms are necessary to analyze these subsistence economies. Special analytical concepts are necessary because social organization and culture—kinship, political organization, religion—affect economic organization and performance so directly and sensitively in non-market systems that only a socio-economic approach which considers explicitly the relationships between economy and society is capable of yielding insights and generalizations of importance (Sahlins 1968:Chap. 5). A special set of questions should be put to primitive economies and the non-commercial sectors of peasant economies: questions about the social aspects of economic organization.

> The ties between producers tend to reach out beyond this common interest in the act of production and its rewards alone. A production relationship is often only one facet of a social relationship . . . Economic relations can be understood only as a part of a scheme of social relations . . . Economic anthropology deals primarily with the economic aspects of the social relations of persons (Firth 1951:136–38).

Polanyi focuses on economy as a set of rules of social organization and on socio-economic structure (organization) rather than quantifiable performance (levels of output; productivity). Moreover, he confines his analysis to primitive and archaic (state-organized, pre-industrial) economies.

The two groups agree that knowledge of economics and of our own economic system, industrial capitalism, should figure explicitly and importantly in economic anthropology. They disagree sharply, however, on the appropriate way to incorporate conventional economics and knowledge of our own economy. The "formalist" group takes what it believes to be the universally applicable concepts of economic theory—scarcity, maximizing, surplus—as that which is to be incorporated in economic anthropology and analyzes the empirical data of primitive and peasant economies in these terms (Pospisil 1963; Firth 1965). They use the leading ideas of elementary economics (Samuelson 1967: Chaps. 1–3) as a guide to analyzing all economies.

Polanyi (1944:Chap. 4), Neale (1957*b*), Fusfeld (1957), and I (Dalton 1961; 1962) describe the salient characteristics of industrial capitalism and economic theory so as to provide a base of contrast with that sub-set of economies we call "primitive." We then show how variants of reciprocity and redistribution act as integrating organizational principles of land and labour allocation, work organization, and produce disposition (Polanyi 1957*a;* 1957*b;* Neale 1957*a*), and how external trade and money uses in such economies are derivative expressions of reciprocal and redistributive modes of transaction (Bohannan 1959; Dalton 1965*a*). Polanyi argues that the concepts of economic theory yield useful insights when applied to our own economy because the institutionalized rules of market exchange and the use of our kind of money and technology induce economizing and maximizing activities; but to employ these terms to analyze the non-market sectors of primitive and peasant economies is as distorting as it would be to use the concepts of Christianity to analyze primitive religions.

The "formalist" group confuses the *ability* to translate any socio-economic transaction or exchange (potlatch, kula, bridewealth) into market terms with the *usefulness* of doing so (Homans 1958; Pospisil 1963). Describing the potlatch as an investment which yields 100 per cent interest (Boas 1897), bridewealth as the price one pays for sexual and domestic services (Gray 1960), and shell transactions on Rossel Island as cash payments for market purchases (Armstrong 1924; 1928), suggests they are basically similar to ordinary commercial transactions in our own economy. These are the analytical views of the anthropologist, his *interpretation* of real world processes which remain the same regardless of what he calls them. Whether it is analytically revealing to interpret the potlatch, bridewealth, and Rossel Island shells in such fashion depends on the folkviews of these events and usages, as well as on the assessment of the differences between these and commercial transactions (Dalton 1961:10–14; 1966).

The Quest for a Universal Theory

There is a deep-seated yearning in social science to discover one general approach, one general law valid for all time and all climes. But these primitive attitudes must be outgrown (Gerschenkron 1954:256).

Those who insist on the applicability of conventional economics to primitive economies are really in quest of a universal theory— a single set of concepts which would yield fruitful insights for all economies, those studied by anthropologists as well as those studied by economists and historians.[4]

> What is required . . . is a search for the general theory of economic process and structure of which contemporary economic theory is but a special case (LeClair 1962:1188).

> What is required from economic anthropology is the analysis of material in such a way that it will be directly comparable with the material of modern economics, matching assumption with assumption and so allowing generalizations to be ultimately framed which will subsume the phenomena of both price and non-price communities into a body of principles about human behavior which will be truly universal (Firth 1966a:14).

The difficulty with this approach is that economic anthropology deals with an extraordinary range of matters in an extraordinarily large set of economies: it is concerned with *structure and performance of both primitive and peasant economies under static and dynamic conditions.* What Firth and LeClair suggest be treated under a single theory is assigned in economics (and sociology) to several sub-fields: price and distribution theory; aggregate income theory; growth theory; comparative economic systems; national income accounting; industrial sociology, etc. In economics we have one set of analytical concepts to answer the question, "What determines prices in U.S. type economies?" And we have a different set to answer the question, "What determines gross national product?"—and yet another to answer the question, "How do we measure national income?" In economic anthropol-

---

4 Clifford Geertz quite rightly points out (in private correspondence) that people confuse the generality of a theory with its ability to be applied universally. Polanyi most certainly is not arguing against generalization or abstract conceptualization; rather, he argues against the position that conventional economics—designed to analyze nationally-integrated, industrial, market economies—provides an adequate conceptual basis for a universally applicable theory of economic structure and process. Specifically, he shows that for economies lacking the salient organizational features of developed capitalism (market integration, machine technology, and the modern kind of money—primitive and archaic economies, in his terms), principles of socio-economic organization exist which require for their analysis conceptual categories different from those of conventional economics (Polanyi 1957a; 1957b; Dalton 1961).

ogy we also need several sets of analytical and measurement concepts because of the several kinds of economies we are dealing with and the different kinds of questions we put to the data.

In summary, those of the thousands of economies studied by anthropologists that are underdeveloped, small-scale market systems—peasant economies (Tax 1963; Firth 1946) can be fruitfully analyzed with the concepts of conventional economics. Moreover, the quantifiable performance of all economies, primitive and peasant included, can be measured in simplified terms analogous to national income accounting terms. But to put interesting questions about the organization of traditional, primitive economies, and primitive and peasant economies undergoing change, growth, and development, requires conceptual categories different from those used in conventional economics.

The Economy:
Individual Behavior vs. Rules of Social Organization

Another underlying difficulty is the existence of two rather different ways of perceiving an economy: one is to concentrate on economic "behavior" of individual persons and the motives that impel the individual behavers, so that the economy is seen as a cluster of individual actors and their motives.

> Economics . . . has long been confidently felt to include a tolerably well-defined type of human behavior. . . . None of these definitions [of economics] covers exactly the same area of behavior as any other. . . . Even economists have long claimed to equate the material side of life with economic behavior. . . . Since this definition does not isolate any type of behavior from any other type. . . . If the unity of economics arises out of the fact that it deals with priced goods, then in some primitive societies it is silly to look for any behavior that can be called "economic". . . . Economics in this view focuses on a particular *aspect* of behavior and not on certain kinds of behavior (Burling 1962:802, 805, 808, 811).

The other approach is to perceive the economy as a set of rules of social organization (analogous to polity and political rules), so that each of us is born into a "system" whose rules we learn. It is from observing the activities and transactions of participants that we derive these systematic rules. This is how Polanyi regards an economy, and, indeed, it is the approach used in comparative economic systems in contrasting the organization (rules) of Soviet and U.S. economies.

Those who perceive an economy as a cluster of individual behavers frequently equate whatever economic activities the behavers undertake with explicit *choice* of those activities, and believe that such choice affirms the economics textbook dictum that in all economies there must be choice of what to produce, how to produce it, and who is to get how much of what is produced. This way of introducing the topics of resource allocation, production functions, and income distribution in industrial capitalism to beginning students in economics is useful because the individual households and firms in national market economies such as our own are confronted with many explicit choices: which of thousands of goods and services to buy; which of hundreds of job markets to enter; which of dozens of products to produce; which of several techniques to use to produce them. These alternative choices are subject to fine calculation because industrial capitalism makes extensive use of money and pricing, and because there are real alternatives among which economic choices can be made without calling down social opprobrium. For example, the American farmer, entirely depending on market sale for livelihood, must choose explicitly how much of each kind of cash crop to grow. The relevant considerations are not personal taste, social obligation, or physical yield, but physical yield times expected money price compared to money costs of production. He makes explicit "economizing" decisions about costs relative to expected market revenue for the several alternative crops he can grow, and the several alternative combinations of resources he can *buy* to grow them. His livelihood depends on such choices.

In subsistence (non-market) economies, the question of choice among real alternatives does not arise in such explicit fashion. A Trobriand Islander learns and follows the rules of *economy* in his society almost like an American learns and follows the rules of *language* in his. An American is born into an English-speaking culture. In no sense does he "choose" to speak English because no real alternative is presented to him. So too, the Trobriander is born into a yam-growing economy. He does not "choose" to plant yams rather than broccoli. The question does not arise in this form, but rather in the form of how much of each of very few conventional crops to plant or how to apportion a given work day to several tasks.

In the Trobriand subsistence economy, labor, land and other resources are not purchased, and produce is not destined for sale to others, so it is personal taste within the *ecological* constraints set by resource endowment, the *technological* constraints set by known techniques of production, and the *social* constraints set by the obligation to provide sister's husband with yams that dictate how much of each crop is to be planted.[5] So too for Tikopia:

> . . . in Tikopia on any given day a man has in theory a choice between working in his orchard and going out fishing, in a canoe or on the reef. It might be held that he will decide according to his preference at the time for an ultimate yield of crops or an immediate one of fish. But in practice his choice may be rigidly determined by social and ritual considerations. The recent death of a man of rank and the taboos associated with mourning may bar him absolutely from any resort to canoe-fishing out at sea, although such may otherwise be his preference and would yield him a greater material return. . . . Moreover, the period of his abstention from canoe-fishing tends to vary directly in accordance with his propinquity of kinship to the dead (Firth 1966:12).

In primitive economies, the constraints on individual choice of material goods and economic activities are extreme, and are dictated not only by social obligation but also by primitive technology and by physical environment. There is simply no equivalent to the range of choice of goods and activities in industrial capitalism which makes meaningful such economic concepts as "maximizing" and "economizing." Nor is there the possibility of fine calculation in monetary terms which pricing allows.

As the literature of theoretical contention in economic anthropology grows, it becomes increasingly clear that those who argue that conventional economics is *applicable* to primitive economies —the Trobriand and Tiv type of economy—have three things in mind:

1. The first is the least difficult to unravel. It is to regard peasant economies as the typical cases to be analyzed in economic

---

[5] Just as an American who somehow chose not to learn English would be severely penalized by the social system in finding jobs, in his ability to communicate with others, etc., so too would a Trobriander be penalized in his society by choosing not to grow yams.

anthropology and to assume that what is true for peasant economies is also true for primitive economies because they are both
within the universe of anthropological interest, and somehow a
single set of concepts and generalizations should apply. Peasant
economies are small-scale, underdeveloped market economies, in
which production for market sale, the use of Western money,
the availability of purchased factors of production, and other
features of market economies are present. The structure and
performance of the commercialized sectors of peasant economies
are amenable to analysis and measurement in conventional economic terms (precisely because money, prices, and markets are
important). But this does not mean that the same is true for
primitive economies—the Trobriands, the Nuer—in which the
crucial features of market organization which allow analysis in
market concepts and measurement in money terms, are absent.

2. The second reason some anthropologists think conventional
economics is applicable to all economies is—to speak bluntly—
due to their imperfect understanding of economic theory and its
concepts. From Goodfellow (1939) and Herskovits (1952), to
Burling (1962) and Cook (1966), there is misunderstanding of
what economists mean by "scarcity," "economize," "maximize,"
and "rational choice." Given cost and demand schedules for a
firm, there is one price-output combination at which a firm
maximizes its profit. This can be shown unambiguously by reference to other price-output combinations for the firm. Anthropologists misuse—or better, mis-translate—this piece of analysis
by erroneously equating all *purposeful* activities with economizing
or maximizing, and then jumping to the conclusion that because
purposeful choices are made in primitive economies, economic
theory must apply.

> Our primary concern in these pages is to understand the cross-
> cultural implications of the process of economizing (Herskovits
> 1952:4).

> From this point of view, we are "economizing" in everything we
> do. We are always trying to maximize our satisfactions somehow,
> and so we are led back to the notion that economics deals not
> with a type but rather with an aspect of behavior. This eco-
> nomic view of society becomes . . . one model for looking at society.
> It is a model which sees the individuals of a society busily en-
> gaged in maximizing their own satisfactions—desire for power,
> sex, food, independence . . . (Burling 1962:817–18).

Such misinterpretations of economic concepts persist because economists who have had occasion to deal with anthropology or primitive societies—Irma Adelman, Joseph Berliner, Everett Hagen, Arthur Lewis—have not addressed themselves to these matters, and the economists who have are associated with Polanyi. Because a Tikopian chooses to fish today rather than to tend his garden does not mean that the economics of Tikopian fishing or gardening is usefully described by linear programming or oligopoly theory.

3. The third way in which it is thought that conventional economics applies to primitive economy is in the measurement of economic performance. Several branches of applied economics and statistics measure production flows (e.g., input-output analysis), and total output and its composition (e.g., national income accounting), for large-scale, nationally-integrated, industrialized economies of both the U.S. and Soviet types. Some kind of measurement of output is possible for any type of economy, no matter how primitive and small, because it is always possible to measure output and performance in terms of the resources used (labor days to build a hut), or in the real terms of the produce forthcoming (tons of yams produced).

Salisbury's book on a primitive economy in New Guinea before and after the introduction of purchased steel axes is cited by Firth (1965) and Cook (1966) as proof of the ability to "apply" conventional economics to a primitive economy because Salisbury does some rather elementary calculations such as the number of man-days of labor required to produce a variety of items (1962: 147). Such calculations can be done for any economy—Robinson Crusoe's, a medieval monastery, an Israeli kibbutz, or Communist China.

If what anthropologists mean by "applying economic theory" is to count the number of yams produced and the number of labour days needed to build a hut, then most certainly economic theory is applicable to all economies. But this is a rather simplistic notion of what "applying economic theory" means.

A prominent national income economist at Cambridge says the following about her experience in measuring subsistence income in rural Rhodesia:

An attempt to examine the structure and problems of a primitive community in the light of the existing body of economic thought raises fundamental conceptual issues. Economic analysis and its framework of generalizations are characteristically described in terms appropriate to the modern exchange economy. It is by no means certain that the existing tools of analysis can usefully be applied to material other than that for which they have been developed. In particular it is not clear what light, if any, is thrown on subsistence economies by a science which seems to regard the use of money and specialization of labor as axiomatic. The jargon of the market place seems remote, on the face of it, from the problems of an African village where most individuals spend the greater part of their lives in satisfying their own or their families' needs and desires, where money and trade play a subordinate role in motivating productive activity (Deane 1953:115–16).

It is true that in attempting to measure economic performance quantitatively, anthropologists put the same questions to small subsistence economies that economists put to our own and the Soviet national economy: What is the total output and its composition for the community? How is income divided? But the absence of cash and pricing means that only crude estimates of output can be indicated—nothing like the detailed components of national income and gross national product for developed economies; and the small number of goods and services produced together with the absence of complicated processes of manufacture and fabrication (the absence of inter-firm and inter-industry transactions in developed economies) means that input-output analysis yields no useful information.

I would agree emphatically that output statistics for subsistence economies are worth having especially in the analysis of community change, growth, and development (Epstein 1962). They would give us additional information, along with knowledge of socio-economic organization, of the pre-modernization economy, as well as rough benchmarks from which to measure growth. I suggest, however, that for traditional, slow-changing, subsistence (and peasant) economies, it is the analysis of socio-economic organization rather than performance that yields insights of comparable interest and depth to those got in analyzing primitive religions, polity, kinship, etc.

Traditional, Subsistence Economies

Cook (1966) criticizes Polanyi and myself for analyzing in detail the structure of traditional subsistence economies such as the

Trobriand Islands in Malinowski's time. In the mid-1960's very few such economies exist intact, almost all of them undergoing various kinds and degrees of economic, social, cultural, and technological change.[6] This kind of complaint seems not to be made in other branches of anthropology: do anthropologists criticize each other for studying traditional political organization or traditional religion because—like traditional economy—they are now undergoing change? Indeed, why study history, then, since it is concerned with forms of social organization no longer in being?

Here we have an example of an odd double standard in anthropology. Anthropologists who would condemn out of hand a theoretical approach which regarded primitive religion or political organization as being simply variants of European religions and polities to be analyzed in the conceptual language of Christianity and democracy, nevertheless approach primitive economy as though it were simply a variant of capitalism to be analyzed in the conceptual language of supply, demand, elasticity, capital, maximizing, (bride) price, etc. (LeClair 1962; Pospisil 1963).

To answer the question specifically: Anthropologists have both old and new reasons to study the organization of traditional, subsistence economies, even in the 1960's when these are changing. One old reason is precisely the same that justifies their studying other aspects of traditional social organization and culture—religion, polity, kinship, language: to find out how these are (or were) organized in as many societies as we can, make analytical generalizations about them, and compare them to our own Western systems. But there are special reasons as well.

Writings in economic anthropology are either descriptive

---

[6] Although, in the mid-1960's, there are very few pure subsistence economies (economies in which commercial transactions are entirely absent), there are a good many primitive economies (especially in Africa) in which half or more of total income comes from subsistence production, and peasant economies in which smaller, but significant amounts of subsistence production are the rule. In the early 1950's, a UN agency reported that ". . . between 65 per cent and 75 per cent of the total cultivated land area of tropical Africa is devoted to subsistence production" (United Nations 1954:13). In the 1960's, the problem of transforming subsistence agriculture in Africa is still very much a matter of concern. See Yudelman (1964); Clower, Dalton, Harwitz, and Walters (1966); Adelman and Morris (1967).

ethnographies or theoretical analyses. The theoretical portion of economic anthropology has been poorly done. I do not mean to suggest that theoretical light began to dawn only with the publication of *Trade and Market in the Early Empires.* Malinowski (1921; 1922; 1935), Mauss (1954), and Firth (1929; 1939; 1946)—to name only the outstanding—have made contributions of great importance. But much was not done, and much of what was done was done poorly. And it is Polanyi's work on modes of transaction, money, markets, external trade, and operational devices in primitive and archaic economies that has begun important new lines of analysis, and, indeed, has allowed us to clear up some old muddles such as "primitive money" (Polanyi 1957; 1968; Dalton 1965), and economic "surplus" (Pearson 1957; Dalton 1960; 1963).

The peoples and communities of Africa, Asia, Latin America, and Oceania traditionally studied by anthropologists are experiencing the several kinds of change entailed in economic development, industrialization, urbanization, and the formation of nation-states. Anthropologists are increasingly concerned with the processes and problems of socio-economic change. There is a rapidly growing literature of theory and case studies (Smelser 1963; Douglas 1965; Brokensha 1966). Indeed, anthropologists have returned to places they did fieldwork in 20 or more years earlier, to study socio-economic change (Firth 1959; 1966).

I suggest that analytical insights and generalizations about change and development have to be based on firm understanding of traditional socio-economic organization (Dalton 1964; 1965*b*). Change is always change of what is; and what is, depends on what has been: "Any planned growth is embedded in a set of institutions and attitudes which come from the past" (Keyfitz 1959:34).

One can illustrate the point from European and American experience. How is it possible to understand the causes and consequences of those New Deal, Fair Deal, or "Great Society" changes in the U.S. economy and their counterparts in the English and Scandinavian welfare states, except by knowing the structure and performance of 19th- and early 20th-century capitalism in Europe and the U.S.? How is it possible to understand the impact of Western money on subsistence economies in Africa unless one first understands the nature of indigenous money and its uses, which, in turn, requires knowing how indigenous economy functioned before the monetary incursion (Bohannan 1959; Douglas 1958)? So too, in order to understand why litigation over land rights sometimes occurs when land is first made subject to contractual purchase and sale, one has to know the nature of land tenure before land was made marketable (Biebuyck 1963).

Processes of modernization—industrialization, the expansion of commercial production—ramify into all segments of society and culture. Many of the anthropological studies being undertaken are addressed to two broad questions, both of which require knowledge of traditional, "pre-modernization" structures: (1) What are those features of traditional social organization, culture, polity, and economy which make for receptivity or resistance to technological, economic, and cultural innovations (Douglas 1965)? (2) What are the "impacts"—processes of sequential change—on traditional social organization and culture when a group undertakes enlarged production for sale, the use of Western money and technology, and incorporates other such innovations (Gulliver 1965; Epstein 1962; Firth and Yamey 1964)?

II. A THEORETICAL FRAMEWORK FOR ECONOMIC ANTHROPOLOGY

A good theoretical framework for economic anthropology should be clear about the similarities and differences between our own economy and primitive and peasant economies, about the relevance of conventional economics to economic anthropology, and it should contain an explicit statement of the matters to be analyzed:

TABLE 1

1. Socio-Economic Structure: Primitive Economies, before modernization
   Peasant Economies, before modernization

2. Economic Performance: Primitive Economies, before modernization
   Peasant Economies, before modernization

3. Socio-economic Organization and Economic Performance in Primitive and Peasant Economies Compared to Industrial Capitalism.

4. Processes and Problems of Socio-Economic Change, Growth, and Development in Primitive and Peasant Communities.

TABLE 2 ECONOMIES OF RECORD AND

| | ECONOMIES OF RECORD | |
| | SMALL-SCALE | |
Primitive and Peasant, Before Modernization	*Primitive and Peasant, Change and Development*	*Utopian*a
Economic Anthropology	Economic Anthropology Applied Anthropology	European and American History
Pre-industrial Economic and Social History (e.g., Europe and Asia)	Economic Development	
	Economic History	

a The important connections between the structure of traditional, primitive economies and utopian communities (Noyes 1870; Nordhoff 1961; Bestor 1950; Bishop 1950) have never been systematically analyzed. Both kinds are small-scale economies whose internal organization is of non-market sorts; where production processes—especially land tenure, work organization, and produce alloca-

I shall discuss some of the conceptual categories I think most useful in economic anthropology, indicate the questions they help answer, and the leading ideas they are associated with (see Tables 2 and 3). In doing so I hope to make several points: to show how much at the beginnings of theoretical analysis we are in economic anthropology; to show what a wide variety of structures, processes and problems are dealt with in the subject; and to suggest lines of analysis and conceptual categories that seem promising.

Economic Anthropology as Part of Comparative Economy

The economies of direct interest to anthropologists are the large set of subsistence and peasant communities in Africa, Asia, Latin America, Oceania, and the Middle East. The focus of analytical interest is either their traditional structure and performance before serious Western incursion (Malinowski 1922; 1935), or matters relating to socio-economic change and development (Epstein 1962; Firth 1966). In either case there is an important literature

SOCIAL SCIENCE SUB-FIELDS

ECONOMIES OF RECORD

NATIONAL

19th-Century Capitalism	*Welfare State and Fascism*	*Communist*
Economic History	Comparative Economic Systems	Soviet Economy[b]
History of Economic Thought	Economic History	Comparative Economic Systems
Classical and Neoclassical Economic Theory	Modern Economic Theory	
Industrial Sociology	Industrial Sociology	Industrial Sociology

tion—express social relationships. It is this feature which makes writers like Nyerere (1964) and Senghor (1964) assert that traditional African communities had a "socialist" ethos.

[b] Soviet economy has developed as a separate field of specialization within economics; see Nove (1962).

outside of anthropology. The fields within economics which provide complementary information are pre-industrial economic history (Postan 1966; Takizawa 1927), comparative economic systems (Grossman 1967; Myrdal 1960; Carr 1951), and the institutional literature of economic development (Lewis 1955; Myrdal 1957; Hagen 1962; Adelman and Morris 1967).

Economic anthropology is best done within a framework of comparative economic systems which draws on all economies of record. The analysis of pre-industrial, developed, and developing economies is now scattered in various branches of economics, history, sociology, and anthropology, all of which contribute information of use to the broad range of topics considered in economic anthropology (see Table 2).

What is an Economic "System"?

One of the many semantic difficulties in economic anthropology is that the word "economy" (like the words "society" and "culture") has no size dimension attached to it. We can speak of the economy of a hunting band comprising a few dozen persons or the economy of Communist China comprising several hundred million.

Whatever the size of the economy it will have several features in common, three of which are of special interest.

1. Whether the human group is called band, tribe, village, or nation, and whether its economy is called primitive, peasant, capitalist, or communist, it consists of people with recognized social and cultural affinities—kinship, religion, language, neighborhood—expressed in some sort of shared community or social life. This means that two kinds of goods and specialist services[7] must be provided for use within the community (however defined): food and other material requisites of *physical* existence, and goods and services for religion, defense, settlement of dispute, rites of passage, and other aspects of *social* and community life. The acquisition or production of material items and specialist services necessary for physical and social existence are never left to chance because neither individuals nor communities can survive without them. It is for this reason that it is useful to regard all communities or societies as having economic systems. The word "system" refers to structured arrangements and rules which assure that material goods and specialist services are provided in repetitive fashion. One task of economic anthropology is to spell out these rules and systematic arrangements for that set of societies of interest to anthropologists.

2. A second similarity among economies is that they all make use of some form(s) of natural resources (land, waterways, minerals), human co-operation (division of labor), and technology (tools, and knowledge of production or acquisition proc-

---

[7] The concept of "services" causes difficulty in economic anthropology (as do the concepts of "capital" and "market") because the term is used to cover a wide range of items or activities in our own economy, only a few of which are found in primitive economies. In our own economy, the term "services" is used to describe ordinary labor, mechanized utilities (telephone and electricity services), the services performed by craftsmen and professional specialists, e.g., dentistry, TV repairs, musicians; and also the functions performed by political and religious office-holders. In our own economy, all but the latter services are organized for purchase and sale. In relation to primitive and peasant economies, I prefer to use the term "specialist services" to refer to those provided by craftsmen, such as blacksmiths, woodcarvers, and dancers, and those provided by persons performing political, religious, and ritual roles.

esses). Each of these features is structured: the use of tools, natural resources, and division of labor require social rules—specified rights and obligations. The rules for the acquisition, use, and transfer of rights to land, we call "land tenure"; the rules specifying human co-operation in production processes, we call "division of labor" or "work organization"; if tools and technical knowledge are important in any economy there will be rules for their acquisition, use, and transfer.

Two general points emerge: when the rules specifying rights of acquisition or usage of any of these components of an economy are expressions of kinship or political relationships, the economic component is inextricably related to the social, and we have a

TABLE 3

ANALYTICAL CATEGORIES AND RELEVANT QUESTIONS
IN ECONOMIC ANTHROPOLOGY

I. TRADITIONAL ECONOMIES

A. *Types*

1. Primitive, without centralized polity (Tiv).
2. Primitive, with centralized polity: chiefdoms, kingdoms, empires (Nupe, Bantu, Inca).
3. Peasant (Malay fishermen, Latin American peasantries).

B. *Analytical Distinctions*

1. Organization
   a. Size of economy; technology; natural resource endowment.
   b. Transactional modes (reciprocity, redistribution, market-exchange; dominant-integrative modes distinguished from petty modes).
   c. Production processes: (1) allocation of resources (land acquisition, use, and transfer; labor acquisition and use; the acquisition, use and transfer of tools and equipment); (2) work organization; (3) disposition of produce; (4) specialist services and their remuneration.
   d. Organization and role(s) of external trade (reciprocal gift trade; politically administered trade; market trade).
   e. Organization and role(s) of internal markets and market places (marketless economies, petty market places, small-scale market-integrated economies; resource markets and produce markets).
   f. Organization of money and money uses (general-purpose and special-purpose monies; commercial and non-commercial

uses of money; relation of money uses to transactional modes).

g. Operational devices: record-keeping, accounting, and measurement devices (quipu strings, pebble counts); devices of culture contact (silent trade, border markets, ports of trade).

h. Prestige economy contrasted with subsistence economy (transactional spheres and conversions; bridewealth; ceremonial transfers; valuables and treasures as special-purpose monies).

i. The relation of economic to social organization (the place of economy in society): social control of resource allocation, work organization, and produce disposition; social guarantee of livelihood through resource allocation and the provision of emergency subsistence.

2. Performance

a. Number of goods and specialist services produced or acquired.

b. Level of output; fluctuations in output; frequency of dearth or famine (emergency devices in dearth or famine: use of trade partners for emergency gifts; use of less-preferred foods; emergency conversions, e.g., sale of treasures and people for food).

c. Distribution of real income: equal or unequal? Why?

d. Distribution of subsistence goods contrasted with distribution of prestige goods (spheres of exchange; conversion between spheres).

C. *Special Problems Relating to Peasant Economies*

1. The nature of market organization and dependence contrasted with national, developed market economies; why "penny capitalism" is an appropriate description of peasant economy.

2. Peasant economy and culture before and after the Industrial Revolution.

3. The mixture of traditional and market economy; of traditional and modern technology; of traditional social organization and culture and elements of modern culture.

4. Peasant economy and society in contrast to primitive economy and society, and in contrast to industrial capitalist economy and society.

II. SOCIO-ECONOMIC CHANGE, GROWTH, AND DEVELOPMENT: SEQUENTIAL PROCESS ANALYSIS

A. *Contexts of change and development: colonialism-culture contact; post-colonial independence-explicit national and village level modernization.*

B. *Types of change*
   1. Degenerative: cultural disruption and absence of substitute forms of organization.
   2. Cash income growth without development: primitive economies becoming peasant; adoption of cash-earning activities with little or no disruption of ordinary life and without concomitant technological and other innovations which diversifies and sustains income growth.
   3. Development: sustained income growth for the local community through integration-economic, political, cultural—into the larger socio-economic unit of which it is a part, without loss of ethnic identity or group malaise.

socio-economic practice, institution, or process. Aboriginal land tenure in parts of Africa are obvious examples, where land is acquired through kinship right or tribal affiliation (Bohannan 1954; Schapera and Goodwin 1937:157). Secondly, what we call economic organization is the set of rules in force through which natural resources, human co-operation, and technology are brought together to provide material items and specialist services in sustained and repetitive fashion.

3. A third similarity is the incorporation of superficially similar devices and practices in economies differently organized. Economies as different as the U.S., the U.S.S.R., and the Tiv make use of market places, foreign trade, monetary objects, and devices for measuring and record-keeping.

In summary, all societies of record—those studied by anthropologists, historians, and economists—have structured arrangements to provide the material means of individual and community life. It is these structured rules that we call an economic system. Economic anthropology delineates these social rules of economy by describing activities and folkviews, and analyzing transactional processes and relationships in the small-scale, pre-industrial communities of the underdeveloped world, and makes comparisons between primitive, peasant, and industrialized developed economies. So too with comparing the components and sectors of economy: the allocation of land and labor, the organization of work, the disposition of produce, and the organization and usage of forms of money, markets, and external trade. There are very important differences among economies, however, differences in structure and in performance, and much valuable analysis lies in contrasting them.

Traditional, Primitive Economies: Structure and Performance[8]

The questions about primitive economies of most interest to anthropologists relate to their organization (structure), and to comparisons of their organization with that of other types of economy (peasant, industrial capitalist). With regard to their performance, one can indicate the relatively narrow range of goods and specialist services produced or acquired. The level of output and fluctuations in output can be measured in terms of quantities produced (Deane 1953; Reynders 1963). Input measures can be devised (Salisbury 1962), indicating amounts of equipment used in production processes and work-days employed, and so arrive at some estimates of productivity. Dietary standards can be scrutinized (Richards 1939). Some impressions of the equality or inequality in real-income distribution can be conveyed. Given the absence of Western money and pricing and the relatively few resources used and goods produced, these measures of performance can only be rough indicators stated in terms of the resource and product units themselves.

The Scale of Primitive Economies

> It is this smallness of scale, so hard for a modern European to grasp imaginatively, which is the fundamental characteristic of primitive life . . . (Wilson 1941:10).

There are some useful distinctions to be made among traditional economies. Much of the literature of primitive economies describes those without centralized polities—"tribes without rulers" —Malinowski's Trobriands being the most minutely described case in the literature. In saying that most primitive economies without centralized polity are small, one means several things: that the economy of the Tiv, the Nuer, or the Trobriand Islanders is small relative to modern, nationally-integrated economies of Europe and America; that most (but not all) resource, goods, and service transactions take place within a small geographical

---

[8] The literature of primitive (subsistence) economies—traditional economies most different from our own—is richest for Africa and Oceania, for small-scale communities rather than kingdoms and empires, and for agriculturalists rather than hunters, gatherers, herders, etc. Malinowski's work (1921; 1922; 1926; 1935; also, Uberoi 1962) is the single best source. On the economies of kingdoms and other politically centralized societies, see Nadel (1942), Maquet (1961), Arnold (1957), and Polanyi (1966).

area and within a community of persons numbered in the hundreds or thousands. It is true that external trade is common and, as with the Kula, sometimes is carried out over long distances. Typically, however, it is intermittent, petty in amount, or confined to very few goods. It is rare (except in peasant economies) for foreign trade transactions to be frequent, quantitatively important, or essential to livelihood.

There are two other ways in which primitive economies are small-scale. Frequently one or two staple items (yams in the Trobriands, cattle among the Nuer) comprise an unusually large proportion of total produce. It is common for these important staples to be produced within the small framework of village, tribe, or lineage. Lastly, a relatively small number of goods and services is produced or acquired—dozens of items and specialist services rather than hundreds of thousands as in developed, industrial economies.

There are mutually reinforcing connections between the size and other aspects of the structure and performance of an economy. Two widely shared characteristics of the small economies anthropologists study are a simple technology (compared to the industrialized economies of the West), and geographical or cultural isolation (again, compared to those of Europe and North America). The absence of sophisticated machines and applied science, and of the extreme labor specialization characteristic of national economies numbering their participants in the millions, means a relatively low level of productivity. Two direct consequences for primitive economies of their simple technology and small size is that their peoples are sharply constrained in production activities by physical resource endowment (ecology), and that their peoples depend greatly on human co-operation for ordinary production[9] processes as well as emergencies such as famine and personal misfortune. Low-level technology combined with small size and relative isolation results in ingrained mutual

---

[9] The extraordinary dependence on immediate physical environment for livelihood made it seem reasonable for an older generation of anthropologists to use classifications such as gathering, hunting, fishing, pastoral, and agricultural "economies". These categories do not classify according to *economic organization,* but rather according to principal source of subsistence, physical environment, and technology. Note that if we used these categories for developed economies, the U.S. and the U.S.S.R. would appear in the same category, both being manufacturing and agricultural "economies".

dependence among people sharing many relationships: those with whom one is economically involved are the same as those with whom one is involved through neighborhood, religion, kinship and polity. The primitive economy in that sense is "embedded" in other community relationships and is not composed of associations separate from these (Dalton 1962; 1964).

> Association is a group specifically organized for the purpose of an interest or group of interests which its members have in common. . . . Community is a circle of people who live together, who belong together, so that they share not this or that particular interest, but a whole set of interests wide enough and comprehensive enough to include their lives (MacIver 1933:9, 10, 12, quoted in Nadel 1942:xi).

Some points may here be underscored: (1) "Primitive" or "subsistence" economies require for the analysis of their *organization* conceptual categories which are socio-economic because material and service transactions are frequently expressions of kinship, religious, or political relationships. (2) Two general features of primitive or subsistence economies are the pervasive social control of production and distribution, and the assurance of subsistence livelihood to persons through the social determination of labor and land allocation and the social right to receive emergency material aid in time of need.

These points have frequently been made before: to Tönnies, primitive economies are *Gemeinschaft* rather than *Gesellschaft;* to Maine, they are characterized by status rather than contract; to Weber and MacIver, they are communities rather than associations; to Karl Polanyi (1944:Chap. 4; 1957), the economy is "embedded" in the society; to Raymond Firth (1951:142), the formula is "From each according to his status obligations in the social system, to each according to his rights in that system."

Primitive economies are so organized that the allocation of labor and land, the organization of work within production processes (farming, herding, construction of buildings and equipment), and the disposition of produced goods and specialist services are expressions of underlying kinship obligation, tribal affiliation, and religious and moral duty. Unlike the economist who can analyze important features of industrial capitalism (such as price and income determination) without considering social relationships, the economic anthropologist concerned with the *organization* of primitive economies finds there is no separate economic system that can be analyzed independently of social organization.

The ways in which tools and implements are acquired, used, and disposed of is another point of contrast between primitive, peasant, and industrial capitalist economies. Typically in primitive economies tools are either made by the user himself, acquired for a fee from a specialist craftsman, or, as is sometimes the case with dwellings, storehouses, and canoes, acquired from a construction group specifically organized for the task. The construction group providing ordinary labor as well as the services of craftsmen specialists is remunerated either by food provided by the host (Thurnwald's *Bittarbeit* and barn-raising in the American West), or with food and luxury tidbits (tobacco, betel), or with these as well as payments in valuables or special-purpose money to the craftsmen-specialists (Dalton 1965*a*). Western cash is not paid. The making of tools, canoes, and dwellings is an occasional event rather than a continuous activity, and the construction workers do not derive the bulk of their livelihood from providing such services. The tools, canoes, and buildings when put to use do not yield their owners a cash income. Typically, the implements are used until they are physically worn out, when they are either repaired or discarded. Unlike some peasant economies (Firth 1946), primitive economies have no second-hand markets for tools and buildings.

Polanyi's analytical distinctions between reciprocity, redistribution, and (market) exchange and their application to specific cases have been written up in detail (Polanyi 1944:Chap. 4; 1947; 1957; 1966; Dalton 1961; 1962; 1965*b*). Unfortunately, they have been misconstrued as applying only to transactions of produce (Smelser 1958; Burling 1962; Nash 1966). These socioeconomic categories apply to inanimate resource and labor allocation and to work organization as well as to produce disposition— to production as well as to distribution of goods and craft services (LeClair 1962). It is misleading to regard "systems of exchange" as something apart from production processes because exchange transactions enter into *each* of the three component processes of production (Dalton 1962; 1964).

Consider any production process: automobile manufacturing in the U.S., yam growing in the Trobriands, collective farming in the U.S.S.R., Malay peasant fishing, or cattle raising among the

Nuer. All these production lines require the allocation of land, labor, and other resource ingredients to the production process; the organization of work tasks within the production process; and the disposition of the items produced. Among the Tiv, acquiring farm land (in accordance with one's lineage affiliation) is as much a "reciprocal" transaction as yam-giving (in accordance with one's *urigubu* obligation) is in the Trobriands.

Primitive States:
Internal Redistribution and External Administered Trade

As in other branches of anthropology, the typical unit of analytical interest in economic anthropology is a relatively small group, the tribe, the lineage segment, the village community. There is a small, internal economy to be analyzed whether our focus of interest is a primitive economy without centralized polity (such as the Tiv), a primitive economy within a centralized polity, such as the local farming communities in Nupe (Nadel 1942), or a peasant economy, such as the Malay fishermen (Firth 1946). To be sure, persons or groups within each of these small economies may carry out transactions with outsiders—external trade, tax and tribute payments to outside political authorities—but it is meaningful to distinguish between internal (local community) transactions and those external to the local group, however defined.

Primitive economies which are part of centralized political authority—what Polanyi called archaic societies and Evans-Pritchard and Fortes (1940) called primitive states—have socio-economic transactions in addition to those found within the local

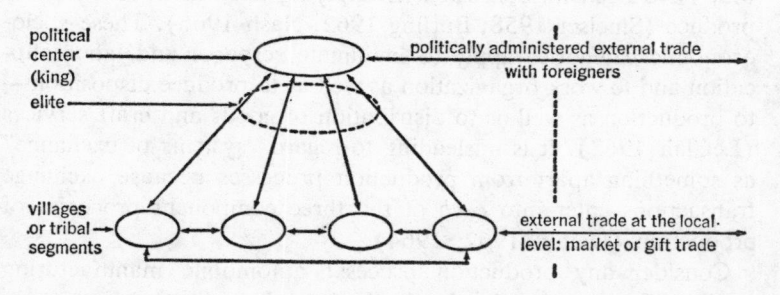

Figure 9   Socio-economic transactions in the primitive economy within a centralized political authority system.

community and between local communities (see Figure 9). These are of two principal sorts, transactions between the political center and its local constituencies, and external trade transactions between the political center and foreigners (Arnold 1957*a;* 1957*b;* Polanyi 1963; 1966). The local constituents pay tribute to the political center—ordinary subsistence goods, luxuries reserved for elite usage, labor for construction projects and military service —and usually receive from the center military protection, juridical services, and emergency subsistence in time of local famine or disaster.

Where there is a centralized political authority, there is a redistributive sector which has no counterpart in primitive economies without a centralized polity (i.e., that are not chiefdoms, kingdoms, or empires). Indeed, where there is an intermediary elite between the king (his royal household economy and his domain), and the villages or tribal segments which express their political subordination through tax and tribute payments and other upward transactions, there are socio-economic sectors that some writers call feudal (Nadel 1942; Maquet 1961), although others question the usefulness of so labeling them (Goody 1963; Beattie 1964).

Peasant Economy

Writers on peasantry (Redfield 1956; Wolf 1966) emphasize the special nature of peasant personality and culture as that which distinguishes peasant from primitive: the semi-isolation from urban culture with which it shares religion and (in Europe) language; that peasants and peasant communities are the rank and file, so to speak, of larger political groupings, so that in Latin America, Europe, and India there are political authorities externally located who exercise some formal political jurisdiction over the peasant villages.

It is important to note that if we confine ourselves to cultural aspects such as religion, language, and political subordination, we can point up what is common to an enormous number of peasantries, and, at the same time justify the use of the special category, peasant culture, by showing it is different in these ways from primitive culture. Trobriand Island culture has none of the characteristics so far enumerated for peasants.

To go further, however, requires some special distinctions because of the long periods of historical time over which groups

called peasant by social analysts have existed intact, and because there are other criteria used to differentiate peasant from
primitive and modern.

One line of demarcation is the Industrial Revolution. Before
the Industrial Revolution occurred in their regions, all peasantries
used primitive technology, differing in no important way from
the technologies used by those groups (Tiv, Lele, Nuer) anthropologists identify as being primitive. Let us call peasant communities as they existed before the Industrial Revolution in
their regions, "traditional" peasantries. Then we can point out
immediately that traditional peasantries, although differing from
primitive societies in those cultural ways specified earlier, were
like primitive communities in their use of simple (machineless)
technology, their small units of production (principally but not
exclusively agricultural) and the relatively few items produced
within a peasant community. In traditional peasantries as in
primitive communities, there is the same reliance upon one or
two staple foodstuffs which comprise a large proportion of total
output, and the same unusually large reliance upon natural resource endowment because of the simple technology used and
the absence of complicated fabrication processes. With regard to
the size of production units, technology, dependence on physical
resource endowment, and the narrow range of items produced,
traditional peasant communities resemble the primitive much
more closely than they do with regard to culture. Moreover,
material performance is roughly the same as in primitive communities, and for the same reasons. The ethnographic record
does not indicate that traditional peasantries were typically less
poor materially than primitive societies.[10]

---

[10] For many traditional peasant economies (village communities), it is
undoubtedly true that real income is no higher than in most primitive
economies. But, aside from difficulties of measuring real output, there are
complicating features of peasant society which make it difficult to say
whether many peasantries had consistently higher levels of output than
is typical in primitive communities. Peasant communities, for example,
seem invariably to be subordinate units of larger political (and religious)
groupings, which means that significant portions of peasant produce and
labor are paid "upward" as taxes, tributes, rents, and tithes. The elite
recipients of such taxes and tributes channelled portions of them into the
creation of churches, palaces, pyramids, armies, etc., some of the services
of which were received back by the local peasant communities. Again, the
slow growth of improvement in agricultural and marketing techniques in

What anthropologists mean by peasant culture is clear; what they mean by peasant economy is sometimes not clear.

By a peasant economy one means a system of small-scale producers, with a simple technology and equipment often relying primarily for their subsistence on what they themselves produce. The primary means of livelihood of the peasant is cultivation of the soil (Firth 1951:87).

But this is a perfect description of the Lele (Douglas 1965), the Tiv (Bohannan 1968), and the Trobriand Islanders in Malinowski's time—all have primitive economies. If we are to make analytical sense of the large literature of economic anthropology we need some finer distinctions.

It is as useful to distinguish between peasant and primitive economy as it is to distinguish between peasant and primitive culture. The *economic* organization of a peasant community has two sets of distinguishing characteristics:

1. Most people depend for the bulk of their livelihood on production for market sale or selling in markets; purchase and sale transactions with cash are frequent and quantitatively important; and, frequently, resource markets are present: significant quantities of labor, land, tools, and equipment are available for purchase, rent, or hire at money price. It is the relative importance of markets for resources and products and of cash transactions that is the principal difference between peasant and primitive *economies*. It is this feature which gives peasant economies their crude resemblance to the least productive of our own farming sectors and which justifies Tax's appropriate phrase, "penny capitalism." But in all other ways relating to productive activities, peasant economies—especially traditional peasantries —more closely resemble the primitive than they do the modern: small-scale, simple technology, a narrow range of output, a few staples comprising the bulk of output, unusual reliance on physical resource endowment because of the absence of applied science and the technology of extensive fabrication; low levels of output —poverty and material insecurity.

2. What strikes the economist is that although the rudi-

---

some European peasant communities for several hundred years before the Industrial Revolution may have given some European peasant communities of say, the 18th century higher incomes than is typical of other peasant and most primitive economies.

ments of capitalist (i.e., market) economy are present and important in peasant communities, they are *incomplete* and *underdeveloped* compared to market organization in a modern national economy. By incomplete is meant that within a given peasant community, some markets may be absent or petty —land may be frequently purchased or rented but labor is not (Chayanov 1966), or vice versa; and that subsistence production may still be quantitatively important in some households. By underdeveloped is meant the absence of facilitative institutions and social capital of advanced capitalist countries: on the one hand, banks, insurance companies, and stock markets; on the other, electricity, paved roads, and educational facilities beyond the elementary school. In peasant communities the extent of economic, cultural, and technological integration with the province and nation is markedly less than is the case with hinterland communities in developed nations.

In summary, peasant society, like primitive society (and also feudalism, *jajmani* in village India, and slavery) is a socioeconomic category (Firth 1964a:17). If we include peasantries of all times and places within our analysis, then it is fair to say that peasant culture is more homogeneous and distinctive than is peasant economy (Fallers 1961). The spectrum of peasantries is wide, and contains varying mixtures of primitive and modern institutions. At one end are those in medieval Europe —the Russian mir, the feudal village (Bennett 1962) and some of present-day Latin America, which are peasant cultures (in religion language, political subordination) with primitive economies (because of the absence of market dependence and cash transactions). There are also cases of peasant economy with a primitive culture, as in the early transition period of African groups enlarging their cash-earning production while retaining their tribal organization and culture (Fallers 1961; Gulliver 1965; Dalton 1964).[11]

---

[11] In this paper I can only call attention to how little work has been done on the economic aspects of peasantry (in the anthropological literature) and suggest that similar cultural features accompany dissimilar economic arrangements in the broad spectrum of peasant societies. There is a great deal more to be said about peasant economy. I am preparing an essay which classifies peasant societies into three sorts. Type I consists of peasant communities which have dependent (non-market) land tenure (such as those under European Feudalism) in which land is acquired by

III. COMMUNITY CHANGE AND DEVELOPMENT

The most promising area for fruitful interchange and collaboration between economics and anthropology is the field of economic development. Most development economists, however, are interested in processes and problems of *national* economic growth and development that have little in common with anthropologists' interests in local community social and economic change. But a growing number of economists are working on matters requiring anthropological insight: creating an industrial labor force, transforming subsistence agriculture (Yudelman 1964), devising policies for investment in educational facilities. Others are devising techniques of measurement and analysis to show the connections between socio-political organization and economic development (Adelman and Morris 1965, 1967). And yet other economists are making use of anthropology, sociology, and psychology to analyze—what is for economists—an unusual range of processes and problems entailed in economic growth and development (Hagen 1962; Myrdal 1957).

Matters relating to what I shall call socio-economic change, growth and development at the local community level conventionally appear in anthropology under the headings of evolution, diffusion of innovations, social change, culture change, culture contact, acculturation, and applied anthropology. There

---

clients from patrons as part of a long-run social and political relationship. Clients reciprocate with obligatory payments of material goods or labor services (farm labor, military labor, road repair, etc.), as well as with more diffuse social and political "payments"—loyalty, respect, homage, ceremonial services. Type II consists of peasant communities of a post-French Revolution sort, in which land tenure is strictly a matter of market purchase (or rental at money price) with no social or political obligations attached to land acquisition or usage. Types I and II refer to communities of long settlement. Type III is a hybrid sort, referring to communities of persons resettled within relatively recent historical times, frequently, as the aftermath of slavery in the Caribbean and the Spanish conquest of Latin America. Kroeber and Redfield, understandably, seized upon cultural attributes to differentiate "peasant" from "primitive" cultures. What remains to be done is socio-economic analysis of peasant groups from an anthropological perspective which takes account of the rich historical literature of European peasantries (e.g., Chayanov 1966) as well as the more recent ethnographies.

are two points about this literature of socio-economic change that I should like to emphasize.

The subject is extraordinarily diverse and complicated. It includes a wide range of complex processes: urbanization, industrialization, commercialization, national integration (cf. Southall 1961, UNESCO 1963). Moreover, these processes take place over much longer periods of time than anthropologists customarily remain in the field, and their analysis requires consideration of the policies of central government which impinge on the small group (village or tribal segment) that traditionally has been the focus of interest in anthropology.

The case studies of socio-economic change reach back to the early days of European colonization of Africa (Schapera 1934; Hunter 1961), Latin America (Chevalier 1963), and Asia (Boeke 1942), when neither political independence was a fact nor economic development of indigenous peoples an explicit intention. The recent case studies are of socio-economic change taking place in villages which are now parts of independent nation-states whose central governments are initiating nation-wide development and modernization. The literature includes cases of piecemeal change, where a new cash crop or a new school or a new religion is introduced in an otherwise traditional community (Dalton 1964), and cases of comprehensive community development, such as the famous case of Vicos (Holmberg *et al.* 1965).

Given the complexity of the processes, the large number and diversity of case studies on record, and the changed political and economic national conditions under which local community development now proceeds, it is not surprising that relatively few theoretical insights and conceptual categories with which to analyze socio-economic change have been contrived. Some notable contributions are Myrdal (1957), Hagen (1962), Smelser (1963), and Adelman and Morris (1967).

Socio-economic change as an anthropological subject is unusual in another way, as well. Many of us who work on problems of development and modernization hope not only to come to understand these processes, but also to use such knowledge to reduce the social costs of economic improvement. Therefore, this extension of the traditional concerns of economic anthropology into processes of socio-economic change and development has policy implications to an extent that is unusual in anthropology (Erasmus 1961; Goodenough 1964; Arensberg and Niehoff 1964).

What is also true is that each of us—the anthropologist, the economist, the sociologist—comes to a novel situation such as change and development in a African village community with two kinds of professional knowledge, the theory of one's subject, and an intimate knowledge of some portion(s) of the real world. The economist (typically) comes with price, income, growth, and development theory, plus his knowledge of the structure and performance of his own and perhaps several other economies. If he is a specialist in economic history or Soviet economy (Gerschenkron 1963), he brings with him knowledge of the sequential processes through which England, Japan, Russia, or the U.S. developed. When he comes to examine local development in an African community, he is struck by similarities to and differences from what he is already familiar with.

First, with the exception of agricultural economics, there is no counterpart in conventional economic analysis to the study of local community change and development. European and American villages and townships—the local community counterparts of the Tiv lineage segment or an Indian village—are never the focus of analytical concern. Economics is about national economies and the component activities of business firms and households thoroughly integrated with their national economy through purchase and sale transactions. Immediately we can feed back into our new concerns knowledge that we know is important from our old ones. Empirically, *how do small groups —the tribe, the village—become part of a regional or national economy?*

Similarly, local community change or development seems never to be a "natural" process of immanent expansion of the village or tribe, but rather the local community's response to incursion from outside itself. Whether it is the Conquistadores' invasion of Peru 400 years ago, or Cornell University's invasion of Vicos 15 years ago, or European colonial incursion into Africa, or the slave-raider, missionary, or merchant who comes, the process of community change starts with impingement from without. Therefore, a second question we can ask of the empirical case studies is, *what is the nature of the initial incursion which starts the processes of socio-economic change, and to what extent does the character of the initial incursion shape the sequential changes that follow?*[12]

Most of the ethnographic case studies fall into one of three broad categories that I shall designate (*a*) degenerative change; (*b*) cash income growth without development; and (*c*) socio-economic development. The three categories—which are really ideal types—are not stages of progression. Moreover, they are clearly overlapping. Some of the empirical literature fits neatly into these categories, some does not. My point is to make sharp analytical distinctions, and to do so I must oversimplify.

Degenerative Change

Much of the early literature of culture contact consists of European and American incursions which produced decimation, misery, and community degeneration among indigenous groups (Rivers 1922; Jaspan 1953).

> Native [Fiji] society [in the 1880's] was severely disrupted by war, by catastrophic epidemics of European diseases, by the introduction of alcohol, by the devastations of generations of warfare, and by the depredations of labor recruiters (Worsley 1957a:19).

By degenerative change I mean severe disruption of the traditional life of a community over several generations with accompanying indicators of novel sorts and frequencies of personal and social malaise. I do not postulate frictionless bliss in the traditional society; but whatever conflicts and malaise were generated by traditional society—warfare, vendetta, sorcery—were coped with by traditional institutions (Malinowski 1959), without prolonged disruption of ordinary life. Where degenerative change occurs, it is, obviously, because the situation is such that traditional institutions designed to deal with traditional sorts of stress and conflict are unable to deal with the novel change because it embodies forces which are at the same time without precedent, irreversible, and overwhelming to traditional organization.

The extreme cases are marked by military conquest and displacement of traditional political authority by conquerers who neither understand nor respect the culture of the society they

---

[12] A third general point of significance I believe to be the time rate of change which is experienced (Polanyi 1944:Chap. 3). This is not, however, independent of the other features of the transformation process.

now control. The indigenous people are unable to resist imposed changes, are prohibited from pursuing rituals or activities which are meaningful and integrative within traditional society, and are made to pursue new activities (e.g., forced labor in mines and plantations) which are not integrative—do not fulfill social obligation and so reinforce social relationships—in traditional society (Steiner 1957).

> For the sting of change lies not in change itself but in change which is devoid of social meaning (Frankel 1955:27).

Degenerative situations and the psychological processes of individual and group reaction to them have caught the attention of many writers, perhaps because the consequences are so dramatic. Having lost the primary ties of meaningful culture, social relationships, and activities (Fromm 1941), and having been forced into meaningless activities and degrading helplessness, individuals and groups react to the bewildering changes with fantasy, aggression, withdrawal, and escape (Hagen 1962:Chap. 17; Smelser 1963). And so we have the ethnography of cultural disintegration, from the Pawnee Ghost Dance to Melanesian Cargo Cults[13] and Navaho alcoholism.

If one examines these cases of degenerative change from the viewpoint of community development, several features stand out:

1. *The nature of the initial incursion.* In cases of severe degenerative change, the initial incursion causes cultural decimation: military conquest, political subjugation, and severe disruption of usual activities. A by-product of the incursion may be material worsening, or, indeed, slight material improvement. But these economic consequences are really beside the point because the force of change is perceived and felt to be deprivation of valued activities and the community's subjugation to militarily superior foreigners with hostile intentions and contempt for indigenous ways. The foreigners may come with the intent to deprive the people of gold or land, but typically it

---

[13] Cargo cults are complicated movements expressing several aspects of fission and fusion. Here, I simply want to emphasize that among other things, they are symptoms of malaise that indicate deep misunderstanding of processes of modernization through which Western goods are acquired.

is not the deprivation of gold or land which causes the deep
disruption.

> Not economic exploitation, as often assumed, but the disinte-
> gration of the cultural environment of the victim is then the
> cause of degradation. The economic process may, naturally, supply
> the vehicle of the destruction, and almost invariably economic
> inferiority will make the weaker yield, but the immediate cause
> of his undoing is not for that reason economic; *it lies in the lethal
> injury to the institutions in which his social existence is embodied.*
> The result is loss of self-respect and standards, whether the unit
> is a people or a class, whether the process springs from so-called
> "culture conflict" or from a change in the position of a class within
> the confines of a society (Polanyi 1944:157. Italics added).

The nature of the initial incursion seems invariably important,
not only to the generation experiencing the initial impact but
also—in its shaping the sequences of socio-economic change
—to successive generations (Hagen 1962). The group's cultural
memory of what they regard as early injustice is long (Schapera
1928), and sometimes is nurtured several generations later (Colson 1949).

2. *The absence of new economic, technological, and cultural
achievement.* The incursion prevents the society from functioning
in customary ways without providing substitute ways which are
meaningful to the people in terms of traditional culture (Steiner
1957; Frankel 1955). It is disintegrative to traditional organization without providing new forms of organization which re-
integrate the society along new lines (Smelser 1963). These are
useful ways to state the problem, but much detailed analysis of
socio-economic change needs to be done: What are the sequential
processes of disintegration and subsequent re-integration? Which
specific features of traditional society are most vulnerable? How
long do these processes take? Under what conditions has re-
integration taken place? We are here concerned with historical
processes to be analyzed in sociological terms. The problems
require explicit concern with long stretches of calendar time and
with sequential process analysis of old and new economy, technology, polity, social organization, and culture.

Degenerative change does not mean that some people believe
themselves to be worse off materially or culturally under the

new conditions. Some people are made worse off by any kind of social change. Rather, it means that the old society ceases to function in important ways, most people perceive the changes as worsenings, and in no important area of social or private life is there widespread absorption of new culture (e.g., literacy), new technology and economy (e.g., new farming methods and enlarged production for sale), of the sorts which create social re-integration. Neither is degenerative change necessarily a permanent state of affairs. Worsley (1957*b*) argues that Melanesian cargo cults, despite their traumatic symptoms of malaise, misunderstanding of European economy, and distorted religiosity, contain the beginnings of wider political organization of an anti-colonial sort which may possibly evolve into more orthodox and productive political activity (see also Hagen 1962).

Growth Without Development

Most of the case studies of community change reported in the literature differ from the one described above in two principal ways. First, the incursion was not severely disruptive of traditional society. The Trobriands (during Malinowski's residence), the Tiv (at the time of Bohannan's fieldwork), and many other groups carried on their traditional activities largely intact for generations after the foreign presence was felt. Second, the peoples became engaged in new cash-earning activities (principally growing cash crops and selling wage-labor), and this was the *only* innovation of importance widely adopted. Subsistence economies became peasant economies as cash earnings and dependence for livelihood on market sale of crops or wage-labor grew, while traditional culture and society remained largely intact (except for those changes induced by the enlarged commercial production or cash-earning).

Here we have the two salient features experienced by a large number of primitive societies: untraumatic incursion which allows ordinary activities, ceremony, and social relationships to continue on much as before; and enlarged cash-earning activities without the concomitant adoption of improved technology, literacy, or any of the other important accoutrements of "modernization" (Gulliver 1965).

I call this situation "cash income growth without development." The community's cash income grows somewhat because of its enlarged sales of crops or labor, but those structural changes in economy, technology, and culture necessary for sustained income growth and the integration over time of the local community with the nation, are not forthcoming. During the period when cash income grows while old culture, values, and folkviews remain initially unchanged (because literacy, new vocational skills, new lines of production, new technology, are not adopted), some characteristic responses are generated:

1. The use of new cash income for old status prerogatives (bridewealth, potlatch).
2. New conflict situations (land tenure litigation).
3. The undermining of traditional arrangements providing material security through social relationships (cash-earning and individualism).

Typically, cash income is earned by individual or household activities rather than lineage or large co-operative group activities (such as canoe building and reciprocal land clearing). Writers on peasant economy (Chayanov 1966; Yang 1945: Chap. 7) stress the economic importance of the *family household* as a production unit for good reasons. The growth of dependence on market sale of labor or crops for livelihood means the lessened dependence on political heads, extended kin, age-mates, friends, and neighbors—in a word, lessened dependence on local social relationships—to acquire labor or land to use in production processes.

The new form of income, Western cash, is utterly different from anything known in traditional marketless economies. It is indefinitely storable, and so provides material security for its individual owner. It can be used to purchase a variety of goods and discharge a variety of obligations which no money-stuff or treasure item does in primitive economy. Not only a potentially enormous range of European imports—gin, tobacco, canned foods, steel tools, crucifixes, transistor radios—school fees, and colonial taxes, but also traditional subsistence goods (foodstuffs), traditional prestige sphere services, obligations, and positions (e.g., bridewealth), and natural resources (land), and labor, all become purchasable or payable with cash. This is what is meant by Western cash being a "general purpose" money (Dalton 1965*a*). The process of acquisition as well as the transactional use or disposition of Western cash in formerly primitive economies breaks down the traditional separation between spheres of subsistence and prestige goods and services (Firth 1958:Chap. 3; Bohannan 1959).

The use of new cash income for old status prerogatives, new conflict situations, and the undermining of traditional arrangements providing material security are related consequences of earning cash income *within an otherwise traditional setting*. For example, that bridewealth has come to be paid in cash rather than, as formerly, in high prestige items such as cows, indicates the great importance placed on cash (and what it will buy and pay for). The *social* consequences of such displacement are several. Consider the contrasting situations before and after cash has displaced traditional valuables as bridewealth. Indigenously, bridewealth in cows could be got by a young man wanting to marry only by soliciting the required cows from kin, friends, elders, chiefs, i.e., by drawing on social relationships and thus creating obligations to repay them (reciprocate) in some form (e.g., labor service, clientship, etc.). After cash becomes acceptable as bridewealth, young men can raise their own cash and pay their own bridewealth, thus weakening their dependence on traditional superiors.

Indigenously, where bridewealth required the payment of prestige goods, the items (such as cows) could be disposed of by the bridewealth recipients in very few ways. Cows (like kula bracelets) could only be exchanged or paid within the prestige sphere which was narrowly circumscribed. But cash received as bridewealth has no such limitations. It can be used for traditional prestige or subsistence goods, or any of the array of new goods. Bohannan (1959) has pointed out the moral ambivalence which results in the changed situation where bridewealth receipts in cash can be spent on goods in a lower prestige sphere.

Socio-Economic Development

Economists can answer the question, "What constitutes successful development?" with little difficulty. Their unit of analysis is the nation-state, and their base of reference is the already developed nations of North America and Europe. The indicators of successful development from the viewpoint of economics are impersonal, having little to do with folk-views, attitudes, social relationships, or culture. Development is characterized in terms of the country's yearly percentage rate of growth in gross national product, the size of per capita income and its distribution, and the use of advanced technology in major production lines.

If anthropologists are asked, "What constitutes successful development?" the answer is more difficult. The anthropologists' unit of analysis is the tribal or village community, not the nation-state[14]; anthropologists are not only concerned with economy and technology, but also with folkviews, attitudes, social relationships, and the rest of culture. And they do not use the already developed nations of Europe and North America as a base of reference for successful development. Moreover, anthropologists are analytically concerned with the wider social process of which economic development is a part, and sensitive to social and cultural costs of economic change.

There is no such thing as a small-scale community's development independent of the larger units of economy and society external to the tribe or village. The several kinds of change that constitute modernization all entail integration with external groupings, i.e., increased dependence upon external groups with whom new economic and cultural transactions take place.

Sustained income growth for the local community requires enlarged production for sale to regional, national, or international markets, and a return flow of consumption goods, producer's goods, and social services (health and education) purchased with the ever-increasing cash income. The community becomes economically integrated (and dependent upon) the regional, national, or international economy through a continual enlargement and diversification of purchase and sale transactions. These can be enlarged and made to grow only with the use of improved technology (tools and technical knowledge) acquired or purchased initially from outside the local community. Moreover, the experience of a significant growth in income seems frequently to be a necessary pump-priming condition if traditional groups are to become willing to take the risk of producing new kinds of crops and goods, or old ones with new, expensive, and unfamiliar techniques of production. Primitive and peasant unwillingness to change production is frequently a sensible expression of their poverty and material insecurity. They cannot afford unsuccessful experiments. The old techniques are not

---

14 Clifford Geertz's work is a notable exception.

very productive, but they keep the people alive. One of the important lessons of the unusual (and unusually quick) development progress in Vicos (Holmberg *et al.* 1965), was that the *Cornell group* assumed the financial risk of planting improved varieties of potatoes. The demonstration effect of the sharp increase in the value product of the new potatoes convinced the people of Vicos to follow suit. A legitimate role for any central government wanting to accelerate local community development is for it to bear some portion of the financial risk of economic and technological innovation.

The local community's integration politically is yet another aspect of community development. But when central government acts only as a tax gatherer, the local community is likely to perceive any governmentally initiated project to expand community output as a device to increase taxes, and therefore to be resisted. Here too there must be demonstration effects: that government can provide the local community with important economic and social services and confine itself to taxing only a portion of enlarged income forthcoming.

Lastly, there is cultural integration with the larger society: learning new language, new vocational skills, literacy, private and public health practices, and acquiring a participant awareness of alternatives, events, and institutions of the larger world.[15]

What perhaps deserves emphasis is that successful development from the economist's viewpoint is compatible with successful development from the anthropologist's viewpoint. Anthropologists are concerned with minimizing the social costs of community transformation, and with preserving the community's ethnic identity in the new society of income growth, machines, and literacy. But we know from examining the sub-cultures in already developed nations, such as Japan, England, the U.S.S.R., and especially the U.S. (with its unusual ethnic diversity), that the retention of identity in both new and old institutional forms is compatible with modern activities. The point surely is to work with those powerful levers of new achievement which the

---

[15] Gunnar Myrdal's point about the mutually reinforcing nature of developmental activities is indispensable for understanding the processes of sequential change, whether they be degenerative, cash income growth, or the structural changes entailed in successful development (Myrdal 1957: Chaps. 1–3).

people themselves perceive as desirable and which induce other positive changes—higher income through new economic and technological performance, and wider alternatives through education. If such developmental achievements are in fact incorporated, those features of traditional culture and social organization incompatible with the new are sloughed off without the personal and community malaise that characterize degenerative change and growth without development.

> Social policy has . . . to assure that the individual in losing both the benefits and the burdens of the old society acquire no weightier burdens and at least as many benefits as he had in his previous station (Okigbo 1956).

CONCLUSION

Karl Polanyi's analytical concepts, insights, and generalizations relate to the socio-economic organization of primitive and archaic economies in which market organization is absent or confined to petty transactions. Here, the components of economy—labor and resource allocation, work organization, product disposition —are expressions of kinship, polity, religion, etc. His analysis is not general in three senses. (1) He did not analyze peasant economies, where market organization, market dependence for livelihood, and the use of Western money are important. (2) He was not concerned with the quantifiable performance of primitive economies, but only with their organization. (3) His analysis of socio-economic change and development was confined principally to Europe (Polanyi 1944:Chaps. 3, 6, 7, 8, 13).

Much of the criticism of his work (and mine) is due to a misunderstanding of the range of economies we are referring to. Several anthropologists who have done fieldwork in peasant economies (Firth 1946), or in primitive economies at the beginnings of commercialization and use of Western money (Salisbury 1962; Pospisil 1963), look for a universal theory. They complain that Polanyi's categories and generalizations (designed for primitive, static economies), do not fit their peasant and changing economies, and so criticism of Polanyi's work ensues.

If, as with Polly Hill, who has written extensively on Ghanaian cocoa farming (1963; 1966), the investigator is interested in peasant economy, cash crops, and economic growth, and particularly with measurable performance rather than socio-economic organization, then he is being rather short tempered when he criticizes those of us who are interested in economies different from those of Ghanaian cocoa farming, and with aspects of economy and society other than measurable performance (Hill 1963*b*).

If, as with Firth and Salisbury, anthropologists are interested in comparative economic performance—how much is produced, how much equipment and labor are used, how income is divided —questions economists put to our own economy, then (in vastly simplified fashion) some of the measurement concepts of conventional economics are usefully applicable, and they fail to understand Polanyi's criticism of conventional economics as inappropriate for analyzing the *structure* of primitive economies.

Some, like Pospisil (1963) and Burling (1962), perceive an economy not as a set of rules of social organization but as economic behavior of individuals and their subjective motivations; when they detect greed and self-aggrandizement they equate these with capitalism and assert that economic "behavior" in primitive societies is the same as in market societies and that Polanyi's conceptual categories are wrong and "romantic" (Cook 1966).

Finally, some anthropologists obliterate all distinctions between descriptive statements, analytical statements, and statements about folkviews, by describing and analyzing the economy, and stating folkviews about it exclusively in market terminology (supply, demand, price, maximizing, capital), and thus quite understandably convince themselves that conventional economics provides all the concepts necessary for economic anthropology (Pospisil 1963).

What must be recognized is that economic anthropology deals with two different sorts of economies, primitive and peasant, under two different sets of conditions, static and dynamic, and with two very different aspects of economy, organization and material performance. Polanyi's theoretical categories are addressed principally, but not exclusively, to the organization of primitive and archaic economies under static conditions. That he did not analyze peasant economies and small-scale economies undergoing change, growth, and development does not vitiate his important contributions to the analysis of non-market economies and the transformations of 18th- and 19th-century capitalism.[16]

To adduce an analogy that illustrates the point: in the Anglo-America of 1933, the topics handled with Marshallian price and distribution theory (Marshall 1920), and its extensions into the analysis of markets in imperfect competition (Robinson 1932; Chamberlin 1933), were the dominant concern of economic theory (the pricing of resources and products under static conditions in market-integrated national economies). In the Anglo-America of 1968, this remains a concern of economic theory but has declined in relative importance as different questions became important and new theories and conceptual categories were invented to answer them: what determines aggregate national output (Keynes 1936)? What determines the rate of growth of aggregate output over time (Harrod 1952; Domar 1957)? Polanyi's system is akin to Marshall's in its traditional concerns.

Moreover, when Soviet economy began to take its present form, beginning in 1928, special concepts and analyses were invented to deal with what is special to Soviet economic organization and performance. So too with the economics of underdeveloped areas. Economists are used to living in several theoretical universes—price theory, income theory, growth theory, development theory, Soviet economy—which overlap only partially. They do not throw out Marshall because he did not answer Keynes' questions; they do not throw out Keynes because he did not answer Harrod and Domar's questions; and they do not throw out any of these market economy theorists because they did not address themselves to issues of collectivization and central planning in Soviet economy. This lesson must be learned in economic anthropology if we are ever to progress beyond the stage where deaf men ceaselessly shout at one another. Like the economists, economic anthropologists are dealing with several aspects of several sorts of economies, and need several sets of concepts to understand and measure them properly.

. . . we have no doubt that the future of economic theory lies not in constructing a single universal theory of economic life but in

---

[16] Much that Polanyi said in *The Great Transformation* (1944) about the social and cultural consequences of the British Industrial Revolution is relevant to current socio-economic change in underdeveloped areas.

conceiving a number of theoretical systems that would be adequate to the range of present or past economic orders and would disclose the forms of their co-existence and evolution (Chayanov 1966:28).

Abstract

While interest in economic anthropology grows rapidly, the creation of a widely accepted theoretical framework is impeded by the persistence—indeed, intensification—of disputes over conceptual issues. Part I of this paper clarifies the issues and explains why controversy persists. Part II attempts to reconcile opposing views by showing how the several different topics that comprise economic anthropology require different sets of analytical and measurement concepts for their fruitful investigation. Part III considers the recent extension of economic anthropology to processes of socio-economic change, growth, and development in communities undergoing "modernization."

To these collective circumstances we have given the name *colonial situation* . . . (1) the domination imposed by a foreign minority . . . acting in the name of a racial (or ethnic) and cultural superiority dogmatically affirmed, and imposing itself on an indigenous population constituting a numerical majority but inferior to the dominant group from a material point of view; (2) this domination linking radically different civilizations into some form of relationship; (3) a mechanized, industrialized society with a powerful economy, a fast tempo of life, and a Christian background, imposing itself on a nonindustrialized, "backward" society . . . (4) the fundamentally antagonistic character of the relationship between these two societies resulting from the subservient role to which the colonial people are subjected as "instruments of the colonial power"; (5) the need, in maintaining this domination, not only to resort to "force," but also to a system of psuedo-justifications [legitimation] and stereotyped behaviors.

G. Balandier

When we undertake the control and education of a backward people such as an African tribe or the natives of New Guinea, we are attempting to produce or to direct changes in their social integration. Our task is to substitute for the existing social structure some other and more complex structure. If we destroy or seriously weaken the existing structure without replacing it by some other more effective, then we only produce social disintegration with all its attendant evils.

A. R. Radcliffe-Brown

Three forces have distintegrated Africa: governmental administration, missionaries, and the new economy. *Ch.-A. Julien*

So a new class arises, who, in the words of one Tswana Chief, are like bats: neither birds nor mice, neither natives nor Europeans.

I. Schapera and A. J. H. Goodwin

. . . he acquired no new skills, merely new vices. *J. H. Boeke*

11 THE SPANISH IN MEXICO AND CENTRAL AMERICA

Eric Wolf

NEW LORDS OF THE LAND

ROYAL COMMAND and supervision ordered not only the relations of New Spain [Mexico and Central America] to Spain, and New Spain to the other Spanish colonies; it also regulated the relation between conquerors and Indians, expecially in the economic realm, between the entrepreneurs-to-be and their laborers. To obtain labor for their enterprises, the colonists at first had recourse to two institutions: the institution of slavery and the institution of *encomienda* or trusteeship. The Spaniards were familiar with slavery as an institution; they had but recently sold into slavery the entire population of the Canary Islands. It seemed natural to them, therefore, to brand and sell as slaves Indians captured in war or received in tribute or condemned to expiate some crime, often enough some infraction of an ill-understood new Spanish law. The Middle American Indians had known a kind of limited slavery in which slaves had been permitted to own property, call some of their time their own, and in which the children of slaves were free. They were confronted now with a new, unlimited slavery in which a human being was treated as a mere commodity, to be sold to mines, sugar mills, and farms, and to be used as an expendable resource.

To receive Indians in *encomienda,* on the other hand, meant that the *encomendero* or trustee received rights to tribute payments and unrestricted personal services from a stipulated num-

SOURCE: Eric Wolf, *Sons of the Shaking Earth,* pages 189–91, 195–232, University of Chicago Press, 1959. Reprinted by permission of the author and publisher.

ber of Indians living in stipulated Indian villages. The institution had prototypes in Castile and perhaps in the *iktá* of Islam, as well as in the perquisites of the Indian chiefs before the Conquest. Yet, in the eyes of the colonist, it was not its medieval provenience which lent merit to the institution; it was rather the opportunity it provided for the organization of a labor force over which he alone would exercise untrammeled sway.

For this reason, both slavery and trusteeship met with royal opposition, for both threatened to raise in the New World the specter of feudalism so recently laid in the Old. The crown, wishing to stand above all men, could not countenance any social arrangement which permitted the re-emergence of power figures who held in their hands combined economic, military, judicial, and social power. In royalist eyes, as Silvio Zavala has said, the nobleman no longer represented a pillar of society, but a source of discord and rebellion. To guard against the rise of combinations of power that could rival the authority of the crown, the king divorced the right to receive Indian tribute from the control of Indian labor. If Indian labor made the wheels turn in this New Spain, then whoever was lord and master of Indians would also be lord and master of the land. With unlimited access to Indian energy, the colonists would soon have no need of Spain or king; hence the crown had to limit this access, supervise it, curtail it. The Indians were thus declared to be direct vassals of the crown, like the colonists themselves. This did not mean that the Indians were to be free to act as they liked, to pursue goals freely chosen with means freely decided upon. It did mean that no private person could lay hands on Indians without prior license from the crown. The Indians were to be royal wards; crown officers would be their tutors upon the road to civilization. These officers would see to it that no Indian remained idle, with satanic thoughts to plague his unoccupied mind. They would work, but they would perform their labor under the watchful eye of royal officers informed of the proper legal prescriptions applying to the particular case.

First, the king abolished all involuntary servitude imposed on individual Indians by individual masters. From 1530 on, Indian slavery was increasingly curtailed; in 1561 the Audiencia of Mexico heard the last cases of slaves to be set free. Only along the northern periphery of New Spain, where Spaniards encountered mobile nomad tribesmen, was slavery maintained as a weapon in the subjugation and pacification of the frontier.

Second, after 1549, the institution of trusteeship no longer included the right to Indian labor. The trustee was to be merely a passive recipient of tribute payments from a given number of Indian villages, but with this tribute—set by royal officials and supervised by the crown—went neither the right to live near his Indians nor to use their labor nor to sit in judgment over them. The trust carried no rights over land. If the crown so desired, it could—and did—allocate land pertaining to one man's Indian villages to another person who applied for a grant of land. Moreover, the grant of tribute was personal and temporary; it applied to the colonist so honored and his son. After the first filial generation, the grant reverted to the king, and the descendants of the original recipient had no claim upon it.

Third, after the middle of the sixteenth century, the crown turned increasingly to a system of compulsory regulated labor, mediated through royal labor exchanges, to fill applications for labor on the part of individuals. In one form or another, this system of regulated labor or *cuatequil* persisted up to the end of the eighteenth century. It bound the employer of Indian labor to pay his workers a standard wage. Labor was to be periodic rather than continuous, allowing workers to return to their native villages after working a stipulated period of time. No more than 4 per cent of the laborers of any community were to be away on outside labor during any given period, nor were they to be taken long distances from their homes. If a trustee wanted Indian labor, he had to hire it from a royal labor exchange at the same price as other men competing for the same precious labor-producing commodity, and no trustee could interfere if a royal officer wished to assign Indians from his tributary villages to the enterprises of another. . . .

It is one of the ironies of the Spanish Conquest that the enterprise and expansion of the colonists produced not utopia but collapse. Like Tantalus reaching in vain for the fruit that would still his hunger and thirst, the conqueror extended his hand for the fruits of victory, only to find that they turned to ashes at the touch of his fingers.

All the claims to utopia—economic, religious, and political

—rested ultimately upon the management and control of but one resource: the indigenous population of the colony. The conquerors wanted Indian labor, the crown Indian subjects, the friars Indian souls. The Conquest was to initiate utopia; instead, it produced a biological catastrophe. Between 1519 and 1650, six-sevenths of the Indian population of Middle America was wiped out; only a seventh remained to turn the wheels of paradise. Like the baroque altars soon to arise in the colony, the splendor and wealth of the new possessions but covered a grinning skull.

Pleaders of special causes ascribed the decimation of the Indian population to Spanish cruelty, but the Spaniards were neither more nor less cruel than other conquerors, past or present. Faced with a large and pliable native population, they perhaps grew accustomed too quickly to the lavish use of Indian services. Yet even the most senseless mismanagement of human resources cannot alone account for such hideous decimation. The chief factor in this disaster appears to have been not conscious maltreatment of the Indian but the introduction of new diseases to which the Indians were not immune. . . . The disease organisms of the Old World were not those of the New, nor the immunities of the New World population those of the Old. Disease and death were thus presented with new victims. From the New World, the Spaniards returned to Europe with but one major disease—syphilis—which in its passage through the new hosts developed a virulence unknown in pre-Conquest America. But in the Indian population of the New World, the disease organisms of the Old World encountered a vast undefended pasture ground. The Spaniards introduced small-pox, which struck in virulent epidemics in 1520, 1531, and 1545; typhoid fever, which brought on epidemics in 1545, 1576, 1735, and twenty-nine times thereafter during the period of Spanish rule; measles, which exploded in a great epidemic in 1595; and—imported apparently in the hold of slave ships from Africa—malaria and yellow fever, the twin scourges of the American tropical lowlands. The Indian population possessed no antibodies against these plagues; they spread without obstruction. . . .

Biological disaster was intensified by economic factors. It appears that at the time of the Conquest population in Middle America had begun to outgrow the available food supply. There

were several severe famines in the valley of Mexico in the course
of the fifteenth century and the prevalence of human sacrifice
would seem to indicate that Indian society had begun to produce
more people than it could integrate into its everyday life. The
introduction of new economic purposes into such a tenuously
poised situation easily tilted the balance against human survival.
For the Spanish Conquest did not merely add the conquerors to
the number of people already living upon the land. As we have
seen, it also altered significantly the relationship between man
and his environment. Spanish economy, indeed western European
economy in general, was inimical to men upon the land. While
Indian cultivation made some intensive use of land, the Spaniards
used land extensively. While Indian economy massed labor in
cultivation, the Spaniards massed animals and tools.

The Indians had possessed no large domesticated animals;
the Spaniards let loose upon New Spain a flood of cattle and
sheep. Encountering a grazing range rich in its original vegetative
cover or fed with the nutriments of cultivated fields, the Spanish
herds multiplied rapidly. Following suit, Indian communities and
Indian nobles also filled agricultural land with livestock. Only
some of this land was land cultivated by the Indian population;
a great deal of new range had probably never been under
cultivation. But even a small amount of land withdrawn from
agriculture had a considerable effect on the distribution of the
Indian population. Livestock-keeping implies a notably more
extensive use of land than cultivation, which can support many
more people per unit of land than pasture range. Nor did
livestock-keeping affect only land in actual cultivation. In many
cases, it engulfed land which the Indians did not farm during
any given year but which constituted the indispensable reserve
in their system of field-to-forest rotation. Occupation of this
reserve imperiled the continued productivity of the field left in
Indian hands and thus also the Indian population which lived
off that land. Sheep produced wool, cattle produced hides; both
produced meat. These products could be sold for good money;
yet the wealth so obtained was won at the expense of hungry
mouths. "Sheep eat men," went the saying when livestock-raising
replaced farming in seventeenth- and eighteenth-century England.
Sheep also ate men in Middle America.

Where the Indians had farmed land with a dibble, the
Spaniards introduced a light plow drawn by oxen and capable

of making shallow furrows and conserving moisture in the soil. With this new instrument, men were probably able to farm land which they had not farmed before: the plow with a metal tip is a much better tool for loosening deep sod and breaking up the tangle of roots and rhizomes than the hoe. Undoubtedly, therefore, the conquerors took under cultivation land which the Indian had not utilized and thus added to the total stock of land available for food production. But in its net effect, the plow also upset the balance of Indian life upon the land. The plow is efficient only where land is plentiful but labor is scarce. Plow agriculture does not produce as much as hoe cultivation on any given unit of land: in modern Tepoztlán, men achieve twice the yield with hoe cultivation as with plow agriculture. Also, plow agriculture means that oxen must be fed, and some land must be devoted to their care. What the plow accomplishes is a saving in labor; the plow performs the work of the hoe cultivator in a third of the time. But it was not labor that was scarce in pre-Conquest Middle America. On the other hand, every unit of land withdrawn from Indian agriculture meant a halving of the food supply produced on that land, and thus a halving also of the population dependent on that food supply. And when that land was planted to wheat to feed the Spanish conquerors rather than the Indian inhabitants of the land, the growing imbalance between man and land was intensified.

Finally, the Spaniards also laid hands on the scarcest and most strategic resource of Middle American ecology: water. They needed water to irrigate their newly plowed fields, to water their stock, to drive the mills that ground their wheat into flour and the mills that fulled their woolens. Sons of a dry land themselves, they were master buildiers of aqueducts and wells; but all too often they appropriated the canals of the native population and impounded the streams behind their own dams. In a country in which a large percentage of the population had depended for their food supply on intensive cultivation made possible by irrigation, this wrecked a pattern of life precariously balanced between sufficiency and starvation. In a population ravaged by disease, such loss of land and water must have had a snowballing effect; it condemned a large percentage of the population to obsolescence and decay.

But the Conquest not only destroyed people physically; it also rent asunder the accustomed fabric of their lives and the pattern of motives that animated that life. Pre-Hispanic society and the new society established by the Conquest both rested on the exploitation of man by man; but they differed both in the means of their exploitation and in the ends to which it was directed. Under the Mexica, a peasantry had labored to maintain a ruling class with the surpluses derived from the intensive cultivation of its fields. But these rulers, in turn, were the armed knights of the sun who labored through sacrifice and warfare to maintain the balance of the universe. In the face of divergent interests, such a society possessed both a common transcendental purpose—to keep the sun in its heaven—and a common ritual idiom for the articulation of this purpose. The society produced by the Spanish Conquest, however, lacked both a common purpose and a common idiom in which such a purpose could be made manifest. It not only replaced intensive seed-planting with extensive pursuits; it also sacrificed men to the production of objects intended to serve no end beyond the maximization of profit and glory of the individual conqueror. Moreover, each group of conquerors—ecclesiastic, official, colonist—pursued a separate and divergent utopia.

Laboring in alien field or mine or mill, bewildered by the conflicting demands upon his loyalty, the exploited Indian could perceive no universal meaning in his suffering. It was not exploitation as such that was new; it was rather that men found no sense of participation in the process to which they offered up their lives. Only the religious forms of the conquerors drew Indian loyalty; around these forms the Indians finally rebuilt their impaired morale. Yet Christianity did not bring salvation for all. Like Carlos Moctezuma, the Indian ruler of Texcoco, executed by the Inquisition for his stiff-necked adherence to the old gods, many Indians could not make the transition from a religion which assuaged fear and guilt through repeated human sacrifice to a view of the world in which salvation was to be assured through the single and unique sacrifice of Christ. Such men, orphaned by the old gods yet unsaved by the new, despaired of the world in which they had to live out their lives.

Many Spaniards, especially the friars, labored valiantly to aid and comfort the Indian sick. Yet it is likely that some of their own cultural practices, introduced into this new cultural medium, proved directly lethal rather than beneficial. The Spanish insistence, for example, that the Indians be concentrated in towns where they could receive the direct benefits of royal law and Christian religion accentuated rather than abated the danger of infection. The friars' battle against the Indian sweat bath, the *temazcalli,* also played a part. Indian use of the sweat bath was a religious rite of purification, carried out under the auspices of the earth goddess. The friars, however, associated bathing with the paganism of the ancient Mediterranean and with the Islamic enemy whom they had just extirpated in southern Spain. They condemned the Indian sweat bath out of religious conviction and in so doing removed still another defense against attacks of germ-borne disease and death.

Yet the labor of these sick and dying Indians was to have made the wheels go round in the new utopia. Without Indian labor, there could be neither silver nor crops for the market. The mines were especially hard hit, for by 1580 they had run out of rich surface deposits. They had begun to work the less accessible ores which required ever new increments of labor. Yields declined steadily from 1600 on. Not until 1690 did mining output again attain the 1560 level. Food supplies underwent a parallel decline. From 1579 to 1700, the colonists found it difficult to obtain adequate food deliveries to towns and mines, except in an occasional bumper year. Spanish cities had to initiate mandatory deliveries from the surrounding countryside and set up public granaries to stockpile grain for resale at fixed prices during lean years. Silk production suffered and declined, as the labor needed during the peak harvesting periods also declined. By 1600 the industry was moribund. Cacao production witnessed a similar fate, as disease and death took toll of the hands required to harvest and process the bean. The decline in mining in turn affected stock-raising, which had counted upon the mines as one of the chief outlets for its multiple by-products. The country faced an emergency; increasingly it abandoned large-scale commercial enterprises in favor of restricted exchange, coupled with production for subsistence purposes. The bubble of unlimited expansion had burst, together with the utopian dream of wealth unlimited.

About 1600, too, the mother country began to suffer the unforeseen consequences of its overseas expansion. Its industry swamped by the gold and silver of the New World, inflation ran rampant, raising prices for Spanish goods at the very same time that purchasing power in the colonies declined toward

the vanishing point. Nor could the mother country absorb the
wool, hides, and dyes which the colony was still able to supply.
Spain and New Spain, linked together by an umbilical cord
from which both were to take rich nourishment, found themselves
trapped in common misfortune.

RETREAT FROM UTOPIA

Had Spain sustained the cumulative development of the sixteenth
century, Middle America might well have achieved a new and
vital synthesis. But the depression of the seventeenth century
put an end to utopian dreaming; the bankrupt dream passed into
receivership. As in past periods of social and political catabolism,
Middle America again retreated into its countryside. The wider
galaxies dissolved once more into their component solar systems
to allow for reintegration on more parochial levels.

In the course of this retreat there emerged two patterns for
such integration: the *hacienda,* the privately owned landed estate
of the colonist, and the tightly knit community of the Indian
peasantry, the *república de indios,* as it is often called in the
colonial records. Each produced its characteristic cultural design, and each imprinted this design so strongly on its carriers
that the outlines of the two patterns are visible in the Middle
American fabric to this day. The purposes which animated the
two institutions were clearly divergent: one was an instrument of
the conquerors, the other an instrument of the conquered. Yet
in their divergence they shared a common denominator. Both
were institutions of retreat, both were designed to stem the
tide of disorder. And both met the challenge of depression in
the same way, for both bought a reduction in the risks of living
at the price of progress.

The colonists had come to America in search of gold and—
through the possession of gold—of liberty. But falling prices in
a depressed market and the catastrophically declining labor force
quickly ended the hopes of limitless wealth and untrammeled self-
determination. As reality encroached upon the utopian dream,
it again forced men to recognize its terms, terms which made
a sack of doubloons in the hand weigh more in the balance
than the hidden treasure of Moctezuma, a string of mules worth
more than the waters of the Fountain of Eternal Youth. Some of
course never acknowledged this confrontation and were lost in

search of their personal El Dorados. Others were deprived of access to legitimate tangible claims or cheated of them: only forty years after the Conquest there were four thousand Spaniards in New Spain without visible means of support. But some there were who through guile or personal energy or bureaucratic favor shouldered aside their competitors and laid hold of the means of production required to support them in the fashion to which they wished to become accustomed. These men—recruited from all manner of men who had come from the mother country —became the members of a new colonial elite.

The characteristic cultural form through which they exercised their domination was no longer the trusteeship over Indians but the outright ownership of land in the hacienda, the large privately owned estate. The title to this land they acquired through purchase, by paying good money into an increasingly depleted royal treasury. The trusteeship had included rights to Indian produce only, and not to land; it had left the trustee passively dependent, at the mercy of royal favor. When a man succeeded in obtaining an outright grant of land, however, he became a director of property he could call his own, property to which he could add, which he might pawn, or which he could sell. To work this new property, the colonists needed labor. This they sought extralegally, by circumventing the royal labor code. The system was deceptive in its simplicity. They invited workers to settle permanently on or near their new estates. The entrepreneur would undertake to pay their tribute to the royal authorities and offer to pay them wages, usually in kind. At the same time, he would grant the worker the right to purchase goods on credit or, as needed, advance him small sums of money. The worker's account would be debited to the extent of the sums involved, in return for a promise to repay the money through labor. Such workers became known as *gañanes, laborios, naborías, tlaquehuales,* or *peones,* the system of labor use *gañanía* or peonage. Upon the twin foundations of landownership and peonage, the colonists thus erected their new economic edifice, the mainstay of their new social order.

Organized for commercial ends, the hacienda proved strangely hybrid in its characteristics. It combined in practice features which seem oddly contradictory in theory. Geared to sell products in a market, it yet aimed at having little to sell. Voracious for land, it deliberately made inefficient use of it. Operating

with large numbers of workers, it nevertheless personalized the
relation between worker and owner. Created to produce a
profit, it consumed a large part of its substance in conspicuous
and unproductive displays of wealth. Some writers have called
the institution "feudal," because it involved the rule of a dominant
landowner over his dependent laborers. But it lacked the legal
guaranties of security which compensated the feudal serf for
his lack of liberty and self-determination. Others have called
it "capitalist," and so it was, but strangely different from the
commercial establishments in agriculture with which we are
familiar in the modern commercial and industrial world. Half
"feudal," half "capitalist," caught between past and future, it
exhibited characteristics of both ways of life, as well as their
inherent contradiction.

Offspring of an economic depression, the hacienda was set up
to feed a limited demand. With its external markets dried up
by an economic downturn and by political weakness in the
mother country, it relied on markets within the colony. In New
Spain, however, only the towns and the mining camps represented
secure outlets for agricultural produce; the Indians of the countryside secured their own foodstuffs and fed themselves. And means of
transportation were neither rapid nor plentiful enough to allow
surpluses from an area with a good harvest to be transferred
quickly to an area of food shortage. Markets were limited not
only by the food habits of the Indian population and by the distribution of the Spanish settlements but also by the limited capacity of any region to absorb its own products. A glut quickly
lowered prices to the point where commercial agriculture met its
ruin. Thus the hacienda played safe by always producing below
capacity. It never staked all or even most of its land on the
vagaries of the market. In times of uncertainty, it could always
fall back on its own resources and feed itself. It possessed its
own defenses, which it never jeopardized.

Inefficient in its use of land, it was yet greedy for it. It
needed and wanted more land, not to raise more crops, but to
take land from the Indians in order to force them to leave
their holdings and to become dependent on the hacienda for
land and work. Once this land was in its possession, the hacienda
readily let it out to the inhabitants of the deprived villages
for farming and stock-raising, but at the price of a stipulated
number of workdays on the cash-crop—producing lands of the

hacienda. Such workers, obtained through indirect means of coercion, constituted the bulk of a hacienda's labor force. They were called *peones baldillos,* because they made use of the hacienda's *baldío* or uncultivated land.

To produce the cash crop, a hacienda would farm only a small portion of its total land resources—its best land—but would do so with an unchanging and antiquated sixteenth-century technology, based on the use of the wooden plow and oxen in the fields and on the water-powered wheel in processing. Its cash crop would be a product of many hands, laboring within the *casco* or core of the hacienda, the sum of many individual efforts each operating at a low level of productivity but considerable in the aggregate through the mere process of addition.

The greater part of this labor was drawn from the non-resident inhabitants of the hacienda's periphery, but the tempo and intensity of the work effort were sustained by a corps of resident laborers, the *peones acasillados.* An *acasillado* had both more rights and more duties than a *baldillo.* Paid in tokens, he could make advance purchases at the store owned and operated by the hacienda, the *tienda de raya.* There he could always obtain maize for himself and his family at lower than market prices. In the highlands, he was entitled to a daily ration of pulque, usually ladled out after a day's work, at the completion of the religious services which peon and owner both attended in the hacienda's chapel. Each man was given a house, and— if he proved faithful and obedient—a plot of land on which he could raise crops for himself. If a man proved properly submissive, moreover, the owner would finance his wedding or a baptism or a religious devotion, or aid him in other times of financial need. To repay these advances, such a worker would then bind himself to work for the owner until the debt was paid, an occurrence not marked by its frequency.

From 1540 on, growing numbers of Indians accepted the liabilities of peonage. Often they welcomed the system as a way of freeing themselves from the increasingly onerous bondage to Indian communities ravaged by death and disease, threatened with loss of land and water, yet all too often required to bear burdens of tribute and labor services assessed on the basis of their past number of inhabitants. Many of the newcomers were attracted also by the novel goods of Spanish manufacture, more accessible through hacienda channels than in the impoverished Indian villages. Extralegal as the system of peonage was, the new worker and his employer soon found themselves partners in a conspiracy to elude royal supervision. Crown officials, aware that they could not stem the tide of peonage, nevertheless strove to limit it by placing a ceiling of five pesos on the sums which could be advanced to any Indian, though they showed no parallel concern for the debt limit of the offspring of mixed Euro-Afro-Indian unions. But soon the new kind of life which developed on the haciendas—favorable to intermarriage and transculturation, providing shared experiences and growing kinship—bound the workers to their common place of residence as much as the accumulating debts bound them to the owner of the hacienda.

Thus the system had advantages for both owner and worker: the owner was guaranteed labor, the worker a measure of novelty, together with security. The system, however, also exacted its social and psychological costs, for—as in all systems of bondage—security was purchased only at the price of liberty. The peon was dependent on the owner, both economically and psychologically. He abrogated his right to decide his own fate; the owner of the hacienda became his guardian and judge, as well as his employer.

Such relations between owner and worker are so different from those to which we are accustomed in modern industrial society that they seem to possess the closeness of personal ties which many tend to miss in present-day life, where superiors and subordinates go their separate, impersonal ways. This has caused some writers to idealize the hacienda, as others have idealized the slaveholding plantation of the ante-bellum South. But there exists a distinction between personal relations, such as those familiar to anthropologists from the study of closely knit small primitive tribes, and personalized relations, in which the relationship bears the guise of a personal relation but serves an impersonal function. Neither hacienda nor slave plantation existed to provide satisfactory relationships between persons. They existed to realize returns on invested capital, to produce profits, functions that take no account of kinship or friendship, of personal needs or desires. The hacienda, like the slave plantation, was a system designed to produce goods by marshaling human beings regardless of their qualities and involvements as persons, an institution of the "technical order," as Robert Redfield has called it, instead of the "moral order." And yet the hacienda personalized many aspects of the relation between owner and worker where modern industrial or commercial organizations substitute the neutral mechanisms of impersonal management through a faceless bureaucracy.

There are relationships which are so basic to all human life that we remain their prisoners as well as their beneficiaries throughout our adult lives. These are the relationships which we experience in growing up in families. When an appropriate situation in adulthood reproduces our infantile condition, we react with emotions learned long ago toward father or mother or siblings, figures often now distant or dead. These emotions provide the fuel for adult institutions which manage to counterfeit the character of the original situation that first produced them. The hacienda achieved this end by elevating the hacienda owner to the role of a stern and irascible father, prepared to guide the steps of his worker-children, ready to unleash his temper and anger upon them when provoked. As long as the worker remained dependent and submissive, he received his just reward: a sum of money, a draft of pulque, a plot for growing corn. When he rebelled against authority, or provoked its anger, he was tied to the whipping post, possessed by every hacienda, and cruelly lashed. Thus the hacienda bound men not only through debts or through force but also through ties of love and hate.

Deprived of their ability to rule their own lives, the workers in turn invested the relation of owner and worker with the elements of personalization. The owner's person became the governor of their lives, their relation with this person the major guaranty of the security and stability on which depended their daily bread and a roof over their heads. Only the owner could materially raise a man's prospects in life, only he could reduce the risks to which the worker was subject. This person, clad in authority and living a life far beyond the reach of his laborers, had to be won over, placated into benevolence, by a show of humility, a pantomime of servitude. The worker not only put his labor time at his owner's disposal; he also offered himself and his family, to secure perhaps yet another advantage in the struggle for support. But each gain of benevolence was achieved only at the expense of competition and conflict with his fellow workers. Where all strove for the same goal, only a few could gain access to the generosity of the master; most remained for life outside the charmed, personalized circle. This competition for imaginary stakes, however, bound the worker with invisible bonds. He set his hopes upon the person of the master. If he succeeded in his ritual pantomime of submission, the master received the credit. If he failed, he blamed himself, or others more successful than he. At the same time, he cut himself off from the others in a like condition.

No human institution, not even the most inhuman, can rely wholly on bayonets; it must build also on the motivations of its participants. On the hacienda, personal motives were harnessed to maintain the regime of labor. Given the appropriate social conditions, men make peons of themselves.

Limited in capital, the hacienda presents a further paradox in the display of power and wealth of its owner: wealth invested in the big house, with its high walls, gateways, courtyards, chapel, jail, and outbuildings; wealth invested in rich clothing and silver trappings for horses; wealth displayed in great feasts and public ostentation. This show of grandeur, however, also had its functions, functions appropriate to the context in which the hacienda arose. It underlined the owner's dominance over his workers, it enhanced his self-esteem, it impressed others. In impressing others, it enshrined an economic purpose, today served by departments of public relations or advertising. A *hacendado*'s display was a public demonstration of his credit rating, an assertion that—in the midst of an economy starved for capital— he deserved credit because his enterprise was capable of generating capital and wealth.

Moreover, such display gave him still another psychological hold over his workers, for it encouraged their vicarious identification with his splendor. Children admire and yet fear an overweening father; they also identify with him. His well-being becomes a symbol of the well-being of the entire family. Overpowered and restrained by him, they also wish to see him acknowledged as powerful by others, to make their own submission seem logical and right. Thus, on the hacienda, workers identified with the figure of the owner. His person became symbolic of the enterprise as a whole, his well-being the justification of their collective effort. Dominated by his will, they yet identified with his mastery, his ability to command respect from others.

His glory became theirs; it furnished the element of drama in their earth-bound and restricted lives.

The hacienda system was here to stay. The dual nature of the hacienda—its ability to retrench in times of adverse markets, its ability to increase production if demand rose—allowed it to adapt even to conditions which differed from those that gave it birth. When the depression of the seventeenth century came to an end in the economic upswing of the eighteenth century, the hacienda, too, participated in the renewed expansion. Peonage, which at the outset had served to bind and hold a labor supply in the face of a diminishing population, became the foundation of an onerous and exploitative system of labor as population again increased. Squads of peons gave rise to peon companies, peon companies to entire armies of peons, all born within the framework of the haciendas and bound to them through debt and past condition of servitude. By the end of the seventeenth century, New Spain was securely in the hands of a class of great landed proprietors, self-made nobles, commanding thousands of dependent laborers, captains of private armies, living in splendid houses, and leading the life of a new aristocracy on horseback, with its display of equestrian skill in competitive games. In sharp contrast with Europe, where a decline of population and an improved technology had freed the feudal serf and turned him into an owner or renter of agricultural property, but much as in Russia during the late eighteenth and nineteenth centuries, the growth of capitalism in New Spain did not produce a greater measure of liberty and freedom for the laborer; instead it sharpened exploitation and increased bondage.

In the retreat from utopia, the strong sought refuge against instability in the control of men and land through the organizational form of the hacienda. But the rest of the countryside, inhabited by the submerged Indian population, witnessed a parallel movement toward consolidation. The Indian, like the Spaniard, sought security, but he had to avail himself of other means.

The Spanish colonist ultimately had access to an apparatus of power managed by others like himself. But the Conquest had deprived the Indian of access to state power. Knowingly, the conquerors had destroyed the connection between the Indian present and the pre-Hispanic past. In dismantling the Mexica state, they had removed also the cortex of the Middle American political organism and severed the nerves which bound communities and regions to the larger economic and political centers. The Indian state was not rebuilt. Royal decree carefully circumscribed the position of the Indian commoners. They were enjoined from wearing Spanish dress and forced to don "Indian" costume, a combination of Spanish and Indian articles of clothing. Indian commoners could not own or use horses and saddles and were prohibited from bearing arms. They had to pay tribute, but, because they paid tribute, they were endowed with economic personality and therefore with judicial personality. They could present their cases in special "Indian" courts and were defined as "free vassals" of the king. They were exempt from military service and from such taxes as the tithe and the sales tax, imposed on Spaniards and others. But legal rights were not accompanied by common political representation. Where Indian officials had once exercised power on the national and regional level, Spanish officials now held sway. The Indian political apparatus had been smashed by the Conquest; and the conquerors were not ill-advised enough to countenance its reconstruction.

With the assumption of power by the Spaniards, the Indian ruling class lost its functions. Some of the chiefs moved to town, adopted Spanish dress and manners, learned to speak Spanish, and became commercial entrepreneurs employing European technology and working land with Indian tributaries and Negro slaves. Spanish law abetted this process by equating them socially with the nobility of Spain and economically with the Spanish *encomenderos*. Since the new law took inadequate account of the pre-Hispanic division between nobility of office and nobility of lineage, granting to all nobles the privileges of hereditary descent, many Indian nobles even added to the pre-Hispanic perquisites of their rank and gained title to lands which had previously belonged either to a community or to a non-hereditary office. Also, the Indian noble who was treated like a Spanish *encomendero* received rights to tribute and personal services and, like other *encomenderos,* began to invest in the process of building capital through capitalist enterprise. Frequently, intermarriage with the conquerors still further dissipated their Indian identity, until they lost touch with the Indian commoners who in the midst of death and upheaval were building a new Indian life in the countryside.

Nobles who remained in the villages, on the other hand,

were reduced by loss of wealth and standing to the position of their Indian fellow citizens. Because his person was still suffused with the magic of past power, a former priest or local chieftain here and there assumed a post in a local community, but he soon lost the ability to command tribute or labor-power to which his ancestors had been accustomed. The new Indian communities were communities of the poor, too overburdened to sustain a class that had lost its function.

With the disappearance of the Indian political elite, there also vanished the specialists who had depended on elite demands: the priests, the chroniclers, the scribes, the artisans, the long-distance traders of pre-Hispanic society. Spanish entrepreneurs replaced the *pochteca;* Spanish artisans took the place of Indian feather-workers and jade-carvers; Spanish priests displaced the Indian religious specialists. Soon there was no longer anyone who knew how to make feather cloaks and decorations, how to find and carve jade, how to recall the deeds of gods and ancestors in days gone by. For a brief period the Indians strove valiantly to learn the new arts of the Mediterranean, and men like Bernardino de Sahagún (1499–1590) and the scholars of the short-lived college of Santiago de Tlatelolco (1536–1606) labored to maintain and enrich the intellectual patterns of Indian culture. But the return to ruralism of the seventeenth century put an end to these hopes and endeavors.

Under the new dispensation, the Indian was to be a peasant, the Indian community a community of peasants. Stripped of their elite and urban components, the Indians were relegated to the countryside. Thus the Indians suffered not only exploitation and biological collapse but also deculturation—cultural loss—and in the course of such ill use lost also the feeling of belonging to a social order which made such poor use of its human resources. They became strangers in it, divided from its purposes and agents by an abyss of distrust. The new society could command their labor, but it could not command their loyalty. Nor has this gulf healed in the course of time. The trauma of the Conquest remains an open wound upon the body of Middle American society to this day.

The strategic unit of the new Indian life was to be not the individual but the Indian community. This the crown protected and furthered, as a double check upon the colonists—ever eager to subjugate the Indians to their exclusive control—as

well as upon the Indians themselves, whose individual freedom
it wished to curb. To this end, it underwrote the legal separateness
and identity of each Indian commune.

Each commune was to be a self-contained economic unit,
holding a guaranteed 6.5 square miles of agricultural land, land
which its members could sell only after special review by the
viceroy. In every commune the duly constituted Indian authorities
would collect the tribute and levy the labor services for which
the members of the commune were to be jointly responsible (not
until the eighteenth century was tribute payment individualized).
A portion of this tribute would go into the royal coffers, but part
of it would be set aside in a "community chest" (*caja de
comunidad*) to finance community projects. Communal officials
were to administer the law through the instrumentality of their
traditional custom, wherever that custom did not conflict with
the demands of church and state. The officers of the crown
retained the privilege of judging major crimes and legal cases
involving more than one community; but the Indian authorities
received sufficient power to guarantee peace and order in the
new communes. The autonomy which the crown denied to the
Indian sector of society as a whole, it willingly granted to the
local social unit.

This model for reconstruction did not envisage a return of the
pre-Hispanic community. Yet so well did it meet the needs
of the Indian peasant that he could take it up and make it his
own. Poised precariously on the abyss of disintegration, the
commune proved remarkably resilient. It has undergone great
changes since the time when it was first constituted in a shattered
countryside three centuries ago, but its essential features are still
visible in the Indian communities today, especially in the southern and southeastern highlands. Thus it is still possible to speak
of this community in the present tense, to regard the present-
day Indian community as a direct descendant of the reconstructed
community of the seventeenth century.

The core of this kind of community is its political and
religious system. In this system, the burden of religious worship
is rotated among the households of the community. Each year,
a different group of men undertakes to carry out the tasks of
religious office; each year a different group of men makes itself
responsible for the purchase and ritual disposal of food, liquor,
candles, incense, fireworks, and for all other attendant expendi-

tures. A tour of religious duty may leave a man impoverished for several years, yet in the eyes of his fellow citizens he has added greatly to his prestige. This spurs men to renewed labor toward the day when they will be able to underwrite another set of ceremonies; and a man will sponsor several such ceremonials in the course of his life. Each tour of sponsorship will add to the esteem in which he is held by his fellow men, until— old and poor—he reaches the pinnacle of prestige and commands the respect of the entire community. The essential element in repeated sponsorship is therefore time: the older a man is, the greater the likelihood that he has repeatedly acted as religious sponsor. Thus old age itself becomes a source of prestige for Indians: an old man is one who has labored in the interests of the community for many years and whose repeated religious activity has brought him ever closer to the state of grace and secular wisdom.

Since all men have an equal opportunity to enlist in carrying the burdens of the gods, and thus to gain prestige, the religious system allows all households to be ranked along a scale of religious participation, prestige, and age. At one end of the scale, the Indians will place the young household which has but recently come into existence and whose head is just beginning to play his part in keeping the balance between community and universe. At the other end, he will place the households of the very old, whose moral ascendancy over the community is very great, owing to their years of faithful service and ritual expenditure.

Certainly this religious pattern has Spanish prototypes in the Iberian *cofradía* or religious sodality, a voluntary association of men for religious purposes. But it is also pre-Hispanic in origin. "There were some," says the Spanish friar Toribio de Benavente of the days before the Conquest, "who labored two or three years and acquired as much as possible for the purpose of honoring the demon with a feast. On such a feast they not only spent all that they possessed but even went into debt, so that they would have to do service a year and sometimes two years in order to get out of debt." In the reconstructed Indian community of the post-Conquest period, this religious pattern was charged with additional functions. It became the chief mechanism through which people gained prestige, as well as the balance wheel of communal economics. Each year, religious participation wipes out considerable sums of goods and money; each year part of the surplus of the community is consumed in offerings or exploded in fireworks to please the saints. The system takes from those who have, in order to make all men have-nots. By liquidating the surpluses, it makes all men rich in sacred experience but poor in earthly goods. Since it levels differences of wealth, it also inhibits the growth of class distinctions based on wealth. Like the thermostat activated by an increase in heat to shut off the furnace, expenditure in religious worship returns the distribution of wealth to a state of balance, wiping out any accumulation of wealth that might upset the existing equilibrium. In engineering parlance, it acts as a feedback, returning a system that is beginning to oscillate to its original course.

The religious complex also has aesthetic functions. The *fiesta,* with its processions, burning incense, fireworks, crowds, color, is not merely a mechanism of prestige and of economic justice. It is also "a work of art," the creation of a magic moment in mythological time, in which men and women transcend the realities of everyday life in their entry and procession through the magical space of the vaulted, incense-filled church, let their souls soar on the temporary trajectory of a rocket, or wash away the pains of life in holy-day drunkenness. For the Indians, time is not linear, as it is for the citizens of the industrialized North Atlantic world, where each moment points toward a future of new effort, new experience, and new goals. The Indian scheme of life moves in an endless round, in which everyday labor issues into the magic moment of religious ritual, only to have the ritual dissolve again into the everyday labor that began the cycle. The Indian community has now forgotten its pre-Hispanic past; its past and its future have merged in a timeless rhythm of alternating mundane and holy days.

The social, economic, aesthetic, and ritual mechanisms of the religious complex do not stand alone. They are part and parcel of a larger system which makes political and religious behavior mutually interdependent. For participation in the religious system qualifies a man also for political office. In Indian eyes, a man who has won prestige for himself by bearing the burden of the community in its relations with the gods is expected and—more than expected—required to assume political office. Thus men who have laid down their burdens as religious sponsors will be asked next to serve as community officials. Qualified for office by past religious participation, they are the ones who transact the business of the community: allocating land, settling boundary disputes, investigating thefts, confirming marriages, disarming disturbers of the peace, dealing with the emissaries of outside power. A man cannot seek political office for its own sake, nor can he bend political power to his individual end. Power is bestowed by the community, and reallocated at intervals to a new group of officeholders. It is the office that governs men, not its occupant. In this democracy of the poor, there is no way to monopolize power. It is divorced from persons and distributed, through election, among all in turn.

The Indian cannot control men; he only wishes to come to terms with them. This process of mutual adjustment has become a group concern. The group counts more than the individual; it limits individual autonomy and initiative. It is suspicious of conflict, tireless in the advocacy of "adjustment." People raised in cultures that thrive on the conflicts of individual with individual would find it difficult to fit into such a community; yet the community can be understood in terms of its context, a larger social order in which men continually fight for power and are ever willing to pay for its fruits the price of their own corruption. In this setting, the Indian community shows great consistency in refusing to play a game that will always seek its first victims among its members. For navigation in troubled water its politico-religious system is a steering mechanism of great resilience.

As the Indian community leveled differences of class, so it obliterated other internal divisions intervening between its jurisdiction and the households that composed it. The diligent ethnologist may still find, among the Otomí-speakers on the fringes of the valley of Mexico, hamlets based on common descent in the male line and enforced marriage outside the community; or patrilineal kinship units sharing a common name, a common saint, and a measure of social solidarity among the Tzeltal-Tzotzil—speakers of Chiapas, though there too they have lost their former exogamy and the common residence which they possessed in the past. But these examples remain the fascinating exceptions to the general rule that, among Middle American Indians as a whole, common territoriality in one community and common participation in communal life have long since robbed such units of any separatist jurisdiction they may at one time have exercised. This holds also for the divisions called *barrios* or sections, which some have traced back to the pre-Hispanic *calpulli* and which in many cases go back to joint settlement in one community—voluntary or enforced—of groups of different origins, in both pre-Hispanic and post-Hispanic times. In most cases these units have simply been transformed into religious sodalities, each concerned with the support of its special saint and socially amorphous in any context other than the religious, although mutual name-calling, backbiting, or slander of one another's reputation may serve to drain off some of the minor irritations of daily life.

It is the household, then, that makes the basic decisions within both the politico-religious and the economic field, the household being usually composed of husband, wife, and children. Such unions are customarily formed through monogamous marriages; polygyny, the marriage of one male to more than one female, occurs but rarely. An unmarried man or woman is not regarded as an adult member of the community and cannot take up his responsibilities in communal life. A person who has lost a marriage partner through divorce or death must remarry before the community will again ratify the social standing he enjoyed before the breakup or end of his marriage. Nor is it marriage alone that bestows full rights of citizenship. A couple must have children to validate their claim to complete adult status; a sterile marriage quickly falls prey to conflict and divorce. Marriage therefore, and a marriage blessed with children, is the common goal of the Indian men and women.

Economically, a marriage is a union of two technological specialists: a male specialist skilled in field labor and house-building, a female specialist skilled in tending the kitchen garden, caring for the small livestock, making pots and clothing, raising children, preparing the daily meal. The functions of the division of labor and of reproduction take precedence in people's minds over marriage as an outlet for sexual impulses. Marriages are often arranged by the parents of the prospective couple, through the services of a go-between. The Indian man seeks a woman to bear his children and to keep up his home: there is little romantic love. Ideally, people conform to strict standards of marital fidelity. In practice, however, there is considerable latitude for sexual adventure outside marriage, and philandering does not usually endanger the bonds of the union. Nor do Indians engage in sexual conquest as a validation of their masculinity; sexual conquest does not add luster to the reputation of the individual. Exploitation of one sex by the other encounters little sympathy, just as political or economic exploitation of one man by another is not countenanced within the boundaries of the community.

Throughout their marriage, the partners retain a rough equality, though, ideally, wives are held subordinate to husbands. Women own the movable goods which they bring with them into the marriage. If a woman owns land, her husband may farm it for her, but the proceeds from the sale of produce raised on such a field is her own, as are the proceeds from the sales of her handicraft products. If she owns livestock, she retains her rights of ownership. In case of divorce, the family herd is divided equally between the divorcing partners. When one of the partners dies, his property is divided equally among the children; the surviving partner retains his share. Women do not occupy political or religious office, but they help their husbands in making the relevant decisions and in carrying out the attendant obligations. Within the home, the woman has a great deal to say, in strongly marked contrast to her non-Indian sister.

Just as the questions of participation in religio-political life are raised and settled within the household, so the day-to-day economic decisions are also made on the household level. It is the household that plants its fields to crops, that sells its maize or chili, that buys the needed kerosene or pottery. It is the men and women of these unit households who handle the money derived from these sales and act as individual economic agents. This apparent contradiction between the behavior of the Indian as a member of his community on the religio-political plane and his behavior as an economic agent has so impressed some observers that they have lost sight of the communal involvements of the Indian and treated him in terms of capitalist economic theory. Indeed, Sol Tax has spoken of the Indians as "penny capitalists," presumably in contrast to more affluent "nickel" or "dime" or "millionaire" capitalists, thus drawing attention at once to his comparative poverty and characterizing his participation in the wider economy as an individual agent, and a capitalist to boot. Certainly the Indian is poor, and no

Middle American Indian community ever existed on a desert
island; it always formed part and parcel of a larger society.
Its economic agents, the members of its households, are subject
to a wider economy and to its laws. For instance, the value
of the money they use and the prices of the commodities
they buy and sell are often influenced, if not directly determined,
by national conditions. The recent inflation, to name but one
case, has affected Indians and non-Indians alike.

But the Indian is not merely quantitatively different in his
economic involvements from other members of society. He differs
qualitatively from the poor non-Indian Mexican or Guatemalan
because he is culturally different from them. Superficially, he may
resemble the individual economic agent of classical economics,
unrestrictedly exchanging goods in a capitalist market. But he is
not a capitalist, nor free of restrictions. His economic goal is not
capital accumulation but subsistence and participation in the
religio-political system of his community. He handles money; but
he does not use money to build capital. It is for him merely one
way of reckoning equivalences, of appraising the value of goods
in exchange. The Indian works first so that he may eat. When he
feels that he has accomplished this goal, he labors to build a
surplus so that he can sponsor a ceremony and gain prestige in
the eyes of his fellow Indians. In the course of his sponsorship,
he redistributes or destroys his surplus by providing displays of
fireworks or dressing the saint's image in a new cloak. Clearly,
the quality of his involvement in the national economy differs
from that of the commercial farmer, industrial worker, or entrepreneur.

Moreover, this pattern of consumption operates within cultural
limitations laid down and maintained by his community. When
we see the solitary Indian bent over his patch of maize, we
seem to see a lone economic agent engaged in isolated production. But this man is enmeshed in a complicated web of traditional
rights to land maintained by his community. Spanish rule granted
each communty sovereign jurisdiction over a well-defined amount
of land. With the passage of time, general communal rights over
land have become attenuated, usually in favor of a mixed system
of ownership, where the richer bottom lands along the valley
floors are now owned by individual members of the community,
while the community retains communal rights over hilly land
and forests. Yet the community still retains jurisdictional rights

over land everywhere, rights which remove land from the category of free commodities. The most important of these rights states that members of the community may not sell land to outsiders. This is usually reinforced by a stringent rule of endogamy, which prohibits members of the community from marrying outsiders and thus endangering the man-land balance. Frequently this taboo is strengthened by other sanctions: the right allowing existing members of the community to glean or the right to graze their livestock on any land within the community after the harvest. Such rights frequently imply sanctions in their turn. A man cannot put a fence around his piece of land or grow crops that mature at variance with the crops of his neighbors. Both land and crops are thus subject to negative limitations, even though the actual process of production is entrusted to the several separate households.

Such limitations also apply to the craft products made in a given community. We may see a woman shaping a pot or a man weaving a hat, and taking pot or hat to market. Again, we apparently see an individual agent engaged in autonomous economic activity. We must however realize that the producer is not "free" to choose the object he wishes to produce and market. What looks like individual craft specialization is but an aspect of a pattern of specialization by communities. There is a general tendency for each community to engage in one or several crafts that are not shared by other communities in its vicinity. Thus, in the Tarascan-speaking area, for instance, Cocucho makes pottery, Tanaco weaves with century-plant fibers, Paracho manufactures wooden objects and cotton cloth, Nahuatzen weaves woolens, Uruapan paints gourds, and Santa Clara del Cobre produces items of beaten copper.

The Indian market is a place where the members of the different communities meet to exchange their products. Such a market brings together a very large and varied supply of articles, larger and more varied than could be sold by any permanent storekeeper in the market town, and does so at prices low enough to match the low income of the Indians. Thus, while the individual producer enters a market that is highly heterogeneous in the variety of goods offered, his particular individual contribution is homogeneous with that of other members of his community. In the characteristic Indian marketing pattern, where the sellers of similar types of objects are arranged together in carefully drawn-up rows, what looks to the casual observer like a mere grouping of individuals is actually a grouping of communities.

We must conclude, therefore, that the Indian's economic involvements are different from those of other participants in the national economy. The individual Indian household is indeed *in* the economy, but not *of* it. For added to the household's general purposes of self-maintenance are the community's purposes aiming at maintaining the Indian social group intact in its possession of land and membership, despite the corrosive influences that continually surround it. A peasantry needs land, and the Indian community defends its land against outsiders through the twin weapons of endogamy and the prohibition of sale to nonmembers. A peasantry faces the risks of class differentiation. As soon as one man accumulates wealth and is allowed to keep and reinvest it, he threatens, in the straitened circumstances of Indian life, to take from others the instruments of their own livelihood. More seriously, wealth breeds power, and power— unless adequately checked—corrupts, stacking the political cards in favor of some men to the detriment of others. Thus the Indian community strives to abolish wealth and to redistribute power. It even frowns on any display of wealth, any individual assertion of independence that may upset the balance of egalitarian poverty. Its social ideal is the social conformist, not the innovator, the controlled individual, not the seeker after untrammeled power. It places its faith in an equality of risk-taking.

It is doubtful whether the Indian community could have achieved these ends by itself alone. Certainly, without the world beyond its confines, it could not have solved its population problem. Each new generation born to it threatens to upset again and again the balance between mouths to feed and land available to feed them. It can solve this problem only by continually exporting population. To stay in the running, it must continually sacrifice some of its sons and daughters to the outside world, thus ever feeding the forces which it attempts to resist. Increasing its own security by exporting people, it at the same time endangers the security of the larger society. Neither Indian peasant nor colonist entrepreneur, the emigrants fall into no ordered category, occupy no defined place in the social order. They become the Ishmaels of Middle America, its marginal men. Cast out into the shadows, with no stake in the existing order, they are forced to seek their own vindication, their place in the sun. If this is impossible within the social framework, then it must needs be against it. Thus the Indian community perpetually creates a body of potential antagonists, ready to invade it and benefit by its destruction.

Without the outside world, moreover, the Indian can never close the ever opening gap between his production and his needs. Robbed of land and water by the Conquest and subsequent encroachment, the Indian community can rarely be self-sufficient. It must not only export people; it must also export craft produce and labor. Each Indian who goes off to work seasonally in other men's fields strengthens his community; each hat, fire fan, or reed mat sold beyond the limits of the community adds to its capacity to resist encroachment. Each Indian who, in the past, enlisted on a hacienda as a *peón baldillo* thus benefited his community. Paradoxically, he also benefited the hacienda that used his labor. Assured of seasonal laborers who would do its bidding at the critical periods in the process of production, the haciendas welcomed the presence of Indian communities on their fringes. For such a community constituted a convenient reservoir of laborers where men maintained their labor power until needed, at no additional cost to the entrepreneur. Suddenly we find, therefore, that the institution of the conquerors and the institution of the conquered were linked phenomena. Each was a self-limiting system, powered by antagonism to the other; and yet their co-existence produced a perpetual if hostile symbiosis, in which one was wedded to the other in a series of interlocking functions.

If colonists and Indians achieved symbiosis, they did not achieve synthesis. While the great landowners secured virtual political and economic autonomy behind the walls of their great estates, they remained ideologically tied to Spain and, through Spain, to Europe. If the Conquest deculturated the conquered, it also affected the conquerors. First it narrowed the range of patterns carried by the newcomers, only to render them doubly provincial in the enforced readaptation to the ruralism of the seventeenth century. If the Conquest ended, once and for all, the isolation of America from the cultural development of the Old World, the ensuing decline of Spain left the new colonies on the margins of the new and larger world into which they had so suddenly been introduced. Here they suffered the fate of any marginal area isolated from its center of cultural productivity.

At the same time, the Conquest cut the lines of communication with the pre-Hispanic past: the conquerors could not take over the culture of the conquered. But neither could they develop a cultural configuration of their own. Communication with Europe remained formalistic and empty. The intellectual and artistic currency of the Old World was sought more for the sake of provincial display than for the sake of a new vital synthesis. Thus, for example, what is astonishing about the colonial architecture of New Spain is not the degree of indigenous influence in its construction but the virtual absence of it. Churches and palaces were built along European lines, even though greater wealth might render them more ornate or though an occasional decorative symbol might betray the hand of an Indian craftsman as yet untutored in the canons of Occidental art. Similarly, New Spain borrowed from Europe the models of sophisticated thought, first the intellectual formulas of the Counter-Reformation, later those of an Enlightenment tempered with Thomism, still later—in rapid succession—the phraseology of Jacobinism, English Liberalism, Comtean Positivism, only to see the European catchwords produce a sterile harvest in the Middle American soil. Thus the society of the post-Conquest period suffered not only from the deepening cleavage between Indian and non-Indian. It also clogged the well-springs of autonomous cultural creativity. Product of the meeting of two cultural traditions, it should have been the richer for their encounter. But design and circumstance both reduced the capacity of each component to quicken and stimulate the other into new cultural growth, and to be quickened in turn by stimuli from outside. Instead of organic synthesis, the meeting of Indian and Spaniard resulted in a social unity that remained culturally mechanical.

12 COLONIALISM AND ECONOMIC GROWTH

Everett E. Hagen

W HILE PHYSICAL CAPITAL useful for economic growth was
constructed in many areas under colonial rule, colonialism caused psychological reactions whose continuing effects
hamper economic growth. Colonial rule caused rather widespread
retreatism, which might be a stage on the road to creativity,
but the severe pressures on the individual that resulted from
the colonial situation also led many individuals to the more
extreme reaction of ritualism. Various forms of group hysteria
that may be referred to collectively as Messianism manifested
the intensity of the stresses. Both among the retreatist and
ritualist individuals and among others not so severely affected
there resulted a rather compulsive clinging to values inimical
to economic growth. After a summary of the pressures exerted
on individuals by colonialism, these phenomena will be discussed
in turn, and then some reactions that somewhat alleviated the
effects.

THE PRESSURES OF COLONIALISM

Colonial rule, wherever it was imposed, created extreme psychological pressures on the subject people not only as a result
of measures which the colonial masters adopted as a matter
of deliberate policy but also inescapably by virtue of what the
colonial administrators were and what their presence in the
colonial area represented.

To begin with, they came unwanted and conquered the society
by force. In doing so they provided an unqualified demonstration

SOURCE: Everett E. Hagen, "Colonialism and Economic Growth," Chapter
17, pages 411–32, *On the Theory of Social Change,* Dorsey Press, 1962. Reprinted by permission of the author and publisher.

that the structure of the native society was of no importance
to them relative to the satisfaction of their own desires—that
in their view the indigenous structure of political and social
power was not worth preserving. In their administration they
disrupted further the overt structure of administrative relationships. They regrouped local governmental areas for the sake of
administrative convenience, provided for choice of legislative or
administrative officials in new ways for convenience or in the
name of advance toward democracy, and modified other traditional political mechanisms to control their functioning. They
had to do some or all of these things to prevent the traditional
channels of leadership from being mechanisms for the organization of resistance to their rule.

There have been partial seeming exceptions, notably leaving
in power the Maharajas in India, local princes in Indonesia,
and some tribal rulers in Africa, under policies of indirect rule.
But surely in such cases the indigenous population was not
deceived. The native rulers were left in nominal possession of
their functions and prerogatives only if they submitted their
exercise of power to the will of the conquerors and turned
over to the conquerors such a share of the material produce of
the society as seemed feasible and was desired. The indigenous
rulers may have submitted to the humiliating procedures of
yielding to alien rule for the sake of their skins, in which
case their continuance in authority was a source of shame to
their subjects, not an evidence of the grace of the colonial
rulers. Even if they continued to function to preserve as much of
the traditional life as they could, their ambiguous position must
have stirred unease. In addition more detailed investigation
would probably show that in all cases the colonial masters
found it necessary to intervene repeatedly by physical force or
threat of force to effect their purposes; the society was not left
intact.

Among the virtually inevitable changes was some disruption
of the economic functioning of the native society. The purposes
of the conquest included economic ones, and, however important
or unimportant they may have been relative to other purposes,
they were not ignored. New taxes were imposed so the necessity
to earn money should impel indigenous workers to present their
produce for sale in the market or to offer their labor to
Europeans who wished to exploit the natural resources of the

country. In the latter case, traditional family and community relationships of great psychological importance, of whose existence the colonial administrators may not have been aware, were disrupted. Ownership of property in fee simple was often introduced under the guise of economic progress and so that Europeans would be able to enter into business operations in the society. Thereby age-old equities in tribal and family wealth and in the inherited use-ownership of property were destroyed, and the social basis of existence in the villages eliminated. More generally, new codes of civil and criminal law were introduced for at least certain purposes. Their introduction destroyed the moral basis for the settlement of some types of disputes among individuals and made it inevitable that, from the viewpoint of the system of values of the traditional society, in some situations inequity and evil would be done.

In some cases religious customs were left alone so far as it was convenient to do so. However, because the Europeans regarded their own culture as superior, they were apt to forbid practices which they regarded as primitive (human sacrifices, the burial of individuals alive under sacred buildings so their spirits may protect the buildings, suicide by a widow on the bier of her husband) but which to the persons they ruled were either demonstrations of their obedience to the desires of the supernatural forces or necessary precautions against supernatural wrath. Even if the Europeans did not forbid such practices, they themselves literally or figuratively desecrated holy ground, as, for example, when they walked on temple grounds wearing shoes. And, as a minimum, the new rulers did not themselves observe the native religion, thereby offending the supernatural spirits and cutting the ties between the society and the supernatural forces at the highest level.

Perhaps equally important, by their very daily existence the colonial masters indicated in countless ways their contempt for the traditional culture. They built their houses differently, used different furniture, wore different clothing, showed repugnance for traditional methods of preparing food, and so on through every aspect of living.

And finally, if these aspects of the behavior of the new masters did not sufficiently suggest to the indigenous people that they were regarded as of little worth, the Europeans taught the lesson unmistakably in the relationships which they established in personal contacts between the two peoples. They regarded the individuals of the subordinated society as inferior not because of what they might or might not do but purely because they were natives. There could be no better evidence than that the word native has become a term of derogation, so that to avoid a connotation of contempt or condescension one must use instead the term *indigenous*. The European colonials would not meet indigenous individuals as social equals (even when those individuals were more liberally educated in Western culture and had better claim to intellectual attainment than the Europeans), excluded them from their homes and their clubs, required them to use terms of address which indicated the inferiority of the speaker, and informed them in a great variety of other deliberate and unconscious ways that they were regarded as unchangeably inferior. The central aspect of the relationship was that the indigenous people were tools being used for the benefit of the Europeans; and no exertion of effort by the individuals at the fringes of European colonial life such as missionaries whose main purpose was to advance the welfare of the subordinated people (or so these individuals believed in their conscious minds) could materially alter this perception.

These results of colonialism are not fortuitous. Many of the acts and attitudes sketched were necessary for the attainment of the avowed purposes for which the colonialists conquered the society: to introduce Western economic practices, to enhance the power and glory of their country, to save the souls of the heathen, and so on. Some which do not seem so are found to be so when we consider the network of actions and relationships necessary to reinforce and secure the effectiveness of certain central actions. The social exclusiveness was justified on the ground that in one's relaxation one wants to associate with one's own kind. The insistence of overt acknowledgment of an inferiority-superiority relationship was said to be necessary to enforce recognition that the Europeans were the rulers and must be obeyed. But, more basically these acts and attitudes were inescapable because of the nature of the colonial relationship. It would have been psychologically impossible for the European elite to live in the role of unwanted intruders in an alien society if they had not persuaded themselves that they were of their essence superior to the conquered people. That is, to suppress their guilt at their aggression, they had to assure and reassure themselves that their culture was superior, presumably because of the biological inheritance which made them superior persons, and that the values and institutions of the natives were of little worth, so that it was justifiable to impose oneself and one's purposes by force. This is the rationale by which any society must assuage its guilt at conquest and control of alien peoples. In addition, the specific individuals who became colonial administrators and businessmen were in the main self-selected, and one of the bases of self-selection was a need structure which was satisfied by the rule of other individuals. After a generation or so the colonialists assured themselves that the indigenous people were grateful for the benefits which had been conferred and wished colonial control to continue. This self-deception was an added defense against guilt at their aggression.

One exception may be noted to this sketch of the personality of colonialists: the colonial administrator who chose that vocation because he was impelled to try to save the indigenous people from the attitudes of his fellow administrators. There were such individuals, their motivation being some degree of rebellion against their own society, some degree of identification with the underdogs, perhaps humanitarianism in some other sense. They were, however, few. Moreover, individuals who objected to their own social system could have opposed it at home; that some such individuals went to the colonies usually implies that they partook of the perception that they were superiors who would lead the benighted natives to more worthy lives. Certainly this was true of missionaries; though their methods were gentler, their disparagement of the native culture was not less extreme than that of the administrators.

The comprehensive derogation thus expressed or implied by colonialism was tempered somewhat by expressed or implied admiration for some qualities of indigenous individuals—their capacity as fighters, their dexterity, and a few others; but these bits of high valuation were almost insignificant offsets to the virtually all-encompassing disparagement.

The low valuation of indigenous individuals manifested by the conquerors would not have mattered if the conquerors had no prestige in the indigenous society. However, the conquerors did have one characteristic conveying tremendous prestige, their overwhelming power. Thus their valuation counted. And even apart from the disparagement they expressed, their disruption of the traditional sources of emotional security created intense stresses.

RETREATISM IN COLONIAL SOCIETIES

When such pressures had persisted for one or two generations, they induced *retreatist* personality in most members of colonial societies. Adults responded to their rage and frustration with behavior in the home which led to *retreatism in their children.*

In many accounts of colonial societies in Asia, in the Middle East, and in North Africa one may read of the *apathy* of the people, of their lack of interest in affairs beyond the immediate circles of their lives. Leaders of Western countries, seeing this apathy, believed that the people of colonial areas had no thoughts or feelings about matters beyond their immediate ken. They believed that tribal or national leaders in the traditional societies who could not be bought might, without much reaction by the people, be replaced by ones who could, and that it was a matter of indifference to the people whether the kept leader pledged the support of his society to one or the other side of an issue. The Western leaders, conceiving the people of colonial societies to be without important values of their own, thought also that they could recognize Western culture as superior to their own if only, like children, they received enough education; and believed, too, that such people were grateful for the blessings that were being conferred upon them.

In country after country, therefore, the Westerners were shocked when, after World War II, the people voted overwhelmingly for independence; and they were still more shocked at the violence with which mobs in many countries manifested their hatred and rage once the circumstances were such that they dared admit these emotions to themselves. These phenomena, as well as the charismatic appeal of leaders like Castro to the simple folk of many countries, are understandable if we recognize that the apathy was not that of brutish unfeeling but that of retreatism, which always masks intense unconscious rage. For generations adults in the society had perceived the contempt of the colonial masters for the values of the society. The deep belief of the indigenous people in those values had conflicted with their respect for or fear of the power of the colonial rulers. The conflict had caused intense anxiety, as well as rage which it was necessary to repress. Children observing this anxiety and humiliation in adults had learned to repress their values, as a defense against pain, but the process had generated rage, none the less intense because it was unconscious. From generation to generation the effect had deepened; retreatism became more complete.

There may have been other causes of retreatism as well. In the discussion in [Hagen 1962:Chapter 19] of the Sioux on two governmental reservations, it is suggested that because their traditional life had been disrupted, their childhood environment provided many conflicting signals to them, in addition to the conflict of values directly resulting from the behavior of the conquerors. It is suggested also that their childhood environment provided them with many motivations which adult life could not satisfy. Both of these results may occur in other colonial societies. Insofar as they do, they add to the pressure on the individual to repress his conflicting values, that is, to become retreatist.

MORE EXTREME REACTIONS

But though retreatism was the most common reaction of colonial subjects to the tensions which developed in the home environment, the behavior of individuals who came most directly under the pressure of almost complete absence of status respect plus almost complete helplessness led to still more extreme ones.

A Scale of Reactions to Derogation

In any environment a child will perceive that sometimes he is only an instrument; that at times powerful and valued others place their convenience before his and use him or ignore him as needed to suit their purposes. This derogation creates anxiety in the child, and he wonders why he is treated thus. Among his responses to this anxiety in the normal case is identification with his parent of the same sex. By identifying himself with his father the son of say four years of age reassures himself that his father does not hate him, that he does not hate his father, that he is attractive to his mother, that he is big, and so on. In this way a child can cope with an occasional sense of being devalued without great hindrance to the development of needs favorable to creativity, that is, to the ability to solve problems with the most efficient use of one's mental capacities.

However, if the disregard by others of one's purposes and values in life is more frequent and more harsh (or, perhaps, if one is more sensitive to it), personality less attuned to coping with the world emerges. With a certain amount of pressure, and certain other specific characteristics of the environment, high need submission-domination and authoritarian personality result; with more pressure and certain other environmental features, values and needs are repressed and retreatism results. In the extreme case, in which the world seems virtually completely hostile to his urges and initiatives, the individual becomes paranoiac. Finding the real world so terrifying as to be intolerable, he refuses to believe that it exists and in desperate fantasy creates for himself a world in which he has a position that makes his existence endurable. Somewhat short of this extreme degree of pressure is the degree which causes the type of personality termed ritualist and, if the pressures impinge on a group rather than an individual, the group behavior known as Messianism. Ritualism and Messianism, which were fairly common in colonial situations, may be thought of as standing between retreatism and paranoia in the scale of reactions.

Identification with the Aggressor

A child experiencing extreme derogation may seek to protect himself by a mechanism known as "identification with the aggressor." It will be useful to discuss this mechanism in general terms before applying it specifically to the colonial case.

The term was first suggested by Anna Freud.[1] Among the half-dozen or more examples that she cites, a trivial one will illustrate the term, that of the small girl, afraid of ghosts and therefore afraid to walk across a dark hall, who solved the problem by pretending each time she crossed the hall that she was the ghost. Another example may illustrate more vividly the nature of the inner behavior of the child who tries to protect himself thus. One of Anna Freud's patients, a boy mortally afraid of being hurt, had been caused pain by his dentist. The boy brought a pocket knife to the next session with Dr. Freud and cut up a rubber ball, cut a string into small bits, and sharpened a pencil incessantly; on a later occasion, when his teacher had accidentally injured him, he came to his therapeutic session wearing a military cap, toy sword, and pistol. He said he "just felt like wearing them today." He was protecting himself from

---

[1] Though she probably had suggested the term earlier, Chapter 9 of her (1937) book presents the discussion of the concept usually referred to.

destruction by trying to persuade himself that he was the destroyer and therefore obviously would not be attacked by the destroyer. In the same way, some children put under extreme pressure by the self-centered and non-loving care of their parents solve this problem by masquerading, so to speak, as one of the parents.

The child masquerades as his parent, but he is not duplicating with pleasure so far as his capacities permit the behavior of someone he loves. His problem is that he is not loved. He lives in terror. He attempts to relieve his terror by persuading himself that he has characteristics identical with the person who has power over him. If he becomes identical with the aggressor, surely the aggressor will not destroy him. But he is not really imitating the quality but only its appearance. The boy did not imitate the dentist's cutting skill in any way that would give him a useful ability; he cut compulsively, ritually, and uselessly except for the function of assuaging his terror. Of course he patterns his behavior after some model around him in his childhood, for except in cases that become psychotic he learns to walk, to talk, to eat in a conventional manner. Presumably he models himself after the least terrifying individual or individuals among those important to him. He acquired no rich sense of nurturance from anyone, for presumably if he had he would have been saved from ritualism, but he finds someone to model his routine behavior after.

Since very little regard for him is manifested by the self-centered father who creates such fear, the child, finding no reason not to believe that his father willingly hurts him, finds no reason to blame himself. Hence all of his rage can be turned outward, and it is intense. At the same time that he slavishly imitates external traits of his father, he hates him with a consuming hatred. But it would be mortally perilous to admit his hatred since he is so completely dependent on the aggressor, his father. Hence he struggles to deny his hatred even to himself. At the same time he struggles with value conflicts. Thus the boy who used his knife to cut, cut, cut was actually tremendously afraid of a knife, and no doubt had to summon up great effort to take the thing in his hand. To do the things he hates and fears but thinks he must do to prevent destruction requires tremendous effort by the individual. The inner struggle drains him of vitality and initiative.

The Colonial Case: Ritualism

In the colonial case the parents' frustrations at their disparaged existence caused the behavior which forced the child to this extreme defense. The father subjected to the most severe withdrawal of status recognition must have reacted with especial severity in his home. Denied other channels for his need dominance and his rage, he must have asserted them in the home with extreme harshness. He must have been so occupied with his rage, humiliations, and bewilderment that he had no capacity to respond to persons around him; he merely ruled them and pushed them out of his way. The perception his children received must have been almost unrelievedly a stark one of a powerful figure who controlled them, who valued them little, and who had his own interests and concerns on which it was dangerous to intrude.

Since we have no direct accounts of such children, we can only reconstruct the childhood behavior from the adult personalities which emerged. The son must have sought in desperation to duplicate some overt aspect of his father's behavior, perhaps his withdrawal from the world and unresponsiveness to things around him. The son dared not direct at his father the rage which filled him, but in his father's rage at the disparaging colonial masters he found a permissible target. The images of the disparaging group that the son perceived at this time in his life were of course very vague and confused ones, consisting largely of something-toward-which-my-father-has-an-attitude. Yet even very early in life he might hate this vague object. He thus served a dual purpose: he could hate, and, at the same time, here was an aspect of his father's attitudes he could identify with, thus protecting himself against his father.

Yet at the same time another motivation impelled him in an opposite direction. If these other persons have more power than his father, perhaps he could protect himself against his father by aligning himself with them instead of hating them. Or perhaps he could do both: both hate them and ape them. His emotional life became confused.

Then, as he moved outside the home and came into more and more actual contact with the power of the colonial elite, he found that in the kind of stimuli they presented to him they resembled his father. They had superior power. And they would no more receive him, regardless of what he did, than would his father. At this point the pattern of behavior he had learned in early childhood suggested to him the threat of complete destruction, complete rejection. But it also suggested a remedy. Using the mechanism of identification with the threatening figures already built into his personality, he now tried to persuade himself that he was just like these new aggressors. By this maneuver he not only warded off this new terror but also lessened his old one; he gained protection from his parents. For he had now become identical with something even more powerful than they.[2]

And so in a Dutch colony in his sports and clothes and speech he might become more Dutch than the Dutch; in a British colony, depending on his social class, he went in for soccer or tennis or golf, and, whatever his class, for physical fitness. If he had the opportunity, he might study in the Western-type schools which the colonial masters established. He might pursue the occupations they approved, becoming, for example, a clerk in their offices. He might become a Christian, a particularly meek and ritualistic Christian.

But even as he masqueraded as one of the aggressors, he was consumed with rage at them which he dared not admit to himself. So, as was true as a child, his energies were forever absorbed in a continuing inner struggle to contain his rage and deal with the conflict within him. The mask-like appearance which characterized many such individuals, presumably the extreme cases, revealed the tenseness of their control; if they gave way an inch to their inner impulses, their self-constraint might break down. Even in the less extreme cases the imitation of Western modes was as if at a distance—as though they did not dare approach too close to being Western. The imitation was a little slavish and intense, a little "tight." Behavior was rote rather than alert. Conflicted and constricted, the individual aped such of the social modes of the colonial masters as were open to him, but with half a heart, no will, bewilderment in his brain, and no initiative and judgment. He would never advance in their world, but he would continue to go through the motions. He is appropriately termed a ritualist.

Many such persons are found in colonial or ex-colonial areas

---

[2] This "overdetermined" characteristic is typical of many psychological mechanisms. They often serve several purposes, including contradictory ones, at the same time.

today. They are clerks in the offices of Western businessmen in colonial areas. They are anxious to succeed, so they think, but something is wrong with their performance. Western businessmen in colonial areas are apt to say, "They are all right as clerks, but they have no head for business." The Westerners think that the characterization applies to all indigenous individuals of the society. Believing this justifies that feeling of innate superiority which, as I have noted, they must have to justify their existence as colonial masters. It does not occur to them to look at the history of the country and wonder how this can be if, as is often or usually true, that history indicates magnificent administrative achievements in war, governmental administration, architecture, engineering, or other activities.

Persons whose personalities partake in considerable degree of identification with the aggressors have sometimes become the first leaders of a colonial country after independence. Sufficiently pursuing identification with the aggressors so that they acquired various European values, but just free enough so that they might speak out for independence, they gained a certain degree of charisma as leaders of the independence movement and so have become leaders of the new nation. However, their values are so mixed that they cannot adequately express the nationalist hatred of the foreigner which the mass of the people feel. Because they cannot, those who are still nationalist leaders today are apt to be replaced, as they age or their initial charisma wears off, by less cultured, more raw and emotional leaders who give vent to the nation's attitudes more effectively. This has been the course of events in Ceylon and Egypt. Some of the pro-French leaders of the African nations that are members of the French community are probably of this conflicted type (others perhaps being merely venal or faithful to the interests of a narrow elite group). Mr. Kasavubu and Mr. Mobutu in the Congo may be conflicted in this way. Certainly a number of leaders in Burma, India, and Pakistan are. Even Mr. Nehru, like the British, speaks patronizingly of the Indians. ". . . My legacy to India? Hopefully, it is 400 million people capable of governing themselves" (Cousins 1961).[3]

It will be surprising if the so-called "moderate leaders" in a

---

[3] Mr. Cousins had suggested that perhaps Mr. Nehru was Gandhi's greatest legacy to India, and had asked Mr. Nehru, "Who is your legacy to India?"

number of the former French colonies are not replaced by more violently anti-Western ones. It would not be surprising to see a parallel development in Burma when U Nu has lost his hold on the people, though that may not occur for so many years that other social currents may determine the country's course by that time. In the complex cultural circumstances of India many other tensions will also affect the course of events, and it would be rash to predict that this sequence will occur; but even there it is a possibility.

Not only the top national leaders but some of their ministers and many of their civil servants at all levels are ritualist in greater or less degree. They entered the civil service in imitation of their European masters. They are excellently trained in European institutions, but many of them are constricted by their inner conflicts. These individuals will faithfully perform routine clerical or ministerial functions, but their lives are essentially imitative and they lack the initiative to meet their countries' complex problems effectively.

Ritualism as Unstable

Ritualism can hardly perpetuate itself. The tensions within the personality of the ritualist are such that the attempts of his children to defend themselves against them may be expected to produce warped, unintegrated personalities in them, but hardly ones with the same malformations as those of the parents. Given a physical environment which in later life confirms the childhood experience, authoritarian personality tends to perpetuate itself since it offers an effective means of coping with interpersonal relationships and the physical world. But ritualism serves a purpose only if there is a harshly dominating personality that must be identified with to avoid self-destruction and that offers a model of power to identify with. The ritualist personality itself does not seem to be such a personality. His personality may be bewildering and confining, and his behavior may cause pain, but he is certainly not powerful.

Ritualism, then, will not produce ritualism. It is an element in a dynamic society, not in a society in equilibrium (though in a society in equilibrium it may appear in an occasional deviant for whom the society has a niche). Ritualism is a characteristic of a process of disruption of equilibrium, a process which may be expected to continue further.

Where the social pressures which led to ritualism continue, retreatism, it seems to me, may emerge.

The ritualist is addicted to order and routine, and his meekness masks inner compulsions. When he becomes a father, the combination, I would suppose, will cause him to dominate his children and to ignore their needs and urges so that they receive the perception, as forcefully as their father obtained it a generation earlier, but not quite in the same way, that the world is unmanageable. While the father of the first generation bludgeoned his children into being merely instruments, the ritualist simply does not respond very much to his children (or to anyone else). He can no more give love freely than he can strike out violently. It seems plausible to suggest that the resulting home environment might readily create a perception in the children that nothing does any good—not obeying, or striking out on one's own initiative, or being aggressive, or identifying with one's parents. This might well be true even if only the father is a ritualist provided that the mother is so submissive in her feminine role that she offers no model of more active (and successful) personality to her children.

It is of particular interest to speculate what the course of change in ritualist personality may be when the social pressures of colonialism have ceased. In ex-colonial societies what personality traits will replace the ritualist ones in the next generation? While the personalities of adults who are ritualist at present will change little, the reduction in social pressures will certainly somewhat alter their behavior in the home. Their children hardly have a traditional personality to fall back on. Will a transition to at least a moderate degree of creativity occur in one generation? Or will the children of these families be ineffective and confused individuals while other families provide the leadership in continuing social change? The latter seems more probable, but the entire subject is so complex that no attempt will be made to explore it here.

Messianism[4]

Even closer to paranoia than ritualism is a group reaction to the psychological pressures of colonialism that I shall term Messian-

---

[4] For discussions of Messianic movements other than the discussions cited below in specific contexts, see: Ames (1957); Linton (1943); Voget (1956); Wallace (1956).

ism, though it does not always involve the belief in a Savior who will save one from one's troubles. Messianism, broadly defined, apparently has appeared in most traditional societies in which an alien power has imposed alien institutions. Suddenly a social movement emerges which embodies the belief that by magic the power of the conquerors can be nullified and the good life restored. The belief is characterized by wishful thinking intensified in desperation to the point of fantasy in which the real is no longer distinguished from the wished for. Under some combination of defense mechanism learned as children and inability as adults to tolerate the crushing weight of the colonial environment, men who previously had been rational citizens peacefully (though resentfully) obeying the colonial commands find the frustrations of reality intolerable. Seeing no rational way to restore an identity for themselves, and unable to live without one, they insist on believing that there is one and find it in magic practices which in moments of lesser pressure they know are of no use.

In Burma, in 1930 and 1931, men in the countryside suddenly believed that incantations and charms would make them immune against the weapons of the English. Armed only with primitive weapons, they marched in a solid phalanx against rifles.[5] In Madagascar, protected from rifle-fire by a bit of wood on a string clenched between the teeth, men charged similarly against European guns.[6] In South Dakota, a generation after the Sioux had been subdued and the buffalo had disappeared from the plains, the Sioux gathered to regain their lands and summon back the buffalo by ritual and dances.[7] The Mau Mau movement in Kenya in the 1950's served several psychological ends by combining Messianism with aggression. In the Southwest Pacific, where the islanders had seen ships and planes pour out supplies during World War II, they believed after the war that if they could cast off the Europeans, ships and planes would appear which would return their native goods to them or would bring them an equitable share of the goods which the Europeans who had destroyed their civilization possessed in such quantities. So they organized in various ways, religious intensity everywhere being a characteristic, to obtain these ends. In New Guinea those

---

[5] A brief account of the movement of which such incidents were a part is presented in Cady, (1958:309–13).

[6] Mannoni, (1956:Chaps. ii and iv, especially p. 149).

[7] Lott, (1959); and see Hagen (1962:Chapter 19).

who lived inland built airstrips in the jungle, and those in shore villages built wharves into the sea and cast their furniture and household equipment into the ocean, waiting thereafter for their magic to bring the ships and planes that should re-equip them.[8] And these are only more or less random examples of what has occurred where the pressure of extreme withdrawal of status respect has made the real world intolerable. It has been suggested to me[9] that a study of the infiltration of European words into native languages has indicated a rough law of the point of cultural pressure at which the life of reality becomes intolerable and Messianic movements tend to appear, but I have not myself seen the evidence in the literature.

It is not unreasonable to suggest that the desire of the leaders of some low-income societies for industrial establishments which are demonstrably grossly uneconomic is a manifestation of the same psychological phenomenon. A steel mill, for example, is a symbol of power. People who have one, it seems, will have power. So the steel mill is built, and the political leaders of the country are impervious to argument that the country lacks coking coal and iron ore and will soon run out of steel scrap, or that these resources are so situated that under the most favorable circumstances, after maximum efficiency has been attained, the steel produced will cost twice the price at which it could be imported. Add perhaps that the funds invested in the plant could instead have been used to produce other goods that would replace imports or increase exports with an efficiency that would raise the level of living. It is not that the leaders are stupid, or that they simply believe that the analyses available to them are imperialist tricks. Rather, they are somehow unable to receive the analyses in their minds; their need for a quick path out of their humiliation to dignity and power is such that it is not possible for them to believe that they cannot achieve the result quickly by magic.[10]

---

[8] For a brief account see Firth, (1951:110–13). Perhaps not all of these movements should be termed Messianic, for not all incorporate belief in a leader, present here on earth, whose magic will make people invulnerable to deadly weapons.

[9] By the late Clyde Kluckhohn, in conversation.

[10] The cultures and personalities of Western societies are not immune to such aberrations. The belief of many Americans after World War II

The belief that one can be rescued from one's troubles by magic of course inhibits intelligent imaginative action to attain economic growth. Messianism is mentioned here both for that reason and because it testifies to the intensity of the psychological pressures created by colonialism.

THE PERPETUATION
OF VALUES INIMICAL TO ECONOMIC GROWTH

This analysis of certain extreme reactions of some groups in colonial societies to severe social pressure may make it easier to understand the more general effects of such pressures among colonial and ex-colonial peoples.

A derogated individual tends to attack both the persons who disparage him and the things they value. For this reason a person with a normal traditional childhood cannot set a high value on using his energies in attacking the problems of industrial production or other varieties of modern business activity. For the Western view that such use of one's energies is a worthwhile way of life and the Western view that the indigenous individuals are

---

that Senator Joseph McCarthy could save the country from Communism, and was doing so, is a case of Messianism. (The degree of attachment of many Americans to Franklin Delano Roosevelt in the 1930's and to General Eisenhower after World War II are not entirely dissimilar phenomena.) In both the American case and the cases in traditional societies, there were pressures that made many individuals extremely anxious. There was bewilderment about the nature of the threat, and lack of perception of any rational solution. Because acceptance of continued anxiety was intolerable, fantasy and belief in a magical solution were resorted to. Senator McCarthy's followers did not regard themselves as resorting to magic. They believed that Communists in the federal establishment did threaten their lives and that Senator McCarthy could find Communists whom the executive officers were unable or unwilling to discover. But this does not distinguish the two cases. Surely the intelligent individuals in traditional societies who resorted to Messianism perceived equally plausible reasons for believing that the method they followed was logical.

World cognition based on more advanced scientific knowledge excludes or curtails the ability to believe in certain types of magical manipulation of the physical world (though the anxious individual can still believe in an invasion by Martians). Yet even up to the present time peoples with the most advanced knowledge have believed in Messianic remedies if the level of their anxiety was sufficiently high.

An early study of a less extreme form of psychological mechanism is William James' "The Will to Believe," in James (1896).

of contemptible intrinsic worth are intertwined; the two were
associated in the colonialists' scheme of values. Accepting the
first involves accepting the European way of life as a frame of
reference, and that involves accepting the second. To do so
would be self-destruction. Hence the indigenous individual clings
to traditional values, not unself-consciously as he would in un-
disturbed traditional society, but compulsively, to protect himself
from the threat to his identity which acceptance of Western values
would constitute. By holding to the idea that physical labor is
demeaning, that an elite individual is interested in humanistic
learning, that one's status determines one's worth, a member of
the traditional elite can protect himself after a fashion from the
derogation of the Westerner. He can tell himself (unconsciously)
that the powerful Westerner's view of the indigenous individual's
worth is not so important after all, since the Westerner by violat-
ing the traditional values proves himself to be of inferior worth.
And for the same sort of reason the nonelite indigenous individual clings with equal compulsiveness to his religious belief,
his view of what type of social structure is good, his traditional
methods.

This is the reaction of the normal traditional individual in a
colonial or newly ex-colonial society toward Western values. That
of a retreatist or ritualist person is similar. The retreatist individual has internalized traditional values even though the conflict
among them is so painful that he has repressed them from con-
sciousness. Thus the values of the colonial masters threaten him
just as they do the traditional individual, and he responds to that
threat with the same defensive maneuver. The ritualist individual
is prepared to ape Western behavior, just as earlier he aped
some threatening characteristic of his father, so that he can try
to persuade himself that since he is like the Westerner, the
Westerner does not really feel contempt for him. However, beneath that external aping he fears the person who derogates him,
just as in infancy and childhood he mortally feared the person
or persons who showed no love for him. The values he holds
to are the ones he found least dangerous in early life. He cannot
productively imitate the persons who threaten him.

Sometimes the controlled appearance of a ritualist is deceptive
to casual observation. Thus it is not always apparent at first
glance whether the diligent colonial student of Western learning
is a person high in need autonomy and need achievement who

is acquiring a useful tool or a ritualist busily but uncreatively strengthening his defense. The similarity, however, is superficial.

Because of the threat posed by the attitudes of Western colonial masters to the identities of indigenous individuals, it is often difficult for a member of a colonial or ex-colonial society to receive technical advice from a Westerner. In the case of American technical aid the problem is intensified by the fact that since World War II American actions that affect the underdeveloped countries have been such as repeatedly to rearouse the sense of humiliation and resentment in the peoples of those countries. In some of our economic aid programs, and even more in our military assistance programs our support of repressive established ruling classes in some countries and our intervention to displace legitimate rulers in one or two others, we have conveyed forcefully to the peoples of those countries the perception that we have no regard for their purposes, even no interest in inquiring what those purposes are, but rather feel justified in flouting their purposes to serve ours.[11]

As a result, with the fibers of their nervous systems, not merely with their minds, many individuals in underdeveloped countries must fear Americans and other Westerners and unconsciously distrust their advice even while apparently listening or watching closely. Would a person who feels contempt for them advise them except in his own interest? And can any action in his interest also be in theirs? Perhaps they fear him especially as he bears gifts, for the colonial administrator often tried to bribe the colonial subject to serve administrative purposes. The defense mechanisms built into the indigenous individual's neural processes rise up to block the processes of his mind when the European advises him. Obviously this sort of attitude is not an absolute bar, but the inhibiting quality of this behavior pattern is no doubt one cause of the ineffectiveness of much technical aid.

Many indigenous individuals, it is true, seek employment in Western business organizations, but close observation will indicate that their behavior is usually ritualist. They seek to identify themselves with European externals; but when they try to function in these positions, their hatred of the underlying European values and the perpetual conflict within them prevent them from functioning successfully. They have "no head for business." It is

---

[11] See the Appendix to this chapter.

plausible to believe that unconsciously they deliberately sabotage the European-type operation. They make mistakes, misunderstand instructions, fail to anticipate needed actions. They do so, I suggest, because they need to protect their identity by demonstrating to themselves that they would not wholeheartedly function as aliens. Or they impose on the operation the traditional interpersonal relationships which one aspect of their value and need structure demands, and the operation fails to function well. Reconciling traditional relationships with the economic and technical requirements may be possible, but it would require an order of creativity which in their conflicted condition they do not possess.

Thus, although colonial rule has laid a material base for economic growth in many countries, it may have created psychological barriers more important in their effects.

A QUALIFICATION:

RIFTS IN THE TRADITIONAL SOCIAL STRUCTURE

One important qualification should be noted to the inability of individuals in traditional societies to share the values of their colonial masters except in a constricted ritualist way. Because of domestic power shifts before any European intrusion, in some traditional societies groups who had once held an accepted place in the society were later denied recognition of the status which they believed was rightfully theirs. When Europeans overthrew the dominant traditional group, the members of some such subordinated groups greeted the Europeans as deliverers. If they did, they may have accepted Western values fairly readily. This reaction occurred in some degree among the Karens, Shans, and Arakanese in Burma, in the Shia sect in Saudi Arabia, among tribal groups in a number of African countries, among important groups in India, and perhaps among groups in many other areas as well. Moreover, if the groups from whom status recognition had been withdrawn have passed through the phase of retreatism and become creative, they may enter effectively upon technological progress.

However, they will not necessarily do so, for two reasons. One is that status recognition may not have been withheld from them for a sufficiently long period to arouse creativity in them. The other is that under the rule of the colonial administrators and businessmen opposing pressures will weigh on them. For the colonial masters indicate extreme disparagement of the values of the subordinated group as well as those of the erstwhile dominant group. Hence the subordinated group is simultaneously attracted and repelled. The resultant impact on them depends on a balance of influences concerning which no general statement can be made, but it is clear that in some situations the subordinated group may seize upon not only Western values but also Western techniques with speed and ingenuity and set economic growth on its way.

India provides an example. Successive waves of invasion and conquest of parts of India and resulting migration and cross-migration within the subcontinent have resulted in complex centuries-old patterns of withdrawal of status recognition, varying over time. Today, as for centuries past, a linguistic-ethnic group that is the dominant elite in one area may be a somewhat derogated minority in another, and a group which by general consensus is the top elite in an area may nevertheless find some aspects of their behavior disparaged by other individuals or groups whose opinion weighs upon them. The situation in India has seemed to me too complex to lend itself to analysis in terms of the analytical model presented in this volume without more intensive examination than it has been possible to give it, but the general observation seems justified that this situation may have produced creative personality in individuals of a number of different groups. India may be ripe for continuing technological progress even though it has very recently come out from under the ordinarily impeding influences of colonial rule; the pertinent question is whether the number of creative individuals produced by the various pressures is great enough.[12]

---

[12] Even if the number is great enough and economic growth proceeds, that fact alone will not assure smooth social change. The creative individuals leading the technological change are members of the elite. The question remains whether they will act so as to convey to the simple folk a sense that they are valued and will do so before the continued derogation of their status to which the simple folk are still subjected, and their suspicions of the European values of national leaders, cause radical political change. (These forces, and not the impression one gains from much popular writing that the Indians will be unhappy if they do not do as well as China, seem to me to be at the core of the political-social problem of India.) While the prospects for social stability seem reasonably good to many observers, one would not wish to make unqualified forecasts.

Even if this is the case, it would be difficult to decide whether on balance colonialism hastened the process of economic growth in India. It may be expected that creative Indian individuals seeking new routes to achievement and status would have established contacts with the West in any event, as they did in Japan and Colombia. Under colonialism they had more extensive contact with many Westerners. Did the greater access to knowledge offset the psychological barriers which the colonial relationship created and the tendency of Western administrators to hamper developments which might compete with their own interests? No one can say with certainty. To the writer it seems likely that even in India colonialism delayed economic growth, but this is a subjective judgment for which no conclusive evidence can be adduced.

IMPLICATIONS FOR THE FUTURE

If colonial rule has had the effects that have been sketched above, what may one conclude concerning the prospects for economic growth in colonial areas, either while they remain colonial or after they obtain their independence?

If the derogation of colonial rule results in retreatist personality after several generations, some individuals with creative personality may emerge in still later generations by the process already sketched by which retreatism leads to creativity. It is to be expected that creative individuals who do emerge while the area is still colonial will not imitate the economic activity of the colonial masters for the same reason that repelled earlier generations: assumption of the master's values will carry with it self-condemnation. They may carry on economic innovation of a distinctly different type, but the situation in which they live is more apt to direct their innovational energies into other activities, such as the attainment of independence.

Even after colonial rule ends, economic growth is not apt to become vigorous until change in personality has occurred. However, it does not follow that a sequence of several generations of personality change must lapse before economic growth will begin. Rather quickly, say in the period between infancy and maturity of one generation, creativity may emerge out of retreatism on a fairly large scale, and the creative individuals may see in economic prowess their best opportunity to prove their worth.[13]

If this analysis is correct, it suggests a minimum lag of say 30 years between the time when independence is assured and the time when economic growth becomes vigorous, and a typical lag somewhat longer. India, however, might be an exception to this generalization because of the quantum of innovational personality channeled toward technological advance that already existed when the British established themselves in the country. Because of it, economic prowess no doubt had a place in the value system of some groups at that time. Hence it was not necessary to react against this value of the conquerors; other values could be identified as the alien and threatening ones. If so, there may have persisted throughout colonial days a stream of economic innovational personality large enough to initiate vigorous economic growth sooner.[14]

APPENDIX: AMERICAN FOREIGN POLICY AND
THE UNDERDEVELOPED COUNTRIES

One of the results of the derogation of individuals of colonial and ex-colonial societies by the colonial rulers is the rage which lies latent in the personalities of many or most individuals in those societies. They do not feel rage in general (there is no such thing) but specifically rage at being used by some person or nation to serve its purposes without regard for their purposes. They rage at being treated as instruments rather than as human beings with their own purposes and values worthy of respect.

Like other important personality characteristics, this tendency to rage must have originated in childhood. Indigenous parents, preoccupied with their frustrations under colonial rule, presumably acted arbitrarily and inconsiderately in the home without

---

[13] In Hagen (1962:Chapter 19) the emergence of creativity among some American Indian leaders is discussed. While their condition is in a sense the archetype of complete colonialism, it differs from the usual case in such important respects—notably immersion in an alien society of overwhelming size, many of whose leaders support their cause—that it would be hazardous to generalize from the American experience to other and more usual colonial situations.

[14] This is admittedly *post hoc* theorizing. It is included to make clear the limits of the generalization stated in this section.

conveying the perception of the rightness of their actions which is conveyed in the traditional situations, and their behavior engendered in their children rage at being treated with disregard of their needs and purposes. As the children grew to adulthood, they experienced again from their European masters the same treatment as instruments, with little regard for their purposes in life. Their rage was confirmed and intensified.

It is appropriately termed an allergy. The reference is of course figurative, but the figure of speech is singularly apt, so close is the parallelism between the reaction of colonial peoples and the physiological one. Most of the societies involved are now free of colonial control, but they are subject to the impact of diplomatic policies of foreign nations; and when any event suggests to the people so sensitized that they are being used by a foreign power to serve its purposes with disregard of their own, a sense of humiliation and rage is re-aroused. The tendency exists among Latin American peoples and in a number of other countries which have long (or always) been free of colonial control, where the elites of these countries have treated the classes below them in a colonial manner.

Since World War II many American actions have aroused this sense of humiliation and resentment in the peoples of most of the economically underdeveloped countries of the world. The result has often been unwitting; in our egocentricity we have not understood that they had purposes different from ours; but this has not lessened the impact. Although this is not the place for a documented account, a brief summary will make clear the nature of the American actions referred to.

In addition to military agreements with countries whose people wanted them, we have made agreements with many whose people did not. For a time we encouraged almost any government that would take our money and munitions to create armed forces of a size that served our purposes and the purposes of that government and the elite classes, but for which the other people of the country saw no need, an undertaking which disrupted families, brought rich and rather arrogant foreigners into the country, and brought on the people danger of a war in which they felt no concern. (That they should feel no concern is shocking to some Americans, but consideration of the history of ex-colonial countries suggests they should be as suspicious of us as the Soviets.)

By our aid we seated more firmly in power ruling groups not selected by the will of the people, some of which groups are in Western terms corrupt, reactionary, insensitive to the needs of the people they rule, and actively oppressive. We supplied these governments arms without pressuring them or effectively helping them to alter the nature of their domestic rule. If we were aware of this effect of our military aid, we regarded it as of less importance than our short-run interest in military security.

In some instances our intervention has been more positive and specific. Because he avowed allegiance to us, we supported a prince in Laos who has no base of popular support; because he was leftist we aided in the deposition in Guatemala of a president legitimately elected who promised eagerly desired land reform; and we aided a plan to overthrow Castro in Cuba because we, and not the people of Cuba, dislike his Communist ties. (We criticize Castro's denial of freedom of speech and action and confiscation of property, but to peasants and workers in Cuba and throughout Latin America denial of these freedoms to elites with whom they feel no empathy must mean little. To them Castro apparently symbolizes primarily social reform and self-respect. And in any event the fact of American intervention probably has more emotional significance to them than any substantive question in Cuba.) Offering economic aid does not offset the rage which these actions arouse; the rage of people who feel humiliated is not dissipated by offering them money. Moreover, in our aid programs we have sometimes put the pocketbook interests of our citizens or our enterprises above what underdeveloped countries regard as their national interest. Of course this is our prerogative, but they feel that we flout their dignity for our profit. Perhaps the example that arouses most emotion in Latin America is our refusal to aid the Brazilian national petroleum enterprise. Latin Americans commonly regard this not as a matter of principle but as a result of the influence in our government of our oil companies and as evidence of our contempt for Latin American wishes.

These comments of course imply no predictions concerning the stability of Castro's position. His internal errors may alienate the people, though his original charisma should survive many errors.

In most of these respects our policies have now been reversed or modified in ways lessening their offensive impact. However, persons who are psychologically allergic remember past humiliations, and react strongly to a few present incidents.

This perception by underdeveloped peoples that we, like their colonial masters, have contempt for their purposes in life or at least have not bothered to understand them has great political and diplomatic significance. It explains actions which have bewildered Americans—some anti-American riots, coolness to Western aims, tendencies to ally with Communist powers. By using countries for our purposes in disregard of theirs we have very probably generated throughout the countries affected and the continents of which they are a part suspicion and hostility vastly greater in significance than the shorter-run purposes we were pursuing. Our actions have helped to assure that if the peoples involved cannot resist these indignities with their own power they will look for support from our enemies, who are not tainted with our historical association with colonialists and who wear the halo of having themselves risen up to overthrow oppressive force. (Their more recent colonialism does not touch the emotions of the peoples of underdeveloped countries, partly because it is repression of peoples with whom the underdeveloped peoples have no empathy and partly because the emotional commitments of the underdeveloped peoples, caused by the Western actions sketched above, predispose them not to believe that it exists.) These reactions of the peoples of underdeveloped countries, rather than the diabolical cunning of Communist agents, are probably the basic reason why the trend in the sympathies of those peoples during the 1950's seems to have been against the United States and the West and toward the Communist powers.[15]

These repercussions of our policies of course strengthen the psychological blocks to effective participation in Western-type economic activity.

---

[15] The evidence of this trend is scattered. I believe, however, that the consensus of responsible reporters who have been in positions to sense the attitudes of the lower classes and the intellectuals in South and Southeast Asia and in Latin America is that the trend is as I have stated it.

To solve their purely domestic problems, people may turn to Communist ideology or leadership even if we do not thus pave the way. The actions I have sketched in the text above are by no means the sole explanation of trends in the attitudes of the people of underdeveloped countries. They are, however, of great importance.

13 COMMUNAL HOSTILITY
TO IMPOSED SOCIAL CHANGE IN
SOUTH AFRICA [1953]

M. A. Jaspan

THIS CHAPTER sets out to provide a brief diachronic account of the social structure of a society—the Ekunene of South Africa—before and after conquest by Europeans. In considering the effects of European conquest, particular attention is directed to the reception accorded by the people to programmes of 'uplift' and development introduced by the European administration and by other agencies.

The people of Ekunene are a section of the South African Bantu-speaking peoples. Their culture, language, and much of their ascertainable history is closely linked to Zulu. Ekunene is the name given by the people to their 'country', a mountainous reservation officially described as a tribal ward of Location No 2, Polela District, Natal.

Ekunene at present comprises an area of approximately 19.7 square miles. Its population, according to the most recent official estimate, was 3,538 in 1938.[1] The density of population was approximately 180 per square mile.

The Ekunene countryside, located about a broken escarpment rising from the Umkomazi River valley in the foothills of the Drakensberg Mountains, is characterized by rolling grassland

---

SOURCE. M. A. Jaspan, "Communal Hostility to Imposed Social Change in South Africa," pages 97–120, in *Approaches to Community Development*, Phillips Ruopp, editor, W. van Hoeve, 1953. Reprinted by permission of the author and publisher.

[1] Report of the Reclamation Committee on Location No 2, Polela District, 1938 (MS.), kindly loaned to me by the Chief Native Commissioner, Natal. In 1949 the Records Clerk at the Polela Health Centre gave 4.200 as the Centre's own most recent population estimate.

with occasional thornbush and thicket in lateral clefts on the hill and mountain slopes. Much of the top-soil is at present severely eroded, some of it so seriously that not even grass will grow in the bald stretches. Numerous water-cloven gullies traverse both the hill-slopes and the more level pastures and fields.

A Government road transport service links Ekunene with Pietermaritzburg, the capital of Natal Province, about 40 miles distant, and with Bulwer, the seat of the Polela Magisterial District, about 10 miles distant.[2]

The Traditional Political and Social Structure of Ekunene

Before Shaka, the great Zulu general, unified the numerous petty chieftaincies in the area now known as Zululand and Natal in the early nineteenth century, Ekunene was an independent political society. Its territory extended north of the confluence of the Tukela and Umzinyathi (Buffalo) Rivers. There was a tradition of past kingship handed down patrilineally for hundreds of years. African informants in Polela, forty years ago, were able to note the names and order of succession of eighteen reigning ancestors of the Chief of Ekunene in 1914 (Bryant 1929:363–88).

According to the principle of primogenital succession from the issue of 'the chief wife' in a polygynous family, the ruler of the royal clan in Ekunene claimed to be the head of the principal or right-hand (*ekunene*) branch of the Dlamini tribe. Consequently his whole section of the original tribe came to be known as Ekunene, or 'they of the righthand branchi'. According to tradition, the tribe was governed by the Chief (*inkosi*)[3], his Great Councillor (*induna*), and by a convocation (*ibandla*) of extended family patriarchs (*abanumzana*). In times of relative peace the Chief maintained his position not solely as a despot, but as the hereditary representative of an aristocratic family closely associated with the history and traditions of the tribe. He was not only the co-ordinator of the machinery of government,

---

[2] From Komkhulu, the 'capital' or Chief's village.

[3] The Zulu term *inkosi* has been variously translated as 'king', 'chief', or 'prince'. Men of Ekunene with whom I discussed the question of apposite translation of this term said that their inkosi was to them as the King of England is to Englishmen. It is customary in South Africa, however, to refer to the inkosi only as a chief.

but the religious leader of his people, constituting in his person, it was believed, the essential temporal link between the spirits of deceased kings and their living subjects. In addition, unless he was a minor, or clearly unsuited to the task, the Chief of Ekunene was the commander of the military forces of the realm.

A considerable body of special ritual values, and some exclusive religious and ritual practices, attached to the person and status of a Dlamini Ekunene king. He was not permitted to come into contact with sick people or corpses, or with people who had any relation of proximity (either through physical contact as neighbours or household members, or through any close degree of kinship, whether affinal or consanguineous) with a recently sick or deceased person. A number of specially chosen attendants administered to his personal and public needs. Such attendants were enjoined to be loyal and obedient to the king in all matters; failure to fulfil such functions properly, or the performance of any actions which aroused suspicion, endangered the life of the servant concerned. Legends and folk-tales about the rivalry that existed between men for appointment to these posts at the court indicates that special privileges and advantages were attached to official posts in the royal service.

Upon his death it was the custom for the Dlamini Ekunene king to be cremated. Everyone else in the tribe was buried at death.[4] When Mafohla, the father of the present Chief, Vusindaba, died, many people said that he was the first ruler of Ekunene to be buried rather than cremated. It is said that the influence of missionaries, exerted through converts to Christianity, constrained his relatives and councillors from disposing of his bodily remains according to custom. In this way, as in so many others, the missionaries are said to have played a part in the general European attack against the culture, traditions, and political independence of Ekunene.

In the traditional social structure the highest status devolved exclusively upon the senior living representative of the main descent line in the ruling clan. Though this rule of succession was founded in custom and sanctioned by law, the brothers of the incumbent not infrequently challenged his position. Sometimes a rival succeeded in usurping the throne. The supporters

---

[4] Except for persons publicly condemned as witches or traitors. After being stoned to death their corpses were thrown into the bush or forest.

of the usurper and their descendants rationalized the act of usurpation by ascribing fictional primogeniture to the usurper. In this way rebellions and political strife could develop and be resolved without the fundamental premises of law and custom being called into question or modified.

At other times, when such conflict developed, the contending lineal factions opposed each other by resort to arms. The outcome of the conflict was by no means certain, depending on numerous circumstances, including the personal qualities of each of the main contenders. Either or neither might win. The conclusion of the conflict almost invariably saw the secession of the losing faction or the division of the tribe into two or more parts. The splinter tribal sections either merged with similar groups or joined integral tribes. This oft-repeated process of bifurcation, a developmental concomitant of the rule of unilateral and primogenital succession, occurred among commoner families also, though to a lesser extent.

The ruling family in Ekunene was and still is the wealthiest in the tribe. Traditionally, riches were measured chiefly by the number of cattle and other stock that a man or group possessed. No one owned more cattle and goats than the Chief; no one had more wives or spears than he. No loyal subject was expected to possess or to have access to medicines and charms more potent than the Chief's.

Traditional African accounts of pre-Conquest social life in Ekunene always notice the large *umuzi* or hamlet, composed of an extended patrifamilial household, that existed in the past. There were no separate farms or disparate habitations consisting of elementary families living in comparative isolation, as there are in Polela today. Nor were widows and deserted wives to be found living with their children in separate *imizi*[5] of their own. The umuzi consisted of a patriarch or headman (*umnumzana*) who stood at the apex of its internal social control system. If his mother was living, she wielded influence and power beyond that of his wives, even his 'great wife'. The mother, or if she was deceased, the 'great wife', was the 'lady of the household' (*inkosikaz' yomuzi*).

The physical plan of the umuzi reflected in its ubiquitous basic pattern the status and social control system of its in-

---

[5] *Umuzi*, household (sing.); *imizi* (pl.).

habitants. A strong circular stockade made of stout poles, brush-wood, and thornbush enclosed a rough circle of beehive-shaped huts of light and portable construction. The main gate of the umuzi (A) was placed furthest away from the section of the principal wife (*ekunene*) (B) and the hut of the headman and his mother (C). (D) was the section of the umuzi occupied by the wife ranking highest after the 'great wife'. Subsequent wives and the wives of married sons of the 'great wife' or other wives were accommodated in huts 'attached' to either (C) or (D) in two arcs extending around the internal circum-ference of the outer stockade towards the main gate. The huts (E) and (F) nearest this gate, and on either side of it, generally housed the adolescent boys and young men of the whole umuzi. This arrangement was believed to favour the defensive needs of the umuzi and to guarantee maximum safety to the um-numzana, to the 'lady of the household', and to other members of the intimate family circle who lived in the rear of the umuzi. The adolescent girls also had their special huts, not far from the boys' quarters. Younger children slept in their mothers' huts. In the centre of the umuzi there was a large cattle byre (*isibaya*) (J), with one or more smaller calf and goat pens leading off it.

There appears to have been no tribal police force, yet there

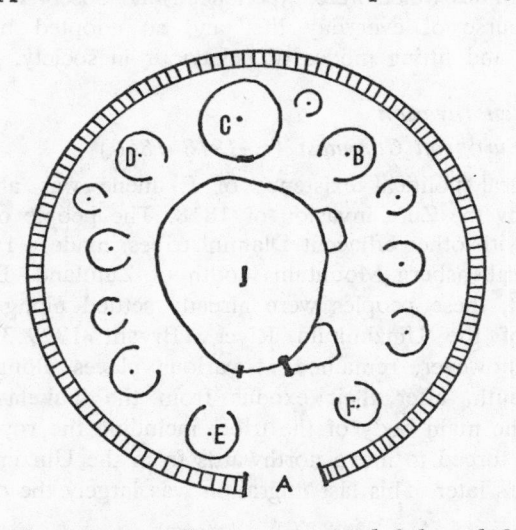

Figure 10 Plan of a pre-Conquest patriarchal household (umuzi).

were bodies such as household and clan councils capable of enforcing sanctions against civil and criminal offenders. Adultery, murder, slander, and theft were all regarded as civil delicts. Household or clan vengeance was frequently resorted to, but was generally limited and directed either by public pressure or the Chief's or induna's authority into the courts, where all efforts were directed towards reconciling the conflicting parties. Witchcraft and disloyalty to the Chief were the only recognised crimes. These were punishable by death.

There is no evidence of there having been a formal educational system, including a regular school of some sort. There is neither a tradition nor a remembrance of circumcision ever having been practised. Girls, however, attended an initiation school (*umgonqo*) soon after attaining puberty.[6] The whole practice of education was (with the exception of the short-term girls' school) informal. Children grew up in age-sets, and were permitted first and enabled later to pursue those activities most beneficial to themselves at each age, and most useful to the economic needs of their parental households. Adults generally took a kindly and indulgent interest in children. In normal domestic life it was an accepted practice for children to be seen *and* heard. Respect for rank and age were, however, implicit in the general body of social values which were experienced and observed by children in the course of everyday life, and so adopted by them as necessary and fitting modes of behaviour in society.

The Shakan Invasion
and the European Conquest (*c. 1818–1850*)

The integral political existence of Ekunene was abruptly terminated by the Zulu invasion of 1818. The people of Ekunene, together with other adjacent Dlamini tribes, made a rapid escape to the Drakensberg Mountains south of Zululand. By 1821, it is thought, these peoples were already settled along the higher reaches of the Umzimkulu River (Bryant 1929:382). Some sections, however, remained at various places along the route to the south, after their exodus from the Tukela-Umzinyathi region. The main body of the tribe, including the royal Ekunene clan, was forced to move northwards from the Umzimkulu about thirty years later. This last migration was largely the consequence

---

[6] Cf. Kohler (1933), for vernacular and translated texts describing traditional girls' initiation practices.

of an unsuccessful struggle with the British colonial administration and with European settlers.[7]

During this period attempts were made to resuscitate the Ekunene state as it was prior to the Shakan invasion. The emergence of a supreme Zulu monarchical state and ruling class, unchallenged by any other tribe or principality in Natal and Zululand, diminished the ritual and patriotic status of the Chief of Ekunene. Militarily, his army and state power were but a shadow of what they were formerly. It was now a refugee society seeking to re-establish itself by perpetuating the external forms of traditional custom and law in new and radically altered conditions. Many of the old ceremonies associated with the agricultural cycle were only partly carried out, and during the years of escape and wandering were often overlooked. The break-up of the tribe into several smaller units, often moving separately or seeking settlement in isolation from one another, led to the emergence of a new class of indunas or powerful abanumzana, who were relatively autonomous in their relationship to the old supreme chief. The basic family and household (umuzi) structure, however, underwent little change at this stage.

European Settlement and Its Consequences

European settlement appears to have begun in about 1870 in the Upper Umkomazi region, where the Dlamini Ekunene people had settled after their migration from the Umzimkulu region. It was viewed with apprehension both by the Chief of Ekunene and his people. Foremost among the European settlers were timber speculators who arrived in the area to clear the local forests of whatever good building and furniture timber could be found.[8] Some of the wood-cutters who operated in the Polela forests could not legally claim any rights to the timber they sent away to Pietermaritzburg, or to the forests where the timber was cut. Resolute action by the Ekunene tribal court led the cutters to seek negotiated 'concessions' from the reigning Chief at bargain prices. The Chief and his council agreed —in return for rifles, liquor, and cash—to the settlement of

---

[7] This traditional account has some corroboration in the recorded material presented by Bryant (1929:388–89).

[8] The timber was required for building purposes, wagon construction, and furniture in the rapidly growing provincial capital at Pietermaritzburg.

certain Europeans in Ekunene. The people believed they were extending rights of usufruct, but not of ownership. When the actions of the settlers appeared to overstep the limits of customary behaviour in respect of communal pasture and forest usage, skirmishes occurred between the people and the settlers. In particular, recurrent friction was generated by the settlers trying to enclose the land they thought most desirable for themselves.

The conflict did not develop on purely localized lines, however. The settlers banded together and called in police or military assistance, as the need for deciding an issue became pressing. The numerous petty tribes and ex-tribal fragments in the area were disunited and could offer no concerted resistance. One by one they were dispossessed of their land and brought into the tax-paying system. In Ekunene much valuable arable land across the Umkomazi was lost, together with the Nkumba, Marwaqa, and other forest areas in the heart of the 'country'. In the period 1875–1885 an increasing number of farmer settlers arrived and took possession of yet more land in and around Ekunene. Local European administration was set up in 1876. From that time onwards there has been a steady diminution of the political power of Ekunene, destroying its independence. These political developments were accompanied by the submergence of most of the distinctive culture of Ekunene, and the dislocation of the traditional closed system of institutionalized social rankings and relationships.

The significant changes in social structure occurred not immediately after the Shakan invasion, but after and as a result of European conquest. The Shakan invasion had not led to any fundamental changes in the techniques of production nor in the pattern of social relationships, for the social and economic system of the Zulu conquerors was hardly different from that of Ekunene. But later, when Europeans began to dispossess the people of Ekunene of their limited arable lands in the mountainous Umkomazi region, land shortage became a key issue upon which relations both within and without the society hinged. Bitter conflict occurred, on the one hand between European settlers and African peasants, and on the other hand between the African peasants themselves. The Chief also entered into the competition for land, and thus became a rival of his subjects. Such competition had not existed in olden Ekunene, where there was no land shortage.

The land shortage and the compulsion to find money with which to pay Government taxes drove men to leave their homes and seek work with Europeans. The necessity of being clothed while in employment, of purchasing food, and the desire for possessing various European commodities created new needs among the Ekunene peasantry. Young men were now able to procure imported material goods which older and more highly ranked men frequently did not have the means to acquire. Patterns of absolute filial obedience began to be supplanted by ambivalent responses which gave rise to conflict. Adult sons began to desert their fathers or to leave the patriarchal household, setting up smaller imizi of their own. The customary modes of showing respect to clan and family elders lost their binding character, since the sanctions which formerly guaranteed their effectiveness could no longer be enforced. The collapse of political power in Ekunene was not followed up by the establishment of a new and positive regime offering an alternative social and moral existence. Instead, the people were left to adjust themselves to a domestic economy impoverished through European spoliation, and to a decaying tribal life which scorned the present and looked back to moral and cultural values of the society before it was conquered. In place of a uniform and integrated moral system buttressed by law and custom, there were now alternative and conflicting possibilities of moral action and response. In this context uncertainty, ambiguity, and ambivalence in social relationships flourished, showing themselves in fear, suspicion, and anxiety.

Modern Political and Social Structure

In matters concerning the ideology of kingship, there is little of the former intense ritual and mythical emphasis on the function and powers of the inkosi. No one now thinks of Vusindaba, the present incumbent of the Dlamini Ekunene royal line, as the king. He is known to be a relatively unimportant and minor chief in the eyes of the European administration; besides, all the inhabitants of Ekunene, like all the citizens of South Africa, are known to be the subjects of the Queen of England.

The principle of primogenital succession and status has now largely lost its traditional significance in the majority of families.

More than 80 per cent of the people are converted Christians and therefore monogamists. With only one wife the conflict over inheritance has become transposed from rivalry between the first-born sons of the different wives and their 'houses', to the opposing claims of the first-born son and the subsequent children. Though primogeniture still determines the *law* of inheritance and succession, in practice most fathers attempt to divide their property between their children before death. Some of these parents favour the alteration of the present customary laws so that property may be equally divided between all the sons, or between all the children. In the Chief's family, however, the importance of the principle persists. The eldest son is jealously guarded, and is subjected to 'strengthening' from the dangers of bewitchment or poisoning by potential enemies or rivals. These latter practices are viewed with impatience by many of his 'progressive' subjects; others smile indulgently at his backwardness and credulity.

The Ekunene section of the Dlamini peoples is now no longer the 'principal' or 'right-hand' branch. The nearby Amakhuze section is now numerically larger and enjoys a higher status, partly as a result of its more vigorous opposition to European government both in the past and present. No one in Ekunene, apart from the Chief and some of his councillors, regarded this shift of political status as a structural inconsistency.

Though there is a tribal court, any subject of the Chief can appeal to the European magistrate[9] at Polela against a judgement of this court. The Chief need not even be given notice of the appeal by the appellant. Furthermore, the Chief's court is not now legally competent to deal with criminal cases, or with civil cases involving Europeans either as plaintiffs or defendants. No European, to my knowledge, has ever appeared as a witness in the tribal court. These factors have combined to reduce the prestige of the tribal court. Some people told me that although in former times strict justice was practised, bribery and corruption now weigh heavily in determining the outcome of a suit. I was unable to validate or reject the correctness of this assertion, but intend to enquire further into the matter during a subsequent field tour.

In the field of ritual there are now few survivals of traditional practice. The first-fruits ceremony has not been practised since

---

[9] In his capacity of District Native Commissioner.

1902, and no one nowadays awaits the Chief's permission to eat new maize or other foods. Furthermore, peasants begin to plough and plant whenever they wish, without awaiting the inception of the seasonal activity at the capital.

The Chief still possesses more livestock—the traditional form of wealth—than anyone else. In a recent legal suit brought against him by some of his subjects, it was claimed that he had used his official position unlawfully to monopolize the grazing rights in a Government-trust farm where grazing is restricted by proclamation. Part of the reaction of the Chief to this unprecedented act of opposing him at a supra-tribal level was to accuse the leaders of the 'opposition' and their sympathizers of attempting to destroy him by sorcery and witchcraft. The Chief has for many years steered clear of the district in which the 'opposition' is centred; he neither eats nor drinks, nor attends any ceremonies or meetings there.

Some of his subjects now have larger cash incomes than the Chief. Most of these subjects have advanced their education considerably further than that of the Chief and the members of his family. They desire to be represented at the meetings and deliberations of the Chief-in-Council, but the latter body has not invited them to do so, nor has the European administration made arrangements for a more representative system of government to be introduced into Ekunene. The Chief, his Councillors, and the conservative section of the tribe are jealous of the material wealth of the rising professional and 'middle' class, and are apprehensive about its claims to greater participation in the formulation of tribal policy and in the government of the tribe generally.

There has been no striking change in the internal production system in Ekunene since European conquest. No industries of any description have been established either in Ekunene or elsewhere in Location No 2, Polela. Within the ward traditional peasant agriculture and animal husbandry are practised. These occupations constitute the backbone of the internal system of production. Because of the land shortage (leading to food shortages and the absence of any kind of surplus produce) and the need to earn money for payment of taxes, educational fees, and imported foodstuffs, the people are constrained to depend for their subsistence, not on their peasant pursuits in Ekunene, but on cash wages earned for the most part outside the Location.

The majority of able-bodied men in Ekunene are employed as unskilled labourers in the service of Europeans, generally a hundred or more miles from Ekunene.

Agriculture is confined to the cultivation of the cereal staples, maize and sorghum, amongst which beans and cucurbits are often undersown. There are no tractors or combines in use. The soil is worked by means of ox-drawn metal ploughs, and in the case of the Chief and a few other relatively well-off men, with harrows and disc cultivators. Many poorer people, especially widows and deserted wives, work the land exclusively by hoe. The severe land shortage has led to the overcropping of existing arable lands, resulting in the rapid and unchecked depletion of soil and vegetation resources referred to above. It has, furthermore, induced men to bring under cultivation areas which were formerly reserved for pasturage, especially the steeper hill slopes.

The increase in the rate of migrant labour in the course of the last half century is closely related to the changed economic needs and social patterns of family life and household organization. Sample studies indicated that there were between eight and eleven times more imizi in 1948 than in 1905. Older men say that their fathers summoned neighbours to beer-drinks and other gatherings by blowing a horn which was heard far down and across the valleys. Nowadays groups of imizi are so closely packed together that one umuzi may be within calling distance of half a dozen others. The average number of inhabitants per umuzi has decreased considerably since 1905, except in the case of the Chief's and some headmen's imizi. In a sample study of two districts of Ekunene I carried out in 1949, the structure of the families composing 170 peasant households was as follows:

Type of family structure	No.	Per cent
Elementary family[1]	87	51.2
Matrinuclear family[2]	42	24.7
Extended patriarchal family or joint fraternal family	36	21.2
Amorphous (bachelors, etc.)	5	2.9
Total no. of households	170	100.0

[1] Composed of a husband and wife and their child(ren).

[2] Composed of a widow or deserted wife or unmarried mother with her child (ren).

The sample indicated that the dominant type of family now-adays is the simple elementary family. Polygynous, patriarchal extended family households have tended to break up, though still 21.2 per cent of the sample fell into this category. Most of the latter, however, were extended only in a horizontal sense, i.e. where married brothers were sharing a joint household. The second largest group is the matrinuclear type, with 24.7 per cent of the total. This type is a modification or incomplete component of the fully constituted elementary family. In the latter 42 households the actual household heads (abanumzana) are women, though the men in the society do not allow them to be considered as such officially.

The changed structure of the majority of families in Ekunene is reflected in the changed patterns of hut arrangement in the umuzi. Nowadays few imizi have a right-hand and a left-hand section; only a handful are built in a circular formation about a central cattle byre, and none of the huts nowadays are shaped like beehives. Almost all huts are built either of brick, concrete blocks, or wattle and daub. Most are conically, but an increasing number are rectangular with internal room divisions.

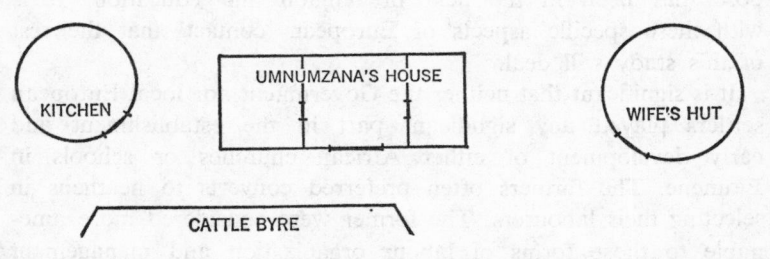

Figure 11 Plan of an elementary family household in Ekunene.

Generally the wife and mother nowadays have increased social responsibility in the home and in communal life. While many of their husbands are cooking and cleaning the homes of their European employers, the wives are felling trees, chopping wood, budgeting for the family, and arranging the children's education, in addition to performing their traditional tasks under the old division of labour (housekeeping and hoeing). A small but growing number of women have, after obtaining a formal educa-tion in mission schools, entered professional life as teachers, health assistants, and nurses. The majority of women, however, are tied to the strenuous task of rearing children in conditions of poverty and malignant malnutrition, and amidst the widespread disruption of those traditional sanctions which guaranteed minimal standards of public and private morality. Medical personnel at the Polela Health Centre[10] believed that there was a greater load of nervous strain upon women than upon men, and that the load is generally increasing. Neurotic illness, in the opinion of responsible persons in the society and of several of the P.H.C. doctors, is widespread in all sections of the society, even among 'progressives' and practising Christians. This latter fact is perplexing and irritating to many European missionaries and educators, because Africans believe these neurotic illnesses are caused by witchcraft or sorcery, things in which practising Christians and educated men are not expected to believe.

The Imposition by Europeans
of Programmes of Social Amelioration

The chief work of planned European intrusion and influence exerted within Ekunene, pursuing a professed ameliorative purpose, has been in the field of religion and education. It is with these specific aspects of European 'contact' that the rest of this study will deal.

It is significant that neither the Government nor local European settlers played any significant part in the establishment and early development of either African churches or schools in Ekunene. The farmers often preferred converts to heathens in selecting their labourers. The former were considered more amenable to those forms of labour organization and management that have evolved on South African farms. Since the earliest times European farmers in Polela have individually and sometimes in organized groups deprecated or distrusted programmes and actions directed towards the extension of education among Africans.

Christian evangelizing activity commenced soon after the arrival of the first missionaries in neighbouring districts. A few

---

10 The Polela Health Centre (P.H.C.), concerned with community health promotion in an area including most of Ekunene, was established by the Union Government in 1940. Its headquarters are within half a mile of Komkhulu, the Chief's village.

settlers had previously converted some of their African labourers. Informants in Ekunene, however, believed that the significance of these early conversions was small because the converts remained 'uneducated people'. This refers to the fundamental linking of religion and education in the minds of the people. Only by grasping the close historical affinity and interdependence of these two cultural forces in their impact upon Ekunene society can the present-day ambivalence of almost all the adults in relation to education be comprehended.

The first Christian missionaries combined evangelism with education. Until recently most people in Ekunene considered a Christian and an educated person to be synonymous. If you wanted to receive an education you had to be a Christian, or at least to adopt the external semblance of a practising Christian. The missionary churches themselves soon realized that the strength of each particular denomination and local station depended more on the kind of social service it could extend to the African community than on any other factor.

In the light of experiences derived from their first contacts with Europeans, the people of Ekunene were ill-disposed towards receiving into their midst any Europeans. Every action of the missionaries was viewed with the utmost suspicion. Every personal 'contact' in Ekunene was regarded as a collaborator and potential enemy of the people. When the missionaries attempted rational argument with the people they usually found that the facts of revelation were treated with matter-of-fact incredulity. Only through offering to educate the people did the first missionaries make any headway whatever. Aged informants told me, in 1949, that the Chief and his Councillors in this period advised their people that since they had been overcome by the military weapons of the white man, they should henceforth try to master his book knowledge and so prepare to overcome their conquerors.

The Presbyterian Church was the first to initiate religious and educational work in Ekunene. The first church-school buildings[11] were erected in about 1905. A few years later the Roman Catholic missionary organization initiated work in Ekunene, start-

---

[11] Nowhere in Ekunene are there any buildings which were constructed or used exclusively as schools. All the five present-day schools are housed in churches.

ing schools and even opening a nunnery[12]. There was a considerable movement away from Presbyterianism towards Roman Catholicism. Later the Anglican and Methodist Churches followed suit in establishing themselves in Ekunene. There was a period of bitter rivalry between the various missions. Although the Presbyterians lost much ground, they still retain considerable influence. Their chief asset is the Presbyterian missionary headquarters in Polela, situated just outside the western boundary of Ekunene. At this centre there is a model primary school, a secondary, and a technical school, objects of high regard to most people in Ekunene. It is instructive to note, however, that owing to the concentration of resources on the development of their central secondary education centre, the Presbyterians have neglected the development of the primary schools within the Location. The result of this policy has been a steady decline in the proportion of Ekunene to non-Ekunene entrants to the post-primary college. The teachers and parents of school children in Ekunene, while desiring the progressive development of the college, are displeased about the backwardness of the schools in the Location. It is said that the missionaries are concerned only with building their own renown; that they behave autocratically and are hostile to Africans in refusing to be guided by the expressed needs of the people, or at least to plan development with, rather than for, the people of Ekunene.

Teachers in Ekunene complain about the severity of the moral code demanded by mission school teachers, the autocratic manner of mission school 'grantees', and the slow progress of extending educational work. All the teachers with whom I discussed the question, with the exception of some Roman Catholic teachers, preferred an exclusively state-controlled educational system to missionary control or surveillance. The missionary programme for the advancement of education is considered sluggish and inadequate to the needs of the community. The mission churches, on the other hand, witnessing a tendency towards the rejection of Christian religion and ideology, are more determined than ever that they should retain control or supervision (in the case of state-aided schools) over the schools in Ekunene. The Christian programme of providing an attractive and needful service for the

---

[12] The nunnery closed down before the outbreak of the Second World War.

people has miscarried. Neither the common people nor the intelligentsia have been able to feel themselves part of the central planning and directing authority of Christian enterprise. The early enthusiasm of the first converts who helped to build the church-schools has passed. It is said that the missionaries themselves have been overcome by the prevalent racialist conceptions of the majority of Europeans in South Africa.

The movement towards a rejection of European and mission control has been growing generally in Natal during the last thirty years at least. Numerous independent or 'separatist' African churches have come into being, many about a nuclear parent church congregation, or centred about a recalcitrant ecclesiastic[13]. In Ekunene, though the success of the separatist and the independent churches has not been as marked as elsewhere, their influence has been felt. The 'Bidiya Church'[14] is said to have been the first independent church in Ekunene which broke away from the Presbyterians. Here a complex association of modified Christian concepts and practices with aspects of ancestor worship has occurred. Bidiya adherents told me that they are the 'true' Christians, since the 'white' missionaries and other 'white' Christians have turned against God and Christ in their treatment of Africans. They assert that all the children of God are equal, but that the 'white' and 'black' members of the 'European denominations' are not treated in this way.

On the whole the separatist churches have achieved even less success than the 'independents' in Ekunene. In the case of the Presbyterian Church, the tendency to fission was forestalled by the official establishment of a separate 'Bantu Presbyterian Church'. This move met with limited success for a few years. But conflict between African ministers of the Church and the European missionaries is still present. The indications in 1948–49 were that it is increasing.

Church attendance everywhere in Ekunene is very small. On some Sundays I have seen less than a dozen men, women, and children at a church service. Some men told me that the church is 'the women's club'. By contrast, a hundred or more people may attend a feast and beer-drink in the same neighbourhood. Most preachers attack the 'backsliding' of their

---

[13] Cf. Sundkler (1948), for a detailed study of the separatist problem.
[14] The word 'Bidiya' is a corruption of 'Presbyterian'.

own adherents, rather than the non-Christian ancestor worshippers, for as we have noted above, more than 80 per cent of the population has been formally converted.

In advancing the work of evangelization, the missionaries have sought to attack and undermine almost all the basic values and customs of pre-Conquest Ekunene society. Sermons from the pulpit, exhortations to the parents of school children, school dramatic performances—all have been used to wage a constant war against the practice of polygyny, girls' initiation, ancestor propitiation, and the holding of traditional ceremonies associated with the life and seasonal cycles. Traditional dress was condemned as the mark of savagery. In political matters the churches did little more than justify the political dominance of Europeans and the poverty of the people in their congested reservation, by referring to the sins of the people before European Conquest, and more especially in the pre-Shakan era.

Although such dogma is unrelated to the central religious themes of Christian belief, it has profoundly influenced the view men have of the worth of their own society and culture. For many years there tended to be a resigned acceptance of the rationale, if not the truth, of this dogma. During the last ten years the growth of industrialism and the African national movement in South Africa have influenced the thinking of both the intelligentsia living in Ekunene and the migrant labourers employed in the cities. Esteem for the values, customs, and traditions of the past, especially the pre-Christian ideology, is being recovered, even among pious Christians. The latter are less afraid to admit a practical toleration or interest in traditionalism (which everywhere conflicts with what is officially described as Christian dogma), and have attempted to justify their attitudes and actions before the enquiring or rebuking missionary. The expulsion from the Protestant Churches of prominent members of the congregation, for sins which are not treated as unethical in the traditional moral system[15], is not uncommon. I was always surprised by the equanimity with which a punished person and other lay members of the congregation accepted the decision of the missionary authorities. In some cases, how-

---

[15] There is only a distant link between religion and ethics in non-Christian life.

ever, expulsion or suspension has not encouraged penitence, but, on the contrary, has stimulated separatism or agnosticism.

The unilateral aspect of the Government's administration in Ekunene has, in matters of education, as in other spheres, induced a characteristic reticence towards the whole ediface of education as it is now constituted. Nevertheless, the overwhelming majority of parents want their children to be educated in schools. They believe that education will enable their children to obtain better jobs and increased incomes. Education is valued and sought after in the belief that it offers some prospect of departure from the chronic poverty, material inadequacy, social dislocation, and cultural vacuity of contemporary life in Ekunene.

The education of the people did not concern the Government in the first years after the administration began to operate effectively in Ekunene. This was regarded as a sphere of endeavour best handled by voluntary agencies, in particular mission churches. The latter undertook the task of educating the people, regarding their work of enlightenment as a sacred trust. Each mission church, as it commenced its educational work in the area, developed a programme of activity (modified subsequently in the light of actual experience, and of the financial resources and broad lines of policy of each of the parent Churches), either implicitly or explicitly. In no single instance where I was able to record the history of the establishment of the five elementary schools in Ekunene was there any evidence of the mission authorities having sought the active co-operation of the Chief or his Councillors in determining how the school should be planned and built, what the curriculum should include, what the specific aim of the education to be provided should be, and so forth. The most that was done was the securing of the Chief's permission to erect a structure (of wattle and daub, or corrugated iron—in four of the five schools), and to convert him and thus win his support for the plans and actions decided upon by the European missionary.

What part in the work of encouraging educational and other 'progressive' works do the 'educated' members of the society take? Most of the men and women who have received a post-primary education at mission schools outside Ekunene[16] have

---

[16] There are no facilities for post-primary education within Ekunene apart from the post-secondary training course for health assistants at the P.H.C.

been attracted by the possibility of obtaining professional employment in or near their homes in Ekunene. Less than a third have been able to do so because of the small number of professional posts available.[17]

Those teachers, health assistants, and others employed in Ekunene place a fundamentally positive evaluation upon many but not all the plans and programmes for social and material amelioration. They oppose the Government's attempts to cull cattle and to impose compulsory 'betterment schemes', which they regard as calculated attempts to impoverish the people. But they support the cause of education, scientific, medical, and health work, agricultural improvement, and soil conservation. In none of these spheres, however, do they consider that genuine concern for the people's welfare and progress are the prime considerations which motivate Government policy and administrative practice. Such concern would inevitably have expressed itself in the principle that the active co-operation of the people through its chosen representatives is a *sine qua non* of progressive social interaction.

Notwithstanding their well-formulated reservations, however, the teachers and other professional workers generally work conscientiously and courageously to make the Chief, his Councillors, and the more conservative members of the community receptive to the work of education, social medicine, and so forth. The reaction to such efforts is ambivalent, as is so much else in the attitudes of the people to the agents and vehicles of social change as it is conceived and practised by Europeans. The teachers and health workers often earn the reputation of being collaborators or traitors. The teachers have defended their actions in supporting the missionaries who built the churches, by pointing out that every additional church has become an additional school. The teachers have also approached the Chief and Councillors with a view to enlisting their support for encouraging better school attendance. Many parents connive at their children playing truant since they do not value the kind of education their children are receiving; others say that the three or four years required in the primary school to acquire the three R's are wasteful; yet others believe that the local schooling is unlikely

---

[17] The proportion employed in Ekunene increased considerably after the establishment of the P.H.C. in 1940.

to equip a pupil for his post-school life. But it is again necessary to stress the fact that everyone I know in Ekunene wants education for their children; many adults want to educate themselves also.[18] Some people, including both educated and 'conservative' individuals, place much faith in the educational and political advantages to be derived from a 'tribal school'. The Chief has been urged to promote the establishment of such a school, but nothing concrete has yet been achieved (October 1952), owing to the organization of the people's forces and resources for other, more important, activities.

In the course of the past five years the Government has grown alarmed about the increasing congestion in the Location, and the accompanying soil erosion and denudation of vegetable resources. Plans have been prepared for the 'rehabilitation' of native agriculture. These are based on a programme of stock culling and pasture control. Fencing and limitation of pastures for stock grazing were introduced some years ago. In most cases the regulations have been systematically flouted. The Government has threatened the offenders, but usually delayed taking punitive action. More recent concrete plans for commencing stock culling have been drawn up. The Magistrate, in his capacity of Native Commissioner, and officials of the Government Native Affairs Department have tried to persuade the people and their representatives of the necessity for agreeing to stock culling. The Africans do not believe, however, that with less stock and fewer grazing rights they will be economically or socially better off. The determination of the Government to impose this 'betterment plan', despite popular opposition, is transforming the character of popular opposition from reticence, negativism, and subtle sabotage to more overt and direct forms of resistance.

---

[18] At least eight adults I knew were pursuing secondary or post-secondary studies by correspondence in 1949.

14 THE DUTCH COLONIAL PERIOD IN INDONESIA: AGRICULTURAL INVOLUTION

Clifford Geertz

Just as the progress of a disease shows a doctor the secret life of a body, so to the historian the progress of a great calamity yields valuable information about the nature of the society so stricken.

Marc Bloch

THE COLONIAL PERIOD: FOUNDATIONS

The Company

A T THE INCEPTION of the colonial period . . . the over-all ecological pattern was fairly well set: on Java, a wet-rice [sawah] agrarian heartland shading off into less developed regions to the west, east, and north; in the Outer Islands, an immense tropical forest worked only here and there by small tribes of swidden farmers.* The first object of interest of the Dutch, as of the Portuguese who immediately preceded them, were the Moluccas, the fabled spice islands; but their attention soon turned toward Java, and it is upon it that they mainly superimposed their colonial economy, turning back again to the Outer Islands only toward the end of the past century.

"Superimposed" is the proper word, because what the Dutch

SOURCE: Clifford Geertz, chapter 4, "The Colonial Period: Foundations," and chapter 5, "The Colonial Period: Florescence," *Agricultural Involution*, University of California Press, 1963. Reprinted by permission of the author and publisher.

* Swidden, or "slash and burn" agriculture, is described in detail in Geertz (1963b:ch. 2.) Ed.

were essentially concerned to do, from 1619 to 1942, was to pry agricultural products out of the archipelago, and particularly out of Java, which were saleable on world markets without changing fundamentally the structure of the indigenous economy. The Netherlands was never able, particularly after William I's attempt to re-absorb Belgium failed, to develop a manufacture export economy even remotely comparable to that of Britain, and so the interest of the Dutch in Indonesia remained overwhelmingly mercantilist to the end. The stimulation in Indonesia of extensive markets for industrial goods, it was feared, would lead only to increased British (or, later, Japanese) influence; the essential economic task was to maintain a decent differential between the import and re-export prices of East Indian agricultural products—a task which implied the developing of Dutch commercial institutions and the discouraging of Indonesian ones.[1] Amid the apparent fluctuations of policy, the colonial period consists, from the economic point of view, of one long attempt to bring Indonesia's crops into the modern world, but not her people.

The means for accomplishing this effort to keep the natives native and yet get them to produce for world markets was the formation of a chronically, and in fact intrinsically, unbalanced economic structure sometimes referred to as "dual."[2] In the export sector, there was administrative capitalism: a system in

[1] The one exception, and that but a partial one, to this generalization was the export of textiles to Indonesia from Twente after 1870. See van Klaaveren (1955:pp. 133–136, 138, 164, 192). Of course, East India products did not have to be carried to Holland before being "re-exported," but could be taken directly to foreign ports (from 1928–1939 about 90 percent of them were—see Boeke 1947:105).

[2] Boeke (1953). The fact that Boeke's theoretical explanations for dualism were largely unsound, his pessimistic assessment of its policy implications arbitrary, and his views concerning Indonesian (or "Eastern") "mentality" fanciful (see Higgins 1956) ought not to obscure the fact, as it sometimes has, that, although mal-integration of labor-intensive and capital-intensive sectors is a general phenomenon, in the Netherlands East Indies economy this mal-integration was present to an extraordinarily high degree; and that Boeke recognized this fact, even if he did not understand the reasons for it, as early as his 1910 Leiden dissertation, long before the modern concern with "factor proportions," "multi-sector models" and "discontinuous investment functions" made it seem like an analytical commonplace. For the half-century debate between Boeke and his critics in Holland, the bulk of it rather beside the point, see *Indonesian Economics* (1961).

which the holders of capital, the Dutch, regulated selling prices and wages, controlled output, and even dictated the processes of production. In the domestic sector there was family-unit agriculture, a little home industry, and some petty internal trade. As the first expanded, stimulated by rising world commodity prices, the second contracted; land and labor were taken out of rice and other village staples and put into sugar, indigo, coffee, tobacco, and other commercial crops. As the first contracted, responding to collapsing international markets, the second expanded, and a steadily growing peasant population attempted to compensate for a lost money income, to which it had become increasingly accustomed, by intensified production of subsistence crops. . . .

East Indian colonial history was marked by a series of politico-economic devices (the East India Company, the Culture System, the Corporate Plantation System) by means of which the European "merchant capitalism" side of the dual economy was to be more efficiently organized for the production and marketing of export crops, and the Indonesian "peasant household" side was to be better protected against the disruptive effects of this large-scale commercial agriculture. Driven on by ever-increasing capital requirements, the Dutch moved from the institutional contrivances of adventurous capitalism in the eighteenth century, to those of state capitalism in the nineteenth, and to those of bureaucratic capitalism in the twentieth. But, as each contrivance or device, building upon the ruins of its predecessor, entailed a yet deeper penetration of the rural economy by Western enterprise, it actually made it more difficult to isolate native life from the economic forces with which such enterprise deals. Modern Indonesia was created both because of Dutch policies and in spite of them.

The Dutch East India Company, the first of these devices, was formed in 1602 as a state-chartered far-eastern trade syndicate with considerable autonomy ("a state within a state") in order to counter the active competition of both Asiatic merchants and other European powers trafficking around the archipelago.[3] At first, the Company was only interested in commerce—in securing

---

[3] The Company's activities were of course not confined to the Indonesian area. The best book on its commercial aspects is Glamann (1958). For its social impact in Indonesia, see Gonggrijp (1957:181–321).

by hook or by crook whatever products might be carried from
places where they abounded to those where they were scarce.
Aside from its depredations in the Moluccas, something of a
landmark in the history of mercantile brutality, its initial impact
was mainly concentrated, therefore, in the passage ports of the
Java Sea, and particularly in those dotting Java's north coast. But,
in an age of rampant mercantilism, the catchword is not "business
is business" but "trade follows the flag": commercial development
implies political expansion. The Company—"tired of the forcing
up of tolls and market taxes and the constant giving of presents
to rulers and lords"—soon turned toward gaining a more comprehensive control over sources of supply (Schrieke 1955:62).
By 1684 it dominated all of Sunda; by 1743 the entire Pasisir
and most of the East Hook; by 1755 the Kedjawén. (The
Moluccas had been in hand since about 1660.) What began as
a trade combine ended, not without struggle, as a sovereign. . . .

The Company, adjusting to local conditions, functioned in
diverse ways in different parts of its realm. But its activities
everywhere worked toward the same end: the reduction of indigenous chiefs to dependents and the substitution of tribute
for trade.

In the Moluccas, the luckless source of cloves and nutmeg, the
Dutch imposed restriction of cultivation, collective punishment
(for "smuggling"), and forced labor exercised through the agency
of humbled native rulers. In the pepper areas, Bantam-Lampong
and, to a lesser extent, central Sumatra, treaties with harbor sultans
established quotas and fixed prices. In the Priangan highlands
coffee gardens were introduced with traditional aristocrats acting
as the Company's labor contractors. Immediately around Batavia
and the adjoining northwest coast, there were nearly a hundred
private sugar estates, leased from local lordlings now converted
to Company employees, the proprietors of which (almost all
Chinese) consequently exercised seignorial rights over the villagers
who chanced to live on them. And in still but half-subdued central
Java were simple levies in rice, timber, cotton thread, beans, and
cash. By the time the Company dissolved in bankruptcy on the
last day of the eighteenth century, it had laid down the general
lines which the Netherlands East Indies economy followed to the
end.

But only the general lines. The Company established the Dutch
presence in the archipelago, introduced a few new cultivations

(mainly coffee; pepper, spices, and sugar preceded it) and devised, in rough form, most of the techniques for skimming cash crops off the surface of an immobilized subsistence economy which later became so useful when Java filled up with peasants. But its impact on the Indonesian ecological pattern as a whole was marginal and unsystematic. It capitalized on it where it could, demanding deliveries, fixing prices, restricting trade but, with a few exceptions, such as the decimation of Banda, it did not attempt to act upon it directly. Its work was pioneering; consolidation of the approach it established came after it with the next major scheme to make Indonesia pay—the Culture System.

The Culture System

The Culture System[4] . . .—the remission of the peasant's land taxes in favor of his undertaking to cultivate government-owned export crops on one-fifth of his fields or, alternatively, to work sixty-six days of his year on government-owned estates or other projects—was only part of a much larger complex of politico-economic policies and institutions. Alongside the mammoth state plantation which this system tended to make of Java, there was a whole series of adjuncts, related systems, and independent growths, so that the picture of the island from 1830 to 1870 is a much more differentiated and much less static one than that which has so often been drawn for us. And yet, in spite of this, in spite of the fact that it never encompassed more than about 6 percent of Java's cultivated land or about a quarter of her people in any one year, and although it was only fully applied for perhaps two decades, van den Bosch's miraculous invention ("less taxes but more Government revenue!" as de Graff exclaims in

---

[4] *Cultuurstelsel.* Properly, this term ought to be Englished as "Cultivation System," but the "Culture System" mistranslation is so embedded in the literature that it seems less confusing to continue to employ it. A great deal has been written about the Culture System (see, for example, the bibliography in Reinsma 1955:183–189), but much of it has been marred by focus on its short-run impact at the expense of its long-run effects, and in particular by an anxious concern with its immediate moral justifiability (or lack thereof) rather than its importance as part of the crystallizing Colonial pattern in Indonesia and the role it consequently played in the formation of modern Indonesian society. The most important exception to this stricture is the discussion by Burger (1939: 117–160).

mock wonder) does define the period (de Graaf 1949:407).
And the period defines the age: ecologically, at any rate, it was
the most decisive of the Dutch era, the classic stage of colonial
history as the Company was the formative.

The System, in this larger sense, was decisive in at least three
ways. By its intense concentration on Java it gave a final form to
the extreme contrast between Inner Indonesia and Outer which
thenceforth merely deepened. It stabilized and accentuated the
dual economy pattern of a capital-intensive Western sector and
a labor-intensive Eastern one by rapidly developing the first and
rigorously stereotyping the second, a gulf which also subsequently
merely widened as Dutch investment grew. And, most important
of all, it prevented the effects on Javanese peasantry and gentry
alike of an enormously deeper Western penetration into their life
from leading to autochthonous agricultural modernization at the
point it could most easily have occurred. Such charges, more
serious than those usually leveled against the System by its enemies (that it was brutal, corrupt or uneconomic), demand, clearly,
both explication and substantiation.

The impact of the Culture System upon indigenous Javanese
agriculture was, of course, mainly exercised through the agency
of the cultivations it imposed as substitutes for money taxes.[5]
Under its aegis, virtually every crop which at the time might
conceivably be grown with profit was attempted: indigo, sugar,
coffee, tea, tobacco, pepper, cinchona, cinnamon, cotton, silk,
cocheneale. . . . Almost all these experiments, save coffee and,
most spectacularly, sugar, eventually failed; but the effect of this
tinkering with the established ecosystems was nonetheless profound. Today almost none of these crops are of central importance in Indonesian exports, which—minerals aside—are
dominated by rubber and copra. But they established the matrix
within which the present farming system, steadily replacing profit-
less crops with profitable ones, matured, and, in fact, over-
ripened.

In these terms, the imposed crops of the Culture System sorted
themselves out into two broad categories: annuals (sugar, indigo,
tobacco), which could be grown on sawahs in rotation with rice;
and perennials (coffee, tea, pepper, and less important cinchona

---

[5] For a history of taxation practices in Java up to 1816, see Bastin
(1957).

and cinnamon) which could not.[6] As a result, these two cultivations developed sharply contrasting modes of interaction with the established biotic communities into which they were projecting, by order of the King. . . .

The two main cultivations, the only ones which occupied much land, absorbed significant quantities of labor, showed important profit, or exercised a lasting influence on the general structure of the peasant economy, were sugar on the annuals side and coffee on the perennials, and they may be taken as type cases.[7]

Sugar demands irrigation (and drainage) and a general environment almost identical to that for wet rice; thus, it was almost of necessity initially cultivated on peasant sawah, for the most part under the one-fifth remission of land-tax procedure.[8] Coffee prefers a highland setting, does not need irrigation, and requires a relatively constant labor force rather than the seasonally variable one of sugar; thus, it was grown on so-called "waste" (that is,

---

[6] This point has been particularly well emphasized by van Klaveren, (1955:18–19, 118, 120).

[7] In 1830, coffee accounted for about 36 percent of Netherlands East Indies exports by value, sugar for about 13 percent; for 1850, the figures are 32 percent and 30 percent; for 1870, 43 percent and 45 percent. Calculated from Furnivall, 1944, pp. 129, 169. For a while, indigo was important, particularly in some dense sawah areas (see, for example, van Doorn 1926:37–38). But it never proved very profitable and eventually became almost completely replaced by sugar as the latter flourished. In 1840 indigo accounted for nearly 9 percent of the export value; by 1870 for about 3 percent (Furnivall, as above), and eventually the invention of synthetic dyes removed it from the scene more or less altogether. Coffee and sugar largely dominated the later phases of the Company period too: see Day (1904:66–70).

[8] In the indirectly ruled principalities of Surakarta and Jogjakarta, to which this procedure did not formally extend, it was cultivated under the seignorial village-lease system (in which the entrepreneurs rented what were essentially political rights over the villages and the villagers who lived in them from the Javanese aristocracy) which had by now migrated from its original foothold on the northwest coast and shifted from Chinese to European hands. In a few special areas, such as the still sparsely settled Surabaja delta, the quasi-private entrepreneurs rented the necessary sawah and hired the required labor from village authorities on a cash-and-carry basis, usually with capital advanced by the government on condition that the crops produced be sold to it at contracted prices. But these latter systems added up to mere variations on the basic approach—the establishment of a symbiosis between the Javanese subsistence economy and the Dutch commercial economy. For a description of these variant arrangements, see Reinsma (1955:125–159).

uncultiv*ated,* not uncultiv*able*) land, for the most part under the labor-tax procedure. Sugar obligations were measured in terms of units of land per village which had to be devoted to its cultivation; coffee assessments were levied in terms of the number of trees each conscripted family had to care for.[9] It would be expected, then, that sugar, integrated into the sawah regime, would become a peasant crop and coffee, isolated from peasant agriculture, would become an estate crop. Instead, however, in the final three decades of the Colonial Period, about 60 percent of Indonesia's coffee production was coming from (almost entirely Outer Island) small holders, and more than 95 percent of her sugar production (still wholly confined to Java) from Dutch-owned corporate plantations.[10]

This paradox dissolves, however, when the mutualistic and "exclusivistic" relationships are considered. In the mutualistic relationship, the expansion of one side, sugar cultivation, brings with it the expansion of the other, wet-rice growing. The more numerous and the better irrigated the terraces are, the more sugar can be grown; and the more people—a seasonal, readily available, resident labor force (a sort of part-time proletariat)— supported by these terraces during the nonsugar portion of the cycle, can grow sugar.

The dynamics on either side of this odd ecological bond support their respective growths. If terracing is improved or extended, because of more and better irrigation, the peasant food production and commercial cultivation can both be increased although they are being grown, so to speak, on the same land. . . .

The pleasing symmetry of this picture assumes that population increase is at least matched by the intensive or extensive growth

---

[9] Van Klaaveren (1955:120). Of course, the relation between labor-force requirements, environmental factors, and the location of the two sorts of cultivation was again a systematic, not a linear one. In part, at least sugar was planted in the lowlands, because that was where the usable population was, coffee in the highlands, because that was where the usable land was. The relative importance of ecological and economic variables in determining the spatial distribution of estate agriculture in Java is difficult to determine with any precision at this late date.

[10] For coffee, Metcalf (1952:70). Small-holder sugar production, because it was so marginal, is much harder to determine precisely; my 5 percent or so estimate is based on the graph on p. 418, of van de Koppel (1946). A discussion of small-holder sugar-growing and the reasons for its weakness can be found in van der Kolff, in Ruopp (1953).

of sawah, and, as we shall see, this eventually came very much not to be the case. It also assumes that the profits to be gained from sugar (or other products) will not prove so fatally attractive as to lead to an overexpansion of its cultivation at the peasant's expense—a danger the government always seems to have realized but not always seems to have been able, or perhaps willing, to avoid. And, more to the immediate point, it assumes that there will be no drift of the market mentality across the export-subsistence line; namely, that Javanese peasants will not themselves replace the cultivation of rice on their lands by smallholder sugar. If they do, the resultant pressure on the subsistence base means that it will be more difficult to conscript peasant land and labor. The workability of the whole mutualistic relationship depends, in short, on each side "doing its job"—the subsistence side feeding the labor force, and the commercial side producing state revenue. . . .

But despite this difference in relationship to existing ecological patterns, annuals and perennials grown under Dutch auspices shared another critical property that peasant cultivations (even when they were the same crops and were grown for the same commercial ends) lacked—they were integrated into a modernizing economy.

This basic difference—a sociological and not an ecological one now—split Netherlands East Indies agriculture into two radically unconformable strata which, despite Boeke's objections, one can only call "native" and "foreign," or, perhaps better, Indonesian and Dutch.[11] For the large-scale, well-capitalized, rationally organized estate agriculture which by 1900 accounted for 90 percent by value of Indonesia's exports (by 1938, after Outer Island small holders got well established, 60 percent), was essentially not part, save in a merely spatial or geographic sense, of the Indonesian economy at all, but of the Dutch (Metcalf 1952:8). The universal practice of colonial historians of opposing the NEI economy as a unit on the one hand to the Netherlands economy as a unit on the other merely obscures this crucial fact. There never really was, even in Company times, a Nether-

---

[11] Some of the "Dutch" side actually came into British, American, etc., hands; by 1937 about a quarter (Allen and Donnithorne, 1957:288). Boeke's desperate attempt to dissociate dualism and colonialism is to be found in his 1953, pp. 18–20 and *passim*.

lands East Indies economy in an integral, analytic sense—there was just that, admittedly highly autonomous, branch of the Dutch economy which was situated in the Indies ("tropical Holland," as it was sometimes called), and, cheek-by-jowl, the autonomous Indonesian economy also situated there. And though, indeed, the two interacted continuously in ways which fundamentally shaped their separate courses, they steadily diverged, largely as a result of this interaction, to the point where the structural contrasts between them were overwhelming. What Boeke regarded as an intrinsic and permanent characteristic of Indonesian (or "Eastern") economic life, "a primarily spiritual phenomenon," was really an historically created condition; it grew not from the immutable essence of the Eastern soul as it encountered the incarnate spirit of Western dynamism, but from the in no way predestined shape of colonial policy as it impressed itself upon the traditional pattern of Indonesian agriculture (Boeke 1953: 14). . . .

Basically, the development of dualism consists of a trend toward fixed (or presumed fixed) technical coefficients of production in more and more capital-intensive enterprises on the one hand, and toward variable ones in more and more labor-intensive activities on the other, together with the peculiarly lopsided pattern of investment, productivity, and employment which flows from this steadily widening disparity (Higgins 1959: 325–340). Despite its formal identity from place to place, the ways in which such a situation can arise historically are very diverse. And as what we are concerned to understand here is not the mere presence but the extraordinary severity of this development so far as Indonesia is concerned (with, so to speak, "runaway dualism"), the nature of Dutch colonial policy, the decisive force on the capital-intensive side, can hardly be irrelevant.

The inability of Dutch private enterprise to provide the capital necessary to exploit Java efficiently was one of the main motivating forces for the institution of the Culture System in the first place (Reinsma 1955:17–21). . . . the Culture System appears to represent the kind of governmental mobilization of "redundant" labor for capital creation projects which has been often proposed and occasionally attempted in underdeveloped areas. Within the framework of the labor-tax system, itself cast in the mold of the traditional corvée powers of the indigenous aristocracy, the government built roads and bridges, expanded irrigation facilities, cleared and improved large tracts of "waste" land, constructed buildings, and generally substituted the labor of the Javanese for the capital Holland lacked in laying the preparative foundations of a very rapidly accelerating, if distorted, process of economic growth. At first, such efforts to accumulate social capital by applying redundant labor to government projects were, like the forced work in cultivation itself, not altogether successful. . . .

From the developmental point of view, therefore, the Culture System represented an attempt to raise an estate economy by a peasantry's bootstraps; and in this it was remarkably successful. Benefiting from the external economies created by the formation of social capital, the forced diffusion of plantation crops and attendant labor skills over the island, and a certain amount of more direct governmental assistance, private enterprises steadily multiplied; soon their returns were great enough that they could provide most of the investment required for the qualitative changes in capital stock, particularly in sugar-milling, which were becoming necessary.[12] As Reinsma has well argued, the protracted "fall" of the Culture System (which lasted from about 1850 to about 1915) and its gradual replacement by the Corporate Plantation System were largely self-generated, because its success in establishing a serviceable export economy infrastructure made private entrepreneurship, originally so hampered by lack of capital, progressively more feasible. . . .

If we look again at the two leading commercial crops of the nineteenth century, coffee and sugar, a somewhat more palpable picture of the developmental pattern appears, which the Culture System "big push" generated (Figure 12).[13] The production of

[12] In 1840, private estates accounted for 17 percent of agricultural export volume, government forced cultivation 78 percent. In 1850, the figures were 26 and 73; in 1860, 58 and 39; in 1870, 43 and 52; in 1873, 72 and 19. Reinsma (1955:157). For a general discussion of "social overhead capital," "external economies," and development, see Higgins (1959: 384–408).

[13] Based on figures in Furnivall (1944:75, 104, 129, 171, 207). The beginning and end points of the Culture System are the conventional ones, and admittedly somewhat arbitrary. No production figures for 1870 are available, evidently.

coffee, the cultivation most immediately affected by the system, rose sharply within ten years of the inception of mass-labor taxation to a new level as it spread extensively over the uncultivated uplands of Java. (In 1833 somewhat more than 100 million trees are said to have existed on Java; two years later, in 1835, about

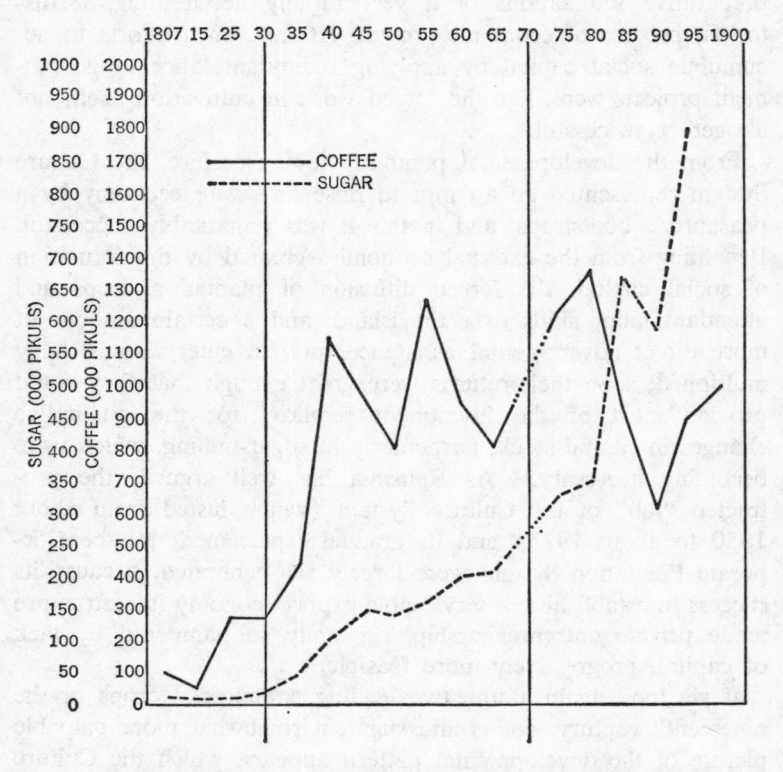

Figure 12 Culture System. Source: J. S. Furnivall, Netherlands India, *Cambridge (England): Cambridge University Press, 1944, pp. 75, 109, 129, 171, 207.*

twice that many, and by 1840–50 more than three times as many.[14]) But, not particularly susceptible to qualitative technical

[14] Van Klaaveren (1955:123). As not even Dutch civil servants can have been so conscientious as to have counted 300 million coffee trees, such figures must, of course, be taken only as general, order-of-magnitude estimates.

improvement, this spread did not continue upward once it reached its approximate limits; having found a higher level, it oscillated around it. (The severe dip in 1880–1890 was due to disease, which was overcome in the 1890's by a shift in species.) For the period of the Culture System proper, roughly the middle half of the nineteenth century, coffee was to Java what textiles were to England—it virtually carried the estate economy, accounting in itself for between a quarter and a third of the Indies' export income.[15]

Sugar production, however, behaved differently. In the first place, it rose less explosively (and also less erratically) under the Culture System, mainly because its advances were based on technical improvements, in both cultivation and milling, which took time and capital to develop. Where the area planted in cane increased only about 18 percent between 1833 and 1861, the production per hectare of refined sugar about tripled.[16] And, unlike the coffee expansion, this growth, once underway, continued at an accelerating rate: by 1900, productivity had doubled again and, now that modern irrigation facilities were appearing in significant quantity, planted area had about tripled, leading to the five-fold output increase shown on the graph.[17] Thus, the role of vanguard industry that coffee played up to about 1880, sugar played for the last quarter of the nineteenth

---

[15] Furnivall (1944). Though price movements obviously shaped this pattern as it developed, they can in no simple way account for it. From 1825 to 1855, the general trend of coffee prices was moderately downward; after 1860 they rose rapidly until 1875, when they plunged downward again, rising once more in 1890–1895 and falling off in 1900 (calculated from Furnivall). Sugar prices were somewhat less fluctuating, at least until 1885, but a similar analysis can be given for them.

[16] Burger (1939:130, 154). On the cultivation side the technical improvements consisted of more intensive planting and care under the so-called Reynoso system; on the milling side of more and more elaborate machinery. Between 1830 and 1839 machinery imports (mostly for sugar) into the Netherlands East Indies averaged 1.48 million guilders annually; 1840–1849, 1.79; 1850–1859, 2.02; 1860–1869, 2.78 (Reinsma 1955: 159). Capitalization was increasing in other crops too: after 1859, the private tobacco grower George Birnie spent more than 500,000 guilders on irrigation works in Djember (Boeke 1953:212–213).

[17] Gonggrijp (1957:121). Gonggrijp's figures do not entirely tally with Burger's, but again the general direction, if not the precise values, is clear enough. For the steady increase in per-hectare refined sugar productivity from about 20 quintals in 1842 to about 165 in 1937, see Koningsberger, in van Hall and van de Koppel (1946:291).

century and into the twentieth, until in 1920 it earned more than a million guilders of export revenue—more than all other products, minerals included, put together.[18]

In sum, if "take-off" is defined as a largely self-generated, relatively sudden transition to sustained economic growth, then there is at least presumptive evidence that something of the sort occurred on the estate side of the dual economy during the Culture System period, or—if the system itself be viewed as merely establishing preconditions—just after it.[19] The fact that the estate sector became progressively more closely integrated into the modernizing Netherlands economy (and progressively segregated from the rigidifying Javanese one) does not mean, as has sometimes been asserted, that it was a simple creation of that economy; it was a creation of Javanese land and labor organized under Dutch colonial political direction. If anything, the flow of support ran the other way: "The true measure of [van den Bosch's] greatness," Furnivall (1944:152) has justly written, "is the renascence of the Netherlands."

The true measure of van den Bosch's malignancy, however, is the stultification of Indonesia. For, although the Javanese helped launch the estate sector, they were not properly part of it, nor were they permitted to become so; it was just something they did, or more exactly were obligated to do, in their spare time. On their own time, they multiplied; and "take-off" on the peasant side was of a less remunerative sort—into rapid and sustained population growth. In 1830 there were probably about 7 million people on Java; in 1840, 8.7; 1850 (when census-taking first became reasonably systematic), 9.6; 1860, 12.7; 1870, 16.2; 1880, 19.5; 1890, 23.6; 1900, 28.4—an average annual increase of approximately 2 percent during seventy years.[20] And, here

---

[18] Furnivall (1944:337). About this time Java was contributing about 10 percent of the world's sugar supply; see graph in Bulletin of the Colonial Institute of Amsterdam, 3:207 (1939).

[19] The "take-off" concept is from Rostow (1960:36–58). However, Rostow's analysis generally ignores the developmental patterns of colonial economies.

[20] Reinsma (1955:175); The Population of Indonesia, p. 22; van Alphen, (1870 second part:68). Not all these sources precisely agree, but the general pattern is about the same. Also, of course, the rate of growth was not steady: in the 1840's when there was famine, the annual increase seems to have sunk to around 1 percent, in the 1850's to have risen to about

too, the pattern once established, persists (though the rate slows):
1920, 34.4; 1930, 41.7. What the precise causes of this "explosion"
were and, particularly, how far it was directly rather than merely
indirectly detonated by Culture System policies, are, reliable
data being scarce, matters of debate. But there is little doubt that
it was during the Culture System period that the saying about the
Dutch growing in wealth and the Javanese in numbers first hard-
ened into a sociological reality. By the end of it, the Javanese
had, as they have today, the worst of two possible worlds: a static
economy and a burgeoning population. . . .

TABLE 1

RELATIONSHIPS BETWEEN WET-RICE PRODUCTION, SAWAH AREA,
HARVESTED SAWAH AREA, PER-HECTARE WET-RICE YIELDS AND
POPULATION IN THE SUGAR AREAS OF JAVA IN 1920
(Indexes only, with all-Java figure set as base)

	Ratio: *Percent of* *wet-rice* *production/* *percent of* *sawah area*	*Ratio:* *Percent of* *wet-rice* *production/* *percent of* *population*	*Percent of* *sawah area* *harvested* *in rice* *(includes* *double* *cropping)*	*Average* *per-hectare* *yields of* *harvested* *(in rice)* *sawah*
The 37 main sugar regencies	107	98	98	110
The 98 main sugar districts	109	100	94	115
The 19 leading sugar districts	113	98	85	128
All-Java (base)	100	100	100	100

Source: Calculated from data in: Landbouwatlas van Java en Madoera,
Mededeelingen van het Centraal Kantoor voor de Statistiek, No. 33, Weltevreden:
1926, Part II, Tables I, III, IV, and V. In Mataram (which in 1920 was
organized slightly differently from the rest of Java), Bantul, Sléman, and Kalasan
have been counted as districts, Mataram itself as a regency.

Whatever the causes, the tie between sugar, wet-rice, and
population density is unmistakable: all three "flourish," if that
is the proper word, together. In Table 1, the main factor which
makes this seemingly contradictory phenomenon possible is revealed: a progressively higher *per hectare* sawah productivity.
Taking Java-wide averages as a base, yields can be seen to rise

3 percent—though it is difficult to tell how much of such variation
stems from irregularities in census-taking. For a review of the development of population surveys in Indonesia, see van de Graaf (1955:138–169).

as one moves to more intensely planted sugar areas, a rise which, especially when combined with the concurrent (but slower) rise in sawah, compensates for the loss of rice land to cane. This, in turn, brings about the more moderate rise in wet-rice production per total sawah area. The question, then, is: why the higher yields?

Two possibilities suggest themselves: (1) sugar tended to be planted in the best rice areas; (2) rice cultivation was more efficiently pursued in the sugar areas. Both of these factors certainly were operative. Given the ecologically specialized, "aquarium" nature of wet-rice growing, it is difficult to distinguish sharply between them because fertility is so closely tied to level of technique rather than merely reflecting natural conditions; the best rice areas are naturally the better-worked areas, and vice versa. As already explained, the ecological requirements for cane and rice are similar, therefore sugar gravitated to the most fertile (i.e., the best-irrigated) sawahs and, by financing water-control facilities, the companies improved and expanded such areas. . . .

As there was virtually no variation in capital inputs in sawah agriculture from one part of the island to another, aside from irrigation works, this greater efficiency in cultivation derived almost entirely from a greater intensification of labor—an intensification made both possible and necessary by the increasing population. The practices have already been mentioned—pregermination, transplanting, more thorough land preparation, fastidious planting and weeding, razor-blade harvesting, doublecropping, a more exact regulation of terrace-flooding, and the addition of more fields at the edges of volcanoes.[21] The concentrative, inflatable quality of sawah, its labor-absorbing capacity, was an almost ideal (in an ecological, not a social, sense) complement to capital-intensive sugar-growing. As Table 1 shows, it enabled the densest regions of Java to keep pace (at least until 1920) with the per-capita output of rice of the island as a whole.

The process resembles nothing else so much as treading water. Higher-level densities are offset by greater labor inputs into the

---

[21] Though they tend to increase labor intensification, such procedures as double-cropping or pushing terraces up mountainsides do not, of course, necessarily increase per-harvested-hectare yields, but increase production mainly by increasing harvested area.

same productive system, but output per head (or per mouth) remains more or less constant from region to region. . . . "Taking all the historical evidence available into consideration, we conclude that per capita food consumption has been maintained through the period of rapid population increase, but it has never risen above a minimal level."[22] Less circumspect, Boeke (1953: 174) summed the whole picture up in a single, mordant phrase: "static expansion."

The superimposition of sugar cultivation on the already unequal distribution of sawah and population over Java left the Javanese peasantry with essentially a single choice in coping with their rising numbers: driving their terraces, and in fact all their agricultural resources, harder by working them more carefully. There was no industrial sector into which to move and, as the returns from cultivation went, in Furnivall's words, to keep the Netherlands from becoming another Portugal, none was developed (Furnivall 1944:151). Coffee-growing was still almost wholly a forced-labor occupation and no real substitute for subsistence cultivation; and the same was true of the other Culture System crops. The Javanese could not themselves become part of the estate economy, and they could not transform their general pattern of already intensive farming in an extensive direction, for they lacked capital, had no way to shuck off excess labor, and were administratively barred from the bulk of their own frontier, the so-called "waste lands" which were filling up with coffee trees. Slowly, steadily, relentlessly, they were forced into a more and more labor-stuffed sawah pattern of the sort the 1920 figures show: tremendous populations absorbed on minuscule rice farms, particularly in areas where sugar cultivation led to improved irrigation; consequent rises in per-hectare productivity; and, with the assistance after about 1900 of an expansion in dry-crop cultivation, a probably largely stable, or very gradually rising, standard of living. Wet-rice cultivation, with its extraordinary ability to maintain levels of marginal labor productivity by always managing to work one more man in without a serious fall in per-capita income, soaked up almost the whole of the additional population that Western intrusion created,[23] at least

---

[22] Hollinger (1953a. See also, Wertheim and The Siauw Giap 1962).

[23] Just what the factors producing the population rise in the nineteenth century were is not quite so clear as the usual references to the removal of Malthus' positive checks would make it seem. Improved hygiene could

indirectly. It is this ultimately self-defeating process that I have proposed to call "agricultural involution."

I take the concept of "involution" from the American anthropologist Alexander Goldenweiser, who devised it to describe those culture patterns which, after having reached what would seem to be a definitive form, nonetheless fail either to stabilize or transform themselves into a new pattern but rather continue to develop by becoming internally more complicated:

> The application of the pattern concept to a cultural feature in the process of development provides . . . a way of explaining one peculiarity of primitive cultures. The primary effect of pattern is . . . to check development, or at least to limit it. As soon as the pattern form is reached further change is inhibited by the tenacity of the pattern. . . . But there are also instances where pattern merely sets a limit, a frame . . . within which further change is permitted if not invited. Take, for instance, the decorative art of the Maori, distinguished by its complexity, elaborateness, and the extent to which the entire decorated object is pervaded by the decoration. On analysis the unit elements of the design are found to be few in number; in some instances, in fact, the complex design is brought about through a multiplicity of spatial arrangements of one and the same unit. What we have here is pattern plus continued development. The pattern precludes the use of another unit or units, but it is not inimical to play within the unit or units. The inevitable result is progressive complication, a variety within uniformity, virtuosity within monotony. This is *involution*. A parallel instance . . . is provided by what is called ornateness in art, as in the late Gothic. The basic forms of art have reached finality, the structural features are fixed beyond variation, inventive originality is exhausted. Still, development goes on. Being hemmed in on all sides by a crystallized pattern, it takes the function of elaborateness. Expansive creativeness having dried up at the source, a special kind of virtuosity takes its place, a sort of technical hairsplitting. . . . Anyone familiar with primitive cultures will think of similar instances in other cultural domains.[24]

---

hardly have played a major role until fairly late. The Pax Nederlandica had perhaps more effect, but probably not so much because so many people had been killed in wars in the precolonial period but because the attendant destruction of crops ceased. Probably most important, and least discussed, was the expansion of the transport network which prevented local crop failures from turning into famines.

[24] Goldenweiser (1936). As his own reference to late Gothic art demonstrates, however, there is nothing particularly "primitive" about this process.

From the point of view of general theory, there is much misplaced concreteness in this formulation; but for our purposes we want only the analytic concept—that of the overdriving of an established form in such a way that it becomes rigid through an inward overelaboration of detail—not the hazy cultural vitalism in which it is here embedded.

The general earmarks of involution that Goldenweiser lists for aesthetic phenomena characterized the development of the sawah system after about the middle of the nineteenth century: increasing tenacity of basic pattern; internal elaboration and ornateness; technical hairsplitting, and unending virtuosity. And this "late Gothic" quality of agriculture increasingly pervaded the whole rural economy: tenure systems grew more intricate; tenancy relationships more complicated; cooperative labor arrangments more complex—all in an effort to provide everyone with some niche, however small, in the over-all system. If the original establishment of terraces in Java's little interior river galleries was but a preliminary sketch of the wet-rice mode of adaptation, and the time of the Javanese states and of the Company saw a filling in of solid compositional substance, the Culture System period brought an overornamentation, a Gothic elaboration of technical and organizational detail. But what makes this development tragic rather than merely decadent is that around 1830 the Javanese (and, thus, the Indonesian) economy could have made the transition to modernism, never a painless experience, with more ease than it can do today. To see how this is so, however, it is necessary to look at the last major colonial device for exploiting the archipelago, the Corporate Plantation System, for it is under its aegis that all the immobilizing processes which the Culture System so powerfully propelled settled into their definitive form.

THE COLONIAL PERIOD: FLORESCENCE

The Corporate Plantation System

The rapid mechanization of sugar-milling in the second half of the nineteenth century steadily made obsolete the Culture System, based on the substitution of (Javanese) labor for (Dutch) capital. With such substitution rendered progressively less practical by technological advance, effective colonial management became less a matter of mobilization of labor and more of regulating the relationship between the highly capitalized sugar "factory," or other crop-processing enterprises, and the peasant village to which it was symbiotically tied.[25]

To this end, the Dutch introduced, in 1870, the Agrarian Land Law. Together with various ancillary enactments, this statute made it possible to transfer direct responsibility for insuring Java's profitability to private enterprises while preventing such enterprises from destroying the village economy upon which that profitability depended. In it, the convenient notion, current since the Raffles interregnum at the beginning of the century, that all uncultivated "waste land" is inalienable state property was for the first time officially codified, making it possible for private plantation concerns to lease such land on a regularized, long-term contractual basis from Batavia and to use such legal titles for the purposes of obtaining credit. Further, the prohibition of outright alienation of peasant land to foreigners embodied in Javanese customary law was given formal legal backing by the government, permitting the systematization of rules and regulations for a similar long-term leasing of it to plantation companies for commercial use by its millions of small-holders. At base, the law which inaugurates the Corporate Plantation period in East Indian economic history, represents one more effort to superimpose commercial economy upon subsistence economy in such a way as to stimulate the first and tranquilize the second.

The immediate beneficiaries of this legal innovation were the individual private Netherlands East Indies planters who had been created by the workings of the Culture System they professed to despise. This was particularly true in sugar, where privately planted cane made up about 9 percent of the total in 1870 and about 97 percent two decades later, though enterprise in coffee, tobacco, and even rice also appeared (Burger 1939:177). But the depression of the middle eighties (coffee prices fell by half, sugar prices by even more) (Furnivall 1944:196), assisted by the onset of crop diseases in both coffee and sugar, wrecked the jerry-built financial structure of the Indies beyond repair. The self-styled "pioneers [and] speculative elements in the Indies itself," whom Reinsma celebrates, were consequently driven into

---

[25] It must be remembered, however, that although sugar production became steadily more capital intensive, it continued to use large quantities of unskilled seasonal labor on the cultivation side of its operations.

the now waiting arms of large-scale Dutch finance, and they soon disappeared into enormous, multi-enterprise, limited-liability corporations rooted firmly in the motherland, or, in some cases, in other European countries. The Amsterdam and Rotterdam merchants of great traffic did not create, as they later came to claim, the Netherlands East Indies estate economy. They bought it—and rather cheaply, considering the social costs of its production—at auction. . . .

Backed by a network of banks—the Java Bank, the Nederlands-Indische Handelsbank, and others, as well as some foreign concerns, such as the Chartered Bank—the corporations diversified plantation production beyond the staple sugar and coffee of the nineteenth century, spread it to restricted parts of Outer Indonesia, built railroads and modern irrigation works, set up agricultural experimental stations to improve yields, and in general created a comprehensive agro-industrial structure probably unmatched for complexity, efficiency, and scale anywhere in the world. By 1938 there were 2,400 estates in Indonesia, equally divided between Java and the Outer Islands, occupying about two and a half million hectares and controlled for the most part by a few large and, "under a coordinating superstructure of large syndicates and cartels," interlocked companies[26]. . . .

Sugar, which remained Indonesia's most important export crop until the thirties, continued its mutualistic relationship with wet rice in but slightly changed guise. As cane was no longer grown on peasant land by government fiat and large-scale "waste-land" tracts suitable for it were scarce, now that Java was so crowded, a complex land-rent system was developed to obtain the use of sawah. A village, sometimes willingly, sometimes coerced by its leaders and local civil servants, contracted a 21½-year lease with an estate. The estate then planted one-third of the village sawah in cane. The cane occupied these fields for about fifteen months; after eighteen months the land was returned to the holders and

---

[26] Van de Koppel (1946). Only about 1.2 million hectares or 47 percent of the land controlled by the estates was actually planted. A systematic, detailed history of the development of corporate enterprise in the Netherlands Indies remains to be written; but a general, rather routine, survey can be found in Allen and Donnithorne (1957 esp. chapter x:181–199). For a literally bird's-eye view of corporation Java around 1927, plus a certain amount of unsystematized data on the various companies, see de Vries, n.d. The internal quotation is from Wertheim (1956:99).

another third of the village's land was taken for sugar, and so on around the cycle. But, as the new cane planting usually took place before the old one was harvested, any particular field was in sugar about a half rather than a third of the time; or to put it aggregatively, an average of about one-half the village's land, now one-third, now two-thirds, was in sugar, and half in peasant crops—either rice, or dry-season second crops such as soya or peanuts. One entire cycle therefore took three years, and seven such cycles could be completed during a single lease-hold. . . .

The product of this complex and intimate interlocking of the rigorous cultivation rhythms of large-scale corporate agriculture and the more pliable ones of traditional household farming was an odd centauric social unit which was neither a proper planta-tion nor yet a peasant community, but different from either of them. The centaur's head was the mill. This heavily capitalized factory in the field (average outstanding investment in a single sugar enterprise seems to have run in the neighborhood of a million dollars during the thirties) with its steam- or electric-driven crushers, filters, centrifuges, evaporators, and vacuum cookers, was run by a European managerial staff of twenty men or so, settled with their families in neat bungalows huddled be-side its walls, and processed the cane production of about a thousand hectares a year.[27] The centaur's body was the peas-antry, upon whom the mill drew not just for land, but for the casual, seasonally extremely variable labor force it needed to clear fields, dig trenches, plant, harvest, carry cane to the mills, and perform countless other occasional tasks connected with the in-dustry. By 1930, sugar concerns were employing more than 800,000 Javanese—men, women, and children—at one point or another during a year; or, as there were some 180 factories, an average of 4,000–5,000 per mill (Allen and Donnithorne 1957; Boeke 1953:141). Clearly, not all the "indirect-rule," "native-welfare," "East-is-East-and-West-is-West" colonial policies in the world could keep an encounter with big business of these dimensions from having a profound effect on rural life. And, as

[27] On sugar-milling technology, see Koningsberger (1946). The invest-ment estimate is based broadly on calculations with the very rough data given in Appendix II of Allen and Donnithorne (1957:288–299), from which source the estimates of European staff and hectarage per mill also come (p. 84).

the leasing arrangement was also applied, in somewhat varying and less penetrating forms, to the commercial cultivation of other annuals—tobacco, cassava, agave, even rice—the effect spread, to some degree, over a fair part of the countryside (Boeke 1953: 91). As van der Kolff has said, in Java the clash of cultures came in the form of a clash of cultivations (van der Kolff 1953).

Even more peculiarly distinctive of the Javanese situation— for the clash of cultivations has, after all, occurred elsewhere, and with perhaps even greater violence—is the fact that this clash took place largely within the context of a well-established, fully crystallized village social system, which though squeezed, de-formed, and enervated was not destroyed by it. The sugar-lease system and, to a lesser extent, the similar practices connected with other crops, did not isolate the disequilibrating forces of commercial capitalism from village life; they introduced them, following the path the Company and the Culture System had blazed, into the very heart of it. Unlike, say, in Jamaica, the sugar industry in Java was not built up on the basis of imported slaves lacking peasant traditions. Unlike, say, in Puerto Rico, it did not forcibly marshal an embryonic peasantry onto enclave plantations and degrade it into a fully proletarianized, essentially landless labor force (Mintz 1956). The Javanese cane worker remained a peasant at the same time that he became a coolie, persisted as a community-oriented household farmer at the same time that he became an industrial wage laborer. He had one foot in the rice terrace and the other in the mill. And, in order for him to maintain this precarious and uncomfortable stance, not only did the estate have to adapt to the village through the land-lease system and various other "native-protection" devices forced on it by an "ethical" colonial government, but, even more com-prehensively, the village had to adapt to the estate.

The mode of its adaptation was again involutional. The basic pattern of village life was maintained, in some ways even strengthened, and the adjustment to the impingements of high capitalism effected through the complication of established insti-tutions and practices. In land tenure, in crop regime, in work organization, and in the less directly economic aspects of social structure as well, the village, "hemmed in on all sides by a crystallized pattern" (to quote Goldenweiser again), faced the problems posed by a rising population, increased monetization, greater dependence on the market, mass labor organization, more intimate contact with bureaucratic government and the like, not by a dissolution of the traditional pattern into an individualistic "rural proletarian" anomie, nor yet by a metamorphosis of it into a modern commercial farming community. Rather, by means of "a special kind of virtuosity," "a sort of technical hairsplitting," it maintained the over-all outlines of that pattern while driving the elements of which it was composed to ever-higher degrees of ornate elaboration and Gothic intricacy. Unable either to stabilize the equilibrated wet-rice system it had autochthonously achieved before 1830, or yet to achieve a modern form on, say, the Japanese model, the twentieth-century lowland Javanese village—a great, sprawling community of desperately marginal agriculturalists, petty traders, and day laborers—can perhaps only be referred to, rather lamely, as "post-traditional."

The durability of the basic framework of the post-traditional rural economy is apparent no matter at which aspect of it one looks. On the side of land tenure, the so-called "communal ownership" systems under which the village as a corporate body exercises various kinds of residual rights of control over fields seem actually to have been strengthened, at least in relative terms, in the sugar-area villages.[28] The need on the mill's side for a simple, flexible, and comprehensive land-owning unit within which cane cultivation could move freely from one block of terraces to the next, unobstructed by a cloud of separate, individualized land rights, and the need on the villagers' side for a reasonably equitable sharing throughout the community of the burdens imposed by the system as it so moved from field to field, made the collective apportionment procedures of traditional communal tenure functional to both parties. . . . In brief, communal tenure allowed the mills to operate in terms of a large-field system appropriate to plantation sugar and, simultaneously, the village to

---

[28] Van der Kolff (1929; van Gelderen 1929). Van der Kolff, in fact, traces the origins of this whole process, too, back into the Culture System period when, "if the indigo and sugar crops were to be a success they had to be grown in rotation on different sites, and since, from the point of view of supervision and irrigation, it was much easier to deal with compact blocks of land, it was to the advantage of the government to regulate matters with a powerful village council rather than with individual landowners" (van der Kolff 1929:111). For a general survey of traditional Javanese tenure systems, see Vollenhoven (1906:604–634). For a more recent discussion, see van der Kroef (1960).

operate in terms of the small-field system appropriate to sawah rice.

In this through-the-looking-glass world, even a major technical innovation in village agriculture—the emergence of unirrigated, annual food crops as true staples alongside paddy—acted more to dampen structural change in the rural economy than to strengthen it. With the exception of soya beans (and, of course, unirrigated rice) all the dry-field annuals which are today important in Java—maize, cassava, sweet potatoes, peanuts—were introduced subsequent to European contact, and their penetration into the by then long-established sawah ecosystem was very gradual. In 1817, Raffles speaks of a recent increase in maize-growing on previously uncultivated poor-soil hill ranges "in the more populous parts of Java . . . where the sawahs do not afford a sufficient supply of rice," but other dry-field crops seem to be of but marginal importance (Raffles 1830:I, 134–137). Cassava began to spread over some less fertile areas in Bantam, Djapara, Semarang, and the Priangan after the experimental station in Buitenzorg imported shoots from Surinam in 1852, but it is only in this century that it has become an important diet item generally.[29] It was, in fact, not until the 1885 depression, when colonial officials actively promoted their use to increase native food production, that such crops—called collectively *palawidja*—began to play a vital role in the peasant economy.[30] By the first decade of this century they had become a fully integral part of village agriculture, both as east-monsoon second crops or sawahs and in crop-and-fallow dry fields, called *tegal*. . . .

. . . What is striking about this development is not how much it affected the general pattern of village economic life, but how little. Agricultural revolutions have been built on less, but in Java thorough-going diversification of traditional monoculture led only to the extension of the already far-advanced involutional process.

The penetration of maize, soyabeans, peanuts, and other crops

[29] Koens (1946). This was not the very first entry of cassava into the archipelago; Rumphius, "the blind seer of Ambon," reports it as early as the seventeenth century from the Moluccas.

[30] De Vries, quoted in Burger (1939:232). Scheltema (1930) quotes a *Koloniaal Verslag* for 1889 which claims that planted rice area increased about 8 percent over the 1817–1878 decade and that of palawidja by 24 percent, almost the whole (23 percent) of the latter increase coming in the form of second-crop planting on sawahs!

into the sawah ecosystem did not change its essential structure. Poured into a rice mold, these crops merely reinforced it. They made it possible to drive a terrace just that much harder, to keep pace with a rising population and, in the sugar areas, with the increasing external pre-emption of village lands, by increasing labor inputs into an already hyperintensive productive system. . . . In short, the result of the expansion of palawidja cultivation was the same as that of virtually every other technological innovation in the peasant sector after about 1830—the maintenance of the marginal productivity of labor at some low but nearly constant (or perhaps gradually declining) figure. It merely gave the multiplying Javanese a bigger pool in which more of them could tread water. . . .

The ecological elasticity of wet rice having at last begun to fail him, the Javanese peasant turned toward diversified dry cropping to eke out, by the most labor-intensive pattern such crops could sustain, his customary meager living. And if one approaches the problem from the consumption side, one comes to the same conclusion as the Dutch agronomist Tergast:

> On densely populated Java the rice production could not keep step [after 1900] with the increase in population. Increasing cultivation of other foodstuffs in rotation with rice and on dry lands has met the rising need for food. Around 1900 the amount of annual per capita quantity available was about 110 kg of rice, 30 kg of tubers, and 3 kg of pulses. Around 1940 this had changed to 85 kg rice, 40 kg maize, 180 kg tubers, and about 10 kg pulses. This change has locally reduced, often seriously, the quality of the diet. Expressed in calories there was little change between 1900 and 1940; the daily menu per capita has been kept on a level somewhat lower than 2,000 calories. That Java, in spite of the heavy population increase and the small possibility of expanding the cultivated area, has been in a position to maintain the calorie level of the diet is due principally to the intensification of rotation on rice fields and more intensive use of the dry lands.[31]

---

[31] Tergast (1950). Of course, Tergast's calculations are merely broad estimates also, perhaps even less precise than the more straightforward estimates of arable land and harvested area. In fact, it seems likely that there was actually a decline in caloric intake between 1900 and 1940. For a summary of other estimates of daily caloric intake (one of which sees it as declining from about 1,850 in 1921 to about 1,750 in 1938 and the other of which sees it as declining from about 2,000 to 1,900 over the same

In addition to land tenure and land use, the involutional process also worked its peculiar pattern of changeless change on the distribution side. With the steady growth of population came also the elaboration and extension of mechanisms through which agricultural product was spread, if not altogether evenly, at least relatively so, throughout the huge human horde which was obliged to subsist on it. Under the pressure of increasing numbers and limited resources Javanese village society did not bifurcate, as did that of so many other "underdeveloped" nations, into a group of large landlords and a group of oppressed near-serfs. Rather it maintained a comparatively high degree of social and economic homogeneity by dividing the economic pie into a steadily increasing number of minute pieces, a process to which I have referred elsewhere as "shared poverty" (Geertz 1965). Rather than haves and have-nots, there were, in the delicately muted vernacular of peasant life, only *tjukupans* and *kekurangans*—"just enoughs" and "not-quite enoughs."

By and large, the set of mechanisms producing this fractionization of output seems to have been centered less on land ownership than on land-working. Equal inheritance, reduction in size of communal shares to permit more shareholders in the same quantity of village land, and within-village bits-and-pieces land sale—all no doubt produced some diminution in the extent of individual holdings. But Javanese farms were small to start with. Though striking local exceptions can be found—again, particularly in the sugar areas where villagers were forced into more extreme measures—there is little evidence for any large-scale secular decline (or increase) in average farm size over Java as a whole during the colonial period. The estimates of mean—and modal—individual holding given by Raffles in 1817 and by Boeke in

period), see van de Koppel (1946). For yet another estimate of quantities of various food crops available per capita from 1913 to 1940 showing a pattern generally similar to Tergast's, see Pelzer (1945:259). In addition, both these calculations and my own analysis in the text omit, mainly because of measurement difficulties, consideration of the extreme intensification of grainless cultivation in house gardens (*pekarangan*), where on an average plot of some thirty square meters a Javanese family may grow literally dozens of different fruits, vegetables, and herbs, and produce, in extreme cases, as much as two-fifths of its caloric intake. See Terra (1946).

1940 run just about the same: slightly under one hectare.[32] The greater part of the dispersion of output, which in the nature of the case must have occurred, seems to have been mediated not through changes in the general structure of proprietary control, but through a marked elaboration and expansion of the traditional system of labor relations—in particular, of the institution of share-cropping.[33]. . .

The productive system of the post-traditional village developed, therefore, into a dense web of finely spun work rights and work responsibilities spread, like the reticulate veins of the hand, throughout the whole body of the village lands.[34] A man will let out part of his one hectare to a tenant—or to two or three —while at the same time seeking tenancies on the lands of other men, thus balancing his obligations to give work (to his relatives,

---

[32] Raffles (1830, I:162; Boeke 1953:52–143). Additional evidence that it was not, in the prewar period at least, changes on the ownership side which facilitated "sharing the poverty" comes from the fact that parceliza-tion—the splitting of single holdings into a large number of very small scattered plots—was not particularly extensive in Java (being about half the level of India or China), nor does it seem to have increased in the immediate prewar period. Further, leaving aside the "Outer Indonesia" region of Preanger only a (very grossly) estimated 2,000 Javanese owned more than 18 hectares of land in 1925 (Scheltema 1931:275). One of the sources of the widespread notion of a radical decrease in average farm size in Java seems to be mere astonishment at its present smallness. Thus Mears (1961) writes: "With the increase in population density on Java, the size of individual holdings has declined to the point where approxi-mately 90 percent of the farmers cultivate less than 1 hectare . . . of land. Almost 70 percent farm less than one-half hectare. Large holdings . . . are the exception with less than one percent of the agricultural holdings ex-ceeding 10 hectares." When it is noted, however, that a survey taken in 1903, when the population was around half what it was in 1958 (and excluding the principalities where farms have always been if anything smaller than average), found that 15.8 percent of the farms were under .18 ha, 32.8 percent under .35 ha, 47.2 percent under .53 ha, 70.9 percent under .71 ha, 89.1 percent under 1.42 ha, and only 3.9 percent over 2.8 ha, the decline, though real, seems a great deal less precipitous and can in no sense account for the absorption of the bulk of the population in-crease into the village economy. Pelzer (1945:166).

[33] For an encyclopedic review of traditional forms of sharecropping in both Inner and Outer Indonesia, see Scheltema, 1931. For a more general discussion of the whole range of types of traditional agricultural labor relations, see deBie (1902:67–74).

[34] In fact, the "share-crop" principle is applied not only to agriculture but also to farm animals. See Scheltema (1931:243–252).

to his dependents, or even to his close friends and neighbors) against his own subsistence requirements. A man will rent or pawn his land to another for a money payment and then serve as a tenant on that land himself, perhaps in turn letting subtenancies out to others. A man may agree, or be granted the opportunity, to perform the planting and weeding tasks for one-fifth of the harvest and job the actual work in turn to someone else, who may, in *his* turn, employ wage laborers or enter into an exchange relationship with neighbors to obtain the necessary labor. The structure of land ownership is thus only an indifferent guide to the social pattern of agricultural exploitation, the specific form of which emerges only in the intricate institutional fretwork through which land and labor are actually brought together.[35] In share tenancy and associated practices the ever-driven wet-rice village found the means by which to divide its growing economic pie into a greater number of traditionally fixed pieces and so to hold an enormous population on the land at a comparatively very homogeneous, if grim, level of living. What elsewhere has been sought through land reform—the minimization of socio-economic contrasts based on differential control of agricultural resources—the Javanese peasant, whose farms were minute to start with, achieved through that more ancient weapon of the poor: work spreading. . . .

Double cropping, more careful micro-regulation of irrigation in and around the terrace, stalk-by-stalk, not to say grain-by-grain, cultivation, reaping and milling methods, developed share-cropping, and other labor innovations all are difficult to abandon once they are firmly instituted. Thus, as the Dutch planter comes to feel that the only possible direction of increased rationalization is in the direction of greater investment in machinery, modern irrigation, scientific experimentation, and so on, the Javanese peasant comes to feel that the only feasible way at least to maintain his living standard, much less raise it, is through more fine-comb agricultural methods, and tends to become increasingly skeptical of the possibilities of improvement through mechaniza-

---

[35] Aside from often applying to the same man at the same time, the terms "landlord" and "share tenant" may even be slightly misleading in their usual connotation in this context where, as Boeke (1953:58) remarks, the cropper is often the stronger part. See also, in this connection, Burger (1930).

tion. Where the plantation sector becomes addicted to capital, the peasant sector becomes addicted to labor—the more they use the more they need. . . . The productive process of the one sector becomes steadily more capital-intensive and that of the other steadily more labor-intensive, until the dualistic gulf which yawns between them seems unbridgeable, as it did to Boeke.

The conservation of traditional land-tenure systems, the assimilation of dry crops to the wet-rice pattern of land use, and the elaboration of established systems of labor relationship are thus all of a piece. They represent a reaction—for all its oft-admired ingeniousness, almost wholly defensive—to the twin pressures of a rising population and a superimposed plantation economy. But they do not exhaust that reaction, for it was as much a cultural and social structural process as an economic and ecological one. The involution of the productive process in Javanese agriculture was matched and supported by a similar involution in rural family life, social stratification, political organization, religious practice, as well as in the "folk-culture" value system—what I have elsewhere called the *abangan* world view—in terms of which it was normatively regulated and ethically justified (Geertz 1960).

Thus, at each stage of the development which we have been following on the level of the rice terrace and the cane field, we could presumably have traced similar processes in the various social and cultural institutions which comprise the backbone of village life. The elaboration of a complex ranking system tied to communal tenure, the fluctuating relationships between kinship, patron-dependent and territorial ties, the vicissitudes of the position of the village headman and his staff, the changing content of village rights as a corporate unit, and even the transformations of the *abangan* "little tradition" as it absorbed into itself a wide range of foreign elements and turned them to its own ends—all these would add substance to the "cultural core" side of our description of the history of a human ecosystem. . . .

Pulled this way and that, hammered by forces over which it had no control and denied the means for actively reconstructing itself, the village both clung to the husks of selected established institutions and limbered them internally in such a way as to permit a greater flexibility, a freer play of social relationships within a generally stereotyped framework. The result was an arabesque pattern of life, both reduced and elaborated, both enormously complicated and marvelously simple: complicated in the diversity, variability, fragility, fluidity, shallowness, and unreliability of interpersonal ties: simple in the meager institutional resources by which such ties were organized. The quality of everyday existence in a fully involuted Javanese village is comparable to that in the other formless human community, the American suburb: a richness of social surfaces and a monotonous poverty of social substance.[36]

---

[36] For discussions of some "suburban" aspects of contemporary Javanese villages, see Jay (1956; Geertz 1959). I have incorporated a few phrases from the latter paper in the paragraph above.

15 THE DISTRIBUTION OF GAINS BETWEEN INVESTING AND BORROWING COUNTRIES [1950]*

Hans Singer

HOW THE IMPORTANCE OF FOREIGN TRADE TO UNDERDEVELOPED COUNTRIES HAS BEEN OBSCURED.

INTERNATIONAL TRADE is of very considerable importance to underdeveloped countries, and the benefits which they derive from trade and any variations in their trade affect their national incomes very deeply. The opposite view, which is frequent among economists, namely that trade is less important to the underdeveloped countries than it is to industrialized countries, may be said to derive from a logical confusion—very easy to slip into—between the absolute amount of foreign trade, which is known to be an increasing function of national income, and the ratio of foreign trade to national income. Foreign trade tends to be proportionately most important when incomes are lowest. Second, fluctuations in the volume and value of foreign trade tend to be proportionately more violent in trade of underdeveloped countries and therefore *a fortiori* also more important in relation to na-

SOURCE: Hans Singer, "The Distribution of Gains between Investing and Borrowing Countries," *American Economic Review, Papers and Proceedings,* May 1950. Reprinted by permission of the author and the American Economics Association.

* The author wishes to acknowledge help and advice received from many friends and colleagues—in particular, Mr. Henry G. Aubrey, Dr. Harold Barger of the National Bureau of Economic Research, Dr. Roberto de Oliveira Campos of the Brazilian delegation to the United Nations, Dr. A. G. B. Fisher of the International Monetary Fund, Prof. W. Arthur Lewis of the University of Manchester (England), and Mr. James Kenny. He also had the inestimable advantage of a discussion of the subject matter of this paper in the graduate seminar at Harvard University, with Professors Haberler, Harris, and others participating.

tional income. Third, and *a fortissimo,* fluctuations in foreign trade tend to be immensely more important for underdeveloped countries in relation to that small margin of income over subsistence needs which forms the source of capital formation, for which they often depend on export surpluses over consumption goods required from abroad.

In addition to the logical confusion mentioned above, the great importance of foreign trade to underdeveloped countries may also have been obscured by the great discrepancy in the productivity of labor in the underdeveloped countries as between the industries and occupations catering for export and those catering for domestic production. The export industries in underdeveloped countries—metal mines, plantations, etc.—are often highly capital-intensive industries supported by a great deal of imported foreign technology. By contrast, production for domestic use, especially of food and clothing, is often of a very primitive subsistence nature. Thus the economy of the underdeveloped countries often presents the spectacle of a dualistic economic structure: a high-productivity sector producing for export coexisting with a low-productivity sector producing for the domestic market. Employment statistics in underdeveloped countries do not adequately reflect the importance of foreign trade, since the productivity of each person employed in the export sector tends to be a multiple of that of each person employed in the domestic sector. Since, however, employment statistics for underdeveloped countries are notoriously easier to compile than national income statistics, it is again easy to slip from the fact that the proportion of persons employed in export trade is often lower in underdeveloped countries than in industrialized countries to the conclusion that foreign trade is less important to them. This conclusion is fallacious, since it implicitly assumes rough equivalence of productivity in the export and domestic sectors. This equivalence may be safely assumed in the industrialized countries but not in the underdeveloped countries.

A third factor which has contributed to the view that foreign trade is unimportant in underdeveloped countries is the indisputable fact that in many underdeveloped countries there are large self-contained groups which are outside the monetary economy altogether and are therefore not affected by any changes in foreign trade. In industrialized countries, by contrast, it is true that repercussions from changes in foreign trade are more widely spread; but they are also thinly spread.[1]

The Drain on the Benefits of Investment. The previously mentioned higher productivity of the foreign trade sector in underdeveloped countries might, at first sight, be considered as a cogent argument in favor of the view that foreign trade has been particularly beneficial to underdeveloped countries in raising their general standards of productivity, changing their economies in the direction of a monetary economy, and spreading knowledge of more capital-intensive methods of production and modern technology. That, however, is much less clearly established than might be thought. The question of ownership as well as of opportunity costs enters at this point. The facilities for producing export goods in underdeveloped countries are often foreign-owned as a result of previous investment in these countries. Again we must beware of hasty conclusions. Our first reaction would be to argue that this fact further enhances the importance and benefits of trade to underdeveloped countries, since trade has also led to foreign investment in those countries and has promoted capital formation with its cumulative and multiplier effects. This is also how the matter is looked at in the economic textbooks—certainly those written by nonsocialist economists of the industrialized countries. That view, however, has never been really accepted by the more articulate economists in the underdeveloped countries themselves, not to mention popular opinion in those countries; and it seems to the present writer that there is much more in their view than is allowed for by the economic textbooks.

Can it be possible that we economists have become slaves to the geographers? Could it not be that in many cases the productive facilities for export from underdeveloped countries, which were so largely a result of foreign investment, never became a part of the internal economic structure of those underdeveloped countries themselves except in the purely geographical and physi-

---

[1] A more statistical factor might be mentioned. Some underdeveloped countries—Iran would be an illustration—excluded important parts of their exports and imports from their foreign trade statistics insofar as the transactions of foreign companies operating in the underdeveloped country are concerned. This is a tangible recognition of the fact that these pieces of foreign investments and their doings are not an integral part of the underdeveloped economy.

cal sense? Economically speaking, they were really an outpost of the economies of the more developed investing countries. The main secondary multiplier effects, which the textbooks tell us to expect from investment, took place not where the investment was physically or geographically located but (to the extent that the results of these investments returned directly home) where the investment came from.[2] I would suggest that if the proper economic test of investment is the multiplier effect in the form of cumulative additions to income, employment, capital, technical knowledge, and growth of external economies, then a good deal of the investment in underdeveloped countries which we used to consider as "foreign" should in fact be considered as domestic investment on the part of the industrialized countries.

Where the purpose and effect of the investments were to open up new sources of food for the people and for the machines of industrialized countries, we have strictly domestic investment in the relevant economic sense, although for reasons of physical geography, climate, etc., it had to be made overseas. Thus the fact that the opening up of underdeveloped countries for trade has led to or been made possible by foreign investment in those countries does not seem a generally valid proof that this combination has been of particular benefit to those countries. The very differential in productivity between the export sectors and the domestic sectors of the underdeveloped countries, previously mentioned as an indication of the importance of foreign trade to underdeveloped countries, is also itself an indication that the more productive export sectors—often foreign-owned—have not become a real part of the economies of underdeveloped countries.

The Nonprogressive Nature of Traditional Investment. We may go even further. If we apply the principle of opportunity costs to the development of nations, the import of capital into underdeveloped countries for the purpose of making them into providers of food and raw materials for the industrialized countries may have been not only rather ineffective in giving them the normal benefits of investment and trade but positively harmful. The tea

---

[2] Often underdeveloped countries had the chance to use royalties or other income from foreign investment judiciously for the transformation of their internal economic structure—a chance more often missed than caught by the forelock!

plantations of Ceylon, the oil wells of Iran, the copper mines of Chile, and the cocoa industry of the Gold Coast may all be more productive than domestic agriculture in these countries; but they may well be less productive than domestic industries in those countries which might have developed if those countries had not become as specialized as they now are in the export of food and raw materials, thus providing the means of producing manufactured goods elsewhere with superior efficiency. Admittedly, it is a matter of speculation whether, in the absence of such highly specialized "export" development, any other kind of development would have taken its place. But the possibility cannot be assumed away. Could it be that the export development has absorbed what little entrepreneurial initiative and domestic investment there was, and even tempted domestic savings abroad? We must compare, not what is with what was, but what is with what would have been otherwise—a tantalizingly inconclusive business. All we can say is that the process of traditional investment taken by itself seems to have been insufficient to initiate domestic development unless it appeared in the form of migration of persons.

The principle of specialization along the lines of static comparative advantages has never been generally accepted in the underdeveloped countries, and it has not even been generally intellectually accepted in the industrialized countries themselves. Again it is difficult not to feel that there is more to be said on the subject than most of the textbooks will admit. In the economic life of a country and in its economic history, a most important element is the mechanism by which "one thing leads to another," and the most important contribution of an industry is not its immediate product (as is perforce assumed by economists and statisticians) and not even its effect on other industries and immediate social benefits (thus far economists have been led to go by Marshall and Pigou) but perhaps beyond this its effect on the general level of education, skill, way of life, inventiveness, habits, store of technology, creation of new demand, etc. And this is perhaps precisely the reason why manufacturing industries are so universally desired by underdeveloped countries: they provide the growing points for increased technical knowledge, urban education, and the dynamism and resilience that goes with urban civilization, as well as the direct Marshallian external economies. No doubt under different circumstances commerce, farming, and plantation agriculture have proved capable of being such growing points, but manufacturing industry is unmatched in our present age.

By specializing on exports of food and raw materials and thus making the underdeveloped countries further contribute to the concentration of industry in the already industrialized countries, foreign trade and the foreign investment which went with it may have spread present static benefits fairly over both. They may have had very different effects if we think from the point of view, not of static comparative advantages, but of the flow of history of a country. Of this latter school of thought the "infant" [industry] argument for protection is but a sickly and often illegitimate offspring.

To summarize, then, the position reached thus far, the specialization of underdeveloped countries on export of food and raw materials to industrialized countries, largely as a result of investment by the latter, has been unfortunate for the underdeveloped countries for two reasons: (1) it removed most of the secondary and cumulative effects of investment from the country in which the investment took place to the investing country; and (2) it diverted the underdeveloped countries into types of activity offering less scope for technical progress, internal and external economies taken by themselves, and withheld from the course of their economic history a central factor of dynamic radiation which has revolutionized society in the industrialized countries. But there is a third factor of perhaps even greater importance which has reduced the benefits to underdeveloped countries of foreign trade-*cum*-investment based on export specialization in food and raw materials. This third factor relates to terms of trade.

It is a matter of historical fact that ever since the seventies the trend of prices has been heavily against sellers of food and raw materials and in favor of the sellers of manufactured articles. The statistics are open to doubt and to objection in detail, but the general story which they tell is unmistakable.[3] What is the meaning of these changing price relations?

The Meaning of Unfavorable Price Relations. The possibility that these changing price relations simply reflect changes in the real costs of the manufactured exports of the industrialized countries relative to those of the food and primary materials of the underdeveloped countries can be dismissed. All the evidence is

---

[3] See United Nations (1949a:II.B.3).

that productivity has increased if anything less fast in the production of food and raw materials, even in the industrialized countries[4] but most certainly in the underdeveloped countries, than has productivity in the manufacturing industries of the industralized countries. The possibility that changing price relations could merely reflect relative trends in productivity may be considered as disposed of by the very fact that standards of living in industrialized countries (largely governed by productivity in manufacturing industries) have risen demonstrably faster than standards of living in underdeveloped countries (generally governed by productivity in agriculture and primary production) over the last sixty or seventy years. However important foreign trade may be to underdeveloped countries, had deteriorated terms of trade (from the point of view of the underdeveloped countries) reflected relative trends of productivity, this could most assuredly not have failed to show in relative levels of internal real incomes as well.

Dismissing, then, changes in productivity as a governing factor in changing terms of trade, the following explanation presents itself: The fruits of technical progress may be distributed either to producers (in the form of rising incomes) or to consumers (in the form of lower prices). In the case of manufactured commodities produced in more developed countries, the former method, i.e., distribution to producers through higher incomes, was much more important than the second method, while the second method prevailed more in the case of food and raw-material production in the underdeveloped countries. Generalizing, we may say that technical progress in manufacturing industries showed in a rise in incomes, while technical progress in the production of food and raw materials in underdeveloped countries showed in a fall in prices. Now, in the general case, there is no

---

[4] According to data of the WPA research project, output per wage earner in a sample of fifty-four manufacturing industries increased by 57 per cent during the twenty years 1919–1939; over the same period, agriculture increased only by 23 per cent, anthracite coal mining by 15 per cent, and bituminous coal mining by 35 per cent. In the various fields of mineral mining, however, progress was as fast as in manufacturing. According to data of the National Bureau of Economic Research, the rate of increase in output per worker was 1.8 per cent per annum in manufacturing industries (1899–1939) but only 1.6 per cent in agriculture (1890–1940) and in mining, excluding petroleum (1902–1939). In petroleum production, however, it was faster than in manufacturing.

reason why one or the other method should be generally preferable. There may, indeed, be different employment, monetary, or distributive effects of the two methods; but this is not a matter which concerns us in the present argument where we are not concerned with internal income distribution. In a closed economy the general body of producers and the general body of consumers can be considered as identical, and the two methods of distributing the fruits of technical progress appear merely as two formally different ways of increasing real incomes.

When we consider foreign trade, however, the picture is fundamentally changed. The producers and the consumers can no longer be considered as the same body of people. The producers are at home; the consumers are abroad. Rising incomes of home producers to the extent that they are in excess of increased productivity are an absolute burden on the foreign consumer. Even if the rise in the income of home producers is offset by increases in productivity so that prices remain constant or even fall by less than the gain in productivity, this is still a relative burden on foreign consumers, in the sense that they lose part or all of the potential fruits of technical progress in the form of lower prices. On the other hand, where the fruits of technical progress are passed on by reduced prices, the foreign consumer benefits along with the home consumer. Nor can it be said, in view of the notorious inelasticity of demand for primary commodities, that the fall in their relative prices has been compensated by total revenue effects.

Other factors have also contributed to the falling long-term trend of prices of primary products in terms of manufactures, apart from the absence of pressure of producers for higher incomes. Technical progress, while it operates unequivocally in favor of manufactures—since the rise in real incomes generates a more than proportionate increase in the demand for manufactures—has not the same effect on the demand for food and raw materials. In the case of food, demand is not very sensitive to rises in real income, and in the case of raw materials, technical progress in manufacturing actually largely consists of a reduction in the amount of raw materials used per unit of output, which may compensate or even overcompensate the increase in the volume of manufacturing output. This lack of an automatic multiplication in demand, coupled with the low price elasticity of demand for both raw materials and food, results in large price falls, not only cyclical but also structural.

The End Result: Maldistribution of Gains. Thus it may be said that foreign investment of the traditional type which sought its repayment in the direct stimulation of exports of primary commodities, either to the investing country directly or indirectly through multilateral relations, had its beneficial cumulative effects in the investing country; and the people of the latter, in their capacity as consumers, also enjoyed the fruits of technical progress in the manufacture of primary commodities thus stimulated and at the same time, in their capacity as producers, enjoyed the fruits of technical progress in the production of manufactured commodities. The industrialized countries have had the best of both worlds, both as consumers of primary commodities and as producers of manufactured articles; the underdeveloped countries have had the worst of both worlds, as consumers of manufactures and as producers of raw materials. This perhaps is the legitimate germ of truth in the charge that foreign investment of the traditional type formed part of a system of "economic imperialism" and of "exploitation."

Even if we disregard the theory of deliberately sinister machinations, there may be legitimate grounds in the arguments set out above for maintaining that the benefits of foreign trade and investment have not been equally shared between the two groups of countries. The capital-exporting countries have received their repayment many times over in the following five forms: (1) possibility of building up exports of manufactures and thus transferring their population from low-productivity occupations to high-productivity occupations; (2) enjoyment of the internal economies of expanded manufacturing industries; (3) enjoyment of the general dynamic impulse radiating from industries in a progressive society; (4) enjoyment of the fruits of technical progress in primary production as main consumers of primary commodities; (5) enjoyment of a contribution from foreign consumers of manufactured articles, representing as it were their contribution to the rising incomes of the producers of manufactured articles.

By contrast, what the underdeveloped countries have to show cannot compare with this formidable list of benefits derived by the industrialized countries from the traditional trade-*cum*-investment system. Perhaps the widespread though inarticulate feeling in the underdeveloped countries that the dice have been loaded against them is not so devoid of foundation after all as the pure theory of exchange might have led one to believe.

It is, of course, true that there are transfer difficulties on the part of the underdeveloped countries which are avoided by production for export directly to the investing countries, but the above analysis may perhaps make a contribution to understanding why this traditional investment system broke down so rapidly and so irreparably in 1929 and 1930. The industrialized countries had already received real repayment from their foreign investments in the five forms described above, and in these ways they may have collected a pretty good return on their investments. When, on top of the returns received in those five forms, they also tried to "get their money back," they may perhaps have been asking (in the economic though not in the legal sense) for double payment; they may have been trying to get a quart out of a pint bottle.

The False Impression of Recent Change in Terms of Trade. There is a fairly widespread impression that this traditional trend toward deteriorating price relations for primary producers has been sharply reversed since pre-war days, although this impression is not as strong now as it was in the middle of 1948. Even if we take that point of time, which represents the peak of postwar primary-commodity prices up till now, a detailed analysis does not bear out the impression that terms of trade have significantly improved in favor of the underdeveloped countries since prewar days.[5]

It may be suggested that the impression that price relations have sharply improved for primary producers can be attributed partly to the abnormal composition of primary-commodity imports into the United States, where coffee plays a predominating part (coffee prices have increased particularly heavily in the immediate postwar period), but specially to the widespread idea that foreign trade between underdeveloped countries and industrialized countries is an exchange of the primary commodities of the former for the capital goods of the latter. In fact, among the imports of the underdeveloped countries capital goods do not generally form the largest category, mainly because the import of capital goods from abroad requires a great deal of comple-

---

[5] For details see the UN study, United Nations (1949a).

mentary domestic investment in those countries for which the domestic finance does not exist or is not mobilized.

The major proportion of the imports of the underdeveloped countries is in fact made up of manufactured food (especially in overpopulated underdeveloped countries), textile manufactures, and manufactured consumer goods. The prices of the type of food imported by the underdeveloped countries and, particularly, the prices of textile manufactures have risen so heavily in the immediate postwar period that any advantage which the underdeveloped countries might have enjoyed in the postwar period from favorable prices realized on primary commodities and low prices of capital goods has been wiped out.

A further factor which has contributed to the impression that relative price trends have turned sharply in favor of primary producers since the war is the deterioration in British terms of trade and the publicity which this deterioration has received because of the strategic importance of the British balance of payments in the network of world trade. It should not be forgotten, however, that the changes in British postwar terms of trade do not merely represent *ceteris paribus* price changes but reflect considerable quantum changes; namely an increase in the quantity exported and a decrease in the quantity imported. It may be suggested, perhaps, that these quantum changes rather than underlying price changes account for the adverse trend before devaluation of British terms of trade. Unless it is to be assumed that the elasticity of demand for British exports is infinite, it is obvious that an expansion in the volume of total exports of manufactured goods by almost 100 per cent will be reflected in lower unit prices for British exports; conversely, the reduction in the quantity of British imports is also reflected in higher prices paid than would otherwise have been the case, partly as a reflection of the diminishing bargaining strength of Britain in consequence of lower imports and partly as a necessary political concession to primary producers to enable them to maintain their incomes in the face of lower quantities sold. The supposition that the changed quantity relations in British trade (as well as deliberate colonial development policies) rather than price changes in world markets are largely responsible for the adverse trend in British terms of trade is greatly strengthened by the fact that other Western European exporters of manufactured goods did not seem to experience any deterioration in their terms of trade but, on the contrary, showed improved terms of trade.[6] The effect of quantum changes on British terms of trade is of course difficult to disentangle statistically. It is more in the nature of a gain missed through inability to exploit the postwar sellers' market price-wise to the full. It is surely a remarkable fact that in a world hungry for capital goods and with its two most important direct industrial competitors eliminated, England should have experienced adverse terms of trade in the years 1945 to 1948.

At this point it may be worth noting the curious ambivalent role which price relations in foreign trade play for the underdeveloped countries. Good prices for their primary commodities, especially if coupled with such a rise in quantities sold as occurs in a boom, give to the underdeveloped countries the necessary means for importing capital goods and financing their own industrial development; yet at the same time they take away the incentive to do so, and investment, both foreign and domestic, is directed into an expansion of primary-commodity production, thus leaving no room for the domestic investment which is the required complement of any import of capital goods. Conversely, when the prices and sales of primary commodities fall off, the desire for industrialization is suddenly sharpened; yet at the same time the means for carrying it out are sharply reduced. Here again it seems that the underdeveloped countries are in danger of falling between two stools: failing to industrialize in a boom because things are as good as they are, and failing to industrialize in a slump because things are as bad as they are.[7] It is no doubt true that failure to utilize high boom export proceeds more determinedly for capital formation because of purely temporary price relations shows a deplorable lack of foresight, but this is hardly very apposite criticism of those underdeveloped countries which rely mainly on private development. All private activity tends to be governed by the price relations of the day.

North America: A Strategic Case. If our view is accepted (namely that the traditional type of foreign investment as it was known prior to 1929 was "foreign" only in the geographical sense and not in the relevant economic sense), does it then

---

[6] United Nations (1949b:II.E.1).

[7] This ambivalence of changing terms of trade has also been stressed in a different context by Lloyd Metzler in his important article (Metzler 1949).

follow that foreign investment has failed to fulfill one of the functions traditionally ascribed to it (and hoped for from it for the future), i.e., to spread industrialization more widely and more evenly throughout the world? It would be premature to jump to this conclusion. What has been maintained in the preceding part of this argument is that past foreign investment and the type of foreign trade which went with it failed to spread industrialization to the countries in which the investment took place. It may be, however, that for a full understanding of the process we have to consider not merely the investing and the invested countries but a third group of countries as well.

It is an interesting speculation that European investment overseas was the instrument by which industrialization was brought to North America. Roughly speaking, the supplies of food and raw materials pouring into Europe as the result of the investment-*cum*-trade system and the favorable terms of trade engendered by this system enabled Europe to feed, clothe, educate, train, and equip large numbers of emigrants sent overseas, principally to the United States and Canada. Thus the benefits to the investing countries of Europe arising out of the system described above were in turn passed on to the United States—the converse of the Marshall Plan—and were the main foundation of the enormous capital formation the result of which is now to be observed in North America. This "macroeconomic" analysis is, of course, in no way contradicted by the fact that the individual migrant was motivated by the prospect of raising his standards of living by the transfer.

Attention may be drawn to the interesting statistical computation of Corrado Gini that even the enormous capital stock characteristic of the United States economy is not more than the equivalent of the burden in consumption goods and in such services as health, education, and other provision for the immigrants—a burden which the United States was enabled to save by shifting it to the European mother countries of the immigrants. Perhaps in the final analysis it may be said that the ultimate benefits of the traditional investment-*cum*-trade system were not with the investing countries of Europe but with the new industrial countries of North America.[8]

---

[8] In more recent years, specially since 1924, United States capital accumulation had of course become quite independent from the original

If this analysis is correct, the industrialization of North America was made possible by the combination of migration and the opening up of underdeveloped overseas countries through European investment and trade. To that extent, Point Four and technical assistance on the part of the United States would be a gesture of historical justice and return of benefits received in the past.

Potential Consequences of This Analysis. Rather than end on a wild historical speculation, it may be useful to summarize the type of economic measures and economic policies which would result from the analysis presented in this paper. The first conclusion would be that in the interest of the underdeveloped countries, of world national income, and perhaps ultimately of the industrialized countries themselves, the purposes of foreign investment and foreign trade ought perhaps to be redefined as producing gradual changes in the structure of comparative advantages and of the comparative endowment of the different countries rather than developing a world trading system based on existing comparative advantages and existing distribution of endowments. This, perhaps, is the real significance of the present movement toward giving technical assistance to underdeveloped countries not necessarily linked with actual trade or investment. The emphasis on technical assistance may be interpreted as a recognition that the present structure of comparative advantages and endowments is not such that it should be considered as a permanent basis for a future international division of labor.

Insofar as the underdeveloped countries continue to be the source of food and primary materials and insofar as trade, investment, and technical assistance are working in that direction by expanding primary production, the main requirement of underdeveloped countries would seem to be to provide for some method of income absorption to ensure that the results of technical progress are retained in the underdeveloped countries in a manner analogous to what occurs in the industrialized countries. Perhaps the most important measure required in this field is the reinvestment of profits in the underdeveloped countries themselves, or else the absorption of profits by fiscal measures and their utilization for the finance of economic development, and the

---

stimulus supplied by immigration, and proceeded without any visible check in spite of a heavy reduction in immigration. The argument put forward here is meant as a historical explanation rather than an analysis of the present sources of capital investment.

absorption of rising productivity in primary production in rising real wages and other real incomes, provided that the increment is utilized for an increase in domestic savings and the growth of markets of a kind suitable for the development of domestic industries. Perhaps this last argument, namely the necessity of some form of domestic absorption of the fruits of technical progress in primary production, provides the rationale for the concern which the underdeveloped countries show for the introduction of progressive social legislation. Higher standards of wages and social welfare, however, are not a highly commendable cure for bad terms of trade except where the increment leads to domestic savings and investment. Where higher wages and social services are prematurely introduced and indiscriminately applied to export and domestic industries, they may in the end turn out to be a retarding factor in economic development and undermine the international bargaining strength of the primary producers. Absorption of the fruits of technical progress in primary production is not enough; what is wanted is absorption for reinvestment.

Finally, the argument put forward in this paper would point the lesson that a flow of international investment into the underdeveloped countries will contribute to their economic development only if it is absorbed into their economic system, i.e., if a good deal of complementary domestic investment is generated and the requisite domestic resources are found.

The most natural way, surely, of encouraging husbandry, is, first, to excite other kinds of industry, and thereby afford the [agricultural] labourer a ready market for his commodities, and a return of such goods as may contribute to his pleasure and enjoyment. This method is infallible and universal.

David Hume

Change is a deliberately vague term. It applies equally to growth and differentiation, to modification of functions, to the . . . destruction of given structures. Social change is a [restructuring] over time, characterized by (a) causes, (b) a certain course of development, and (c) certain results . . . To proceed beyond the description of change to an explanation of it, it is necessary to formulate refutable statements about the variables on which these three dimensions depend, i.e., to formulate theories.

Wolfgang Zapf

. . . a good theory . . . makes possible generalizations that bring together and explain empirical observations not previously seen to be related to one another.

Meyer Fortes

16 MECHANISMS OF CHANGE AND ADJUSTMENT TO CHANGE[1]

Neil J. Smelser

INTRODUCTION

A THOROUGH analysis of the social changes accompanying economic development would require an ambitious theoretical scheme and a vast quantity of comparative data. Because I lack both necessities—and the space to use them if I possessed them—I shall restrict this exploratory statement in two ways. (*1*) Methodologically, I shall deal only with ideal-type constructs, in Weber's sense; I shall not discuss any individual cases of development, or the comparative applicability of particular historical generalizations. (*2*) Substantively, I shall consider only modifications of the social structure; I shall not deal with factor-allocation, savings and investment, inflation, balance of payments, foreign aid, size of population, and rate of population change—even though these variables naturally affect, and are affected by, structural changes. These omissions call for brief comment.

Max Weber defined an ideal-type construct as a

> one-sided accentuation . . . by the synthesis of a great many diffuse, discrete, more or less present and occasionally absent *concrete individual* phenomena, which are arranged . . . into a unified *analytical* construct. In its conceptual purity, this mental construct cannot be found anywhere in reality (Weber 1949:90, 93).

SOURCE: Neil J. Smelser, "Mechanisms of Change and Adjustment to Change," pages 32–54, *Industrialization and Society*, B. F. Hoselitz and W. E. Moore, editors, Unesco/Mouton, 1963. Reprinted by permission of the author and publisher.

[1] I am grateful to Professors William Petersen, Herbert Blumer, Reinhard Bendix, and Kingsley Davis of the University of California, Berkeley, for critical comments on an earlier version of this essay.

The analyst utilizes such ideal constructs to unravel and explain a variety of actual historical situations. Weber mentions explicitly two kinds of ideal-type constructs—first, "historically unique configurations," such as "rational bourgeois capitalism," "medieval Christianity," etc.; and second, statements concerning historical evolution, such as the Marxist laws of capitalist development (Weber 1949:93, 101–3). While the second type presupposes some version of the first, I shall concentrate on the dynamic constructs.

"Economic development" generally refers to the "growth of output per head of population" (Lewis 1955:1). For purposes of analyzing the relationships between economic growth and the social structure, it is possible to isolate the effects of several interrelated technical, economic, and ecological processes that frequently accompany development. These may be listed as follows: (*1*) In the realm of technology, the change *from* simple and traditionalized techniques *toward* the application of scientific knowledge. (*2*) In agriculture, the evolution *from* subsistence farming *toward* commercial production of agricultural goods. This means specialization in cash crops, purchase of non-agricultural products in the market, and often agricultural wage-labor. (*3*) In industry, the transition *from* the use of human and animal power *toward* industrialization proper, or "men aggregated at power-driven machines, working for monetary return with the products of the manufacturing process entering into a market based on a network of exchange relations" (Nash 1955:271). (*4*) In ecological arrangements, the movement *from* the farm and village *toward* urban centers. These several processes often, but not necessarily, occur simultaneously. Certain technological improvements—e.g., the use of improved seeds—can be introduced without automatically and instantaneously causing organizational changes;[2] agriculture may be commercialized without any concomitant industrialization, as in many colonial countries (Boeke 1942:76–89); industrialization may occur in villages (Nash 1955; Herman 1956; Aubery 1957); and cities may proliferate even

---

[2] W. H. Beckett (1953:138–43), for instance, distinguishes between "technical improvement" and "organizational improvement" in agriculture. For an analysis of the interplay between technological advance and productive reorganization during the Tokugawa period in Japan, see Rosovsky (mimeographed:7–17).

where there is no significant industrialization (Hodgkin 1957:ch. 2). Furthermore, the specific social consequences of technological advance, commercialized agriculture, the factory, and the city, respectively, are not in any sense reducible to each other. (Hoselitz 1955; Davis and Golden 1955).

Despite such differences, all four processes tend to affect the social structure in similar ways. All give rise to the following ideal-type structural changes, which have ramifications throughout society: (*1*) Structural differentiation, or the establishment of more specialized and more autonomous social units. I shall discuss the occurrence of this process in the different spheres of economy, family, religion, and stratification. (*2*) Integration, which changes its character as the old social order is made obsolete by the process of differentiation. The state, the law, political groupings, and other associations are particularly salient in this integration. (*3*) Social disturbances—mass hysteria, outbursts of violence, religious and political movements, etc.—which reflect the uneven advances of differentiation and integration, respectively.

Obviously, the implications of technological advance, agricultural reorganization, industrialization, and urbanization differ from society to society, as do the resulting structural realignments. Some of the sources of variation in these ideal patterns of pressure and change are described in the next paragraphs.

a) Variations in pre-modern conditions. Is the society's value system congenial or antagonistic to industrial values? How well integrated is the society? How "backward" is it? What is its level of wealth? How is the wealth distributed? Is the country "young and empty" or "old and crowded"? Is the country politically dependent, newly independent, or completely autonomous? Such pre-existing factors shape the impact of the forces of economic development (Kuznets 1955; 1954; Gerschenkron 1952; Linton 1952; Aitkin 1959).

b) Variations in the impetus to change. Do pressures to modernize come from the internal implications of a value system, from a wish for national security and prestige, from a desire for material property, or from a combination of these? Is political coercion used to form a labor force? Or are the pressures economic, as in the case of population pressure on the land or that of loss of handicraft markets to cheap imported products? Or do economic and political pressures combine, as, for example, when a tax is levied on peasants that is payable only in money? Or are the pressures social, as they are when there is a desire to escape burdensome aspects of the old order? Factors like these influence the adjustment to modernization greatly (Staley 1954: 21–22; Rostow 1960; Moore 1951:ch. 2–4; Hoselitz 1955: 177–79).

c) Variations in the path toward modernization. Does the sequence begin with light consumer industries? Or is there an attempt to introduce heavy, capital-intensive industries first? What is the role of government in shaping the pattern of investment? What is the rate of accumulation of technological knowledge and skills? What is the general tempo of industrialization? These questions indicate elements which affect the nature of structural change and the degree of discomfort created by this change (UN 1955a:ch. 1; Kindleberger 1958:184–85, 315–16; Buchannan and Ellis 1955:275 ff.; Kuznets 1954:21–22).

d) Variations in the advanced stages of modernization. What is the emergent distribution of industries in developed economies? What are the emergent relations between state and economy, religion and economy, state and religion, etc.? While all advanced industrialized societies have their "industrialization" in common, uniquely national differences remain. For instance, "social class" has a different social significance in the United States than in the United Kingdom, even though both are highly developed countries.

e) Variations in the content and timing of dramatic events during modernization. What is the import of wars, revolutions, rapid migrations, natural catastrophes, etc., for the course of economic and social development?

These sources of variation render it virtually impossible to establish hard and fast empirical generalizations concerning the evolution of social structures during economic and social development.[3] Therefore, my purpose here is not to search for such

---

[3] For instance, Blumer (1960:9) has questioned the generalization that "early industrialization, by nature, alienates and disaffects workers, makes them radical, and propels them to protest behavior." He even concludes that "industrialization . . . is neutral and indifferent to what follows in its wake." If one searches for specific generalizations like those Blumer has rejected, of course, he will inevitably be disappointed. One must not conclude, however, that the establishment of ideal-type constructs about the consequences of industrialization, and their use in interpreting national experiences are fruitless.

generalizations, but rather to outline certain ideal-type directions of structural change that modernization involves. On the basis of these ideal types, we may classify, describe, and analyze varying national experiences. Factors like those indicated above determine, in part, a nation's distinctive response to the universal aspects of modernization; but this in no way detracts from their universality. While I shall base my remarks on the vast literature of economic development, I can in no sense attempt an exhaustive comparative study.

STRUCTURAL DIFFERENTIATION IN PERIODS OF DEVELOPMENT

The concept of structural differentiation can be employed to analyze what is frequently termed the "marked break in established patterns of social and economic life" in periods of development (Kuznets 1954:23). Simply defined, "differentiation" is the evolution from a multi-functional role structure to several more specialized structures. In illustration, we may cite here three typical examples. During a society's transition from domestic to factory industry, the division of labor increases, and the economic activities previously lodged in the family move to the firm. As a formal educational system emerges, the training functions previously performed by the family and church are established in a more specialized unit, the school (Smelser 1958:ch. 9–11). The modern political party has a more complex structure than do tribal factions, and the former is less likely to be fettered with kinship loyalties, competition for religious leadership, etc.

Formally defined, then, structural differentiation is a process whereby

> *one* social role or organization . . . differentiates into *two or more* roles or organizations which function more effectively in the new historical circumstances. The new social units are structurally distinct from each other, but taken together are functionally equivalent to the original unit (Smelser 1958:2).

Differentiation concerns only changes in role structure. It must not be confused with two closely related concepts. The first of these involves the cause or motivation for entering the differentiated role. Someone may be motivated to engage in wage-labor, for instance, by a desire for economic improvement, by political coercion, or indeed by a wish to fulfil traditional obligations (e.g., to use wages to supply a dowry). These "reasons" should be kept conceptually distinct from differentiation itself. The other related concept concerns the integration of differentiated roles. For example, as differentiated wage-labor begins to emerge, there also appear legal norms, labor exchanges, trade unions, and so on, that regulate—with varying degrees of success—the relations between labor and management. Such readjustments, even though they sometimes produce a new social unit, should be considered separately from role specialization in other functions.

Let us now inquire into the process of differentiation in several different social realms.

Differentiation of Economic Activities

In underdeveloped countries, production typically is located in kinship units. Subsistence farming predominates; other industry is supplementary but still attached to kin and village. In some cases, occupational position is determined largely by an extended group, such as the caste.[4]

Similarly, exchange and consumption are deeply embedded in family and village. In subsistence agriculture, there is a limited amount of independent exchange outside the family; thus production and consumption occur in the same social context. Exchange systems proper are still lodged in kinship and community (e.g., reciprocal exchange), and stratification systems (e.g., redistribution according to caste membership), in political systems (e.g., taxes, tributes, payments in kind, forced labor).[5] Under these conditions, market systems are underdeveloped, and the independent power of money to command the movement of goods and services is minimal.

As the economy develops, several kinds of economic activity are removed from this family-community complex. In agriculture, the introduction of money crops marks a differentiation between the social contexts of production and of consumption. Agricultural wage-labor sometimes undermines the family production unit. In industry, several levels of differentiation can be identified. Household industry, the simplest form, parallels subsistence agriculture in that it supplies "the worker's own needs, unconnected

---

[4] Boeke (1942:8–9, 32–34); Hagen (1957:195); Maden (1951:813–21); Dowd (1957). For qualifications on the degree to which caste dominates occupation in India, see Davis (1951:163 ff.).

[5] See, Polanyi, Arensberg, and Pearson (1957); Smelser (1959); Boeke (1942:36–39); Solomon (1957:131 ff.).

with trade." "Handicraft production" splits production and consumption, though frequently consumption takes place in the local community. "Cottage industry," on the other hand, often involves a differentiation between consumption and community, since production is "for the market, for an unknown consumer, sold to a wholesaler who accumulates a stock."[6] Finally, manufacturing and factory systems segregate the worker from his capital and not rarely from his family.

Simultaneously, similar differentiations emerge in the exchange system. Goods and services, previously exchanged on a non-economic basis, are pulled progressively more into the market. Money now commands the movement of increasingly more goods and services; it thus begins to supplant—and sometimes undermine—the religious, political, familial, or caste sanctions which had hitherto governed economic activity (Bailey 1957:4–5). This is the setting for the institutionalization of relatively autonomous economic systems that exhibit a greater emphasis on values like "universalism," "functional specificity," and "rationality."[7]

Empirically, underdeveloped economies may be classified according to the respective distances they have moved along this line of differentiation. Migratory labor, for instance, may be a kind of compromise between full membership in a wage-labor force and attachment to an old community life. Cottage industry introduces extended markets but retains the family production fusion. The employment of families in factories maintains a version of family production. The expenditure of wages on traditional items, like dowries, also manifests the half-entry into the more differentiated industrial-urban structure.[8] The causes of such partial differentiation may lie in resistance on the part of the populace to give up traditional modes, in the economics of demand for handmade products, in systems of racial discrimination against native labor, or elsewhere.[9] In any case, the concept

---

[6] These "levels," which represent points on the continuum from structural fusion to structural differentiation, are taken from Boeke (1942:90).

[7] Levy (1952). The pattern variables of T. Parsons are also relevant, discussed in Parsons (1951:58–67). For applications of the pattern variables to economic development, see Theodorson (1953).

[8] Examples of these compromises may be found in Moore (1951:29–34; 1957:79 ff.); Richards (n.d.:ch. 5); Myers (1958:52, 175); Rottenberg (1957:150–51); Aubrey (1957); Doucey (1954); Balandier (1955:60–61); Smelser (1958:ch. 9); Herman (1956).

[9] Non-economic barriers are discussed at length in Moore (1951:ch.

of structural differentiation provides a yardstick for discerning the distance that the economic structure has evolved toward modernization.

Differentiation of Family Activities

One consequence of the removal of economic activities from the kinship nexus is the family's loss of some of its previous functions, and its thereby becoming a more specialized agency. As the family ceases to be an economic unit of production, one or more members leave the household to seek employment in the labor market. The family's activities become more concentrated on emotional gratification and socialization. While many halfway houses, such as family hiring and migratory systems, persist, the trend is toward the segregation of family functions from economic functions (for case studies see Levy 1949, and Smelser 1958).

Several related processes accompany the differentiation of the family from its other involvements. (*1*) Apprenticeship within the family declines. (*2*) Pressures develop against nepotism in the recruitment of labor and management. These pressures often are based on the demands of economic rationality. The intervention frequently persists, however—especially at the managerial levels—and in some cases (e.g., Japan), family ties continue to be a major basis for labor recruitment. (*3*) The direct control of elders and collateral kinsmen over the nuclear family weakens. This marks, in structural terms, the differentiation of the nuclear family from the extended family. (*4*) An aspect of this loss of control is the growth of personal choice, love, and related criteria as the foundation for courtship and marriage. Structurally, this is the differentiation of courtship from extended kinship. (*5*) One result of this complex of processes is the changing status of women, who generally become less subordinated economically, politically, and socially to their husbands than they had been under earlier conditions.[10]

2–4). On the persistence of handicrafts, see Minkes (1953:156–58); Herman (1956); Uyeda (1938:84–112).

[10] Kindleberger (1958:59 ff.); Moore (1951:29–34, 71–75); Frazier (1955:76–83); UNESCO (1956:108–9, 115–17, 187, 216–20, 369–72, 616 ff.); El Daghestani (1954); Siegel (1955); Stein (1955); Elkan (1956); Byers (1958:177); Linton (1952); Belshaw (1957:88 ff., 191 ff.); Orde Browne (1933:100–5).

In such ways, structural differentiation undermines the old modes of integration in society. The controls of extended family and village begin to dissolve in the enlarged, complicated social setting which differentiation creates. Thereupon, new integrative problems are posed. We shall inquire presently into some of the lines of integration.

Differentiation of Religious Systems

Because of Max Weber's monumental thesis linking ascetic Protestantism and capitalism,[11] a disproportionate amount of attention has been devoted to the initiating role that *formal* religious values play in economic development. Although much excellent work has been done in this area (Bellah 1957; Geertz 1955), insufficient emphasis has been given to the important role of secular nationalism in the industrial takeoff.

> With the world organized as it is, nationalism is a *sine qua non* of industrialization, because it provides people with an overriding, easily acquired, secular motivation for making painful changes. National strength or prestige becomes the supreme goal, industrialization the chief means. The costs, inconveniences, sacrifices, and loss of traditional values can be justified in terms of this transcending, collective ambition. The new collective entity, the nation-state, that sponsors and grows from this aspiration is equal to the exigencies of industrial complexity; it draws directly the allegiance of every citizen, organizing the population as one community; it controls the passage of persons, goods, and news across the borders; it regulates economic and social life in detail. To the degree that the obstacles to industrialization are strong, nationalism must be intense to overcome them (Davis 1955; Gerschenkron 1952; Rostow 1960).

In fact, nationalism seems in many cases to be the very instrument designed to smash the traditional religious systems—those like, e.g., the classical Chinese or Indian—which Weber himself found to be less permissive than Protestantism for economic modernization.

On the other hand, nationalism, like many traditionalistic religious systems, may hinder economic advancement by "reaffirmation of traditionally honored ways of acting and thinking," (Hose-

---

[11] Weber's relevant works include (1948, 1951, 1958). For secondary treatments, see Parsons (1937:ch. xiv and xv) and Bendix (1959).

litz 1953) by fostering anti-colonial attitudes after they are no longer relevant,[12] and, more indirectly, by encouraging passive expectations of "ready-made prosperity" (Van der Kroef 1956). We can distinguish among these contrasting forces of "stimulus" and "drag" that such value systems bring to economic development by using the logic of differentiation in the following way.

In the early phases of modernization, many traditional attachments must be modified to permit more differentiated institutional structures to be set up. Because the existing commitments and methods of integration are deeply rooted in the organization of traditional society, a very generalized and powerful commitment is required to pry individuals from these attachments. The values of ascetic and this-worldly religious beliefs, xenophobic national aspirations, and political ideologies (like, e.g., socialism), provide such a lever. Sometimes these diverse types of values combine into a single system of legitimacy. In any case, all three have an "ultimacy" of commitment, in whose name a wide range of sacrifices can be demanded and procured.

The very success of these value systems, however, breeds the conditions for their own weakening. In a perceptive statement, Weber notes that, at the beginning of the twentieth century, when the capitalistic system was already highly developed, it no longer needed the impetus of ascetic Protestantism (Weber 1948: 181–82). By virtue of its conquest of much of Western society, capitalism had solidly established an institutional base and a secular value system of its own—economic rationality. Its secular economic values had no further need for the "ultimate" justification they had required during the newer, unsteadier days of economic revolution.

Such lines of differentiation constitute the secularization of religious values. In the same process, other institutional spheres—economic, political, scientific, etc.—become more nearly established on their own. The values governing these spheres are no longer sanctioned directly by religious beliefs, but by an autonomous rationality. In so far as this replaces religious sanctions, secularization occurs in these spheres.

---

[12] Cf., for example, the Indonesian expulsion of needed Dutch teachers and engineers. It has been maintained that the upsurge of regionalism in India has led to a deterioration of English as a linguistic medium for education in Indian universities. See Harrison (1960).

Similarly, nationalistic and related value systems undergo a process of secularization as differentiation proceeds. As a society moves increasingly toward more complex social organization, the encompassing demands of nationalistic commitment give way to more autonomous systems of rationality. For instance, the Soviet Union, as its social structure grows more differentiated, is apparently introducing more "independent" market mechanisms, "freer" social scientific investigation in some spheres, and so on.[13] Moreover, these measures are not directly sanctioned by nationalistic or communistic values. Finally, it seems reasonable to make the historical generalization that, in the early stages of a nation's development, nationalism is heady, muscular, and aggressive; as the society evolves to an advanced state, however, nationalism tends to settle into a more remote and complacent condition, rising to fury only in times of national crisis.

Hence there is a paradoxical element in the role of religious or nationalistic belief systems. In so far as they encourage the breakup of old patterns, they may stimulate economic modernization. In so far as they resist their own subsequent secularization, however, these same value systems may become an impediment to economic advance and structural change.

Differentiation of Systems of Stratification

In analyzing systems of stratification, we concentrate on two kinds of issues.

   a) Are ascribed qualities subject to ranking? Ascription focuses
      primarily on those aspects of the human condition that
      touch the biological and physical world—kinship, age, sex,
      race or ethnicity, and territorial location. To what extent is
      status determined by birth in a certain tribe? in a certain
      family? in a certain ethnic group? in a certain place—a
      region of the country or "the wrong side of the tracks"?
      Some ascription exists in all societies, since the infant in the
      nuclear family always and everywhere begins with the
      status of his parents (Davis 1957; Parsons 1954). The
      degree to which this ascribed ranking extends beyond the
      family varies from society to society. In our own ideology,
      we minimize the ascriptive elements of class and ethnic

---

[13] For discussion of the balance among political and other elements in Soviet society, see Bauer et al. (1957).

membership; but in practice these matter greatly, especially for Negroes.

b) The degree to which all positions in society (occupational, political, religious, etc.) are consequences of status ascribed from birth. For example, the American egalitarian ideology places a premium on the maximum separation of these positions from ascribed categories; but in fact, family membership, minority-group membership, etc., impinge on the ultimate "placing" of persons. In many non-industrialized societies, the link between ascription and position is much closer. Criteria like these reveal the degree of openness, or social mobility, in a system.

Under conditions of economic modernization, structural differentiation increases along both dimensions discussed.

1. Other evaluative standards intrude on ascribed memberships. For instance, McKim Marriott has noted that, in the village of Paril in India,

> Personal wealth, influence, and mortality have surpassed the traditional caste-and-order alignment of kin groups as the effective bases of ranking. Since such new bases of ranking can no longer be clearly tied to any inclusive system of large solidary groupings, judgments must be made according to the characteristics of individual or family units. This individualization of judgments leads to greater dissensus [*sic*]. (Marriott 1953; UNESCO 1956:152; Coleman 1958:70–73.)

Of course, castes, ethnic groups, and traditional religious groupings do not necessarily decline in importance *in every respect* during periods of modernization. As political interest groups or reference groups for diffuse loyalty, they may become even more significant.[14] As the sole bases of ranking, however, ascriptive

---

[14] In some cases, these ascriptive pegs become the basis for political groupings long after the society has begun to modernize. See Jacoby (1949:27–28, 50, 76, 91–93, 123–25, 248), Coleman (1958:332–67). Harrison has argued that the present significance of caste in India is "if anything, stronger than before," but that this significance appears as competitiveness in the new political arena of the country (Harrison 1960: chap iv; also Davis 1951:171). William Petersen has suggested that, in the advanced society of Holland, a process of "pillarization" has occurred, in which semi-ascribed religious groups have become the major focus of political and social competition.

standards become more differentiated from economic, political, and other standards.[15]

2. Individual mobility through the occupational hierarchies increases. This is indicative of the differentiation of the adult's functional position from his point of origin. In addition, individual mobility is frequently substituted for collective mobility. Individuals, and no longer whole castes or tribes, compete for higher standing in society. The phenomenon of growing individual mobility seems to be one of the universal consequences of industrialization. After assembling extensive empirical data on patterns of mobility in industrialized nations, Lipset and Bendix conclude that "the overall pattern of [individual] social mobility appears to be much the same in the industrial societies of various Western countries."[16] Patterns of class symbolization and class ideology may, however, continue to be different in industrialized countries.

THE INTEGRATION OF DIFFERENTIATED ACTIVITIES

One of Emile Durkheim's remarkable insights concerned the role of integrative mechanisms during periods of growing social heterogeneity. Attacking the utilitarian view that the division of labor would flourish best without regulation, Durkheim demonstrates that one concomitant of a growing division of labor is an *increase* in mechanisms for co-ordinating and solidifying the interaction among individuals whose interests are becoming progressively more diversified.[17] Durkheim locates this integration largely in the legal structure; however, similar kinds of integrative forces can be discerned elsewhere in society.

Differentiation, therefore, is not by itself sufficient for modernization. Development proceeds as a contrapuntal interplay between differentiation (which is divisive of established society) and integration (which unites differentiated structures on a new basis). Paradoxically, however, the course of integration itself produces

---

[15] For a study of the cross-cultural similarity in the ranking of industrial occupations in developed countries, see Inkeles et al. (1957).

[16] Lipset and Bendix (1959:13 ff.). Of course, the transition from collective to individual mobility is not instantaneous. See Marriott (1953: 153) and Davis (1955).

[17] Durkheim (1949:ch. iii–viii). A recent formulation of the relationship between differentiation and integration may be found in Bales (1950).

more *differentiated* structures—e.g., trade unions, associations, political parties, and a mushrooming state apparatus. Let us illustrate this complex process of integration in several institutional spheres.

Economy and Family

Under a simple kind of economic organization, like subsistence agriculture or household industry, there is little differentiation between economic roles and family roles. All reside in the kinship structure. The *integration* of these diverse but unspecialized activities also rests in the local family and community structures, and in the religious traditions which fortify both.

When differentiation has begun, the social setting for production is separated from that for consumption; and the productive roles of family members are isolated geographically, temporally, and structurally from their distinctively familial roles. This differentiation immediately creates integrative problems. How is information about employment opportunities to be conveyed to working people? How are the interests of families to be integrated with the interests of firms? How are families to be protected from market fluctuation? Whereas such integrative exigencies had been faced by kinsmen, neighbors, and local largesse in pre-modern settings, modernization creates dozens of institutions and organizations designed to deal with the new integrative problems—labor recruitment agencies and exchanges; labor unions; government regulation of labor allocation; welfare and relief arrangements; co-operative societies; savings institutions.[18] All these involve agencies which specialize in integration.

Community

When industrialization occurs only in villages, or when villages are built around paternalistic industrial enterprises,[19] many ties of community and kinship can be maintained under the industrial conditions. Urbanization, however, frequently creates more anonymity. As a result, in expanding cities there often emerge voluntary associations—churches and chapels, unions, schools, halls, athletic clubs, bars, shops, mutual-aid groups, etc. Sometimes the growth of these integrative groupings is retarded because of the

---

[18] Smelser (1958:ch. xii–xiii); Parsons and Smelser (1956:ch. iii); Nash (1955:275); Mehta (1958:20–23).

[19] Smelser (1958:99–108); Myers (1958:52–54); Stein (1955).

movement of migratory workers,[20] who "come to the city for
their differentiation" and "return to the village for their integration." In cities themselves, the original criterion for associating
may have been the common tribe, caste, or village; this criterion
sometimes persists or is gradually replaced by more "functional"
groupings based on economic or political interest.[21]

Political Structure

In a typical pre-modern setting, political integration is closely
fused with kinship position, tribal membership, control of the
land, or control of the unknown. Political forms include chieftains,
kings, councils of elders, strong landlords, powerful magicians
and oracles, etc.

As social systems grow more complex, political systems are
modified accordingly. Fortes and Evans-Pritchard have specified
three types of native African political systems. These, listed in
terms of their respective degrees of differentiation from kinship
lineages, are as follows: (*1*) small societies in which the largest
political unit embraces only those united by kinship—thus political
authority is conterminous with kinship relations; (*2*) societies in
which the political framework is the integrative core for a number
of kinship lineages; and (*3*) societies with a more formal administrative organization. Such systems move toward greater differentiation as the society's population grows and economic and
cultural heterogeneity increases (Fortes et al. 1940:1–25). In
colonial and recently-freed African societies, political systems have
evolved much further; parties, congresses, pressure groups, and
even "parliamentary" systems have emerged.[22] In describing the
Indian village, Marriott speaks of the "wider integration of local
groups with outside groups" (Marriott 1953:152). Sometimes
such wider political integration is, like community integration,
based on extension and modification of an old integrative principle. Harrison has argued that modern developments in India

---

[20] Orde Browne (1933:112–16); Doucy (1954:446–50); Elkan (1956:
ch. ii–iii).

[21] UNESCO (1956:84–85, 105, 120–21, 128–30, 220–21, 373–77, 469–
73); Forde (1955:119–21); Hodgkin (1957:85 ff.); Hoselitz (1955:183);
Coleman (1958:73–80); Harrison (1960:330–32).

[22] Apter (1956); Hodgkin (1957:115–39); Almond and Coleman
(1960).

have changed the significance of caste from the "traditional village extension of the joint family" to "regional alliances of kindred local units." This modification has led to the formation of "new caste lobbies" which constitute some of the strongest and most explosive political forces in modern India (Harrison 1960:100 ff.). We shall mention some of the possible political consequences of this persistence of old integrative forms later.

We have indicated the ways in which differentiation in society impinges on the integrative sphere. The resulting integrative structures attempt, with more or less success, to co-ordinate and solidify the social structure which the forces of differentiation threaten to fragment. In many cases, the integrative associations and parties are extremely unstable: labor unions turn into political or nationalistic parties; religious sects become political clubs; football clubs become religious sects; and so on (Hodgkin 1957). This fluidity indicates the urgent need for reintegration during rapid, irregular, and disruptive processes of differentiation. The initial response is a trial-and-error type of reaching for many kinds of integration at once.

We have outlined some structural consequences of technological advance, agricultural commercialization, urbanization, and industrialization. We have analyzed these consequences in terms of differentiation and integration. The structural changes are not, one must remember, a simple function of industrialization alone. Some of the most far-reaching structural changes have occurred in countries where industrialization has hardly begun. For instance, colonialism or related forms of economic dominance create not only an extensive differentiation of cash products and wage-labor, but also a vulnerability to world price fluctuations in commodities (Jacoby 1949:ch. i; Emerson et al. 1942:135–36; Mosk 1950:3–17). Hence many of the structural changes already described, and the consequent social disturbances to be described presently, are characteristics of societies which are still technically pre-industrial.

DISCONTINUITIES IN DIFFERENTIATION AND INTEGRATION:
SOCIAL DISTURBANCES

The structural changes associated with modernization are disruptive to the social order for the following reasons:

a) Differentiation demands the creation of new activities, norms, rewards, and sanctions—money, political position, prestige based on occupation, etc. These often conflict with old modes of social action, which are frequently dominated by traditional religious, tribal, and kinship systems. Traditional standards are among the most intransigent obstacles to modernization; and when they are threatened, serious dissatisfaction and opposition to the threatening agents arise.

b) Structural change is, above all, *uneven* during periods of modernization. In colonial societies, for instance, the European powers frequently revolutionized the economic, political, and educational frameworks; but they simultaneously encouraged or imposed a conservatism in traditional religious, class, and family systems.

The basic problem in these [colonial] societies was the expectation that the native population would accept certain broad, modern institutional settings . . . and would perform within them various roles—especially economic and administrative roles—while at the same time, they were denied some of the basic rewards inherent in these settings . . . they were expected to act on the basis of a motivational system derived from a different social structure which the colonial powers and indigenous rulers tried to maintain (Eisenstadt 1957:298).

In a society undergoing post-colonial modernization, similar discontinuities appear. Within the economy itself, rapid industrialization—no matter how co-ordinated—bites unevenly into the established social and economic structures (Bauer and Yamey 1957:64). And throughout the society, the differentiation occasioned by agricultural, industrial, and urban changes always proceeds in a seesaw relationship with integration: the two forces continuously breed lags and bottlenecks. The faster the tempo of modernization is, the more severe the discontinuities. This unevenness creates *anomie* in the classical sense, for it generates disharmony between life experiences and the normative framework which regulates them (Durkheim 1951:Book II, ch. v).

c) Dissatisfactions arising from conflict with traditional ways and those arising from *anomie* sometimes aggravate each other upon coming into contact. *Anomie* may be partially relieved by new integrative devices, like unions, associations, clubs, and government regulations. However, such innovations are often opposed by traditional vested interests because they compete with the older undifferentiated systems of solidarity (Davis 1955:296 ff.). The result is a three-way tug-of-war among the forces of tradition, the forces of differentiation, and the new forces of integration (E.g., Jaspan 1953). Under these conditions, virtually unlimited potentialities for group conflict are created.[23]

Three classic responses to these discontinuities are anxiety, hostility, and fantasy. If and when these responses become collective, they crystallize into a variety of social movements —peaceful agitation, political violence, millenarianism, nationalism, revolution, underground subversion, etc.[24] There is plausible—though not entirely convincing—evidence that the people most readily drawn into such movements are those suffering most severely under the displacements created by structural change. For example:

[Nationalism appeared] as a permanent force in Southeast Asia at the moment when the peasants were forced to give up subsistence farming for the cultivation of cash crops or when (as in highly colonized Java) subsistence farming ceased to yield a subsistence. The introduction of a money economy and the withering away of the village as the unit of life accompanied this development and finally established the period of economic dependence (Jacoby 1949:246).

Other theoretical and empirical data suggest that social movements appeal most to those who have been dislodged from old social ties by differentiation without also being integrated into the new social order.[25]

Many belief systems associated with these movements envision the grand, almost instantaneous integration of society. Frequently, the beliefs are highly emotional and unconcerned with realistic policies. In nationalistic movements in colonial societies, for instance, "the political symbols were intended to develop new,

---

[23] E.g., the conflict between migratory workers and full-time resident workers; see Elkan (1956:23–24).

[24] For theoretical discussions of this relationship between strain and disturbance, see Parsons et al. (1955:ch. ii and iv); Smelser (1958:ch. ii, ix–x).

[25] Emerson et al. (1942:25–29); Eisenstadt (1957:294–98); Kornhauser (1959:Parts II–III); Lipset (1960:ch. ii); Watnick (1952).

ultimate, common values and basic loyalties, rather than relate to current policy issues within the colonial society." (Eisenstadt 1957:294). Furthermore, belief systems of this kind reflect the ambivalence that results from the conflict between traditionalism and modernization. Nationalists alternate between xenophobia and xenophilia; they predict that they will simultaneously "outmodernize" the West in the future and "restore" the true values of the ancient civilization; they argue both for egalitarian and for hierarchical principles of social organization at the same time (Matossian 1958). Nationalism and related ideologies unite these contradictory tendencies in the society under one large symbol. If these ideologies are successful, they are then often used as a means to modernize the society and thus to erase those kinds of social discontinuity that caused the initial nationalistic outburst.

Naturally, early modernization does not inevitably produce violent nationalism or other social movements. Furthermore, when such movements do arise, they take many different forms. Below are listed the five factors which seem most decisive in the genesis and molding of social disturbances.

1. The scope and intensity of the social dislocation created by structural changes. "The greater the tempo of these changes . . . the greater the problems of acute mal-integration the society has to face."[26]

2. The structural complexity of the society at the time when modernization begins. In the least developed societies, where "the language of politics is at the same time the language of religion," protest movements more or less immediately take on a religious cast. In Africa, for instance, utopian religious movements apparently have relatively greater appeal in the less developed regions; whereas the more secular types of political protest, like trade union movements and party agitations, have tended to cluster in the more developed areas (Hodgkin 1957:95 ff.; Coleman 1958:38 ff.). The secularization of protest increases, of course, as modernization and differentiation advance.

3. The access that disturbed groups have to channels that influence social policy. If dislocated groups have access to those responsible for introducing reforms, agitation is usually relatively peaceful and orderly. If this avenue is blocked—because of either the isolation of the groups or the intransigence of the ruling

---

[26] Eisenstadt (1957:294); Coleman (1957:42 ff.); Hodgkin (1957:56).

authorities—demands for reform tend to take more violent, utopian, and bizarre forms. This is the reason that fantasy and unorganized violence are likely to cluster among the disinherited, the colonized, and the socially isolated migrants.[27]

4. The overlap of interests and lines of cleavage. In many colonial societies, the social order broke more or less imperfectly into three groupings: (*a*) the Western representatives, who controlled economic and political administration, and who were frequently allied with large local landowners; (*b*) a large native population who—when drawn into the colonial economy—entered it as tenant farmers, wage-laborers, etc.; (*c*) a group of foreigners—Chinese, Indians, Syrians, Goans, Lebanese, etc.—who fitted between the first two groups as traders, moneylenders, merchants, creditors, etc. This view is oversimplified, of course; but several colonial societies approximated this arrangement.[28] The important structural feature of such an arrangement is that economic, political, and racial-ethnic memberships *coincide* with each other. Thus, *any* kind of conflict is likely to assume racial overtones and to arouse the more diffuse loyalties and prejudices of the warring parties. Many colonial outbursts did, in fact, follow racial lines (Emerson et al. 1942:141–43; Jacoby 1949: ch. iii). In so far as such "earthquake faults" persist after independence has been attained, these societies will probably be plagued by similar outbursts (Van der Kroef 1954; Harrison 1960:ch. iii–vi). If, on the other hand, the different lines of cleavage in the society criss-cross, the society is more nearly able to insulate and manage specific economic and political grievances peacefully (Lipset 1960:ch. iii).

5. The kind and amount of foreign infiltration and intervention on behalf of protest groups.

STRUCTURAL BASES FOR THE ROLE OF GOVERNMENT

Many have argued, on economic grounds, for the presence of a strong, centralized government in rapidly modernizing societies. Governmental planning and activity are required, for example, to direct saving and investment, to regulate incentives, to encourage

---

[27] Barber (1941:663–69); Niebuhr (1929); Holt (1940:740–47); Sundkler (1948); Worsley (1957).

[28] Emerson et al. (1942:136–40); Hodgkin (1957:60–75); Robequain (1944:79–88); Furnivall (1948:116–23); Machlup (1936:140–46).

entrepreneurship, to control trade and prices, etc. (Spengler 1955). To their arguments, I should like to add several considerations that emerge from the analysis of structural change during periods of rapid development.

a) Undifferentiated institutional structures frequently constitute the primary social barriers to modernization. Individuals refuse to work for wages because of traditional kinship, village, tribal, and other ties. Invariably, a certain amount of political pressure must be applied to loosen these ties. The need for this pressure increases, of course, in proportion to rate of modernization desired.

b) The process of differentiation itself creates conditions demanding a larger, more formal type of political administration. Thus, another argument in favor of the importance of strong government during rapid and uneven modernization is based on the necessity to accommodate the growing cultural, economic, and social heterogeneity, and to control the political repercussions of the constantly shifting distribution of power accompanying extensive social reorganization.

c) The probability that periods of early modernization will erupt into explosive outburst creates delicate political problems for the leaders of developing nations. We shall conclude this essay on the major social forces of modernization by suggesting the kinds of government that are likely to be most effective in such troubled areas. First, political leaders can increase their effectiveness by openly and vigorously committing themselves to utopian and xenophobic nationalism. This commitment is a powerful instrument for attaining three of their most important ends. (*1*) They can enhance their own claim to legitimacy by endowing themselves with the mission of creating the nation-state. (*2*) They can procure otherwise unobtainable sacrifices from a populace which may be committed to modernization in the abstract, but which resists making concrete breaks with traditional ways. (*3*) They can use their claim to legitimacy to repress protests and to prevent generalized symbols, such as communism, from spreading to all sorts of particular grievances. However, these political leaders should not take their claim to legitimacy too literally. They should not rely on their nationalistic commitment as being strong enough to enable them to ignore or smother grievances completely. They should "play politics," in the usual sense, with aggrieved groups, thus giving these groups access to responsible political agencies, and thereby reducing the conditions that favor counter-claims to legitimacy. One key to political stability seems to be, therefore, the practice of flexible politics behind the façade of an inflexible commitment to a national mission.

CONCLUSION

I have attempted to sketch, in ideal-type terms, the ways in which economic and social development are related to the social structure. I have organized the discussion around three major categories: differentiation, which characterizes a social structure that is moving toward greater complexity; integration, which in certain respects balances the divisive character of differentiation; and social disturbances, which result from the discontinuities between differentiation and integration.

Four qualifications must be added to this analysis. (*1*) I have not tried to account for the determinants of economic development itself. In fact, the discussion of differentiation, integration, and social disturbances has presupposed a certain attempt to develop economically. However, these three forces condition the *course* of that development once it has started. (*2*) For purposes of exposition, I have presented the three major categories in the order restated above. However, this ordering must not be inferred to mean that any one of the forces assumes causal precedence in social change. Rather, they form an interactive system. Disturbances, for instance, may arise from discontinuities created by structural differentiation; but these very disturbances may shape the course of future processes of differentiation. Likewise, integrative developments may be set in motion by differentiation; but they, in their turn, may initiate new lines of differentiation. (*3*) Even though the forces of differentiation, integration, and disturbances are closely linked empirically, we should not "close" the "system" composed of the relationship among the three forces. Differentiation may arise from sources other than economic development; the necessity for integration may emerge from conditions other than differentiation; and the sources of social disturbances are not exhausted by the discontinuities between differentiation and integration. (*4*) The "all-at-once" character of the transition from less differentiated to more differentiated societies should not be exaggerated. Empirically, the process evolves gradually and influences the social structure selectively. This essay has emphasized various halfway arrangements and compromises in order to illustrate this gradualness and irregularity.

17 THE PRINCIPLE OF CIRCULAR AND CUMULATIVE CAUSATION

Gunnar Myrdal

THE VAGUE NOTION OF THE VICIOUS CIRCLE

A LMOST ALL students of problems connected with under-development and development will be found, in one connection
or another, to have made a reference to the "vicious circle".
Professor C. E. A. Winslow, for instance, in a book devoted to the
economics of health, points out: Winslow (1951:9; see also Myrdal
1952).

> It was clear . . . that poverty and disease formed a vicious
> circle. Men and women were sick because they were poor; they
> became poorer because they were sick, and sicker because they
> were poorer.

Winslow thus points to a circular and cumulative process, continuously pressing levels downwards, in which one negative factor
is, at the same time, both cause and effect of other negative
factors.

In the same spirit, Professor Ragnar Nurkse (1952; cf Nurske
1953), when giving the 1952 Commemoration Lectures in Cairo,
referred to the "vicious circle of poverty" and explained:

> The concept implies, of course, a circular constellation of
> forces tending to act and react upon one another in such a way
> as to keep a poor country in a state of poverty. Particular in-
> stances of such circular constellations are not difficult to imagine.
> For example, a poor man may not have enough to eat; being
> under-nourished, his health may be weak; being physically weak,

SOURCE: Gunnar Myrdal, "The Principle of Circular and Cumulative
Causation," chapter 2, in *Economic Theory and Underdeveloped Regions*
(American edition entitled *Rich Lands and Poor*), 1957. Reprinted by
permission of the English publisher, Gerald Duckworth & Co. Ltd., and
of the American publisher, Harper & Row.

his working capacity may be low, which means that he is poor,
which in turn means that he will not have enough to eat; and so
on. A situation of this sort, applying to a country as a whole, can
be summed up in the trite proposition: "a country is poor because
it is poor".

Quite obviously a circular relationship between less poverty, more
food, improved health and higher working capacity would sustain
a cumulative process upwards instead of downwards.

The whole American folklore built around the tendency for
people to want to jump on the bandwagon is centred around a
conception of an upward spiral. So is, of course, also the expression in America which is so typical of their optimistic go-getting
culture: "nothing succeeds like success". To this, which is by
itself so eminently true, must be added, in order to preserve the
balance, a reminder of the truth also of the traditional idea of
the "vicious circle" downwards: nothing fails like failure.

As so often is the case, the Bible gives a perfect expression of
this ancient folk wisdom:

> For unto every one that hath shall be given, and he shall have
> abundance: but from him that hath not shall be taken away even
> that which he hath.[1]

In this admirable statement the truth is seen that the cumulative
process goes in both directions. And there is voiced also an understanding of the fact, which in our analysis will be given much
importance, namely that the cumulative process, if not regulated,
will cause increasing inequalities.

STABLE EQUILIBRIUM A FALSE ANALOGY

In this book I shall attempt to give a more definite formulation
to this vague idea of the circular causation of a cumulative
process. It is my conviction that this idea contains *in nuce* the
approach to a more realistic analysis of social change—indeed a
vision of the general theory of under-development and development which we are all yearning for.

---

[1] St. Matthew, xxv:29; cf. xiii:12. Cf. the folksy American expression:
"Them as has gits." A peasant in Southern Portugal was heard saying:
"Those who have something here, get everything, but those who have not
anything, get nothing."

Expressed first in negative terms, my starting point is the assertion that the notion of stable equilibrium is normally a false analogy to choose when constructing a theory to explain the changes in a social system. What is wrong with the stable equilibrium assumption as applied to social reality is the very idea that a social process follows a direction—though it might move towards it in a circuitous way—towards a position which in some sense or other can be described as a state of equilibrium between forces. Behind this idea is another and still more basic assumption, namely that a change will regularly call forth a reaction in the system in the form of changes which on the whole go in the opposite direction to the first change.

The idea I want to expound in this book is that, on the contrary, in the normal case there is no such tendency towards automatic self-stabilisation in the social system. The system is by itself not moving towards any sort of balance between forces, but is constantly on the move away from such a situation. In the normal case a change does not call forth countervailing changes but, instead, supporting changes, which move the system in the same direction as the first change but much further. Because of such circular causation a social process tends to become cumulative and often to gather speed at an accelerating rate.

A social process can, of course, be stopped. One possibility is that new exogenous changes may occur which have the direction and the strength necessary to bring the system to rest. The position of balancing forces which thus becomes established is, however, not a natural outcome of the play of the forces within the system. The position is, furthermore, unstable. Any new exogenous change will by the reactions in the system again start a cumulative process away from this position in the direction of the new change.

Alternatively, the position of rest may have been achieved by policy interferences, planned and applied with the intention of stopping the movement. This is, of course, the very opposite of a natural tendency towards equilibrium, endogenous to the system.

This general characterisation of a process of social change refers to the normal case; I shall be discussing at the end of the next chapter the exceptions where countervailing tendencies are at work.

AN ILLUSTRATION: THE NEGRO PROBLEM IN AMERICA

I once carried out a comprehensive study of the development problem of one particular group of people: the Negro population in the United States (Myrdal 1944). It was during this study that I first came to realise the inadequacy of the equilibrium approach, and to understand that the essence of a social problem is that it concerns a complex of interlocking, circular and cumulative changes. I was gradually moved to make this thought the main hypothesis of my study. My purpose in now referring back briefly to this study is to give greater concreteness to the circular mechanism in a cumulative process of social change.

The American Negro people are not confined to one single geographic district where they are alone by themselves. But they are nevertheless cut off from the rest of the American population, and are bound together in a distinctly separate social group, with a community of worries and a common destiny. This relative social isolation is effected by the American version of the institution of colour caste.

Behind the colour line the Negro people live a life almost as separate as if they were on an island with restricted communications with the mainland. They have developed an entire class structure of their own. The caste disabilities reflect themselves in the fact of a greater concentration of the Negro population in the lower social strata, and also in lower levels of all economic and social indices for comparable strata. The unity of interests and aspirations in this social group is just as great as that existing in any under-developed country or region.

The relative status of the Negro people in America in the late 'thirties and early 'forties, when I made my survey, had been rising since the great national compromise in the 1870's, after the Civil War and Reconstruction, but not very rapidly and there had even been some retreats.

The prevailing views on the Negro problem among social scientists were mostly framed in terms of static equilibrium and *laissez-faire*, and demonstrated rather faithfully the general tendency towards social fatalism which is inherent in this approach. Mistrust of the efficiency of "interferences" with the social process— such as, for example, efforts towards educating the white people to broader views, campaigns for giving Negroes legal redress through the courts, and legislation, "movements", and "reforms" —characterised the approach, and was felt to bear the mark of hardboiled scientific objectivity in contradistinction to the credulity of the do-gooders.[2] The practical conclusion tended to be that the rise in Negro status would continue to be, as it had been for generations, a very slow and uncertain process, largely outside the grip of intentional policy measures: "state-ways cannot change folk-ways".[3]

In my study I reached the conclusion that the national compromise which had reigned for such a long time was approaching its end. "Ten years from now this (past) period in the history of inter-racial relations in America may come to look as a temporary interregnum. The compromise was not a stable power equilibrium." (Myrdal 1944:1014). More positively, my conclusion was that "not since Reconstruction has there been more reason

---

[2] Nevertheless, the social scientists of this period—though often asserting in all good faith that their findings and teaching could not have any great practical effect on the development of inter-racial relations in America—were all the time efficiently bringing together and organising the rational arguments for a fundamental social change. Indeed, they were making it increasingly difficult for educated white people to continue to hold some of the sterotyped opportunistic views which were basic to segregation and discrimination. It is my conviction, for which I have given the evidence in the book referred to above, that the work of American social scientists during the pre-war period contributed mightily towards producing the driving forces for the dynamic development of inter-racial relations which began to gather increased momentum some ten years ago.

[3] This *laissez-faire* approach in the tradition of William Sumner—with still older moorings in the natural law philosophy which, with all the enthusiasm for fact-finding, has a particularly strong hold in America—was often connected with a vague philosophy of economic determinism. In the pre-war period, it presented itself in two versions with many intermediary positions: a radical Marxist version, where the expectation was an economic revolution which would change everything and even eradicate race prejudice; and, much more commonly, a conservative liberalistic version, according to which no such revolution was to be expected and, consequently—as the assumption in that version too was that no significant change can be brought about except by tackling the "basic factor", the economic system—the situation would remain pretty well as it was and that, anyhow, there was not a great chance for the reformers to alter much. The one-factor theory thus strengthened the equilibrium approach and its inherent fatalistic tendency and stood in the way of a rational conception of circular inter-dependence leading to cumulative dynamic development, implying chances also for magnified effects of purposely induced changes.

to anticipate fundamental changes in American race relations, changes which will involve a development toward the American ideals" (Myrdal 1944:xix). This great, dramatic break in the social development of American society has since actually happened. A student who has sometimes been wrong in his forecasts of the future will be excused for pointing to a case when he was right.

CIRCULAR CAUSATION

I want now to sketch in its barest outlines the social theory or methodological hypothesis that I used in this particular study.[4]

In its simplest form the explanatory model can be reduced to two factors: "white prejudice", causing discrimination against the Negroes in various respects, and the "low plane of living" of the Negro population. These two factors are mutually inter-related: the Negroes' low plane of living is kept down by discrimination from the whites while, on the other side, the Negroes' poverty, ignorance, superstition, slum dwellings, health deficiencies, dirty appearance, bad odour, disorderly conduct, unstable family relations and criminality stimulate and feed the antipathy of the whites for Negroes.

White prejudice and low Negro standards thus mutually "cause" each other. If at a point of time things tend to remain about as they are, this means that the two forces balance each other: white prejudice and the consequent discrimination against the Negroes block their efforts to raise their low plane of living; this, on the other hand, forms part of the causation of the prejudice on the side of the whites which leads them to discriminatory behaviour.

Such a static "accommodation" is, however, entirely fortuitous and by no means a stable equilibrium position. If either of the two factors should change, this is bound to bring a change in the other factor, too, and start a cumulative process of mutual interaction in which the change in one factor would continuously be supported by the reaction of the other factor and so on in a

---

[4] The rest of this section contains a condensation of the methodological argument in the book cited and particularly Chapter 3, Section 7, "The Theory of the Vicious Circle", pp. 75 ff., and Appendix 3, "A Methodological Note on the Principle of Cumulation", pp. 1065 ff., in Myrdal (1944).

circular way. The whole system would move in the direction of the primary change, but much further. Even if the original push or pull were to cease after a time, both factors would be permanently changed, or the process of interacting changes would even continue without any neutralisation in sight.

Both the two factors are composite entities. On the one hand, the Negro's plane of living is an amorphous concept definable only in terms of a number of components—employment, wages, housing, nutrition, clothing, health, education, stability in family relations, law observance, cleanliness, orderliness, trustworthiness, loyalty to society at large, etcetera—which are all inter-related in circular causation. A rise in any single one of the components would tend to raise all the others and thus, indirectly as well as directly, result in a cumulative decrease in white prejudice, with new effects back on the Negro plane of living itself.

The other factor, white prejudice, is an equally composite entity, as "attitudes" always are: a combination of right and wrong beliefs and heterogeneous valuations. And it is equally unstable. For experience shows that if, by some chance, discrimination in a particular field of social contact is increased or decreased, the psychological force behind it, i.e. prejudice, tends to change so as to support actual behaviour. This too fits into the general pattern of circular causation.

The point is not simply that "many forces are working in the same direction." They are, in fact, not doing so. In general there are periods when opposing forces balance one another so that the system remains in rest until a push or a pull is applied at one point or another. When the whole system starts moving after such a shock the *changes* in the forces work in the same direction, which is something different. And this is so because the variables are so interlocked in circular causation that a change in any one induces the others to change in such a way that these secondary changes support the first change, with similar tertiary effects upon the variable first affected, and so on.

THE SCIENTIFIC PROBLEM

The circular causal inter-relation between all the factors in the development of a population group like the American Negroes gives sense to the general notion of the "status" of the group— in essentially the same way as the inter-relation between prices gives sense to the notion of the "price level"—and an index of this status could be constructed, and would have meaning as measuring in time or space the general tendency of the system. The main scientific task is, however, to analyse the causal inter-relations within the system itself as it moves under the influence of outside pushes and pulls and the momentum of its own internal processes.

In a realistic study the system becomes, of course, very much more complicated than any abstract model. In the case of the Negro problem, for example, each of the elements of the main factors in the situation—the low Negro plane of living and white prejudice—needs to be studied intensively with reference to other variables such as region, social class, age, sex, and so on. The scientific ideal is not only to split the factors into their elements and to arrange them in this way, but to give for each of the elements quantitative measures of its ability to influence each of the others, and to be influenced itself by changes in other elements within the system or by changes in exogenous forces.

The outside forces in the study in question are essentially the whole surrounding national community. Some of these outside forces, e.g. the business situation and employment opportunities, are subject to violent short-term changes. Others are more constant determinants, for instance the complex of inherited ideals which I called "the American Creed" in my study, and the institutional and political framework as it is influenced and activated by those ideals. The outside forces push and pull the system continuously, and at the same time change the structure of forces within the system itself.

The time element is of paramount importance, as the effects of a shock on different variables of the system will be spread very differently along the time axis. A rise in employment, for instance, will almost immediately raise some levels of living; but a change in levels of education or health is achieved more slowly, and its effects on the other factors are delayed, so that there is a lag in the whole process of cumulation.

Ideally the scientific solution of a problem like the Negro problem should thus be postulated in the form of an inter-connected set of quantitative equations, describing the movement —and the internal changes—of the system studied under the various influences which are at work. That this complete, quantitative and truly scientific formulation is far beyond the horizon does not need to be pointed out; but in principle it could be made, and I submit that the working out of such a complete and quantitative solution should be the aim of our research endeavours even when they have to stop far away from the ideal.

If the realism of the hypothesis of circular causation is accepted, certain general conclusions can be drawn which it is worth while to spell out already at this point. To begin with, it is useless to look for one predominant factor, a "basic factor" such as the "economic factor."[5] When studying the Negro problem or any other social problem under this hypothesis it becomes, indeed, difficult to perceive what precisely should be meant by the "economic factor" as distinct from the others, and still less understandable how it can be "basic," as everything is cause to everything else in an interlocking circular manner.

For similar reasons, the application of this hypothesis moves any realistic study of under-development and development in a country, or a region of a country, far outside the boundaries of traditional economic theory. This is because of necessity the study becomes concerned also with all the so-called "non-economic factors" which the classical economists lumped together in such concepts as "the quality of the factors of production" and "the efficiency of production" and usually kept outside their analysis.

It is important to keep in mind that, if the hypothesis of cumulative causation is justified, an upward movement of the entire system can be effected by measures applied to one or the other of several points in the system; but this certainly does not imply that from a practical and political point of view it is a matter of indifference where and how a development problem is tackled. The more we know about the way in which the different factors are inter-related—what effects a primary change of each factor will have on all the other factors, and when—the better we shall be able to establish how to maximise the effects of a given policy effort designed to move and change the social system.

Nevertheless, it is unlikely that a rational policy will work by changing only one factor. Thus, though this theoretical approach

---

[5] We might in this connection note that there has been much unconscious application of Marxian economic determinism, particularly in the American sociological literature, sometimes of a kind that Marx and Engels would have been tempted to characterise as "vulgar Marxism".

is bound to suggest the impracticability, in the political sphere, of all panaceas, it is, on the other hand, equally bound to encourage the reformer. The principle of cumulation—insofar as it holds true—promises final effects of very much greater magnitude than the efforts and costs of the reforms themselves. The low status of the Negro is, for instance, tremendously and self-perpetuatingly wasteful all round—their low educational standard causes low productivity, health deficiencies and low earnings, and these again keep down the educational standards, and so on.

The cumulatively magnified final effects of a push upward when wisely applied to the relevant factors is, in one sense, a demonstration, and also a measure, of the earlier existing "social waste". In the end, the cost of raising the status of the Negro will not involve any "real net cost" at all, but instead result in great "social gains" for society. The definition of these political concepts, based on explicit value premises, must be conceived of in the dynamic terms of circular causation of a cumulative development.

This is, indeed, the principle by which an under-developed country can hope to "lift itself by its shoe strings"—if it can only manage to accomplish what Professor W. W. Rostow calls the "take-off into sustained growth" (Rostow 1956:25–48) and afford the sacrifice of waiting for the full returns of its policy efforts.

ARGUMENTUM AD HOMINEM

I started this chapter by referring to the floating, vague notion of the "vicious circle" and by citing folklore and the Bible. I feel, indeed, very much in line with ordinary common sense when I stress that in the normal case circular causation is a more adequate hypothesis than stable equilibrium for the theoretical analysis of a social process.

John Maynard Keynes had some basis for his famous dictum that usually "the practical men" are unknowingly "the slaves of some defunct economist" when they express general opinions. They then often think in the metaphysical terms of the doctrines and predilections of economic theory. But in their own sphere of activity they act on better assumptions.

Every successful businessman has the principle of the cumulative process as a built-in theory in his approach to practical problems; otherwise he would not be successful. A politician would be a failure if he did not bring the cumulative effects into his calculations. The whole philosophy of the professional philanthropists is imbued with this hypothesis.[6]

I go further and feel inclined to think that Keynes' accusation of traditionalism could be directed with even more justice against the economists themselves, particularly since the duty would clearly have been ours to liberate not only our own thinking but also that of the general public.

Practical men have been ahead of theory in monetary matters, to choose a more specific case. It is a fact that the new and dynamic approach, which was opened up by Knut Wicksell, followed by many others—among them, of course, most prominently Keynes—and which has reshaped such a large part of short-term economic theory as well as economic policy, was totally original only to the theoreticians with their usually unquestioning acceptance and belief in J. B. Say's law of the necessary equilibrium between total demand and total supply.

Laymen have, of course, never believed in that law; they have always known that demand could fall short of, or exceed, supply, and that in the former case business was booming while it was falling off in the latter case. And Wicksell's new approach only spelled out in clearer terms vague ideas held by bankers, businessmen and political leaders upon the basis of which they had always been acting—though on a more general plane, where they were only talking and at most demonstrating their prejudices, they usually felt happy to fall in with the false doctrines and predilections of the theoreticians.

---

[6] In fact, the best formulation I have found of the working of the cumulative process in the field of the Negro problem was given by one of the wisest heads of foundations in America, the late Edwin R. Embree (1931: 200) of the Rosenwald Fund: "There is a vicious circle in caste. At the outset, the despised group is usually inferior in certain of the accepted standards of the controlling class. Being inferior, members of the degraded caste are denied the privileges and opportunities of their fellows and so are pushed still further down and then are regarded with that much less respect, and therefore are more vigorously denied advantages, and so around and around the vicious circle. Even when the movement starts to reverse itself—as it most certainly has in the case of the Negro—there is a desperately long unwinding, as a slight increase in goodwill gives a little greater chance, and this leads to a little higher accomplishment, and that to increased respect, and so slowly upward toward equality of opportunity, of regards, and of status." The vaguely implied notion that circular causation retards the speed of progress is, however, wrong.

18 REGIONAL ECONOMIC INEQUALITIES

Gunnar Myrdal

A SIMPLE ILLUSTRATION

I HAVE SUGGESTED that the principle of interlocking, circular inter-dependence within a process of cumulative causation has va-lidity over the entire field of social relations. It should be the main hypothesis when studying economic under-development and development.

Suppose that in a community an accidental change occurs which is not immediately cancelled out in the stream of events: for example, that a factory, where a large part of the population gets its livelihood, burns down and that it becomes clear that it would not pay to rebuild it, at least not in that locality. The immediate effect of this primary change is that the firm owning it goes out of business and its workers become unemployed. This will decrease incomes and demand.

In its turn the decreased demand will lower incomes and cause unemployment in all sorts of other businesses in the community which sold to, or served, the firm and its employees. A process of circular causation has so been started with effects which cumu-late in the fashion of the "vicious circle".

If there are no other exogenous changes, the community will be less tempting for outside businesses and workers who had con-templated moving in. As the process gathers momentum, busi-nesses established in the community and workers living there will increasingly find reasons for moving out in order to seek better markets somewhere else. If they do, this will again decrease

SOURCE: Gunnar Myrdal, "The Drift Towards Regional Economic In-equalities in a Country," chapter 3, in *Economic Theory and Underdevel-oped Regions* (American edition entitled *Rich Lands and Poor*), 1957. Re-printed by permission of the English publisher, Gerald Duckworth & Co. Ltd., and of the American publisher, Harper & Row.

incomes and demand. It will usually also change the age structure of the local population in an unfavourable direction.

To throw light on the mechanism of this cumulative causal sequence, let us watch the behaviour of one single factor and let us choose one a little outside: the local tax rate. I shall assume that local taxation is either, as in Scandinavia, levied directly on incomes or, as in many other parts of the world, indirectly related to them. As the income basis narrows, the tax rate will have to be raised.

The higher tax rate, in its turn, will itself act as an extra incentive for businesses and workers to leave the community, and as a disincentive keeping out those who otherwise might have considered moving in. This then, in a second round, will again decrease incomes and demand and, consequently, cause the tax rate to move still further upwards, having much similar effects again. Meanwhile the less favourable age distribution will have not only contributed to lower taxable income per head, but also raised the relative need for public welfare services.

If in this situation the local authorities, because of the rising tax rate, are moved to lower their standards in various public services—such as the provision of schooling for children, homes for the aged, roads, and the like—the rise of the tax rate may be retarded but only at the expense of making the community less attractive for businesses and workers in another important respect.

Should the tax rate before the first change have reached a stationary level, it is now not moving towards this level as an equilibrium—or any other stable level—but continuously away from the initial state of balancing forces. And this movement itself is all the time causing new changes which push the tax rate still higher, and so on and so on. This simple model of circular causation with cumulative effects, released by a primary change, is, I believe, more typical of actual social processes then the intersection of the demand and supply curves at an equilibrium price which has become symbolic of much of our reasoning in economic theory.

If, nevertheless, in well-organised welfare states the local tax rate does not continue on that adventurous course but is prevented from rising too much, and if also the community is restrained from lowering the standards of public services too much, this has quite another explanation than the play of market forces:

namely the fact that national legislation has been enacted for the specific purpose of stopping such a cumulative process by subsidising from the common purse any individual community which for reasons outside its own command has got into financial difficulties, and at the same time prescribing certain minimum standards for public services.

Indeed, the modern highly integrated national states in the one-sixth of the non-Soviet world which is well off and rapidly progressing have furnished themselves with a most complex network of systems of regularised public interferences of all sorts which have the common purpose of counteracting the blind law of cumulative social change, and hindering it from causing inequalities between regions, industries and social groups [see Myrdal 1960]. To this question of the countervailing changes induced by organised society I shall come back in the next chapter.

In my example the primary change was an adverse one. The cumulative process, however, also works if the initial change is for the better. The decision to locate an industry in a particular community, for instance, gives a spur to its general development. Opportunities of employment and higher incomes are provided for those unemployed before or employed in a less remunerative way. Local businesses can flourish as the demand for their products and services increases. Labour, capital and enterprise are attracted from outside to exploit the expanding opportunities. The establishment of a new business or the enlargement of an old one widens the market for others, as does generally the increase of incomes and demand. Rising profits increase savings, but at the same time investments go up still more, which again pushes up the demand and the level of profits. And the expansion process creates external economies favourable for sustaining its continuation.

The local tax rate—the factor I picked out for a closer view on the causal inter-relations in a downward cumulative process—can be lowered, and the amount and quality of public services enhanced: both changes will make the community more attractive to businesses and workers for this reason also, with the result that the local finances will again be boosted, with similar results on the tax rate and public finances, and so on.

These fiscal effects of localised expansion may be reduced as a result of interferences by the state in the form of schemes for inter-regional equalisation built into the taxation system; but as in the present chapter I am still considering only the free play of the market forces I shall neglect this possibility for the moment.

THE PLAY OF THE MARKET FORCES WORKS TOWARDS INEQUALITY

A cumulative process of the same general character, going downwards or upwards as the case may be, will also be generated by a change in the terms of trade of a community or a region, if the change is large and persistent enough or, indeed, by any other change having as its effect a substantial decrease or increase in the inter-related economic quantities: demand, earning power and incomes, investment and production. The main idea I want to convey is that the play of the forces in the market normally tends to increase, rather than to decrease, the inequalities between regions.

If things were left to market forces unhampered by any policy interferences, industrial production, commerce, banking, insurance, shipping and, indeed, almost all those economic activities which in a developing economy tend to give a bigger than average return—and, in addition, science, art, literature, education and higher culture generally—would cluster in certain localities and regions, leaving the rest of the country more or less in a backwater.

Occasionally these favoured localities and regions offer particularly good natural conditions for the economic activities concentrated there; in rather more cases they did so at the time when they started to gain a competitive advantage. For naturally economic geography sets the stage. Commercial centres are, of course, usually located in places where there are reasonably good natural conditions for the construction of a port, and centres for heavy industry are most often located not too far away from coal and iron resources.

But within broad limits the power of attraction today of a centre has its origin mainly in the historical accident that something was once started there, and not in a number of other places where it could equally well or better have been started, and that the start met with success. Thereafter the ever-increasing internal and external economies—interpreted in the widest sense of the word to include, for instance, a working population trained in various crafts, easy communications, the feeling of growth and elbow room and the spirit of new enterprise—fortified and sustained their continuous growth at the expense of other localities and regions where instead relative stagnation or regression became the pattern.

MIGRATION, CAPITAL MOVEMENT AND TRADE: THE "BACKWASH EFFECTS"

It is easy to see how expansion in one locality has "backwash effects" in other localities. More specifically the movements of labour, capital, goods and services do not by themselves counteract the natural tendency to regional inequality. By themselves, migration, capital movements and trade are rather the media through which the cumulative process evolves—upwards in the lucky regions and downwards in the unlucky ones. In general, if they have positive results for the former, their effects on the latter are negative.[1]

The localities and regions where economic activity is expanding will attract net immigration from other parts of the country. As migration is always selective, at least with respect to the migrant's age, this movement by itself tends to favour the rapidly growing communities and disfavour the others.

In the historical epoch—which is only just now coming to its end in the very richest and most advanced countries—when birth-control is still spreading to lower economic and social strata,[2] the poorer regions will also have a relatively higher fertility. This adds its influence to that of the net emigration in making the age distribution in these regions unfavourable; in the longer run it may also cause a less favourable relation between total working population and resources. The poverty in rural regions of Europe during the long period of net emigration to the industrial centres —and to America—has a main explanation in the unfavourable age distribution there, caused by migration and in part also by higher fertility rates.

Capital movements tend to have a similar effect of increasing inequality. In the centres of expansion increased demand will spur investment, which in its turn will increase incomes and demand and cause a second round of investment, and so on.

---

[1] This statement will be qualified in the next section but one.

[2] When this process is completed, the average fertility might well be rather high or at times even rising; but it is positively, and not negatively, correlated to economic and social status.

Saving will increase as a result of higher incomes but will tend to lag behind investment in the sense that the supply of capital will steadily meet a brisk demand for it. In the other regions the lack of new expansionary momentum has the implication that the demand for capital for investment remains relatively weak, even compared to the supply of savings which will be low as incomes are low and tending to fall. Studies in many countries have shown how the banking system, if not regulated to act differently, tends to become an instrument for siphoning off the savings from the poorer regions to the richer and more progressive ones where returns on capital are high and secure.

Trade operates with the same fundamental bias in favour of the richer and progressive regions against the other regions [see the essay by Singer]. The freeing and widening of the markets will often confer such competitive advantages on the industries in already established centres of expansion, which usually work under conditions of increasing returns, that even the handicrafts and industries existing earlier in the other regions are thwarted. The hampering of industrial growth in the poorer southern provinces of Italy, caused by the pulling down of internal tariff walls after Italy's political unification in the last century, is a case in point which has been thoroughly studied: industry in the northern provinces had such a lead, and was so much stronger that it dominated the new national market, which was the result of political unification, and suppressed industrial efforts in the southern provinces.[3]

As industrialisation is the dynamic force in this development, it is almost tautological to state that the poorer regions remain mainly agricultural: the perfection of the national markets will

---

[3] The process was conditioned and encouraged by the liquidation of the political and administrative centres in Southern Italy, while those in Northern Italy, which at that time more than now were tools in the hands of the industrial interests there, gained hegemony over the whole country. The unification of Italy was in reality very much a conquest and an annexation of Southern Italy by the stronger North. The role of the state in the cumulative process will be discussed in the next chapter. Another example on a still larger scale is the long economic stagnation after the Civil War up till the Second World War of the Southern states of the United States. As I shall argue in Chapter 5 (Myrdal 1957) this systematic bias of trade as between regions forms also part of the mechanism of exploitation in the economic relations between a metropolitan country and its colonies.

even, as I have just mentioned, tend to frustrate earlier beginnings of industrial diversification in agricultural regions. In the backward regions of Southern Europe about three quarters of the population get their livelihood from agriculture. In these regions also, not only manufacturing industry and other non-agricultural pursuits but agriculture itself show a much lower level of productivity than in the richer regions.[4]

THE "NON-ECONOMIC FACTORS"

The cumulative processes towards regional inequality work through many causal chains usually not accounted for in our theoretical analysis of the play of market forces. I have already referred to selectivity in migration and the effects of poverty on fertility.

If left to themselves, those regions which had not been touched by the expansionary momentum could not afford to keep up a good road system, and all their other public utilities would be inferior, thus increasing their competitive disadvantages. Railways would be built so as to meet the effective demand for transport, i.e. without much consideration of the needs of those regions.

On the same assumption the poorer regions, unaided, could hardly afford much medical care and their populations would be less healthy and have a lower productive efficiency. They would have fewer schools and their schools would be grossly inferior—in Southern Europe the population of the poorer regions is actually still largely illiterate.

The people living there would on the average be believers in the more primitive variants of religion, sanctioning traditional *mores* by taboos and functional magic, and they would be more

---

[4] Part of the stronger competitive position of industry in Northern Italy at the time of Italy's political unification was based on the fact that it also had a more developed agriculture.

Professor Jacob Viner (1953:52) makes the plausible point that ". . . the real problem in poor countries is not agriculture as such, or the absence of manufactures as such, but poverty and backwardness, poor agriculture and poor manufacture". This is supposed to be a criticism of Professor Raul Prebisch and others who have urged industrialisation as the necessary mainstay in a programme of economic development. As his argument is narrowly static, Viner, however, misses entirely the point that industrialisation is intended to rectify an economy in imbalance and to give a dynamic momentum.

superstitious and less rational generally. Their entire systems of valuations would take on such an imprint of poverty and backwardness that they would become even less susceptible to the experimental and ambitious aspirations of a developing society.

All these frustrating effects of poverty, operating through other media than those analysed by traditional economic theory, are interlocked in circular causation, the one with the others and all with the biases I referred to in the working of migration, capital movements and trade. The opposite effects of rising economic levels in the centres of expansion are in a similar fashion also interconnected in a circular causation, continuously sustaining further expansion in a cumulative fashion.

Economic theory has disregarded these so-called non-economic factors and kept them outside the analysis. As they are among the main vehicles for the circular causation in the cumulative processes of economic change, this represents one of the principal shortcomings of economic theory. As I pointed out in Chapter 2 [see previous reading] and shall further pursue in Chapter 11 (Myrdal 1957) it explains largely why this theory was unable to state the dynamic problems of economic under-development and development—or, to formulate it differently, how this theory managed to avoid stating those problems.

For easy reference I shall refer to all relevant adverse changes, caused outside that locality, as the "backwash effects" of economic expansion in a locality. I include under this label the effects *via* migration, capital movements and trade as well as all the effects *via* the whole gamut of other social relations exemplified above; and the term refers to the total cumulated effects resulting from the process of circular causation between all the factors, "non-economic" as well as "economic".

It should be pointed out in this connection that all history shows that the cheap and often docile labour of under-developed regions does not usually attract industry. The few examples where the labour supply has been effective in bringing industry to backward regions—the movement of textile industry from New England to the Upper South in the United States is one case— are rather in the nature of exceptions to a general rule. There are so many forces working in the opposite direction, among them the external economies in the established centres of economic expansion. Ordinarily it is labour which has to move to the localities of rising demand and there make the difficult effort of adjustment to the different ways and values of an expanding society.

THE "SPREAD EFFECTS"

Against the backwash effects there are, however, also certain centrifugal "spread effects" of expansionary momentum from the centres of economic expansion to other regions. It is natural that the whole region around a nodal centre of expansion should gain from the increasing outlets of agricultural products and be stimulated to technical advance all along the line.

There is also another line of centrifugal spread effects to localities farther away, where favourable conditions exist for producing raw materials for the growing industries in the centres; if a sufficient number of workers become employed in these other localities even consumer goods industries will be given a spur there. These, and also all other localities where new starts are being made and happen to succeed, become in their turn, if the expansionary momentum is strong enough to overcome the backwash effects from the older centres, new centres of self-sustained economic expansion.

The spread effects of momentum from a centre of industrial expansion to other localities and regions, operating through increased demands for their products and in many other ways, weave themselves into the cumulating social process by circular causation in the same fashion as the backwash effects in opposition to which they set up countervailing changes. They represent a complication of the main hypothesis that in the normal case the changes in other factors which are called forth as reactions by a change in one factor, always tend to move the system in the same direction as the first change.

In no circumstances, however, do the spread effects establish the assumptions for an equilibrium analysis. In the marginal case the two kinds of effects will balance each other and a region will be "stagnating". But this balance is not a stable equilibrium, for any change in the forces will start a cumulative movement upwards or downwards.

In reality, the expanding stagnating and regressing localities are arranged in a fairly continuous series on different levels, with all possible graduations between the extremes. Insofar as in the aggregate all the dispersed industrial advances amount to something considerable, economic standards in the whole country are given a lift.

It is quite possible that all the regions in a country may be inside this margin of balancing forces—if the initial starts are many and strong and successful enough and if the centrifugal spread effects work relatively effectively. The problem of inequalities then becomes a problem of the different rates of progress between regions in the country. But ordinarily, even in a a rapidly developing country, many regions will be lagging behind, stagnating or even becoming poorer; and there would be more regions in the last two categories if market forces alone were left to decide the outcome.

Even in such countries as the United States or Sweden, where in the last century business enterprise has been able to exploit a particularly favourable situation as regards natural resources, and where other unusually advantageous conditions for economic growth have also been present, not least in the general cultural situation, developments have not been such as to draw the whole country into a more or less equal and simultaneous expansion process. A closer view reveals great disparities. In the United States, for example, almost the whole of the region usually referred to as the South was until recently largely a stagnating one. Similarly, the emergence some generations ago of the great new opportunities in agriculture on the Western frontier left large rural areas in New England in a decay from which some of them have not yet emerged.

A country where, on the contrary, few starts are being made and/or where the starts do not happen to result in a substantial and sustained increase in demand, incomes, investment and production, becomes an under-developed country. Even there, however, as in several Latin American countries, there are usually localities and regions which are advancing industrially.

TWO BROAD CORRELATIONS

The Secretariat of the United Nations' Economic Commission for Europe has for several years devoted increasing attention to the empirical study of the problem of regional development and under-development in various European countries. The results so far reached have been published in the annual *Economic Surveys of Europe*. In 1955 a more comprehensive analysis of these problems was contained in a separate chapter of the Survey.[5] From this study I want only to quote two main conclusions.

The first one is that in Western Europe disparities of income between one region and another are much wider in the poorer countries than in the richer ones. If we use such a simple measure of regional inequality as the proportion of the total population of a country living in regions where the average income is less than two-thirds of the national average, we find that this proportion amounted to only a few per cent in Great Britain and Switzerland, to some ten per cent in such countries as Norway and France, and to about one-third in Italy, Turkey and Spain.[6]

The second conclusion is that while the regional inequalities have been diminishing in the richer countries of Western Europe, the tendency has been the opposite in the poorer ones.

A large part of the explanation for these two broad correlations may be found in the important fact that the higher the level of economic development that a country has already attained, the stronger the spread effects will usually be. For a high average level of development is accompanied by improved transportation and communications, higher levels of education, and a more dynamic communion of ideas and values—all of which tends to strengthen the forces for the centrifugal spread of economic expansion or to remove the obstacles for its operation.

The neutralisation of the backwash effects, when a country reaches a high level of development where the spread effects are strong, will itself spur on economic development, and so become an important factor in the cumulative process. For with the extinction of abject poverty on a large scale goes a fuller utilisation of the potentialities of the human resources in a nation. This is one of the reasons why rapid and sustained progress becomes an almost automatic process when once a country has reached a high level of development.

In contrast, part of the curse of a low average level of development in an under-developed country is the fact that the spread

---

[5] "Problems of Regional Development and Industrial Location in Europe" *Economic Survey of Europe in 1954*, Geneva, 1955, pp. 136 ff.

[6] Not only the inequalities within each country but also the differences in relative inequality between countries would have appeared much greater, if the administrative division into regions used for the tabulation had been more adequate to the problem studied.

effects there are weak. This means that as a rule the free play of the market forces in a poor country will work more powerfully to create regional inequalities and to widen those which already exist. That a low level of economic development is accompanied as a rule by great economic inequalities represents itself a major impediment to progress. It tends to hold the under-developed countries down. This is one of the interlocking relations by which in the cumulative process "poverty becomes its own cause".

I cannot overcome the temptation to repeat my quotation from the Bible: "For unto every one that hath shall be given, and he shall have abundance: but from him that hath not shall be taken away even that which he hath." That there is a tendency inherent in the free play of market forces to create regional inequalities, and that this tendency becomes the more dominant the poorer a country is, are two of the most important laws of economic under-development and development under *laissez-faire*.

In this chapter I am disregarding interferences by the state. In the next chapter, where I discuss the role of the state, my general point is that the activity of the state will tend rather to support those forces which result in the two broad correlations which I have been discussing.

EXAMPLES OF OTHER COUNTERACTING CHANGES

There are a great number of complications and qualifications that in a more elaborate analysis would have to be fitted into the model I am outlining of circular causation of a cumulative social process. They are all related to exceptions from the hypothesis that the causation is circular.

If there are counteracting changes the cumulative effect will be weakened and the process may even be stopped altogether. But even in the accidental event that the forces come to balance each other, the assumption for an equilibrium analysis will ordinarily not be established, for the balance will be unstable. On both sides of such a fortuitous balance the system will entail a cumulative process in the causation of which, however, not all changes are unidirectional and connected.

Among counteracting changes there are those which may be recognised as "external dis-economies", if the term be allowed. There may be factors inherent in the situation of a centre of economic expansion which tend to retard or, when it has reached a certain level of development, even to reverse the cumulative process, by causing an increase in public expenditure and perhaps in private costs, because industry and population become too concentrated. Once again this can be stated in the homely terms of folk wisdom: "Trees can never grow as high as heaven."

To the same category would belong the depressing effects of decreasing demand in a "maturing economy", if this pessimistic theory, cultivated during the Great Depression, particularly in America, were correct—which, however I doubt, except in very special circumstances.

It may also be that in a centre of expansion wages and the remuneration of other factors of production will be driven up to such a high level that other regions get a real chance to compete successfully. Or a prolonged period of economic expansion may have saddled a prosperous region with a very large stock of old capital equipment which it is tempting not to discard as rapidly as would be advantageous in a period of swift technological development. Moreover, a country which, thanks to an early start, has for some time enjoyed a quasi-monopolistic position may find that the spirit of enterprise and risk-taking has been damaged.[7]

In the opposite case, a downward cumulative process may also give rise to endogenous countervailing forces and come to a halt. The cruel Malthusian checks of classical population theory —a rise in death rates when population increase had pressed down consumption below the subsistence level—were examples of such countervailing changes. These checks set a limit beyond which regression could not proceed and thus established a lower limit to the process. Assuming a permanency in the forces operating in the direction of economic regression, equilibrium at this low level would indeed for once be a stable one. The recent explosive development of medical science, making the prevention of death even at exceedingly low standards of living a rather easy and inexpensive matter, has tended to weaken the population checks, and thus moved the stagnation equilibrium to a much more depressed level of human misery.

---

[7] An analysis of these and other factors which may retard an expansionary movement, as they operated in Europe in the period between the two world wars, is contained in Svennilson (1954).

Naturally, in the short run, in all countries and in all regions at all times the equilibrating interplay of countervailing changes in demand, supply and price—to which economic theory has devoted such a disproportionate amount of attention—will be operating more or less according to that theory. This interplay, however, usually represents only the ripples on the surface.

In general, changes of anticipation consequent on more primary changes tend rather to push a cumulative process in the same direction; this agrees with the main hypothesis. Thus, already an expectation on the part of the white population that the Negro plane of living will rise normally tends to decrease white prejudice. In certain regions of the South in America and, in particular, among the poor whites who compete most closely with the Negroes, such an expectation may, however, at least for a time, instead cause rising resentment and increased prejudice, which then introduces an opposite secondary reaction but, of course, no equilibrium.

When rising prices cause people to expect further price increases, this will normally induce them to buy more and sell less, so that the primary tendency of the prices to rise will be strengthened, and this agrees with our hypothesis of circular causation. Indeed, it was mainly to the part played by anticipations in the cumulative movement of an economy away from price stability that Wicksell attributed the acceleration of the process in its later stages.[8] But, of course, it is possible that people may be so conditioned by theory or earlier experience that they will expect that after a rise in prices there will follow a fall; this then, of course, has the contrary effect.

A realistic study of any social process will have to reckon with a great variety of differently inter-related changes in response to a primary change, and I do not deny that sometimes those changes are inter-linked in such a way as to counteract each other. Nevertheless, I believe that when main trends over somewhat longer periods are under consideration, the changes will in the main support each other and thus tend to be cumulative in their net effects.

---

[8] Wicksell's policy goal of a constant price level was not to be expected as an outcome of the play of the forces in the market but as a result of intentional monetary policy.

CHANGES IN GENERAL BUSINESS CONDITIONS

It has to be remembered, however, that long-term changes are nothing more than the cumulative results of a succession of short-run changes, among which are the short-term fluctuations in the general business conditions of a country. A boom implies a generalised spur to expansion over the whole economic field. It will perhaps usually have its most powerful effects in the established industrial centres, but may induce a number of new starts in other localities or encourage lagging activity—the result of earlier starts, which were losing momentum—to continue. A boom will probably always increase the relative strength of the spread effects. A depression will decrease it.

Changes in general business conditions are traditionally dealt with as "the business cycle problem" and this tradition has continued long after these changes seem to have lost every appearance of being cyclical. This is, of course, due to our recognition that there are in the system self-generating changes of the countervailing type, though not contained in the same time-space, and this is also my reason for referring to the problem in the present section. Business cycle research has been dominated by the time series: interest has been focused on the aggregate changes from one point or period of time to another, while disregarding the differences in geographic space and even the changes in time of these spatial differences.

I believe that more intensive research on the changes in general business conditions, focused more specifically on their consequences for economic development, would be rewarding. This would imply research on the differences between localities and regions, as those differences change under the influence of the play of forces in the market during changes in general business conditions.

19 SOCIAL STRUCTURE AND ECONOMIC PROGRESS [EUROPE, 1951]

John E. Sawyer

I T HAS long been customary for the opening chapter of economics textbooks and the opening lecture of elementary courses to make a formal bow to the importance of "noneconomic" factors. This ritual has tended, however, to have about the same relation to what follows thereafter as the opening prayer of a national political convention has to the subsequent activities on the convention floor.

For more than a century the primary focus and the very great achievements of economics have centered about an increasingly sophisticated analysis of relationships held to be "internal" to economics. While the wisest observers of economic behavior have been deeply aware of the social context, the major effort of the science has tended to remain within certain assumptions of the late Enlightenment from which it sprang, as to the relation of economic processes to the more general frame of social action. These powerful simplifications and the techniques they have facilitated have greatly contributed to the successes of economics in developing a "new mechanics" of prices and costs, allocation and distribution. They have, however, limited the kinds of questions that economics has either asked or been able to answer.

The massive social upheavals of the last twenty years have forced to the fore new questions not answerable within these traditional restrictive assumptions. Wars, depression, and the extraordinary ventures in which the United States has engaged (such as the European Recovery Program, Point Four, and the

SOURCE: John E. Sawyer, "Social Structure and Economic Progress: General Propositions and Some French Examples," *American Economic Review, Papers and Proceedings,* May 1951. Reprinted by permission of the author and the American Economic Association.

like) have made it increasingly evident to economists and states-
men alike that the institutional context cannot be taken as constant or assumed away and that economic activity and economic
progress are not simply a function of tools and resources, capital
and markets. The big questions of the day concerning economic
growth and development cannot be answered without increasing
attention to what have been considered noneconomic categories
or without recognizing the extent to which economic activities,
while powerfully molding the social forms and class relationships
of a society, are themselves a function of the total social structure.

In gross terms, of course, the importance of the wider institutional context has long been accepted. Marx and others have
emphasized the basic institutional conditions of capitalist development—transferability of property, mobility of resources, free
labor, a rational-legal political frame, and the like. But less generally appreciated have been the ways in which the formal and
informal social structure persistently shapes the behavior for all
economic actors.

In this paper I want to do two things: First, to suggest a
way of approaching these questions, indicating some of the sorts
of problems that need to be examined; second, to illustrate the
kind of influences at work, using examples from within that
fraction of the globe that has shared the basic institutional developments of modern capitalism, notably the French example.[1]

I

Forced back into sociocultural categories we rapidly discover how
little we know of them, of the mechanisms through which they
operate, or of how to incorporate such categories of explanation
into the systematic analysis of economic processes. We do not
yet have the social theory or understanding of the human personality adequate to demonstrate precise interrelationships among
all these variables. The newer social sciences, however, offer useful concepts and ways of getting considerably closer to the processes by which patterns of motivation and behavior are shaped.

One of the most useful of these approaches—so-called "func-
tional-structural" analysis, as developed in contemporary sociol-

---

[1] At the request of the editor I have omitted here a range of references
to people and sources given in two closely related and more extended
papers noted below.

ogy—focuses attention on the extent to which social action tends to be "structured," both as to ends and means. Any society necessarily institutionalizes particular goals and values, patterns of social relationship, and ways of doing things requisite to the continued operation of that social system; in sociological language, it prescribes patterns of normative conduct in a system of structured roles. Where these patterns of working and living, acting and reacting, seeking and believing become so widely accepted as "legitimate" that conformity with them is generally expected and is supported by moral sanctions, they can be called the "institutions" of that society. In any going society these institutions are highly interdependent. The patterns of family relationships or of social rankings or ultimate values, for example, necessarily bear in upon patterns of economic activity.

From birth the human individual is molded toward conformity with these institutions through the process of socialization. Family, neighborhood, school, and all the rest bring him in substantial measure to internalize those goals and relationships, those ways of feeling and behaving that make up the bulk of the informal social structure; and a variety of sanctions, ranging from police action to the most subtle forms of social pressure, continuously urge conformity to established ways. It is in terms of his particular social structure—its institutionalized rankings and values and patterns of conduct—that the individual normally seeks approval, recognition, and reward.

The economic actor, then, must be seen as oriented to a comprehensive institutional system in relation to which he acts and aspires. Only in reference to this total social situation can the utilities and disutilities involved in any specific decision or course of action be meaningfully calculated. Insofar as action is to be analyzed in terms of rational choices among alternatives, the concept must, as a first requirement, be broad enough to embrace the full range of social rewards and penalties, the sum of satisfactions in relation to this total social situation; and, at a more complicated level, it must eventually be radically deepened to comprehend the working out of compulsive behavior through institutionalized channels.

It is evident that different institutional systems will be more or less encouraging or discouraging to particular patterns of economic activity. A community whose systems of beliefs and statuses, for example, give high reward and recognition to worldly achieve-

ment will get more in the way of economic enterprise than one
otherwise oriented. This approach, while clearly not offering
quantitative solutions, provides some sort of frame for comparative analysis of the ways in which given social structures are
differentially favorable to the kind of economic development
with which we are here concerned.

II

A wide range of comparative studies will be needed in the effort to
bring any precision to the effect of social structure on economic
behavior. Investigations involving extreme contrasts—industrial
America and Brahman India—can open up the widest questions
of orientation and stratification; but the more extreme the differences in the total historical and institutional setting, the more
difficult it is to establish precise correlations. Studies involving
much closer comparisons—such as those among the countries of
Continental Europe or of the Western Hemisphere, or between
Boston and Chicago, or perhaps even Rochester and Buffalo—
may in the long run prove most significant in clarifying the problem. These finer analyses, however, will require the sharper use
of sharper tools and a wealth of information not now available.

For our purposes there are advantages to selecting examples,
from Western Europe and, where Europe's diversity forces choice,
to focusing on the French case. An area of immediate practical
concern with which some familiarity can be assumed (not yet
quite true of the various Bongo-Bongo's), Europe has shared with
us a basic range of Western institutional developments; and
yet it is a society with differences from the United States sufficiently clear to allow of the sort of comparative generalizations
necessary in so brief a paper. (In making these implicit comparisons with American development we are, of course, quite
arbitrarily isolating one factor from the gross differences in location, size, resources, rates of growth, etc., that have together made
for a fundamentally different economic history.

Looked at on any relative scale European institutions stand
out over the past five hundred years as having been exceedingly
favorable to economic progress. Europe, after all, gave rise to
modern capitalism and to the industrial age—a perspective that
must be borne in mind in any examination of this kind. Yet

industrial capitalism came in Europe into a relatively stabilized society with unusually explicit cultural traditions, and with a highly elaborated social structure compounding important survivals from each of the great prior social orders that had arisen on successive economic foundations in the European past. From each of these eras and institutional systems the countries of modern Europe have inherited a mixed legacy. Our interest here is in the economic drag, the rigidities and resistances to economic development in this heritage—both as significant to the European future, and as an illustration of the ways in which social structure pervasively and persistently shapes economic activity.

For it seems evident beyond argument that while recognizing the force of Marx's insight, we must modify the metaphor: the new forms have never fully emerged from the womb of the old. New modes of production have everywhere disrupted the existing social order and created new class and power relationships and forms of their own, but they have nowhere succeeded in eliminating important conflicts and contradictions inherited from the pre-existing social structure. The new has grown within what it only partially destroyed. In this sense it could be argued that, for the social revolutionary, the brutalities of Lenin and Stalin perhaps reflect a social diagnosis more accurate than that of Marx; while new economic processes indeed produce basic social changes, probably nothing short of large-scale liquidations can totally destroy an institutional inheritance. For as long as man's habits and memories and ideals carry forward past patterns, this heritage exerts a lasting impress on the subsequent evolution of the social order.

The problem of assessing the impact of this heritage on modern European economic growth is not a simple one. Variations of considerable significance exist between nations and within nations, and the influence has not been wholly unfavorable to economic development. The German case, for example, illustrates particularly well the ways in which a relatively unbroken feudal heritage while containing deep resistances to capitalism can also carry forward certain institutional patterns that serve the needs of a rapid industrialization. This can be seen directly in the relation of the large estate system to labor availabilities and similar points, quite apart from the mixed insight and aristocratic preference in Schumpeter's thesis regarding bourgeois dependence on a

landed ruling class. A whole series of comparative studies is
needed to explore these issues. France offers a useful place to
begin.

III

Perhaps more than any other nation, France has experienced to
the full the major sequence of social orders of the European past:
the feudal system; the *ancien régime* dominated by the centralized,
military monarchy and a surviving aristocracy; petty bourgeois,
commercial capitalism, and the institutions of the French Revolutionary settlement. A brief paper cannot attempt to analyze the
institutional characteristics of these or evaluate the impact of their
survivals.[2] It can at best suggest the kind of relationships involved. This we will attempt by first reviewing in highly generalized terms certain institutional patterns inherited from each
epoch; and then indicating ways in which they have adversely
affected economic development.

From the system of institutions associated with feudalism and
manorialism have come those patterns that probably most distinguished the social structure of the old world from that of the
new. From this age, modern France has inherited patterns of
social stratification that the Revolution and Republic have never
completely eliminated. A society historically rooted in knight-
hood, seigneurial agriculture, and dependent tenure tended to
establish as permanent a system of social rankings based on birth
and place, not simply dividing men into the larger categories of
those who prayed, fought, and worked, but institutionalizing an
elaborate hierarchy of hereditary statuses. To birth and status
it also tied property, occupation, training, and social function
in the widest sense. The craftsman or villager as well as the
count tended to identify himself, his skills, and his heirs with a
given place in the social hierarchy.

The prevailing system of ideas and religious beliefs powerfully
mobilized sentiments for traditionalism, community, and personal
relationships as against change, mobility, and enterprise. It taught
that this system of things represented not simply what was, but

---

[2] I have attempted somewhat fuller annotated discussions of these institutional conflicts in France in two related papers: Sawyer (1951a;
1951b).

what ought to be—that the whole architectonic structure was of divine design, and acceptance of one's station and lot in this world a part of the Christian duty. Poverty for the masses of men was assumed, and charity its only relief. The lay elite, geared to values of land and family, arms and honor, by reason of its prestige in the social scale helped fix a set of attitudes that was generally inhospitable to the market and the merchant. These patterns of stratification and their institutional ramifications, though legally eliminated and in some measure socially repudiated since 1789, have remained unevenly but widely diffused in the social structure of modern France.

Many of these so-called "feudal" patterns were also reinforced by institutions subsequently associated with the centralized monarchy and its attendant aristocracy. From this epoch we might select for our purposes those patterns that institutionalized national power and national glory as ultimate ends of the social effort. Spelled out in terms that emphasized the army, the state, the church, the court, the arts, these patterns extended the prestige of crown and court to the elite services—military, diplomatic, judicial, and financial—and gave important social recognition to the professions and the arts. Business activity tended to be judged and regulated in terms of its relation to the ends of national power and glory, and came in significant degree both to fear an irresponsible fisc and yet look to the state for direction and protection. Even a Colbert was unable to raise the prestige of trade against an aristocracy that elaborated the privileges and vanities of rank as its functions diminished. The tastes and habits of this increasingly self-conscious elite spread patterns of consumption favoring personal service, the château, leisure, and the graces, and giving prestige to the skills of the craftsman, the individualized product of high excellence, the personal relationship in production and exchange.

Over and against these patterns there had grown up during the centuries since the revival of trade and the towns another set of institutions associated with peasant ownership, petty-bourgeois commerce, and bourgeois thrift. Breaking through in the French Revolution, these patterns have become established in France to a degree probably unequaled anywhere else in Europe. The political and social boldness of the revolutionary ideology and settlement was matched by an economic caution. It enshrined the little man, the little economic unit, the little economic aspiration. The lower middle classes—artisan, tradesman, petty official —mightily reinforced by the establishment of a system of peasant proprietors, have written their goals and interests into the institutions of the Republic. While many of these patterns have naturally been favorable to capitalism, the cluster on which we are here focusing—the institutionalization of the small unit, in the peasant farm, the craft shop, the *boutique*—has in its turn established patterns unfavorable to industrial development. These are visible in all fields—primary, secondary, and tertiary.

IV

Broadly speaking, institutional survivals from this historical past have operated against economic development in two main ways: First, by sustaining a range of rigidities to the free flow of men and resources obstructing the full exploitation of productive techniques; and, second, by focusing the efforts and aspirations of men in greater measure on goals and values other than those of increasing material welfare. (Whether this be good or bad is quite outside our immediate problem.) Let us look at their effect on various economic actors and activities.

At the upper end of the business scale these patterns of stratification and social values have operated against aggressive and creative entrepreneurial exploitation of such opportunities as have existed—an effect of considerable economic significance, given the kind of private enterprise economy still prevailing in France. They have limited entrance into business leadership, regularly sending the elite of influence, intellect, and education into the professions, state services, and other careers outside of business, while significantly restricting access to the higher economic levels to those having the proper kinship connections. They have weakened the incentives to aggressive, innovating entrepreneurship and provided only limited social rewards to the successful self-made man (who, significantly, is not only assumed to have been a less frequent phenomenon, but typically has tried to hide rather than boast of his rise from humble origins). Moreover, a status system less oriented about business success and money income as a symbol thereof has partially undercut the force of the particular rewards that capitalism had to give. Perhaps most fundamental of all, the French businessman has never been able to identify himself with national goals—

to share that sense of carrying forward a great social effort that has so fortified his American counterpart.

Traditional patterns have also strengthened and legitimized tendencies to the habitual, to continuing with old methods, products, and customers, to remaining within the circular flow. The large range of French business that has remained family business has been typically preoccupied with assuring the status of the family over time, maximizing security and continuity rather than any combination of more dynamic objectives. Inherited emphasis on community and tradition have also provided a set of social attitudes favorable to "acts in restraint of trade." They have facilitated the practice of regulating an industry or a market so as to preserve the community of producers or sellers—to each according to his station—and have worked against the aggressive use of competitive advantage, to a degree that has conspicuously restricted the process of creative destruction so central to *The Theory of Economic Development* (Schumpeter).

If the businessman and the cautious French investor have failed to seek new combinations and the manufacturer to exploit the possibilities of industrial production, their behavior is at least partially analyzable in terms of the effect of social structure on them and in turn on the behavior of French workers, customers, and retailers.

At the bottom of the scale, inherited patterns and horizons have operated to restrict the participation of the French working class in the process of economic development. Still living within horizons of a divinely sanctioned Malthusianism, of a stratified social order in which the masses of men were forever to live at the margin in inferior status, French workers have never really been able to conceive of the possibility of an ever expanding economy or of steadily increasing worker standards of living. They have tended to cling to traditionalisms, to old skills and relationships identified with a given status, to particularistic attachments to place and occupation. These patterns have strengthened familiar resistances to mobility, to the changes involved in increasing productivity, to the working of the impersonal market mechanism, to the demands of large-scale organization and industrialism. Inherited institutional patterns have also powerfully contributed to the fundamental class antagonisms of modern France. Sharing in widely diffused anticapitalist sentiments deriving in part from feudal roots, offered limited chance of economic advancement as a class or of social mobility as individuals, often resentful of their social inferiority in the land of *liberté, egalité, fraternité,* skeptical of ever winning a better life within the given social structure, French workers have in significant numbers repudiated the existing system.

Inherited patterns have also profoundly affected the consumer and the nature of the market in ways unfavorable to industrial development. The upper-class consumer, responding to a scale of values that gave highest prestige to luxuries, quality, individualized products, and hand skills, has tended to resist the standarized outpouring products of mass production. Even in such an American staple as cigarettes, the producer and retailer have had to recognize consumption tastes reflecting traditional regional and class lines. Inherited consumption patterns have also emphasized leisure and personal service rather than durables and the newest factory-made gadgets. The French customer has resisted the invasions of advertising and installment buying, and has shown a persistent preference for the personalized exchange relations he has enjoyed with that extraordinary institution, the typical French retailer. The large masses of consumers have not had the income to provide much in the way of effective demand and have themselves tended to live within traditional class consumption lines even when experiencing increased prosperity.

French commerce has never developed the kind of distribution system organized about the principles of volume and turnover necessary to exploit the potentials of industrial production. To this result social patterns have significantly contributed. In the traditional scale of things, retail trade had the lowest prestige of all the major forms of economic activity, and the business of catering to the popular purse has rarely drawn resources or enterprise. Meanwhile, under the Republic the small retail outlet has been institutionalized as a symbol of petty-bourgeois independence. Its cautions, conservatisms, inefficiencies, and utter disinterest in volume, cost analysis, or the whole merchandising operation have choked the channels of trade for as long as it has charmed its customers. Politically strong enough to check the spread of chain and department stores, protected by law, habit, and ideology, its reign still seems unchallenged.

Finally, in agriculture, land holdings in parts of France divided to this day into small scattered strips of medieval origin testify to the grip of the past. The French peasant shed little but his seigneur and his dues in 1789; his attitudes toward land, family, status, and continuity changed little. These patterns have made for an intensified traditionalism, a resistance to new techniques, to large-scale agriculture, and mechanization—a tenacious cling-ing to land held over generations even under conditions of rural poverty. The revolutionary settlement institutionalized a system of peasant proprietors that has to this day kept surplus labor on the land and protected small, unprogressive units that are at once economically inefficient and politically invulnerable.

Other examples could be cited: in accounting practices, tax evasion, investment habits, the particular importance of minorities in economic life. Perhaps, however, even so generalized and in-complete a discussion has been able to suggest ways in which inherited institutional patterns have influenced economic activity and major economic actors—entrepreneur, investor, worker, con-sumer, retailer, farmer. In isolating here the factor of social structure we are not, of course, asserting its primacy in the social process or its adequacy as an explanation of the lag in French economic development. Resources, markets, war, for example, remain fundamental. We are insisting only on the direct relevance of the total social structure to economic activity, and on the need of its further analysis in relation to economic processes if we are to get at the big questions of economic progress.

20 RURAL ECONOMIC ORGANIZATION
[EUROPE, 1930]

P. A. Sorokin, C. C. Zimmerman, and C. J. Galpin

A. INTERNAL ORGANIZATION OF THE FAMILY FARM
BEFORE AND AFTER THE DEVELOPMENT OF
MONEY ECONOMY AND URBANIZATION

I. DIFFERENCES IN ECONOMIC ORGANIZATION

THE CHAPTER on the family stressed the fact that familism was the heart and soul of rural institutional organization as it existed previous to any considerable development of urbanization and money economy. The first conspicuous proof of the validity of this statement is found in the character of rural economic organization in the stage preceding great urbanization and the development of a money economy. This organization was essentially familistic. Peasant agricultural enterprise was family enterprise, the family being proprietor, laborer, and manager. The satisfaction of the needs of the family was practically the sole object of running the farm, and the whole organization of peasant economy was adapted to this need. The size of the holding, the kind of crops produced, the division of labor were all dependent, for the most part, upon the size of the family and its consumption needs; and everything was organized in such a way that the family itself was able to satisfy all its needs in respect to food, beverages, clothing, shelter, and tools by the utilization of its own forces. Thus the family tended to be a self-sufficient economic world. The mutual fusion of the family and the farm was so great that the terms "household" and "hearth" were equally applicable to the peasant family and to the peasant farm, and it was impossible to regard one as separate from

SOURCE: P. A. Sorokin, C. C. Zimmerman, and C. J. Galpin, "Rural Economic Organization," chapter 11, pages 124–37, Volume II, *A Systematic Source Book in Rural Sociology* (3 volumes), University of Minnesota Press, 1930. Reprinted by permission of the publisher.

the other. This familistic trait of peasant economy determined practically every detail of its organization. It caused peasant economy to assume forms very different from those of business enterprises, particularly modern capitalistic nonfamily farm enterprises.

With the development of money economy and urbanization the familistic traits of the peasant farm enterprise have tended to fade, though familism still survives [1930] to a greater extent in the economic organization of the typical family farm than in the nonagricultural industrial enterprise or in the capitalistic nonfamily farm enterprise. The subsequent readings describe the situation in detail. Here we will limit the discussion to a brief enumeration of some of the principal differences between the economic organization of the typical peasant family farm before the development of a money economy and that of the typical capitalistic agricultural enterprise without familistic traits. These differences reveal what changes take place in the economic organization of the farm in its transition from a self-sufficient family economy to a money economy.

1. The object of the agricultural business is different in the two cases. A capitalistic agricultural entrepreneur organizes his enterprise and invests his capital in it in order to obtain a reasonable return on the capital invested. The typical peasant, on the other hand, carries on farming because it is the most convenient, sometimes even the only possible way for him to obtain a minimum of subsistence for himself and his family. This difference in purpose has important results. The capitalistic type of farming ceases to be justifiable as soon as the profit, that is, the interest on the capital, falls below that which could be obtained from the same capital and entrepreneural ability applied to other industries. Where family or peasant farm economy prevails and more remunerative occupations cannot be entered easily, a low profit does not prevent the continuation of farming activity. Naturally a peasant would like to have a good return on his investment, but he regards it as worth continuing so long as his efforts and those of his family yield some return and supply them with their essential needs.

2. The clear-cut capitalistic farm enterprise is usually a large-scale enterprise; it utilizes more capital, more land, and more labor than the family or peasant enterprise.

The work is done by hired labor, the proprietor performing only the organizational functions [while in the family or peasant farm economy] the work is done exclusively, or at least mainly, by the peasant and his family. . . . Of course, even on very small farms the personal labor of the owner sometimes plays no important part. Such are farms of peasant families that for various reasons have lost all their working hands. But such peasant farms should be regarded as decaying farms and for this reason they neither represent an exception to the above-mentioned difference nor do they have any particular interest from the standpoint discussed (Brutzkus 1923:237–38).

3. In a capitalistic enterprise labor and capital are mobile and are not bound to the land, while in a peasant or family farm organization these elements are much more closely bound together, much less mobile. Not only in the past, but even at the present time, peasant farm economy has been peasant family economy.

The history of a peasant farm enterprise is at the same time that of a peasant family. It begins with the separation of the newly married couple from the paternal family. They usually do not have much capital but have energy and the capacity for work. In the course of their work their labor gives results, but at the same time the couple is more and more burdened with children. At this stage of the family the couple has to work more strenuously in order to get the necessary means of subsistence. The situation of the family improves as the children grow and become helpers and finally mature workers (Ibid.:244).

This is the most prosperous period in the history of the peasant family. Presently, however, the grown-up children marry and start their own farms, and the cycle begins over again. This indicates that the character of the peasant economy is determined by the character of the peasant family. The amount of land, the character of the farming, the expense budget, the amount of labor expended by the peasants, and the amount of cattle and inventory are all determined, for the most part, by the size and composition of the peasant family and by its consumption needs. When its members do not emigrate or enter other occupations, an increase in the size of the family leads to an increase of its land and produce— through the renting or buying of additional land; through the redistribution of land in the peasant land communities, so as to increase the portion of the communal land allotted to the growing families and decrease the portions allotted to the diminishing families; and, finally, through an increase of the efficiency of the labor of the peasant; a decrease in the size of the family leads to a decrease of the amount of land at its disposal. The papers of Makaroff and Tschaianoff describe in detail this process of the adjustment of peasant farm economy to the size, composition, and needs of the family. They leave no doubt that the peasant farm organization and the peasant family are inseparably bound together. And "the smaller the opportunity for the surplus peasant population to leave the land and be absorbed in city industries, the more conspicuously are these family traits of peasant economy expressed."

This close connection between the organization of the farm and the size and composition of the family does not exist in a capitalistic enterprise. As a rule capitalistic economy is not determined by the size and composition of the family of the capitalistic entrepreneur; its working hands are hired hands; its size and character are determined by the conditions of the world market and the whole machinery of capitalistic economy.

4. Capitalistic agricultural organization has as its aim production for the world market and not primarily for the family of the entrepreneur. Hence its production is determined not by the consumption needs of the family of the entrepreneur but by the demands of the world market. The form of a peasant economy, on the other hand, is determined chiefly by the consumption needs of the family; and the more "natural" the economic conditions of the area or the country, the more is this true.

From the qualitative standpoint the consumptive characteristic of peasant economy is manifest in the fact that opportunities for enrichment and accumulation of wealth are less developed than in capitalistic economy. Because of the monetary character of profit in capitalistic economy and the possibility of expansion through a larger investment of capital without additional expenditure of labor on the part of the entrepreneur himself, the size of his family does not affect the possibilities for enrichment and the accumulation of wealth. In order to secure expansion in a peasant economy, it is necessary to increase the limited labor efforts of the family; a part of the income, moreover, is received not in money but in the form of natural products, which can be accumulated only to a certain limit and which often have no significant market value.

Of course these peculiarities of peasant economy tend to become less pronounced as the connection between the world market and peasant economy becomes closer. In the United States they have been obliterated to a great extent, but they have not entirely disappeared even there (Ibid.:245–47).

In Europe this consumptive character of peasant economy is still in evidence. In various parts of Russia from 40 to 90 per cent of the produce of the peasant farm is consumed by the peasant family and only from 10 to 60 per cent is sent to market.[1] In Switzerland, in the period from 1904 to 1906, about 27 per cent of the produce of the peasant farms was consumed in its natural form by peasant families; on small peasant farms (those from 3 to 5 hectares) this percentage increased to 33 (Laur 1909). In 1926 peasant families consumed 31 per cent of the entire produce of the smaller farms and 18 per cent of that of the larger farms.[2] There is scarcely any doubt that these consumptive traits of peasant economy are destined to become less pronounced with the intensification of the connection between peasant economy and the world market, as is shown by the situation in the United States. Nevertheless, it is doubtful if they will be obliterated entirely. Some portion of the unmarketable natural products will continue to be used and consumed by the peasant family.

5. Finally, peasant farmer economy is, as has been mentioned, a labor economy carried on exclusively, or at least mainly, by the labor of the peasant farmer family itself. The typical capitalistic economy is carried on with hired labor. To a capitalist, land is merely the means of obtaining the maximum profit, and everything is done to increase that profit. If the introduction of better machinery, for instance, will reduce his expenses, particularly wages, and increase his income, the entrepreneur will make the change, although it may produce unemployment among the people who have worked on his land and hence reduce their total income. To a peasant, land is fundamentally the means of utilizing the labor of his family and of thus obtaining the necessary means of subsistence. In other words, the purpose of capitalistic economy is to obtain the maximum profit on invested capital; farmer and

---

[1] A. V. Tschaianoff, *Fundamental Ideas and Forms of Peasant Cooperative Organization* (Russ.), pp. 88 ff.; *Materials of Land Evaluation in Vologda Province* (Russ.), II, 225. [Chayanov 1966].

[2] *Statistisches Jahrbuch der Schweiz*, 1927, Bern, p. 154.

peasant economy has the added purpose of obtaining a return for the labor invested in agricultural enterprise. This aspect of "returns" on his economic activity is rather more important to the peasant than the aspect of profit. Professor Laur, Professor Brdlík, and many Russian investigators have shown this point clearly. The following data for Switzerland illustrate the difference in respect to profits in the two types of economies (Laur 1909:97).

COMPARISON OF PROFITS IN PEASANT AND CAPITALISTIC ECONOMIES
OF SWITZERLAND [1904–1906]

Size of Farm in Hectares	Per Cent of Labor by Farm Family	Wages to Members of Family		Profit on Capital Invested on Basis of 4 Per Cent Interest	
		Francs	Per Cent of Total Income	Francs	Per Cent of Total Income
3–5	90	1,727	61.0	1,103	39.0
5–10	80	2,340	54.4	1,965	45.6
10–15	71	2,817	49.2	2,912	50.8
15–30	54	2,946	41.9	4,091	58.1
30–70	39	2,273	25.2	6,764	74.8

According to these data, in Switzerland, where land values are very high and the investment of capital is considerable, 60 per cent of the incomes from farms of 3 to 5 hectares consists of wages for the labor of the farmer and his family, and only 39 per cent consists of profit on the capital invested. On the larger and more capitalistic farms, which use a greater proportion of hired labor, the situation is reversed and profit on capital composes the principal portion of the total income, while wages for the work of the family occupy a much less important place. In the still smaller landholdings of the peasants of China, India, Russia, and Japan the relative importance of the wage element in the income from farming is even greater.

This presents to the peasant economic tasks that are considerably different from those of the capitalistic enterpriser and give to peasant economy a different organization. Suppose that some Swiss peasant farm of 5 to 10 hectares becomes capitalistic in its character. Suppose that through such reorganization labor expenses are cut in half, reduced by 1,200 francs, let us say, while at the same time the gross income from the farm decreases by only 700 francs. This means that the net profit of the capitalist increases by 500 francs. It is evident that such an organization is more profitable for the entrepreneur and preferable from his standpoint. But is it preferable also from the standpoint of the peasant? Assuming that the entrepreneur of such a reorganized farm is a peasant, his profit on his capital is increased by 500 francs, but his income in the form of wages for his labor is decreased by 1,200 francs. This means that his total net income is decreased by 700 francs. If the peasant were sure that his labor, which yields him 1,200 francs when applied in farm work, could be profitably applied somewhere else and would bring him 700 francs or more, he would have reason to reorganize his farm along capitalistic lines. If such a certainty is absent, and if, as is the case in many countries, it is difficult to "invest his labor" elsewhere, outside his farm, he has a valid reason for preferring the noncapitalistic organization of his farming. Though his profit on the capital invested will be smaller, his total income will be greater, because he will receive more remuneration for the labor of himself and his family to compensate for the slight loss in profit (Brutzkus 1923:256 ff.).

A series of investigations conducted in Czechoslovakia by Brdlík and in Russia by Makaroff, Tschaianoff, Tschelinzeff, and others have yielded similar results.

The above discussion shows that the internal organization, or the "soul," of the typical peasant economy as it existed before the development of money economy was radically different from the general organization of any business enterprise and of modern nonfamily farming. While the latter are almost free from familism, the former was merely the family in its economic aspects.

II. RESULTS OF THE TRANSITION
FROM FARMER PEASANT TO CAPITALISTIC ENTERPRISE

We have already mentioned the fact that the development of money economy and of urbanization tended to weaken the family and familism and consequently to efface the familistic traits of the economic organization of modern farmer peasant enterprises and cause it to approach the form of capitalistic farm enterprises. Instead of using the help of the family to produce almost all the principal necessities for its own consumption, the modern farmer . . . produces primarily for the market, and he is thus forced to produce what is demanded by the market rather than what is necessary for the family. This has led to a series of very important changes in farmer peasant economy.

1. In the first place, family clothing, beverages, some types of food, furniture, carts, the principal tools, and many other articles are no longer produced by the family for the satisfaction of its own needs, because the low cost of making these objects in factories has made such a division of labor more profitable. Many subsidiary industries previously carried on by the farmer peasant family have also been abandoned by it. Hence the first effect of urbanization on farmer peasant economy has been to produce a shift from an all-embracing and many-sided economy to a specialized type.

2. The second effect has been to create further specialization in the production of agricultural products themselves according to the demands of the market. The increasing division of labor and the improvement of the means of transportation have forced farmer peasants to limit production to those agricultural products that may be produced most cheaply under the existing natural conditions and sold most profitably under existing demands of the market, regardless of their use by the farmer peasant family itself.[3] As a result, general farming has been abandoned in many places in which it has been shown to be more or less unprofitable. Many areas especially suited to the production of a particular farm product, such as wheat, potatoes, flax, chickens, butter and milk, or cattle, began to specialize in the production of a single commodity and to curtail their production of others, even though they were necessary for the sustenance of the farm family itself. The farm family began to buy these other products in the market with the money obtained from the sale of a particular agricultural product. At the present a considerable number of farmers in the United States buy canned food instead of producing it on their own farms. Such specialization has naturally narrowed the many-sided character of farm economy and farm work still more and has led to a division of labor between the farmer peasants of various areas. While almost all farmer peasant economic enterprises of the past were somewhat similar in that all were self-sufficient and aimed first of all to produce the things necessary

---

[3] For an analysis of the factors influencing choice of production, see Black (1926). Here are mentioned only the major considerations without reference to minor ones.

for their own living in large enough quantities to meet the demands of the family, the modern farm economic enterprises, by virtue of their specialization, differ widely in various places. Instead of an undifferentiated type of farmer, we have the dairy farmer, the poultry farmer, the wheat farmer, the cattle-breeder, the cattle-feeder, the fruit-raiser, the beekeeper, and so on. Each of them produces a commodity for which there is demand, in such quantities as the market dictates. Most of the necessities of the farm family are purchased in the market with the money obtained from the sale of particular products raised on the farm.

3. The transition from farm economy to money economy has naturally been accompanied by a series of other changes. The farmer or peasant has become more deeply involved in the money economy and the world market. Whereas conditions and changes in the demand and supply of the market concerned him only remotely in the past, they affect him incomparably more at the present moment. He tends to become more and more an entrepreneur who produces for the world market, and as a result he must study world market conditions, their fluctuations, and the principles of money economy and of contemporary economic organization. Otherwise he is doomed to fail. Since his economic activity must be adapted to ever changing conditions, he is forced to give up to an increasing extent his traditional ways of farming and to replace them by the rational (the new, flexible, and changing) ways advised by his experience and by science. Like any other entrepreneur, he is in greater need of credit than before, a need that involves him more and more in the whole mechanism of contemporary money economy, brings him nearer to the world market and the market nearer to him, breaks his economic isolation and independence, and forces him to fight for the organization of credit facilities. The farmer has now entered into the *roundabout* capitalist type of production.

4. We must also take into consideration the effects of the growing use of agricultural machinery—threshing rigs, combines, tractors, stationary gas engines, plows, and so on, all of which are produced by city industries and purchased on the market by the farmer. Thus, as a producer and as a consumer, as a buyer and as a seller, he becomes more and more entangled in the money economy and more and more dependent upon the world market. The fact that a portion of agricultural production (machine production and so forth) is carried on in the factories of the city

naturally impels farmers to create economic organizations among themselves that can protect and promote their interests as producers and consumers, as buyers and sellers. Hence the recent appearance and growth of many forms of farmer peasant cooperative organizations to serve these purposes. (See the paper of Emelianoff in the readings.)

These are the principal changes that the development of a money economy and urbanization have produced in the internal organization of peasant farmer economy. In their totality they tend to obliterate the familistic traits that formerly dominated it and to shape it along the lines of the modern business enterprise free from all traces of familism. The soul, the formative principle of the inner organization of the farm enterprise, tends to become quite different from what it used to be.[4] Since the family has tended to weaken with the development of money economy and urbanization (see the chapter on the family), such a transformation of rural economy is a natural result of this fundamental process.

B. ORGANIZATION OF EXTRAFAMILIAL ECONOMIC INSTITUTIONS BEFORE AND AFTER THE DEVELOPMENT OF MONEY ECONOMY AND URBANIZATION

I. Characteristics of Early Extrafamilial Organizations

Although the family farm tended to be self-sufficient before the development of money economy, actually it was not entirely so. Each family necessarily had some economic relations with other families of the community—there was some exchange of com-

---

[4] For a further development of this point, see John D. Black, *op. cit.;* Werner Sombart, *Das Wirtschaftsleben im Zeitalter des Hochkapitalismus,* Munich and Leipzig, 1927, pp. 969 ff., 1020 ff.; Fritz Beckmann, "Der Bauer im Zeitalter des Kapitalismus," *Schmollers Jahrbuch,* 1927, Leipzig, pp. 49–91; Albrecht, *Grundriss der Sozialökonomik,* IX Abteilung, I Teil, pp. 56 ff.; Leon E. Truesdell, *Farm Population of the United States,* Washington, 1926, chap. i; Charles J. Galpin, *Rural Life,* New York, 1918; Joseph Weigert, *Untergang der Dorf-Kultur,* Munich, 1930, pp. 20 ff.; Norman S. and Ethel C. Gras, *The Economic and Social History of an English Village,* Harvard University Press, 1930, pp. 680–701 and *passim;* Edvard Bull, *Vergleichende Studien über die Kulturverhältnisse des Bauerntums,* Oslo, 1930, pp. 25 ff.; Eli F. Heckscher, "Natural and Money Economy," *Journal of Economic and Business History,* III, 1–30 (November, 1930).

modities, some borrowing and lending, some mutual assistance in agricultural work and on the occasion of such important events as death, birth, marriage, calamity, disaster, or sickness. Furthermore, the families of the community, as one collective unit, had several general economic interests in common, such as the protection of their interests from encroachment by outsiders, the care of community paupers and other charity work, the institution of various measures for protection against fire, inundation, drought, and so forth. Finally, in certain aggregates the existence of community landownership and joint tenancy made necessary the very close cooperation of all the families of the community. Thus in the rural population there existed, side by side with the family household, several extrafamilial economic associations and institutions for the greater satisfaction of the needs of the family.

These extrafamilial economic organizations were also characterized by familistic traits. They were constructed along the lines of an enlarged family; indeed, they often were associations of several related families. In other cases they were composed of families of neighbors united by a number of ties into a friendly cumulative group intimately known to one another and bound into one solidary body similar to that of related kinsmen. Many other traits of such associations of cultivators were more or less familistic. Their cooperative unions were usually local; they were primary groups whose members knew each other personally; they were united on the basis of family or friendship ties, and an outsider or unknown person could not be a member. They were primarily mutual aid associations, the principal object being to give help to the relative, friend, or neighbor who needed it. Help given by a member to others insured him the others' assistance when he needed it.

Considerations of profit played either no part or an unimportant one. Most of the forms of mutual economic help yielded no formal monetary or economic remuneration to the helpers. When remuneration was given, it was something without pecuniary value, as, for instance, a meal served to the villagers after they had helped with certain work. No formal rules existed as to when, for what remuneration, and to what extent a villager should lend his assistance. Among the members of a family such formalities are absent and unnatural, for normally each member helps the others as much as necessary, regardless of the amount of exertion and sacrifice entailed and without any formal contract as to the amount of remuneration to be received. The same principle of familism was characteristic of the relationships of the extrafamilial cumulative rural communities. If the worker in a family died suddenly and the family could not carry on its agricultural work, the villagers collectively did the work; if a peasant decided to build a house and needed hands, the villagers came and helped him, their only pay being the meals they received from him while they were working; the experienced peasant women served as nurses during childbirth. There was the same type of mutual help in many other cases and on many other occasions, of which the Russian peasant *pomochi* (help) and similar institutions and customs among practically all agricultural populations before the development of money economy furnish hundreds of illustrations.

We may summarize by saying that the extrafamilial rural economic associations of the stage we are considering were familistic in character; consequently they were local, primary, based on family relationship or friendship, nonpecuniary, informal, mutually benevolent. Each was a kind of mutual aid society composed of the members of a large family rather than an organization of strangers united only by profit-making motives, such as are the economic organizations of a period of money economy. The subsequent readings dealing with extrafamilial economic organizations among Chinese cultivators give more detailed illustrations of this characteristic. The essential traits of these Chinese organizations exist, with some variations, among most of the agricultural peoples who are not yet deeply involved in money economy.

II. Changing Character of Extrafamilial Economic Organizations

The internal structure of rural extrafamilial economic organizations has naturally undergone considerable change with the development of money economy and urbanization. They have tended to lose their familistic soul and the other traits that have been associated with it. The basis of locality in the cumulative community has tended to be replaced by a basis of occupation unlimited by territory; the primary character of the association, by the secondary; its small size, by the nation-wide scale; and the personal acquaintance between the co-members, by a purely formal affiliation of a multitude of people belonging to the same class and having similar economic interests. Informality has given way to the organization of cooperative societies having formal constitutions and rules and to formal contractual relationships in which the privileges and duties of members are definitely outlined. Naturally pecuniary motives have become increasingly important and have tended to become the dominant, sometimes the only, reason for the existence of organizations. Their structure, their technique, and their functions have tended to become identical with those of thousands of other economic associations of urban people. The peasant and the farmer, deeply involved in the mechanism of money economy, have been forced to forsake their previous forms of economic organization and to use the forms and the techniques typical of urban economic organizations.

Extrafamilial economic organizations of peasants and farmers exist today principally in the form of various kinds of cooperative associations, which embody the essential traits of modern economic organizations in general. Professor Emelianoff's paper gives an analysis of their economic characteristics. He shows that they differ widely from earlier familistic organizations, and he explains why they appeared relatively recently and why they originated in connection with the Industrial Revolution and the development of money economy. The modern cooperative organization is the form cultivators must adopt to serve their economic needs under the new economic conditions.

Thus, in the field of the family farm, as well as in that of the extrafamilial economic organization, the transition from natural to money economy has been similar to that from rural to urban conditions. It has manifested itself mainly in the disappearance of the formative principle of familism and many other traits associated with it. If we remember that the transition from rural to urban conditions has also been the transition from the cumulative rural community to functional associations and from the strong to the weakened family, the evolution of rural economic organizations appears but a logical aspect of the great and complex process of the social transformation of the basic forms of the social organization of mankind. It is in complete harmony with these fundamental changes. . . .

21 THE AGRARIAN ORIGINS OF MODERN JAPAN

Thomas C. Smith

INTRODUCTION

. . . taking the country as a whole [agricultural changes] fell mainly in the Tokugawa period [1600–1868], and their central feature was a shift from cooperative to individual farming. At the beginning of the period, farming was generally carried on through the cooperation of families organized into actual or putative kinship groups, who to some extent shared land, labor, animals, tools, and even food and housing. By the end of the period, however, such cooperation had largely disappeared. Although it lingered on for a generation or more in isolated places, in the end the individual family nearly everywhere clearly emerged as the center of production organization and economic interest.

This mighty change is easier to describe than explain, but if one of its causes may be singled out as especially important, it must be the growth of the market, with all that implies about changes in men's ways and ideas. More than any other influence the market lifted economic life in the village out of the context of traditional social groupings. Economic exchange, which had been merely an aspect of social relations, a necessary concomitant of kinship, became increasingly independent of social organization and created values of its own. Thereafter what goods and services men gave and received, on what occasions and in what amounts, was less a matter of obligation than whether the price was right.

This was a disruptive tendency in a society based even among the peasants on a hierarchy of birth. Economic life in the village

SOURCE: Thomas C. Smith, *The Agrarian Origins of Modern Japan* (excerpts from the Introduction, and chapters 3, 5, 6, 7), Stanford University Press, 1959. Reprinted by permission of the publisher.

had been organized around lineages, which provided a distributive as well as a productive system; now it ignored or worked against them. As family gain became the chief end of economic activity, new productive energies were released and income was more and more distributed without regard to status. Old wealthy families laden with prestige came on hard times; new cadet lines added field to field, moving into the landlord class. Thus the power of status, traditionally defined, was greatly reduced, and new routes were opened to social position and political power. The results were far-reaching. Peasant society took on an unprecedented mobility of which the effects were felt far beyond the boundaries of the peasant class; agriculture became competitive, productivity increased, commercial and industrial activity in the countryside flourished; there were even profound shifts of political power in many villages. . . .

[DEPENDENT] LABOR SERVICES

. . . *nago** accounted for a large fraction of the peasant population in the seventeenth century, and seem to have been present

---

* [*nago:* dependent laborers owing service to the household of their master who gave them land; theirs is a diffuse, socio-economic relationship of a master-client sort (see Smith 1966:ch. 2). ". . . in Kyushu *fudai* [hereditary servants] who were given land were called '*nago*' . . . [and] were also thereupon considered branch families. A government compilation of the customary law in the early Meiji period [1868–1912] makes a similar statement: 'In the countryside servants are sometimes given a share of the [land-] holding of the master and made branch families (*bekke*); such branches, *which are called nago*, do so many days of labor a month in perpetuity for the master's family.'" Smith (1966:23) sums up the situation with regard to landholding families and the several sorts of dependent, client-laborers they retained: ". . . the extended family, which constituted the labor force on large holdings, consisted of three elements: the nuclear family in the center, affines and cognates in the next circle, and servants and *nago* in the third. Servants were taken into the family as children, educated in its values, and, later, through the dynamics of natural growth and differentiation in the family, often established as branch families. Since upon receiving land *fudai* [hereditary servants] became indistinguishable from *nago*, and in many cases were even designated as *nago*, it is probable that a large part of the *nago* class sprang from hereditary servants. If so, *nago* were not an outside element taken into the family to meet a temporary labor shortage, but one that the family itself produced, and the relationship between them and the holder must have been similar to that of branch and main families." Ed.]

in some numbers everywhere in the country, except perhaps in a few scattered areas of commercial farming. Cultivating the land in close dependence on certain large holders—whom we shall call *"oyakata"*[1] to distinguish them from ordinary holders without *nago*—*nago* families were not autonomous farming units. They and their *oyakata* were cooperators who together formed an important element of the agrarian system and a pervasive and influential social relationship in the village. Any description of their relationship should begin with an account of its economic basis; since something has already been said on this subject from the *oyakata's* side, we shall look at it now chiefly from the *nago's*.

Nago had access to land only in the form of allotments from the *oyakata,* on whom they were usually also dependent for the necessary means of working land—among others, housing, tools, animals, compost, fuel, fodder, and water. Access to village common land and water was a right associated with the holding of arable, and since *nago* held land only by private arrangement with the *oyakata,* they had access to communal resources in his name only. With the market in a rudimentary state of development, moreover, materials taken from the common were essential to the self-sufficient farm economy. From the common came wood to repair the peasant's house and farm tools, twigs and dead branches to keep his family warm through the winter, grass and leaves for compost. If any one of these was more important to him than the others, it may, surprisingly, have been compost, owing to the intensive character of Japanese farming, which planted fields year after year to the same crop without rest. Water was another critical communal resource to which the *oyakata* gave access; it came through his irrigation rights and often even from his very ditches. In that case the *nago* could not transplant rice seedlings until the *oyakata* had finished his planting and could release water, thus synchronizing the work of the two and encouraging the exchange of labor for tools and animals. . . .

. . . *Nago* no doubt themselves owned the simplest farm tools; but for tools with expensive iron parts, which could not be made

---

[1] *"Oyakata"*—one who takes the role of parent—was perhaps the commonest term for such holders; the corresponding term for *nago* was *"ko-kata,"* or *"child."*

in the village, let alone fashioned at home, they had to rely on
the *oyakata*. And the same was true of draft animals; even
if the initial cost of a horse or bullock was not prohibitive,
the size of allotments made animals an uneconomic investment.[2] Yet for certain farm operations they were indispensable.
. . .

Nago in these areas managed to survive in large numbers
because labor services, which were essential to holder cultivation,
were indirectly compensated. Merging with the family labor force
on workdays, *nago* received their meals from the *oyakata's* kitchen
along with *genin** and others;[3] it might almost be said that on
such occasions *nago* temporarily became family members, re-
verting to *genin* status. The stipulated annual number of workdays for *nago* varied sharply from one place to another, from
one or two in some localities to as many as two hundred in others;
and in many cases no maximum was fixed at all, the number
depending wholly on the *oyakata's* needs. But since, for obvious
reasons, the need for labor services was reduced as *nago* were
assigned tenant land by the *oyakata*, and since tenancy appeared
on a significant scale only with the growth of trade and industry,
one may take upward of thirty or forty days as typical of the
seventeenth century. Where workdays were considerably fewer,
they represented a more advanced phase of economic development. Workdays, then, were a major source of *nago* income in

---

2 Such scattered data as exist on the animal population show that draft
animals averaged less than one per family in most villages; their ownership, however, was heavily concentrated in the hands of large holders. For
example, in 1679, there were 39 holders and 34 work animals in a village
in Shinshū—an average of nearly one per family; but the two largest
holders in the village owned four animals each.

* [*genin*: poor persons distantly related to families whom they joined
as agricultural servants. See Smith (1966:ch. 2). "*Genin* typically came
from families whose size had outrun the resources of their small [land-]
holdings . . . the person sent out as a *genin* typically joined a family
larger than his own, and in doing so not only made his own smaller and
simpler but made the other larger and more complex. This is not to say
that he became immediately and in all respects a member of the new
family, but in time he did so to some degree—especially if he were a
fudai, or hereditary servant." (Smith 1966:12, 13). Ed.]

3 In some cases at least, the adult *nago* were accompanied on workdays
by their children, who did not work but nevertheless ate; Professor Ariga
reports a case of this kind in which the *oyakata* normally provided four
meals on workdays.

the early Tokugawa period and were probably willingly given for that reason.[4] Thus in the seventeenth century, resources flowed continuously from the *oyakata's* farm to the *nago's* allotment and back again in different form: capital in many shapes going one way, labor the other. This exchange was the visible mark of economic interdependence; but interdependence went even further. Since the *oyakata's* animals and implements and the *nago's* labor could be used on but one farm at a time, there was a kind of breathing, organic unity between the two farming units, one resting when the other worked. (For a vivid illustration, see [Smith 1966] Chapter 4, note *n* on page 47.) . . .

The *oyakata* loaned his *nago* suitable clothing for dress occasions, gave them cast-off furniture and cooking utensils, and in modern times paid the doctor when they fell ill, perhaps counting the payment a loan, though at the same time neither expecting nor pressing for repayment. In other words, he treated the *nago* very much as he would a needy kinsman.

More important, however, he helped *nago* survive the ever-recurring crop failures that were the marks of agricultural backwardness, and which hit everyone periodically but hit the weak most often and hardest. Custom and self-interest, both, obliged the *oyakata* to open his storehouse at such times, to provide his *nago* with food and seed until the next harvest lest he be thought pitiless for thus driving them onto the highways in search of sustenance and a more reliable protector. If that happened, it was usually because famine conditions prevailed and the *oyakata* was himself short of food. Except for such times when no one was safe from hunger, *nago* had greater security than many small holders; indeed, small holders frequently gave up their land to an *oyakata* in return for the protection *nago* status afforded.

The continuous exchange between *oyakata* and *nago* of labor, capital, food, and protection for labor was unlike the exchange familiar to modern economies; it was an economic exchange in the guise of a social relationship, not a direct exchange of economic values defined by an impersonal market. For one thing, there were no individual transactions to which prices might apply;

---

4 In addition to workdays, there were a number of festivals during the year when *nago* were usually given food and drink at the *oyakata's* house; this was also the practice on the occasion of marriages, births, and deaths in the *oyakata* family.

there was only a continuous trading of certain resources for others that was felt to be equitable in the long run, though not exactly or in any particular time period. For another, there was no market to price diverse commodities in a common unit, so precise comparisons of value could not be made nor accounts struck, even had this been thought desirable. Something nevertheless kept the exchange tolerably equitable from the point of view of the participants, or it could not have been sustained, as it was, generation after generation. The governing factor was the reciprocal obligations of kinship or kinlike relations, which were not only understood and observed by both parties but insisted upon by community opinion. . . . Far from being a means of payment for land, then, labor services were clearly part of a far-reaching system of personal obligation. . . .

It frequently happened that individual *oyakata* held considerably more *nago* than the cultivation of their respective holdings could conceivably have required. Why? One suspects that in such cases family growth, through the proliferation of *genin,* had conspired to produce more *nago* on some holdings than were needed. But however that may be, it is clear that *nago* were often maintained by virtue of an obligation to keep them rather than for strictly economic reasons.

Nago, generally, perhaps even universally, owed their respective *oyakata* certain services in addition to workdays. Although these services varied endlessly in detail, all had one feature in common: unlike labor services, they had little or no economic value, consisting of ritual acts unmistakably expressing personal subordination. . . .

In the annual cycle of ceremonies that described the orbit of family and village life, there were many occasions that called for ceremonial services to the *oyakata.* These occasions differed considerably from one locality to another, as did the form of the ceremonies themselves. But there were two occasions that seem universally to have called for such services and to have been most elaborately observed: New Year's and All Souls' (*bon*). A common feature of these two occasions, indeed the central element of both, was in the rites performed to ancestors. Not only were *nago* required to be present at these rites in the *oyakata's* home, but they often had an active role in them. . . .

Oyakata-nago relations changed very little so long as the village economy remained largely closed to outside market influences;

the same crops were tilled in the same way, and there was very little change in the stock of possessions of individual families. But conditions became less stable as trade and industry began to modify the self-sufficient agrarian economy. This development generally belongs to the late Tokugawa period, but even in the seventeenth century it was already a powerful force in some areas, and at least dimly felt in others.

The growth of rural trade and industry brought two significant though very gradual changes in the economic position of the *nago* class. Of both, the immediate cause was a steady increase in the price of labor, a phenomenon characteristic of periods of economic growth. One change was that *oyakata* were obliged to give land in increasing amounts to *nago* as tenants, in order to hold them on the land against the pull of rising wages in the town—a practice also encouraged by the fact that, with *genin* becoming more expensive and difficult to find, *oyakata* could work less and less land themselves. The second change was the *nago* families could now increasingly supplement their farming income by working at domestic handicrafts, or other part-time employment. No sudden improvement in the *nago's* position occurred, nor were all *nago* equally affected, but for some there was for the first time hope of achieving a significant measure of economic independence.[5] . . .

Here and there, wherever tenancy was spreading, the vital integration of *nago* and *oyakata* farming was gradually disrupted. One mark of the disruption was the reduction of labor services, to which even the *oyakata* could have no objection, for he had less land to work than before and he must give the *nago* more time to farm as a tenant. The upshot was that the *nago* was increasingly self-employed, and he increasingly sought rewards for his labor on his own land, rather than on the *oyakata's*. Very slowly, out of the matrix of the *oyakata's* holding, the *nago* with his allotment and tenant land was emerging as an autonomous producer.

Growing economic competence eventually brought a change in *nago* legal status. *Nago* were registered neither as holders of land nor as family heads, being subordinate to the *oyakata* in both respects. This system of registration greatly simplified administration; it not only reduced the number of holders and

---

[5] For fuller discussion of the transformation of *nago* worked by the market, see [Smith 1966:Chapter 9].

family heads to be dealt with but, by making *oyakata* responsible for their *nago,* avoided dealing with a class of peasants who were so to speak neither socially nor economically competent. . . .

One consequently finds evidence throughout the Tokugawa period of the elevation of *nago* to the status of separate families and independent holders.[6] It is even possible occasionally to follow, from one village register to a subsequent one, the progress of an individual *nago* to holder status.[7] We should not imagine, however, that such advancement occurred on a massive scale—it happened sporadically. Nor should we suppose that it greatly altered the *nago's* relations with his *oyakata,* for such relations were economic and social as well as legal. The achievement of economic and social autonomy was a gradual process which legal autonomy, an either-or matter, cut across midway. On the day after registration as a holder, the former *nago* was as dependent on the *oyakata*—for housing, for land as a tenant, for capital, for everything except his allotment—and as tightly bound to him by obligations recognized by the community as he had been the day before.[8] This is broadly hinted in the fact that he often continued performing labor services, that the very persons recently named "holder" in one document were sometimes designated in other contemporaneous documents as *"nago,"* that persons recently raised from *nago* status were often not granted full political rights in the village.[9]

---

[6] An edict of Hideyoshi, apparently applying only to certain parts of the Kinai, stipulated that persons holding even cultivation rights be registered as holders. This order has been widely interpreted as having transformed *nago* into holders throughout much of the Kinai. Professor Araki offers evidence of a somewhat similar development in the Kantō. In still another area, the lord of Sendai in 1717 ordered that *nago* in his domain be given full title to their allotments and thereby made "new holders".

[7] A population register of 1650 for a village in modern Hyogo Prefecture, for example, lists five persons as *"kerai"*—another of the common local terms for *nago*—who are entered in a land register of 1656 as holders.

[8] This is obvious from the size of holdings belonging to former *nago;* for example, five who became holders between 1650 and 1656 in a village in modern Hyogo Prefecture held land yielding 5.8 *koku,* 1.05 *koku,* 0.34 *koku,* 0.09 *koku,* and 0.06 *koku* respectively. [1 *koku*=4.96 bushels of rice or rice equivalents. Ed.]

[9] As in a village in Awa Province: there a land register of 1612 listed four holders whose names, nevertheless, bore this notation: *"Genin,* not qualified to serve as village elder."

Not only, then, were *fudai** continuously entering the *nago* class from the bottom; after 1650, *nago* at the top were moving into the holder class. In doing so, they shed *nago* legal status but carried *nago* social and economic relations with them into the holder class. That is, the obligations to an *oyakata* were not peculiar to *nago:* they might be found also among the holder class. This begins to suggest that the familial organization of farming was not confined to large holdings, but extended beyond them, to form a network of relations encompassing the entire range of holdings from large to small.

THE ORGANIZATION OF POLITICAL POWER

It is evident that we must think of the seventeenth-century village as consisting, not of a number of autonomous farming units, but of clusters of mutually dependent ones. Outside the areas of commercial farming, all these groupings were very similarly organized, each consisting of a large holding and a number of smaller dependent ones (including *nago* allotments, which may be considered holdings from the economic point of view). The size of individual groups varied considerably, ranging from as few as three or four families to as many as 15 or 20; but whatever the number, the group duplicated in miniature the hierarchical economic and social structure of the village.

As cooperative economic units, the groups performed a number of indispensable functions for their members. They mobilized labor for tasks that recurred more or less regularly which no family could cope with individually; when a house was to be built, or a thatch roof was to be replaced, or fields were damaged by flood and needed repair, each family in the group provided

---

* [*fudai:* hereditary servants. See Smith (1966:ch. 2). *"Fudai* were acquired for the most part in two ways: either they were born of *fudai* who were already held, or they were acquired by purchase or gift from poor families with a surfeit of members . . . Many [*fudai*] were the sons and daughters of impoverished holders who had given them away or more likely, sold them, usually as children when they were most burdensome and could make no resistance. All parental rights were surrendered along with the child in such cases . . . fudai [were] similar to kin of the master in that they might be given land—or cultivation rights—and made branch families by him; . . . in acquiring land they also assumed a status in relation to the master very similar to that of *nago*." (Smith 1966:13, 14, 22.) Ed.]

labor regardless of who happened to benefit at the moment. The group also provided the framework for day-to-day cooperation in farming, especially between the largest and the smallest holdings. For the large holding provided a pool of capital, of tools, animals, seed, food, fertilizer, storage space, and so on, which the small holding drew on from time to time; the small in turn furnished the large holding with labor when needed. Thus, although in a sense the small holding was worked as an adjunct to the large holding it also gave it crucial support. Through cooperation the group as a whole attained a degree of self-sufficiency that was impossible for any of its members alone—a self-sufficiency imposed by physical isolation and the rudimentary state of the market.

One function of the group that deserves special notice was to provide a single, large labor force for the spring planting. Even in the Tokugawa period, rice was not sown directly in the fields but was started in special beds from which the seedlings were later transplanted. This hard, slow work had to be performed within the exceedingly short period when the seedlings could be transplanted without dangerously interrupting their growth. Since enormous quantities of water were required to work the soil to the consistency of a thick paste preparatory to receiving the young plants, and since few fields could be given the necessary amount of water simultaneously, it was necessary to flood and plant fields one after another in rotation. This reduced the period allowed for planting any one field to a matter of a few hours. To accomplish the planting in the allotted time required a labor force far larger than the individual family could muster. And the various lineages in the village—main family, branches, and pseudo-branches—provided stable groupings for performing this critical work. Mobilizing all its adult members for the planting, the group moved with the water from field to field, without regard for individual ownership; not only did this permit fields to be planted in the extremely short time water was available to each, but it added to the sociability of this exhausting and otherwise wholly disagreeable task. Needless to say, the power to refuse a family this help and sign of solidarity gave the group enormous power over its members. . . .

In areas where economic life had been little affected by outside influences, however, lineage groups functioned very much as they must have nearly everywhere several centuries ago—mobilizing labor for house raising, reroofing, road building, planting and harvesting, and providing a mechanism for day-to-day co-operation. . . . Survival of the lineage group adds details to our knowledge of its social functions. Where its economic functions were still strong, the group had a highly developed social side. Members celebrated or mourned together at births, weddings, funerals, and numerous annual festivals, and although persons outside the group might also participate in the activities on such occasions, the primary roles were reserved for members of the lineage. These recurring events underline the solidarity of the group. . . .

The head of a lineage enjoyed a politically powerful position in the village for obvious reasons. Lineage groups were units of social and economic life, clusters of interdependent interests that clung together with great force and were broken up only when the competitive inducements of trade began, much later, to dissolve the internal ties. . . .

. . . The political power of a family depended solely on the size and discipline of its lineage in relation to others; but this is not quite correct—other, related points of support must be mentioned. The most important of these was the restriction of village office to certain prominent families who perforce included the heads of lineages and in some cases no one else. . . .

Nearly every village had its *kyūka*, or "old families," and its "new families" who were variously called *shin'ya, shintaku, shimban, kitarimono*. These were not merely descriptive terms but designations of differential status and rights that applied more or less permanently.[10] . . .

A village headman, writing on the conduct of his office in the early nineteenth century, emphasized the political significance of family age, stating that "old families should be selected [by a headman as subordinates] . . . for, however prosperous a family

---

[10] The Meiji compilation on customary law affords many examples of discrimination against newly established families. For instance: "In Awa . . . the farmers dislike to own descent from a new family, and so . . . younger sons do not start new families but take the succession of a family about to become extinct." Or: "The new householder [in Noto Province] pays from 3 to 5 yen to the village as 'face money.' . . . " Or again: "The house of the new family [in Tamba Province] may be covered with straw-thatch only, not with reed-thatch or with tiles." (Wigmore, *Private Law*, V, 99, 103–4.)

may be, if degree is overlooked, things will not go well." This view was widely held and commonly enforced as part of the village constitution. . . .

But if the line between "old" and "new" was drawn differently from one place to another, all villages appear to have drawn it under force of the same compelling circumstance. That circumstance was having reached limits placed on the growth of the village by the amount of available resources, especially in the form of common land and water sources. Until these limits were reached, new families might be created with the same rights in the community as existing families; but once these resources were fully employed, or nearing that stage, no new share could be created without diminishing the actual or future value of existing shares.[11] Rather than suffer this loss existing families restricted or prohibited altogether the creation of new families who could claim shares. . . .

There were three usual methods of filling the office of headman: election, rotation, and inheritance, in order of increasing exclusiveness. The least common of the three was election, which seems to have been confined to villages where traditional status patterns had broken down under the impact of commercial farming—a modern feature of agrarian life. In most traditional villages the role of headman either was hereditary within a single family and the office was handed down from father to son with the family headship, or it rotated at regular intervals among a few qualified families only. . . .

It was of considerable importance to the authority of privileged families, of course, that the lord did his utmost to support and exalt the position of village officials. He could not do otherwise; the collection of taxes, the maintenance of peace, the security of administrative centers—all depended ultimately upon the self-discipline of thousands of autonomous villages, in which the most effective advocates of obedience were the local headmen. In all parts of the country, therefore, the lord sought to lift the head-

---

[11] The author of the "Minkan shōyō" tells us how villages tended to expand until they pressed severely against their resources: "As to the origin of villages, one or two families usually settle where the land is good, and fields are brought under the plow surrounding the dwellings of the settlers. Gradually a village forms; new houses are built among the existing ones, new fields are opened up, and land previously neglected, such as valley bottoms and marsh, is filled in, ditches and ponds are built and new fields are developed until not an inch of land is left. . . ."

man above the ordinary peasants, with the intent of assuring his loyalty and at the same time impressing the rest of the village with the dignity and authority of his office. Thus, for example, the headman and his family were permitted to wear silk and certain articles of dress considered especially elegant, to live in large and elaborately decorated houses, and sometimes even to wear swords and take surnames—all of which were forbidden the peasants generally.

The lord also constantly exhorted the peasants to look upon the headman as a parent, to give him love and respect—but above all obedience. He himself stood ready to give the headman every help including the support of troops if necessary . . . To appeal for such intervention was a confession of inability to get along otherwise—a confession that reduced the headman's value by exposing him to the ruling class as ineffectual and to the villagers as the lord's agent. Rather than thus isolate himself from the approval of village opinion, many a headman in a crisis sided with the village against his lord though the decision to do so often meant almost certain death. Throughout the Tokugawa period, but especially in the first half when the solidarity of the village had not yet been widely disturbed by the influence of competitive farming, many peasant uprisings were led, not by outcasts and ne'er-do-wells, but by headmen.

This brings us to another point of support for the power of the leading families of the village: the solidarity of the community itself. For it was essential to their power that they be able to speak with the voice of the village—on behalf of the sanctity of tradition, communal interests, and other similarly approved public goals. If politics is the art of transforming private interests into the public good, rarely have the conditions for its successful practice been so favorable as in the Japanese village before the advent of trade. This is best seen perhaps in the headman's discharge of his office. . . .

Geographically isolated from all but a few neighbors, farming communities since prehistoric times have been compact settlements whose families, linked to one another by innumerable ties of kinship, and trusting for protection in the same local gods, were huddled together physically. This afforded mutual comfort in the face of a menacing natural environment, and enabled them to help one another in their work and in conditions of famine, sickess, and death. But all such factors somehow still do not adequately explain the most important social characteristic of the Japanese village, its fierce and pervasive sense of solidarity.

The urgent sense that the village was a group that could tolerate no genuine internal differences, even in intimate matters of family concern, was evinced in more ways than can be discussed here. It was manifest in the legal personality that history had given the village: its competence to make contracts, borrow money, sue and be sued, and its collective responsibility in matters of taxation and criminal law. The solidarity was acted out annually in collective rites to the community deity who protected his "children," not as individuals, but as members of the community, whose priestly officials were automatically also the village's secular leaders. It was evident in community exclusiveness: in rules against the sale of land to outsiders; against the settlement of outsiders without consent within the village precincts; in the endless disputes and law suits between villages over water rights and wasteland; in the village rule of endogamy except for high-placed families who had to go outside the village to find marriage partners of comparable family rank.

The striving for solidarity was not least evident in the way personal affairs were often given a public character lest they otherwise lead to deviant opinion or behavior.[12] . . . the village was armed with very powerful weapons to bring about conformity. Gossip, by which the humiliation of deviant behavior or opinion was made generally known, usually sufficed to secure conformity; but if not some mild form of public censure normally would. The villagers had innumerable ways of expressing disapproval—placing a mark on a man's door, for instance, or assembling at his gate and beating on pots and pans in unison. But occasionally when harrying did no good sterner measures were taken, leading by degrees to ostracism and expulsion from the village—the severest punishments that could be inflicted.

---

[12] The following quotation is part of an agreement signed by all the holders of a village in 1831 is an example: "Poor harvests have continued for several years now and the harvest this year was especially bad. The villagers have therefore talked together and agreed as follows:

"1. At the wheat planting and when planting vegetables, *sake* will not be brought out to the fields to give those working there a noontime sip as in the past. . . .

"2. When weeding or otherwise tilling rice, even when help is being received with such work, no one may take any refreshment but tobacco or tea; it is strictly forbidden to bring rice or *sake* to the fields. . . ."

So severe were these punishments that the mere threat of them could scarcely fail to have effect. Banishment drove a man onto the highway without property or credentials, so that he must soon starve or run afoul of the law. Significantly, banishment was not confined to serious offenses, but might be invoked for any wrong-doing persisted in—the purposeful flouting of opinion apparently being as serious as any crime.[13] Ostracism was scarcely less cruel than banishment; the entire village severed relations with an offender against its norms, and in some cases even forced him to live at a distance. No one would greet him on the road or help him in any way except in the case of fire or death; he could not buy in the village store, the local doctor or midwife would not respond to his call, his children could not be members of the village youth group (*wakashū*). In the isolated settlements of the Tokugawa period the utter withdrawal of the sympathy of neighbors was more than most men could stand.

Once the village official was armed with the support of public opinion, therefore, his authority was very nearly absolute; he needed no help from the lord. His problem was rather to guide opinion to a desired consensus. In doing so he was aided by the urgent desire of the community to reach *some* consensus (a force that could also be dangerous) and by the opportunity his position gave him for influencing others. He was head or stood close to the head of a lineage whose support he could expect, and as a large holder he probably also had persons outside his lineage who were dependent on him as tenants, or for water or for the use of animals. These could be counted on to support him unless some stronger claim on their loyalties was exerted from another quarter. He was linked by marriage to other families similarly placed in the village since marriage generally occurred between families of equal status.[14] . . .

---

[13] Thus, in village law codes listing a large number of prohibitions, many quite trivial, one frequently finds such statements as : "If anyone should violate these regulations he will most certainly be expelled from the village . . ."; or again, "If any violation occurs . . . the culprit's ears will be cut off and he will be driven from the village."

[14] This is shown by the fact that the only circumstance recognized in most traditional villages for marrying outside the village was inability to find a marriage partner of equal family rank inside. A report by the headman of a Tosa village in 1857 tells us that in inquiring about a prospective bride from another village the first question asked was about her family's status.

Above all, the headman must maintain a solid front with the other leaders of village opinion, taking full account of their views, dignity, and interests, always compromising with them rather than risking a breach. . . . Abhorring dissonance, the village went to surprising lengths to avoid any open conflict of opinion; as recently as the postwar period, for instance, one village assembly was in the habit of meeting privately the day before its scheduled public meeting, in order that decisions on the latter occasion might be unanimous. We see this same concern for public harmony in the advice of our headman about dealing with boundary disputes; he recommends that the disputing parties be brought together and persuaded to compromise their differences—significantly, nothing is said about discovering the right of the matter or seeing justice done. Only after a compromise had been reached—which is to say, after the matter had been settled—should the headman give an order! . . . .

But not everyone could act for the community. Those few who could were qualified to do so because they stood each at the apex of a system of farming, kinship, and property rights that knitted a group of families together in intricate interdependence.[15] The political power of the heads of these groups was merely one aspect, in practice undifferentiated from the others, of the paramountcy of each in his group. When these leading families were in agreement, their decision had behind it all the weight of their several groups, now acting as one. And such families did habitually act together, for uniting them were marriage ties, class interest, and a common concern in preserving the authority of the community.

THE GROWTH OF THE MARKET

There were scattered islands of commercial farming in Japan from very early times, but as late as 1600 peasants still typically

---

[15] The dependence of political power in the village on economic and social power—or rather the single identity of all three—is well illustrated by the fact that in at least some villages today there are in effect two different systems of offices. One is that prescribed by law and within whose competence all matters involving the village with higher administrative organs fall, and the other is a system of traditional offices with traditional titles which has authority over such internal matters as the law is not concerned with—for instance, quarrels between neighbors or within families, village festivals, and the morals of young people.

produced to feed and clothe themselves, to pay taxes in kind, and to store whatever surplus there might be in good years against the certain crop failures of the future. But rural life changed rapidly after the Tokugawa conquest, as people became used to peace, transport improved, and the warrior class was removed from the fastness of the countryside to castle towns. The islands of commercial farming expanded, ran together, and began to fill in the surrounding sea of self-sufficient economy.

How great was the change in the two hundred years or so after 1600 is suggested by the pace of urban growth. Town life dates from at least the eighth century in Japan. But as late as the second half of the sixteenth century, when overseas trade flourished as never before, there were no more than two or three population centers that justly deserved the name "city". . . .

Then, in the two centuries after 1600, urban population grew with astonishing speed, increasing more than in the previous millennium. Edo, no more than a fishing village in 1590, grew into a vast and crowded city of more than half a million by 1731, when it was perhaps the world's largest city. Osaka and Kyoto grew less rapidly, but both had populations of 400,000 or more by 1800; together with neighboring Sakai and Fushimi they comprised an urban center of nearly a million people. . . .

Enormous quantities of grain, fish, timber, and fibers were required to feed, clothe, and shelter the growing population of the towns. Most of it came by way of local markets and merchants from Japanese farming and fishing villages, since foreign trade contributed almost nothing. What a task and what opportunities were set for villages which in the eighteenth century had produced little or nothing for sale! And what social adjustments were required to meet the challenge successfully! Not the least of these was to make farming far more specialized, for the country could no longer afford the gigantic waste of peasants all growing the same crops and therefore nearly everywhere growing some of them inefficiently.

The waste and inefficiency had been inevitable so long as urban population was inconsiderable and the opportunity to buy and sell was very limited. Then each region, village, and holding tended to produce what it needed, which was what all the others needed too. Everywhere rice and the lesser grains were the staples; they were supplemented only by a bit of fruit and vegetables grown for family consumption, a fiber crop for clothing, and perhaps some tobacco if soil and climate permitted. In the late Tokugawa period one still found villages with the characteristic subsistence pattern of cropping. But by the beginning of the nineteenth century this stage was long past. Except in notably backward places —wild and remote valleys, isolated promontories, areas cut off by poor soil from the main stream of economic development— peasants by then typically grew what soil, climate, and price favored, regardless of what they themselves happened to need. If a family were short of food or of critical raw materials as a result, it made no difference since nearly anything was available in the local market, supplied with commodities from places scores or even hundreds of miles away. . . .

One must be careful not to exaggerate the degree of commercial farming anywhere. It is clear from Professor Furushima's figures that as late as the early Meiji period [1868–1912] one cannot speak of farming as predominantly commercial even in

PERCENTAGE OF CASH CROPS BY DISTRICT, 1877

	All Agricultural Products (in yen)	Cash Crops (percent)	Number One Cash Crop (percent)
Kinai	14,858,779	25.8	11.9
Sanyō	15,605,320	13.7	7.6
Kyūshū	23,800,176	10.2	3.5
Shikoku	19,426,756	12.0	3.0
Kantō	26,939,263	14.7	4.2
Hokuriku	18,999,313	12.0	3.3
Tōsan	35,463,319	26.8	14.8

the Kinai. In that region, rice accounted for 60 percent of all farm products in 1877—evidence of a still high degree of peasant self-sufficiency.[16] But there were enclaves where commercial farming was highly developed. In several counties of Kawachi and Settsu provinces, for instance, cotton alone accounted for between 40 and 50 percent of all farm products (by value), and in one county cotton, vegetables, and indigo together accounted for 61 percent. Differences were no doubt equally great

---

[16] Because a very high percentage of rice on most holdings went for taxes or was consumed at home—a condition still found in some places today; see [Smith 1966:ch. 13].

from one village to another, for here as elsewhere commercial farming mingled with the farming typical of an earlier era, the one often within a few miles of the other.[17]

As commercial farming spread, so of course did the use of money. Not that money was anything new to the peasant. A Korean ambassador in the fifteenth century marveled at the use of money everywhere in rural Japan: everyone would accept it, beggars and prostitutes would take nothing else, and the way-farer need carry nothing more than a full purse. But the ambassador must have stayed on the main roads, for in the back country he would have found money less common. Ogyū Sorai, with his keen eye for signs of social change, tells us that coins were a curiosity outside the towns until the Genroku period but since then had come into use everywhere, even in the loneliest mountain hamlets. . . . there can be no doubt that a momentous change, signified by the use of money, was taking place in the economy in the first half of the eighteenth century.

The very landscape testified to the change. New markets were springing up everywhere and established ones were growing to new size; by the late Tokugawa period these markets, usually held at ten-day intervals, were to be found even in remote and backward districts. There were a score or so of such markets in most provinces by the early eighteenth century, some dating back a century or more but the majority apparently of more recent origin. The peasant could buy everything he needed in them; a list of commodities regularly sold in a market established in Takada village (Aizu *han*) in 1665 included cloth, harnesses, cotton, paper, rice, soybeans, firewood, hoes, hoe handles, sickle handles, winnowing baskets, looms, tobacco, grain, vegetables, mortars, straw hats, and straw matting—in addition to items offered for sale only occasionally. It is significant that the regular commodities were all articles in daily use among the peasants; gone were the luxury goods commonly found in local markets before the Tokugawa period when warriors and their households had been a conspicuous feature of village life.

Scattered about the country were hundreds of tiny markets like

---

[17] Even today one can pass quickly from villages where commercial farming is highly developed to villages where it is meager, for example by descending from the train that follows the Ki River and proceeding by bus up nearly any of the narrow valleys that run back into the mountains on either side.

the one in Aizu, serving an area within a radius of perhaps four
or five miles, selling a bit of everything. Less numerous, but
perhaps more important in knitting the country together economically, were larger markets each dominated by a single commodity that drew buyers from all over. Such a place was the
great silk market at Fukushima about 1818:

> The first great market of the year in Fukushima opens on the
> 14th of the sixth month. During the night of the 13th peasants
> gather with their silk from a distance of many miles around and
> wait for the market to open at dawn. Buying and selling begins
> on the 14th and continues for two watches. During this time,
> about one hundred horseloads of silk amounting to 3,600 *kan*
> weight are sold for fifteen or sixteen thousand *ryō*. . . . The
> sellers, who number several thousand, have their silk examined
> for quality and weighed and are paid accordingly. Nowhere in
> the country is there a market where so much money changes
> hands as here. . . .

Cottage industry was of course no new feature of village life;
peasants had always made things for use in their homes, and
over the centuries they had nurtured to maturity a tradition of
skill that could sometimes be turned to account in the market
place. Nobody objected to such industry; but Tōzan and nearly
every other warrior objected fiercely to domestic industry that
produced chiefly for the market, prospering (they thought) at
the expense of agriculture. After all, there was just so much
labor, and if it was used for industry, agriculture was bound to
suffer: it was as simple as that. . . .
But the urban monopoly could not last. With the growth of city
population and the spread of money in the country the consumption of silk increased enormously, and along with other industries
the silk industry jumped the neat channels decreed for it by guild
organization and government statute, and moved increasingly
from the town to the village. City artisans of course did not
disappear and they even continued to monopolize some branches
of production; but by the end of the Tokugawa period the industry as a whole was rurally based.[18] In the emerging mass

---

[18] Contemporary writers typically saw this as a threat to the towns
generally rather than merely to some groups in the towns. Takemoto
Ryūhei, for example, wrote: "In recent years, small shops and small merchants have greatly increased in rural areas, which is the reason for the
luxury there and the impoverishment of the towns."

market price made all the difference, giving rural producers a decisive advantage, for they were less encumbered than urban producers by guild restrictions and were nearer to raw materials and water power. Moreover their labor costs were far more elastic since they did not demand a livelihood from industry, merely part-time employment to fill the lulls in farming. . . .

Rarely if ever did industry displace agriculture in importance in the local economy, but sometimes it became equally important, giving rise to villages that might fairly be called semi-industrial. . . . In some counties of Kawachi and Settsu provinces, cotton accounted for between 40 and 50 percent of the value of all agricultural products, and where cotton was grown it was generally also ginned. Nor was ginning the only important industry in the region around Osaka. Cotton spinning and the maufacture of vegetable oil were nearly as important. In Yamato Province, for instance, there were 208 licensed oil makers in 1773, many of them using water power and producing up to 20 or 30 *koku* of oil annually. In addition there were a great many illicit producers, if we may judge from the complaints against them by those with licenses, and from the fact that the licensing system broke down toward the end of the Tokugawa period because it could no longer be enforced. . . .

The organization of local industry varied widely, many different historical stages being simultaneously spread over the countryside. There had been a time when peasants typically grew their own raw materials and worked them through numerous processes to a finished product ready for the consumer; but this early stage of organization was no longer characteristic of most regions, though it persisted everywhere to some degree. By the latter part of the eighteenth century, production was typically broken into separate operations performed by different families, so that each product ready for the consumer stood at the end of a rather long series of market transactions.[19] . . .

---

[19] Contemporaries were quite aware of the changes that were taking place in the organization of industry. An edict of 1835 in the Kiryū fief described the growing division of labor in the silk industry as follows: "In former times the peasants and their wives and daughters raised silkworms, reeled silk yarn from the cocoons, and wove the yarn into cloth as an occupation in their spare time. But in recent times, industry having become more and more prosperous, there has developed a large class of silk-yarn wholesalers (*ton'ya*) who have quit raising cocoons and buy silk yarn from families in their own districts and others."

The more a peasant family bought and sold, the larger the area of its economic life that was lifted out of the context of custom-bound social groups and subjected to the impersonal decrees of the market. How far economic activity had been transferred to the market place by the late Tokugawa period is difficult to say. The best indicators are probably the family budgets cited by Tokugawa administrators to illustrate conditions among the peasantry. Though these were rarely actual budgets, they were made up for illustrative purposes by persons who knew their subject, and they therefore throw considerable light on the economy of individual holdings. Consider the example given below, which purports to be the budget of a family on a rather large holding in Settsu Province at the end of the eighteenth century.[20]

Farming on this holding was evidently less commercial than on many holdings in the area; for one thing, the holding was planted less heavily than most to cotton[21]—the prime cash crop throughout the Kinai and of all crops the one requiring the heaviest applications of fertilizer.[22] Second, this holding had an unusually

---

[20] *Income*

   1. from 2.5 *chō* of paddy

	rice	51 *koku*
	wheat	28.5 *koku*
	straw	312 *momme* of silver

   2. from 4.5 *tan* of unirrigated fields

	cotton	120 *momme* of silver
	vegetables	462 *momme*

   3. from handicrafts

	cotton weaving, "straw work," straw matting	295 *momme*

Expenditures

	land tax	19.5 *koku* of rice
	miscellaneous	551 *momme* of silver
	fertilizer	2.077 *momme* of silver
	tools	491 *momme*
	wages of hired hands	730 *momme*
	food	16.5 *koku* of wheat
	food	3.33 *koku* of rice
Balance		Surplus of 250 *momme*

[21] In 1877, cotton accounted for 37.2 percent of the value of all crops in the county where this holding was located; note that on this holding cotton brought less than the straw from rice and wheat.

[22] According to a contemporary treatise, cotton required approximately 100 percent more fertilizer than rice.

high proportion of paddy land planted exclusively to rice and wheat (as a winter crop). The family was consequently not only self-sufficient in food but able to pay the entire land tax in kind, even though in this area a large part of this tax was commonly paid in money. It will be perceived, then, that this holding was by no means an extreme example of involvement in money economy, but the contrary. . . .

The budget shows money expenditures under four headings—tools, fertilizer, labor, and miscellaneous. Tools were the smallest of the four, followed by "miscellaneous"—a category of un-specified content which, judging from the items commonly ap-pearing in other budgets, probably included expenditures for so-cial occasions, transport, animal rental, and articles of daily use such as salt, tea, vegetables, cooking oil, lamp oil, charcoal, firewood, pots and pans, soy sauce, fans, perfume, medicine, headgear umbrellas, candles, dye, bedding, leather, rope. Per-haps, just as the writers of the time contended, the peasant was less self-reliant than his grandfather had been, but life was manifestly easier for him, too.

Commercial fertilizer was the largest item of money expendi-ture, accounting for over half the total. At first glance this is a surprisingly high percentage, for the area planted to cotton was small; but the budget may have been intended to reflect the exhaustion of sources of natural fertilizer, since this condition was widespread in the Kinai.[23] The enormous growth of popu-lation in the century and a half after 1600 had pushed terraces higher and higher up the hillsides; and this movement was fur-ther encouraged by the spread of cash crops, which on the whole were less dependent than rice on water. Since these crops gen-erally required intensive fertilization, they not only helped destroy the sources of natural fertilizer but very seriously increased the demand on them. There was therefore a constellation of powerful forces drawing holdings into dependence on commercial fertilizers.

Our Settsu holding, then, was by no means untypical. Records of the port of Osaka show that fertilizer was the third largest item (by value) of 119 imports in 1714. . . .

---

[23] Many Kinai villages were totally without land for collecting leaves and cutting grass by the early Meiji period. The exhaustion of sources of natural fertilizer was occurring elsewhere, judging from budgets from other areas which show nothing so consistently as relatively large sums spent for fertilizer.

Labor ranked second in the Settsu budget as an item of money expenditure, and this was its position in most budgets of the time. Surplus labor was increasingly finding employment in trade, handicrafts, and transport. *Nago* and the older types of *genin* were accordingly disappearing, and less free forms of labor were being driven out by more free. This transformation was accompanied by a considerable increase in the price of labor. Local documents were crowded with references to wages, and district administrators were forever complaining of the high costs of labor, predicting the certain ruin of agriculture as a result. Nor did the complaints and forebodings come exclusively from areas where industry was expanding; they were also heard from such remote places as Tōhoku, whence it seems that labor was migrating seasonally and even permanently in search of employment. . . .

. . . a vast number of large and middling farmers . . . employed one or several hired hands from spring through fall, taking on still others at the peak periods of work. Small holders of course rarely hired labor and then for no more than a day or two at a time, but such holders were scarcely less affected than the larger ones by the development of wage labor. It was now much easier than ever before to turn spare time and surplus family labor to immediate account. For many small holders wages earned by part-time work in the neighborhood were an important source of money income, and in some villages peasant families appeared who lived almost entirely by working for wages. Employment for wages clearly served the same economic function of complementing the income of small holdings that labor services had earlier, but the social results were strikingly different. . . .

Valuable as budgets and village reports are for the history of agriculture, they yield only fragmentary data. To follow through time an individual holding we must turn to agricultural diaries. Most such diaries are too terse[24] or short to be of use, but in 1942 Professor Toya found in a village in Musashi Province a diary that was extraordinarily full and covered an exceptionally

---

[24] The peasant, to whom writing came hard, typically recorded in a diary only what he could not trust himself to remember. Thus if he were keeping a particularly full record, a man would probably note every year what crop he planted to each field, how much the field yielded at the harvest, the amount and variety of the seed he used—all significant facts he would soon forget. But rarely would he note the size of each field since that did not change from year to year, and without this datum the other figures must be used with extreme caution.

long period. At the time of discovery the diary had been kept continuously by successive heads of the same family since 1720 —a period of 222 years—and in addition to daily entries it contained a continuous year-end record of yields! . . . .

When the journal opens in 1720, the Ishikawa family was scarcely in touch with the market. It grew tobacco, beans, potatoes, cotton, and cocoons—all cash crops—but in very small quantities which were probably consumed at home rather than sold. For the rest the family grew grains clearly meant for food: chiefly rice, wheat, barley, and millet. The high degree of self-sufficiency this pattern of cropping suggests did not last out the century, however. A notable shift toward commercial farming occurred when silkworms began to be raised in quantity on the holding in the last decade of the century. Part of the worms were sold for cash, but part were kept for the production of cocoons and silk yarn. Since the Ishikawa lived very near Hachioji, one of the most important silk markets of the time, it is no wonder that they developed an interest in sericulture and silk reeling.

As the family devoted more and more of its land and labor to sericulture, certain of the old subsistence crops inevitably disappeared. Rice, wheat, barley, and millet continued to be cultivated in approximately the same amounts as in the early eighteenth century. But hemp, which replaced cotton as a fiber crop in 1769, was dropped in 1781, and after that date cloth was apparently bought with cash from the sale of cocoons and raw silk, instead of made at home as before. Tea disappeared as a crop in 1750, tobacco in 1827, and taro in 1868—all having first undergone a gradual restriction of acreage. These changes in cropping reflect a shift away from subsistence to commercial farming, and we are therefore not surprised to find that the journal recorded more and more trips to nearby markets as time passed—two in 1728, 17 in 1824, 24 in 1840, and 16 in 1867.

Changes in the use of labor and in methods of cultivation accompanied or followed changes in cropping. In 1728, 45 man-days were spent gathering firewood, but only eight were used in this work in 1804; by that time the family presumably bought most of its fuel. There was also a shift from natural to commercial fertilizers, dried fish replacing grass gathered on the mountainside. The labor saved by this shift was employed in new tasks; in the care of the cocoons and in silk reeling, of course, but also in more intensive cultivation. For instance, no weeding was recorded at all in 1728, but weeding was repeated several times in 1867, and the use of commercial fertilizers meant more intensive fertilization. These and other improvements that may be inferred brought a rise in yields. The greatest increase came as a result of a shift from dry to wet rice in the early eighteenth century, but increases in other major crops, though less dramatic, were considerable.

This brief history of the Ishikawa holding illustrates how pervasive change was, once started. It started but never ended with closer relations to the market, for buying and selling were merely surface indications of changes that went to the very heart of peasant life. Crops, labor organization, farming techniques, even the view men took of such things as wealth, work, and neighbors changed with the altered relation to the market. . . .

AGRICULTURAL TECHNOLOGY

We often think of Japanese agriculture as having been static or nearly so until very recent times; many statements to this effect may be found in both Western and Japanese authorities. But the fact is that it underwent notable technological (though not mechanical) changes long before the modern period. Between 1600 and 1850 a complex of such changes greatly increased the productivity of land, altered that of labor both in specific operations and over all, and contributed to lasting changes in agrarian institutions. The writers of the day gave no picture of order and permanence but one of incessant flux.

Few changes were the result of inventions; most resulted from the spread of known techniques from the localities in which they had been developed to areas where they were previously unknown or unused. How the spread occurred is not known in detail although it is obvious that growth of the market played an important role, breaking down local barriers, transporting ideas and objects from place to place wherever merchants traveled. But never does the mere availability of a new technique assure its adoption; men must first be convinced of its value or at least persuaded to try it, and where there is no margin for failure and any departure from tradition seems to invite disaster, that requires a formidable intellectual leap. . . . Trade with the outside world was continually diminishing the power of custom and magic in village life, breathing into farming a new spirit of enterprise. . . .

There is ample evidence of the fact of a new attitude toward change, though the reason for it remains obscure. Receptivity to the new and tolerance of the unknown and untried are particularly noticeable in the agricultural treatises which, after about 1700, were ardently reformist and empirical. . . . educating the peasant in better ways of farming: explaining the growth patterns of different crops, the proper planting and harvesting times, the characteristics of various soils, the effects of fertilization and weeding—always with a view to increasing crop yields and cash income. . . .

The wellspring of incentive was the enrichment of the family, not individual gain—much less the welfare of society or the state. No innovation that failed to appeal to the interest of the family could win acceptance, nor could any that did appeal fail of acceptance in the long run. It is no accident, then, that the technical changes of this period tended to strengthen the solidarity of the nuclear family and its role in farming.

All of the important innovations in farming increased the productivity of either land or labor or both. Commercial fertilizers— chiefly dried fish, oil cakes, and night soil collected in towns and cities—were perhaps the most important of all innovations in raising yields. Not that these fertilizers were unknown before the Tokugawa period, but they were confined to villages located on the outskirts of towns or near the seacoast where the frontiers of farming and fishing met. It was only with the development of inland transport and the spread of local markets during the seventeenth and eighteenth centuries that commercial fertilizers penetrated the interior of the country and the deep hinterland of towns. Rarely did they entirely supplant manure, grass, leaves, and ashes gathered from waste and forest land, but we have seen that by the early nineteenth century they came to supplement them importantly almost everywhere.

The peasant must initially have had misgivings about exchanging hard-won cash for dried fish or night soil; but he did not have to be taught the value of fertilizer, only its new and unfamiliar forms. From the beginnings of rice culture, fields in all parts of the country had been planted year after year to the same crop without rest, and the peasant knew from oral tradition and personal experience that only the most intensive fertilization could sustain this exhausting regime. Besides, natural fertilizers were nearly everywhere perennially in short supply as a result of the intense demand for them.[25] Even in heavily wooded or mountainous country where the supply was more than ample, the peasants' ability to exploit this natural bounty was severely limited by the vast amount of labor that cutting and carrying grass and leaves required, particularly as such work fell mostly at the planting.[26] No wonder nearly everyone looked with favor on fertilizers that came ready to use in straw bags and were available in whatever quantity the purse could stand. . . .

The new fertilizers not only raised crop yields, but also permitted more intensive use of the land. Natural fertilizers were generally insufficient to sustain more than a single crop a year, but with the advent of commercial fertilizers, double and even triple cropping became common wherever winters were not too harsh and soils were sufficiently drained for a winter crop. Of course multiple cropping neither doubled nor trebled the yield of a holding; usually not all fields could be sown to a second crop, and wheat and vegetables, the favorite winter crops, did not yield as heavily as summer rice. On the other hand, whatever they did yield (minus seed and fertilizer) was a net gain; and in the event summer crops were already sufficient to provide food and pay taxes in kind, the winter and spring crops could be sold. The income could then be used to buy tools, animals, and more fertilizer, giving a further impetus to productivity, or at least helping to sustain it at the new level.

A second technical development of great importance was the increase in the number of plant varieties. Professor Tōhata and his associates have calculated from the names of seeds appearing in literary sources that the number of rice varieties increased from 177 in the early seventeenth century to 2,363 by the middle of

---

[25] Since natural fertilizers all came ultimately from the same source, the supply of one could not be increased except at the expense of others: if a peasant cut more grass for compost, for instance, he necessarily reduced the supply of manure (and perhaps starved his work animal into the bargain).

[26] A village report (*meisaichō*) from Kōzuke Province in 1780 gives one an idea of the immense labor the use of natural fertilizers required, stating that between 70 and 80 horseloads of cut grass were required per *tan* of paddy and about 30 horseloads per *tan* of upland. Thus a holding of 10 *tan* divided equally between the two types of land would need about 525 horseloads!

the nineteenth. . . . Almost all of the detailed records of farming show the peasant planting four, five, or six varieties of rice each year, and almost every year some variety not planted before appeared and one of the old ones was dropped, sometimes with a notation that it had not done well. Although the peasant had no word for it, perhaps, he was consciously experimenting to find the variety best suited to each of his fields. Occasionally the records give us information that points unmistakably to higher yields as a result of his efforts. An agricultural diary from Tōhoku, for example, shows a persistent testing, adopting, and discarding of varieties of rice between 1808 and 1866, and during this period the date at which the harvest was completed was pushed back from the sixth to the twenty-third day of the ninth month, lengthening the growing season in this northern country by 17 days!

One of the most impressive technical achievements of the Tokugawa period was the extension of irrigation.[27] Part of this vast work consisted of the construction of thousands of small wells, ponds, ditches, and devices for lifting small amounts of water, but much of it was on a very large scale—great arterial ditches carrying water a score of miles or more, drainage and embankment works that for the first time made arable the rich alluvial soil along the lower courses of the larger rivers, and so on. . . .

The conversion of dry fields to paddy naturally brought a sizable gain in crop yields. Although the magnitude of the increase varied from place to place, it is worth recalling that rice yields on the Ishikawa holding eventually rose about 100 percent as a result of a shift from dry to wet rice, which suggests how great the increase might be at times. But higher yields were by no means the only result of new irrigation works, and not all of the results

---

[27] Two factors particularly contributed to the rapid development of irrigation in the Tokugawa period. One was the development of engineering, which enabled arable to be extended into the lower courses of great rivers subject to frequent flood. Another was the availability of private investment funds, especially during the last half of the period. How important the latter may have been is suggested by data from Ise Province, where most new irrigation works during the Tokugawa period were undertaken after 1700 and were financed mainly by merchants, landlords, and peasants who had presumably grown rich and adventurous on the profits of trade.

were beneficial. Sources of firewood, fertilizer, and fodder were progressively depleted as the cultivated area (with the aid of new irrigation works) encroached on meadow, forest, and waste. Peasants nearly everywhere complained of the loss in this way of valuable communal resources. But though they complained of the loss, and individual peasants may have been ruined by it, on balance it was undoubtedly beneficial for farming, for the diminution of communal resources tended to weaken collective control over farming and to release new individualist energies.

The possibility of specialization—that is freedom from the necessity of cultivating uneconomic crops—was a major contribution of the market to productivity. An illustration: in Wakae county, Kawachi Province, growing conditions were generally unfavorable to rice; not only was summer rainfall in normal years light and water for irrigation scant, but the soils of the county tended to be light and sandy, quite different from the heavy, sticky soil rice likes best. Nevertheless, at the beginning of the Tokugawa period rice had been widely grown in Wakae for food and to pay taxes in kind. But from the early seventeenth century, cotton, a relatively new crop to Japan, gradually displaced rice until by 1877, 28 percent of paddy land and 58.8 percent of upland in the county was planted to it. Cotton flourished under local growing conditions; it was easily marketed in nearby Osaka and brought a good price. There can be no doubt therefore that this shift in cropping was a net economic gain—for individual holders, for the region, and for the country as a whole.

There were numerous other technical changes during the Tokugawa period that deserve at least passing mention. In the early decades of the period, rice seedlings were commonly planted in the ground more or less haphazardly, but by the nineteenth century care was being taken to plant them in evenly spaced rows. This uniformity assured the maximum number of plants to a field without crowding, and encouraged more intensive weeding by permitting a flat-bottomed weeder to be run between the tidy rows without injury to plants. By the nineteenth century greater care was also being taken to level paddy fields so the plants would stand in water at a uniform depth; this made irrigation far more effective and allowed water to be used to protect plants against low temperatures. Also, as time passed, seeds were more commonly soaked in water to bring them to the sprout before planting, thus lengthening the growing season; oil was more widely used as an insecticide, and a crude rule-of-thumb crop rotation came to be commonly practiced on unirrigated fields.

Although techniques of seed selection were known earlier, they were much more widely used in the Tokugawa period than before. One method of selection was to suspend seeds in a salt solution to separate the heavier seed from the lighter; another (which could be combined with the first) was to use as seed the grain produced by the hardiest plants. In addition to increasing yields these techniques reduced the amount of seed sown, probably between 20 and 50 percent.[28] But more important in the long run than economizing on seed was the contribution that seed selection made to the development of new plant varieties; in fact, until the beginning of scientific plant breeding, most new domestic varieties of rice must have been by-products of seed selection. . . .

The journal of a family in Aki Province gives annual production data for five fields of constant size during the period 1787 to 1888. On all five fields yields rose significantly: on the three that were planted throughout the period to one crop (rice) the decennial average of production rose between 50 and 71 percent; on one of the other two fields the increase was even greater. This field was planted to rice continuously from 1787 through 1856; taking 1787–97 as the base period, the decennial average ran 100, 148, 168, 203, 212, 195, 195 . . . One must remember, too, that there were very important gains in productivity that were not reflected in crop yields at all, such as those from crop substitutions and the more intensive use of land by double cropping. . . .

Technical innovations during the Tokugawa period increased not only per-acre yields but per-acre labor requirements as well. Not that all innovations had the effect of intensifying the use of labor, but this was undoubtedly the over-all effect on most holdings. One important reason for this was that innovations rarely if ever came singly; they hung together in clusters by a kind of inner logic; one innovation brought others in its train, and often could not be adopted independently of them. For example:

---

[28] An eighteenth-century treatise gives as normal two or three *shō* of seed per *tan* of land for rice, but in 1809 we find a family in Aizu (incidentally, with rising rice yields) sowing one *shō* per *tan!* A family in Shinano achieved a 30 percent reduction in rice seed between 1796 and 1799 while reducing the area planted to rice by only 8 percent.

multiple cropping required more intensive fertilization, which in turn was facilitated by animal plowing to turn the soil more deeply than was possible with spading and so permit heavier applications of fertilizer without damage to plants; and animal plowing was exceedingly difficult without improved drainage, which made it possible to dry the ground in the spring so as to offer less resistance to the plow; and so on. Other "clusters" of innovations might be cited. Through such linkages of interdependence the ultimate effect of even individual labor-saving innovations was often to intensify the use of labor.

Commercial fertilizers are an illustration. Insofar as they replaced natural fertilizers they saved an enormous amount of labor. They drastically reduced and might entirely eliminate the work of cutting and hauling grass from the mountainside, then trampling it into the plowed and flooded fields; moreover, this labor was saved at the planting, when the work load reached its annual peak and time and human energy were most precious. How great was the potential for saving at this season may be judged from the fact that in the seventeenth century about ten man-days per *tan* of paddy were spent in cutting grass and composting fields prior to planting. But this is only part of the story. Multiple cropping was a common result—indeed often the chief aim—of the adoption of commercial fertilizers; and insofar as it was, the new fertilizers added more labor to farming than they saved, though it should be noted that the addition came mostly at a time when employment was otherwise slack.

Another illustration is the *semba-koki,* the only important mechanical innovation in farming during the Tokugawa period. Significantly this device first appeared about the Genroku period (1688–1703) in the area of commercial agriculture around Osaka and thereafter spread gradually to other parts of the country. It consisted of a wooden frame with a protruding row of long teeth at first made of bamboo but later of iron, between which the rice stalks were drawn to strip away the grain. This replaced the earlier technique of drawing the stalks with one hand between two large chopsticks (*koki-hashi*) held in the other. One contemporary source has it that the *semba-koki* was ten times as fast as the chopsticks. This may be an exaggeration, but it is evident that the new tool was the far more efficient, and moreover it could be used by hands that were not sufficiently strong or skilled to operate the clumsy chopsticks. Thus it not only saved labor at the harvest—another peak of labor demand—but made new sources of family labor available. Still, the end result was not always a saving of labor; for by releasing labor at this particular season the *semba-koki* often made it possible, for the first time, to plant a winter crop hard on the fall harvest.

More or less permanent changes in cropping occurred on thousands of holdings during the Tokugawa period, and they generally brought an increase in per-acre labor requirements. The changes were chiefly of two kinds: the substitution of rice for an unirrigated crop, and the substitution of a cash crop for a subsistence crop. With the expansion of irrigated acreage, low-yielding crops were commonly replaced by rice, which was the most labor-intensive of all food crops and when planted to a previously unirrigated field required the upkeep of new ditches, terraces, and embankments, thus adding appreciably to the labor load. The chief cash crops (cotton, tobacco, sugar cane, indigo) were all labor-intensive,[29] and they tended to supplant on upland fields crops that were notably less so.

Some technical changes during the Tokugawa period added wholly new operations to farming (at least on individual holdings), without eliminating others. New irrigation works are an excellent example, but there are many others. Seed selection, the treatment of seeds before planting, planting in evenly spaced rows, more intensive weeding, the adoption of insecticides, the use of irrigation as a protection for plants against frost—all were important changes of this kind. Some new crops had a similar effect. At least one that was rapidly spreading—mulberry—could be added to a holding without necessarily reducing or eliminating other work; for the trees might be planted on the borders between fields or on odd plots of ground not otherwise used; or, of course, leaves for feeding the silkworms could be bought from others. . . .

The most radical effect of technical change, of which all others were in a sense merely functions, was a trend toward smaller farming units. This seems a natural and even inevitable development if one assumes for the moment that the small nuclear

---

[29] The only actual figures available on labor requirements of cash crops are for cotton and indigo, which required 40–60 and 75–100 man-days respectively per *tan* of land as compared with about 40 for rice, and rice was far more labor-intensive than the crops actually replaced on upland fields.

family was the unchanging, ultimate integer of peasant society. With the progress of agricultural technology, it took less and less land to support this family, which because of new labor-intensive techniques could anyway work less land than before. . . .

. . . technical change on balance, made the operations of farming more intricate. Far from simplifying and making more uniform the multitude of tasks that confronted the labor force (as mechanical innovations presumably would have done), innovations actually increased the demands made on every farm worker. They demanded of him more specialized knowledge and skill, more attention to detail, the exercise of more initiative and judgment. Weeding, seed selection, planting in rows, the use of strong and costly fertilizers, the leveling of fields, the use of water as protection against frost—these and many other operations depended for their effectiveness on the alertness, effort, and skill of individual workers. To speak metaphorically, rather than impelling farming forward to a manufacturing stage of production these operations served to strengthen its handicraft character. The increasing emphasis in farming on just such operations put the larger labor force at an ever greater disadvantage in competing with the small one. The large labor force with its hereditary servants and *nago,* its part-time workers and degrees of family membership, was a loosely organized and relatively heterogeneous social group. By contrast the small labor force, which in most cases coincided precisely with the nuclear family, was tight, disciplined, and socially homogeneous. It consequently not only could supervise its members more successfully, but could rely on them to a far greater degree for spontaneous effort since it gave them stronger and more immediate incentives. Under the circumstances, technical innovations brought the opposite of the economies of scale we tend mistakenly to associate with *all* technological advance; that is, beyond a certain small size, the larger the farming unit the more inefficient it was likely to be.

The second factor, which increased the effect of the first, was a secular rise in the cost of labor. The continuously rising remuneration of labor outside the family acted as a disintegrative force on the large, heterogeneous labor force. Its social bonds were already relatively weak and now gave way before the pull of high wages outside. As this group consequently began to dissolve, it became even less competent than before to meet the challenge of an agriculture becoming steadily more individualized; so it slowly made way for a smaller unit of organization. . . .

The social counterpart of this development was the slow but steady dissolution of the extended family into its nuclear constituents. We shall give some attention to the details of this process later; but it will not be difficult to understand it in principle now if one keeps in mind that the extended family was a product of the older mode of cultivation. Just as that mode had required a large family organization, so the shift on large holdings to tenant cultivation now required a small labor force. With the trend to tenant cultivation in full tide, the *raison d'être* of the extended family disappeared. . . .

. . . in Japan the trend toward *smaller* units of farming made mechanization virtually impossible; it kept the agricultural population a relatively homogeneous class of small peasant farmers despite the presence of landlords and obvious differences of wealth; it preserved the organic unity of the village community despite the growth of a nonfarming population within it; it enhanced rather than diminished the role of the family in farming; and it maintained the farming population at a constant level, and so at a very high ratio to urban population despite industrialization. . . .

22 ECONOMIC DEVELOPMENT AND SOCIAL CHANGE IN SOUTH INDIA

Scarlett Epstein

A GREAT DEAL has been heard about 'changeless India' and about the 'timeless and changeless Indian village'. If this book does nothing else it should at least dispel this naïve notion. In my review of events which occurred in Wangala and Dalena during the past 25 years I have demonstrated that villagers were not slow to react to new economic opportunities. In fact they were no slower than farmers the whole world over. 'Most of the farmers of the world are not motivated by abstract ends or speculative results. . . . For them "seeing is believing". . . . The distrust of new and untried ways is an obverse of the faith in the known, that which with all its ups and downs, has supported the society since time immemorial' (Mead 1953:198). Both Wangala and Dalena villagers accommodated themselves relatively quickly to the new economic environment created by irrigation in the area. I have shown how irrigation integrated villages into a regional economy and how the different roles Wangala and Dalena occupied within the wider economy set each village on a different path of development.

The decision to irrigate the Mandya region did not originate in any source indigenous to the villages. Rather it was the Government of Mysore which planned the irrigation of a certain area in order to increase the productivity of the land. Similarly, it was Government initiative which underlay the further efforts required to bring about the economic expansion of the region by setting up a sugar factory at Mandya and by making the town the headquarters of a separate District Administration. In this re-

SOURCE: Scarlett Epstein, "Conclusion: Economic Development and Social Change," and "Appendix 1," pages 311–46, in *Economic Development and Social Change in South India,* Manchester University Press, 1962. Reprinted by permission of the author and publisher.

spect then the changes I have described for Wangala and Dalena are not unique or of local interest only; they are representative of the increasing modern tendency whereby new economic potentials created by Government result in the incorporation of subsistence economies in the wider cash economy. In this final chapter therefore I shall discuss the general principles underlying the social changes that occurred in Wangala and Dalena.

In the preceding chapters I discussed *how* Wangala and Dalena changed since irrigation reached the area. Here I shall analyse *why* certain changes occurred in Dalena and not in Wangala, and beyond this *why* the two villages changed as they did.

In much of anthropological literature, social change is analysed as it has arisen in situations of culture contact which involved the diffusion of an alien more advanced culture among 'primitive' peoples (see Malinowski 1945; Gluckman 1958; Mead 1956). Such diffusion may be in terms of technology, religion or political institutions. In all such work there is a distinction drawn, explicitly or implicitly, between change in which basic elements of the society alter, and change in which social action, while not repetitive, does not alter the basic social forms (Firth 1954:17).

In my own study, which is one of the effects of economic engineering rather than of culture contact or diffusion, I found that some aspects of social structure changed while others remained the same, and that some aspects of culture changed while others persisted. To explain this uneven change I find I must further distinguish between different types of structural relations and different aspects of culture. Arising out of the discussion in the preceding chapters I have categorised structural change into economic, political, ritual, familial and organisational change according to the functional relations involved. Cultural change I shall discuss in terms of change in economic and prestige values. I have chosen these aspects of culture out of a great variety, firstly, because I regard them as major determinants of social behaviour, and secondly, because these were the aspects of culture which changed or were responsible for some structural change in the two villages under discussion.

Since unrestricted social mobility is usually regarded as essential to an expanding economy, it would be very interesting to know how far caste values are tied to economic relations and will change with the latter, and how far they are independently perpetuated through the educational pattern. In order to give a clearer picture of caste values we would require a close study of the education children receive in their homes and at school, and of how far differentiation of castes is inculcated into the mind of the young through listening to religious stories or watching religious dramas. Thus a study of villagers' caste values would have to include an analysis of personality formation. Unfortunately, lack of time prevented me from carrying out such analysis of caste values.

> All peoples, civilised as well as primitive, are obliged to make a selection and rank certain objects and certain modes of conduct as more desirable, more agreeable or more worthy than others. Each society has such set orders or preferences usually referred to as its system of values. (Values formally defined are preferences regarding objects and actions in their social context.) The value scales are imposed upon members of the group by the ordinary process of social conditioning, and what attracts or repels one person tends also to attract or repel his fellows. (Hogbin 1958:58)

Values then are responsible for the direction of social behaviour; if values change, social behaviour will also change. However, since a change in social behaviour usually involves a change in different aspects of culture as well as a change in several types of structural relations, it is difficult to allocate it to any one of our categories. For instance, if we observe that sons cease to work for their father's estates and rather work as casual labourers for other farmers, this would involve, according to our categories, a change in prestige and economic values as well as a change in economic and familial relations. Therefore although the categories of structural and cultural changes are interconnected, for analytical purposes I propose to discuss each category separately. I do not claim to cover all types of structural relations, nor all aspects of culture. For instance, I shall not discuss change in religious beliefs because this was not an important variable in the culture change which occurred in the two villages under discussion. Except for the few Muslim families in Wangala, inhabitants of both villages were Hindus before irrigation reached Mandya area and they are still adhering to the same religious faith. They did not change their religious beliefs, only their religious practices changed, and these I shall discuss under the heading of 'ritual change'.

Thus I am aware of the limits to the application of our categories of social change to other such studies. But since social behaviour has so many different aspects I find it impossible to deal with all of them and restrict my discussion to those which are relevant to an understanding of social change in Wangala and Delena.

STRUCTURAL CHANGE

(a) Economic Change

By economic change I mean a change in economic roles and relations. Both Wangala and Dalena have undergone considerable economic development during the past 25 years, that is to say in both villages the output of goods and services has increased considerably with the same or greater labour input. Both villages have changed from subsistence to cash economies, but the resultant economic changes were quite different in Dalena and Wangala. Wangala's economy has remained wholly agricultural, while Dalena's has diversified. At this point I am not dealing with the reasons for this different kind of economic development, only with the actual facts of it. The reasons will become apparent when I deal with cultural changes. For the present it suffices that while Wangala remained a discrete agricultural economy, Dalena's diversification led to its closer integration into the regional economy. Some Dalena men took up employment in the town, some became contractors for the Public Works Department, bought carts for hiring out, or bullocks for trading, while yet others bought land or worked as agricultural labourers in neighbouring villages. Dalena's agricultural village system was thus hinged on to the wider industrial and commercial system. The Wilsons have observed that as the range of relations increases, the degree of dependence upon neighbours and contemporaries diminishes (Wilson & Wilson 1954:86). Thus as Dalena men increased the range of their economic relations, the interdependence between farmers and their agricultural labourers decreased and consequently the hereditary economic relations between Peasant masters and Untouchable clients disappeared.

Individuals act in their self-interest as they perceive it and are usually unconscious of the social relations which affect and help to determine their behaviour, or of the effect their behaviour has in turn on social relations. When Dalena Peasant farmers ceased to give to their Untouchable clients the customary annual reward they thought they were doing this merely to save what they had come to regard as uneconomic expenditure. They were not aware that they were terminating an economic relationship, nor did they realise that they had been prompted to do this by the increased range of their economic relations.

The major part of Dalena's economic structure was incompatible with the new economic environment in which Dalena men now operate and therefore most economic relations changed. It would have been uneconomic for Dalena farmers to employ their Untouchable clients on wet lands in neighbouring villages, because of the time wasted in walking to and from the lands. At the same time it would have been impossible for Untouchables to work for farmers outside their own village whilst remaining committed to labour for their Peasant masters whenever the latter required their services. The employment of men outside their own village was thus incompatible with the indigenous employment structure and therefore hereditary employment relations gave way to impersonal ones.

Yet some aspects of the customary economic structure still persist unchanged. For instance, when Dalena Peasants broke off their hereditary economic relations with one of the Washermen because he had offended a man of their own caste, they did not dispense with these hereditary relations but merely transferred them to another Washerman. In this case economic relations remained unchanged, and only the personnel involved changed. The extension of economic ties by Dalena men outside their own village did not affect the customary relations between Peasants and Washermen. Peasants still require the services of a Washerman and the Washerman still wants to get his food by washing clothes for Peasants. Thus the tithe relationship between Peasants and Washermen is not incompatible with the new economic situation in Dalena and so far it persists.

Similarly, the economic role of women is unaltered in the new system. They continue to operate in the customary subsistence farming economy. Their continued work on the land is not merely compatible with the new economic system, it is in fact essential to sustain it. If wives ceased to work the village dry lands, their menfolk would have less spare time to seek employment outside their village, or to cultivate their wet lands. Even if farmers employed more Untouchable women, rather than use their own wives for the agricultural work, they would still have to devote more time to the cultivation of their village dry lands, for they would have to supervise their paid labourers. It is, in short, the continued agricultural labour of their wives that enables Dalena men to participate in the wider cash economy. Dalena women still continue to pay for goods and services in kind rather than in cash; they pay the Potter, who comes from a neighbouring village, in quantities of ragi or paddy. Very rarely does a Dalena women venture to purchase goods at Mandya fair; she leaves the cash purchases to her husband. This division of labour between husband and wife is quite compatible with the participation of Dalena men in the wider cash economy and therefore traditional economic relations between them have persisted in the changed economic environment.

Thus we see that incompatibility provides a clue to change. Incompatibility causes friction and leads to change. Conversely, compatibility may ensure the continued functioning of customary relations. In my analysis of economic development in Wangala I have shown how irrigation raised the whole economy to a higher level at one stroke. In spite of the change from subsistence to cash, Wangala remained a wholly agricultural economy. Therefore, its employment structure remained unaltered. Peasant farmers now require more labour, so they employ their Untouchable clients and their Peasant debtors for more days per year. The greater labour requirements for cash cropping can be quite easily met under the traditional system of hereditary economic relations. The unilinear economic development in Wangala set up no incompatibility, no friction between new wants and old ways, in the indigenous employment structure, which therefore persists. But not only do they require the same type of agricultural labour; Wangala Peasants still need the same services for their Functionaries. Therefore, when the indigenous Blacksmith desired to sever his hereditary bonds with Peasant households, he was made to provide a substitute before the *panchayat* agreed to release him from his obligations. As in the case of the Dalena Washerman, Wangala Peasants retained the economic relationship, while allowing the personnel to change.

The persistence of a rural economy in itself, however, does not ensure the absence of economic change.

The potato and the pig, for instance, when introduced among the Maori of New Zealand radically altered the economic structure. They reduced the amount of labour put in on other crops, and on fowling; they altered the production balance between men and women, they gave commoners a chance of earning relatively higher incomes and elevating themselves in the social scale; they even helped to change the scheme of ritual by reducing the amount of economic magic demanded. Together with other factors, such as the musket, they were the basis for important structural changes in Maori society. (Firth 1951:85)

Thus we see that although the Maori remained a wholly rural society the introduction of new crops radically changed the economic structure. Probably the most important factor in this change was the redistribution of wealth. If irrigation of Wangala lands had brought about a reallocation of economic resources, this would have undoubtedly caused friction in the traditional economic organisation and led to its change. But far from upsetting it, irrigation in fact emphasised the existing economic differentiation and economic relations could continue unaltered.

The economic role of wives is the only part of Wangala's economic structure which has changed since the advent of irrigation. Wangala husbands can devote all their time to the cultivation of their village lands. It became a matter of prestige for a husband to relieve his wife of the duties of helping him cultivate his lands. The continued agricultural labour of wives was incompatible with the new status criteria and therefore economic relations between husband and wife changed.

Though the change from subsistence to cash economy has integrated Wangala into the wider cash economy, the resulting economic relations are so tenuous that they hardly affected the indigenous economic structure. As producers Wangala's economic relations are almost confined to Mandya's sugar factory which, since it occupies a monopsonistic position *vis-à-vis* the farmers, is able to dictate the conditions of the contract for the cultivation of cane. On the other hand, as consumers, Wangala villagers purchase goods from so many different sources that no formalised economic relations result. Such formalised economic relations remain confined to the village and as we have seen these have hardly changed.

The point of theoretical interest emerging at this stage of the discussion is that economic development may occur without any change in economic roles and relations, provided it does not result in a reallocation of resources or in an increased range of economic relations. Far from undermining the economic structure of any society such economic development may even strengthen the existing pattern of economic relations.

(b) Political Change

By political change I mean change in political roles and relations. In Dalena there have been radical political changes. *Panchayat* members are no more necessarily lineage elders; Peasants are no more the arbitrators in intra-Untouchable disputes. Dalena villagers working in the Mandya sugar factory participated in a strike and quite a number of villagers attended a meeting held in Mandya to protest against the reorganisation of Mysore State. Their many links with the wider economy have brought about an awareness of wider political issues.

The increased economic mobility created by economic diversification led to a redistribution of wealth, which became incompatible with political leadership based on the hereditary principle. The new magnates sought political expression for their newly acquired economic status and the poorer hereditary lineage elders had no power to oppose this quest. This development preceded the first *panchayat* election under the new democratic legislation. Dalena villagers had already begun to accept the idea that political office need not be hereditary and therefore the elections legalised the already established departure from a strictly hereditary political system. Dalena's elected *panchayat* is a far less effective council than its traditional *panchayat* used to be. Cases formerly settled by the *panchayat* are nowadays taken to the courts in Mandya.

In short, in Dalena economic diversification led to a close integration into the wider economy and subsequently also into the wider body politic. The increased range of economic relations increased the range of political relations.

By contrast, Wangala displays no such change in formalised political relations. The village *panchayat* still consists of hereditary lineage elders and continues to settle most disputes between villagers. Peasant masters are still arbitrators for their Untouchable clients. The new democratic legislation did not affect the functioning of the indigenous hereditary *panchayat,* because it was introduced into a system of unchanged economic roles and relations. The reserved seats for Untouchables remain a fiction as long as Untouchables continue in a dependent economic relationship on their Peasant masters. If the new democratic legislation had been accompanied by a redistribution of land in favour of Untouchables, it would probably have been effective in bringing about Untouchable representation in the *panchayat*. As it was, political legislation did not aim at any economic change and was therefore ineffective.

The only change in Wangala's political relations occurred in the sphere of factions. Two of the structurally younger but economically powerfully lineages have combined against two of the politically and ritually dominant, but economically declining lineages. Factions in Wangala provide a mechanism whereby economic status may be translated into political influence. But since irrigation emphasised the existing economic differentiation rather than increased economic mobility and since it also strengthened the villagers' uniform interest in farming, Wangala's factions are not rigidly opposed. In this they differ from Dalena where factions display the basic cleavage between innovators and conservatives and where economic diversification has increased economic mobility. Economic change in Dalena was followed by political change, whereas the persistence of Wangala's economic structure was responsible for the persistence of its political structure.

(c) Ritual Change

By ritual change I mean a change in traditional religious ritual roles and relations. In Dalena the break in the traditional economic relations between Peasant masters and their Untouchable clients led to a severance of ritual relations between the individual households involved. Since the Peasant master refused to give his Untouchable client the customary annual reward, the latter refused to perform his customary ritual services for the former. In a society such as Dalena where every service demands a reward, it would have been unreasonable to expect Untouchables to continue their ritual services to their Peasant masters after the latter had broken off economic relations with them. Thus nowadays an Untouchable no longer carries the torch ahead of a Peasant funeral or helps to build a canopy for the wedding in his master's household. Yet the ritual relationship between Peasants and Untouchables as groups is still effective. Untouchables continue to act as drummers at village festivals. The continued group relationship between Peasants and Untouchables is in accordance with the holding of Government-granted land by Untouchables as a reward for services to the village as a whole. Furthermore, Untouchables perform their duties as a group because they are scared of Peasant violence. In the Mandya area clashes have occurred between Peasants and Untouchables. However, as fewer and fewer village ceremonies are being performed in Dalena, the significance of this group relationship is declining.

Dalena Peasants still have their customary ritual relations with their Functionaries. The Barber and Washerman continue to perform important ritual services in Peasant life-cycle rituals. These ritual relations are in line with the continued hereditary economic relations between Peasants and Functionaries. Though ritual still plays an important part in the life-cycle of individual Peasants its importance in economic life is declining. While most farming activities are highly ritualised, non-farming activities are not ritualised at all. After every harvest each lineage performs a thanksgiving ritual to the lineage deity on the land of the lineage elder. By contrast, no ritual is performed when a factory worker receives his wages or a contractor his pay. As more non-farming activities assume importance in Dalena, the prominence of traditional ritual in economic activities is declining. Altogether the prominence of ritual in village life is decreasing. The rigid faction opposition between innovators and conservatives prevents the celebration of joint village festivals. During the whole of my stay in Dalena I did not see a single ceremony performed by all villagers jointly. The discussion over joint village ceremonies always broke down over the refusal of innovators to participate. For these innovators, economic success rather than ritual roles is the ultimate criterion of social status. They are therefore not interested in participating in village ceremonies.

In Wangala, where the economy is still wholly rural, ritual occupies a dominant role in economic activities. Here ritual status is still the ultimate determinant of social status. Since ritual status is always hereditary, at least in theory, while economic status may be acquired, there is always a tendency for men to try and translate their newly gained economic status into ritual status through exerting political influence. I have described how factions lead to the duplication of ceremonies in the village and thus to the creation of new ritual offices (Epstein 1962:132–34). Thus in Wangala we find an increase in the number of intra-Peasant ritual relations, while ritual relations between Peasants and their Untouchable clients and their Functionaries continue unaltered. Peasants still pay their annual reward to their Untouchable clients and their Functionaries and these two dependent groups continue to perform their ritual services in Peasant ceremonies.

There has therefore been some ritual change in both villages, but while the change in Wangala was intra-caste and resulted in an increased number and intensity of ritual relations among Peasants, in Dalena the change was inter-caste, resulting in a disappearance of ritual relations between Peasant masters and their Untouchable clients.

(d) *Familial Change*

By familial change I mean change in relations within the family. I have argued for both Wangala and Dalena that the conversion from a subsistence to a cash economy led to the breakdown of the joint family unit among Peasant farmers. 'It can be stated as a theorem valid in a high percentage of cases, that the greater the opportunity for profit in any social cultural situation, the weaker the ties of extended kinship will become' (Linton 1952: 84).

Thus economic development, whether or not it brings about economic changes, will almost invariably result in the breaking up of joint family ties. The partitioning of joint families affects the relationship between father and sons. Under the joint family system in Wangala and Dalena sons showed extreme respect to their father; now that the custom of partitioning has been adopted many more quarrels arise between father and sons. The sons assume an attitude of greater independence once they realise that they have a right to become independent farmers as soon as they are married and able to set up their own *ménage*. At the same time the relationship between brothers has also changed. Younger brothers showed greater respect to their elder brother as long as he was or was expected to be, the manager of the joint estate. Tupa, the young Wangala Peasant who quarrelled with his father over his share of the family estate and joined the faction in opposition to his own lineage, is an extreme example of the disrespect shown by a man to his father and brother (See Epstein 1962:129). The public condemnation of his action, on the other hand, illustrates the value Wangala villagers still attach to lineage unity.

Greater economic independence affected the respect shown by

men towards their father and brothers. It also affected the relationship between husband and wife in Wangala. Buffaloes and money-lending give Wangala wives an independent source of income, which makes them less subservient to their husbands. Wangala husbands are faced with a dilemma: on the one hand the life they provide for their wives is a major determinant of their own social status; on the other, if they release their wives from agricultural labour and provide them with buffaloes as an independent source of income, wives become less obedient to their husbands. Wangala women have learned to operate in a cash economy; they go to the weekly fair at Mandya where they purchase the household requirements and where some of them sell the butter they have made out of buffalo milk. The money earned from such sales they keep for extras for themselves or their children, whereas the household requirements are purchased with money provided by the husband. Dalena women are far less independent than their Wangala sisters. They still function in the customary subsistence economy and continue to work the lands of their husbands. Status criteria in Dalena are unaffected by the sort of life a husband provides for his wife. Women are in fact the pillars of the traditional village farming economy. Even the richest man's wife works on his fields. Because economic relations between husband and wife are unchanged, familial relations between them are also unaltered; the wife shows her husband the customary respect. By contrast, in Wangala where the wife occupies a new economic role familial relations are also changed and the wife is much less subservient to her husband.

(e) Organisational Change

By organisational change I mean a change in the principles of social organisation. In Wangala the hereditary principle is still basic to the social organisation. Office as a lineage elder or *panchayat* member is still hereditary; likewise, relations between Peasant masters and Untouchable clients are also hereditary, as are those between Peasants and Functionaries and between creditors and debtors. The hereditary principle is quite compatible with Wangala's economic system in which economic status is largely inherited. A man's economic status is determined by the size of the ancestral estate and the number of heirs that have to share it; personal initiative can hardly help to raise his economic status. Although the relative economic status of successive generations of households may be quite different, this has nothing to do with the personal ability and efforts of the particular householder, but rather is a result of the accidents of birth and death. The five present magnates in Wangala were all fortunate in being sole heirs to their ancestral estate. Since heredity continues to determine the economic status of households in Wangala, it also continues to be the general principle of social organisation.

Another aspect of the hereditary principle is the personal element in the relationship between the members of different social groups. This personal element creates emotional attachments between the parties to such a hereditary relationship. For instance, the hereditary relations between Peasant masters and their Untouchable clients bridge the gulf between castes and Untouchables by giving each Peasant master a personal interest in the well-being of his Untouchable client. Conversely, the Untouchable client develops an emotional attachment to his Peasant master and takes a personal interest in the cultivation of his master's lands or in the performance of rituals in his master's household, quite apart from his obligations.

However, the hereditary principle of social organisation is only compatible with a closely integrated society, in which economic, political and ritual relations are concentrated within the boundaries of the village. Once the range of these relations is extended beyond the limits of the particular society, the dependence on fellow-villagers will diminish and the personal element in the indigenous relationship will give way to an impersonal one. This is what happened in Dalena, where participation in the regional economy has increased economic mobility. Personal ability and drive rather than the size of the ancestral estate or the number of heirs with whom it must be shared became the effective determinant of economic status. The growth of the competitive spirit is seen in the elimination of the hereditary relations between Peasant masters and Untouchable clients. Though in the traditional system too, labourers were distinguished into good and bad, the personal performance of the labourer is now the chief criterion: the better the worker, the more he is sought after. In turn competition amongst the Untouchables themselves has undermined their unity and prevented any combined protest against the system of untouchability itself.

The greater economic mobility created by Dalena's economic diversification has similarly undermined the traditional principles of political organisation. Some of the *panchayat* members are no longer elders of lineages. Hereditary claims to political office now yield before the power exerted by newly established magnates. Furthermore, the principle of group mobility in the political sphere has disappeared in favour of mobility of the individual household. In Wangala, the magnate who sought political office had to get his lineage raised to the status of 'major' lineage before his membership of the *panchayat* was generally recognised. By contrast, in Dalena a magnate's economic power has become generally accepted as sufficient qualification for political office.

Yet agnation remains an important principle of political organisation in both villages. In Wangala and Dalena factions are organised on the basis of lineage, and so is membership of the *panchayat*. The introduction of the new competitive principle and the persistence of the agnatic principle cause an inconsistency in Dalena's present social organisation. This gives rise to friction on the one hand and allows for political manipulations by individuals adhering to opposing principles of social organisation, on the other.

Dalena's radical economic change, its integration into the regional economy, undermined the very principles on which its society had been organised; the absence of such economic change allowed the hereditary principle to continue unchallenged in Wangala.

CULTURAL CHANGE

(a) Change in Economic Values

Wangala villagers give farming the dominant place in their system of economic values. To be a farmer used to be, and still is, the ultimate aim of every Wangala villager. Land yields food and food is essential to life. However, farming is not merely an economic activity, or a means of making a living, it is rather a way of life. Each farmer develops an emotional attachment to his soil, and so long as he can make a 'reasonable' living by working his lands, he will continue to be a farmer. Irrigation increased the income a farmer can derive from his lands and therefore strengthened the value he attaches to farming. This largely explains why Wangala survived as a wholly rural economy, in spite of the opportunities offered in the regional economy. The ownership of even a small fraction of an acre keeps a Wangala man from moving out of his village, as we saw even in the case of a craftsman such as the Goldsmith (see Epstein 1962:82). And even the landless seem to prefer agricultural labour to any other type of work. They have grown up in the rural environment with its personal relations between farmer and labourer and prefer the relative security these offer to the hazards of life in the town. On the other hand, it must be noted here that a concerted policy on the part of the sugar factory and the Administration in Mandya to employ landless Untouchables from surrounding villages would no doubt have attracted Wangala's Untouchables to employment in the town. However, the discrimination against Untouchables in Mandya reduced their employment possibilities in the town and they have therefore remained in their villages. Wangala Untouchables are very disgruntled with their poverty, but they all cherish the secret hope that one day they too will become farmers of standing. None of them complains about his inability to get a job in the town. The only employment they seek is work on the factory plantation. Thus the value attached to farming has percolated through even to the poorest Untouchables. As long as population pressure does not force some of Wangala's villagers off the land, they will continue their agricultural activities, and will continue to give farming highest preference in their system of economic values.

In Dalena, too, villagers used to attach highest value to farming. But as they saw irrigation making their neighbours richer, while their own lands remained dry, they decided that they too would participate in the economic expansion of the region in whatever way they could. Thus they began to attach higher value to increasing their income than to farming. Yet farming is still the ultimate aim of every Dalena man, even if at present he is a factory worker. All hope to accumulate sufficient money to buy land and become full-time farmers. Even though they are aware of the shortage of land, each hopes that he at least will be fortunate enough to acquire land, once he has saved sufficient money to purchase it. The persistence of the value attached to farming reflects both the instability of the wider economy and the resistance to changes in value. Villagers realise that income from non-agricultural sources depends on the continued expansion of the wider economy, whereas land will always yield food. They well remember the years when the sugar factory in Mandya closed down and they were all thrown back on dependence for their livelihood on their lands. Thus in terms of the wider economy the value Dalena villagers attach to farming is quite consistent with their experience; only in terms of the village economy, with its shortage of land, is it inconsistent. However, the system of economic values held by many generations in Dalena's past, and inculcated into villagers during their childhood, is not so easily eradicated or changed. The resistance to a change in economic values appears to be a general social phenomenon. The value attached to landholding in Britain led the new industrialists of the Industrial Revolution to invest in large estates. It took many years before the old economic values were displaced by new ones. There appears to be a time lag between a change in the economic environment and in the economic values held by individuals in a society. Thus we may expect that the value Dalena villagers still attach to farming will give way in the future to a preference for employment in the town. In the meantime the contradictory pull of the value attached to earning money and the preference given to farming causes some curious inconsistencies in their behavior pattern. For instance, factory workers are all envied for their jobs by their fellow-villagers, while they themselves all want to become full-time farmers. These factory workers introduce new prestige criteria into the village on the one hand; on the other, their desire to become farmers prompts them to perpetuate the traditional village system. Chennu, the factory worker who had bought himself a gold watch and a bicycle, thereby showing the urban influence on his behaviour, yet desired to become a medium in the traditional religious system of the village, whereby he perpetuated customary beliefs (see Epstein 1962: 302). Indeed, all the factory workers in Dalena support the conservative faction. It is this persistence of the value attached to farming that is largely responsible for the fact that Dalena has not been swallowed up in the wider system but continues to have a social identity of its own. Once villagers give higher preference to working in the town than to being farmers, Dalena will probably become a dormitory for men working in Mandya, provided the regional economy continues to expand.

Thus we can see that, given the difference between wet and dry lands, the system of economic values determined the type of economic development which took place in Wangala and Dalena. The persistence in the preference given to farming by Wangala villagers led to the development of a wholly rural economy, while the greater value attached to earning money by Dalena villagers led to the diversification of their economy. Yet the high priority Dalena men still give to farming indicates that there is a time lag between a change in the economic environment and in economic values, which slows down the rate of social change. The value attached to farming strengthened Wangala's traditional economic system and delayed the breaking up of Dalena's social system.

(b) Change in Prestige Values

Economic development has considerably increased the strife for prestige in Wangala and even more so in Dalena. Both societies are used to a rank-conscious caste system. It is not surprising therefore that when increased economic mobility led to a challenge of those with ascribed status by those with achieved status, the struggle for prestige became intensified. The different criteria of prestige employed in the two villages reflect the different type of economic development they have undergone. Dalena's economic diversification led to greater economic differentiation and thus to the development of more and more refined criteria of prestige, arising out of the contact with the town. Dress has become an important criterion of prestige. The richest Dalena men wear fine, clean shirts over a dhoti even on ordinary working days, while the poorest still wear only a loincloth. The richest Dalena men have to dress better in order to impress officials in the administration in Mandya whom they approach for contracts, or farmers from other villages where they hold land. The two Dalena men who are employed as clerks in Mandya wear western-style suits when they go to work. Thus the prestige accorded by dress arises out of the different economic activities performed by Dalena men. In Wangala rich and poor alike work on the land and use tattered cotton shirts and shorts for everyday wear. Here uniform occupation has prevented dress from becoming an important criterion of prestige except on special occasions such as village festivals or weddings.

Expenditure on sundries in Dalena displays similar differentiation to clothing. The richest Dalena men smoke cigarettes and pay frequent visits to Mandya coffee shops where they drink coffee or tea and take sweet or curried relish. The poorest still only chew betel leaves and nuts. The prestige accorded by dress and expenditure on sundries clearly reflects the impact of the town on Dalena villagers. The urban influence is also noticeable in the number of English words used by Dalena men. By using English words those who have contact with the town want to distinguish themselves from mere country yokels. Thus men with urban contacts always refer to the last house in a street as *'coneh lasht maneh'*, *coneh* being the vernacular word for last and *maneh* for house. In this expression they use the English as well as their own vernacular word to denote the term 'last'. In other instances, such as *'clean illa'*, meaning 'it is not clean', they simply substitute an English word for their own vernacular one. All Dalena villagers have adopted English words for foreign innovations, such as *rodu* for road, *bassu* for bus, *hotelu* for coffee shop, *party* for faction, and *chairman* for the village political leader. Wangala villagers use the same English terms to denote foreign concepts, but indigenous ones like 'last' and 'clean' they express in their own vernacular. English is the language spoken by officials in the town through contact with whom many English words find their way into Dalena's vocabulary. Wangala villagers have fewer contacts of this kind and therefore less occasion to pick up as many English words as Dalena villagers. Thus the use of English words has become a prestige criterion in Dalena because of its many links with the town, whereas this is not true of Wangala with its concentration on peasant values and activities.

Yet Wangala's prestige system too shows signs of urban influence. The hiring of a jeep for the bridal procession through the village, or the provision of a Western-style jacket and shoes for the bridegroom's outfit, are examples of the cultural impact of the town on the village. That the urban influence is mostly displayed at weddings, which otherwise are celebrated in the traditional manner, indicates an assimilation of new to customary types of behaviour, rather than a displacement of old by new patterns of behaviour.

Increased expenditure on weddings in Wangala expresses a concern for prestige in a closely-knit community. By contrast Dalena villagers have so many different links with surrounding villages and Mandya that the struggle for status within the traditional, closely integrated, village system has lost some of its importance to them. In their eyes, items which are readily transportable, and which can easily be shown off outside their own village, award prestige. These items, such as dress, pens, pencils, gold watches, or bicycles, will yield prestige to their owner in a wider sphere of social contacts and not just in his own village. Accordingly, rather than introduce novel items into the traditional wedding procedure, which after all would yield prestige only among a very limited number of people, Dalena villagers prefer to spend money on purchases of items which they can display easily on visits to neighbouring villages and to Mandya.

Similarly, the prestige value Wangala villagers attach to men relieving their wives of agricultural labour on their own lands expresses a preoccupation with prestige in an integrated society. For the sort of life a man provides for his wife can be regarded as a matter of prestige only by those people who can actually observe it. By contrast, Dalena men's manifold links with the regional economy have increased the range of people among whom they seek to establish their status. Therefore, quite apart from the economic necessity of Dalena wives still working their husband's land, it would yield them prestige only among their fellow-villagers if they were to relieve their wives from agricultural labour. To impress Mandya officials and farmers from neighbouring villages they have to wear fine clothes, smoke cigarettes, own a gold watch and a bicycle.

The type of home a man owns is a matter of prestige in both villages. The poorest villagers, who live in mud huts with thatched roofs, look up to those who live in mud houses with tiled roofs, and these in turn look up to those who have built new houses. In Wangala, however, all new houses are still built in the customary style; the family shares the living space inside the house with its farm animals. Although villagers always admire the city-type house none has ventured yet to imitate it. The farmer's emotional attachment to his farm animals makes it inconceivable that he live separated from them. This attachment seems to be a common occurrence in rural communities. In the Chinese village described by Martin Yang, cattle are classified as members of the household and have a day set aside for the celebration of their birthdays (Yang 1945:47).

However, once farmers begin to trade in cattle, the attachment lessens, and they are more ready to accept housing innovations. For instance, Dalena villagers all build their new houses in a new style with separate cattle sheds and partition for bathrooms. But they do not copy the city-type house; instead they have developed a compromise between the traditional village type and the new city-style house. 'Any innovation, no matter how far-reaching the implications and how great the pressures for its acceptance, will be projected against existing cultural patterns and will consequently undergo a reinterpretation to bring the new cultural elements into consonance with the total way of life of the group' (Herskovits 1956:454).

The persistence of the traditional type of house in Wangala and the introduction of a new compromise style in Dalena demonstrate two important principles of cultural change. Firstly, the principle of cultural inertia by which customary forms of behaviour will continue unless acted upon by a strong external force; and secondly, the reinterpretation of new cultural elements to bring them into line with the total behavior pattern of the group.

Wangala villagers continue building their new houses in the traditional style because the impact of urban values was not strong enough to eradicate the villagers' attachment to their farm animals. By contrast, Dalena villagers all build their new houses in a new style, because firstly they do not keep their farm animals long enough to become attached to them, and secondly they have been so much exposed to urban influences that the imitation of urban living has itself become a prestige criterion. Yet a straightforward copying of the city-style house would have contravened the whole pattern of behaviour of Dalena villagers; they are still farmers and have to have cattle sheds, and they still like to collect rainwater through a central square opening in the middle of the roof. Furthermore women, being more conservative than men because they are less subject to external influences, still prefer to cook in the old type of kitchen. I have mentioned earlier the one two-storey city-type house in Dalena built by an emigrant son for his mother and brothers (see Epstein 1962:195). It is used mainly for storage, while the family itself lives in the back portion. The persistence of these traditional ways is reflected in the style of the house itself which embodies features of the traditional as well as of the urban type of house.

Dalena men adopt habits and manners which confer prestige beyond the boundaries of the village, but they also compete for prestige among themselves. Traditional values still remain significant in this contest as we saw in the case of Chennu who sought to become a medium. But what is important here is that mediumship, for example, yields prestige only among the conservative faction. The progressive faction does not regard ritual status within its own Peasant caste as a criterion of prestige. It considers economic assets as according the highest prestige; the headman is looked up to by followers of his faction because he is one of the richest men in the village and has installed electricity in his house and bought some furniture such as a table, chairs and a wooden cot. Since economic differentiation in Dalena coincides with caste differentiation there is no challenge to the prestige ranking of castes, and the struggle for prestige goes on within the Peasant caste itself.

In Wangala ritual status is still the ultimate criterion of prestige between castes and within the Peasant caste. The two Untouchable households who live in mud houses are looked up to by their fellow-Untouchables who live in mud huts, but not by Peasants who live in mud huts. In this case ritual differentiation outweighs economic differentiation.

Ritual status within the Peasant caste is, at least in theory, strictly hereditary. Thus the prestige structure is influenced by the hereditary principle operating in Wangala society. The fact that the leaders of the progressive faction try to create new hereditary ritual offices speaks for the high prestige attaching to ritual status. Yet, in Wangala too, the standard of living is a prestige criterion; the rice-eater has more prestige than the ragi-eater; the man who smokes cigarettes has higher prestige than the one who only smokes country cigarettes. This co-existence of a ritual and economic aspect to prestige introduces an element of flexibility into the prestige structure and makes it impossible to talk of clear-cut prestige classes. The hereditary executant of a ritual office will be accorded prestige by virtue of his ritual performances; he need not be a wealthy man with a new house or celebrate his son's wedding with great expenditure. On the other hand, the Peasant who has no ritual office but who spends lavishly on the wedding of his son will also be regarded as a man of prestige. The newly introduced economic criteria of prestige undermine the rigid ritual prestige structure of the past.

Economic development has effected a change in prestige values in both Wangala and Dalena, because the higher incomes allow for greater refinement in prestige criteria. But whereas in Wangala the ritual aspect is still the ultimate criterion of prestige, in Dalena the economic aspect has become dominant in prestige rating. We have seen that Dalena's greater economic differentiation and integration into the wider economy have led to the displacement of the ritual by the economic aspect of prestige. Conversely, Wangala's greater isolation and economic uniformity is responsible for the persisting dominance of ritual criteria in prestige rating.

CONCLUSION

In the preceding analysis of the elements of structural change in Wangala and Dalena I have argued that economic development need not necessarily produce economic change. Only where the new economic system was incompatible with features of traditional economic organisation did we find a change in economic roles and relations. But wherever there was such economic change we also found corresponding changes in political and ritual roles and relations as well as in the principles of social organisation. Thus we have established a positive correlation between economic, political, ritual and organisational change, with economic change being the determining variable.

Economic development led to the disappearance of the joint family unit in both Wangala and Dalena. Familial change may thus occur quite independently of any other structural change, whereas we have seen a consistency in economic, political, ritual and organisational change.

Finally, in my analysis of cultural change I have tried to show how the persistence of economic values delayed social change. I have also argued that economic development results in some change in prestige values and the latter are influenced by the principles on which the society is organised, as well as by its economic structure. Thus I have drawn certain functional relations between economic development and the different aspects of structural and cultural change. These functional relations can be traced out in the social events which occurred in Dalena and Wangala during the past 25 years. The possible general validity of these functional relations has to be tested by many more studies of economic development and social change.

APPENDIX

POPULATION, BY AGE AND SEX

| | | Wangala | | | | Dalena | | |
Age	Male	%	Female	%	Male	%	Female	%
0–4	93	18·50	73	15·10	58	15·90	54	15·90
5–14	111	22·10	118	26·90	88	24·00	60	17·60
15–24	104	20·70	112	24·60	65	17·90	80	23·60
25–34	80	15·90	65	14·30	70	19·10	54	15·90
35–44	57	11·40	42	9·30	36	9·80	31	9·00
45–54	35	6·90	32	7·00	28	7·60	35	10·10
55 and over	23	4·50	13	2·80	21	5·70	27	7·90
Total	503	100·00	455	100·00	366	100·00	341	100·00

HOUSEHOLDERS' FARM WAGES AND PROFITS PER ACRE OF PADDY

| | Wangala | | Dalena | |
Rs.	No.	%	No.	%
(Loss)–0	2	4	1	3
0–40	6	12	2	6
40–80	8	15	—	—
80–120	9	17	7	22
120–160	13	25	4	12
160–200	7	13	5	15
200–400	4	8	7	21
400 and over	3	6	7	21
Total	52	100	33	100

PER ACRE OF SUGARCANE

| | Wangala | | Dalena | |
Rs.	No.	%	No.	%
200–400	4	9	1	9
400–600	8	18	2	18
600–800	4	9	1	9
800–1,000	7	16	3	28
1,000–1,200	13	30	1	9
1,200 and over	8	18	3	27
Total	44	100	11	100

PER ACRE OF JOWAR

Rs.	Wangala No.	%	Dalena No.	%
(Loss)–0	1	6	5	12
0–20	2	13	14	33
20–40	2	12	5	12
40–60	4	25	13	31
60–80	6	38	1	2
80 and over	1	6	4	10
Total	16	100	42	100

PER ACRE OF DRY AND WET RAGI

Rs.	Wangala Dry ragi No.	%	Wet ragi No.	%	Dalena Dry ragi No.	%
(Loss)–0	—	—	—	—	7	17
0–40	2	8	—	—	8	19
40–80	3	12	—	—	18	43
80–120	6	24	—	—	8	19
120–160	8	32	—	—	1	2
160–200	6	24	—	—	—	—
200–240	—	—	2	22	—	—
240–280	—	—	1	12	—	—
280–320	—	—	2	22	—	—
320–360	—	—	2	22	—	—
360 and over	—	—	2	22	—	—
Total	25	100	9	100	42	100

AVERAGE AGRICULTURAL CAPITAL
AND ANNUAL INDIRECT COST PER ESTATE

	Wangala Rs.	*Dalena* Rs.
(1) Agricultural capital	660	370
(2) Interest p.a.	79	44
(3) Depreciation p.a.	47	28
(4) Maintenance p.a.		
(a) subsistence	144	80
(b) cash	24	18
(5) Indirect cost		
(2+3+4) p.a.	294	170

NOTE: Agricultural capital includes the value of draught animals as well as all farming tools and equipment, but excludes land.

DISTRIBUTION OF AGRICULTURAL CAPITAL PER ESTATE

Rs.	*Wangala* %	*Dalena* %
0–200	19	33
200–400	17	37
400–600	9	7
600–800	11	9
800–1,000	24	9
1,000–2,000	9	5
1,200 and over	11	—
Total	100	100

NOTE: Agricultural capital includes the value of draught animals as well as all farming tools and equipment, but excludes land.

AVERAGE VALUE OF LIVESTOCK OF VARIOUS KINDS PER HOUSEHOLD

	Wangala Rs.	%	*Dalena* Rs.	%
Bullocks (pair)	203	59	105	40
Cows (pair)	43	12	82	31
Buffaloes	77	22	29	11
Sheep	20	6	38	14
Goats	3	1	10	4
Total	346	100	264	100

INCIDENCE OF ANIMAL OWNERSHIP OF VARIOUS KINDS
AND AVERAGE VALUE PER HOUSEHOLD

Kind of livestock	*Wangala* No. of holding HH.	Average value per holding HH.	*Dalena* No. of holding HH.	Average value per holding HH.
		Rs.		Rs.
Bullocks	102	382	57	281
Cows	58	144	83	151
Buffaloes	72	265	33	135
Sheep	29	143	57	103
Goats	19	26	43	36

DISTRIBUTION OF THE VALUE OF DOMESTIC LIVESTOCK IN ALL VILLAGE
HOUSEHOLDS

Households

Value of domestic livestock	*Wangala* No.	%	*Dalena* No.	%
Rs.				
Nil	52	27	24	16
0–300	56	29	71	46
300–600	44	23	47	31
600–900	25	13	7	4
900–1,200	10	5	1	1
1,200 and over	5	3	3	2
Total	192	100	153	100

AVERAGE VALUE OF NON-PRODUCTIVE PROPERTY PER CONSUMPTION UNIT

	Wangala Rs.	%	*Dalena* Rs.	%
Personal property	79	17	81	16
House	341	74	378	74
Household chattels	42	9	54	10
Total	462	100	513	100

SOURCES OF AVERAGE NON-PRODUCTIVE PROPERTY PER CONSUMPTION
UNIT

| | Wangala | | Dalena | |
	Rs.	%	Rs.	%
Home-produced	20	4	14	3
Barter	2	—	1	—
Gift	295	64	259	50
Cash purchase	145	32	239	47
Total	462	100	513	100

DISTRIBUTION OF VALUE OF PROPERTY PER CONSUMPTION UNIT IN
SAMPLE HOUSEHOLDS

Non-productive

| | Households | | | |
| | Wangala | | Dalena | |
Value Rs.	No.	%	No.	%
0–200	16	25	9	19
200–400	17	27	20	42
400–600	7	11	7	14
600–800	14	21	2	4
800–1,000	5	8	2	4
1,000 and over	5	8	8	17
Total	64	100	48	100

PERSONAL

| | Households | | | |
| | Wangala | | Dalena | |
Value Rs.	No.	%	No.	%
0–40	20	31	10	21
40–80	12	19	23	48
80–120	20	31	7	15
120–160	7	11	1	2
160–200	3	5	4	8
200 and over	2	3	3	6
Total	64	100	48	100

HOUSE PROPERTY

| | Households | | | |
| Value Rs. | Wangala | | Dalena | |
	No.	%	No.	%
0–200	30	47	25	52
200–400	11	16	7	15
400–600	12	19	5	11
600–800	7	11	2	4
800–1,000	2	4	4	8
1,000 and over	2	3	5	10
Total	64	100	48	100

HOUSEHOLD CHATTELS

| | Households | | | |
| Value Rs. | Wangala | | Dalena | |
	No.	%	No.	%
0–20	11	17	7	15
20–40	25	39	16	33
40–60	20	30	12	25
60–80	5	9	4	8
80–100	1	2	2	4
100 and over	2	3	7	15
Total	64	100	48	100

SOURCES OF AVERAGE MONTHLY INCOME PER CONSUMPTION UNIT

Cash

| | Wangala | | Dalena | |
	Rs.	%	Rs.	%
(1) Manufacturing and trading profits	1·00	4	5·00	23
(2) Rents and interest	1·00	4	2·00	10
(3) Crop sales	14·50	65	5·00	21
(4) Animal products	1·00	4	2·00	10
(5) Crafts	0·50	2	—	—
(6) Wages (agricultural)	4·00	17	2·00	9
(7) Wages (non-agricultural)	—	—	3·00	14
(8) Miscellaneous	1·00	4	3·00	13
Total	23·00	100	22·00	100

ALL SOURCES

	Wangala		Dalena	
	Rs.	%	Rs.	%
Subsistence	9·00	28	12·00	33
Barter	0·50	2	1·50	4
Gifts	0·50	1	0·50	1
Cash	23·00	69	22·00	62
Total	33·00	100	36·00	100

DISTRIBUTION OF TOTAL MONTHLY EXPENDITURE

Sample households

Monthly expenditure per consumption unit	Cash expenditure				Overall expenditure			
	Wangala		Dalena		Wangala		Dalena	
Rs.	No.	%	No.	%	No.	%	No.	%
0–5	1	2	2	4	—	—	—	—
5–10	7	11	7	15	—	—	—	—
10–15	18	28	16	33	5	8	1	2
15–20	19	30	11	23	10	16	9	19
20–25	9	14	5	10	12	19	8	16
25–30	9	14	2	4	12	18	11	23
30–35	1	1	2	4	14	22	8	17
35–40	—	—	—	—	4	6	3	6
40 and over	—	—	3	7	7	11	8	17
Total	64	100	48	100	64	100	48	100

DISTRIBUTION OF MONTHLY EXPENDITURE PER CONSUMPTION UNIT
IN SAMPLE HOUSEHOLDS

Food and clothes

Households

Monthly expenditure per consumption unit	Food				Clothes			
	Wangala		Dalena		Wangala		Dalena	
Rs.	No.	%	No.	%	No.	%	No.	%
0–5	—	—	—	—	52	80	34	71
5–10	13	22	4	8	12	20	9	19
10–15	20	31	21	44	—	—	5	10
15–20	20	31	15	32	—	—	—	—
20–25	10	14	3	6	—	—	—	—
25–30	1	2	3	6	—	—	—	—
30 and over	—	—	2	4	—	—	—	—
Total	64	100	48	100	64	100	48	100

SUNDRIES AND HOUSEHOLD OVERHEADS

Households

Monthly expenditure per consumption unit	Sundries				Household overheads			
	Wangala		Dalena		Wangala		Dalena	
Rs.	No.	%	No.	%	No.	%	No.	%
0–2	17	27	14	29	5	8	2	4
2–4	29	45	21	44	46	75	38	79
4–6	15	23	6	13	12	16	8	17
6–8	3	5	2	4	1	1	—	—
8–10	—	—	2	4	—	—	—	—
10 and over	—	—	3	6	—	—	—	—
Total	64	100	48	100	64	100	48	100

INTEREST

Households

Rs.	Wangala		Dalena	
	No.	%	No.	%
Nil	3	6	5	10
0–2	41	63	27	57
2–4	18	28	9	19
4–6	1	2	3	6
6–8	—	—	1	2
8 and over	1	1	3	6
Total	64	100	48	100

DISTRIBUTION OF MONTHLY INCOME PER CONSUMPTION UNIT IN SAMPLE HOUSEHOLDS

From manufacturing and trading profits

Households

Rs.	Wangala		Dalena	
	No.	%	No.	%
Nil	57	89	32	67
0–5	3	5	5	11
5–10	1	2	4	8
10–15	2	3	1	2
15–20	1	1	2	4
20 and over	—	—	4	8
Total	64	100	48	100

FROM CROP SALES

Households

Rs.	Wangala No.	%	Dalena No.	%
Nil	17	27	30	63
0–5	2	3	10	21
5–10	6	9	5	10
10–15	12	19	1	2
15–20	8	12	1	2
20–25	7	11	—	—
25 and over	12	19	1	2
Total	64	100	48	100

FROM ANIMAL PRODUCTS AND MISCELLANEOUS SOURCES

Households

	Animal products				Miscellaneous sources			
	Wangala		Dalena		Wangala		Dalena	
Rs.	No.	%	No.	%	No.	%	No.	%
Nil	44	69	25	52	37	58	25	52
0–2	8	12	7	15	18	28	4	8
2–4	9	14	4	8	5	8	6	13
4–6	2	3	4	8	3	5	5	11
6–8	1	2	6	13	—	—	3	6
8 and over	—	—	2	4	1	1	5	10
Total	64	100	48	100	64	100	48	100

FROM INTEREST

Households

Rs.	Wangala No.	%	Dalena No.	%
Nil	43	67	30	63
0–5	16	25	10	21
5–10	4	6	5	10
10–15	1	2	1	2
15 and over	—	—	2	4
Total	64	100	48	100

FROM AGRICULTURAL AND NON-AGRICULTURAL WAGES

	Households							
	Agricultural wages				*Non-agricultural wages*			
	Wangala		*Dalena*		*Wangala*		*Dalena*	
Rs.	*No.*	*%*	*No.*	*%*	*No.*	*%*	*No.*	*%*
Nil	29	46	21	44	61	95	23	48
0–2	5	9	11	23	2	3	6	13
2–4	10	14	9	19	1	2	6	12
4–6	6	9	3	6	—	—	3	6
6–8	4	6	—	—	—	—	1	2
8–10	2	3	2	4	—	—	3	6
10 and over	8	13	2	4	—	—	6	13
Total	64	100	48	100	64	100	48	100

DISTRIBUTION OF MONTHLY DEFICIT PER CONSUMPTION UNIT
IN SAMPLE HOUSEHOLDS

	Households			
	Wangala		*Dalena*	
Rs.	*No.*	*%*	*No.*	*%*
Nil	42	63	28	58
0–2	8	13	6	13
2–4	8	12	10	21
4–6	3	6	4	8
6 and over	3	6	—	—
Total	64	100	48	100

DISTRIBUTION OF MONTHLY SAVINGS PER CONSUMPTION UNIT
IN SAMPLE HOUSEHOLDS

	Households			
	Wangala		*Dalena*	
Rs.	*No.*	*%*	*No.*	*%*
Nil	25	39	20	42
0–4	13	20	12	25
4–8	9	14	6	13
8–12	6	9	4	8
12–16	3	5	1	2
16–20	1	2	—	—
20–32	3	5	—	—
32 and over	4	6	5	10
Total	64	100	48	100

23 A FACTOR ANALYSIS OF MODERNIZATION IN VILLAGE INDIA*

Irma Adelman and George Dalton

INTRODUCTION

THERE DOES NOT now exist a field of study which analyzes the economic and social processes that are transforming village communities in the developing world, and relates village to national development. Yet policies to increase agricultural productivity and inculcate attitudes and skills favorable to new economic and cultural achievements at the village level are important in developing countries.

There are three basic obstacles which must be surmounted in studying micro-development. First, the communities undergoing socio-economic changes are many and widely different. Studies of individual villages based on sustained fieldwork can provide us with insights into the process for specific communities,[1] but the conclusions reached cannot readily be generalized to other villages because of the extraordinary range of variation among them. Second, statistical information on village economic structure and

*We are grateful to the National Science Foundation for supporting this research under grant GS1235 and to the Council of Intersocietal Studies of Northwestern University for financing a trip to India to check the results of the statistical analysis. We are indebted to Clarence Gulick, Robert Edminster, David Hopper, Wolf Ladijinsky, John Mellor, Ronald Ridker, Abraham Weisblat, and Clifton Wharton, Jr. for their constructive comments, and to Dylis Rennie and Joyce Nussbaum for their research assistance. Professor Mellor has kindly allowed us to quote some of his comments on this paper as plausible alternative or supplementary interpretations.

[1] See for example T. S. Epstein, *Economic Development and Social Change in South India*, Manchester University Press 1962. F. Bailey, *Caste and the Economic Frontier*, Manchester University Press 1962. John W. Mellor et al., *Developing Rural India*, Cornell University Press 1968.

performance is scarce and often of dubious accuracy. Third, there are no theories generating models of sequential change and development at the village level which are theoretically persuasive and amenable to policy implementation. Agricultural economists, anthropologists, and rural sociologists usually concern themselves with the introduction of innovations piecemeal and emphasize different aspects of the transformation process, even though they recognize that the effectiveness of modernization policies is influenced by many disparate, mutually interacting, forces. Development planners who must devise policies to apply at the village level therefore have no knowledge of the functional relationships among variables of the kind available to planners working on macro-economic development.

In this paper we attempt to overcome some of these difficulties in analyzing village development in India. Of the many forces at work, we try, by statistical means, to isolate the few that are most important, explain their operation, and indicate their policy uses.

DATA

The data for the research described in this paper are taken from village surveys carried out by the Indian government in representative villages in each of the 15 states between 1960 and 1962, as part of the overall Census of India for 1961.[2] The purpose of the village surveys was to obtain comparable information on the structure and performance of village communities. The published results contain statistics on income, landholdings, educational and transport facilities, etc., as well as verbal descriptions of village history, caste composition, and styles of life.

Of the three hundred village surveys available in the summer of 1967, we chose a representative sample of 108. The number of villages from each state included in our sample is proportional to the rural population of that state. We also chose our sample so as to reflect the full range of variation in village development contained in the original studies.

We were able to include in our analysis only those variables for which data were given in the published surveys. We had to leave out an index of ecological conditions, for example, because information on rainfall, soil quality, sub-soil, water, etc., was

---

[2] Census of India, 1961, Part VI, Village Survey Monographs (Monographs on selected Villages) and District Census Handbooks.

not reported. An index of household wealth had to be excluded since it would have required data on savings, consumer durables, holdings of jewelry and other real assets which were not consistently reported. Nor were we able to include data on family planning programs or data which would enable us to evaluate the effectiveness of land reform legislation.

Several variables were discarded from the study because they lacked systematic association with any other included variable. Among these were indicators of peasant indebtedness (the amount of household debt, the ratio of debt to income, and the proportion of debt incurred for productive purposes), and of the quality of health facilities. Finally, we omitted a variable describing the type of religion because it proved impossible to define it in a manner which is both conceptually appropriate and capable of implementation with our data sources.

Definition of Variables and Method of Classification

We ranked the 108 villages with regard to each of 17 variables. Where the information or concept were not specifiable in numerical terms, we grouped the villages into three, four, or five ranked categories depending upon the fineness of the survey data. In most cases, numerical scores were assigned to the ranked groups according to the scale described in I. Adelman and C. T. Morris, *Society, Politics and Economic Development*, pp. 14–15. Experiments with alternative scales (logarithmic and squared) indicated that the results were insensitive to the scale chosen.

1. *Population.* Villages were ranked according to the number of households, which ranges from 932 to 8, with a mean of 158 households.

2. *Number of Castes.* This indicator ranks villages into five categories according to the number of named caste groups resident in the village. The top group consisted of villages having more than 15 castes (the highest number being 26 castes). The second, third and fourth groups contained villages with 12–14, 8–11 and 1–7 castes respectively. The lowest group was composed of villages with predominantly tribal organization in which castes are unimportant.

3. *Extent of Commercialization.* This indicator groups villages into one of three sets, high, medium and low, depending upon the proportion of yearly village produce which is sold to markets. The top group contains villages which sold over 50 per cent of

production; villages in the lowest group sold less than 25 per cent of their output. The proportion of total output sold ranged from 100 per cent to 0.

4. *Quality of Agricultural Technology.* This composite index ranks villages according to the proportion of arable land which is irrigated and the proportion of farm households which use chemical fertilizer or pesticides. The per cent of cultivated land under irrigation ranged from 0–100 per cent, with a mean of 24.3 per cent and a mode of 0 per cent. Villages were also divided into three groups according to the per cent of their households using improved tools, chemical fertilizers, and pesticides.[3]

5. *Location and Access to Transport.* This indicator also is a composite of several data series: quantity and quality of village access to transport facilities (all-weather roads, bus service, railway service), and the distance of the village from towns and cities. Villages were divided into four groups according to the following criteria: in the first group villages were six miles or less from a town, had access to an all-year motorable road and to frequent bus services and were within six miles of a railroad. In the second group, villages were ten miles or less from the nearest town with access to an all-year motorable road, or within five miles of a railroad. Villages in the third group were fifteen miles or less from a town, had no access to an all-year motorable road and no railroad within five miles. In the fourth group the villages were more than fifteen miles from a town and ten miles from a railroad and had no access to an all-year motorable road.

6. *Awareness of Social Legislation.* One of the very few indicators of social attitudes we could contrive from the survey information was the extent of awareness in the village of legislation on social issues. This index was based on the per cent of villagers

---

[3] Professor Mellor comments: "With respect to your definition of agricultural technology there is a small problem in that . . . the irrigation variable is essentially a physical given over which the individual household has relatively little control whereas the use of fertilizer is one on which the individual household has a substantial amount of control. In both respects this must be qualified of course because with certain types of small-scale irrigation such as wells, the household does have a fair amount of control and likewise physical conditions may in some cases be quite unsuited to the use of fertilizer leaving in fact very little control by household. Thus there is substantial contrast in general in the nature of control over these variables. Nevertheless I think you have chosen the two most important variables here."

who were aware of legislation introduced since independence prohibiting untouchability. The range was from 100 per cent to 3 per cent, with a mean of 38.1 per cent, and median and mode of 25.0 per cent.

7. *Education.* This variable is a composite (determined by factor analysis) of four "primary" variables: (1) the per cent of children aged 5 to 14 who attended school, which ranged from 0 to 89 per cent with a mean of 32.5 per cent; (2) the per cent of female children aged 5 to 14 in school, which had a mean of 18.3 per cent and a mode of 5 per cent and ranged from 0 to 75 per cent; (3) the number of literate males over 14 expressed as a percentage of all males over 14 (mean 30.6 per cent and range 0 to 81 per cent); and (4) the educational facilities available in and near the village. The type of school (primary or secondary) and proximity to the village were taken into account when dividing villages into four groups for this last indicator.

8. *Family Household Type.* This variable ranks villages according to the proportion of simple households (i.e., containing one married couple with their unmarried children) in the village. This percentage had a mean value of 48 per cent and ranged from 92 per cent to 6 per cent.

9. *Female Child Marriage.* This variable ranks villages by the number of married females who are less than 14 years old, expressed as a percentage of the total number of females under 14 in the village. The percentage ranged from 0 to 37 per cent, with a mean of 3.8 per cent.

10. *Per Cent of Low-Caste Households.* The number of people belonging to low castes expressed as a percentage of the total village population, ranged from 0–100 per cent, with a mean of 29 per cent and median and mode of 11 per cent.

11. *Cooperative Membership.* The number of village households which were members of multipurpose cooperative societies was expressed as a percentage of all the village households. The range was 0 to 78 per cent, with a mean median and mode of 20.5, 2.5 and 0.

12. *Income.* This variable combines two aspects of village income: the average monthly income per household and a measure of extent of inequality in income distribution. The latter was indicated by the per cent of households in the village with average monthly incomes below 50 Rupees.

Average monthly incomes range from 20 to 213 Rupees, with

a mean of 80.9 and median of 72. The per cent of households in each village earning less than 50 Rupees per month had a mean of 40.7 and ranged from 0–95.

13. *Land Per Capita.* This indicator classifies villages according to the quantity of arable land per capita (the total amount of land used for farming divided by the village population). The arable land per capita ranged from 0.1 acre to 9.2 acres. The distribution of land holdings has two modes—1.2 and 3.7 acres, and a mean and median of 1.85 and 1.2 respectively.

14. *Community Development Activity.* Villages were divided into four groups according to the number and size of development projects undertaken by the community. These ranged from villages which had undertaken more than four substantial projects (e.g., building new roads or schools) to villages where no community projects had been undertaken.

15. *Employment in Agriculture.* For each village, the number of people aged 15 to 59 who were employed in agriculture was expressed as a percentage of all people in that age group. The percentage ranged from 0–99, with a mean and a mode of 56.0 per cent.

16. *Per Cent of Households Owning Land.* Villages were classified according to the percentage of households owning some farmland. The percentage varies from 14 to 100 with mean, median and mode of 71.9, 80.0 and 100. (The data were not available to calculate a frequency distribution of land ownership by amounts of land held.)

17. *Per Cent of Tenant Farmers.* This variable classifies villages according to the percentage of households who lease land from owners or who work land they do not own on a share-cropping arrangement. The mean percentage was 20 per cent and ranged from 0 to 100.

THE STATISTICAL TECHNIQUE

Factor analysis[4] requires no pre-existing theory of functional relationships; it can handle masses of diverse data relating to a

---

[4] For full explanations of the technique see I. Adelman and C. T. Morris, *Society, Politics and Economic Development,* The Johns Hopkins Press, Baltimore 1967, H. H. Harman, *Modern Factor Analysis,* University of Chicago Press, Chicago 1960 and L. L. Thurstone, *Multiple Factor Analysis,* University of Chicago Press, Chicago 1961.

large number of social and economic characteristics and communities; and is not sensitive to the scale chosen for the quantitative specification of the variables. Factor analysis therefore helps circumvent many of the difficulties inherent in the study of micro-development.

This technique uses an analysis of variance to group variables into a few clusters (Factors) according to the closeness of the linear relationship between the variables. The mathematical principles by which each cluster or "Factor" is formed from the observable variables are as follows: (1) Those variables that are most closely intercorrelated are combined within a single Factor. (2) The variables assigned to a given Factor are those that are most nearly independent of the variables assigned to the other Factors. (3) The Factor sets are derived so as to maximize the percentage of the total variance attributable to each successive Factor (given the inclusion of the preceding Factors). (4) The Factors are independent (uncorrelated with each other). The number of Factors is determined by the criterion that the last Factor extracted explain at least 5 per cent of the overall inter-village variance.

Factor analysis does not allow us to attribute cause and effect. It does, however, permit us to delineate the *underlying regularities* in a complex mass of data by extracting from a larger set of variables the *mutual interdependence* among the subsets of characteristics comprising each Factor.

The results of the Factor analysis are summarized in Table 1. Each entry in the table (or matrix) shows the importance of the influence of the Factors (or columns) on the variables (rows). More specifically, each entry or "Factor loading," is the net correlation between a Factor (set) and a single observed variable.

The Factor loadings may be interpreted more familiarly in terms of the squares of the entries in the Factor matrix. Excluding the last column, which will be explained later, the square of each entry in the matrix represents the proportion (percentage) of the total unit variance of each variable which is explained by each Factor, after allowing for the contributions of the other Factors. The first row of the table, for example, shows that 49 per cent ($=.702^2$) of the variation in population among villages is explained by Factor 1, an additional 9 per cent each ($=.290^2$ and $.290^2$) by Factors 3 and 4, while the net contribution of Factors 2 and 5 is less than 1 per cent.

The right-hand column of the table gives the sum of the squared Factor loadings, or the "communality" of each variable. The communality indicates the proportion of the total unit variance explained by all the common Factors taken together and is therefore analogous to R^2 in regression analysis. The communality of village population for example is

$$(.702)^2+(.044)^2+(-.290)^2+(.290)^2+(-.045)^2=.664$$

That is, 66 per cent of the variation in population size among villages is associated with the six common Factors extracted from the seventeen variables included in our analysis. The six influences associated with population in Factor 1 account for roughly 70 per cent ($=^{49}\!/_{66}$) of the "explained" intervillage variation in population.

In addition to indicating the weight of each Factor in explaining the observed variables, the matrix of loadings provides the basis for grouping the variables into common Factors. It is this power to extract statistically cohesive sets of social and economic forces which vary together systematically that makes the technique of Factor analysis of interest to social scientists analyzing development and modernization. Each variable may reasonably be assigned to that Factor with which it has the closest linear relationship, i.e., where it has the highest loading. Once variables have been assigned to Factors, each Factor may be "identified" by giving a reasonable explanation of the underlying economic and social forces which it represents.

Table 1 is arranged so that variables with their highest loadings in Factor 1 are listed first, followed by variables with their highest loadings in Factors 2 through 5 consecutively. The bold print marks off the factor sets to which each indicator is assigned.

THE RESULTS OF THE ANALYSIS

The economic characteristics which have their highest loadings in Factor 1 are the population of the village, the extent of commercialization of productive output, the quality of agricultural technology, and the nearness of villages to towns and transport facilities. The social characteristics are the number of castes, the extent of awareness of social legislation and the level of educational attainment of the village.

Villages which score high on Factor 1 have relatively large

TABLE 1
ROTATED FACTOR MATRIX
FOR 17 ECONOMIC AND SOCIAL VARIABLES

Economic and Social Indicators	Rotated Factor Loadings					
	F_1	F_2	F_3	F_4	F_5	R^2
1. Population	.702	.044	−.290	.290	−.045	.664
2. Number of Castes	.820	−.199	−.113	.026	−.061	.730
3. Commercialization	.665	.124	.149	−.337	.000	.593
4. Level of Agricultural Technology	.706	.048	.247	.047	.039	.566
5. Transport and Location	.608	.116	.171	−.043	−.338	.528
6. Awareness of National Social Legislation	.540	.383	.096	−.310	−.079	.550
7. Education	.522	.413	.143	.157	−.105	.499
8. Family Type	−.231	.666	−.225	−.053	−.250	.613
9. % Female Children Married	−.193	−.797	−.060	−.079	.028	.682
10. % Low Caste	.012	−.043	.815	.076	.053	.676
11. Cooperative Membership	.118	.009	.825	−.107	−.155	.731
12. Income	.402	−.084	.037	−.577	.023	.503
13. Land per capita	−.148	.049	.073	−.689	.410	.672
14. Community Development Activities	.326	.123	.280	.474	.244	.484
15. % Employment in Agriculture	−.154	−.242	−.096	.054	.742	.645
16. % Land Owners	−.203	−.358	−.075	−.145	.668	.643
17. % Tenant Farmers	−.084	−.111	−.053	.086	−.773	.627

populations stratified into many castes. They use more modern agricultural techniques and sell a high proportion of their output to nearby, easily accessible towns. They are also more aware of national legislation concerning untouchability and have better educational facilities, more school age children in school, and a higher incidence of literacy. By contrast, the villages which score low on Factor 1, have small populations and few castes, use traditional agricultural techniques, produce principally for their own consumption rather than for market sale, are distant from towns and cities, and have poor access (or none at all) to modern means of transport. They are also less aware of national social legislation, have fewer educational facilities and are less educated. Theirs is a profile of traditional economic and cultural isolation and self-sufficiency—the absence of integrative interactions with the larger economy and society.

Factor 1 represents the extent of village level economic and social modernization. Two of the variables, population and number of castes, indicate the scope for economic specialization and division of labor. The larger the village population and the number of castes, the greater the local supply of labor and the capacity for occupational specialization. A large population moreover means greater effective demand in the local market. The extent of commercialization, the quality of agricultural technology, and the quality of access to towns and transport facilities (the other three economic characteristics which cluster in Factor 1), indicate the extent to which local communities are economically integrated with the regional and national economy. Greater commercialization means that a larger proportion of village producers are selling to markets outside the village. A higher level of agricultural technology involves greater use of purchased inputs (e.g., fertilizer). Nearness to towns and transport facilities gives superior access to markets external to the village in which to sell produce and buy consumer's and producer's goods, as well as wider occupational alternatives. Villages that ranked high on commercialization, agricultural technology, and nearness to transport facilities and towns, are facing outward economically; they are coming to depend on impersonal market forces and on economic opportunities and facilities external to the village.

Extent of awareness of social legislation, and extent of education also appear in Factor 1, which suggests that those villages which face outward economically are also culturally more closely linked with the external world. Economic contact breeds cultural contact. The larger, more commercialized and better located villages tend also to receive relatively more educational facilities, and to make fuller use of the facilities provided.

Our measure of income and its distribution has an important secondary loading (16 per cent of variance) in Factor 1. That higher, more evenly distributed income associates with higher village scores on Factor 1 probably reflects the fact that three of the component variables of Factor 1 are the usual targets of agricultural extension and regional development activities: to provide social overhead capital, to enlarge production for sale and to provide better transport facilities to link villages to cities and to market towns. But the association is not very strong, an indication that as of 1961, the base line of our data, intervillage differences in technology, commercialization, and transport and location still largely reflected historical conditions long in existence in India rather than recently initiated agricultural policies. Irrigation had been started as long as a century back; fertilizer use was still low and, for technical reasons, could be intensively used only where irrigation assured abundant and certain supply of water. Irrigated, more productive land was also settled more densely, leading to larger villages and more castes. The economic and social characteristics which associate in this Factor therefore represent a slowly changing low level static equilibrium.[5]

The Second Factor

Factor 2 characterizes the extent of traditional social arrangements in the village. Villages with high scores on this Factor have a *large* proportion of nuclear (as compared to extended) family households and a *small* proportion of girls under the age of 14 who are married. The more traditional villages have a larger proportion of joint family households and a higher frequency of child marriage.

We note that awareness of national social legislation (5 per cent of variance), extent of education (16 per cent of variance) and per cent of landowners (13 per cent of variance) have secondary associations with Factor 2. Traditional villages have not

---

[5] We are indebted to Hopper and Weisblat for this point.

only a high proportion of joint family households and frequent child marriages, but also a high percentage of landownership, and little education and awareness of national social legislation.

It appears that ownership of land tends to keep extended families together in order to avoid uneconomical fragmentation of plots. This socially retarding influence is reinforced by the land reform legislation, which sets ceilings on legally permissible amounts of land owned according to family size. Material incentives therefore tend to encourage landowners to retain the joint family.[6]

Factor 1 explains 24 per cent of overall intervillage variance in the extent of economic and socio-cultural modernization. Factor 2 accounts for only 12 per cent. This, together with the low average levels of social development represented in our data (the average village in the sample still had 52 per cent of joint families and 5.3 per cent child brides) implies that actual social change in Indian villages had lagged behind economic and attitudinal change.

The Third Factor

Variables which appear in Factor 3 are the proportion of the total which low-caste households comprise in the village, and the proportion of households which belong to cooperatives. Villages that score high on this Factor have a high proportion of low-caste households, and a large percentage of households who are members of cooperatives. This Factor explains 10 per cent of the overall variance in all characteristics among villages.

There are several possible explanations for the association shown in Factor 3. Governmental authorities may have deliberately established cooperatives in areas densely populated by low-caste villages. It has been suggested to us that high caste land-owning minorities, who dominate villages politically, may have induced their low-caste dependent clients to form cooperatives in order that the village receive some material benefits that the government provides through the cooperatives. The material benefits received in these paper cooperatives then accrue largely to the high caste persons.[7]

---

[6] This point is stressed by Epstein *op. cit.*

[7] Professor Mellor comments: "It was my impression although I have not seen statistical evidence to support it, that this is particularly true of the

The Fourth Factor

Income, land per capita, and (with a negative correlation) the extent of community development activities undertaken cluster in Factor 4. That income has its highest loading in the fourth rather than the first Factor suggests that (as of 1961) income differences between villages were not as great as other differences, and were neither as strongly nor as systematically related to the other economic indicators of development as were the indicators which cluster in Factor 1. The principal reason for income differences among Indian villages appears to be differences in amount of land cultivated. Since our data are for 1961, technology had been largely static for a long time. Both the quality of technology and land tenure arrangements have therefore tended to adjust to the inherent productivity of land, with the result that income differentials are more the consequence of differences in relative abundance of land than of technological or economic improvements. It is reassuring that income has its second highest loading in the economic modernization Factor 1, and that the extent of commercialization and awareness of social legislation have high secondary loadings in Factor 4, the income Factor. This suggests that village income is responsive to the policy programs to improve agriculture: commercialization of production, improvements in irrigation and in the use of fertilizer, and the provision of farm to market roads. As of 1961, these programs were not the primary influences upon intervillage income differentials because there was little improved technology to be disseminated[8] and much of it required an expensive package of complementary resources.

---

credit cooperatives which are the most numerous types of cooperatives. The higher caste people dominate them and pull most of the, what is in effect, subsidized credit for their own purposes. Perhaps high caste people are more likely to organize, join and dominate cooperatives if there are a lot of low caste people in the community."

[8] This point is stressed by Mellor, Hopper and Weisblat. For a discussion of agricultural technology, see W. D. Hopper, "The Mainsprings of Agricultural Growth," Dr. Rajendra Prasad Memorial Lecture to the 18th Annual Conference of the Indian Society of Agricultural Statistics, 28–30, 1965 and T. W. Schultz *Transforming Traditional Agriculture* (Yale University Press, 1964).

The Fifth Factor

Factor 5, which accounts for 12 per cent of the overall inter-village variance, describes the type of land tenure and the extent to which land resources allow agricultural specialization. Villages that have a high proportion of households owning land (and therefore relatively few tenant farmers), have many people employed full-time in agriculture as well as a relatively large amount of land per capita. By contrast, the low-scoring villages have little land per capita, a smaller proportion of land owners, a higher proportion of tenant farmers, and a greater than average percentage of households supplementing their agricultural income with non-agricultural employment.

Professor Mellor tells us that the positive association of larger plots, more frequent land ownership and greater reliance on agricultural employment, probably arise because

> where the soil is highly productive as in the alluvial deltaic areas, there is a tendency for sharply rising production functions relating labor input and output. This provides a basis for labor productivity way beyond the subsistence requirements of the labor force which, in turn, provides a basis for a landlord class living off of the land and labor of others. Such landlordism will be associated with high population density and small farms, both tracing from the high productivity of the land base. Where there is a prosperous landlord class of this type one would expect them to demand a number of services beyond those in agriculture and, hence, to have a substantial amount of nonagricultural employment.

When the land base is adequate, moreover, fewer households need to supplement their low agricultural incomes with secondary and tertiary employments outside of agriculture.

It is not surprising that the four variables which portray the nature of the agricultural base of the villages should associate together in a single Factor. But given the overwhelmingly agricultural character of village India, it is surprising that this Factor is the weakest of the five—it explains less variance among villages than the first four Factors. It is also surprising that forces of agricultural dynamism such as better agricultural technology, greater commercialization, and higher incomes should have relatively small associations with the characteristics of land. (Their loadings in Factor 5 are only .039, .000, and .023, implying neg-

ligible correlations with this Factor.) These findings support the
contention of W. Neale that the nature of agrarian tenure has not
been a primary obstacle to increasing agricultural productivity and
income in the past. The absence of a strong association between
land tenure, income and technology might also mean that tenant
farming tends to occur where ecological conditions favor the
use of advanced technology, the latter factor more or less balancing the former.[9]

FACTOR ROWS

The Factors that affect each variable and the extent of their
influence are shown in the rows of Table 1. We comment here
only on these rows which yield additional information on the
relationships between the variables.

Income

A profile of high income villages would include the following
characteristics in order of importance: a relatively high amount
of land per capita (in Factor 4), a high degree of commercialization (Factors 1 and 5), better than average performance in adopting improved agricultural technology (Factor 1), a relatively
large number of castes (Factor 1), more awareness of national

---

[9] W. C. Neale, *Economic Change in Rural India: Land Tenure and
Reform in Uttar Pradesh,* 1800–1955 (New Haven: Yale University Press,
1962).
Professor Mellor writes: "I would argue that the highly productive land
will also be land which is more responsive to your primary measure of
agricultural technology, namely fertilizer use. It is also more likely to be an
irrigated area and also likely to respond better to irrigation. Thus where a
tenancy is more viable then it is likely to find the practices by which you
measure agricultural technology as being profitable also. It, of course, does
not necessarily follow that tenancy is either favorable or unfavorable to
modern agricultural technology. One might argue, for example, that tenant
farming was unfavorable. However, tenant farming tends to occur where
other conditions are more favorable towards advanced technology, the latter
factor more than balancing the former. Having said this, however, I
would agree that the nature of agrarian tenure has not been a primary
obstacle to technological change and increasing productivity in Indian
agriculture. At the present time, however, we may be seeing the beginning
of some major social and income distributional problems arising from
tenancy in those areas in which it is still prevalent."

social legislation (Factors 4 and 1) and a higher than average level of educational achievement (Factor 1).

The close relationship between more land per capita and higher average income probably reflects the prevailing condition of low-level traditional technology of Indian agriculture as of 1961. As indicated earlier, where the use of artificial fertilizers and contrived irrigation is sparse, and technology is relatively stationary, income differentials are more likely to be primarily the result of the amount of arable land per person available to be worked.

As of 1961, programs to commercialize production and to improve technology and access roads, while responsible for some of intervillage variance in income, were not the most important influences upon income differentials among villages for two major reasons: (1) the technology differentials reflected in our data were largely historical differences, long in existence, and were all within the framework of traditional (rather than modern) agriculture, and (2) the available spectrum of technology required an expensive package of complementary innovations and was not very profitable.

Agricultural Technology

The quality of agricultural technology bears no systematic relationship to the agricultural characteristics included in Factor 4 but relates instead to commercialization, size of village, and nearness to transport facilities and towns included in Factor 1 (55 per cent of variance). These associations indicate that by 1961, reforms in land tenure had had considerably less impact on technical innovations in Indian agriculture than had commercialization and the creation of farm-to-market roads. However, as pointed out to us by Professor Mellor:

> Your data show that improvements in agricultural incomes and agricultural methods are not associated with the tenure system when studied on a cross-sectional basis. However there may be a number of other factors such as the profitability of new methods and the basic productivity of land which are associated with the tenure system. Thus it may well be that where the land reforms were effective in India they brought about tenure changes which did bring about income increases greater than would otherwise have occurred and improvements in agricultural methods greater than would otherwise have occurred.

Extent of Commercialization

The extent of commercialization has considerable weight in three of the five Factors, which confirms findings elsewhere that growth in market activities is a particularly powerful solvent of traditional society.[10] Increased commercialization means greater dependence on market sales, a corresponding reduction in production for self-use, and thereby an increase in the proportion of cash receipts to real income. Increased dependence on market sale for livelihood increases the sensitivity of production decisions to market prices. Farms thereby become integrated into the larger regional and national economy because they increase and contract production of specific cash crops in response to price changes. The receipt of cash income enables producers to purchase technologically superior inputs such as pesticides and chemical fertilizers, from the national economy. In addition, farmers are able to make economic decisions on the basis of cost accounting and to hire seasonal wage labor on short-run, cash-wage terms, instead of through long-run master-client dependency relationships. On the household budget side, cash income widens the range of choice of consumption goods, allows modern forms of savings to take place, and makes possible the purchase of services such as education, which enable people to move out of the traditional village-bound culture and economy.

Several of these effects are captured in Factor 1 (45 per cent of variation in extent of commercialization), which reflects interrelatedness among increased commercialization, more economic specialization, enlarged use of modern (purchased) agricultural technology, superior access to transport facilities and towns and higher village income. In addition, ten per cent of the variance in extent of commercialization is associated directly with the income Factor (4).

On the other hand, we find that the extent of commercialization does not vary with the amount of land per capita and the nature of land tenure (Factor 5). This lack of association is rather surprising. It probably reflects the low grade technology employed in 1961: differences in size of land holdings and in type of land tenure largely compensated for variations in eco-

---

[10] See "Introduction" in P. Bohannan and G. Dalton, Editors, *Markets in Africa;* also Ch. 6 in T. Smith, *The Agrarian Origins of Modern Japan* (1959), 297–338.

logical conditions, so that larger land holdings did not tend to generate a greater proportion of marketable produce.

Transport and Location

Access to transport facilities and to towns is recognized in the literature on development as a powerful force for inducing modernization. Better transport facilities allow goods and people to become outwardly mobile. Opportunities are created for new occupational choices, new earnings from market sale, and for imports of producer and consumer goods into the hinterland. The economic integration of villages into the national economy leads to the diversification and enlargement of commercial and cultural transactions between the village and the outside world.

The force of these remarks is shown in our Factor analysis which indicates that 36 per cent of the total variance in transport and locational advantages is associated with the economic and social modernization Factor (Factor 1). This association may arise because larger, more commercialized villages have a greater effective demand for roads and therefore tend to be better served by transport facilities, or because better access to transport and towns itself constitutes an important modernizing force inducing more economic and cultural interaction with the rest of the economy. The effect of transport and location is also evident from the association in Factor 5 of relative isolation with higher dependence on agriculture. This association which accounts for only 10 per cent of variance is probably best explained by the relatively limited employment opportunities outside of agriculture in inaccessible villages.

Employment in Agriculture

Sixty-five per cent of the variance in agricultural employment is associated with the full set of 17 variables. Fifty-five per cent of this variance is associated with the components of Factor 5, which describe the nature of the agricultural base. It is not surprising that villages tend to specialize according to comparative advantage; those with better conditions for agriculture have more people engaged in agriculture.

The low statistical correlation between agricultural employment and Factor 1 is noteworthy. Apparently, the better located, highly commercialized, more technologically advanced villages do not differ significantly from their opposites with regard to the proportion of households engaged in agriculture. This lack of significant correlation between agricultural and other aspects of modernization is probably due to the relative infrequency of livelihood alternatives outside of agriculture. Although it is common for village households to supplement their agricultural income with subordinate occupations, these are usually not sufficiently remunerative to allow villages to move out of agriculture completely.

Land Per Capita

The amount of available land worked per capita is dependent on the quality of land. With low-level technology and a massive population, Indian villages are in a Malthusian and a Ricardian universe: population density varies directly with the capacity of land to produce subsistence requirements and the more inherently productive land is cultivated more intensively.

Land per capita has its greatest secondary loading in Factor 5 (16 per cent of variance), indicating a relationship between the amount of land available, the extent of employment in agriculture and the prevailing system of land tenure. These associations probably capture the results of an historical adjustment to subsistence production and to the absence of real economic alternatives that characterize traditional systems: economic and institutional arrangements in agriculture have adjusted to ecological and technological differences in the productivity of land.

Awareness of National Social Legislation

The extent of awareness of national social legislation is the only attitudinal characteristic we were able to include in our analysis. It is probably a proxy for other changes in attitudes which we were unable to capture with our data sources.

Twenty-six per cent of the variance in awareness of national social legislation is associated with variance in the economic development indicators of Factor 1. This interaction may arise either because the wider horizons represented in the attitudinal changes induce greater economic integration or because the transformations of the type represented in Factor 1, which tend to integrate the village into the larger economy, also tend to expand the desire for outside information.

Fifteen per cent of the variance in awareness of national social legislation (regarding untouchability) among villages is associated with the social change indicators of Factor 2. Villages in which a high proportion of the population is aware of national social legislation tend also to have a high percentage of nuclear families and a low incidence of child marriages. To some extent, therefore, change in attitudes and in social activities vary together. The limited interaction between them in our data suggests that changes in social modernization lag significantly behind changes in attitudes.

Another nine per cent of the variance in awareness of national social legislation is associated directly with income change in Factor 4. Differences in attitudes towards modernization and economic activity interact to some extent with actual incomes. Attitudes towards untouchability, which are reflected in this variable, may lead to differences in extent of observance of the traditional ritual constraints on economic occupations. These restrictions lead to a suboptimal distribution of factors of production, which on the average is reflected in somewhat lower incomes. Alternatively, causality may work in the opposite direction. Caste restrictions are in some sense a socio-religious mechanism for sharing unemployment and underemployment; prosperity permits a relaxation of these arrangements. Regardless of the direction of causality, however, the weakness of the association between income and strength of caste restrictions suggests the existence of long time lags in the mutual feedback process, or of little actual change in the potentially causal variable, or some combination of the two.

Education

Our variable indicating the extent of educational facilities and their effectiveness (as measured by adult literacy and per cent of school age children in school) associates most closely with economic and attitudinal modernization as summarized in Factor 1. An examination of the simple correlations of education with the variables in Factor 1 suggests, however, that this association arises primarily because large villages also tend to be better endowed with educational facilities rather than because of the association of education with the more dynamic economic and social variables.

There are also discernible associations between educational achievements and Factors other than the one to which it is assigned. The strongest (16 per cent) is a positive relationship with Factor 2, which suggests that social modernization is associated with attitudinal changes induced by education.

Family Household Type

In India, the traditional mode of family household organization is the extended family (three generations with or without collateral relatives living together). The literature on this point stresses that the extended household is an economic unit of peasants working cooperatively for subsistence and that the extended household tends to give way to the nuclear family household once cash earnings grow and alternative modes of employment emerge. Our analysis supports these views (see Factor 2). Where there are many nuclear households and infrequent child marriages, there is less land ownership and greater awareness of national social legislation.

Number of Castes

The fact that the number of castes has its highest loading in the economic modernization Factor is one indication of the influence of the caste system on economic progress in India. Since different castes are associated with different skills, a larger number of castes permits a greater division of labor and more occupational specialization. Because all castes are permitted to engage in agriculture, and the number of castes is correlated with the size of the village, a larger number of castes indicates the availability of a greater locally mobile pool of labor. This is an important matter because improved agricultural technology such as increased irrigation and the use of fertilizer requires greater labor inputs.

The number of castes present in a village is not simply a proxy for the size of population. The two variables have different signs in one of the five Factors, and the magnitude of their Factor loadings differ in the other three.

Proportion of Low Caste Households

The absence of systematic relationships between density of low caste households and Factors other than 3 implies that villages with a relatively large proportion of low caste households are neither better nor worse off than other villages with regard to income and other positive attributes of welfare and modernization. The probable reason for this is the greater geographic and occupational mobility of low caste households.

Membership in Cooperatives

It is noteworthy that the frequency of membership in cooperatives is associated only with Factor 3. Evidently, as of 1961, cooperatives had not yet contributed significantly to economic development and to social modernization. There are several possible explanations. The cooperative movement might have been too recent for its effects to be evident by 1961. It is also possible that the crude fact of membership in cooperatives is not in itself meaningful; that what is required instead is an indicator of the effectiveness of cooperatives. Rural cooperatives may not in themselves moreover, be sufficient to generate conditions for an agricultural transformation without strong supporting technical agricultural services, and without accessible markets for the product.[11] Most agricultural innovations require a set of several innovations introduced simultaneously: to use chemical fertilizer profitably requires more water and more labor to be employed per acre. Therefore, "threshold effects" are likely, with sharp and discrete improvements in productivity following the introduction of such a package of innovations, rather than a slow growth in productivity following the introduction of a single innovation. We cannot tell from our analysis whether the institution of cooperatives is inappropriate to conditions in India or whether there simply was not available in 1961 any significant quantity of improved seeds, chemical fertilizer, rural credit, etc., for cooperatives to acquire and disseminate to members.

Community Development Activities

The negative association between community development activity and income in Factor 4, which reflects the compensatory character of the program, also suggests that, as of 1961, community development efforts had not been very successful in raising village incomes. Many reasons could account for the ineffectiveness of this program. (1) The institution of community development may be inherently unsuited to inducing rural economic modernization in India; or (2) while the institution is, in principle, suitable, its implementation had been defective (the quality of extension agents was below par, the nature of technical support services was defective, the emphasis of the programs on

---

[11] Mellor et al., *Developing Rural India,* suggests that many cooperatives in India are ineffective.

physical accomplishments was misguided, etc.); or (3) the community development programs were operating below the threshold level of effectiveness (too few agents per farmer, too short a span of time for the effectiveness of their programs to manifest itself, too little credit to disburse at too high a cost, etc.); or (4) community development programs, to be effective, require complementary resources or activities which at the time were not available (profitable technologies, rural education, etc.). Intensive micro-research is required to decide which combination of these explanations is relevant.

CONCLUSION

The factor analysis of 17 variables relating to 108 villages in India is an attempt to identify the more important forces at the village level in economic development and cultural modernization.

India

Our data refer to rural India as of 1961 when deliberate policies of agricultural development and cultural modernization had just begun to have discernible effects. The differences between economically progressive and backward villages were largely the result of an historical adjustment to superior growing conditions and access to urban markets, rather than the result of recently initiated development programs.

Our factor analysis points up the importance of various economic forces to village modernization. Factor 1, which explains most of the intervillage variance, includes the extent of commercialization, the quality of agricultural technology and nearness to transport and cities. The importance of economic forces is shown also in the relationships between Factor 4 and the variables in Factor 1. These indicate that commercialization and improvements in agricultural technology, by 1961, had some effect on income although their effect was still overshadowed by the weight of history. Nevertheless, the economic associations in Factor 1 and 4 suggest that rural development policy in India can profitably be concerned with conventional economic programs—farm to market roads, agricultural extension services, the development of profitable technologies[12] and the fostering of commercial crops.

---

[12] This point is stressed by Mellor, who writes: "I would state that the most important feature of rural development policy should be policy con-

Giving up traditional social practices in village India seems to lag behind economic improvement and behind changes in social attitudes. Our indicators of social change (movement to nuclear households and decline in female child marriage) appeared in the second Factor, and accounted for only half as much variation among villages as the indicators of economic and cultural modernization in Factor 1. Economic improvement had not yet induced much social change. Indeed, economic incentives worked to keep the extended family together.

The influence of caste in our study appears in the awareness of social legislation prohibiting untouchability, in the number of castes per village, and in the per cent of village population composed of low castes. The factor analysis suggests that the weaker the caste system the higher the level of income and development, and that the income and modernization position of the untouchables are equivalent to those of other rural Indians: the simple correlation between per cent of low caste persons in a village and village income is .09!

There is evidence in our study that cooperatives and community development efforts had little positive effect on the rural economy as of 1961. These programs had very weak associations with rural economic modernization, commercialization, agricultural technology, and rural incomes.

The evidence on land reform is mixed. Types of land tenure do not appear to influence agricultural incomes or agricultural technology. There is, however, a significant association between larger farms and higher than average income per head.

In summary our study suggests that future prospects for rural development in India are mixed. On the one hand, there is evidence that rural modernization is responsive to economic policies such as improvements in farm to market roads, the dissemination of agricultural technology, and greater commercialization. On the other hand, such rural development policies encouraging co-operatives, community development blocks, and land reform seem ineffective. There is also evidence that the

---

cerned with generating highly profitable new technologies. One of the great problems with rural development in the periods to which your data refer is the lack of profitable technology available to villagers. In the late '60s we have begun to see some highly profitable new technologies coming out of research programs which were generated in an earlier period."

social transformation of rural India has barely begun, and that
the caste system and traditional attitudes continue to exercise a
retarding influence on economic modernization.

Micro-Development

Unlike parts of Africa and Oceania, village India contains peasantries with centuries of contact with commerce, cash, and colonial
administration. The larger culture and society in India included
centralized government, literacy, and cities; wide areas of common language and religion also mark off traditional peasant
India from tribal culture. The historical preparation of India for
modernization and development is therefore closer to that of
Europe and Japan than to Africa or New Guinea.

Although traditional peasantries have a headstart on tribal
societies, their problems and processes of village transformation
have much in common.

The more "traditional" is an Indian village community, the
more its economy resembles a pre-colonial village in Africa or
New Guinea. The constraints imposed by simple technology,
ecological dependence, physical and economic isolation (and
therefore smallness of scale) are similar. The self-sufficiency of
their subsistence economies represents a historical accommodation to the severe economic, technological and geographical conditions of life; villagers depend upon local ecology, technology,
and social organization for material survival. The extreme social
stratification of the caste system in India expresses the mutual dependence of villagers in securing livelihood. In Africa, similar ecological, technological, and economic conditions were coped with
principally through kinship arrangements or Chieftainship. Mutual dependence for survival there too ramified into all village
institutions: economy, religion, friendship, age-sets, family,
lineage, neighborhood; everyday life as well as ceremony reinforced it.

In India, population density, land tenure arrangements, agricultural technology, and family and caste have all adjusted to
superior ecological and locational advantages. Disparities among
villages in per capita income are not very large and are explained
primarily by differences in natural resource endowments. The
family and caste relationships evolved are risk-sharing devices
designed to distribute the proceeds of uncertain, low-income activities in a way which assures survival. Such adjustment of

economy to society remains intact only as long as agricultural technology remains static, and opportunities to earn livelihood outside of agriculture, are few.

The redirection of village communities away from activities and institutions designed for survival to those which make for income growth and cultural modernization poses a "dilemma of transition." The old systems of mutual dependence worked for untold centuries to keep people alive in conditions of harsh uncertainty, when drought or flood or the ravages of war meant hunger or worse. The activities and institutions which bring economic development and cultural modernization require and reward an entirely different underlying principle: dependence on impersonal transactions and institutions outside the village. These take the form of regional, national and international markets for village sales and purchases, and regional or national governments for the provision of technical and social services. The dilemma of the transition is how to contrive institutional devices to assure material security to peasants willing to undertake risky and expensive innovations, so that failure will not starve or impoverish them.

Our work suggests that the interaction between economic and social change during the process of transition occurs in the following fashion. First, economic and technological improvement tends to erode the material security rationale underlying the traditional social institutions such as caste and the joint family household. Economic modernization also tends to induce changes in social awareness and attitudes. Together these create a new perception of traditional social institutions, whose costs are now felt to outweigh their benefits. The eventual result is to change social institutions. The beginnings of such a sequence of change in India are discernible.

24 VICOS: A PEASANT HACIENDA COMMUNITY IN PERU

Allan R. Holmberg

PERU: THE HISTORICAL SETTING FOR CHANGE

FEW NATIONS of Latin America can point to a more ancient and distinguished cultural heritage than Peru, where the beginnings of civilization go back many centuries. The earliest remains show that more than 5,000 years ago the irrigated valleys of the desert coast—the "fertile crescent" of the New World—already supported settled and industrious populations. Gradually, as these valleys came to support larger and larger populations through the development of irrigation and agriculture, distinctive civilizations and even empires grew strong. Indeed, long before the arrival of the Spaniards, there were large and thriving urban centers in most of the oases of the desert coast. The city of Chan Chan for example, the capital of the Chimu empire, whose vast remains lie well preserved just outside the modern city of Trujillo, is estimated by archaeologists to have had a population of some 200,000 inhabitants.

Parallel developments were also taking place in the intermontane valleys of the Andes, as evidenced by the massive ruins of Chavín de Huántar, which lie on the east slopes of the Cordillera Blanca, in north-central Peru. In the first half of the fifteenth century, however, the situation changed drastically. A relatively small and well-organized group, now known as the Incas, who had previously been confined to a small region of mountain valleys in southern Peru, began a period of warlike expansion which, in less than a hundred years, established their

SOURCE: Allan R. Holmberg, "Changing Community Attitudes and Values in Peru: A Case Study in Guided Change," pages 63–107, in *Social Change in Latin America Today,* Random House, for the Council on Foreign Relations, 1960. Reprinted by permission of the Council on Foreign Relations.

rule from Ecuador in the north to Chile in the south, and from coast to jungle. The Inca empire had from six to eight million subjects within its domain, the richest and the most populous state in pre-Columbian America. Its capital, Cuzco, then a city of over 200,000 people, is a striking monument to the Incas' power and wealth.

After overthrowing this great Indian empire, the Spaniards, bent on exploiting Peru for the crown and themselves, gradually wrought profound changes in the patterns of life which they found there. Peru was stripped of much of its manpower and wealth, and Spanish colonial institutions were implanted firmly throughout the realm. The new rulers imposed a rigid class system, with a small Spanish elite at the top and a great mass of Indians at the bottom. The new landowners introduced a highly commercialized economic system based on the use of money and on competition in the international market, where no market had existed before, and they consolidated their power through the *encomienda,* or entail, and later through the *hacienda,* or plantation estate. By these changes the original population was reduced to a state of social and economic disrespect which persists to the present day. Both the empire of the Incas and that of the Spaniards were rigidly stratified along class lines. Thus, the concept of a natural and hierarchical ordering of society, based on an aristocratic tradition, has been an all-pervasive and dominant theme throughout the history of Peru. The masses of the people, whether Indian or *mestizo,* have been ruled by a small and dominant minority, often with an iron hand. No change that has yet occurred, unless it be the new technological revolution now taking place, has done much to alter this basic fact.

In spite of recent changes, Peru as a whole represents a fairly rigidly stratified social system. Out of a total population of over nine million people, more than three million are still classified as Indians. Most of them follow a way of life derived from the pre-Spanish era, modified, of course, by the aftereffects of colonial rule which assigned the Indians to the lowest status within the caste-like social structure. In this respect, the Andean countries, particularly Ecuador, Peru, and Bolivia, stand somewhat apart from the other nations of South America. Moreover, unlike Mexico and more recently Bolivia, Peru has undergone no sharp break with its traditional past in the form of a profound political and social revolution. In it, political power is still closely held and social changes are affecting the various segments of the people and the various regions of the country at widely differing rates of speed and impact.

THE GEOGRAPHICAL SETTING AND SOCIAL CHANGE

As a habitat for man, Peru has been abundantly blessed and mightily cursed by nature. It contains majestic mountains and fertile valleys, interspersed with barren wastes and impenetrable jungles. On one point there is substantial agreement. Peru is a land of fantastic geographic and climatic contrasts among and within its three principal geographic areas—the coast, the mountains, and the jungle.[1]

The coastal plain is a vast desert. Because of cold offshore currents in the Pacific, the prevailing westerly winds lose their moisture before they reach the shore, and the trade winds from the east discharge theirs before crossing the maritime range of the Andes. Consequently, that part of Peru lying between the coast and the higher peaks of the coastal range, a strip of about 1,400 miles in length and from 20 to 80 miles in width, is rainless the year around.

Nevertheless, the coast is the most important part of Peru, economically, socially, and politically. The Pacific offers ready access to the outside world while the Andes provide the rich, silt-bearing rivers which irrigate large, fan-like valleys of the desert coast and make this region the most productive agricultural area of Peru. Some forty or more of these valleys, divided by barren wastes of twenty to fifty miles in width, crisscross the coastal plain. For lack of water, however, only about 5 per cent of the desert coast, which in turn constitutes only about 10 per cent of the total area of the country, is actually under cultivation.

From the coastal plain, and sometimes directly from the sea, rises the Andean mountain chain, covering about 40 per cent of the total area. By almost any standards the Andes constitute a formidable barrier to human habitation and economic development, for the arable part, or *sierra,* consists of a series of inter-montane valleys, whose floors are at about 8,000 feet in altitude, overtowered by the high wall of the Andes. The even loftier

---

[1] For a useful review of geographic and demographic factors, see Ford (1955).

altiplanos, or high plains, at 12,000 feet or more, are suitable for little except grazing.

A third geographical area, the *montaña,* or jungle, covering about 50 per cent of the total area, encompasses the eastern foothills of the Andes and some parts of the Amazon flood plain. Belonging to the Amazon drainage basin, the whole area, potentially rich in natural resources, lacks both the communications and population necessary for its further development. It is the home of aboriginal tribes of the Amazon basin. Historically, this has been the least significant geographical area of Peru.

POPULATION DISTRIBUTION AND SOCIAL STRUCTURE

Peru is a nation of relatively unintegrated plural societies. The Quechua and Aymara Indians, for example, are but two examples of fragmented social communities, separated from each other and from the nation as a whole by geographic, linguistic, and cultural differences. More significant for our discussion are two major groupings, *mestizos* and Indians. The coast, which contains about 25 per cent of the total population, is almost exclusively a *mestizo* area; it is rapidly moving toward a commercial agricultural and industrial economy, with a mobile social structure founded on an essentially dynamic system of values. In many respects, it is not unlike some parts of the United States.

The inter-Andean valleys and the high plains of the mountain areas, on the other hand, contain a high percentage of Indians, as well as lower-class *mestizos;* this population lives by traditional subsistence farming, under a fairly rigid social structure founded on an essentially static and fixed system of values. Between these two worlds, *mestizo* and Indian, a rather sharp division of culture and outlook, which grew up during colonial times, persists down to the present day. In language, social and political organization, and values, the two groups, although dependent on each other, represent quite distinct modes of life. This fact constitutes one of the major dilemmas now faced by Peru in striving for national unity and social and economic progress—goals which are given constant lip service, at least, by middle-class policy-makers.

In Peru the distinction between *mestizos* and Indians is attributed in part to an imputed racial inferiority of the Indian, derived from colonial times. However, over the past four hundred years, the population has become pretty thoroughly mixed biologically. In Peru today, as in other "Indian" countries of Latin America, the assignment of an individual to the subordinate group is not determined primarily on the basis of physical characteristics such as skin color, as in the case of the Negro in the United States. It rests largely on a configuration of cultural characteristics, among which language, dress, and manners are most important. A person who speaks an Indian language, wears homespun dress, and chews coca will be classed as an Indian. If the same person speaks Spanish, wears Western dress and does not chew coca he may be classed—depending on other characteristics such as family name, occupation, education, and wealth—as either *mestizo* or white. In a biological sense, at least, Peru has no racial problem. Its so-called "racial" problem is largely a cultural one.

The problem of achieving a homogeneous national culture is further complicated by the factor of geographical and cultural regionalism. If there are sharp differences between coast and *sierra,* the same is also true of the inter-Andean valleys, which differ greatly in population and culture because of the barriers which the Andes pose to ready communication between them. Historically, this has resulted in a considerable proliferation of local differences in language and culture within both Indian and *mestizo* groups. Even within the two major Indian languages, Aymara and Quechua, the latter contains a number of mutually unintelligible dialects.

The wide span of cultural differences is reflected in and reinforced by the distribution of the *mestizo* and Indian populations. About 70 per cent of the total population of Peru is rural. On the other hand, Lima, with its port, Callao, is the only city of major commercial, industrial, and political importance. Other urban centers, with few exceptions, are little more than farming towns or mining centers. By and large, the *mestizos,* most of whom belong to the lower class, predominate in departmental, provincial, and district capitals of both the coast and the *sierra.* The Indian population, on the other hand, is concentrated on large *haciendas* or in so-called indigenous communities of the highlands, often isolated physically from the *mestizo* world. Of a total of about three million Indians in Peru, roughly one million live as landless *peones* on *haciendas,* one million as small but independent farmers in indigenous communities, and one million detached from the land as workers in mines and *mestizo* villages or as migrant laborers and servants. While most of the Indians live separated from the *mestizos* by caste barriers and physical isolation, the *hacienda* Indians probably occupy the lowest position, economically and socially, of all Indian groups. At the top of the status hierarchy, and centered on the coast, stands a very small upper-class elite which is considered white.

At least in part because of this hierarchical ordering of society, which has remained until recently in a kind of static equilibrium, the relations of the individual to the community and of the community to the nation are very different from those which are considered customary in the United States and in some other Latin American nations. Dependence and submission, rather than independence and freedom, characterize social relations within the community and these same themes tend to govern relations between the community and the nation. In other words, at one level the *mestizo* is *patrón* of the Indian; at another, the government is *patrón* of the community. 'The close holding of power, characteristic both of the *patrón-peón* system and of dictatorial governments, has tended to forestall and discourage any local initiative for change. Moreover, since many governments in Peru —like many *patrones* of *haciendas*—have often played far from beneficent roles, community attitudes toward government like those of *peón* toward *patrón,* have frequently been hostile and aggressive.

PRESENT TRENDS OF CHANGE

The traditional system is now being subjected to many inroads. Today there are few communities that have not been touched, however lightly, by the technological revolution. Coca-Cola, the tin can, penicillin, and even the wrist watch and radio have penetrated to the most remote *haciendas* of the Andes. More important, there has been going on a shift of political power from the landowning aristocracy of the older type to a more commercially minded *hacendado* and a new entrepreneurial class. This has been matched by a shift in ideology, away from the maintenance of the *status quo,* toward the demand for a more mobile society, one which can eventually provide sources of skilled labor and a solid market for manufactured goods. Industrialization, of course, has been responsible for most of these changes and demands.

For better or worse, however, the effects of these changes have thus far been confined largely to the coastal region—to the big-scale commercial *haciendas* and the urban centers. In the *sierra* changes are much less apparent. The coast has been and is the high-status area of Peru; Lima is the Mecca of prestige, power, and wealth. To gain stature in the social system, a Peruvian literally comes down from the heights of the Andes, he does not go up. Apart from a business venture or a week end in the mountain air, there is little movement of a permanent nature from coast to *sierra*. Such a shift can bring on not only physical *soroche* (mountain sickness), but "social *soroche*" as well. On the other hand, as a Peruvian comes down from the mountains and takes root in the coastal area, he not infrequently forgets all about the mountain valley where he grew up.

This raises what is perhaps Peru's most serious social issue. Frequently referred to as the "Indian problem," it might better be called the problem of the *sierra* or the mountain region as a whole, for it involves *mestizos* as well as Indians. The *sierra* is still the backbone of the Peruvian nation, almost as much as in Inca and colonial times. It contains Peru's major resources, natural and human.[2] Yet, by comparison with what the *sierra* has contributed and could contribute to the nation as a whole, it has received relatively little in return. Most of its wealth and its best manpower are siphoned off to the coast. In my opinion, until new attitudes toward the *sierra* are accepted both in the *sierra* and on the coast, particularly new attitudes toward the indigenous population, Peru is destined to remain a relatively "underdeveloped" nation.

Of course, many changes have recently been taking place in some types of *sierra* communities. Since the 1930's, and indeed even before that, an active program of road-building has greatly lessened the isolation of the highlands from the coast. It is possible now to go by car and truck to most *mestizo* towns and villages of the highlands, even though they are often cut off in the rainy season. Although trade has increased greatly between highlands and coast, most of the many changes that have followed have been technological, not social or ideological, in character. The

---

[2] I have not considered the *montaña,* or jungle, region because it is still largely unpopulated, and mass migrations to it are not likely to take place in the immediate future. Much capital will be needed to develop this area.

one exception has been the tenure of the APRA party.[3] Although APRA took important steps toward breaking the caste barriers, spreading power more widely, reforming the land system, and promoting higher standards of living and education among Indians and lower-class *mestizos,* it was overthrown before it could consolidate these gains. Since the failure to bring social change to the most numerous, isolated, and depressed groups, the processes of change have reverted to the traditional social channels and therefore are felt primarily in *mestizo* communities. The gap between social groups is widened in turn by the fact that influences coming from the coast to the highlands are carried there largely by *mestizos* who subscribe to upper-class values, among which "keeping the Indian in his place" ranks high. Consequently, Indian communities, particularly *hacienda* communities, have remained much the same.

One by-product of the growing contacts of *mestizo* highland villages with the coast deserves special mention. Increased geographical mobility has led many young *mestizos,* both men and women, to leave their *sierra* villages for greener pastures in urban centers and on the coast. In one such *mestizo* village a community study found relatively few people between sixteen and forty.[4] As no one is left except the Indians to do the work, *mestizo* villages in the *sierra* have come to depend more and more on the surrounding Indian population.

More and better roads have, of course, also had their effects on Indian villages. Though in the highlands most large *haciendas* and many Indian communities still lack roads to connect them with the highway system, they all have access to some market town which is tied in with it. Yet, the greatly increased geographical mobility of the Indians has had little effect on their highland communities. The explanation is not far to seek. It is possible, though not easy, for an Indian to move to the coast and become assimilated in *mestizo* society. Within the *sierra,* however, it is much more difficult for him to lose his identity as an Indian. Strong pressures operate within and between both castes, Indian and *mestizo,* to keep him in his place.

---

[3] Alianza Popular Revolucionaria Americana, the party headed by Victor Raúl Haya de la Torre; the latter has recently been in Peru again after a long period of exile.

[4] See Humberto Ghersi, *El indigena y el mestizo en la communidad de Marcara,* Ph.D. thesis, University of San Marcos, Lima, 1954.

Frequently an Indian who has lived on the coast as a worker or a soldier, has enjoyed a higher standard of living and a period of freedom from the rigid pattern of village custom, and has learned Spanish and adopted new values and attitudes, finds himself in a situation of considerable conflict when he returns to his highland village. He is no longer satisfied to conform to Indian standards, yet he is not accepted by *mestizo* society. Within his Indian community, where standing is based on age and wealth, he finds no channels through which to express his coast-acquired enlightenment and skills. Within *mestizo* society, where prestige is based largely on descent, he is again assigned to the lower caste.

What can the "displaced" Indian do? He can go native again, sometimes under worse conditions than before because pressure on the land has been mounting. He can return to the coast. There, because of increased immigration and the lag in economic development, opportunities for employment better than he can find in the highlands have been steadily falling behind the growing demand. As a result, while individual Indians are being increasingly assimilated into the national society, the communities from which they come remain much the same. This situation is likely to prevail unaltered until some direct attack is made on the traditional caste structure. Only then will it be possible to foster social and cultural change among the Indian population in their own villages.

Perhaps the greatest barrier to any change in this social system is the persistence in the *sierra* of an outmoded but powerful institution, the *haciendas* or latifundia. In many respects this institution, which governs the lives of more than one million Indians, does not differ substantially from what it was in Spain of the Middle Ages. Yet, there is encouraging evidence that, where Indians live under conditions of greater independence and freedom as they do in indigenous non-*hacienda* communities, changes in attitudes, values, and behavior are occurring at a faster rate. In many non-*hacienda* villages, which have owned their own lands from pre-Columbian times and have enjoyed a large measure of local autonomy, the spirit of community solidarity and cooperation is fairly strong.

This does not hold true for the *haciendas,* in which the individual's sense of responsibility to the group and the continuity of effective local leadership were largely destroyed under the colonial regime. In terms of fostering a modern and even democratic development, the non-landlord Indian communities do not present nearly as great or as many problems as do the *haciendas* or the *mestizo* villages, for their built-in traditions of responsible local leadership enable them to act as a group. When they feel threatened by the outside world, they can defend themselves jointly against it; when attracted by it, they have group mechanisms for adjusting to the desired change.[5] This is in sharp contrast to the *hacienda* system where the *patrón* alone holds the reins of power and where his interests are strongly opposed to those of the group, or even to *mestizo* villages over which the national administration exerts a centralized control, sometimes with a very strong hand.

In order to catch up with the modern world, Peru must break the chain of dependency relationships that bind all levels of the present social structure. Both the caste structure of the society and the latifundia system of the *sierra* are destined to disappear. In fact, they are already doomed. The question is whether they will disappear in a fairly gradual and orderly manner, as has happened in many parts of the coast, or whether this change will take place suddenly and by more drastic means, as in Mexico and Bolivia.

Present trends indicate that Peru may succeed in gradually assimilating the Indian and other depressed populations into the

---

[5] Perhaps a note of caution should be injected at this point. There exists in Peru and abroad a somewhat distorted image of the indigenous peoples of the Andes as fundamentally cooperative and among whom the group spirit runs high. In this view, some four hundred years of harsh and brutal exposure to the outside world have done little to upset the collectivistic patterns which were a heritage of pre-Columbian times. The evidence usually cited is that over one million Indians still live in "indigenous communities" where they share and share alike, and that even on *haciendas* cooperative patterns are the rule. Actually this is not so. Present research indicates that, while it is true that the indigenous populations are united to a man when it comes to defending the group against the outside world, for example against an encroachment upon their lands, internally they are little influenced by a spirit of group loyalty or altruism. Individualism runs high in most indigenous communities, particularly in *haciendas*. Social responsibilities seldom extend beyond immediate kinship groups. For this reason, it is likely that the differential distribution of such values as power and wealth is as marked in most Indian communities as in the population at large. This appears to be the case at least in most areas where modern research has been carried out.

wider national community by peaceful means if the government
continues a policy of giving more and more active encouragement
to the *sierra* in education, health, and economic development. If
these policies are not continued and strengthened, there may well
arise a pan-Indian or pan-peasant movement, as in Bolivia, which
would usurp the power of government and initiate drastic reform.
In this connection, it is significant that in Peru the strongest
center of Communist activity is in Cuzco, the former capital of
the Inca empire.

PERU'S INDIAN PROBLEM

Valiant efforts have been made and are being made by the
national government, as well as by international and private
agencies operating in Peru, to offset the dangers of the unbalanced development of some regions to the neglect of others.
The *sierra* has long been recognized as a problem, and the
montaña has been pictured, quite unrealistically, as a future paradise. Yet, both the financial resources available and the training
of the people have been sadly inadequate to foster the industrial
development of any but the coastal regions, with the exception
of some mining areas, which, however, contain a relatively small
part of the total population.

It has been relatively easy to modernize and industrialize the
large *haciendas* of the coast. As a result of the improved standards
of living and education, the people of this area have largely
assimilated the values of a modern industrial society, at least
to a point where they can now move ahead under their own
steam as rapidly as economic factors will permit. The plain fact
of the matter is, however, that the coast does not have the immediate economic potential to absorb the accelerating migrations
from the *sierra* that have been taking place in recent years. Both
the push exerted by pressure on land in the *sierra* and the pull
of the positive attractions of the coast, with its higher wages and
better standards of living, have created an unbalanced type of
development within Peru as a whole, a situation that gives rise to
great concern. So grave has this problem become, in fact, that a
few years ago the national congress gave serious thought to
prohibiting further migrations from the highlands to the coast.
However unrealistic this attempt at a solution would be, policy-
makers have come increasingly to recognize that, if Peru is to

achieve any kind of integrated development as a nation, more attention must be paid to the neglected areas, the highlands and the jungle.

Peru's basic problems in developing its vast jungle areas are going to be technical and economic in character. What they need above all is more people and more capital. Given the economic situation of Peru, these are not likely to be supplied in the directly foreseeable future. The *sierra* also suffers from overpopulation, as well as from a lack of capital, but in addition its people are poorly equipped to face the stresses of adjusting rapidly to the industrial influences exerted by the coast. Herein lie difficulties of the greatest magnitude. Recent governments, it is true, have recognized that the maldistribution of population cannot be solved solely through migration to the coast. Through encouraging private investment in the overpopulated *sierra*, backed by the state-owned Santa Corporation, the Peruvian government is trying to create many new jobs in the valleys of the *sierra*, especially in processing locally produced commodities and in small-scale industries.

Nevertheless, the success of new developments in industry and agriculture in the mountain areas will depend primarily on the ability of the Indian and *mestizo* subsistence farmers, often landless, to make a reasonably satisfactory adjustment to a new way of life based on commercial agriculture and industry. Now living under the domination of whites and *mestizos,* the Indians are too poor to buy land, even when it comes on the market, and the land on which they live has been steadily declining in fertility. In many instances, they are obliged to work off tenant obligations without pay. They are badly undernourished and are without health and educational facilities. Many are victims of coca and alcohol.

These and other frustrating conditions have combined to produce in the Indian communities deep-seated attitudes of distrust, fear, suspicion, and even hate toward the outside world. Precisely because of these attitudes, they have so far resisted and are likely to go on resisting the halfhearted, piecemeal, unintegrated attempts at modernization which have been initiated thus far by more "enlightened" *hacendados* and industrialists or by the Peruvian government. The plain fact is that social and economic conditions among the highland populations, especially the Indians, have reached such an alarming state that only a large-scale and well-coordinated effort to promote change can enable them to find a place in the modern world, by making them a productive force in an emerging democratic society.

Studies that have been made of highland communities in Peru clearly support the logic of undertaking a broad and integrated approach to change among the Indians. In fact, this is the only approach with much promise of winning enthusiastic acceptance among the Indians. Beneath a profoundly pessimistic outlook on life, derived from long experience, they feel strongly the need for, and desire, drastic changes in many aspects of their present mode of life. Fortunately, they are not completely apathetic to the broader outside world, nor to the hope that they may soon be given an opportunity to improve their lot within the nation. This hope is clearly reflected in the vigor with which they occasionally defend what few rights they now possess and by the diligence, dignity, and pride with which they assume obligations of leadership and responsibility in their own society. It is likely that, given opportunities to develop a more progressive and optimistic outlook on the world, the Indians will adjust fairly rapidly to modern conditions and will assume a productive and responsible place in Peruvian national life. Actually, the hope of the Andean countries, not only Peru but Bolivia and Ecuador as well, lies in the mountain regions with their masses of hard-working peasants. It is no less true, however, that, unless the Indian populations are increasingly provided with opportunities and assistance in changing their way of life and improving their lot markedly, present conditions of unrest and dissatisfaction can lead to more and bloodier revolutions, as has happened in Bolivia, or, at the least, to extreme and continuing conflicts in the process of their adjustment to modern life.

A PILOT ATTEMPT AT SOCIAL CHANGE[6]

To document the problems and potentials of social change among the Indians of Peru, it may be helpful to review one current attempt to incorporate a community of *hacienda* Indians into a more modern way of life, one which will also be in keeping with the *sierra* environment. In 1952, in collaboration with the In-

---

[6] Some of the findings have been treated elsewhere. See Holmberg (1955), and Whyte and Holmberg (1956).

digenous Institute of Peru and with the support of the Peruvian government, Cornell University undertook a systematic program of research and development in order to determine how an Indian population would respond to a concerted effort to introduce it to a more modern way of life. The community selected was Vicos, a *hacienda* situated in an inter-Andean valley, Callejón de Huaylas, about 250 miles northeast of Lima. Known for its conservatism and its hostility to the outside world until 1952, this *hacienda* had undergone little change since it was first established in the colonial period, over four hundred years ago.

Surrounded by snow-capped peaks, some of which rise to over 20,000 feet, the *hacienda* of Vicos has a land area of about 35,000 acres, of which some 7,000 are now under cultivation or are used for grazing. It is rocky and hilly, with elevations of about 9,000 to 14,000 feet. The lower slopes of the *hacienda* are used principally for farming, the most important crops being maize, potatoes, barley, wheat, beans, and quinoa. The higher slopes are utilized solely for pasturing animals, particularly cattle and sheep.

Like some two or three hundred similar properties, Vicos belongs to the state and until recently was leased out to the highest bidder at public auctions held every ten years. Attached to the land, but owning none of it, were some 1,850 Quechua-speaking Indians, in over three hundred families, most of whom live on small and scattered subsistence farmsteads on the lower slopes of the *hacienda,* constituting roughly 90 per cent of the arable land. The remaining 10 per cent of the land, or about five hundred acres, was formerly farmed for commercial purposes by the lessee of the *hacienda.* The necessary Indian labor was supplied without charge, except for a small gratuity to buy coca. By custom one adult member of each household was obligated to pay a labor tax of three days each week to the *hacienda* in return for the right to occupy a small plot of land supposedly sufficient to support his family. In addition to the labor tax, which also involved the unpaid use of the Indians' domestic animals, the *peones* were obligated by turn to supply the *hacienda* and its employees with certain free services as cooks, grooms, watchmen, shepherds, and servants. For failing to fulfill these obligations a *peón* could be dispossessed of his tools, his animals, or his plot of land.

Until the Cornell group assumed responsibility for the administration and development of Vicos, power—economic, political, and judicial—was completely concentrated in the hands of a single individual, the *patrón*. Thus the fate of each *peón* depended almost completely upon him. Theoretically, he held control of all the lands of the *hacienda* and of all of the people living within its boundaries. In this respect the *patrón* was not unlike a feudal baron. Actually, about the only area of life on which his authority did not impinge was that of religion, for which the parish priest and Indian officials were responsible. This does not mean that the Indian community had no organization of its own. A local mayor, who also appointed a number of assistants, was selected annually by a process which may be loosely termed an election. But the responsibility and authority of these village officials did not go much beyond the conduct of religious life within the community. They had little or nothing to say in matters of secular concern, which remained exclusively the province of the *patrón*.

As a result, positions of responsibility in public affairs were lacking in the life of Vicos, adequate leadership did not develop, almost no public services were maintained, and the community was in a highly disorganized state. Apart from alliances with immediate kinship groups and a common devotion to religious practices, particularly the *fiesta* of the local saint, there were almost no values that were widely shared among the members of the Vicos community. At the same time standards of living were at a bare minimum.[7] Health and nutritional levels were extremely low.[8] Educational facilities and consequently skills were

---

[7] Surveys indicate that the differential distribution of the lands among the Indian population at Vicos was very great. Many families held less than an acre while others farmed as much as thirty or forty acres. The per capita distribution of crop land among the Indian population is about an acre, at least one-half of which is on rocky and upland soil. Cited from an unpublished manuscript by Robert Stevens of Cornell University on agricultural production on the Hacienda Vicos, 1954.

[8] Recent studies by Dr Carlos Collazos and collaborators (1953) indicate that the Indians of Vicos have a per capita consumption of about 1,500 calories per day. This is only about 70 per cent of the recommended minimum for reasonably good health. In addition to caloric deficiency, nutrition surveys indicate that the Indians have an extremely low intake of calcium and vitamin A. All families at Vicos consumed less than 75 per cent of the recommended amounts.

On some aspects of health in the highlands of Peru, see E. H. Payne, L. Gonzáles-Mugaburu, and E. M. Schleicher, "An Intestinal Parasite Survey in the High Cordilleras of Peru," *American Journal of Tropical*

almost completely lacking. Cooperation within the community was the exception rather than the rule, and resistance to the outside world was high. Attitudes toward life were static and pessimistic. Such, in fact, were the conditions prevailing among the Indian population of Vicos when the Cornell group assumed control. Similar conditions are found on many *haciendas* and in many Indian communities of the highlands.[9]

Changing this state of affairs, without a large investment of resources or without a revolution, would seem at first glance to be an almost insoluble problem. To be sure, it was and still is no easy task. Yet it is not as hopeless as it might seem. In the case of Vicos, at any rate, it has been possible, on the basis of careful studies carried out in advance of initiating any action, to design a modest program of technical assistance and education which has gained fairly wide acceptance and has helped to awaken most members of the community to new opportunities for improving their lot through their own efforts. I must again stress, however, that only a broad and integrated approach to problems of development made it possible to reach the desired goals of higher standards of living, social respect, and a self-reliant and enlightened community which can eventually take responsibility for the direction of its own affairs as a functioning part of the nation. Under this approach, every effort was made to tackle each problem in terms of understanding and respecting the local culture, the only basis on which lasting changes can be understood by the community as desirable and can be accepted by it.

From the beginning the Vicos project has been conducted with a minimum of outside personnel and funds.[10] Except for

---

Medicine and Hygiene, July 1956, pp. 696–698. These investigators found a very high rate of such parasites as pinworm, roundworm, and amoebic dysentery on the Hacienda Vicos and in other communities of Callejón de Huaylas. Recent investigations at Vicos by Dr. Marshall Newman of the Smithsonian Institution indicate, however, that Indians have a very low rate of heart disease and high blood pressure, characteristic of modern civilization (personal communication).

[9] See, for example, William W. Stein, *Hualcan: An Andean Indian Estancia*, Ph.D. thesis, Cornell University, Ithaca, N.Y., 1955.

[10] Most of the funds for research and development at Vicos have been provided by grants from the Carnegie Corporation of New York to Cornell University. In addition, the author has received special research funds from the Wenner-Gren Foundation for Anthropological Research, Inc., and the Social Science Research Council. The Peruvian government has also been most generous in its support of the project and in supplying

graduate students engaged exclusively in research, and agencies of the Peruvian government normally operating in the area, not more than two North Americans and two Peruvians have at any time been concerned directly with the administrative and developmental aspects of the Vicos program.

On the basis of preliminary anthropological and technical studies and after consultation with the residents of the *hacienda* concerning their needs and hopes, it was possible to initiate a unified program of change centered on three major areas of development: economics and technology, nutrition and health, and education. To these should be added a fourth area, that of social organization, although, because of the deeply ingrained nature of the *hacienda* system, it was neither desirable nor feasible to move rapidly in this area at the outset. In all these areas of activity some people in Vicos felt the need for improvement; hence, they were responsive to suggestions for innovation. In fact, these were also areas in which change was absolutely necessary if the research and development program was to reach its two fundamental goals: changing the initial and predicted image of the project members from one of hostile *patrones* to that of friendly consultants and observers; and developing within the community independent and dynamic problem-solving and decision-making organizations which could gradually assume the responsibilities of leadership in public affairs in a rational and humane manner and along democratc lines.

To promote movement toward these general ends, the project leaders designed a great many specific steps. In the first place, many of the abuses under the traditional *hacienda* system could be eliminated from the very start. Interviews with a large sample of villagers showed, for example, that the obligations which were most irksome to the Indians were not, as might be expected, the three-day labor service which they rendered for the right to use their plots of land. They were, rather, the additional unrecompensed services they had to provide to the *hacienda* and its employees. Under previous administrations, for example, a man

───────────────────────────────
technical and scientific personnel. Particular thanks are due to the following people, all of whom at one time or another have been associated with the Cornell-Peru project: Dr. Carlos Monge M., president of the Indigenous Institute of Peru and co-director of the project; Dr. William C. Blanchard, Dr. Humberto Ghersi, Sr. Enrique Luna, Dr. William Mangin, Miss Joan Snyder, and Dr. Mario Vázquez.

might suddenly be called out for a tour of duty as a shepherd for the *hacienda,* or a woman as a cook, just when their services were most urgently needed at home. In such matters abuses had apparently been frequent in the past and feelings in the community ran high. Under a more enlightened approach it proved possible to abolish these free services and to hire paid employees, training them to assume a genuine responsibility for their new jobs. One example will illustrate the kind of change that was introduced.

On the upper part of the *hacienda* is a large grazing area known as the Quebrada Honda. This is a glaciated canyon which provides the only route to other valleys across the mountains from Vicos. Here both the *patrón* and the Indians traditionally grazed their cattle. The canyon served also as a public trail, and since distances were great it was customary for pack trains coming to and from a mining area over the passes (a three-day journey) to spend at least one night in the Quebrada Honda. For the right to pasture their animals there, muleteers were required to pay a small fee to the *hacienda,* and the collection point was at the narrow mouth of the canyon, which also served as a check point to prevent the theft of cattle. Traditionally, *peones* had to perform a period of free duty at this post, but, since this gave them no rewards, abuses were rife. "Deals" were made with muleteers; cattle were stolen; and animals were allowed to despoil fields. All this caused considerable loss to the *hacienda* and to the Indians themselves, much more than was gained by the tax. Simply by placing at the check point an Indian employee who then received the toll as his income, it was possible to reduce this loss to a minimum. Actually it resulted in a saving for the *hacienda* and for the Indians as well.

In addition to eliminating the worse direct abuses of the *hacienda* system, it was necessary to take positive steps toward solving other problems, first of all in the sphere of economic life. Unless the output of the Indian households and the *hacienda* fields could be raised substantially, it would not be possible to support the institutions necessary for the adjustment of Vicos to modern life except on a welfare or gift basis, and this is not a likely prospect in Peru, considering the state of its economy and the nature of its power structure. Nor would a welfare approach lead to a solid type of development, rooted in the desires and responsibilities of the community itself.

In the area of economic activity positive steps could be and were taken, for the desire to improve the community's livelihood existed, at least in a dormant state. Wealth is held in high esteem in the Indian community. Unlike *mestizo* communities, in it the genealogical factor is of little or no significance in assigning positions of prestige in the social structure. To accumulate wealth in an agrarian society like Vicos, however, the peasant must work hard and also be frugal. It is through physical labor that he gains dignity and it is through frugality that he accumulates wealth. These values, too, contrast sharply with those of *mestizo* society, in which people go to extreme limits to avoid the indignity of physical labor and attach a high value to conspicuous consumption.

This does not mean that an Indian is willing to labor long and well under all conditions. In most instances he will do so only when he is working for himself or within his own culture. When working outside this framework, under conditions in which he is held in disrespect and generally receives little in the way of reward, he usually tries to get by with as little effort as he can. This was true under the traditional *hacienda* system at Vicos, and labor productivity was much lower on *hacienda* fields than on the Indians' individual plots. As economic rewards to the Indians have increased, as well as their self-respect, the improved productivity has more than offset the cost of the additional investments required.

Today, the "miracles" of modern science make it possible to increase agricultural output sharply, even in the steep and rock-strewn fields of the Andes, as has been proved at Vicos. Poor soil was not the only factor responsible. Seed had degenerated; inherited techniques, such as row spacing, were outmoded; adequate fertilizers were unavailable; the use of insecticides against plant diseases was unheard of. The motto at Vicos was, as it still is in most of the mountain areas of Peru, "plant and pray"— a formula that has not always produced very good crops.

At just about the time the Cornell-Peru project was being launched at Vicos, the potato crop, the Indians' mainstay, had failed because of a blight which affected the entire region. On the basis of good technical advice,[11] it was found not only that

---

[11] Supplied by the Servicio Cooperativo Interamericano de Producción de Alimentos, a branch of the Institute of Inter-American Affairs.

this blight could readily be controlled but that the potato crop could be greatly increased by following a few simple rules: adequate preparation and fertilizing of the soil; healthy and disinfected seed; proper weeding and cultivation; and periodic spraying with insecticides. Presented with this formula for increasing their potato yields, the Indians did not immediately scramble to adopt the practices suggested. Many were too poor to purchase the necessary supplies. Others had no land to plant. Still others— in fact, most of the people, including local Indian leaders—were suspicious of any advice or aid that came from the outside.

In the end, the Cornell project worked out a plan by which the Indians could buy the necessary supplies on credit, paying it off at the end of the season with a share of the crop. This arrangement was sufficiently attractive to a small group of Indian families so that some new agricultural practices were at least initiated within the community. Actually, yields of healthy potatoes more than doubled the first year, with the dramatic result that the new practices were adopted by almost all Indian families within the next two years. Today it is almost impossible to find anyone who plants by the old traditional methods. Since then, it should be added, Vicos has become the largest producer of potatoes in the region; yields have increased, in some instances as much as 400 per cent. In short, potatoes, in addition to serving as a main subsistence item, have also become a commercial crop, providing Indian families with much-needed cash to buy other necessities.[12]

This is simply one example of what can be done through a bootstrap operation to raise both the economic level of the Indian household and the production of food. When we examine the important increases in food production which can be brought about in Peru and elsewhere through the patient and careful introduction of more modern methods, the *sierra* of Peru no longer stands out as the area of poor resources that it has always been considered. The Vicos experience indicates so far that dramatic results can be achieved at a relatively small cost. They can

---

[12] A full account of this experiment can be found in Mario Vázquez, *A Study of Technological Change in Vicos, Peru*, M.A. thesis, Cornell University, Ithaca, N.Y., 1955. In 1958, the community of Vicos sold 262,000 kilograms of potatoes on the Lima market and with the profits made a substantial down payment on the purchase of the *hacienda* lands. In addition, it is now conducting its own Point Four program in several other communities, to pass on the improved techniques to its neighbors.

be attained, however, only if careful attention is given, not only
to the problem of modern techniques, but also to the people and
their culture. For this reason, from the very start the Cornell-
Peru project has given careful thought to the problem of developing a spirit of independence, responsibility, and leadership
in community affairs—a spirit that had never existed before except in the sphere of religious life.

TOWARD NEW COMMUNITY LEADERSHIP

When the Cornell-Peru project first assumed control at Vicos,
the making of decisions in most matters of secular concern was
almost wholly vested in one individual, the *patrón,* who was not
a member of the Indian community. On the *hacienda* the direct
supervision of work was in the hands of six Indian leaders or
foremen, called *mayorales,* traditionally appointed by the *patrón.*
Although selected to represent the *patrón's* interest, they were
also people of status in the community at large, particularly in
those districts from which they came and in which they had direct
supervision of the labor force. Most of them had previously
occupied important positions in the politico-religious hierarchy
of the Indian community through which prestige and power are
gained. All of them were old men, hence highly respected in the
traditional community.

The project was concerned with transferring power to the community, not with retaining it, as in the traditional *hacienda* system.
As a first step, it was necessary to establish some local group,
as representative as possible, with which it could share the power
of making decisions. Because of their knowledge, experience,
and prestige, the body of *mayorales* was selected to assist the
project in directing the economic and social affairs of the *hacienda,* for example, in settling conflicts over land and cattle. As
this group developed greater skill, more and more responsibility
was delegated to it. The project leaders met in weekly session
with these six men; with friendly guidance and encouragement,
they soon began to take a perspective somewhat broader than
their original vested-interest or "dog-eat-dog" outlook on *hacienda* and community affairs. In addition to these sessions, all
decisions made by this group were discussed with the labor force
as a whole so that necessary modifications could be made in the
interests of the community at large.

'Through the use of these and similar methods, together with positive advice and assistance in matters of economic development and social respect, of health and education for all members of the community, the way was cleared to promote better understanding and greater self-reliance and to seek out reasonable solutions to community problems. Over several years a number of groups have been organized and trained to assume creative leadership in various aspects of life, including economic development, nutrition and health, education, and political affairs. These groups gradually learned to assume more and more responsibility for community affairs and developed a growing ability to work together without serious frictions. Finally, in 1957, when the project had prepared the ground for giving up its control of the *hacienda,* that control could then be transferred completely to an elected body of proven leaders. The Vicosinos had come of age, not without turmoil and strain.

NEW GOALS IN EDUCATION AND HEALTH

Perhaps the most significant change that has occurred at Vicos is that education for the children and for the villagers has now become both a possibility and a goal. In the whole process of changing practices and perspectives within this peasant community, education and enlightenment have played the key role. It was assumed from the very beginning of the project that, without a carefully designed program of education, both formal and informal, it would be impossible either to establish or perpetuate whatever changes were proposed, in ways of work or of thinking. For this reason a basic rule in the Vicos experiment has been to find out first what the community aspired to achieve and then, through the formation or strengthening of local groups, as in the case of the *mayorales,* to place these goals in a broader setting, so that in achieving them the community would also be building a body of knowledge, skills, and attitudes which would in turn foster in it a solid and self-reliant growth. In the long run this kind of growth can only take place through education in the broad sense of the word.

Something of the educational problem in the *sierra,* as well as the significance of education for the future development of the Indians of Peru, can be gleaned from a brief review of the Vicos experience. When a member of the Cornell-Peru project first came to study Vicos in 1949, he found that a primary school had already been in operation for the past nine years. Yet he was unable to find a single child of primary-school age who could read or write, either in Spanish or in his own tongue. A little Spanish was spoken by a mere handful of young men, most of it learned during their army service.

On investigation, the reasons for this situation soon became apparent. For one thing, under the traditional *hacienda* system, no support was given by the owner to education. *Hacienda patrones* were concerned not with developing an enlightened population but with maintaining the *status quo*. For them, children were a source of unskilled labor which might be lost once they were given the opportunity to learn new skills and acquire new values.

In the second place, the parents of the children resisted the idea of providing an education for their children. To a certain extent this was attributable to defects in the national educational system as well as to the conditions in which it functioned under the traditional *hacienda* system. In Peru, Indian villages such as Vicos are frequently supplied with unprepared and ineffective teachers who are not qualified for a teaching post in an urban center. Conversely, such teachers often seek appointments to Indian areas in order to retain their professional status as teachers. Even if the teachers are conscientious in their efforts, they frequently come into conflict with *patrones* and are not given any facilities to live and work. More often, perhaps, being *mestizos,* they share the prejudices of the outside world and thus tend to treat Indian children as inferior and put them to work as servants and gardeners instead of teaching them badly needed skills. An Indian parent who observes these abuses—and they occur frequently—sees no reason to send his children to school, particularly when their labor is badly needed at home.

At Vicos, the teaching post and facilities were so inadequate that only the poorest teachers accepted an appointment there. The children who actually attended school had to sit on the ground in an outside and drafty corridor of a crumbling adobe building where the teacher herself lived in poverty and misery. In any single year the total school population had never exceeded fifteen to twenty pupils out of a possible 350, and none of them had ever had more than a year or two of the poorest possible training. Moreover, it was almost unheard of to send a girl to school. No wonder the process of learning was not highly valued! In the traditional *hacienda* system there was simply no place or need for education, as can be clearly seen by the following figures on the state of education at Vicos in the latter part of 1951:

Had not gone to school	1,576
Were going at the time	36
Could read and write (very poorly)	5

It may be added that of the 36 pupils then at school many had been encouraged in this by the influence of the Cornell-Peru project, which had only recently been initiated.

The first efforts at education, in any formal sense, were directed toward improving the facilities and training available for children as well as for younger adults. First, the leaders of the project had to win some measure of confidence within the community, largely through the visible rewards of economic progress and through the spirit of mutual respect fostered by sharing the making of decisions. Only then did they begin holding numerous meetings with parents, Indian leaders, and teachers to discuss the building of a school which would be adequate to provide at least a primary education for all children of the community. At the same time, abuses in the old system, such as absenteeism of teachers and the use of pupils as servants, were abolished. New rewards for good attendance were provided. Since many children had to come from as far away as a half-hour on foot, a school lunch program was initiated to provide better nutrition. Since many of the Indian families were desperately poor, this in itself may have provided the primary stimulus for more than tripling the school population after the first year of the lunch program.

Other means of support for schooling were found gradually. The Ministry of Education sent more and better teachers. The community set about building a new schoolhouse. By the end of the second year, the first wing of a modern school had been finished. By the end of the third year, a second wing was being built, including a spacious auditorium which is now used also for community functions.

All labor for this development, and a large part of the material, much of it made locally, were provided by members of the Indian community, organized, supervised, and trained by project personnel. Many new building skills were thus added to the occupational inventory of the community. One assumption that we made in planning the project was that, unless most members of the community made some contribution to the construction of the new school, few of them would have any interest in putting it to use. 'The more members who pitched in to help build it, the more who would feel entitled to a return on their investment in the form of sending their children to school. This assumption was borne out, as shown in the records of school attendance from 1951 to 1957:

Year	School Attendance	Number of Teachers
1951	14–18	1
1952	30–35	2
1953	35–60	2
1954	85–90	3
1955	110–120	5
1956	180–190	7
1957	200–250	7

By 1958 over 250 pupils were registered in the school, and the number of teachers had increased to eight.

In Vicos there are actually two schools in operation, one for girls and one for boys. Although the ratio of boys to girls is still about three to one, nevertheless a large proportion of both boys and girls have had several years of continuity in their education, a thing which was previously almost unheard of. The classification of the school has also been changed. Starting at a primary level, it has been raised to a pre-industrial category. This means that technical training is provided in agriculture and the industrial arts, in addition to the regular curriculum of Peruvian primary schools. An adult education program has also been initiated through which younger adults are rapidly becoming literate and acquiring useful skills needed for providing a more enlightened leadership in the direction of community affairs. In 1957, a *núcleo escolar,* a kind of central school, was formed at Vicos, which also provides educational services to nearby communities.

In terms of the future, one of the most important results of the program at Vicos is that the educational process is becoming a fully accepted value within the community. One index of this is the change which has been taking place in the parents' own behavior and attitudes. Not only are they sending their children to school increasingly, in some instances at a considerable sacrifice, but they are growing prouder of their children's attainments. I remember well one father who pointed with great pride to a letter he had just received in the handwriting of his own son, who had been to school at Vicos and was then on a vacation visit to another part of the country. Previously all such letters had been written by scribes.

The parents have shown in still other ways their changed attitude toward education. They are attending school events in steadily increasing numbers, until the graduation exercises have become a kind of secular *fiesta*. A few parents have taken responsibility for helping the teachers stimulate a wider interest in education throughout the community. There has been some success in forming a committee of parents and teachers for maintaining and improving school facilities. While the school has been transferred to the jurisdiction of the Ministry of Education, the responsibility for running and improving it is entirely in the hands of the community.

The acceptance of education as a value is also reflected in the behavior of the school children at Vicos. In many instances the acquiring of skills has enabled them to enjoy new prestige at home and to compete successfully in the outside world. This in turn has led to an increasingly optimistic outlook on life and on their prospects for the future. Perhaps more than any other aspect of the Vicos program, the school has become a symbol of progress and of hope for the future. As it happens, no other community of the region, and few rural communities anywhere in Peru, can boast of comparable educational facilities. These accomplishments—and they have for the most part been self-made —have rightly become a source of pride to the Vicosinos and of envy and respect by their neighbors. The Peruvian government has done much (even though it has only made a start) to encourage these developments. If they are continued on a much larger scale in the *sierra*, Peru will soon obtain its reward in the form of enlightened and responsible citizens who will make positive contributions to the national life.

One further area of development to which our pilot project gave special attention is that of health. Some indication has been given (footnote 8, p. 532) of the low levels of health and nutrition that prevailed in Vicos when the project began; and the age-old habit of coca chewing presented special problems.[13] At least in the field of health, substantial changes have taken place. In collaboration with the United Nations and the Peruvian Ministry of Health, a twice-weekly clinic was inaugurated at Vicos; it has raised standards of well-being considerably and has almost eliminated the most infectious diseases. Contrary to early expectations, there has been little resistance to the acceptance of modern medical practices or even to the purchase of modern drugs. As an outgrowth of this program, the Vicosinos, in collaboration with a neighboring Indian community, Recuayhuanca, have constructed a "sanitary post" or clinic at which basic medical services are now available.

THE END OF THE "HACIENDA" SYSTEM AT VICOS

Perhaps the most significant development that has occurred at Vicos since the research program was begun in 1949 is that, after four hundred years of peonage under the *hacienda* system, the Vicosinos have now become the masters of their own destiny and of their own land. Helped along the road by an integrated program of change, one based on the felt needs of the people, the community is now approaching a level of social maturity at which its further development would be held back by a continuation of the *hacienda* system. When this had come to be clearly recognized by both the community and the government, plans were elaborated to enable the Vicosinos to purchase the lands on which they had lived as serfs ever since the Spanish conquest. Their new-found stature in freedom was symbolized by an event of great significance. In October 1956, democratically, by a direct vote of all its adult citizens, the people of Vicos elected their own delegates to assume the direction and management of community and *hacienda* affairs. Since that time, the *peón* system

---

[13] See, for example, UN Economic and Social Council (12th sess.), *Official Records: Special Supplement I, Report of the Commission of Enquiry on the Coca Leaf*, E/1666 (New York: Author, 1950). In my opinion the conclusions of this report are not based on the best scientific evidence. For one thing, preliminary field studies of Vicos indicate that the social aspects of coca chewing are more important than had been previously believed. Moreover, the habit is not as vicious as has been thought. It is likely that, as health and nutritional levels rise, the chewing of coca will pretty much cease to be a problem.

of obligatory labor has been abolished and the Vicosinos now pay taxes on their land. At least one community of the *sierra* has thus taken a new lease on life.

With the transfer, in October 1957, of the *hacienda* lease from the Cornell-Peru project to the community of Vicos, the leaders of the project withdrew from direct control or even supervision of its affairs. After centuries of serfdom the Vicosinos are now masters of their lands and their affairs. The former leaders of the project are available to offer advice when it is requested, for its field director, Mario Vázquez, is continuing his researches into the processes of change and I have also visited Vicos almost every summer. Now, as prior to 1951, the project is concerned with studying the process of social change, not directly with engineering it.

The results of self-rule and self-reliance have been strikingly demonstrated at Vicos since 1957. In the first year after "independence," production doubled, with a substantially smaller labor force. The year 1959 saw a further rapid improvement. With the increased resources now available to them, the Viscosinos are taking up many new projects, this time completely on their own. They are improving access roads to get their produce to market, working out better marketing and transportation arrangements and developing a better water supply. They are better fed, clothed, shod, and housed. It is truly hard to recognize in the new Vicos the bedraggled and hopeless village where our project first began its studies in 1949.

This does not mean that all the problems of Vicos have been solved. Obviously, much remains to be done there and in other parts of the *sierra* where poverty and disease, illiteracy and injustice, are still rife. But the experience of the Cornell-Peru project clearly indicates that the people of the *sierra,* once given proper encouragement, advice, and respect, can do much by themselves to better their lot. Certainly the Vicosinos, given the baseline from which they began, have made great strides toward shaping and sharing positive human values—freedom, respect, enlightenment, and well-being. Given the opportunity, other peoples of the *sierra* can do the same.

Peru's policy-makers have, as I reported above, given their encouragement and support to the Vicos experiment from its inception in 1951, and they have followed its progress with keen interest. Now they are working to multiply its benefits. In the past three years, convinced that the integrated or multifacet approach to social and economic development and self-respect offers the most effective means of arousing the *sierra* people, with their excellent human potential, to develop the spirit and the habits of community self-improvement, the Peruvian government has been engaged in launching five similar pilot projects in key areas of the country. In this expanding effort to crack the crust of centuries and release human energies and hopes, the Indigenous Institute of Peru and the Ministries of Education, Health and Agriculture, as well as United Nations and inter-American agencies, are playing an active part. Some of the leaders of the new projects first studied *sierra* life at Vicos and first learned there how to work with an Indian community to meet its great needs. As at Vicos, each project is based, first, on a careful field study of the community and, second, on the nurturing of responsibility and initiative within the community itself, rather than importing some alien and transitory institutions from without.

A POSITIVE APPROACH FOR THE FUTURE[14]

What generalizations can be drawn from the experience of Vicos, and what are some of its policy implications? One basic conclusion is that, contrary to a widely held opinion in Peru and elsewhere, the indigenous populations of the *sierra* have a great potential for development and for becoming a progressive and dynamic part of the Peruvian nation. Moreover, the process of modernization within this long-isolated population can take place without the loss of certain fundamental and positive values that are deeply ingrained in Indian society: respect for work, frugality, cooperation.

Our experience at Vicos indicates that, if granted respect, the Indian will give respect. If allowed to share in the making of decisions, he will take responsibility and pride in making and carrying them out. The fundamental problem of the *sierra* is largely a problem in human relations: that of improving social relations between *mestizos* and Indians and incorporating both groups into a modern way of life. This calls for a policy not

---

[14] The writer wishes to acknowledge the collaboration on this section of Miss Joan Snyder, formerly a research associate of the Cornell-Peru project.

simply of technological and economic intervention, as has largely been the approach in the past, but also of cultural or educational intervention. Only this approach can open the way to a broadening of horizons in both groups and ultimately a basic change in the present caste structure and in social values. An approach to the *sierra* people along these lines can lead them into a dynamic and progressive society, more like that of the coast, and ultimately will foster a more balanced development of Peru as a nation.

INTERDEPENDENCE OF ECONOMIC AND SOCIAL CHANGE

In the past it has been the assumption of technical aid programs, such as those of the U.S. International Cooperation Administration, that the introduction of technological changes will by itself bring about a broader outlook on the part of the people aided, thus helping to incorporate the community into the larger nation. Experience shows that this is not always the case. It has become increasingly apparent that the acceptance of new technology does not foretell its later use; it does not necessarily promote the broader development of the community or lead to a change in values on the part of its members.

More often than not, increased economic benefits are channeled through traditional value and social systems, intensifying old imbalances. In the *sierra* of Peru, this means, for example, that additional income derived from economic development may be spent in gaining prestige through staging more elaborate religious *fiestas* rather than be put to productive uses. The offering of technical aid alone has, in fact, often resulted in arousing the expectations of more technical help to come and in developing highly opportunistic attitudes on the part of the recipients. Certainly this has been the case in many communities of Peru where the older, paternalistic type of social structure still prevails.

Although there are evident trends toward a wider sharing of power, as attested by the increasing control of the government by the middle segments of society, older and hostile images of national government, derived from the concentrated holding and misuse of power by the privileged few, still persist in most *mestizo* and Indian villages of Peru. Consequently, many sincere attempts, even on the part of the present government, to initiate change at the local level meet with little cooperation or success. At the same time, most of the underdeveloped communities of

Peru hold what are, by our standards at least, unreal images of what the government can and should do for them. Particularly among the *mestizos,* community expectations of what a government can and will do for them in the fields of education and health, economic and social development, and public sevices, are far in excess of what even the most benevolent *patrón* (except perhaps in oil-rich Venezuela) could possibly provide. Yet there is little willingness on the part of local communities to assume responsibilities for reaching these strongly desired goals.

The gap between aspiration and action cannot be explained by poverty alone. It is due as much to the failure of the ambition to achieve desired changes, despite much lip service given to it, to take firm root in community feeling and action. How best to bring this about still constitutes a major question for both research and policy. One thing is certain. The traditional paternalistic type of social and political structure must be overcome if the *sierra* communities are to be incorporated into the nation, but this alone will not assure their developing along democratic lines or for the best interest of the nation.

For the kind of development that calls upon the local community to help itself, rather than wait passively for help from above, the absolutely essential conditions, in addition to programs of technical and economic assistance, are: an improved standard of living, the effective functioning of the community within the larger environment, and a program of cultural or educational intervention. There must also be a deliberate attempt to develop local leaders who will remain identified with the future of their own village and who will find their deepest satisfaction in promoting its progress. Otherwise, potential leaders of the *sierra* will continue to be siphoned off to the coastal area, as they become aware of the opportunities for upward social mobility that exist outside their mountain valleys.

The experience at Vicos shows that much can be done to strengthen the economic life of the *sierra.* By introducing more modern methods and techniques, agricultural production can probably be doubled or tripled in most of its regions. So far, except for the state-owned Santa Corporation, little or nothing has been done to develop small local industries in the *sierra,* although they could absorb much of the population that now migrates year by year to the coast. Just one example. On even the poorer lands of the *sierra* it is possible to grow fiber crops for the production of rope and bagging; in many areas, in fact, there are enough fiber plants growing wild to support a small industrial operation. Yet Peru does not have a single factory for these products and actually imports them at high cost from abroad. The *sierra* holds a similar potential for the industrial processing of fruit, meat, and dairy products.

Much good work along this line has been and is being done outside the *sierra* by the Institute of Inter-American Affairs, under its bilateral agreements with the Peruvian government, as well as by the Pan American Union and the United Nations and its subsidiaries. Unfortunately, too little work has been done with the smaller farmers or the Indians. Most of these efforts have been concentrated on the large *haciendas* and on commercial farmers, who are easier to reach but who constitute only a small part of the total population.

DEVELOPMENT OF LEADERSHIP

In the promotion of social rather than merely economic change, the problems are more complex but far from insoluble. Indeed, at a number of key points in *sierra* society even a relatively modest amount of progress may stimulate a self-propelling and dynamic series of further changes. One of these key points is the development of community solidarity and community leadership. In most rural communities there is a growing body of people who have had contact with the outside world—particularly the younger men who have worked in the coastal regions or done their military service there—and these people are highly critical of the traditional village authorities. Through their experience with life outside their narrow valleys, these young men have taken on many of the values of a national society, and they cannot find fulfillment for them within the traditional village hierarchy.

Probably the only means by which this can be done is to find ways of identifying the prestige of the individual with his role in improving the welfare of the village as a whole. To achieve this, several other changes will be required. At present, neighborhood and kinship ties are far stronger than any feeling of internal unity within the Peruvian village. To overcome this, an essential first step is to promote a sense of loyalty to the community, thus cutting across the lines of neighborhood and kinship groups and stimulating an awareness that the welfare of the individual depends in some measure on that of the entire community. One way to do this is to foster the development of local organizations to deal with issues that affect all families, regardless of local affiliation or status, such as school and health care. Another way lies in promoting recreational and athletic events that attract a wide participation. Many of these occasions, for example, the staging of dramas or chorales, can perhaps be linked to the major religious *fiestas*, which now draw a large though decreasing attendance.

To understand its own problems and opportunities, the *sierra* village needs to know much more about the towns and villages of its own area so as to copy useful changes more rapidly and to develop a spirit of emulation. The isolated village will then see that its problems are not unique and will understand better which things it can do for itself and in which it can reasonably expect aid from the central government.

In order to develop a greater degree of community solidarity, it is essential to strengthen the role of local leadership so as to make it representative of the community as a whole. In the traditional *hacienda* or Indian community the range of activities of the village authorities should be broadened to include all functions which are of importance to all members of the community. To the traditional ritual activities, with their stress on age and the dignity of office, must be added an enlarged responsibility for new activities carried on for the active benefit of the entire community. To promote cohesion and avoid the paralysis of dissension, it is important, among people of the *sierra*, to build up the prestige of holding office. Placing new responsibilities on local authorities for a growing variety of activities will enhance their stature both in their dealings with the outside world and in their leadership with the community.

It is also important to broaden the number and functions of positions of leadership in the villages, in order to provide active roles to a larger proportion of their members. This can help the people to see that authority is the responsibility and the right of all, not the privilege of a small group representing particular interests. This change can be used to give active roles of leadership to the large number of individuals who have had wide experience outside their valleys. As the *sierra* villages enter the path of modernization, the functions of their leaders are also altering, and this requires a change in the qualities of experience and outlook expected of them.

RELATIONS BETWEEN "MESTIZOS" AND INDIANS

The barriers to communication between Indians and *mestizos* are a major factor isolating the Indian villages from the influences of the outside world. The dominant *mestizo* group, standing between the Indians and the nation, has served to block communication, not to facilitate it. Even a partial lowering of this barrier would lead to an increased involvement and participation by the Indian communities in the national society. Furthermore, no effort to develop the well-being of the indigenous villages and to retain potential leaders within their *sierra* villages can work if by staying there they must also remain forever at the bottom of the social ladder.

One approach to improving intergroup relations stresses the need for changing the behavior of the minority or depressed group, with the expectation that this will gradually modify the attitudes of the majority or dominant group. The assumption made is that present attitudes stem from the behavior of the minority and that altering this behavior will result in removing the prejudices of the majority group. It can, however, be argued on strong grounds that the unfavorable attitudes of the dominant group are often transmitted from one generation to the next without reference to the actual situation and that the "improvement" of the minority group will not necessarily create a more favorable attitude toward it. Indeed, the emphasis placed upon improving the status of the minority may actually cause the dominant group to feel that its superior position is being threatened and it may react even more negatively to evidences of that improvement.

An alternative approach is to tackle the problem of changing the attitudes of the majority group. The variety of techniques which have been studied range from formal programs of education to the creation of situations in which contact takes place between members of the two groups either voluntarily or under some degree of compulsion. Many of these methods have created more favorable attitudes toward the minority group. In such an approach, however, too little attention is paid to effecting changes within the minority. In the *sierra* of Peru, for example, it will be necessary to bring about changes in the behavior of both *mestizos* and Indians.

Still a third approach is to create new situations for which there is no set pattern of behavior, and in which each person must decide for himself how to act. In making his decision, the individual takes into account a number of new factors present, apart from his general attitude toward the minority group. These new factors may include the appropriateness or inappropriateness of discrimination as applied in other situations, the need for securing the co-operation of the other person, the relevance of laws or strongly held values forbidding discriminatory behavior, or the presence of other people who would disapprove of such conduct.

Whatever approach is stressed, it is clear that, as the process of modernization gets under way, a great improvement can be brought about in relations between *mestizos* and Indians in the *sierra*. This can be hastened, however, if new situations are arranged so as to bring members of both groups together in a way that will minimize discriminatory behavior. This is possible in schools, in developmental projects, in recreational events, and so forth, provided they are based on real needs of both Indians and *mestizos* and therefore elicit the cooperation of both groups in order to achieve shared ends.

OPENING NEW CHANNELS OF COMMUNICATION

A third broad area, highly significant for the future development of the *sierra,* is that of establishing better channels of communication with the outside world. This is essential if the Indian villages are to learn to deal effectively with the wider community, to utilize its resources for their own development, and to develop self-reliance and local initiative in support of desired changes.

Physical access of the mountain villages to the outside world is improving rapidly through the construction of roads and the increasing use of trucks and buses, but the channels of information are still very circumscribed. Orders and communications of various sorts are delivered to the local communities from district and provincial offices, without producing much effect, and the officials almost never visit the villages or explain the administration's purposes to the peasants. While the villagers have frequent contacts with nearby towns for purposes of trade or *fiestas,* the effects of this are slight because of the social distance separating Indians and *mestizos.* In these contacts, the Indians, being kept in an inferior positon, can seldom learn anything new.

Channels of information can be broadened in a variety of ways. The improving of communications media involves more than simply teaching people to read and write, or imparting information through the written word. Many isolated villagers of the *sierra* have not learned to look at photographs in such a way as to grasp their full meaning. For example, the showing of a public health film at Vicos revealed that the picture had failed to convey its intended message, for each scene was understood as a separate incident. The audience was wholly unable to see any connection between the film and its own life, and it misunderstood any features that were not completely realistic. When lice were depicted as larger than life, the conclusion was that they were an entirely different sort of animal. Except for religious *fiestas,* few rural villagers have seen any variety of drama, and the functioning and purpose of radios are known only to a few individuals. While radio, newspapers, and films may play a leading role in the process of accelerated modernization—and the establishing of regional newspapers and radio stations would be a major step forward—in the early stages only patient face-to-face explanation and demonstration can provide effective channels of communication.

While there are many other aspects of community development that can be tackled in any program of induced social change, giving special attention to the three key areas—economic life, leadership, and communications—has the advantage of bringing about other changes. Increased economic contacts between the village and the outside world will lead to a growth of knowledge about outside markets, more effective techniques, use of available resources, and opportunities for putting special skills to work. Widening the channels of communication with the outside will make the rural villagers better aware of the governmental services that are available to them and will encourage them to play a more active role in their dealings with local, provincial, and national governments. Similar gains can be expected in other areas of *sierra* life, in health and nutrition, in recreation and artistic expression.

THE ROLE OF U.S. POLICY

In the effort to help the depressed strata of Peru's population achieve their new aspirations, the United States has a key role to play. Economic cooperation between it and Peru has, to be sure, contributed to awakening the peasant and Indian populations to the idea of change. But this in itself is not enough, if Peru is soon to attain political stability, a broadening democracy, and a balanced development of the entire nation. Too much of U.S. economic aid and technical assistance—and, in my opinion, Peru has been helped far too little—has been channeled into the traditional social structure from the top. Too large a share of it has been directed to the large *haciendas* and urban centers of the coast, where the aristocratic tradition and paternalistic system are still strong, and too little to the people of the *sierra*. Because it has been easier to work with the dominant and educated groups, U.S. and other outside aid has not had the desired effect, that of enhancing the capacities of large numbers of the Peruvian people to produce more wealth and thus to share broadly in the benefits of economic and cultural development.

Any sound policy of economic aid, as Chester Bowles (1957:45) has written, in addition to "creating more wealth . . . must place heavy emphasis on the development among the workers and peasants of a healthy, cooperative attitude toward their national governments and their communities." The counterpart of this is that strong emphasis must also be placed on developing among policy-makers healthy and cooperative attitudes toward the workers and peasants. For Peru, this means that these large groups must be allowed and encouraged to take increasing responsibility for the direction of their own affairs and to enjoy the benefits of modern development.

Any sound program of economic aid, as Bowles goes on to point out, "requires steady progress toward three essential objectives without which political stability . . . will almost certainly fail to develop: (1) a recognizable increase in economic output; (2) a sense of widespread personal participation in the creation of this increase; (3) a public conviction that the fruits of the increase are being fairly shared, with injustice steadily lessening."

Toward the first of these objectives, Peru has recently made great strides. To reach the other two, it still has a long way to go. These are the neglected areas of development to which policy-makers must direct more attention. A broad program of exchange of ideas and of education is needed to aid in filling the gap. Such a program can help the people of Peru, and many other countries —for Peru merely provides a case study in the potentialities for social development—to achieve a wider sharing of power and wealth, of enlightenment and social respect. At the same time, a program of this integrated type, supplementing the now tradi-tional contributions to economic development, can do more than any other to promote genuine understanding and enduring friend-ship between the two peoples.

25 VICOS: THE INTERPLAY
BETWEEN POWER AND WEALTH[1]

Mario C. Vázquez[2]

T HE OBJECT of this paper is to describe the relationship between wealth and power in Vicos during recent times.

WEALTH AND POWER

BEFORE THE INTERVENTION OF THE CORNELL PERU PROJECT

In the course of our studies carried out from 1949 to 1951
(Vázquez:1952) it was found that Vicos was characterized by
a predominantly subsistence economy. Savings and profits were
the prerogative of the few, who owned great numbers of livestock
especially cattle. Large amounts of cash could be obtained quickly
only by selling livestock to dealers outside the manor. The
relatively few families who did possess cattle to sell were regarded by their fellow serfs as "rich" although no serfs could
be regarded as very well-to-do in terms of the national economy.

Those who had no cattle to sell obtained cash in the form of
daily wage work from Thursdays through Saturdays in neighboring
towns where salaries were low because of the superabundance of
Vicosinos seeking work during those three days of the week.

SOURCE: Mario C. Vázquez, "The Interplay Between Power and Wealth,"
American Behavioral Scientist, Volume III, No. 7, March 1965, pages
9–12. Reprinted by permission of the publisher, Sage Publications, Inc.

[1] This paper (Comparative Studies of Cultural Change) was prepared
under contract AID/csd-296 with the Office of Technical Cooperation
and Research of the Agency for International Development. The data
analyzed were collected under the direction of Professor Allan R. Holmberg with grants from the Carnegie Corporation of New York and an
anonymous donor. The conclusions are those of the author, and do not
necessarily reflect opinions or policies of any supporting agency or organization.

[2] Research Associate, Department of Anthropology, Cornell University,
and Research Coordinator for the Cornell Peru Project in Peru.

Others migrated seasonally to the plantations of the Coast as contract laborers. Others served as harvest nomads in the upper Casma River valley, exchanging their labor for a share of the grain harvest, paid in kind. Finally, on Sundays the women obtained a few soles in cash by selling eggs, cheese, etc., and by hiring out as domestic servants to the Mestizos. A few men sold baskets, charcoal, and glacial ice.

Thus the principal source of serf wealth, and its primary symbol among the serfs, was the number of head of cattle that each family possessed. Cattle constituted the only marketable property available to the Vicosinos for sale at a given moment. Since Vicos was a manor operated under a peonage system, houses, trees, other improvements and lands which constitute a source of wealth and a form of savings in free societies had value in name only. They could be transferred only by the operator of the manor and not by the serfs even though the latter had actually constructed the dwellings they occupied. The serfs were mere usufructuaries during the time that they carried out their manorial obligations of working three days per week for the overlord of the manor.

According to the census taken of the Vicos population by the Cornell Peru Project at the beginning of 1952, and utilizing the local criterion of wealth, which is the number of animals owned, twenty-eight families or 7.7 per cent of the total number of families at that time were found to be wealthy. That is, they owned more than eleven head of cattle or of their equivalent in other animals, reckoned in terms of sales prices (Vázquez: 1957) rather than grazing units.

The wealthy Vicosinos were considered specially privileged individuals because they were lucky, and enjoyed divine protection which caused their herds to increase and made them successful in other activities. This was the case in the realm of agriculture, where the crops of the rich were superior as a rule to those of other farmers, because their animals were utilized more opportunely to fertilize their fields (which have probably been under continuous cultivation for at least 3,000 years and therefore require fertilization to yield well), and in the operations of plowing and planting. In the latter tasks, the animal owners naturally had first call on the power of their beasts. Also, the wealthy farmers could obtain the supplemental human labor necessary to cultivate their fields at the proper time in exchange for lending their oxen or beasts of burden to those without these animal resources. In addition to all this advantage, the wealthy farmers had more time free to tend personally to their crops and animals, while those who lacked animals had to wait upon the grace of the wealthy before they could initiate their own plowing and planting, and at the same time they had to obtain cash by hiring out by the day in order to provide for the primary subsistence needs of their families.

Besides being considered as people blessed by fortune, the wealthy were viewed by their fellow serfs as constituting the highest status social group within the manor. They were regarded as "the powerful ones," and "the monied ones," or "the cattle barons." Of course, their status was higher if they were elders and had occupied positions of local authority. They were then the *"yayas,"* the men with the highest prestige, the most power and authority, whose opinions were in many matters decisive during discussions of the internal affairs of the serf population.

Class distinctions obliged the wealthy to possess certain objects symbolic of their status, to behave differently, and to accept the responsibilities of fictive kinship and local authority. If they did not, they became subject to the social controls of satire and hostility. So the wealthy had to dress better than their inferiors, and to own at least two sets of clothes, to possess homes with several rooms made of sun-dried bricks and roofed with clay tiles, and closed by wooden doors made by professional carpenters. The wealthy had to disdain serving as daily wage workers in neighboring towns or Coastal plantations, to participate as functionaries in the local religious festivals and those of the nearby towns, to accept positions of local authority in the administration of the manor and its serf population, and to accept the responsibilities of sponsoring weddings, etc.

The factor that imbued the wealthy with the greatest social visibility and power was not their possession of a large number of animals *per se,* nor the bearing of the rich man, but rather their ability to have cash on hand ready to be used at a moment's notice. That is to say that they should have had the ability to carry out any kind of transaction and so to dominate by means of their money those situations that might affect them or their families, and to "assist" the needy by granting them loans.

The Vicosinos knew that with cash in hand they could obtain better prices in commercial transactions, whether buying or selling.

Thus, in selling cattle the wealthy owner held out for the best offer, while the poor owner was apt to sell at lower prices, being pressed for cash. In the same fashion, the wealthy person obtained the best discounts while making purchases, especially in the case of peripatetic peddlers, who preferred to sell on a cash basis and not on credit, which was the traditional practice.

The wealthy stood out, and they demonstrated their superiority over other individuals by acting as the local bankers. They were able to grant loans to those who needed money. The loans were granted under diverse terms—with or without interest, over a fixed or an indefinite time period—with the arrangements subject to the type of relationships that existed between the lender and the borrower.

A loan granted by a rich Vicosino did not constitute a simple monetary transaction with its corresponding paperwork, but was rather the beginning of a state of dependency of the borrower toward the lender, and it lasted for the entire period during which the debt had not been paid. By virtue of having loaned a sum of money varying between fifty and five hundred soles (between two and twenty dollars at current exchange rates), the rich man felt that he had the right to use the person of his debtor, who became his permanent *minka* or unpaid laborer, for his various enterprises. Should the debtor fail to do the bidding of the lender, he was obligated to return the amount of the loan plus any accrued interest. Usually this was done through the local Indian authorities, whose intervention was in itself embarrassing, and a bad precedent for the debtor, since upon its being made public that he was a bad risk, he could no longer obtain loans from other serfs.

The power of the wealthy Vicosinos was not limited only to other serfs, but extended to the manor overlords and overseers and to the Mestizos living in neighboring towns. In several instances, the wealthy obtained land from the manor above and beyond what the other serfs received, in exchange for animals or money that they turned over to the overseers or employees of the manor. These transactions were frequent when the rich man held a job with the manor administration such as straw boss, *repuntero,*[3] etc. In the case of Mestizo authorities under whose

---

[3] *Repuntero:* A person assigned by the manor administration to care for the herds in the pasturelands and/or collect grazing fees from drovers for outside livestock pastured on manor lands.

jurisdiction the Vicosinos found themselves, it was common knowledge that the wealthy Indians were never punished. On the contrary, the Mestizo authorities usually favored them, and thus the sons of the wealthy were not pressed into military service, although it was legally compulsory for Peruvian citizens.

In fact, giving gifts or bribes to the authorities was institutionalized. It had acquired a Quechua term, and was known as the *"senyi."* The Vicosinos who could best satisfy such Mestizo demands were the wealthy. Some of them had established symbolic kinship ties with a number of key authorities, such as the clerks who held permanent positions.

THE CORNELL PERU PROJECT
AND THE INTRODUCTION OF TECHNOLOGICAL CHANGE

Between 1952 and 1956, as part of its study on culture and technological change, the Cornell Peru Project introduced into Vicos, with regard to the economic sphere in terms of its practical objective of improving the standard of living of the Vicos serfs, modern techniques of agricultural production including new varieties of seed for the locally important crops such as potatoes and maize. At the same time, the medieval system of servitude and peonage, which has kept the Vicosinos in the status of serfs since Spanish colonial times, was gradually abolished (Holmberg:1956). Then, when the Indians took over direction of their own affairs, the obligation to work three days each week for the management disappeared.

Between 1957 and 1962, the Cornell Peru Project supported the Vicosinos in their effort to buy the estate of Vicos and to become its proprietors, which culminated in the purchase completed on July 13, 1962. At the same time that it sponsored the change in land tenure, the Cornell Peru Project assisted in a democratic reorganization of the process of public decision-making by the former serf population. Vicos is now directed by a Governing Council whose members are elected by the people in ten electoral zones. At the present time, the Vicos community is a type of production enterprise organized along cooperative lines, in which its members receive the major economic benefits.

The Cornell Peru Project fostered greater contact between Vicosinos and the outside world. Thus, the Project supported and reinforced the initiation of new programs of development tending to consolidate the communal economy as a production enterprise, as well as that of each one of its members. Among these programs, several deserve mention:

a) The installation of communal workshops. Initiated by the Cornell Peru Project and carried out under the direction of the Ministry of Labor and Indian Affairs for the teaching of sewing and the use of sewing machines. In addition to the apprentice training they received, the participants have made 844 garments, during 1964.

b) The Credit Cooperative. In November, 1963, under the guidance of a specialist from the National Agricultural University in Lima, a credit cooperative was established. It now commands a capital of S/.21,666.95 (or $812.00) and has granted loans in the amount of S/.40,400 (or $1,513.00). This cooperative is developing a new type of saving in cash, outside the family, with truly striking results.

c) The hotel at Chancos. In 1963 the hotel at Chancos, located at the boundary of the Vicos community, was re-opened. It is operated under the direction of a Peace Corps Volunteer and one of its aims is to provide work opportunities for the youth of Vicos. Eight young Vicos men have participated in operating the Chancos installation since its reopening.

d) The forestation program. Begun in April 1964, under the direction of the Forestation Administration of the Ministry of Agriculture, this program has financial backing from the Alliance for Progress of the United States. The work is directed by trained technicians from the Peruvian Ministry of Agriculture. The program consists of establishing a stand of several million eucalyptus trees. The proceeds of the harvest of these plantings is to be divided between the Ministry of Agriculture and the Vicos Community in the ratio of three to seven parts, respectively.

The Vicosinos who are now participating in the operation of the Chancos hotel and thermal baths and in the forestation program receive the highest salaries paid in the entire valley where Vicos is located. This income is causing important changes in the traditional relationship between wealth and power in Vicos.

WEALTH AND POWER IN 1964

As already mentioned, the Cornell Peru Project was initiated with the explicit practical objective of improving the standard of living of the Vicos population (Holmberg:1952). That original goal has been achieved. Vicos is no longer, in 1964, a society with essentially a subsistence economy. It is far exceeding its former little-more-than subsistence agricultural structure, because both the community as a farm enterprise and the majority of its members work the land not only for the sake of subsistence, but also for commercial purposes. At the same time, the Vicosinos devote themselves to other economic activities that are new sources of monetary income.

Economically, the Vicosino no longer depends solely on the agricultural production of his farm plots or on the sale of his livestock, or, in the absence of these, on the daily wages earned in neighboring towns and the plantations on the Coast.

In 1964, the Vicosinos are in effect shareholding members of a production enterprise called the Andean Community of Vicos. This organization operates with its own capital of approximately S/.1,200,000 (or $45,000.00) created during the last seven years through the commercial exploitation of community held farm lands in Vicos. Seventy per cent of this capital has been utilized to pay for the purchase of the Vicos estate. Its total price of S/.2,000,000 (or $75,000.00) will be paid to the former owner in 1965, with the aid of a loan for half this amount already made to Vicos by the Government of Peru for this purpose in 1962.

Besides accumulating capital toward the purchase of the Vicos estate itself, the Vicosinos each year participate in the distribution of a certain percentage of the community farm enterprise harvest. Thus in 1964, 93 per cent of the families were beneficiaries of 25 per cent of the gross production of potatoes on the communal lands (87,768 kilograms of potatoes). This made it possible for 65 per cent of the families to sell the potatoes raised on their own farm plots through the community farm enterprise marketing program in the national capital. These families earned an average income of S/.1,000 ($37.50) from the sale of their agricultural products. These and other families sold additional potatoes directly to Mestizo buyers who sought them out in Vicos, to buyers in the capital city of the department where they hauled them, and to local storekeepers who have established fictive kinship relations with Indians.

In addition, 75 per cent of the families purchased the total grain production of the community farm enterprise in maize, wheat and barley, at prices lower by 20 per cent to 50 per cent than those current in the regional market.

Twenty per cent of the Vicos families also have an income of from eight to thirty soles ($0.30 to $1.12) a day by virtue of wages received by some of their members who work in the forestation program or in the Chancos hotel. At the moment, this figure must have risen to about 87 per cent, since the massive transplanting of 1,500,000 eucalyptus seedlings is now being carried out. Later on, 15 per cent of the Vicos labor force will be required for ten consecutive years up to the first harvest, at which time possibly a greater number of workers will be needed.

Twelve per cent of the Vicosino families participate in the credit cooperative. The members deposit their savings monthly and most of them have already obtained loans for the purchase of sewing machines, tools, musical instruments, business inventories, etc.

Finally, there is one Vicosino resident in Vicos who is an employee of the national government who annually earns more money (S/.25,000) than the richest Vicosino of the traditional type of the locality, who sells a yearly average of five head of cattle for an approximate cash income of S/.15,000.

Despite the increase of the daily wage rate from twelve to fifteen soles for men and from five to eight soles for women in neighboring towns in the last few years, few Vicosinos accept these jobs. They prefer to work on their own farm plots cultivating potatoes, and currently in the national forestation program. On the other hand, it should also be mentioned that in the year 1964 several Vicosinos have returned from the Coast to live in Vicos, in continuation of a current of return migration that began some years ago with the improvement of the Vicos economy (Vázquez:1963). They have become steady workers in the forestation program and in the Chancos hotel.

From the preceding, it is concluded that the Vicosinos have been freed by the Cornell Peru Project not only from the manor system and peonage, but also from the conservative plutocracy upon which most of them depended by virtue of having solicited or needing to solicit monetary loans, which all but converted them into serfs of the wealthy for as long as the loan was not repaid.

As a consequence of the previously outlined changes, there may now be observed:

a) An increase in commercial activity in Vicos and the region. In 1953, thirty-two persons devoted themselves to the resale of merchandise obtained in Carhuaz and Marcara. In 1963, seventy-eight persons sold a greater variety of articles, acquired for the most part in Huaraz at lower prices, or purchased from Huaraz wholesalers, who deliver the merchandise to Vicos.

b) The use of personal capital for the cultivation of potatoes using new seed potatoes and guano fertilizer.

c) The purchase of chickens for breeding purposes and of cattle, donkeys and horses of high quality, which are used not only to move the internal agricultural produce of Vicos, but also are hired out to pack ore from nearby mines to trucking terminals.

d) The increased purchase of cotton clothing, and manufactured cloth for making clothing for women and children.

e) The acquisition of modern appliances, tools, and furnishings such as sewing machines, bicycles, radios, record players, musical instruments, tables, chairs, cots, trunks, etc.

f) The utilization of Mestizo style materials in house construction, as in using plaster to whiten the walls, and ceramic roof tiles purchased in the valley outside Vicos.

g) The formation of new institutions such as the St. Andrew's Band of Vicos, the Community Cooperative, the Vicos young men's soccer club, etc.

h) The participation of youths and poor individuals in local government, with single prerequisite of obtaining a majority of the votes of their fellows.

CONCLUDING REMARKS

Finally, in summary it may be said that before the Cornell Peru Project intervened in Vicos, 52 per cent of the families were poor (Vázquez:1957) with extremely limited sources of income. Wealth in the form of livestock and the money accumulated by their sale was in the hands of only 7.7 per cent of the families. Now, however, wealth in the form of monetary income is within the reach of essentially all Vicosinos.

Although the majority of the Vicosinos still lack the animals to fertilize and cultivate their fields, they now have the cash with which to hire draft animals, and to purchase natural and chemical fertilizers and seeds. Approximately 70 per cent of the families no longer have to beg the wealthy few to lend them money because, in addition to their traditional sources of income, they receive income from the cash sale of their commercial agricultural products, and in the form of wages for work that they obtain in the programs sponsored by their own community, and now by the national government. Now there also exist in situations such as the credit cooperative and the communal sewing workshops, means of saving which permit them to invest in the purchase of more foods, clothing, and modern commodities of diverse uses, including capital goods such as a truck and sewing machines.

It should also be mentioned that in the sector that does not participate actively in this technological progress, there are still poor men and widows who continue to depend on the traditional rich to whom they are subordinated not only for economic reasons, but also by kinship ties.

In conclusion, wealth, which gave a small group of Vicosinos the power to exercise several types of economic oppression and to dominate most individuals in the serf population through reprisals and moral sanctions, is now represented in the form of money coming from new sources of income and is shared by the majority of Vicosinos. They are gradually freeing themselves from their oppressors and at the same time participating in the economic life of the region and of the country. And a new type of formal power has been created, represented by the Governing Council of the community, which is proving its improved wealth position by purchasing the former estate lands, and is responsible for the various programs for the development of Vicos.

26 RISK, UNCERTAINTY, AND THE SUBSISTENCE FARMER

Clifton R. Wharton, Jr.

VILLAGE-LEVEL economies operate much as self-contained, self-sufficient economic enclaves with communal goals, institutions and processes, designed far more for the preservation of human life than for development. Since in its earliest phases, sedentary agriculture is a productive process whose product may be eaten by the producer, there is inevitably a strong attachment by the peasant farmer to the goals, institutions, and processes associated with the economy, society, and polity of the village.

Despite the almost infinite variety of village-level institutions and processes to be found around the world, they have three common characteristics which are pertinent to change: 1) they have historically proven to be successful, i.e., the members have survived; 2) they are relatively static, at least the general pace of change is below that which is considered desirable today; and 3) attempts at change are frequently resisted, both because these institutions and processes have proven dependable and because the various elements constitute something akin to an ecologic unity in the human realm.

THE RESPONSIVENESS OF SUBSISTENCE FARMERS

The earliest characterizations of subsistence or traditional farmers described them as technologically backward, with deficient

SOURCE: Clifton R. Wharton, Jr., "Risk, Uncertainty, and the Subsistence Farmer: Technological Innovation and Resistance to Change in the Context of Survival," a paper read at the Joint Meetings of the American Economic Association and the Association for Comparative Economics, Chicago, Illinois, December 1968. The excerpts reprinted here comprise one-third of the original paper, and are reprinted by permission of the author.

entrepreneurial ability, and with limited aspirations. The influence of limited aspirations is best summarized in the colonial stereotype of the "lazy natives" who refuse to work for an income beyond what they require for their subsistence. Economists labeled such behavior the "backward bending supply curve of labor." Other social scientists, more culturally sensitive and empathetic, viewed such behavior as merely instances where non-economic variables dominated and swamped economic factors favorable to economic maximization.

Interestingly these early views of limited or negative peasant responses to economic opportunity were held by many individuals who were witnesses to or participated in instances of massive "response" by subsistence and peasant farmers to improved economic opportunities. During the colonial period, in most instances, the economic opportunity was the dynamic development of new markets in the metropolitan country for the beverages, food and industrial raw materials which could be produced in the colony. Some but not all of the rapid dynamic response in these cases could be explained by the coercion of colonialists, or by the development of infra-structure facilities by the colonial power, or by a crop's promotion by organized interest groups.

More recently, the idea of an economically inert peasantry has been seriously challenged. First, there are those economists led by Professor Jones [1960] and Professor T. W. Schultz [1964], who find ample evidence that subsistence farmers *are* economic men who do maximize in the utilization of their available economic resources *given* the available technology. Such farmers may be operating at low absolute levels of production but nonetheless they are optimizing at the ceiling of the available technological possibilities. This group argues that what is fundamentally lacking is improved technology. The obvious solution under such circumstances is to give first priority to the development of new technology to alter the production possibilities.

Second, a large number of economists have been conducting rigorous empirical research to determine whether or not such farmers respond to economic incentives. Despite the varieties of empirical and analytical measures used and crops involved, the overwhelming evidence indicates that subsistence and semi-subsistence farmers do in fact respond to economic incentives. They increase the production of those crops whose relative economic returns have improved, and decrease those which have become disadvantageous. Some of the observable response has come as a result of greater intensification in the use of available resources without any significant alteration in the existing technology; others have come through the adoption of new techniques and practices.

Despite all this new evidence, there is equally ample evidence, usually in semi-anecdotal or case study form, where farmers have seemingly not responded to an "obvious" economic opportunity. Explanations of such cases vary. Some analyses rely upon non-economic explanations—the indigenous culture militated against the new practice; there were serious religious prohibitions which would prevent the adoption of a new technology; higher production would disrupt the fabric of the traditional society. Others find that upon closer examination the economic advantages turned out to be illusory—the landlord secured all the gain; the moneylender skimmed off the cream; the government guaranteed price was not in fact paid; the cost structure made the new innovation unprofitable.

The current pressures of burgeoning population on world food supplies have heightened the need for more rapid economic responsiveness and the more rapid adoption of new technology. Improved understanding of the resistances to adopt or to respond are becoming critical. One set of explanatory variables which deserves more rigorous study is the influence of risk and uncertainty juxtaposed against the subsistence levels of living and production of such farmers. Risk factors are not predominant or exclusive influences in the adoption process; it is merely that their greater specification will facilitate their inclusion with other equally important factors.

THE CAUSES OF RISK AND THE SOURCES OF UNCERTAINTY

A basic distinction relevant for the decision-making framework of the subsistence farmer is between: 1) those future events to which he can assign probabilities based upon past experience or personal knowledge; and 2) those future events to which he cannot assign probabilities, or where the probabilities offered are not derived from his personal experience but are based on external knowledge provided by others.

Even the most illiterate peasant farmer has a knowledge of the probabilities which attach to his current, traditional practices. These relate to three major sources of year to year variability. First, the farmer faces *yield variability*. Actual field or barn yields obtained are a function of a wide range of variables —sunshine, humidity, rainfall and even their incidence and timing during the cropping season; pests such as birds, rats, worms; blights, fungi and viruses; and even the unpredictable acts of God and man such as wars, insurrections, and revolts. Second, there is *cost variability*. Even in subsistence and semi-subsistence type agriculture there are inputs required for production which are purchased—ranging from minor farm tools and fertilizer to oxen rental and hired labor. Whether or not actual cash is employed in the payment process is inconsequential. The critical issue is the variability in the incidence of such costs. The typical farm decision-maker faces expenses which tend to fall into two categories: those which are subject to his decision-making control, and those which are outside his control. In both cases, predictable and unpredictable probabilities are involved, i.e., risk and uncertainty. Family labor is fundamentally subject to the control of the farm decision-maker, but its utilization is affected by illness and even the availability of off-farm employment. The costs of farm product processing such as milling, off-farm storage, transport to market and interest on loans are outside his control, although knowing what these costs were in previous years helps him in formulating the probabilities. Third, there is a *product price variability*. Choice of crop and crop combinations as well as intended levels of output are based upon price expectations. The divergence between expected prices when crop choice and planting decisions are made and actual prices after harvest may be considerable, both positively or negatively.

The critical element is that these three variabilities combine in any given crop period to affect the net return to the farm family. The extent to which the farmer can reduce unintended fluctuations in each category is quite limited, but every effort is made to reduce those subject to his control. Historical knowledge on the past variabilities in each does exist, and he takes these into account—whether it is distrust of assured government prices, or fear of a locust cycle.

INTERACTION OF RISK, UNCERTAINTY
AND SUBSISTENCE ON TECHNOLOGICAL INNOVATION

Any new technology or practice has associated with it some expected probabilities for yields per acre and consequent income figures. Extension workers or salesmen who are promoting new techniques often present them in terms of average (sometimes maximum) yields obtained at an experiment station. But the typical subsistence farmer has his own subjective rate of discount for such probabilities. He has learned from bitter experience to be wary of new methods which *as he sees them* have been insufficiently adapted and evaluated for his particular situation, and which may not perform in his fields as promised. The farmer, in deciding whether to adopt an innovation, may be seen as making a choice: on the one hand he estimates the most probable yield from a new technique, and the range of variability around this expected figure; on the other hand, he uses as a basis for comparison the expected yield from the familiar method he has been using, and the much narrower range of variability around that expected level. In short, he compares not only the levels of expected net yields, but also the reliability with which these yields can be expected, as he sees it.

Let us assume we are dealing with a subsistence farm family which consumes, say, 80 percent of its production in the average year. This consumption is fairly constant; in good years the farmer may have some surplus produce to sell, and in bad years little or none, but at least his family is fed. Such a consumption level can be regarded as his minimum subsistence level, i.e., a level he will strive not to fall below. This definition of a minimum subsistence level is not purely physiological: the farmer's notion of a minimum is likely to be somewhat above that which will barely sustain life, but below the level of nutrition adequate for maintenance of a desirable standard of physical exertion. Farmer's ideas of minimum tolerable levels may vary quite a bit from place to place, from farmer to farmer, and through time. But, when a farmer's output comes close to what he considers as his minimum standard, then his behavior as a producer is affected.

When the subsistence farmer confronts a possible innovation, he will be concerned with two questions: 1) Will the new method, taking its probable costs into account, produce an expected yield appreciably higher than his old method? 2) Is there a reasonable probability that something will go wrong, and that the new method will result in a net yield below his minimum subsistence level? *Even if the answer to (1) is yes, he will not change his method unless he can also answer (2) in the negative.* Thus, the closer his current output is to his minimum subsistence level, the more conservative he is likely to be. The more unfamiliar the proposed innovation and/or the change agents concerned with it, the more cautious will be the farmer's approach.

However, if he can be convinced that the new method is not only better but reliably so, and that its probable negative variability will still leave him better off than he was before, then he is most likely to make the change. A good illustration of this point may be seen in the table below, where objective figures on variability (cross sectional) are presented: although the farmers' subjective estimates of variability cannot be recorded, the impact of experiences in various places should bring these subjective estimates close to the objective realities.

EXAMPLE OF RICE YIELDS

The recent experience with the new rice varieties from the International Rice Research Institute is perhaps indicative. The rapidity with which the new varieties (especially IR-8 and IR-5) have been spreading in Asia refutes the stereotype of the non-economic peasant. The Philippines has been a rice importer—some 230,000 tons annually from 1961 to 1967. The very rapid adoption of the new high-yielding varieties first introduced in 1966 has already made the Philippines self-sufficient in rice for the first time in recent history.

The statistical variance in yields per hectare associated with the newer varieties is considerably larger than with the traditional varieties. If the average yields for the new and old varieties had been fairly similar, then the average farmer would probably have resisted adoption. What is especially significant in the present case is not merely that the average yields with the new varieties are higher, but that the negative standard deviation for the new varieties is *higher* than the average yields of the old traditional variety.

AVERAGE YIELDS OF IR-8 AND LOCAL RICE VARIETIES
IN THE PHILIPPINES, DRY AND WET SEASONS 1966–67*
(Metric Tons per Hectare)

	$-SD_X$	$\overline{X}$	$+SD_X$
Dry Season			
IR-8	3.24	5.86	8.48
Binato	1.51	3.17	4.83
Wet Season			
IR-8	2.59	4.49	6.39
Local	1.00	2.32	3.64

* Data supplied by the International Rice Research Institute, Los Banos, The Philippines.

This helps to explain the startling phenomenon currently taking place with the "Green Revolution"—the rapid adoption of the new high-yielding varieties of wheat and rice (Wharton 1969a).

SOME PUZZLES AND PARADOXES EXPLAINED

The above analysis may help to explain a few puzzles and paradoxes commonly encountered with technological innovation in the developing world.

Differential adoption within same community. In many agricultural areas, one can find farmers who have adopted a new innovation coexisting with neighboring farmers who have failed to adopt even though the latter see the new technology every day and are aware of it. "Demonstration effects" and "neighbor effects" seem to have no impact.

Food staple vs. non-food staple variations. A common experience is a differential resistance to technological adoption between staple and non-staple food crops. Technological innovation tends to move more rapidly among farmers specializing in non-food staples (especially commercial crops) than is true with food staples.

The "dual farmer." One frequently encounters farmers who grow both a food staple and a non-food staple. They are willing to innovate or to employ a new technology with a commercial crop but persist in traditional practices with the food staple.

New crops vs. old crops. Another common observation has been that the introduction of new crops requiring new technology seems to be easier than changing the technology of a traditional, well-established crop.

In each of the four cases, a good deal of the variation in adoption can be attributed to the relationship between subsistence standards of living, and the expected variability in output of the food staple under the new technology. In the first case, for example, the non-adopters are most frequently those farmers who are less commercial (both in product and input) and whose resources relative to their minimum subsistence standard of living are extremely close. Where the proposed innovation and its associated variability exceeds the minimum subsistence level, as was the case with the new rice varieties in the Philippines, then adoption proves to be swift.

Some further implications of this analysis may be outlined. Given a close historical relation between annual food output and a farm family's minimum subsistence level, the degree of risk aversion—and thus the extent of resistance to innovations—will be *reinforced* by five factors:

1. the greater the concentration on food crop(s) on the farm;
2. the lesser the availability of other food sources;
3. the lesser the opportunities for alternative employment of family labor, or of other farm resources;
4. the tighter the capital rationing facing the farmer, and the higher the interest rate he must pay;
5. the closer the value of the family's minimum subsistence level is to the value of the family's net worth (assets minus debts).

PROGRAM AND POLICY IMPLICATIONS

If risk and uncertainty are as important in the context of subsistence as indicated, then certain steps are required to assure a greater rapidity and extent of adoption of new technology.

1. Information on the variability of any new technology is as important as its average performance. Any determination of the economic feasibility of a new practice or technique should pay equal, if not more, attention to the variability in yields, especially the lower deviations as they relate to minimum subsistence standards of living of potential innovating farmers.

2. In developing new technologies, agricultural research organizations should recognize the importance which subsistence farmers

attach to the variabilities associated with any possible innovation. Plant breeders, for example, should pay greater attention to those specific characteristics which may help to reduce negative deviation and offer greater dependability.

3. Where only a narrow range covers the minimum subsistence standards, levels of living, and physiological minima, programs designed to diffuse new technology need to pay much greater attention to methods for "risk insurance" or assuring the peasant who innovates that failure (i.e., an output falling below his minimum subsistence standard) will not result in a major penalty, viz. loss of life or loss of property or indebtedness. Existing social structures and institutions (viz. extended family) which already provide some degree of "risk insurance" should be recognized as such and wherever possible treated as complementary to any new insurance system.

4. Methods of technological introduction and trial in a peasant community should recognize that in the early stages the typical farmer attaches a subjective variability to the expected yield of the new technology which is considerably wider than the true one. Extension and information measures should concentrate just as much on reducing this subjective variability in the minds of potential innovators as on spreading knowledge about the average or maximum yields. Assurance as to the dependability of the practice or technology may be more important to the peasant farmer than its dramatic output possibilities.

27 SMALLHOLDER AGRICULTURE
IN EASTERN NIGERIA *

C. Davis Fogg

AGRICULTURE is the economic mainstay of nearly all of the underdeveloped nations of tropical Africa. For example, over 50 percent of Nigeria's gross national product is attributed to agriculture, and 85 percent of her foreign exchange earnings come from the export of primary produce. If development is to take place, it is obvious that major reliance must be placed on the agricultural sector. In recognition of this fact, approximately 14 percent of the £676 million 1962–68 Nigerian National Development Plan expenditure is devoted to agriculture.

Economists recognize that emphasis must be placed on productive agriculture, not only to increase per capita income and to create markets for industrial goods, but to maintain or increase export earnings needed to finance the import of capital goods needed to stimulate the hoped-for industrialization of the country. Seventy-five percent of the population of Nigeria is involved in farming, and 98 percent of the export crops are produced by subsistence or small-scale farmers on holdings giving extremely poor yields. It follows that this vast amount of underutilized manpower and land should be tapped to accelerate the economic development of Nigeria. My purpose here is to examine the means available to develop the agricultural sector and to note the social and economic barriers standing in the way. I will limit my comments for the most part to Eastern Nigeria, although the

SOURCE: C. Davis Fogg, "Economic and Social Factors Affecting the Development of Smallholder Agriculture in Eastern Nigeria," *Economic Development and Cultural Change,* Volume 13, No. 3, April 1965, pages 278–92. Reprinted by permission of the author and the publisher (the University of Chicago Press).

* The opinions expressed in this article are the author's own and are not necessarily the views of the Government of Eastern Nigeria.

comments are applicable to the southern part of Nigeria and to many tropical African countries having similar economic conditions.

The nature of tropical agriculture in underdeveloped countries has received frequent and intensive attention by a number of people. I intend here only to summarize the cogent points.

Agricultural production in Eastern Nigeria may be typified in the following ways:

1. *Scarce and fragmented land.* Each farm family has an average of one to two acres under production at any one time. Frequently the holdings are scattered and a farmer holding two acres may have five different plots dispersed over a radius of one to five miles from his village.[1]

2. *Individual and communal ownership of land.* In Ibo society the ownership of land is divided between the individual family and the community. The family always retains title to the homestead (compound) and traditional family farmland surrounding the compound. The community may "own" more extensive farm

---

[1] This is not necessarily true in all parts of Eastern Nigeria. For example, the average acreage available to the farmer in Calabar, Ogoja, and Abakaliki provinces is considerably higher than that in the rest of the region. Accurate statistics on land use, however, are difficult to obtain. Bulletin No. 5 of the 1959–60 Agricultural Sample Survey of Eastern Nigeria (Lagos: Federal Office of Statistics, 1961) states that Ogoja and Abakaliki provinces have 1.5 acres per adult male farmer while the most densely populated area (Uyo province) has only 0.7 acres per farmer. As the accuracy of the statistics can be questioned because of the limited sample taken by the survey team, I think it sufficient to say that the *average* farmer in Eastern Nigeria has the right to work one to two acres of land at any one time.

This, however, says nothing about the distribution of land rights among farmers. Some wealthy farmers own considerably more land than the average, and it is not unusual to find an individual or family with the right to farm 5 to 10 acres. For example, in 1962, when the government announced that it was prepared to supply subsidized planting materials to replant 10,000 acres of oil palm, with high yielding varieties, 20,000 acres were immediately offered by farmers who had consolidated plots measuring 5 or more acres. The Ministry of Agriculture anticipates no difficulty in finding enough farmers with five or more consolidated acres to plant 60,000 acres of oil palm, 100,000 acres of rubber, and 20,000 acres of cocoa during the 1962–68 Development Plan period.

land removed from the village itself. The communal land is apportioned to families by agreement within the village. Where land is particularly scarce, ownership by a family tends to become permanent and communal land disappears.

3. *Low productivity.* Tropical soils are poor, resulting in poor yields and long fallow cycles of five to seven years. Poor planting varieties are often used and perpetuated by consumption of the best produce and the saving of the worst for "seed" material. Fallow cycles are decreasing because of population pressure on the land, and productivity is therefore decreasing even further in many areas of the country. Fertilization, pest control, and selective use of planting stock is seldom practiced.

4. *Subsistence production.* Each family produces primarily for its own consumption and sells produce in the market only if a surplus is harvested. A recent survey showed that 80 to 90 percent of the food consumed by an average family was produced by that family.

5. *Cash crops.* As noted above, few people produce with the sole intention of selling in the market. One natural crop, oil palm, has a ready export market, and farmers sell large amounts of surplus palm oil and kernel to the Marketing Board's agents for export. I would guess the 85 to 90 percent of Nigeria's exportable palm oil is supplied by small holders having less than an acre under oil palm. Most of the palm oil comes from unproductive wild palms. A few farmers grow recently introduced cash crops such as cocoa and rubber.

Approximately 98 percent of Eastern Nigeria's exports of palm oil, palm kernel, and cocoa are produced by smallholders. Only 2 percent of produce exports can be attributed to plantations and large-scale holdings.

6. *Internal market for food crops.* The population of Nigeria is shifting rapidly to urban areas. A recent survey indicated that 80 to 95 percent of the primary school leavers from densely populated rural areas of Nigeria take semi-permanent residence in urban areas. As this shift increases and as more people take up non-farm occupations, there will be an expanding internal market for food crops. Urban market prices have shown marked increases in the last two years indicating increasing shortages of basic foodstuffs. If urban industry is to be encouraged, attendant increases in food production must follow.

Although the physical resources of the country are poor, productivity can be vastly improved through the introduction of modern farming techniques. Although it is impossible to greatly increase the amount of arable land, land substitutes such as fertilizers, new plant varieties, and improved cropping practices can bring about substantial increases in production and large decreases in the proportion of land that must remain in fallow. Fertilizers alone have produced average increases in yield as high as 60 percent in some basic foodstuffs, and spectacular increases as high as 339 percent have been noted.[2] Chemical spraying can, for example, double the production of Amazon type cocoa. Indeed, without reducing the amount of land fragmentation and without introducing mechanization, the production of the agriculture sector could be substantially increased. Large increases are possible only if information, materials, and incentives are widely distributed throughout the economy. As in all underdeveloped countries, it falls on the government to provide the stimulus and "seed" capital necessary to develop productive agriculture.[3]

APPROACHES TO AGRICULTURAL DEVELOPMENT

There are five basic approaches to agricultural development being tried or considered in Eastern Nigeria. They are: (1) commercial plantations; (2) nucleus plantations; (3) settlement schemes; (4) smallholder "investment" schemes; (5) smallholder "improvement" schemes.

---

[2] See Mann (1963). The study gives the results of fertilizer trials conducted on yam, cassava, maize, and rice in Eastern Nigeria from 1947 to 1960. Increases in yields varied of course with the crop, soil type, and amount and type of fertilizer used in the trials. For example, the application of 2.14 cwt. of 10N:10P:20K granular fertilizer to cassava produced increases in yield ranging from 8 to 116 percent, with an average yield increase of 62 percent. Maximum increases in yields obtained with other crops were (a) rice—75.8 percent in response to mixed non-granular fertilizers; (b) maize—339 percent in response to Nitrogen; (c) yam—71.3 percent in response to Nitrogen.

The yields obtainable by the average farmer would, of course, be less than those noted in the supervised field trials but would still be high enough to warrant government expenditure on schemes designed to stimulate the proper use of fertilizers.

[3] For an interesting discussion of the organizational problems bearing upon an effective transfer of scientific knowledge from the research stage to production, see Hill and Mosher (1963).

Commercial plantations involve large-scale planting (a minimum of 5,000 to 10,000 acres) and processing of export crops such as cocoa, oil palm, and rubber. Plantations usually use mechanized planting, maintenance, and harvesting where possible.

A nucleus plantation combines a commercial plantation and a settlement scheme. The "nucleus" contains processing facilities and a commercial plantation run with paid labor. Smallholders are given small plots around the nucleus on which to build a house, grow subsistence crops, and grow the cash crop being produced by the central plantation. The nucleus plantation as planned in Eastern Nigeria and as operated in Uganda and Kenya either processes and markets the smallholder's produce for a fee or contracts to buy the produce at a fixed price.

Settlement schemes involve the resettling of a large number of farmers into one consolidated planting area. Each farmer is allocated land for housing, subsistence crops, and a commercial crop. Each settlement has centralized processing facilities for the commercial crop. In Eastern Nigeria the government provides the social services. The settlers are given a loan for their house, land, and living expenses, which must be repaid after their crops come into bearing.

Smallholder schemes do not attempt large-scale land consolidation, but work with the land that the individual or community already has. Investment type schemes try to persuade the farmer to plant commercial crops that take more than a year to mature. Thus, rubber, cocoa, and oil palm, which require five to seven years to come into production, are typical investment crops. In Eastern Nigeria the farmer is paid a subsidy in the form of planting materials, fertilizers, and cash. The subsidy is intended partially as (1) an inducement, (2) compensation for loss of income from land temporarily taken out of production, and (3) a contribution toward the cost of planting and maintaining the new acres. The farmer is usually required to plant a minimum number of acres (five in Eastern Nigeria), and he forfeits his subsidy if his acreage is not maintained according to the instructions of the government.

Improvement schemes attempt to improve existing acreages through the introduction of one or more of the following: (1) improved planting materials, (2) improved cropping practices, or (3) fertilizers. For purposes of definition in this paper, I will assume that improvement schemes apply only to crops having a maturity cycle of less than 12 months, such as yam, cassava, and cocoa yam. Since the payback period is usually less than a year, cash subsidies to the farmer are not required.

ECONOMICS OF AGRICULTURAL DEVELOPMENT SCHEMES

Table 1 gives output/input ratios for plantation, settlement, smallholder investment, and smallholder improvement schemes under conditions operating or contemplated in Eastern Nigeria. The output/input ratios for nucleus plantations are about the same as those of regular plantations and are therefore not listed separately.

TABLE 1

OUTPUT/INPUT RATIOS FOR PLANTATIONS, SETTLEMENT,
SMALLHOLDER (INVESTMENT) SCHEMES, AND SMALLHOLDER
(IMPROVEMENT) SCHEMES

Type	*Output: input*	*Output: govt. input*	*Cash income—farmer: cash outlay—farmer*
	(1)	(2)	(3)
1. Plantations			
oil palm	2.3:1	2.3:1	—
cocoa	1.7:1	1.7:1	—
rubber	1.4:1	2.8:1	—
2. Settlement schemes			
oil palm, rubber	2.3:1	4–6:1	5–6:1
3. Smallholder (investment) schemes			
oil palm	7:1	26:1	5.5:1
cocoa	2:1	27:1	n.a.
rubber	3:1	37:1	6.0:1
4. Smallholder (improvement) schemes			
yams	2.9:1	6.4:1	5.3:1
cassava	3.8:1	8.4:1	6.9:1
cocoa	2.9:1	6.4:1	3.8:1

Column 1, Output/Input Ratio for the Economy: The output/input ratio as defined below gives us some measure of the benefit of a scheme to the economy as a whole. Output/input ratios such as these can be used in evaluating alternative investment possibilities. The output-input ratio was calculated by valuing output at world prices (for export crops) or average market prices (for subsistence crops) and dividing by the total cost of all factors of production and marketing. The input figure includes (1) all production and maintenance costs including paid labor or the imputed cost of the smallholder's labor; (2) transport and handling cost to market or port; (3) cost of processing (if any); (4) depreciation of the estimated value of the land for investment crops. No attempt was made to discount the income and expenditure streams to take account of the time value of money.

Column 2, Output/Government Input Ratio: Output was calculated as described above with the exception noted in (d) below. The ratio essentially measures the addition to GNP per unit of government expenditure on a given scheme. Government inputs include the following:

(a) *Plantation schemes:* The government "share" of expenses in plantations is assumed to be the product of the plantation expenses and the percentage government ownership. For oil palm and cocoa plantations, the government of Eastern Nigeria would be forced to subscribe 100 percent of the capital because of artificially low Marketing Board prices. The return to the economy as a whole for oil and rubber plantations is attractive. The profit, however, is taken by the Marketing Board which maintains a large differential between the f.o.b. world price and the price paid to producers. The crops are therefore unattractive to private investors. Rubber is not under the control of the Marketing Board, and the government might therefore be able to attract 50 percent private participation in rubber plantations. In this case, only 50 percent of the cost and depreciation inputs are attributed to government input.

(b) *Settlement schemes:* Although settlers on the Eastern Nigeria Farm Settlements will have to pay back money advanced to them for subsistence, housing, land, and land development, the government will still have to bear the cost of agricultural extension services, administrative staff, schools, hospitals, roads, water supply, and other amenities. Government input includes the estimated cost of these amenities and services.

(c) *Smallholder (investment) schemes:* Eastern Nigeria is currently operating investment type planting schemes for oil palm, cocoa, and rubber. The government input for all three schemes includes the cost of extension services, planting stock, subsidized chemicals and fertilizers, and cash compensation. With the exception of extension services and subsidies on cocoa spraying chemicals, the government contribution ends before the crops come into full bearing. The out-of-pocket cost of the schemes to the government runs from 13 to 18 pounds per acre planted (excluding the cost of extension services and administration).

(d) *Smallholder* (*improvement*) *schemes:* Improvement schemes assume that the crop to be improved is already being planted by the farmer. The output figure under this type of scheme is therefore incremental output, that is, the value of the additional produce obtained by adopting new methods. For cocoa, this entails spraying against fungus and pests. For yam and cassava, the improvement is the use of simple fertilizers. None of the improvement schemes cited here involves the introduction of new varieties of plant.

Eastern Nigeria currently is operating a cocoa improvement scheme. The government, at present, does not have a scheme to improve subsistence crops such as yam and cassava. The cost data for the latter came from Ministry of Agriculture field trial data and not from actual experience with an improvement scheme. It is assumed that the government subsidizes fertilizers and chemicals to the extent of 33⅓ percent.

Column 3, Cash Income to Farmer/Cash Outlay by Farmer: This ratio is useful in determining whether or not the scheme will be economically attractive to the farmer. Cash income is calculated using the price that the farmer is likely to receive for his produce. In the case of Marketing Board crops, this is substantially less than world or market price. In the case of subsistence crops, the price received by the farmer would be the local market price less transport costs and middleman's profit. As the latter costs are unknown, the average market prices were used for calculating the farmer's income from rubber, yam, and cassava. The cash outlay by the farmer includes nominal labor costs, cost of fertilizers and implements, and processing charges.

References and Accuracy of the Data:

(a) *Plantation schemes:* The figures are based on the operating experience of the Eastern Nigeria Development Corporation and are therefore reliable. Marketing costs were obtained from the annual reports of the Eastern Nigeria Marketing Board.

(b) *Settlement schemes:* The data for settlement schemes was taken from a project description and costing provided by the Eastern Nigeria Ministry of Agriculture. The Ministry had not fully costed the farm settlement schemes, nor has the government yet decided precisely which cost is to be borne by government and which by the settlers themselves. The output/input ratios are therefore educated guesses.

(c) *Smallholder* (*investment*) *schemes:* The figures are based on excellent project descriptions and costings prepared by the Eastern Nigeria Ministry of Agriculture and should therefore be accurate. An additional reference was "Economic Analysis of Tree Crops

Schemes (Oil Palm, Cocoa and Rubber)," prepared by the Ministry of Economic Planning, Enugu.

(d) *Smallholder (improvement) schemes:* The figures for the cocoa improvement scheme were obtained from the references cited in (c) above. The data for the yam and cassava improvement schemes was taken from "Fertilizer Use in Eastern Nigeria," by Dr. W. S. Mann, Ministry of Agriculture, Enugu, March 1963.

(e) *General references included:*

(1) Eastern Nigeria Marketing Board Reports, 1959–62.

(2) Tables of costs of establishment, maintenance, and harvesting of cocoa, rubber, and oil palm prepared by the Eastern Nigeria Ministry of Agriculture.

(3) Costs of cocoa production in West Africa distributed by Cadbury Fry, Ltd.

(4) P. N. C. Okigbo, *Nigerian National Accounts, 1957* (Enugu: Government Printer, 1962).

(5) *Agriculture Sample Survey, 1959* (Lagos: Federal Office of Statistics, 1961).

(6) Draft copy of a paper on the pattern of food consumption in an Eastern Nigerian Village, by Dr. W. S. Mann, Ministry of Agriculture, Enugu.

(f) It should be emphasized that the costs for the smallholder (investment) and the settlement schemes are based on government projections rather than actual operating experience. The schemes began operating in mid-1962 and it is too early to tell if the cost projections are accurate and the incentives given to farmers sufficient to make the schemes a complete success.

Column 1 of Table 1 gives output/input ratios calculated for the economy as a whole. The output is priced at the world price (for export crops) or market price (for local crops), and the inputs include all costs to the market (or port), including the imputed cost of the farmer's labor and the cost of government extension services.

Column 2 gives the output/government input for each type of scheme. Output is priced at world or market price, and government input includes all costs to government. In the case of the smallholder schemes, this includes costs of subsidies and agricultural extension services.

Examination of Table 1 shows that smallholder investment and smallholder improvement schemes offer the greatest economic return to the economy as a whole. Settlement schemes run a close second, according to the costings provided by the government of

Eastern Nigeria. I should note, however, that settlement schemes in Africa have been generally unsuccessful, and costs are usually far greater than anticipated by the sponsoring government. The most important conclusion derived from Table 1 is that the smallholder schemes (particularly the investment type) show the highest economic output per unit of government input—an extremely important consideration in underdeveloped countries where government capital is so limited. The smallholder schemes, of course, show a high output to government input because: (1) they mobilize resources not otherwise available for productive investment, that is, farm labor, peasant savings, inefficiently used land, etc.; (2) the productivity of peasant land can be vastly improved by application of a few simple, proven agricultural techniques, as mentioned above; (3) there is an absence of the large overhead investment in housing, social amenities, transport facilities, and administrative staff found in the plantation and settlement-type schemes.

One can argue that the productivity of peasant holdings can be even further improved by land consolidation that allows more economical use of labor and elementary mechanized planting and harvesting. While this is true, the gains to be had by mechanization and—in many instances—consolidation can be considered at a later stage of agricultural development when marginal increases (10 to 15 percent) in food and export crop production become important.

While risking oversimplification, we might postulate that agricultural development in areas similar to Eastern Nigeria should be divided into the following stages:

Stage 1: Smallholder Development

Primary emphasis would be on the introduction of elementary agricultural techniques to peasant farmers, village cooperatives, and community agricultural efforts. The increase in productivity and attending increase in GNP will generate capital that can be used to (1) diversify the agricultural sector, (2) finance the initial development of industry, and (3) lift agricultural production to a level where larger-scale efforts described under Stage 2 can be started.

The gains possible under smallholder development can be seen from the following example: Assume that country X has a GNP of £1,000,000,000, 70 percent of which can be attributed to the agricultural sector. If we assume that an average increase in production of 100 percent is possible and that 30 percent of the agricultural sector can be improved in the first 10 years of development, the annual addition to GNP at the end of 10 years will be £210,000,000. This is approximately equivalent to a growth in GNP of 2 percent per year.

Stage 2: Continuation of Smallholder Development and Introduction of Larger Production Units

As smallholder productivity improves and when the majority of the willing or physically accessible peasant farmers have been approached, the government might shift its emphasis to the encouragement of larger consolidated production units. This, however, is not to say that plantation development and development of consolidated holdings should be neglected during the early stages of a country's agricultural development. On the contrary, plantations are often useful in attracting foreign capital, securing export earnings, providing research and nursery facilities, and providing training grounds for agricultural extension staff. Trial consolidation schemes are useful for demonstration purposes and for building up a reservoir of knowledge that can be applied on a mass scale at a later stage of development. Development of peasant holdings is difficult because of the attitude changes necessary in the farmer if he is to accept agricultural methods deviating from time-honored practices. We will therefore examine the incentives for, and barriers to, smallholder development.

ECONOMIC INCENTIVES

Empirical evidence shows a fairly high degree of economic motivation among the various tribes in Eastern Nigeria. For example, in the early 1950's, when commodity prices were high, farmers planted about 20,000 acres of cocoa. Cocoa was not a crop that was traditionally planted or one which had been introduced previously, and the acreages were planted with little promotion on the government's part. Much the same was true of cashew in the late 1950's and more recently of poultry production. Where the promise of economic return was high enough, farmers tried new and unproven crops.

The various tribes of the Eastern Region—and the Ibo, in particular—apparently did, and still do, place high value on material wealth. When Europeans came to trade in slaves and later in oil palm along the coast of Nigeria, they found the native traders good businessmen and were able to obtain fewer concessions from them than in most places on the West Coast of Africa. Today the Ibos are well known throughout Nigeria and the Cameroons as clever and able traders.

While it is difficult to trace the origin of economic motivation, it is interesting to speculate on the reasons for its existence in terms of the traditional society in the eastern region. I will speak in terms of the Ibo tribe (the predominant tribe and that which I know best), but the influences I think are equally valid for most of the earlier trading tribes inhabiting the coastal areas of the region.[4]

There was and is no over-riding religious or feudal authority binding the Ibo-speaking peoples together. While some tribal groups have common gods, each village and sometimes individuals have more important gods of their own. The cultural or authority unit has always been a relatively small extended family unit or village. Ibo society is notable for the almost complete absence of strong natural chiefs or rulers. A few villages or tribes have them but most do not. There are titled men of nominal power in the villages (called Ozo), but these men buy their titles—they are not hereditary.[5]

The picture that one gets of pre-colonial society in the eastern region is one of small splintered tribal groups, insecurity against invasion, and constant change as power shifted from one tribal group to another or even from one group to another within a single community. The men of acquired wealth seem to have been the men of power. I suppose that wealth afforded a man or family some degree of protection since he was probably able to buy off his enemies or amass arms and people to defend his family or wage war on neighboring tribes. Being accustomed to

---

[4] For a history of the development of trade in the Niger Delta area see Dike (1956).

[5] Strong traditional rulers exist, however, among the Yoruba of the western region and the Hausa and Fulani in the northern region. It is suggested that the absence of strong hereditary leaders in Ibo territory might be an inducement to development. It would seem to be in the interest of strong traditional leaders, particularly in the northern region, to inhibit development to allow power to remain in the hands of a select traditionally-minded few.

change and interested in material wealth, the eastern region tribes were quick to take advantage of trade in slaves and palm oil and exhibited economic intuitions that are even more pronounced today.

Given the fact that people react positively to economic incentives and are willing to accept change when the incentive is high enough, we can postulate that the degree of acceptance of new agrarian techniques partially depends on (1) the magnitude of monetary return, and (2) the timing of the return.

Judging from interest rates in the local money markets, we can infer that the average peasant farmer would require a 70 to 100 percent return to his cash capital input to induce him to use changed agricultural techniques. His cash output/input would have to be at least 2:1. In improvement schemes, I would estimate that the average farmer would have to expect a doubling in output before he could be induced to try new techniques. Referring back to column 3 of Table 1, we can see that the smallholder and settlement schemes would seem to offer sufficient cash return to induce the farmer to change his ways.

The timing of the return is also important. The more rapid the return, the more likely the farmer is to change his ways. While investment schemes pay off more handsomely in the long run, the improvement schemes usually pay off during one planting-harvesting season. The improvement schemes would therefore have more appeal to the illiterate with limited land and capital to invest.

ECONOMIC BARRIERS

Economic barriers to successful smallholder schemes might be summarized as follows:

1. *Limited government capital.* Smallholder development involves large expenditures on training, extension personnel, materials, and cash subsidies to farmers. Most foreign aid agencies are unwilling to finance "local" expenditure, and the brunt of the cost of smallholder schemes will have to be borne from local resources.

2. *Scarce capital among peasant farmers.* The farmer himself will have to contribute the bulk of the capital and recurrent costs of both improvement and investment type smallholder schemes. His contribution usually takes the form of land, labor, and some

cash needed to purchase planting and maintenance materials. Some farmers are too poor to make even the most nominal contribution. In other cases, the social calls on the farmer's capital (contributions to societies, school fees of relatives, and so forth) are too large to permit him to finance or use improved agricultural techniques.

3. *Market imperfections.* Economic incentive is normally provided through the market price mechanism. In Eastern Nigeria, the small farmer is sometimes isolated from the main produce markets by the trader who partially or wholly absorbs urban market price increases into his profit. The farmer therefore may not be aware of the most profitable or even a profitable crop. The price passed on to the farmer may not be enough to induce him to plant or improve crops that would normally offer the rates of return mentioned above.[6] The small farmer is therefore often at the mercy of the produce wholesaler. Lack of inexpensive transport facilities and efficiently organized marketing channels accounts for the imperfection.

4. *Limitations of land.* The average farmer produces almost exclusively for his family's consumption and only sells extra produce (if any) in the market. Where land is extremely scarce, the peasant farmer will be reluctant to attempt any new or unproven crops or techniques that might fail and endanger his food supply. Change can only take place therefore where there is some "risk" capital in the form of excess land.

5. *Labor limitations:* Although most underdeveloped countries abound in underemployed labor 95 percent of the year, labor becomes scarce during the limited time periods suitable for planting and harvest. This is particularly true where agricultural holdings are far from the farmer's dwelling or are fragmented and the individual plots located far from each other. The farmer usually draws labor from his immediate family, and transportation time

---

[6] When the profit margin is too low, farmers may not even harvest producing acreages. This reportedly happened in 1962 when the price paid to producers of palm oil fell to a new low. Some farmers did not make the effort to harvest fruits from inconveniently located trees and in some cases only harvested enough to meet their own requirements for consumption.

In all fairness it must be mentioned that increases in local consumption and smuggling across borders were other factors which helped lower the quantity of palm oil sold to the Marketing Board.

to and from farm plots often limits the amount of land that one family can tend or develop.

Labor shortages will probably grow more acute on small farms in the near future as the younger generations leave for the cities to find work more in keeping with their expectations for themselves.

The above factor would seem to point to the need for land consolidation and, in some cases, labor-saving mechanization. I believe, however, that the government will be able to find a sufficient number of consolidated smallholdings with adequate labor to fully utilize the capital available for agriculture in the early stages of development.

6. *Lack of efficient processing facilities.* Export crops such as oil palm, cocoa, coffee, and rubber require elementary processing before they can be marketed. The price received for the crop depends on the quality of the processed product, and nominal inexpensive improvements in the processed product can bring large price increases to the producer. This is particularly true for consumables such as cocoa, tobacco, and coffee, where the taste of the final product is largely dependent on the quality of the initial processing. At present, the processing techniques used by the small producer are crude and produce a mediocre product. Simple improvements in existing processing techniques could produce a larger quantity of a top quality product.[7] Improvement of rural processing techniques must therefore go hand in hand with improved production techniques if the producer is to be given the fullest price incentive to improve and expand his production.

7. *Limiting factors of time and distance on extension agents.* Where the farmer's plots are fragmented or relatively inaccessible because of poor transport facilities, the extension agent is forced to waste a good deal of time in transit between plots and different farmers. When high quality extension staff is limited, as it is bound to be in the early stages of a country's development, smallholder schemes will have to concentrate on holdings which

---

[7] It should be noted that West German development after the war was based on a ruthless pushing for production and minimization of social expenditure to create the economic base for later development of social services. For details see Wallich (1958). Hirschman's discussion of social overhead versus directly productive investment in economic development is also relevant. See Hirschman (1958).

are (a) readily accessible, and (b) of reasonable size. In Eastern Nigeria, the farmer must be located close to a road and must hold at least five acres of consolidated land before the government will allow him to participate in the schemes.

As transport facilities improve and as more extension agents become available, the less accessible and smaller farmers can be approached and consolidated schemes started for farmers having less than the minimum economic acreage. Voluntary consolidation is encouraged of course by setting a lower limit on the number of acres needed for participation in a smallholder scheme.

SOCIAL BARRIERS TO SMALLHOLDER DEVELOPMENT

1. *Inertia and fear of failure.* Farmers are reluctant to change their way partially because of inertia and partially because of the fear that new methods might fail and leave their families short of food or income. This factor will grow in importance as the limited amount of under-utilized land is forced to support a growing population. Indeed, the very necessity to support more people builds the farmer's resistance to change. This in turn reinforces the potential vicious circle of growing population and steady or declining percapita food production.

2. *Fear of loss of prestige through failure.* The Ibo culture will not bring negative social sanctions against a farmer who wishes to try new agricultural techniques that have a potentially high economic return (except in a few areas where planting a certain crop is against the wishes of a village god). A farmer who tried new techniques and failed, however, would be called a fool and would lose a good deal of face in his community. The fear of failure and the attendant loss of face might therefore be a strong deterrent against change to a farmer well-rooted in his community.

3. *Bias against agriculture.* Largely due to widespread primary education throughout the southern part of the country, traditional values are rapidly breaking down. While this makes the youth receptive to change, the new transitional value system looks down upon agriculture as a vocation. The young Nigerian has rejected the most obvious traditional value—life tied to the land—for presumably glittering city life. Even the youth who has failed to obtain work in the cities is reluctant to return to his home and

take up farming. Return would be an admission of both the individual's failure and the failure of his new adopted way of life to provide for him. Only the repeated failure of school leavers to find jobs in the cities will drive the present generation back to the farm. In the meantime, the government will have to rely on the established farmer to begin agrarian reforms.

Perhaps primary and secondary school leavers in 1970 will be more receptive to agricultural vocations if (a) agricultural education improves at the primary and secondary school levels, (b) young school leavers recognize the failure of their predecessors and revise their expectations to a level more in keeping with their education and abilities, and (c) the government is able to make agriculture economically attractive.

4. *Short time horizon.* Because the African has been largely concerned with day-to-day, planting-season-to-season activities and welfare, the concept of investment for future returns is difficult to sell. A shilling in hand now is worth considerably more to the average farmer than a pound several years hence. The time horizon lengthens with the level of education and the amount of capital available (in terms of land, cash, and expendable family labor). Investment type smallholder schemes should therefore be attractive to the more educated, wealthier farmer. Only the improvement-type schemes that have a rapid pay-off would be attractive to the farmer with a limited time horizon and relatively limited capital.

5. *Non-economic calls on capital.* Social calls on an individual's capital makes it difficult for him to accumulate enough capital to start or sustain an investment in agriculture. According to his ability to pay, the individual must educate and support his family and relatives and contribute to various local societies and community development efforts. While this represents a highly organized social security system, the system stifles investment by those who have the most capital, are most knowledgeable, and are most capable of seeing the value of longer term investments. In addition to family and community calls on capital, the individual often needs to acquire the physical trappings of wealth: a radio, a bicycle, and so forth, depending on his income. While social pressures will continue to drain investable capital, more and more Nigerians are limiting financial aid to their immediate family. I would expect this trend to continue.

TACTICS FOR DEVELOPMENT OF SMALLHOLDER AGRICULTURE

In conclusion, I would like to suggest development tactics not previously mentioned that might circumvent or overcome the social and economic barriers to smallholder development.

A. Optimum Use of Capital

There is little that can be done to immediately increase the amount of capital available to the government for agricultural development. Assuming that tax revenue has been maximized, the government will have to spend the limited funds available in the most productive manner. The small farmer, of course, also has limited capital. The government will therefore have to provide economic incentives above those provided through the market in the form of subsidies.

The government can and should make planting materials, fertilizers, and insecticides readily available at a reasonable price. It might also be necessary to give guarantees or payments against temporary income losses incurred by the use of new methods, the planting of new crops having long maturity cycles, or the failure of the crops and methods introduced. Limitations on government funds, however, precludes the giving of large subsidies to a large number of people. It therefore follows that the government must spread its "seed capital" by obtaining the largest possible contribution from the farmer himself.

As a first step, then, subsidies might be scaled to the minimum necessary to attract farmers who are relatively wealthy in terms of land and cash. As the economy grows and tax revenues increase, the government can better afford to increase subsidies to the poorer farmer and mount more expensive consolidation schemes.

Such tactics will make the rich richer and might be unpalatable to those who believe that the most poverty-stricken should be the first to benefit from government economic aid. If scarce capital is first given to the poorest farmers, little sustained economic growth will ensue. The poor can contribute little capital to match the government money and they would be prone to spend increases in income on consumption rather than investment.

Subsidies of course should be partially or wholly withdrawn from farmers when their new crops come to fruition and when they are able to bear the full economic cost of the scheme. Governments must avoid paying recurrent subsidies to those who do not need them.

B. Improved Marketing Facilities

Normal extension of road transport facilities will help bring the farmer closer to the urban markets, allow him to sell his produce at a more favorable price, and encourage the supply of reasonably priced food stuffs to the growing urban population. Governments can further aid smallholders by encouraging cooperative marketing of produce. Village cooperatives should bring down produce transport costs and eliminate a number of the middle-man traders who tend to isolate the small farmer from the lucrative markets.

In addition, the introduction of simple storage facilities and techniques should help the farmer obtain a better price for his goods. With adequate storage facilities, the farmer could sell his produce after the harvest season is well over and obtain a price 25 to 100 percent higher than that prevalent during the harvest period. Traders often increase their profit by the same means.

C. Processing Facilities

Governments should develop and introduce small-scale processing techniques and equipment for the use of the small producer. If the equipment is expensive, government loans will have to be made available and processing cooperatives encouraged.[8]

D. Price Controls

Many underdeveloped countries have marketing boards which control producer prices and provide facilities for the purchase, grading, sale, and evacuation of export produce. Marketing boards can be used to (a) tax produce by accumulating reserves that will later be spent on development projects or added to a country's general revenue, (b) stabilize produce prices and use

---

[8] For example, the government of Eastern Nigeria will make credit available to farmers and cooperative societies to enable them to purchase hydraulic presses for the processing of palm oil. The presses are considerably more efficient than the traditional screw press and should return from 75 to 150 percent per annum to the owner if properly used. One thousand presses will be distributed during the 1962–68 development plan period. The cost of the press to the farmer will be approximately £500, including ancillary equipment and a contract for free service for the first few years of operation.

reserves to adjust price incentives to the average farmer, or (c) implement a revenue plus stabilization policy that falls between the two previously mentioned extremes.

Where marketing boards exist, the government concerned must be extremely careful not to set producer prices so low that they heavily tax the farmer and discourage smallholder production. For example, a government could easily work against itself inadvertently if it required its marketing board to contribute to general revenue and in turn used the revenue to subsidize or stimulate agricultural production. The marketing board might have to set its producer prices far below the world price and would substantially discourage future production if the long-term supply curve for the commodity in question is very price elastic. Produce marketing board prices and pricing policies must therefore be considered together with other factors when designing incentive policies for smallholder schemes.[9]

---

[9] The Eastern Nigeria Marketing Board seems to have adapted a middle-of-the-road policy with respect to the controlled producer price of palm oil, cocoa, palm kernels, and a few minor crops. For example, the Board contributed over £11,000,000 to Eastern Nigeria's development effort between 1954 and 1961 and has promised to contribute at least another £2,300,000 toward the finance of the 1962–68 Development Plan. The Board also increased its reserve position from £8,300,000 in 1956 to £15,900,000 in 1960. The reserve at this time was equal to about three-quarters of the Board's gross annual volume and provided a reasonable good hedge against decreases in world commodity prices. In 1961, the Board appropriated about £5,000,000 to contribute to various development projects, thereby allowing its reserves to drop to about £11,500,000. Because of decreased reserves, the poor world price outlook for palm oil and kernels, and, perhaps, increased pressure to contribute to the 1962–68 Development Plan, the Board dropped the 1962 producer price for oil 16 percent to £40 per ton and the producer price for kernels 14 percent to £25 per ton. The volume of special grade oil sold to the Board summarily dropped from 128,000 tons to 99,000 tons, indicating that the supply of palm oil to the Marketing Board might be price elastic in the short run. The volume of oil sold to the Board recovered to about 115,000 tons in 1963 but still failed to reach the record levels of about 135,000 tons in 1958–60 when the producer price was £50 to 47/15. The lowered volume could, of course, be due to the lower producer price, inclimate weather during the growing season, or increases in local consumption. It is impossible to divide responsibility between the three factors.

Price decisions made by the Marketing Board in the next few years may, however, substantially affect the future production of export commodities in Eastern Nigeria. This will depend upon the long-term price elasticity of palm produce and cocoa. The Ministry of Agriculture is currently sub-

Where marketing boards have been in operation for a number of years, there should be enough price and production data to allow economic analysis. With a reasonable analysis in hand, the government can set an optimum producer price—either to maximize production or to maximize marketing board profits. In either event, the price decisions should be put on a rational basis.

E. Overcoming Social Barriers

Social barriers to agricultural development are as difficult to overcome as they are to identify. We can, however, list the following tactics that should be useful in the early periods of development:

1. For investment type schemes, identify and work with farmers who have risk capital in the form of land, cash, available labor, and social prestige within their peer group.
2. Improvement type schemes can be opened to all classes of farmers as long as their land is accessible and not extremely limited.
3. For all types of schemes, one must identify the individuals who are receptive to change. They will frequently be established farmers with some education, capital, and prestige in his village. Alternatively, the individual might be considered a deviant by his own society and might have little to lose by trying new agricultural techniques. The easiest group to identify and work with, of course, are those who have previously tried and accepted new crops or techniques.

The paramount question facing a number of countries today is how to induce the younger generation to remain on or go back to the farms. Part of the answer lies in making agriculture economically attractive. The addition of required courses in agriculture in primary and secondary schools would at least familiarize the younger generations with agricultural techniques and the economic benefits of farming.

How one can change the younger generations' negative attitudes

---

sidizing palm and cocoa production through its smallholder planting schemes. If the Marketing Board sets the producer price too low, the government may fall short of her agricultural targets. Should this happen, the government will have inadvertently worked against itself by using the Marketing Board as a taxation device to collect revenue for development, which in turn required a low producer price, which in turn discouraged the very production that the government was collecting revenue to stimulate.

toward agriculture is a difficult question to answer. I fear that only continued time and frustration will drive unemployed school leavers back to the farm. Until agriculture is accepted as an acceptable vocation, the economy's growth will be impeded.

CONCLUSION

In the preceding pages, I have briefly presented the economic and social factors affecting the development of smallholder agriculture.

To my mind, the economic factors are of greatest importance if only because they are readily identifiable and more easily manipulated than the social factors. Although social barriers to development may be overriding in select cases, one can generally (at least in Eastern Nigera) find enough predominantly economically motivated people to absorb the capital set aside by the government for agricultural development.

To date, economists and sociologists have largely neglected the study of smallholder agriculture per se and concentrated on the larger and more spectacular settlement and consolidation schemes. If development is to be accelerated in the agriculturally based economics, then more attention must be paid to smallholder agriculture—the potential gains are too large to overlook.

28 REPORT ON THE INDUSTRIALISATION OF THE GOLD COAST [GHANA, 1953]

W. Arthur Lewis

INDUSTRIALISATION starts usually in one of three ways: (1) with the processing for export of primary products (agricultural or mineral) which were previously exported in a crude state; or (2) with manufacturing for an expanding home market; or (3) with the manufacture for export of light manufactures, often based on imported raw materials.

PROCESSING MATERIALS FOR EXPORT

The classical example of this first case is the growth of British industry in the 16th and 17th centuries. In 1500 England was still an exporter of raw materials, mainly raw wool. Successive English monarchs strove to build up local manufacture of woollen cloth, and by 1650 the export of wool had been almost completely replaced by an export of cloth.

The main difficulty in the way of capturing the processing of raw materials, and thus of getting the consuming countries to import a finished product instead of its raw materials, lies in the superiority of the consuming countries as centres for manufacturing. This superiority is based both on long experience and also on the scale and variety of their manufacturing industries, which is the secret of efficient production. This superiority was an obstacle even four centuries ago, when England was trying to wrest the processing of her own raw material from the more highly developed Netherlands. To-day, the gap between industrialised

SOURCE: W. Arthur Lewis, "Report on the Industrialisation of the Gold Coast," Accra, Government Printing Department, 1953. The excerpts reprinted here comprise one-fourth of the original Report, and are reprinted by permission of the author.

and undeveloped countries is even wider than it was then, and therefore the obstacles to successful competition are even greater.

In this competition the undeveloped country relies usually on two advantages: (a) low labour cost, based on low wages, and (b) an advantage in transport cost, if the material loses weight in the course of processing. Low wages are not the same as low labour cost. In comparison with the United Kingdom, labour cost is lower on the Gold Coast only if the difference in wages is great enough to offset the difference in productivity. The result varies very much from industry to industry. The difference in wages is fairly constant: money wages of unskilled labour are about four times as high in the United Kingdom as they are in the Gold Coast. So the wage cost of manufacturing is lower in the Gold Coast wherever it takes less than four men to do a job that one man would do in the United Kingdom. There are a great many occupations where the advantage in wage cost lies with the Gold Coast. This advantage then helps to offset the disadvantage in other costs—bigger fuel bills, greater cost of supervision, greater costs of maintaining equipment and so on—which every Gold Coast Industry has to bear. . . .

THE HOME MARKET

It is more usually an advantage in transport costs which decisively favours the processing of raw materials on the spot. This advantage arises in the case of those raw materials which lose weight in the process of manufacture. For example, since it takes four tons of bauxite to make one ton of aluminium, transport charges are saved if bauxite is turned into aluminium on the spot, instead of being transported as bauxite to the country where the aluminium will be used. Similarly, it is cheaper to transport sawn timber than the equivalent logs, steel than the equivalent iron ore, sugar than the equivalent sugar cane, and so on. It is not, on the other hand, cheaper to transport cloth than the equivalent cotton, because very little fibre is lost in the process of manufacture. Neither is it cheaper to transport soap to the consuming market, rather than the equivalent oils, or rubber tyres rather than the equivalent latex.

One raw material which is always lost in the process of manufacture is fuel. If fuel is available side by side with the material which is to be processed, the producing country has thus a double advantage over all consuming countries which do not have their own fuel. A source of fuel is not always important, because some commodities supply their own fuel, in the form of waste. Thus, sugar factories, sawmills, and palm oil factories are usually self-sufficient in fuel. However, where coal or oil has to be burnt, a raw material producing country is at a disadvantage if it is short of coal or oil, because the processing of raw materials frequently makes heavy demands on fuel. These demands may be so heavy that even a weight losing material is drawn to the fuel instead of the fuel to the material. In spite of the fact that it takes four tons of bauxite to make one ton of aluminium, the bauxite is usually carried to the fuel and not the fuel to the bauxite; similarly, iron ore is more usually carried to coal than coal to iron ore.

The decisive factor locating the processing of raw materials is thus, to summarise, usually not low wage cost, but loss of weight in the process of manufacture. Thus it is not surprising that in the Gold Coast the chief cases in which processing before export occurs are the timber industry, where up to 40 or 50 per cent of the weight of the log is waste in sawmilling, the palm oil industry, where the waste, by weight, is even greater, and the removal of precious stones from the useless ores in which they are buried, where the waste is greater still. . . .

Apart, however, from environment, wage cost, and transport cost, the prospect of manufacturing for the home market is dominated by one other consideration, namely the size of the local market in relation to the minimum size at which production can be done economically. The size of the local market for manufactures depends, given the size of the population, upon how rich or poor the people are. In poor countries the local market for manufactures is very small because the people spend the largest part of their income upon food and housing, and have only a small surplus available for expenditure on manufactures. Most of this surplus has to be spent on clothes, and the clothing industries are almost the only ones which have any chance of success.

The development of manufacturing for the home market therefore essentially depends upon improving the productivity of other economic activities. As the incomes derived from agriculture, from mining and from other activities grow, the local market for manufactured commodities grows automatically, and this is what makes possible the creation of factory industries catering for a local demand.

From this point of view, the most usual path to progress is increasing efficiency in the production of food. In very poor countries nearly the whole of the population is required in agriculture just to produce enough food for the country. As efficiency in food production grows, the proportion needed to produce food diminishes. In fact the simplest index to productivity in a country is to ask what proportion of the population is needed in agriculture to produce enough food for the whole country. In the richest countries, such as the United Kingdom, the United States of America and Australia, the answer is 12 per cent to 15 per cent, whereas in most under-developed countries 60 per cent or more of the people are required in agriculture to produce a standard of feeding only half as good as that which the more efficient countries produce with 12 per cent of their populations.

Ever-increasing productivity in agriculture affects manufacturing favourably in two ways. First, as the farmer's production grows, he has an ever-increasing surplus to offer in exchange for manufactures; ever-increasing productivity in agriculture means an ever-increasing market for manufactures. And secondly, as productivity grows, and the proportion of the population required in food production falls, labour becomes available for manufacturing industry.

In unenlightened circles agriculture and industry are often considered as alternatives to each other. The truth is that industrialisation for a home market can make little progress unless agriculture is progressing vigorously at the same time, to provide both the market for industry, and industry's labour supply. If agriculture is stagnant, industry cannot grow.

In the Gold Coast there is very little sign of an increase in agricultural productivity, except in so far as the improvement in the world price of cocoa since the war is an increase in agricultural productivity. Physical production per man, outside the cocoa industry, is probably constant, and in the cocoa industry it is probably declining. According to the Government Statistician, about half the adult male population of the Gold Coast is engaged in food production (excluding cocoa, which absorbs only one-third as many). This half of the economy is almost certainly stagnant.

The most certain way to promote industrialisation in the Gold

Coast is to lay the foundation it requires by taking vigorous measures to raise food production per person engaged in agriculture. This is the surest way of producing that large and ever-increasing demand for manufactures without which there can be little industrialisation.

There are two ways of increasing production per man in agriculture. One way is to increase the yield per acre; the other way is to increase the number of acres worked per man. To increase the yield per acre is usually the cheaper way. It requires first that there should be research, to breed the most productive seeds and livestock, to discover the best use of fertilisers, to determine approximate crop rotations, and so on. The Gold Coast Department of Agriculture has done some work in these spheres, and has no doubt made the best use of the scanty resources at its disposal. But, in one sense, the surest way to industrialise the Gold Coast would be to multiply by four or five the resources available to the department for fundamental research into food production. And then, as the results become available, to multiply five-fold the funds available for extension work in the villages. . . .

MANUFACTURING FOR EXPORT

The countries which are best suited to capture export markets for finished commodities are those which possess cheap fuel and weight-losing raw materials. There are, however, countries which have built up industrialisation on the basis of exporting, without possessing these advantages. Japan, Hong Kong and Puerto Rico are outstanding examples, Lacking fuel and raw materials, these countries have concentrated on importing raw materials which are light in relation to their value (so that transport cost is small), and which use little fuel in the process of manufacture. Textile fibres, rubber, leather and paper are the most important materials in the categories.

A country which lacks advantageous natural resources can compete effectively in foreign markets only on the basis of low labour costs. This way of earning a livelihood appeals, therefore, only to countries where the population is so large in relation to natural resources that even the least remunerative occupations must be fostered. The Gold Coast is not in this position. Though wages are low in comparison with the United Kingdom, they are

high in comparison with wages in other undeveloped countries. There is an abundance of land, and an acute shortage of labour. Countries which cannot feed their people from their own soil must export manufactures in return for food, or face starvation, and they must keep their wages down to whatever level will permit them to compete with more efficient producers. . . .

THE HOME MARKET

. . . apart from bauxite, the processing of raw materials does not offer any immediate prospect of increased local manufacturing on a significant scale. If there is to be significant industrialisation, it must be for the home market. As we have already seen, all manufacturing in the Gold Coast is subject to environmental handicaps, which may be offset by low wage costs in whole, in part, or not at all. In addition, industries are favoured or disadvantaged according to the nature and location of their raw material, according to their fuel requirements, according to how capital intensive they are and according to the size of the local market. . . .

Industrialisation for the home market usually begins with the manufacture of textiles, since consumers at low income levels spend more upon textiles than upon all other manufactures combined. Indeed, industrialisation cannot begin to offer substantial employment unless it makes considerable inroads into the market for textiles. . . .

If textiles are the most important of the consumer goods, metals are the basis of producer goods, entering into all kinds of equipment. The total importation of metals even exceeds the total importation of textiles, respectively in 1950 £13,750,000 and £12,980,000. Any country can take up textile manufacture, but no country can become mainly dependent upon manufacturing activity if it does not have the resources necessary for producing metals, namely ores and cheap power. The Gold Coast seems likely to become a great producer of aluminium, but it has not the resources to be a great producer of iron and steel, which is what the home market consumes.

One does not, however, need to have ores in order to have some metal manufacture. Ores are needed for the primary processes of making pig iron or steel, or ingots of copper or other metals, for the primary processes are characterised by great loss

of weight. The finishing processes, however, involve little loss of weight, beyond the fuel used. It is therefore possible to import pig iron, or raw steel or other metals, and to manufacture finished goods. Even at this stage, however, a country is at a disadvantage if it has also to import fuel. If cheap power becomes available, a fairly large industry can be created in the Volta area, based on imported metals. One has in mind such products as rainwater pipes, cooking stoves, cisterns, bath tubs, iron posts, building materials, buckets, iron drums, bedsteads, lamps, chains, nails, implements and tools, springs, nuts and bolts and small articles generally. . . .

FOREIGN ENTERPRISE

In any country the early stages of industrialisation are usually the work of foreigners, because usually only they have the knowledge and the capital. This was true of the industrialisation of Britain from the fifteenth century to the seventeenth, when the foundations of later greatness were being laid, and it is true of every modern industrial country since that time, except the U.S.S.R. The U.S.S.R. relied on foreigners for knowledge, but supplied the capital herself, by squeezing it out of her farmers. Japan used both foreign knowledge and foreign capital, but the very unequal distribution of income in the country enabled her wealthy classes to supply a much greater proportion of the required capital than is possible in more egalitarian countries. There is no question that industrialisation is impossible in the Gold Coast without bringing in the knowledge of expatriates; the question is only on what terms they come in, and how much of their own capital they may invest. . . .

To the extent to which industrialisation is financed from domestic savings, it is, in the ultimate analysis, the farmers who provide the wherewithal. In Japan, this was accomplished by levying high taxes and rents upon them; and in the U.S.S.R. it was accomplished by an inflationary process, with the prices of manufactures rising faster than food prices, to the farmers' disadvantage. It is, however, one thing to prise capital out of the farmer when his productivity is increasing year by year, and quite a different matter to prise it out of a stagnant agriculture. In Japan, in the period 1880 to 1920, the yield of an acre of agricultural land increased on the average by 1·3 per cent per

annum and the output per person engaged in agriculture increased even faster than this, namely by 2·4 per cent per annum. When such rapid agricultural progress is taking place, it is not very difficult to get a lot more capital out of the farmers, and still leave them with an annually rising standard of living. Much is talked about the speed of Japanese industrialisation; but it is not generally realised that what really made this possible was the spectacular increase in agricultural productivity which was taking place at the same time.

We return thus to a point which . . . has already [been] made: the secret of industrialisation is a rapidly progressing agriculture, and, more particularly, since food production is the major part of agriculture, the number one priority in a programme of economic development is measures which increase food production per head. Without such measures, a country like the Gold Coast cannot spare the labour for industries, cannot find the capital for them, and has too small a market to support their output.

All the same, if it were desired to exclude foreign capital altogether from manufacturing industry, it would not be altogether impossible to squeeze another £3,000,000 a year out of the people of the Gold Coast, even with agricultural productivity stagnant. They would not like it, and would show their dislike of any Government which persisted in such a policy, but presumably if all political leaders were united in backing such a policy they might get away with it. The alternative is to rely, instead, to a considerable extent on foreign capital.

Foreign capital is unpopular in all countries which are or have been in colonial status. This is mainly because in such countries the foreigners do not get assimilated into the population. The Dutchman or Frenchman who started a new industry in Tudor England became an Englishman in due course. His children grew up in English schools (such as there were), inter-married, and lost their foreign allegiance. Similarly, the Englishman who went to America, or to Australia, was soon absorbed, and he or his family ceased to be foreign. This process of assimilation does not occur when the immigrant differs in race, in religion, and in ways of living from the people amongst whom he comes. He lives differently, and does not inter-marry. Whether his family settles in the country, as the Chinese do in South-east Asia, or goes back home, as English men do in West Africa, he remains

a foreigner, and attracts the fears and dislike which the human race seems everywhere to feel for outsiders and for other non-conformers.

Indeed, it is often the case that foreigners are content with smaller profits than domestic capitalists; the latter are inclined to look mainly for quick, 100 per cent returns, and to shun investments where one may have to wait a long time to get one's money back. All private capital invested in undeveloped countries expects to make large profits, whether it be domestic or foreign. This is because the risk of investing in such countries is greater than the risk of investing in the developed countries, where the factors which determine profitability are better known, and more easily controlled.

In any case, from the point of view of economic development what matters with profits is not how large they are, but how much goes out of the country. For profits which are reinvested in the country raise the general standard of living. There is a greater presumption that domestic profits will be reinvested than there is that foreign profits will be reinvested in the country, and since reinvested profits are the main source of savings in any country, this difference is important. But the difference is not always large. Many foreign capitalists automatically reinvest their profits in the country, and indeed there is no reason why they should not do so if the country continues to offer opportunities for economic expansion. It is probable that a large proportion of the foreign-owned capital now in the Gold Coast consists simply of profits made there and reinvested.

Assuming that foreign capital is required, the alternative to permitting foreign enterprise is that the Government should borrow abroad, presumably at a rate of interest lower than the profits that foreign entrepreneurs would want, and should either operate factories itself, or lend the money to African entrepreneurs. Most governments, however, need all the money that they can raise, whether by loan or by taxes, for the more urgent purpose of expanding the public services. This purpose is more urgent in a double sense. It is more urgent because the expansion of the public services is necessary if other economic activities are to be developed, so that a government is likely to contribute more to development if it expands the public services generally than if it uses the same money to build a factory. And it is more urgent also in the sense that no one but the government can expand the public services, whereas if the government does not build factories, others will. No government is so rich that it does not have to choose between alternative ways of spending money. Even the Gold Coast Government, which seems rich to its citizens, is really very poor. If the Government were to set out to give the Gold Coast the educational system which it needs, this alone would swallow all the funds at its disposal, let alone if it were also to try to provide water supplies throughout the country, adequate medical services, properly surfaced roads, telephones, and other public utilities. There is no doubt in the writer's mind that the Gold Coast Government can do more for development by spending its money on expanding the public services, which are woefully inadequate, and on quadrupling that part of its agricultural services which relate to food production for the local market, than it can do by operating factories. If the Government were determined to exclude private foreign capital, it would be better to postpone industrialisation rather than to divert money to it from these more urgent purposes. For the present the Government should confine its ownership of factories to the inescapable minimum. What this inescapable minimum is, we discuss in later sections.

Besides, even if the money were available, industrialisation cannot proceed without the knowledge of foreigners. In some cases this can be hired, either by hiring individuals in the market, or by employing an experienced firm as managing agents. But in other cases, such as the manufacture of aluminium, there is no way of starting the industry without the full participation of foreign capital and enterprise.

Development, like anything else, has a price. The question is not whether there are disadvantages, but whether the benefit exceeds the cost. Even when foreigners make large profits they are still contributing to development, not only by means of the wages, taxes, and other expenses that they incur, but also because they train labour and impart commercial experience to the general population.

The most serious indictment that can be levied against foreign capitalists, in economic terms, is not that foreign shareholders receive dividends, but that the foreigners are often reluctant to train up people in the secrets of their craft. For usually the foreigner's most useful contribution to a country is not his capital, but the new techniques which he brings. If these new techniques

are dispersed among the people progress is rapid, and the country soon becomes independent of foreign patronage. But if they remain the monopoly of a few foreigners, development must be slow.

The foreigner's most useful craft in these days is not scientific information, but managerial experience. Science and technology are taught in schools, and the local people can study them in their own or foreign universities. The craft of business management, however, can be learnt only in managing business. If no one will employ the local people above the level of clerks, they cannot learn how to manage industrial businesses for themselves, and their economic affairs will always be dominated by foreigners. This is the reason why the foreigners, in those countries where they refuse to be assimilated, are usually most careful to exclude local people from managerial positions. It is also the reason why most colonial countries, as soon as they become independent, pass legislation or take other steps to compel foreign firms to open up managerial positions to local people. But even non-colonial countries have taken such measures; thus, when foreigners brought new trades to England in the sixteenth and seventeenth centuries, the patents of monopoly which they were granted usually included the condition that the foreigner must train a number of Englishmen in his craft within a stipulated period.

Whatever the foreigner's faults may be, the fact remains that the Gold Coast needs him more than he needs the Gold Coast. Foreign capital does not need the Gold Coast. If all the foreign capital now in the Gold Coast were driven out, it would have little difficulty in being absorbed elsewhere, for the simple reason that the Gold Coast is a very small place relatively to the world as a whole. There are many places within the sterling area crying for capital—England herself, not to mention Australia, the Rhodesias, Ceylon and elsewhere. The Gold Coast cannot gain by creating an atmosphere towards foreign capital which makes foreigners reluctant to invest in the Gold Coast.

Terms must be reached which are acceptable to both sides. The Government should decide on what terms foreign capital will be acceptable, should announce these terms definitely, and should abide by them. The issues which have to be decided are (i) from what industries foreign capital will be excluded altogether, (ii) whether foreign capitalists will be required to have African partners, (iii) what rules are to regulate employment, (iv) whether profits or prices are to be regulated; (v) whether capital and profits can be freely transferred, and (vi) what is to be the procedure on nationalisation.

1. *Exclusion.*—Certain countries have excluded foreign capital altogether from certain sectors of the economy. Ownership of land or of mineral rights is a common exclusion, not only in West Africa, but also in Asia and in Latin America. Our interest, however, is only in factory industries. Here there are two possible classes of exclusion, industries which are reserved to the government, and those which are reserved to African enterprise.

Most governments now reserve "public utilities" exclusively for public operation. The definition of a public utility is based upon two concurrent characteristics. The industry must be one whose products are consumed by very wide sections of the community. And it must be one which is most economically conducted as a monopoly, or at any rate on a scale of production so large that the producer would have power to exploit the consumer. There are obvious candidates for inclusion in this category, such as electricity or railway transport. Other borderline candidates remain subject to dispute—such as steel or cement. . . .

2. *Partnership.*—The Government of India has announced that it will look most favourably upon foreign capitalists when they propose to operate in partnership with Indian capital (private or public). This partnership may take the form merely that local capitalists, or the Government, are to participate in the capital, or it may take the form that local capitalists are also to participate managerially.

Managerial participation is most valuable to the country, since its nationals in this way gain the best experience, and are thus able to launch out on their own. It would, however, be very irksome to foreign capitalists to be told that they must always act in partnership with local capitalists. This would certainly drive some away, and prevent others from coming. To insist on participation in capital is less irksome, but is also less useful, and hardly worth embodying into an edict. . . .

It is also surprising that more foreign firms do not make it easy for Gold Coast Africans to buy their shares. It is to the interest of foreign firms in the Gold Coast to do all that they can to identify African interests with their own, in order to diminish the suspicion which foreign enterprise everywhere attracts and the peculiar risks of discrimination which it therefore runs.

3. *Employment.*—Since the foreigner's greatest contribution is to train up domestic entrepreneurs, no foreigner should be allowed to operate in the country if his prejudices are such that he denies superior employment to the local people. Many countries have passed legislation to this effect, and the Gold Coast should do the same. The law would apply to any industrial firm, within five years of the passing of the law, or five years of the firm coming into operation, whichever is the later. It would apply to senior appointments, say to persons whose taxable income exceeds £600 a year. It would require that within five years one quarter of persons holding such appointments must be Gold Coast Africans. And it would apply to all firms employing fifty persons or more. A period of grace is needed to enable the firms to select and train Africans for superior jobs. The percentage of Africans to be employed need not be set beyond a quarter, since this percentage is large enough to wither away reluctance to employ Africans which has been founded only on prejudice. . . .

It is . . . most important to encourage firms to reinvest their profits in the country—not necessarily in the same industry—because profits are the major source of saving in any economy. Industrial countries encourage reinvestment by taxing distributed profits more severely than they tax undistributed profits; but this does not work in dependent countries, partly because the effect of double taxation arrangements is to nullify tax exemptions, and partly because the distinction one wishes to make is not between distributed and undistributed profits, but between profits reinvested in the country and profits transferred abroad (whether distributed or reinvested abroad). It may be possible to create legal distinctions between profits transferred abroad, profits held idle in the country, e.g. in cash, and profits reinvested in the country, but it would take much ingenuity to devise practicable distinctions. In any case, the attitude of the Government should be not to prohibit transfers, but merely to make reinvestment attractive. . . .

So many countries restricted transfers during the nineteen-thirties, because of shortage of foreign exchange, that foreign capitalists have become wary of making investments unless the Government pledges itself not to restrict transfers. The Gold Coast Government should give this pledge.

4. *Nationalisation.*—Every capitalist would like to have a guarantee that his firm will not be nationalised. In these days no

government can usefully give a pledge that subsequent government will not nationalise an industry. What the Government can do, however, is to give an undertaking that if a firm is nationalised, it will be paid fair compensation. Presumably such a guarantee is at present implicit in the reserve powers of the Governor. It would be better enshrined in the constitution, as it is in the constitutions of the United States of America, and of India. . . .

PUBLIC OWNERSHIP

We have already argued that the Gold Coast Government is so short of money that it should be reluctant to take on the ownership and operation of industrial undertakings, except where this is inescapable. It may be inescapable in two cases, in public utilities, and for purposes of pioneering.

In the case of public utilities, which we have defined to include all important monopolies, public ownership is one way of protecting the consumer against exploitation, but it is not the only way. The alternative way is to leave the industry in private hands, but to control its prices or profits, and its conditions of sale. There is no point in entering into controversial discussion here of the appropriate place to draw the line between public ownership and private enterprise. Every government has its own philosophy in accordance with which it draws this line where it thinks fit.

From the point of view of economic development, public ownership as a means of pioneering is much more interesting. In countries where entrepreneurs lack experience or confidence, there is a case for the government to lead the way by establishing industries with its own money, and to show that they can be operated successfully; in the expectation that it can withdraw from industry once the pioneering stage is over. The great exponent of this technique was Japan. There, between 1870 and 1900, the Government started one industry after another, and there is hardly a major industry in Japan to-day which was not initiated under government ownership. There was, however, no intention of permanent ownership; once the factory had become a going concern, the Government sold out, and turned its attention elsewhere. Also the Japanese Government was quite willing to make loans or subsidies to private entrepreneurs where it thought that this would serve the same pioneering purpose. . . .

AFRICAN ENTERPRISE

To train up African enterprise must naturally be one of the major objectives of economic policy. The role of the foreigner is that of the tutor: a sometimes likeable but usually tiresome fellow, from dependence on whom one wishes to escape at the earliest possible moment. As in politics, so also in economic life, the test of maturity is that the country can proceed on its own without needing any significant foreign help. That is why foreign business men should not be allowed in the country unless they play their part in training Africans to do their job, and this is why, in one sense, the crucial test of an industrialisation policy is not how rapidly it increases employment or output, but how rapidly it builds up African enterprise. This conclusion does not stem from any emotional attitude towards foreigners, who are neither better nor worse than the indigenous people, and neither more nor less lovable; even if we look at the matter on its most pedestrian level, there are simply not enough foreigners available to initiate all the development of which the Gold Coast is possible, so progress must be slow unless the African people learn to start and to run things for themselves.

African entrepreneurship is deficient in technical knowledge, in managerial capacity, and in capital. Of these three, the easiest to remedy is the deficiency of technical knowledge. For this can be learnt in technical schools and universities, or by placing Africans in foreign firms, at home or overseas, to learn the necessary techniques. Besides, technique can usually be hired. African business men should not hesitate to employ expatriates who have special knowledge: some already do so, and more should follow their example. For an African to hire a European (or Indian or Japanese or whomsoever has the skill) should be regarded neither as treachery to the racial cause nor as a source of added prestige; it is often simply the quickest way to establish an African business on a sound foundation.

Lack of managerial capacity is more difficult to remedy. The requirements of business management are five-fold. First, there is the management of physical resources—factory layout, the organising of a smooth flow of work through the factory, materials handling, care of machinery. Secondly, there is the keeping and use of records—of stocks, orders, costs, debits and credits. Thirdly, there is the management of men—selection of staff, discipline, loyalty, *esprit de corps,* delegation of duties and authority. Fourthly, there is the commercial sense, which cuts out waste, adjusts the use of resources to the flow of output, knows what prices to pay or to charge, and knows how to buy and to sell. And finally, there is the sense of integrity, without which a firm cannot acquire reputation or goodwill, and without which it cannot therefore last.

These requirements are listed because their importance is frequently overlooked. It is a common error, in undeveloped countries, to believe that entrepreneurship requires mainly technical knowledge and capital. The truth is the reverse: if people really have managerial capacity they will in most cases be able to find technical knowledge and capital to work with. What makes a business successful is the efficiency of its management, for, given this, all else will follow.

Management is one of the highest of the arts, because of its simultaneous demands upon character, upon intelligence, and upon experience. Deficiencies in management are therefore difficult to remedy. Some of the requirements can be taught in business schools, such as the tricks of factory layout, or of conducting interviews, or of keeping books. But much can be learnt only by experience. And those requirements which depend on personality and upon character can be met only by people whose outlook on life is appropriate.

Because business management has to be learnt so largely on the job, the Germans sent large numbers of their young people to work in England in the last quarter of the nineteenth century, in firms where they could acquire some administrative experience. Their example was followed a little later by Japan, whose young people were sent similarly to Germany and to the United States. The Gold Coast should follow suit by placing young people in firms in Britain, or, if colour prejudice stands in the way of this, by sending them to India, or to Japan, or to the United States, or any other country which will agree to have them. On their return a few may go into business on their own; but most of them will find employment in existing firms, African or European; or else in the ever expanding government service, which also demands administrative capacities.

African enterprise cannot be built up simply by lending Africans money. To lend money to entrepreneurs who lack managerial capacity is merely to throw it down the drain. What potential African industrialists lack is not primarily money; it is rather technical knowledge, and experience of factory organisation. If the government lends money it should do this only as a supplement to rendering technical and managerial assistance. In fact, the loan should be made only on condition that the borrower is willing to accept some measure of supervision. In some other countries, where money is lent to small business men, the lending agency stipulates that one of its officers becomes a director of the company to which money is lent, with power to veto certain transactions; in other cases it is content merely to have powers of inspection, and to give advice. In the Gold Coast a lending agency should have a staff of persons with managerial experience, who keep in the closest touch with all borrowers, partly to ensure that the loan is used for the purpose for which it is given, and partly to advise generally. . . .

PROBLEMS IN MANUFACTURING

Public Services.—A factory needs adequate and cheap supplies of electricity, water and gas, and adequate telephone and transport facilities. At present none of these public services is either adequate or cheap. Gas is not provided at all, and will not be provided until urban incomes are large enough to make profitable the provision of domestic supplies. All the other services are being extended and improved, under the Development Plan. Whether supply will catch up with demand, at present rates of growth, the writer cannot say; but this is certainly the intention of present proposals. Inadequate public supplies is at present a major obstacle to further industrialisation; some factories cannot get the water they would need for extensions; others cannot get space on the railways; many have to generate their own electricity, which always costs more than would extending the public service. If the best way to promote industrialisation is to have an agricultural policy which raises output and income per head, then the next best way is to have an adequate framework of public services. . . .

The advantage of [the Government] buying up large areas for industrial estates extends far beyond the conferment of a secure title. An even more important advantage is that factories are concentrated together. This concentration appeals to the town planner, who in any case desires to separate residential from industrial areas. But it appeals just as much to the industrialist because of the economies which result from having factories close together. The cost of supplying all public services is reduced—water, electricity, railway facilities, and so on. A general engineering service is more easily provided. The sale to each other of by-products and of components is more easily organised. A labour market develops. It is much easier to create the framework required for industrialisation if factories are together than if they are scattered all over the place.

The disadvantage of congregating factories is, of course, the political objection raised by towns in which special facilities are not provided. There is always some demand that new factories should be sited all over the country, and even in the heart of the countryside, so that everyone may have an equal chance of industrial employment. Such a demand simply fails to take account of the substantial economies of industrial concentration, economies whose appeal is to be seen in the fact that it is usually the largest industrial concentrations that grow fastest. This demand can most easily be conceded in rich countries, where industry is already well established, and which can therefore afford the risk of penalising new industrial growth. But in countries where manufacturing is just starting, it is best to make the most of the advantages of concentration, and to leave the dispersal of industry to a later stage when manufacturing is a well established and rapidly growing activity. This is not to say that anyone should be prohibited from setting up outside an industrial centre if he so desires; some factories are attracted to particular spots by what they offer in labour, or raw materials, or water, or climate, or otherwise. It is merely an argument for providing a small number of centres where those factories which gain from concentration may have the opportunity of doing so. . . .

SUBSIDISATION

Should the government subsidise or protect manufacturing industries which could not otherwise pay their way? It is generally agreed that a government ought to give temporary assistance to new industries to help them to find their feet, if it is convinced that they will be capable of standing on their own after an initial short period of running it. Should it also permanently assist industries which would otherwise never be able to pay their way?

Permanent protection is justified in overpopulated countries, but not in the Gold Coast. In some countries the population is so large that the area available for agriculture can be cultivated by a fraction of the available rural population. Any useful work which can be found for the surplus population adds to national output. Entrepreneurs will not employ the people unless the value of the work done is at least equal to the wage, whereas employment is worth while so long as it adds anything to natural output, even though the addition is less than the wage. In such countries as India, Japan, Jamaica, or Egypt, industrialisation is a substitute for unemployment, and is necessarily one of the two major objectives of economic policy, the other objective being to maximise the output of agriculture. . . .

. . . Factories are gregarious because they use common facilities, and because they trade with each other. The more factories there are, the cheaper it is to supply them with electric power, specialised transportation facilities, gas, engineering repair facilities, and so on. Also, the more factories there are, the more they lean on each other, one buying the by-products of another, which would otherwise waste; or providing for the other services without which the other could not continue. The efficiency of an industrial system is therefore a function not only of the length of time for which it has been in existence, and not only of the size of each factory, but also of the number and diversity of its factories. Hence, it may be sensible to establish a number of factories which would not pay by themselves, because the existence of these factories makes it possible for others to get services economically, and because the growth of the system as a whole eventually makes profitable parts of it which could not have stood by themselves.

The argument of the last paragraph supports general protection for industry, but supports it only in those countries where rapid industrialisation can be expected (usually for an export market) because the country has resources specially favourable to industrialisation (including cheap labour in an over-populated country). In such countries a relatively short period of general protection (say 20 years) may see an enormous increase of industry, sufficient to put manufacturing squarely upon its feet.

This is not the case with the Gold Coast, which has none of the resources that specially favour manufacturing (apart from aluminium), and in which therefore the growth of manufacturing will be limited by the slow growth of home demand due to the stagnation of agricultural productivity. For some time to come manufacturing will be peripheral to the economy as a whole, and there will be no case for measures which could be justified only if a tremendous increase in manufacturing were likely to be achieved.

We are left, then with the following conclusions. (1) There is always a case for temporary assistance, to set an industry upon its feet. (2) Industries which employ mainly women are specially worth attracting, even to the extent of some protection. And (3) manufacturing industry as a whole is worth some support, because of the uncertainty of agricultural prices, but this argument must not be pressed very far. . . .

CONCLUSIONS AND RECOMMENDATIONS

Measures to increase the manufacture of commodities for the home market deserve support, but are not of number one priority. A small programme is justified, but a major programme in this sphere should wait until the country is better prepared to carry it. The main obstacle is the fact that agricultural productivity per man is stagnant. This has three effects. First, the market for manufactures is small, and is not expanding year by year, except to the extent of population growth; consequently it would take large subsidies to make possible the employment of a large number of people in manufacturing. Secondly it is not possible to get ever larger savings out of the farmers, year by year, to finance industrialisation, without at the same time reducing their standard of living; hence industrialisation has to depend on foreign capital, and large amounts of capital for this purpose could be attracted only on unfavourable terms. And thirdly, agriculture, because it is stagnant, does not release labour year by year; there is a shortage of labour in the Gold Coast which rapid industrialisation would aggravate.

Number one priority is therefore a concentrated attack on the system of growing food in the Gold Coast, so as to set in motion an ever increasing productivity. This is the way to provide the market, the capital, and the labour for industrialisation. Priority number two is to improve the public services. To do this will reduce the cost of manufacturing in the Gold Coast, and will thus automatically attract new industries, without the government having to offer special favours.

Very many years will have elapsed before it becomes economical for the government to transfer any large part of its resources towards industrialisation, and away from the more urgent priorities of agricultural productivity and the public services. Meanwhile, it should support such industrialisation as can be done on terms favourable to the country. That is to say, it should support industries which can be established without large or continuing subsidies, and whose proprietors are willing to train and employ Africans in senior posts. Because industrialisation is a cumulative process (the more industries you have already, the more new industries you attract) it takes time to lay the foundations of industrialisation, and it would be wrong to postpone the establishment of any industry which could flourish after a short teething period. . . .

In order to carry out such a programme the government should:

1. establish an Industries Division in the Department of Commerce . . .
2. announce its willingness to give limited aid, by way of temporary protection or subsidy, to newly established factories in the industries listed as "favourable" or "marginal" . . .
3. announce its attitude to foreign enterprise; welcoming such enterprise, especially if it enters into partnership with the Government or with African enterprise; guaranteeing free transfer of profits and dividends, and fair compensation independently determined if nationalisation takes place; and safeguarding the employment of a proportion of Africans in senior posts . . .
4. arrange for suitably qualified Africans to be employed temporarily in industrial undertakings in other countries . . .
5. arrange a conference of persons engaged in labour management in the Gold Coast, or interested in the subject, with a view to initiating further research and teaching . . .
6. decide to accord priority to industry over domestic consumption in the extension of public services which are in short supply . . .
7. abolish import duties on industrial raw materials . . .

8. purchase land, outside Kumasi and Accra, for development as industrial estates . . .
9. promote and aid the establishment of a first class hotel in Accra . . .
10. set aside funds (*a*) for developing industrial estates, including building factories to be leased . . . ; (*b*) for lending to small African firms, under strict supervision; (*c*) for lending to or investing in large scale enterprise . . . ; (*d*) for operating government factories, either for pioneering purposes, or as public utilities . . .
11. increase the staff of the Industrial Development Corporation, and charge it with the duties listed in [this report] and with the general duty of aiding African enterprise . . .

REFERENCES CITED

Adelman, Irma
  1961. *Theories of Growth and Development* (Stanford: Stanford University Press).
Adelman, Irma, and Morris, Cynthia Taft
  1965. "Factor Analysis of the Interrelationship between Social and Political Variables and Per Capita Gross National Product," *The Quarterly Journal of Economics*, 89:555–78.
  1967. *Society, Politics, and Economic Development* (Baltimore: Johns Hopkins University Press).
  1968a. "Performance Criteria for Evaluating Economic Development Potential: An Operational Approach," *Quarterly Journal of Economics*, Vol. LXXXII, May.
  1968b. "An Econometric Model of Socio-economic and Political Change in Underdeveloped Countries," *American Economic Review*, December.
Aitken, H. G. J., ed.
  1959. *The State and Economic Growth* (New York).
Allan, W.
  1965. *The African Husbandman,* (London and Edinburgh: Oliver and Boyd).
Allan, W., Gluckman, M., Peters, D. U., and Trapnell, C. G.
  1948. "Land Holding and Land Usage among the Plateau Tonga of Mazabuka District," *Rhodes-Livingstone Papers*, No. 14.
Allen, G. C., and Donnithorne, A. G.
  1957. *Western Enterprise in Indonesia and Malaya* (New York: Macmillan).
Almond, G. A., and Coleman, J. S.
  1960. *The Politics of Developing Areas* (Princeton).
Ames, N. M.
  1957. "Reaction to Stress: A Comparative Study of Nativism," *Davidson Journal of Anthropology*, Vol. III, No. 1, Summer.
Apter, David E.
  1956. *The Gold Coast in Transition* (Princeton).
  1960. "The Role of Traditionalism in the Political Modernization of Ghana and Uganda," *World Politics*, XIII:45–68.
Arensberg, Conrad M.
  1937. *The Irish Countryman* (Cambridge: Harvard University Press).
Arensberg, Conrad M., and Niehoff, Arthur H.
  1964. Introducing Social Change (Chicago: Aldine).

Armstrong, W. E.
   1924. "Rossel Island Money: A Unique Monetary System," *Economic Journal*, 34:423–29.
   1928. *Rossel Island* (Cambridge: Cambridge University Press).
Arnold, Rosemary
   1957a. "A Port of Trade: Whydah on the Guinea coast," *Trade and Market in the Early Empires*, K. Polanyi, C. M. Arensberg, and H. W. Pearson, eds. (Glencoe: The Free Press).
   1957b. "Separation of Trade and Market: Great Market of Whydah," *Trade and Market in the Early Empires*, K. Polanyi, C. M. Arensberg, and H. W. Pearson, eds. (Glencoe: The Free Press).
Aubrey, H. G.
   1957. "Small Industry in Economic Development," L. W. Shannon, ed., *Underdeveloped Areas* (New York).
Bailey, F. G.
   1957. *Caste and the Economic Frontier* (Manchester).
Balandier, Georges
   1955. "Social Changes and Social Problems in Negro Africa," in C. W. Stillman, ed., *Africa in the Modern World* (Chicago).
   1956. "Le contexte socio-culturel et le cout social du progrès," *Le "Tiers-Monde": Sous-developpment et developpement* (Paris: Presses Universitaires de France).
   1958. "Sociologie des regions sous-developpées," *Traite de Sociologie*, Vol. 1, G. Gurvitch, ed. (Paris: Presses Universitaires de France).
Bales, R. F.
   1950. *Interaction Process Analysis* (Cambridge, Mass.).
Baran, Paul A.
   1956. *The Political Economy of Growth* (New York: Monthly Review Press; London: Calder).
Barber, B.
   1941. "Acculturation and Messianic Movements," *American Sociological Review*, VI, No. 5.
Barlow, Frank
   1961. *The Feudal Kingdom of England, 1042–1216* (1st ed. 1955) (London).
Barth, Fredrik,
   1963. *The Role of the Entrepreneur, in Social Change in Northern Norway* (Bergen, Oslo: Norwegian Universities Press).
   1964. "Capital, Investment, and the Social Structure of a Pastoral Nomad Group in South Persia," *Capital, Saving, and Credit in Peasant Societies*, R. Firth and B. Yamey, eds. (Chicago: Aldine).
   1965. "Economic Spheres in Darfur," paper presented at ASA Conference on Economic Anthropology (Oxford, 1965). Reprinted in Firth, 1968.
   1966. *Models of Social Organization*, Royal Anthropological Institute Occasional Paper, No. 23.
   1967. "On the Study of Social Change," *American Anthropologist*.

Bartram, William
1958. *The Travels of William Bartram,* Francis Harper, ed. (New Haven: Yale University Press).
Bascom, W. R.
1951. Social Status, Wealth and Individual Differences Among the Yoruba, *American Anthropologist,* 53:491–505.
Bastin, J.
1957. *The Native Policies of Sir Stamford Raffles in Java and Sumatra* (Oxford: Oxford University Press).
Bauer, P. T., and Yamey, B. S.
1957. *The Economics of Underdeveloped Countries* (Chicago).
Bauer, Inkeles, and Kluckhohn
1957. *How the Soviet System Works* (Cambridge, Mass.).
Beattie, J. H. M.
1959. "Checks on the Abuse of Political Power in some African States," *Socioloqus,* IX:97–115.
1964. "Bunyoro: An African Feudality?" *Journal of African History.* Reprinted in Dalton 1967.
Beckett, W. H.
1953. "The Development of Peasant Agriculture," in *Approaches to Community Development,* P. Ruoppe, ed. (The Hague: van Heuve).
Beidelman, T. O.
1959. *A Comparative Analysis of the Jajmani System* (New York: J. J. Augustin).
Bellah, R. N.
1957. *Tokugawa Religion* (Glencoe, Ill.).
Belshaw, Cyril S.
1965. *Traditional Exchange and Modern Markets* (Englewood Cliffs: Prentice-Hall).
Belshaw, Horace
1956. *Population Growth and Levels of Consumption,* (Allan and Unwin).
1957. "Some Social Aspects of Economic Development in Underdeveloped Areas," in Shannon 1957.
Bendix, R.
1956. *Work and Authority in Industry: Ideologies of Management in the Course of Industrialization* (New York: Harper).
1959. *Max Weber* (New York).
Benedict, Ruth
1956. "The Growth of Culture," *Man, Culture and Society,* H. Shapiro, ed. (New York: Oxford University Press).
Bennet, H. S.
1962. *Life on the English Manor, 1150–1400* (Cambridge: Cambridge University Press).
Bestor, A. E., Jr.
1950. *Backwoods Utopias* (Philadelphia: University of Pennsylvania Press).

Biebuyck, Daniel, ed.
1963. *African Agrarian Systems* (London: Oxford University Press).
Bishop, Claire
1950. *All Things Common* (New York: Harper).
Black, John D.
1926. *Introduction to Production Economics* (N.Y.).
Bloch, Marc
1933. "Feudalism, European," in the *Encyclopaedia of the Social Sciences*.
1961. *Feudal Society*, French ed., 1939–40 (London).
1966. *French Rural History* (London: Routledge & Kegan Paul).
Blumer, H.
1960. "Early Industrialization and the Labouring Classes," *The Sociological Quarterly*, Vol. 1, No. 1.
Boas, Franz
1897. "The Social Organization and the Secret Societies of the Kwakiutl Indians," *Report of the U. S. National Museum for 1895* (Washington, D.C.).
Boeke, J. H.
1910. "Tropische-Koloniale Stadhuishoudkunde" (Amsterdam dissertation).
1942. *The Structure of Netherlands Indian Economy* (New York: Institute of Pacific Relations).
1947. *The Evolution of the Netherlands Indies Economy* (Haarlem: H. D. Tjeenk Willink).
1953. *Economics and Economic Policy of Dual Societies* (Haarlem: H. D. Tjeenk Willink, New York: Institute of Pacific Relations).
1954. "Capitalist Development in Indonesia and Uganda: a Contrast," *International Social Science Bulletin*, Vol. 6, No. 3.
Bohannan, Paul
1954. *Tiv Farm and Settlement* (London: H.M.S.O.).
1957. *Justice and Judgement Among the Tiv* (New York: Oxford University Press).
1959. "The Impact of Money on an African Subsistence Economy," *The Journal of Economic History*, 19:491–503.
Bohannan, Paul, and Bohannan, Laura
1968. *Tiv Economy* (Evanston: Northwestern University Press).
Bohannan, Paul, and Dalton, George, eds.
1962. *Markets in Africa* (Evanston: Northwestern University Press).
Bohannan, Paul, and Dalton, George
1965. "Introduction," in *Markets in Africa* (New York: Natural History Press).
Boulding, Kenneth
1957. "The Parsonian Approach to Economics," *Kyklos*, 10:317–19.
Boutruche, Robert
1959. *Seigneurie et féodalité* (Paris).
Brokensha, David W.
1966. *Social Change at Larteh, Ghana* (Oxford: Clarendon Press).

Broom, Leonard, Siegel, B. J., Vogt, E. Z., and Watson, J. B.
1954. "Acculturation: An Exploratory Formulation," *American Anthropologist*, 56:973–1000.

Browne, G. St. J. Orde
1933. *The African Labourer* (London).

Brutzkus, B. D.
1923. *Ekonomia selskago khosiaistva* (Agricultural Economics) (Berlin). German translation: *Okonomie der Landwirtschaft*, 1923 (Berlin).

Bryant, A. T.
1929. *Olden Times in Zululand and Natal* (London).

Buchanan, N. S., and Ellis, H. S.
1955. *Approaches to Economic Development* (New York).

Bultot, F.
1954. *Saisons et Periodes Sèches et Pluvieuses au Congo Belge et au Ruanda-Urundi* (Bruxelles: Publications de l'Institute National pour l'étude agronomique du Congo Belge).

Burger, D. H.
1939. *De Ontsluiting van Java's Binnenland voor het Wereldverkeer* (Wageningen: H. Veenman).

Burling, Robbins
1962. "Maximization Theories and the Study of Economic Anthropology," *American Anthropologist*, 64:802–21.

Busia, K.
1951. *The Position of the Chief on the Modern Political System of Ashanti* (London: Oxford University Press for the International African Institute).

Cady, John F.
1958. *A History of Modern Burma* (Ithaca, New York: Cornell University Press).

Cancian, Frank
1966. Maximization as Norm, Strategy, and Theory: A Comment on Programmatic Statements in Economic Anthropology, *American Anthropologist*, 69:465–69.

Carr, E. H.
1951. *The New Society* (London: Macmillan).

Chamberlin, E. H.
1933. *The Theory of Monopolistic Competition* (Cambridge: Harvard University Press).

Chayanov, A. V.
1966. *The Theory of Peasant Economy*, Daniel Thorner, Basile Kerblay, and R. E. F. Smith, eds. (Homewood, Illinois: Richard D. Irwin).

Chenery, Hollis B.
1965. "Comparative Advantage and Development Policy," in *Surveys of Economic Theory*, Volume II, *Growth and Development* (New York: St. Martin's Press).

Chevalier, François
1963. *Land and Society in Colonial Mexico* (Berkeley: University of California Press).

Chilver, Mrs. E. M.
  1960. "'Feudalism' in the Interlacustrine Kingdoms," *East African Chiefs*, Audrey Richards, ed. (London).
Clower, Robert, Dalton, G., Harwitz, M., and Walters, A. A.
  1966. *Growth Without Development: An Economic Survey of Liberia* (Evanston: Northwestern University Press).
Coleman, J. S.
  1958. *Nigeria: Background to Nationalism* (Berkeley and Los Angeles: University of California Press).
Colson, Elizabeth
  1949. "Assimilation of an American Indian Group," *Human Problems in British Central Africa* (*Rhodes-Livingstone Journal*), 5:1–13.
  1958. "The Role of Bureaucratic Norms in African Political Structures," in *Systems of Political Control and Bureaucracy in Human Societies*, Verne F. Ray, ed. (Seattle Proc. A. Eth. Soc.).
Cook, Scott
  1966. The Obsolete "Anti-market" Mentality: A Critique of the Substantive Approach to Economic Anthropology," *American Anthropologist*, 68:323–45.
Coulborn, R., and Strayer, J. R.
  1956. *Feudalism in History*, (Princeton: Princeton University Press).
Cousins, Norman
  1961. "Talk with the PM," *Saturday Review*, May 27.
Dalton, George
  1959. "Robert Owen and Karl Polanyi as Socio-economic Critics and Reformers of Nineteenth Century Capitalism," unpublished Ph.D. dissertation, University of Oregon.
  1960. "A Note of Clarification on Economic Surplus," *American Anthropologist*, Vol. 62, No. 3 (June).
  1961. "Economic Theory and Primitive Society," *American Anthropologist*, Vol. 63, No. 1 (February).
  1962. "Traditional Production in Primitive African Economies," *The Quarterly Journal of Economics*, 76:360–78.
  1963. "Economic Surplus Once Again," *American Anthropologist*, Vol. 65, No. 2 (April).
  1964. "The Development of Subsistence and Peasant Economies in Africa," *International Social Science Journal*, 16:378–89.
  1965a. "Primitive Money," *American Anthropologist*, 67:44–65.
  1965b. "Primitive, Archaic, and Modern Economies: Karl Polanyi's Contribution to Economic Anthropology and Comparative Economy," *Proceedings of the 1965 Annual Spring Symposium of the American Ethnological Society* (Seattle: University of Washington Press).
  1965c. "History, Politics, and Economic Development in Liberia," *Journal of Economic History*, 25:569–91.
  1966. "Bridewealth versus Brideprice," *American Anthropologist*, 68:732–37.
  1967. *Tribal and Peasant Economies: Readings in Economic Anthropology* (New York: Natural History Press).

1968a. *Primitive, Archaic, and Modern Economies: Essays of Karl Polanyi* (New York: Anchor Books).

1968b. "Economics, Economic Development, and Economic Anthropology," *Journal of Economic Issues* (June).

1968c. Review of: *Primitive and Peasant Economic Systems*, by Manning Nash (San Francisco: Chandler, 1966), *American Anthropologist*, 70:368–69.

1969a. "Economics, Anthropology, and Economic Anthropology," in *Anthropology and Related Disciplines*, Otto von Mering, ed. (Pittsburgh: University of Pittsburgh Press).

1969b. "Traditional Economic Systems," in *The African Experience*, edited by John Paden and Edward Soja (Evanston: Northwestern University Press).

1969c. "Theoretical Issues in Economic Anthropology," *Current Anthropology*, 10:63–101.

1970. "The Economic System," in *A Handbook of Method in Cultural Anthropology*, R. Naroll and R. Cohen, eds. (New York: Doubleday).

Dandekar, V. M.

1962. "Economic Theory and Agrarian Reform," *Oxford Economic Papers*, 14:69–80.

Davidson, Basil

1961. *Black Mother* (London).

Davis, K.

1951. *The Population of India and Pakistan* (Princeton, N.J.).

1955. "Social and Demographic Aspects of Economic Development in India," in Kuznets, *Economic Growth*.

1957. *Human Society* (New York).

Davis, K., and Golden, H. H.

1955. "Urbanization and the Development of Pre-Industrial Areas," *Economic Development and Cultural Change*, III, No. 1.

Day, C.

1904. *The Dutch in Java* (New York: Macmillan).

Deane, Phyllis

1953. *Colonial Social Accounting* (Cambridge: Cambridge University Press).

deBie, H. C. H.

1902. *De Landbouw der Inlandsche Bevolking op Java* (Batavia: Kolff).

de Graaf, H. J.

1949. *Geschiedenis van Indonesie* (s'Gravenhage: van Hoeve).

de Vries, H. M.

n.d. *The Importance of Java Seen from the Air* (Batavia: Kolff).

deWilde, John C. et al.

1967. *Agricultural Development in Tropical Africa* (Baltimore: Johns Hopkins University Press).

Dike, K. O.

1966. *Trade and Politics in the Niger Delta 1830–1885* (Cambridge: Oxford University Press).

Dobb, Maurice
1946. *Studies in the Development of Capitalism* (London: Routledge & Kegan Paul).

Doke, C. M.
1931. *The Lambas of Northern Rhodesia* (London: Harrap).

Domar, Evsey D.
1957. *Essays in the Theory of Economic Growth* (New York: Oxford University Press).

Doucey, A.
1954. "The Unsettled Attitude of Negro Workers in the Belgian Congo," *International Social Science Bulletin*, VI, No. 3:442–51.

Douglas, Mary
1951. "A Form of Polyandry among the Lele," *Africa*, Vol. 21.
1954. "The Lele of the Kasai," *Africa Worlds*, D. Forde, ed. (London: Oxford University Press).
1957. "The Pattern of Residence Among the Lele," *Zaire*, Vol. 11.
1958. "Raffia Cloth Distribution in the Lele Economy," *Africa*, Vol. 28. Reprinted in Dalton 1967.
1959a. "Age Status Among the Lele," *Zaire*, No. 13.
1959b. "The Lele of the Kasai," in *The Church and the Nations*, A. Hastings, ed. (London: Sheed & Ward).
1962. "Lele Economy Compared with the Bushong: A Study in Economic Backwardness," in *Markets in Africa*, P. Bohannan and G. Dalton, eds. (Evanston: Northwestern University Press).
1965. "The Lele—Resistance to Change," in *Markets in Africa*, P. J. Bohannan and G. Dalton, eds. (New York: Natural History Press).

Dowd, D. F.
1957. "Two-thirds of the World," in *Underdeveloped Areas*, L. W. Shannon, ed. (New York).

Duby, Georges
1968. *Rural Economy and Country Life in the Medieval West* (London: Edward Arnold Publishers).

Durkheim, E.
1949. *The Division of Labor in Society* (Glencoe: The Free Press).
1951. *Suicide* (Glencoe: The Free Press).

Easton, David
1959. "Political Anthropology," in *Biennial Review of Anthropology, 1959* (Stanford).

Edel, Matthew
1967. "Jamaican Fishermen: Two Approaches in Economic Anthropology," *Social and Economic Studies*, Vol. 16, No. 4 (December).
1969. "Economic Analysis in an Anthropological Setting: Some Methodological Considerations," *American Anthropologist*, Vol. 71, No. 3:422–33.

Eicher, Carl K.
1967. "The Dynamics of Long-Term Agricultural Development in Nigeria," *Journal of Farm Economics*, Vol. 49, No. 5 (December).

Eisenstadt, S. N.
1957. "Sociological Aspects of Political Development in Underdeveloped Countries," *Economic Development and Cultural Change,* V, No. 4.

El Daghestani, K.
1954. "The Evolution of the Moslem Family in the Middle Eastern Countries," *International Social Science Bulletin,* VI, No. 3.

Elkan, W.
1956. *An African Labour Force* (Kampala, Uganda).

Embree, E. R.
1931. *Brown America: The Story of a New Race* (New York: Viking Press).

Emerson, R., Mills, L. A., and Thompson, V.
1942. *Government and Nationalism in Southeast Asia* (New York).

Epstein, T. Scarlett
1962. *Economic Development and Social Change in South India* (Manchester: Manchester University Press).
1967. "Productive Efficiency and Customary Systems of Rewards in Rural South India," in *Themes in Economic Anthropology,* R. Firth, ed. (London: Tavistock).

Erasmus, Charles J.
1961. *Man Takes Control* (Minneapolis: University of Minnesota Press).

Evans-Pritchard, E. E.
1940. *The Nuer* (Oxford: Clarendon Press).
1954. "Introduction," in *The Gift,* by Marcel Mauss (Glencoe: The Free Press).
1961. *Anthropology and History* (Manchester).

Fallers, Lloyd A.
1956. *Bantu Bureaucracy* (Cambridge).
1961. "Are African Cultivators to Be Called 'Peasants'?" *Current Anthropology,* 2:108–10.

Fallers, Margaret C.
1960. *The Eastern Lacustrine Bantu,* International African Institute Ethnographic Survey of Africa, East Central Africa, Part XI.

Fals Borda, Orlando
1965. "Violence and the Break-up of Tradition in Colombia," in *Obstacles to Change in Latin America,* C. Veliz, ed. (London: Oxford University Press).

Fanon, Frantz
1959. *L'An V de la Révolution Algérienne* (Paris: Maspero).
1959. *Les Damnes de la Terre.* (Paris: Maspero).
1965. *The Wretched of the Earth* (London: MacGibbon and Kee).

Fei, John C. H., and Ranis, Gustav
1964. *Development of the Labor Surplus Economy: Theory and Policy* (Homewood, Illinois: Richard D. Irwin, Inc.).

Firth, Raymond
1929. *Primitive Economics of the New Zealand Maori* (London: Routledge & Kegan Paul).
1939. *Primitive Polynesian Economy* (London: Routledge & Kegan Paul).
1946. *Malay Fishermen: Their Peasant Economy* (London: Routledge & Kegan Paul).
1951. *Elements of Social Organization* (London: Watts and Co.).
1954. "Social Organisation and Social Change," *Journal of the Royal Anthropological Institute.*
1957. "The Place of Malinowski in the History of Economic Anthropology," in *Man and Culture: An Evaluation of the Work of Bronislaw Malinowski,* R. Firth, ed. (New York: Harper Torchbooks).
1958. "Work and Wealth of Primitive Communities," in *Human Types,* revised edition (New York: Mentor Books).
1959. *Social Change in Tikopia* (London: George Allen and Unwin).
1964a. "Capital, Saving, and Credit in Peasant Societies: A Viewpoint from Economic Anthropology," in *Capital, Saving, and Credit in Peasant Societies,* R. Firth and B. Yamey, eds. (Chicago: Aldine).
1964b. *Essays on Social Organization and Values* (London: Athlone Press).
1965. Review of: *Kapauku Papuan Economy,* by Pospisil (Yale University Publication in Anthropology No. V), *American Anthropologist.*
1966a. *Primitive Polynesian Economy,* revised edition (London: Routledge & Kegan Paul).
1966b. *Malay Fishermen: Their Peasant Economy,* 2nd edition (London: Routledge & Kegan Paul).
1967. ed. *Themes in Economic Anthropology* (London: Tavistock).
1969. "The Influence of Social Structure upon Peasant Economies," in Clifton R. Wharton, Jr., ed., *Subsistence Agriculture and Economic Development* (Chicago: Aldine).
Firth, Raymond, and Yamey, B.
1964. *Capital, Credit, and Savings in Peasant Societies* (Chicago: Aldine).
Fogg, C. Davis
1965. "Economic and Social Factors Affecting the Development of Small-Holder Agriculture in Eastern Nigeria," *Economic Development and Cultural Change,* 13:278–92.
Forde, Daryll
1937. *Habitat, Economy, and Society* (London: Methuen).
1955. "The Social Impact of Industrialization and Urban Conditions in Africa South of the Sahara," *International Social Science Bulletin,* VII, No. 1.
Fortes, Meyer
1953. "The Structure of Unilineal Descent Groups," *American Anthropologist,* 55:17–41.

1953. "Analysis and Description in Social Anthropology," *The Advancement of Science,* No. 38 (September).

Fortes, M., and Evans-Pritchard, E. E., eds.
1940. *African Political Systems* (London).

Foster, G. M.
1953. "What Is Folk Culture?" *American Anthropologist,* 55:159–73.
1965. "Peasant Society and the Image of the Limited Good," *American Anthropologist,* 67:293–315.

Frankel, S. H.
1955. *The Economic Impact on Under-developed Societies* (Cambridge: Harvard University Press).

Frankenberg, Ronald
1967. "Economic Anthropology: One Anthropologist's View," in *Themes in Economic Anthropology,* R. Firth, ed. (London: Tavistock).

Frankfort, H., ed.
1949. *Before Philosophy* (Penguin).

Frazier, E. F.
1955. "The Impact of Colonialism on African Social Forms and Personality," in Stillman 1955.

Freud, Anna
1937. *The Ego and the Mechanisms of Defense,* translated from the German (London: Hogarth Press).

Fromm, Erich
1941. *Escape from Freedom* (New York: Rinehart).

Furnivall, J. S.
1944. *Netherlands India* (Cambridge: Cambridge University Press).
1948. *Colonial Policy and Practice* (Cambridge).
1957. *An Introduction to the Political Economy of Burma,* 3rd edition (Rangoon: Peoples Literature Committee and House).

Fusfeld, Daniel B.
1957. "Economic Theory Misplaced: Livelihood in Primitive Society," in *Trade and Market in the Early Empires,* K. Polanyi, C. M. Arensberg, and H. W. Pearson, eds. (Glencoe: The Free Press).

Fustel de Coulanges, N. D.
1891. *The Origin of Property in Land,* trans. Margaret Ashley (London).

Ganshof, F. L.
1952. *Feudalism* (Belgian edition 1944) (London).

Geertz, Clifford
1956a. "Religious Belief and Economic Behavior in a Central Javanese Town: Some Preliminary Considerations," *Economic Development and Cultural Change,* 4:134–58.
1956b. *The Social Context of Economic Change* (Cambridge, Mass.).
1959. "The Javanese Village," in *Local, Ethnic and National Loyalties in Village Indonesia,* G. W. Skinner, ed. (New Haven: Yale University Cultural Report Series, Southeast Asia Studies: 34–41).
1960. *The Religion of Java* (Glencoe: The Free Press).
1962a. "Studies in Peasant Life: Community and Society," in *Biennial*

Review of Anthropology for 1961, Bernard J. Siegel, ed. (Stanford: Stanford University Press).

1962b. "Social Change and Economic Modernization in Two Indonesian Towns: A Case in Point," in *On the Theory of Social Change*, by Everett E. Hagen (Homewood, Illinois: Dorsey Press).

1963a. *Peddlers and Princes* (Chicago: University of Chicago Press).

1963b. *Agricultural Involution* (Berkeley: University of California Press).

Georgescu-Roegen, Nicholas

1960. "Economic Theory and Agrarian Economies," *Oxford Economic Papers*, 12:1–40.

1969. "The Institutional Aspects of Peasant Communities: An Analytical View," in Clifton R. Wharton, Jr., ed., *Subsistence Agriculture and Economic Development* (Chicago: Aldine).

Gerschenkron, Alexander

1952. "Economic Backwardness in Historical Perspective," in *The Progress of Underdeveloped Areas*, B. Hoselitz, ed. (Chicago).

1954. "Social Attitudes, Entrepreneurship, and Economic Development," *International Social Science Journal*, 6.

1962. *Economic Backwardness in Historical Perspective* (Cambridge: The Belknap Press of Harvard University Press).

Glamann, K.

1958. *Dutch Asiatic Trade, 1620–1740* (The Hague: Nijhoff; Copenhagen: Danish Science Press).

Gluckman, Max and others

1948. *Land-holding and Land-Usage Among the Plateau Tonga*. Rhodes-Livingstone Paper No. 14.

Gluckman, Max

1954. *Rituals of Rebellion in South-East Africa* (Manchester).

1958. *Analysis of a Social Situation in Modern Zululand*, Rhodes-Livingstone Paper No. 28.

Gluckman, Max, and Cunnison, I. G.

1962. "Foreword," in *Politics of the Kula Ring*, by J. P. Singh Uberoi (Manchester: Manchester University Press).

Godelier, Maurice

1965. "Objet et Méthode de l'Anthropologie Économique," *L'Homme*, 5(2).

1966a. *Rationalité et Irrationalité en Économie*. (Paris: Francois Maspero).

1966b. "Systeme, Structure et Contradiction dans Le Capital," *Les Temps Modernes*, 246.

Goldenweiser, A.

1936. "Loose Ends of a Theory on the Individual Pattern and Involution in Primitive Society," in *Essays in Anthropology Presented to A. L. Kroeber*, R. Lowie, ed. 99–104 (Berkeley: University of California Press).

1937. *Anthropology*.

Gonggrijp, G.
1957. *Schets Ener Economische Geschiedenis van Indonesie*, 4th printing (Haarlem: Bohn).
Goodenough, Ward Hunt
1964. *Co-operation in Change* (New York: Russell Sage Foundation).
Goodfellow, D. M.
1939. *Principles of Economic Sociology*. (London: Routledge).
Goody, Jack
1962. *Death, Property and the Ancestors* (London).
1963. "Feudalism in Africa?" *Journal of African History*, 4:1–18.
Gough, Kathleen.
1968. "Anthropology: Child of Imperialism," *Monthly Review*, 19(11).
Gould, H. A.
1958. "The Hindu Jajmani System," *Southwestern Journal of Anthropology*, 14:428–37.
Gouldner, Alvin
1960. "The Norm of Reciprocity: A Preliminary Statement," *American Sociological Review*, XXV.
Gourou, P.
1951. *Notice de la Carte de la Densité de la Population au Congo Belge et au Ruanda-Urandi* (Bruxelles: Institute Royal Colonial Belge).
1955. *La Densité de la Population Rurale au Congo Belge, etc.* (Brussels: Acad. Roy. Sci. Col. Mem. 8,1,2).
Government of India
1954. *Evaluation Report* (Delhi: Planning Commission).
Graaf, E. A. van de
1955. *De Statistiek in Indonesie* (s'Gravenhage: van Hoeve).
Gray, Robert F.
1960. "Sonjo Pride-price and the Question of African 'Wife Purchase,'" *American Anthropologist*, 62:34–57.
Griliches, Zvi
1958. "Research Costs and Social Returns: Hybrid Corn and Related Innovations," *Journal of Political Economy*, Vol. 66, No. 5 (October).
Grossman, Gregory
1967. *Economic Systems* (Englewood Cliffs: Prentice Hall).
Gruchy, Allan G.
1966. *Comparative Economic Systems* (Boston: Houghton Mifflin).
Gulliver, P. H.
1965. "The Arusha—Economic and Social Change," in *Markets in Africa*, P. J. Bohannan and G. Dalton, eds. (New York: Natural History Press) (Reprinted from 1962 edition, Northwestern University Press).
Hagen, Everett E.
1957. "The Process of Economic Development," *Economic Development and Cultural Change*, V, No. 3.
1962. *On the Theory of Social Change: How Economic Growth Begins* (Homewood, Illinois: Dorsey Press).

632   *References Cited*

Harris, M.
  1959. "The Economy Has No Surplus?" *American Anthropologist,*
  Vol. 61, No. 2.
Harrison, S. E.
  1960. *India: The Most Dangerous Decades* (Princeton, N.J.).
Harrod, R. F.
  1952. "An Essay in Dynamic Theory," in *Economic Essays* (New
  York: Harcourt, Brace).
Hart, C. W. M., and Pilling, A. R.
  1960. *The Tiwi of North Australia* (New York: Holt, Rinehart, and
  Winston).
Herman, T.
  1956. "The Role of Cottage and Small-Scale Industries in Asian
  Economic Development," *Economic Development and Cultural
  Change,* IV, No. 4.
Herskovits, Melville J.
  1940. "Anthropology and Economics," in *The Economic Life of Primitive Peoples* (New York: Knopf).
  1938. *Dahomey* (New York: J. J. Augustin).
  1941. "Economics and Anthropology: A Rejoinder," *Journal of Political Economy,* 49:269–78; reprinted in *Economic Anthropology*
  (New York: Knopf, 1952).
  1952a. *Economic Anthropology* (New York: Knopf).
  1952b. "The Problem of Adapting Societies to New Tasks," *The
  Progress of Underdeveloped Areas,* B. F. Hoselitz, ed. (Chicago:
  University of Chicago Press).
  1956. "African Economic Development in Cross-Cultural Perspective,"
  American Economic Review.
Higgins, B.
  1956. "The 'Dualistic Theory' of Underdeveloped Areas," *Economic
  Development and Cultural Change,* 4:99–115.
  1959. *Economic Development* (New York: Norton).
Hill, E. F., and Mosher, A.
  1963. "Organizing for Agricultural Development," in Vol. III of
  *The United States Papers Prepared for the United Nations Con-
  ference on the Application of Science and Technology for the
  Benefit of the Less Developed Areas* (Washington, D.C.).
Hill, Polly
  1963a. *Migrant Cocoa Farmers of Southern Ghana* (Cambridge: Cambridge University Press).
  1963b. "Markets in Africa" (a review article), *The Journal of Modern
  Africa Studies,* Vol. 1, No. 4.
  1965. *A Plea for Indigenous Economics: The West African Example,*
  Working Papers of the Economic Development Institute 5 (Ibadan:
  Economic Development Institute, University of Ibadan).
  1966. "A Plea for Indigenous Economics," *Economic Development
  and Cultural Change,* 15:10–20.

Hirschman, Albert O.
1958. *The Strategy of Economic Development* (New Haven: Yale University Press).

Hobsbawm, Eric
1964. "Introduction," in *Pre-capitalist Economic Formations,* by Karl Marx (London: Lawrence and Wishart).

Hodgkin, T.
1957. *Nationalism in Colonial Africa* (New York).

Hogbin, Ian H.
1951. *Transformation Scene* (London: Routledge & Kegan Paul).
1958. *Social Change* (Watts).

Hollinger, W.
1953. "Indonesia, Quantitative Studies 2, The Food Crop Sector," Center for International Studies, Massachusetts Institute of Technology (dittoed).

Holmberg, Allan R.
1952. "La Realización del Proyecto de Antropológica Aplicada en la Zona de Vicos, Marcara, Anchash," *Peru Indigena,* Vol. 2, No. 4.
1955. "Participant Intervention in the Field," *Human Organization* (Spring).
1956. "From Paternalism to Democracy: The Cornell Peru Project," *Human Organization,* Vol. 15, No. 3:15–18.
1965. "The Changing Values and Institutions of Vicos in the Context of National Development," *American Behavorial Scientist* VIII:3–8.

Holt, J. B.
1940. "Holiness Religion: Cultural Shock and Social Reorganization," *American Sociological Review,* V, No. 5.

Homans, George C.
1940. *English Villagers of the Thirteenth Century* (Cambridge: Harvard University Press).
1958. "Social Behavior as Exchange," *The American Journal of Sociology,* 62:597–606.
1964. "Bringing Men Back In," *American Sociological Review,* 29:808–18.

Hoselitz, B. F.
1953. "Non-Economic Barriers to Economic Development," *Economic Development and Cultural Change,* I, No. 1:9.
1955. "The City, the Factory, and Economic Growth," *American Economic Review,* XLV, No. 2.

Hoyt, Robert S.
1961. *Feudal Institutions: Cause or Consequence of Decentralization?* (New York).

Humphreys, S. C.
1969. "History, Economics and Anthropology: The Work of Karl Polanyi," *History and Theory,* 8, No. 2.

Hunter, Monica
1961. *Reaction to Conquest* (London: Oxford University Press).

Inkeles, A., and Rossi, P. H.
  1957. "National Comparisons of Occupational Prestige," *American Journal of Sociology*, LXI, No. 4.
Ivens, W. G.
  1927. *Melanesians of the Southeast Solomon Islands* (London: Kegan, Paul, French, Trubner).
Jacoby, E. H.
  1949. *Agrarian Unrest in Southeast Asia* (New York).
James, William
  1896. *The Will to Believe and Other Essays in Popular Philosophy* (New York: Longmans Green & Co.).
Jaspan, M. A.
  1953. "A Sociological Case Study: Communal Hostility to Imposed Social Changes in South Africa," in *Approaches to Community Development*, Phillips Ruopp, ed. (The Hague: van Hoeve).
Jay, R.
  1956. "Local Government in Rural Central Java," *Far Eastern Quarterly*, 15:215–27.
Johnson, C. E.
  1956. African Farming Improvement in the Plateau Tonga Maize Area of Northern Rhodesia," Bull. No. 11, Lusaka (Dept. of Agr.).
Jones, William O.
  1961. "Food and Agricultural Economies of Tropical Africa: A Summary View," *Food Research Institute Studies*, Vol. II:3–20 (Stanford University).
Joy, Leonard
  1967a. "One Economist's View of the Relationship Between Economics and Anthropology," in *Themes in Economic Anthropology*, R. Firth, ed. (London: Tavistock).
  1967b. "An Economic Homologue of Barth's Presentation of Economic Spheres in Darfur," in *Themes in Economic Anthropology*, R. Firth, ed. (London: Tavistock).
Kaberry, Phyllis
  1940–41. "The Abelam Tribe, Sepik District, New Guinea: A Preliminary Report," *Oceania*, XI.
Kaplan, David
  1968. "The Formal-Substantive Controversy in Economic Anthropology: Some Reflections on Its Wider Implications," *Southwestern Journal of Anthropology*.
Keyfitz, Nathan
  1959. "The Interlocking of Social and Economic Factors in Asian Development," *The Canadian Journal of Economics and Political Science*, 25:34–46.
Keynes, John Maynard
  1936. *The General Theory of Employment, Interest, and Money* (New York: Harcourt, Brace).
Kindleberger, C. P.
  1958. *Economic Development* (New York).

Knight, Frank
1941. "Anthropology and Economics," *Journal of Political Economy*, 49:247–68; reprinted in *Economic Anthropolgy*, by M. J. Herskovits (New York: Knopf, 1952).

Koens, A. J.
1946. "Knolgewassen," in *De Landbouw in den Indischen Archipel*, C. J. J. van Hall and C. van de Koppel, eds., 163–240 (IIA). (s'Gravenhage: van Hoeve).

Kohler, M.
1933. *Marriage Customs in Southern Natal* (Pretoria).

Kolff, G. H. van der
1929. "European Influence on Native Agriculture," in *The Effect of Western Influence on Native Civilizations in the Malay Archipelago*, B. Schrieke, ed., 103–125 (Batavia: Kolff).
1953. "An Economic Case Study: Sugar and Welfare in Java," in *Approaches to Community Development*, by P. Ruopp, 188–206 (The Hague and Bandung: van Hoeve).

Koppel, C. van de
1946. "Eenige Statistische Gegevens over de Landbouw in Nederlandsch-Indie," in *De Landbouw in den Indischen Archipel*, C. J. J. van Hall and C. van de Koppel, eds., 361–423 (I). (s'Gravenhage: van Hoeve).

Kornhauser, W.
1959. *The Politics of Mass Society* (Glencoe, Ill.).

Kroeber, A. L.
1948. *Anthropology* (New York: Harcourt, Brace and Co.).

Kroef, J. M. van der
1960. "Land Tenure and Social Structure in Rural Java," *Rural Sociology*, 25:414–30.

Kuznets, S.
1954. "International Differences in Income Levels: Some Reflections on Their Causes," *Economic Development and Cultural Change*, II, No. 1.
1955. "Problems in Comparisons of Economic Trends," *Economic Growth: Brazil, India, Japan*, S. Kuznets, W. E. Moore, and J. J. Spengler, eds. (Durham, N.C.).

Leach, E. R.
1960. "The Sinhalese of the Dry Zone of Northern Ceylon," in *Social Structure in Southeast Asia*, G. P. Murdock, ed. (Chicago: Quadrangle Books).

Le Chau
1966a. *Le Viet Nam Socialiste: Une Economie de Transition* (Paris: Maspero).
1966b. *La Révolution Paysanne du Sud Viet Nam* (Paris: Maspero).

LeClair, Edward E.
1962. "Economic Theory and Economic Anthropology," *American Anthropologist*, 64:1179–1203.

LeClair, Edward E., Jr., and Schneider, Harold K.
1968. *Economic Anthropology: Readings in Theory and Analysis* (New York: Holt, Rinehart, and Winston).

Levin, Jonathan V.
1960. *The Export Economies* (Harvard University Press).

Lévi-Strauss, Claude
1954. "Economic Motivation and Structure in Underdeveloped Countries," *The International Social Science Bulletin*, Vol. 6, No. 3.
1960. "L'Anthropologie Sociale Devant l'Histoire," *Annales*, 4.

Levy, M. J., Jr.
1949. *The Family Revolution in Modern China* (Cambridge, Mass.).
1952. "Some Sources of the Vulnerability of the Structures of Relatively Non-Industrialized Societies to Those of Highly Industrialized Societies," in Hoselitz, *The Progress of Underdeveloped Areas* (Chicago).

Lewis, Timothy
1956–1957. "Seebohm's Tribal System in Wales," *Economic History Review* (2nd Ser.), X:16–33.

Lewis, W. Arthur
1953. *Report on the Industrialisation of the Gold Coast* (Accra; Government Printing Department).
1954. "Economic Development with Unlimited Supplies of Labour," *The Manchester School of Economic and Social Studies*, 22:139–91.
1955. *The Theory of Economic Growth* (London: Allen and Unwin).
1958. "Unlimited Labour: Further Notes," *The Manchester School of Economic and Social Studies*, 26:1–32.
1962. "Foreward," in *Economic Development and Social Change in South India*, by T. Scarlett Epstein (Manchester: Manchester University Press).

Lienhardt, R. Godfrey
1956. "Religion," in *Man, Culture, and Society*, Harry L. Shapiro, ed., (New York: Oxford University Press).

Linton, Ralph
1940. "A Neglected Aspect of Social Organization," *American Journal of Sociology*, Vol. 45.
1943. "Nativistic Movements," *American Anthropologist*, Vol. XLV.
1952. "Cultural and Personality Factors Affecting Economic Growth," *The Progress of Underdeveloped Areas*, B. F. Hoselitz, ed. (University of Chicago Press).

Lipset, S. M.
1960. *Political Man* (Garden City, N.Y. Doubleday).

Lipset, S. M., and Bendix, R.
1959. *Social Mobility in Industrial Society* (Berkeley and Los Angeles).

Lloyd, P. C.
1955. "The Yoruba Lineage," *Africa*, 25:235–51.

Lombard, J.
1957. "Un Système Politique Tradionnel de Type Féodal: Les Bariba du Nord-Dahomey. Aperçu sur l'Organisation Sociale et le Pouvoir Central," *Bull. I.F.A.N.*:464–506.
1960. "La Vie Politique dans une Ancienne Société de Type Féodal: Les Bariba du Dahomey," *Cahiers d'Études Africaines*, III:5–45.

Lott, Milton
1959. *Dance Back the Buffalo* (Boston: Houghton Mifflin).

Lynn, C. W.
1937. *Agriculture in North Mamprusi,* Bull. No. 34 (Accra: Dept. Of Agric).

Machlup, F.
1936. "Three Economic Systems Clash in Burma," *Review of Economic Studies,* III, No. 2.

MacIver, R. M.
1933. *Society, Its Structure and Changes* (New York: R. Lond and R. R. Smith).

Maden, B. K.
1951. "The Economics of the Indian Village and Its Implications in Social Structure," *International Social Science Bulletin,* III, No. 4.

Maine, Sir Henry
1883. *Dissertations on Early Law and Custom* (London).

Mair, Lucy P.
1961. Clientship in East Africa," *Cahiers d'Études Africaines,* II: 315–25.
1962. *Primitive Government* (London).

Maitland, F. W.
1897. *Domesday Book and Beyond* (Cambridge).

Malinowski, Bronislaw
1921. "The Primitive Economics of the Trobriand Islanders," *Economic Journal,* 31:1–15.
1922. *Argonauts of the Western Pacific* (London: Routledge).
1935. *Coral Gardens and their Magic,* Volume I (New York: American Book Company).
1937. "Anthropology as the Basis of Social Sciences," in Cattel, Cohen, and Travers, eds., *Human Affairs* (London: Macmillan).
1945. *The Dynamics of Culture Change* (Yale University Press).
1959. *Crime and Custom in Savage Society* (Paterson: Littlefield, Adams) (first published in 1926).

Mann, W. S.
1963. *A Study in the Economics of Fertilizer Use in Eastern Nigeria,* Technical Bulletin No. 5, Eastern Nigeria Ministry of Agriculture (Enugu, Nigeria, March).

Mannoni, (Dominique) O.
1956. *Prospero and Caliban: The Pyschology of Colonization,* trans. Pamela Powesland (New York: Frederick A. Praeger, Inc.).

Mao Tse-tung
1954. *How to Analyse the Classes in the Rural Areas,* Selected Works, Vol. 1 (London: Lawrence and Wishart).

Maquet, Jacques
1954. *Système des Relations Sociales dans le Ruanda Acien* (Tervuren).
1961a. *The Premise of Inequality in Ruanda* (London: Oxford University Press).
1961b. "Une Hypothèse pour l'Étude des Féodalités Africaines," II: 292–314.

Marglin, Stephen A.
1965. "Insurance for Innovators," Appendix B in David Hapgood and Max F. Millikan, eds., *Policies for Promoting Agricultural Development* (Cambridge, Mass.: Center for International Studies, Massachusetts Institute of Technology, January).

Mariner, William
1827. *An Account of the Tongan Islands in the South Pacific Ocean,* 3rd edition, Joyn Martin, ed. (Edinburgh: Constable).

Marriott, McKim
1953. "Social Change in an Indian Village," *Economic Development and Cultural Change,* I, No. 2.
1955. "Little Communities in an Indigenous Civilization," in *Village India,* McKim Marriott, ed., American Anthropological Association Memoir 83:171–222.

Marshall, Alfred
1920. *Principles of Economics,* 8th edition (London: Macmillan).

Martin, K., and Knapp, J.
1967. *The Teaching of Development Economics* (Chicago: Aldine Press).

Marx, Karl
1953. "Einleitung zur Kritik der Politischen Oekonomie," in *Grundrisse der Kritik der Politischen Oekonomie* (Berlin: Dietz).
1956. *Die Deutsche Ideologie,* (trans. in *Karl Marx: Selected Writings in Sociology and Social Philosophy,* by T. B. Bottomore and Maximilen Rubel (London).
1961. *Economic and Philosophic Manuscripts of 1844* (Moscow: Foreign Languages Publishing House).
1964. *Pre-capitalist Economic Formations* (London: Lawrence and Wishart).

Matossian, M.
1958. "Ideologies of Delayed Industrialization," *Economic Development and Cultural Change,* VI, No. 3.

Mauss, Marcel
1954. *The Gift: Forms and Functions of Exchange in Archaic Societies* (Glencoe: The Free Press).

McClelland, David C.
1961. *The Achieving Society* (Princeton, N.J.: Van Nostrand Co.).

Mead, M.
1953. *Cultural Patterns and Technical Change* (UNESCO: Mentor, N.Y.).
1956. *New Lives for Old* (New York: William Morrow & Co.).

Mears, L. A.
1961. "Economic Development in Indonesia Through 1958," *Ekonomi dan Keuangan, Indonesia,* 14:15–57.

Mehta, A.
1958. "The Mediating Role of the Trade Union in Underdeveloped Countries," *Economic Development and Cultural Change,* VI, No. 1.

Mellor, John W.
1963. "The Use and Productivity of Farm Family Labor in Early

Stages of Agricultural Development," *Journal of Farm Economics,* Vol. 45, No. 3 (August).

Mellor, John W. et al.
1968. *Developing Rural India* (Ithaca: Cornell University Press).

Metcalf, J.
1952. "The Agricultural Economy of Indonesia," Monograph 15, U. S. Department of Agriculture, Washington, D.C.

Metzler, Lloyd
1949. "Tariffs, Terms of Trade and Distribution of National Income," *Journal of Political Economy* (February).

Millikan, Max F., and Hapgood, David
1957. *No Easy Harvest* (Boston, Mass.: Little, Brown).

Minkes, A. L.
1953. "A Note on Handicrafts in Underdeveloped Areas," *Economic Development and Cultural Change,* I, No. 2.

Mintz, S.
1956. "Cañamelar: The Sub-culture of a Rural Sugar Plantation Proletariat," in *The People of Puerto Rico,* J. Steward, ed. (Urbana: University of Illinois Press).

Miracle, Marvin P.
1962. "African Markets and Trade in the Copperbelt," in *Markets in Africa,* P. Bohannan and G. Dalton, eds. (Evanston: Northwestern University Press).
1968. "Subsistence Agriculture: Analytical Problems and Alternative Concepts," *American Journal of Agricultural Economics,* Vol. 50, No. 2 (May).

Moore, Barrington, Jr.
1967. *Social Origins of Dictatorship and Democracy: Lord and Peasant in the Making of the Modern World* (Boston: Beacon).

Moore, Wilbert E.
1951. *Industrialization and Labor* (Ithaca and New York).
1955. "Labor Attitudes Toward Industrialization in Underdeveloped Countries," *American Economic Review,* 45:156–65.

Mosher, Arthur T.
1966. *Getting Agriculture Moving* (New York: Praeger).

Mosk, S. A.
1950. *Industrial Revolution in Mexico* (Berkeley and Los Angeles: University of California Press).

Myers, C. A.
1958. *Labor Problems in the Industrialization of India* (Cambridge: Harvard University Press).

Myint, Hla
1964. *The Economics of the Developing Countries* (London: Hutchinson).
1965. "Economic Theory and the Underdeveloped Countries," *The Journal of Political Economy,* LXIII:477–91 (October).

Myrdal Gunnar
  1944. *An American Dilemma. The Negro Problem and Modern Democ-*
    racy (New York: Harper).
  1952. "Economic Aspects of Health," Chron. World Health Organisa-
    tion, Geneva, 6, No. 7–8.
  1957. *Rich Lands and Poor* (New York: Harper).
  1960. *Beyond the Welfare State* (New Haven: Yale University Press).
Nadel, S. F.
  1942. *A Black Byzantium: The Kingdom of Nupe in Nigeria* (Lon-
    don: Oxford University Press).
Nash, Manning
  1955. "Some Notes on Village Industrialization in South and East
    Asia," *Economic Development and Cultural Change*, III, No. 3.
  1966. *Primitive and Peasant Economic Systems* (San Francisco, Cali-
    fornia: Chandler Publishing Company).
Neale, Walter C.
  1957a. "Reciprocity and Redistribution in the Indian Village," in *Trade*
    and Market in the Early Empires, K. Polanyi, C. M. Arensberg, and
    H. W. Pearson, eds. (Glencoe: The Free Press).
  1957b. "The Market in Theory and History," in *Trade and Market in*
    the Early Empires, K. Polanyi, C. M. Arensberg, and H. W. Pearson,
    eds. (Glencoe: The Free Press).
Nicolai, N.
  1952. "Problemes du Kwango," *Bulletin de la Societe Belge d'Études*
    Geographiques, Vol. 25, No. 2.
Nicolai, N., and Jacques, J.
  1954. *La Transformation du Paysage Congolais par le Chemin de Fer,*
    L'Exemple du B. C. K., Acad. Roy. Sci. Col. Brussels, Sect. des Sce.
    Natu. et Med. Mem. in 8, XXIV, L.
Niebuhr, H. R.
  1929. *The Social Sources of Denominationalism* (New York).
Nordhoff, Charles
  1961. *The Communistic Societies of the United States* (New York:
    Hilary House) (first published in 1875).
Nove, Alec
  1962. *The Soviet Economy* (New York: Praeger).
Noyes, John Humphrey
  1870. *American Socialisms* (Philadelphia: J. B. Lippincott).
Nurkse, Ragnar
  1952. *Some Aspects of Capital Accumulation in Underdeveloped Coun-*
    tries (Cairo).
  1953. *Problems of Capital Formation in Underdeveloped Countries*
    (Oxford).
Nyerere, Julius K.
  1964. "Ujamaa," in *African Socialism*, W. H. Friedland, C. G. Rose-
    berg, Jr., eds. (Stanford: Stanford University Press).
Okigbo, Pius
  1956. "Social Consequences of Economic Development in West Africa,"
    Annals of the American Academy of Political Science: 125–33.

Owen, Robert
1927. *A New View of Society* and other writings (New York: Dutton, Everyman ed.).
Panel on World Food Supply
1967. *The World Food Problems*, A Report of the President's Science Advisory Committee, The White House, Washington, D.C. (May).
Parsons, T.
1937. *The Structure of Social Action* (New York).
1951. *The Social System* (Glencoe: The Free Press).
1954. "An Analytical Approach to the Theory of Social Stratification," *Essays in Sociological Theory*, revised edition (Glencoe, Ill.).
Parsons, T., and Smelser, N.
1956. *Economy and Society* (Glencoe, Ill.).
Payne, Gonzáles-Mugaburu, and Schleicher
1956. "An Intestinal Parasite Survey in the High Cordilleras of Peru," *American Journal of Tropical Medicine and Hygiene* (July).
Pearson, Harry W.
1957. "The Economy Has No Surplus: Critique of a Theory of Development," in *Trade and Market in the Early Empires*, K. Polanyi, C. M. Arensberg, and H. W. Pearson, eds. (Glencoe: The Free Press).
Pelzer, K. J.
1945. *Pioneer Settlement in the Asiatic Tropics* (New York: Institute of Pacific Relations).
Pfanner, David E.
1969. "Case Study: A Semi-Subsistence Village Economy in Lower Burma," in Clifton R. Wharton, Jr., ed., *Subsistence Agriculture and Economic Development* (Chicago: Aldine).
Pirenne, Henri
1936. *Economic and Social History of Medieval Europe* (London: Routledge & Kegan Paul).
Pitt-Rivers, J. A.
1954. *The People of the Sierra* (London: Weidenfeld and Nicolson).
Polanyi, Karl
1944. *The Great Transformation* (New York: Rinehart).
1947. "Our Obsolete Market Mentality," *Commentary*, 13:109–17. Reprinted in Dalton, 1968a.
1957a. "Aristotle Discovers the Economy," in *Trade and Market in the Early Empires*, K. Polanyi, C. M. Arensberg, and H. W. Pearson, eds. (Glencoe: The Free Press). Reprinted in Dalton, 1968a.
1957b. "The Economy as Instituted Process," in *Trade and Market in the Early Empires*, K. Polanyi, C. M. Arensberg, and H. W. Pearson, eds. (Glencoe: The Free Press). Reprinted in Dalton, 1968a.
1960. "On the Comparative Treatment of Institutions in Antiquity, with Illustrations from Athens, Mycenae, and Alalakh," in *City Invincible*, C. H. Kraeling and R. M. Adams, eds. (Chicago: The University of Chicago Press). Reprinted in Dalton, 1968a.
1963. "Ports of Trade in Early Societies," *Journal of Economic History*, 23:30–45. Reprinted in Dalton, 1968a.

1966. *Dahomey and the Slave Trade* (Seattle: University of Washington Press).

1968. "The Semantics of Money Uses," in *Primitive, Archaic, and Modern Economies: Essays of Karl Polanyi*, G. Dalton, ed. Garden City, N.Y.: Doubleday, Anchor Books).

Polanyi, K., Arensberg, C. M., and Pearson, H. W., eds.

1957. *Trade and Market in the Early Empires* (Glencoe: The Free Press.

Pollock, F., and Maitland, F. W.

1898. *The History of English Law*, 2 vols., 2nd edition (Cambridge).

Pospisil, Leopold

1958. *Kapauka Papuans and Their Law*, Yale University Publications in Anthropology, No. 54 (New Haven: Yale University Press).

1963. *Kapauku Papuan Economy*, Yale University Publications in Anthropology, No. 67.

Postan, M. M.

1966. *The Agrarian Life of the Middle Ages*. Volume I of The Cambridge Economic History of Europe, 2nd edition (Cambridge: Cambridge University Press).

Potekhin, I. I.

1960. *On Feudalism of the Ashanti*, paper read to Twenty-fifth International Congress of Orientalists, Moscow.

Priestley, M. J. S., and Greening, R.

1956. *Ngoni Land-Utilization Survey 1954–5* (Lusaka: Government Printing).

Pulleyblank, E. G.

1958. "The Origins and Nature of Chattel Slavery in China," *Journal of Economic and Social History of the Orient*, 1.

Quiggin, A. H.

1949. *A Survey of Primitive Money* (London: Methuen & Co.).

Raffles, T. S.

1830. *The History of Java*, 2 vols. (London: John Murray).

Rattray, R. S.

1923. *Ashanti* (London).

1929. *Ashanti Law and Constitution* (London).

Read, K. E.

1959. "Leadership and Consensus in a New Guinea Society," *American Anthropologist*, LXI.

Redfield, Robert

1947. "The Folk Society," *American Journal of Sociology*, 52:293–308.

1956. *Peasant Society and Culture* (Chicago: The University of Chicago Press).

Rees, Morgan A. M.

1958. *An Economic Survey of Plateau Tonga Improved Farmers*, Bull. No. 14 (Lusaka: Dept. of Agric).

Reinsma, R.

1955. *Het Verval van het Cultuurstelsel* (s'Gravenhage: van Veulen).

Reynders, H. J. J.

1963. "The Geographical Income of the Bantu Areas in South Africa," in *African Studies in Income and Wealth,* L. H. Samuels, ed. (Chicago: Quadrangle Books).

Richards, Audrey I.

1939. *Hunger and Work in a Savage Society* (London: Oxford University Press).

1948. *Land, Labor and Diet in Northern Rhodesia* (London: Oxford University Press).

1960. "Social Mechanisms for the Transfer of Political Rights in Some African Tribes," *J. R. Anthrop. Inst.,* XC:175–90.

1961. "African Kings and their Royal Relatives," *J. R. Anthrop. Inst.,* XCI:135–50.

Rivers, W. H. R.

1912. "The Disappearance of Useful Arts," in *Festskrift Tillegnad Edvard Westermarck,* Helsingfors, 109–30.

1922. *Essays on the Depopulation of Melanesia* (Cambridge: Cambridge University Press).

Robbins, Lionel

1935. *An Essay on the Nature and Significance of Economic Science* (London: Macmillan).

1968. *The Theory of Economic Development in the History of Economic Thought* (New York: St. Martin's Press).

Robequain, C.

1944. *The Economic Development of French Indo-China* (London).

Robinson, Joan

1932. *The Economics of Imperfect Competition* (London: Macmillan).

Rogers, Everett

1960. *Diffusion of Innovations* (Glencoe: The Free Press).

Rosenberg, Nathan

1964. "Neglected Dimensions in the Analysis of Economic Change," in *Explorations in Social Change,* G. K. Zollschan and W. Hirsch, eds. (New York: Houghton Mifflin).

Rostovtzeff, M.

1953. *The Social and Economic History of the Hellenistic World,* 3 vols. corr. edition (London: Oxford University Press).

Rostow, W. W.

1956. "The Take-off into Sustained Growth," *Economic Journal* (March).

1960. *The Stages of Economic Growth* (Cambridge: Cambridge University Press).

1963, ed. *The Economics of Take-off into Sustained Growth* (London: Macmillan).

Rottenberg, Simon

1957. "Income and Leisure in an Underdeveloped Economy," in Shannon 1957.

1958. "Review of *Trade and Market in the Early Empires,* K. Polanyi, C. M. Arensberg, and H. W. Pearson, eds. (Glencoe: The Free Press, 1957)," *American Economic Review,* 48:675–78.

Rounce, N. V.
  1946. *The Agriculture of the Cultivation Steppe of the Lake, Central, and Western Provinces* (Salisbury: Longmans, Green for Dept. of Agric., Tanganyika).
Rubin, Vera
  1962. "Cultural Change," in *Biennial Review of Anthropology for 1961*, Bernard J. Siegel, ed. (Stanford: Stanford University Press).
Ruopp, Philipps, ed.
  1953. *Approaches to Community Development* (The Hague: van Heuve).
Ruttan, Vernon W.
  1959. "Usher and Schumpeter on Invention, Innovation, and Technological Change," *Quarterly Journal of Economics*, Vol. LXXIII, No. 293 (November).
Sahlins, Marshall D.
  1958. *Social Stratification in Polynesia*, American Ethnological Society Monograph (Seattle: University of Washington Press).
  1960. "Political Power and the Economy in Primitive Society," in *Essays in the Science of Culture in Honor of Leslie White*, G. Dole and R. Carneiro, eds. (New York: Crowell).
  1962a. "Review of *Sociological Aspects of Economic Growth*, by B. F. Hoselitz (Glencoe: The Free Press, 1960)," *American Anthropologist*, 64:1063–73.
  1962b. *Moala* (Ann Arbor: University of Michigan Press).
  1963. "Poor Man, Rich Man, Big-Man, Chief: Political Types in Melanesia and Polynesia," *Comparative Studies in Society and History*, 5:285–303.
  1965. "On the Sociology of Primitive Exchange," in *The Relevance of Models for Social Anthropology*, M. Banton, ed. (London: Tavistock).
  1968. "Tribal Economics," in *Tribesmen* (Englewood Cliffs, N.J.: Prentice-Hall).
Salisbury, Richard F.
  1962. *From Stone to Steel* (London: Cambridge University Press).
  1966. "Anthropology and Economics," paper presented at the annual meetings of the American Anthropological Society, Pittsburgh (November). (To appear in *Anthropology and the Neighboring Disciplines*, Otto von Mering, ed., Pittsburgh: University of Pittsburgh Press, in press.)
Samuels, L. H.
  1963. *African Studies in Income and Wealth*, (Chicago: Quadrangle Books).
Sawyer, John E.
  1951a. "Strains in the Social Structure of Modern France," in *Modern France: Problems of the Third and Fourth Republics*, E. M. Earle, editor, (Princeton).
  1951b. "The Entrepreneur and the Social Order: France and the United States," in *Men in Business: Studies in the History of Entrepreneurship*, Wm. Miller, ed. (Cambridge).

1951c. "Social Structure and Economic Progress," *American Economic Review*, 41:321–29.

Schapera, I.

1928. "Economic Changes in South African Native Life," *Africa*, I:170–88.

1934. *Western Civilization and the Natives of South Africa* (London: George Routledge and Sons).

1956. *Government and Politics in Tribal Societies* (London: Watts).

Schapera, I., and Goodwin, A. J. H.

1937. "Work and Wealth," in *The Bantu-Speaking Tribes of South Africa*, I. Schapera, ed. (London: Routledge & Kegan Paul).

Scheltema, A. M. P. A.

1930. De Sawahoccupatie op Java en Madoera in 1928 en 1888. Korte Mededeelingen van het Central Kantoor voor de Statisiek. Buitenzorg.

Schlippe, P. De

1956. *Shifting Cultivation in Africa: The Zande System of Agriculture* (London: Routledge).

Schrieke, B.

1955. *Indonesian Sociological Studies, Part I* (The Hague and Bandung: van Hoeve).

Schultz, T. W.

1964. *Transforming Traditional Agriculture* (New Haven: Yale University Press).

Seebohm, Frederic

1883. *The English Village Community* (London).

1895. *The Tribal System in Wales* (London).

1902. *Tribal Custom in Anglo-Saxon Law* (London).

Seers, Dudley

1963. "The Limitations of the Special Case," *Institute of Economic and Statistics Bulletin*, 25:77–98 (Oxford).

Sen, Amartya K.

1966. "Peasants and Dualism with and Without Surplus Labor," *Journal of Political Economy*, Vol. LXXIV, No. 5 (October).

Senghor, Leopold S.

1964. *On African Socialism* (New York: Praeger).

Service, Elman

1966. *The Hunters* (Englewood Cliffs, N.J.: Prentice-Hall).

Shackle, G. L. S.

1949. *Expectations in Economics* (Cambridge: Cambridge University Press).

1961. *Decision, Order, and Time in Human Affairs* (Cambridge: Cambridge University Press).

Sharp, R. L.

1952. "Steel Axes for Stone-age Australians," *Human Organization*, Vol. 11:17–22 (Summer).

Siegel, B. J.

1955. "Social Structure and the Economic Change in Brazil," in Kuznets, 1955.

Simpson, Lesley Byrd
1950. *The Encomienda in New Spain* (Berkeley and Los Angeles: University of California Press).
Singer, Hans
1950. "The Distribution of Gains Between Borrowing and Lending Countries," *American Economic Review* (May).
1952. "The Mechanics of Economic Development," *The Indian Economic Review* (August).
Sinha, D. P.
1967. "The Phariya in an Intertribal Market," *Economic and Political Weekly*, 2:1373–78.
1968. *Culture Change in an Intertribal Market* (New York: Asia Publishing House).
Smelser, Neil J.
1958. *Social Change in the Industrial Revolution* (London: Routledge & Kegan Paul).
1959. "A Comparative View of Exchange Systems," *Economic Development and Cultural Change*, vii, No. 2.
1963. "Mechanisms of Change and Adjustment to Change," in *Industrialization and Society*, B. F. Hoselitz and W. E. Moore, eds., UNESCO-Mouton.
1965. *Reading on Economic Sociology* (Englewood Cliffs, N.J.: Prentice-Hall).
Smith, M. G.
1956. "Segmentary Lineage Systems," *Journal of the Royal Anthropological Institute*, 88, Part 2:39–80.
1960. *Government in Zazzau* (London).
Smith, Thomas C.
1959. *The Agrarian Origins of Modern Japan* (Stanford: Stanford University Press).
Solomon, M. R.
1957. "The Structure of the Market in Under-developed Economies," in Shannon, L. W., ed., *Underdeveloped Areas* (New York).
Southall, Aidan W.
1956. *Alur Society* (Cambridge).
1961. ed. *Social Change in Modern Africa* (London: Oxford University Press).
Spengler, J. J.
1955. "Social Structure, the State, and Economic Growth," in Kuznets, Moore, and Spengler, eds., *Economic Growth: Brazil, India, Japan* (Durham, N.C.: Duke University Press).
Spicer, Edward
1952. *Human Problems in Technological Change* (New York: Russell Sage Foundation).
Spindler, Louise S. and Dalton, George
1959. "Culture Change," in *Biennial Review of Anthropology for 1959*, Bernard J. Siegel, ed. (Stanford: Stanford University Press).

Srinivas, M. N.
1959. "The Dominant Caste in Rampura," *American Anthropologist,* 61:1–16.
Staley, E.
1954. *The Future of Underdeveloped Areas* (New York).
Stein, S. J.
1955. "The Brazilian Cotton Textile Industry, 1850–1950," in Kuznets, 1955.
Stein, William
1955. *Hualcan: An Andean Indian Estancia,* Ph.D. thesis, Cornell University, Ithaca, N.Y.
Steiner, Franz
1957. "Towards a Classification of Labor," *Sociologus,* 7:112–29.
Stenton, F.
1961. *The First Century of English Feudalism, 1066–1166,* 1st edition 1932 (Oxford).
Stephenson, Carl
1942. *Mediaeval Feudalism* (Ithaca).
1954. *Mediaeval Institutions* (Ithaca).
Stevenson, H. N. C.
1943. *The Economics of the Central Chin Tribes* (Bombay).
Stolper, G.
1966. *Planning Without Facts* (Cambridge: Harvard University Press).
Strayer, Joseph R.
1956. "Feudalism in Western Europe," in *Feudalism in History,* Rushton Coulborn, ed. (Princeton).
Sundkler, M.
1948. *Bantu Prophets in South Africa* (London).
Svennilson, Ingvar
1954. *Growth and Stagnation in the European Economy,* United Nations' Economic Commission for Europe (Geneva).
Sweezy, Paul, ed.
n.d. *The Transition from Feudalism to Capitalism* (London: Arena).
Takizawa, Matsuyo
1927. *The Penetration of Money Economy in Japan and Its Effects upon Social and Political Institutions* (New York: Columbia University Press).
Tawney, R. H.
1967. *The Agrarian Problem in the Sixteenth Century* (New York: Harper) (first published London, 1912).
Tax, Sol
1963. *Penny Capitalism* (Chicago: The University of Chicago Press) (first published in 1953).
Tergast, G. C. W.
1950. "Improving the Economic Foundation of Peasant Agriculture on Java and Madoera (Indonesia)," unpublished mimeographed paper, trans. by the International Bank for Reconstruction and Development.

Terra, G. J. A.
　1946. "Tuinbouw," in *De Landbouw in den Indischen Archipel,* C. J. J. vanHall and C. van de Koppel, eds.: IIA:622–746 (s'Gravenhage: van Hoeve).

Theodorson, G. A.
　1953. "Acceptance of Industrialization and Its Attendant Consequences for the Social Patterns of Non-Western Societies," *American Sociological Review,* Vol. 18, No. 5:477–84.

Thomas, Elizabeth Marshall
　1959. *The Harmless People* (New York: Knopf).

Thompson, E. A.
　1952. "Peasant Revolts in Late Roman Gaul and Spain," *Past and Present,* 2:11–23.

Thurnwald, Richard
　1932. *Economics in Primitive Communities* (London: Oxford University Press).

Torday, E.
　1925. *On the Trail of the Bushongo* (London: Seeley, Service & Co., Ltd.).

Turner, V. W.
　1957. *Schism and Continuity in an African Society* (Manchester: Manchester University Press).

Uberoi, J. P. Singh
　1962. *The Politics of the Kula* (Manchester: Manchester University Press).

UNESCO
　1956. *Social Implications of Industrialization and Urbanization South of the Sahara* (Geneva).
　1963. *Social Aspects of Economic Development in Latin America* (New York).

United Nations
　1949a. *Relative Prices of Exports and Imports of Under-developed Countries,* Dept. of Economic Affairs, Sales No. II.B.3.
　1949b. *Economic Survey of Europe in 1948,* Dept. of Economic Affairs, Sales No. II.E.1.
　1950. Economic and Social Council (12th Sess.), Official Records: Special Supplement I, "Report of the Commission of Enquiry on the Coca Leaf," E/1666 (New York).
　1954. *Enlargement of the Exchange Economy in Tropical Africa* (New York: United Nations).
　1955a. Department of Economic and Social Affairs, *Processes and Problems of Industrialization in Underdeveloped Countries* (New York).
　1955b. "Problems of Regional Development and Industrial Location in Europe," *Economic Survey of Europe in 1954* (Geneva).

Uyeda, T.
　1938. *The Small Industries of Japan* (Shanghai).

van Alphen, H.
　1870. *Java en het Kultuurstelsel* (s'Gravenhage: van Stockum).

Vandenplas, A.
　1947. *La Température au Congo Belge,* Pub. Minis. Colon.

van der Kroef, J. M.
  1956. "Economic Developments in Indonesia: Some Social and Cultural Impediments," *Economic Development and Cultural Change*, IV, No. 2.
  1960. "Minority Problems in Indonesia," *Far Eastern Survey*, XXIV.
van Doorn, C. L.
  1926. *Schets van de Economische Ontwikkeling der Afdeeling Poerworedjo (Kedu)* (Weltevreden: Kolff).
van Gelderen, J.
  1929. "Western Enterprise and the Density of Population in the Netherlands Indies," in *The Effect of Western Influence on Native Civilizations in the Malay Archipelago*, B. Schrieke, ed.:85–102 (Batavia: Kolff).
van Klaveren, J. J.
  1955. *The Dutch Colonial System in Indonesia* (Rotterdam(?): no publisher).
Vansina, Jan
  1954. "Les Valeurs Culturelles des Bushong," *Zaire*, No. 9 (November).
  1956. "Migration dans la Province du Kasai," *Zaire*.
  1957. "L'État Kuba dans le Cadre des Institutions Politiques Africaines," *Zaire*, Vol. 11.
Vayda, Andrew
  1969. *Environment and Cultural Behavior: Ecological Studies in Cultural Anthropology* (New York: Natural History Press).
Vázquez, Mario C.
  1952. "La Antropología Cultural y Nuestro Problema del Indio," *Peru Indigena*, Vol. 2, No. 5–6:7–151.
  1955. *A study of Technological Change in Vicos, Peru*, M.A. thesis, Cornell University, Ithaca, N.Y.
  1957. "Cambios en Estratificación Social en una Hacienda Andina," *Peru Indigena*, Vol. 6, No. 14–15.
  1963. "Proceso de Migración en la Comunidad de Vicos, Ancash," in H. F. Dobyns and M. C. Vázquez, eds., *Migración e Integración en el Peru* (Lima: Editoral Estudios Andinos, Monografía Andina No. 2:93–102).
Viner, Jacob
  1953. *International Trade and Economic Development* (Clarendon Press, Oxford).
Vinogradoff, P.
  1892. *The Villainage in England* (London: Oxford University Press).
  1911. "Comparative Jurisprudence," article in *Encyclopaedia Britannica*, 11th edition, Vol. 15:580–87.
  1920. *Outlines of Historical Jurisprudence*, Vol. I, *Introduction—Tribal Law* (London).
Voget, Fred W.
  1956. "The American Indian in Transition: Reformism and Accommodation," *American Anthropologist*, Vol. LVII.
  1963. "Cultural Change," in *Biennial Review of Anthropology for 1963*, Bernard J. Siegel, ed. (Stanford: Stanford University Press).

Vollenhoven, C.
1906. *Het Adatrecht van Nederlandsch-Indie* (Leiden: Brill).
Von Neumann, J., and Morgenstern, Oskar
1964. *Theory of Games and Economic Behavior* (New York: John Wiley).
Wallace, Anthony F. C.
1956. "Revitalization Movements," *American Anthropologist,* Vol. LVIII.
1966. *Religion: Anthropological View* (New York: Random House).
Wallich, Henry C.
1958. *Mainsprings of The German Revival* (New Haven: Yale University Press).
Watnick, M.
1952. "The Appeal of Communism to the Underdeveloped Peoples," in B. F. Hoselitz, *Progress of Underdeveloped Areas* (Chicago).
Watson, William
1958. *Tribal Cohesion in a Money Economy* (Manchester: Manchester University Press).
Weaver, Thomas F.
1968. "The Farmers of Raipur," in John W. Mellor et al., *Developing Rural India* (Ithaca, N.Y.: Cornell University Press).
Weber, Max
1924. *Gesammelte Aufsatze zur Sozial und Wirtschaftsgeschichte* (Tübingen).
1947. *The Theory of Social and Economic Organization,* translated by A. M. Henderson and Talcott Parsons (New York: Oxford University Press).
1949. *The Methodology of the Social Sciences* (Glencoe, Ill).
1950. *General Economic History* (Glencoe: The Free Press).
1951. *The Religion of China* (Glencoe: The Free Press).
1958a. *The Religion of India* (Glencoe: The Free Press).
1958b. *The Protestant Ethic and the Spirit of Capitalism,* trans. by T. Parsons (New York: Scribner).
Wertheim, W. F.
1956. *Indonesia in Transition* (The Hague: van Hoeve).
Wertheim, W. F., and The Siauw Gap [Sic]
1962. "Social Change in Java, 1900–1930," *Pacific Affairs,* 35:223–47.
Wharton, Clifton R., Jr.
1963. "The Economic Meaning of Subsistence," *Malayan Economic Review,* Vol. 8, No. 2 (October).
1969a. "The Green Revolution," *Foreign Affairs* (April).
1969b. ed. *Subsistence Agriculture and Economic Development* (Chicago: Aldine).
Whyte, William, and Holmberg, Allan
1956. "Human Problems of U. S. Enterprise in Latin America," *Human Organization* (Fall).
Wilson, Godfrey
1941. *An Essay on the Economics of Detribalization in Northern Rhodesia,* The Rhodes-Livingstone Papers, No. 5.

Wilson, Godfrey and Monica
   1954. *An Analysis of Social Change* (Cambridge University Press).
Winslow, C. E. A.
   1951. *The Cost of Sickness and the Price of Health,* Monograph Series, No. 7 (Geneva).
Wiser, W. H.
   1958. *The Hindu Jajmani System* (Lucknow: Lucknow Publishing House).
Wolf, Eric R.
   1955. "Types of Latin American Peasantry," *American Anthropologist,* 57 (3).
   1959. *Sons of the Shaking Earth* (Chicago: The University of Chicago Press).
   1966. *Peasants* (Englewood Cliffs, N.J.: Prentice-Hall).
Wolff, P.
   1961. "L'Étude des Économies et des Sociétés Avant l'Ère Statisque," in *L'Histoire et ses Méthodes,* C. Samaran, ed. (Paris).
Worsley, Peter
   1957a. *The Trumpet Shall Sound: A Study of "Cargo" Cults in Melanesia* (London: MacGibbon and Kee).
   1957b. "Millenarian Movements in Melanesia," *Rhodes-Livingstone Institute Journal,* 18–31.
   1964. *The Third World* (London: Weidenfeld and Nicolson).
Yamey, B. S.
   1964. "The Study of Peasant Economic Systems: Some concluding Comments and Questions," in *Capital, Saving and Credit in Peasant Societies,* Raymond Firth and B. S. Yamey, eds. (Chicago: Aldine).
Yang, Martin C.
   1945. "The Family as a Primary Economic Group," in *A Chinese Village* (New York: Columbia University Press).
Yengoyan, A.
   1966. "Ecological Analysis and Traditional Agriculture," *Comparative Studies in Society and History,* 9:105–16.
Yudelman, Montague
   1964a. *Africans on the Land* (Cambridge: Harvard University Press).
   1964b. "Some Aspects of African Agricultural Development," in *Economic Development for Africa South of the Sahara,* E. A. G. Robinson, ed. (London: Macmillan).